FROM PATMOS • TO PARADISE

A COMMENTARY ON REVELATION

STEWART CUSTER

BJU PRESS

GREENVILLE, SOUTH CAROLINA

Library of Congress Cataloging-in-Publication Data

Custer, Stewart, 1931-

    From Patmos to paradise : a commentary on Revelation / Stewart Custer.

      p. cm.

    Includes bibliographical references and indexes.

    ISBN 1-59166-194-3 (hard : alk. paper)

      1. Bible. N.T. Revelation—Commentaries. I. Title.

    BS2825.53.C87 2004

    228'.077—dc22   2003025115

American Standard Version (ASV). © 1901, by Thomas Nelson and Sons, © 1929 by International Council of Religious Education.

English Standard Version (ESV). Scripture quotations are from The Holy Bible, English Standard Version, copyright © 2001 by Crossway Bibles, a division of Good News Publishers. Used by permission. All rights reserved.

The International Inductive Study Bible, New American Standard Bible (NASB). Scripture taken from the New American Standard Bible Copyright © 1960, 1962, 1963, 1968, 1971, 1972, 1973, 1975, 1977 by The Lockman Foundation. Used by permission.

New English Translation (NET). Copyright © 1997-2001 by Biblical Studies Press, L.L.C. and the authors. All rights reserved.

The New Jerusalem Bible, Reader's Edition. Biblical text © 1985 by Darton, Longman and Todd Ltd and Doubleday, a division of Bantam Doubleday Dell Publishing Group, Inc.

New Revised Standard Version (NRSV). © 1989, Division of Christian Education of the National Council of the Churches of Christ in the United States of America.

The NIV Study Bible (NIV). Scripture taken from the HOLY BIBLE, NEW INTERNATIONAL VERSION, Copyright © 1973, 1978, 1984 International Bible Society. Used by permission of Zondervan Bible Publishers.

Interior images: Marshall Neal, pp. xxxiv–xlviii (Seven Churches),
Craig Oesterling, pp. xxxiv–xlvi (stones)
Map and medallion art: James Hargis

From Patmos to Paradise: A Commentary on Revelation
Stewart Custer, Ph.D.

© 2004 BJU Press
Greenville, South Carolina 29614

Printed in the United States of America
All rights reserved

ISBN 1-59166-194-3

15 14 13 12 11 10 9 8 7 6 5 4 3 2 1

Dedicated to
my dear son,
Steven,
who may well
live to see
the Blessed Hope
fulfilled

TABLE OF CONTENTS

PREFACE TO THE READER

This commentary has been the intention of the author ever since he began teaching courses in Old Testament and New Testament prophecy in 1960. He has taught the exposition of the Book of Revelation as well as the exegesis of the Greek text to seminary students; he has expounded Revelation to his congregation more than once over the years. He has spoken on Revelation in Bible conferences in many different churches. He is convinced that the key to understanding the book is faith in the verbally inspired text of God's holy Word. The reader should come to Scripture seeking the meaning that John, the original author, had in mind, not bringing his private opinions to foist on the text. This commentary seeks to provide pastors and sincere believers in Christ help in perceiving the meaning of Revelation and the complex interpretations that have been drawn from it. It will draw upon the reverent comments of preachers and writers of the past, from the early comments of Victorinus to contemporary authors. It will be very sparing in referring to the critical writers who think that doubt is the key to understanding the Bible. When Martin Rist in the liberal *Interpreter's Bible* suggests that Revelation is a work of fiction designed to make emperor worship abhorrent and martyrdom popular (vol. 12, p. 354), there is no spiritual benefit to the hungry-hearted believer. The reader who is interested in such comments may find a bibliography of critical interpreters beginning on page 299. Many pastors and Bible teachers who consult such skeptical works often cannot find anything that they would like to share with a congregation. The author trusts that this commentary will be a spiritual blessing to every reader, even as John prayed for his readers (Rev. 1:3). He hopes that when the reader sees that the word *blessed* occurs seven times in Revelation, he does not see merely dry statistics, but a seven-point sermon outline. The fact that God is called *Almighty* nine times in Revelation (Rev. 1:8 note) is a theme that can be pursued with great spiritual benefit. The theme of "Jesus Christ" fills the pages of Revelation. It is a wonderfully complex picture of the Lord, the future, the world, and the heart of the believer. On every page the author has provided the lovely phraseology of the King James Bible, the beautiful precision of the Greek text (the author's own translation), and, thanks to a university library and to a computer, information from an array of commentaries and sermons on Revelation. May God bless every reader of this commentary. May each one see "in the midst of the seven lampstands one like the Son of man" (Rev. 1:13).

Special thanks go to Miss Suzette Jordan for her patient editorial wisdom; to Dr. Ron Tagliapietra for the Herculean task of checking every last Greek word and reference; and to Mr. James Hargis for the chart and the beautiful medallions that organize the sections of the book; and special thanks to Dr. Marshall Neal for his beautiful color photos of Patmos and the seven cities of Asia Minor.

Bob Jones University
Christmas 2003

INTRODUCTION

The Book of Revelation is the capstone of the Word of God. It gathers up the truths of all the rest of Scripture and organizes them into the plan of God for the ages. It shows us the divine purpose in permitting good and evil to wage war against one another. God is the holy and righteous King, who will defeat all His foes and will bring His redeemed people into His eternal kingdom of peace and glory. He will care for His people as a loving bridegroom cares for His cherished bride. But He will also defeat all the powers of evil and will assign them the punishment appropriate for their evil deeds. When He has finished His mighty work, all the universe will know that He has done all things well.

Authorship. The beloved disciple, John, had pondered these things for many years. He had heard the command of the Lord Jesus to "search the scriptures" (John 5:39). He had done so with zeal and diligence. Now he writes as the inspired penman of the Spirit, weaving into his language hundreds of allusions to the OT books that he knew so well. He identifies himself as "John" (Rev. 1:4). He is the last surviving apostle, already identified in the Book of Acts (Acts 3:1). He humbly refers to himself as "your brother and companion in tribulation" (Rev. 1:9). But he writes with the certainty that his words are the word of the Living God, who will hold all men responsible to obey (Rev. 22:18–19). Liberal commentators may argue that some unknown "John" wrote Revelation (Shirley Jackson Case, *The Revelation of John*, pp. 201–2; James Moffatt, *The Expositor's Greek Testament*, vol. V, p. 323), but their arguments are not convincing. The earliest church traditions identify the author of Revelation as John the Apostle (Justin Martyr, *Dialogue with Trypho the Jew*, p. 81, c. A.D. 150; Irenaeus, *Against Heresies*, IV, pp. 14, 2; Clement of Alexandria, *Who Is the Rich Man That Shall Be Saved?* p. 42; Tertullian, *Against Marcion*, II, p. v, c. A.D. 200; Origen, *De Principiis* I, iii, p. 10, c. A.D. 225; Hippolytus, *Treatise on Christ and Antichrist*, pp. 36–42, A.D. 236). The Muratorian Fragment (c. 170) lists Revelation as canonical and names John as the author. The first person known to have denied apostolic authorship is the heretic Marcion. Victorinus (died in persecution in A.D. 303), the earliest commentator on Revelation whose work has survived, named John the Apostle as author in his comments on Revelation 10:3–4. Perhaps the most important testimony (and earliest) is an indirect one. Eusebius, the church historian, testified concerning Papias that he was "an ancient man who was a hearer of John and a companion of Polycarp" (*Ecclesiastical History*, iii, 39, 5f.). Eusebius went on to describe the five books that Polycarp wrote, in which he clearly identified John the Apostle as the author of Revelation. Now Eusebius was a symbolic interpreter and did not like the Book of Revelation because it taught the Millennium, but he would not deny that John the Apostle wrote it. One of Eusebius's contemporaries did question John's authorship. Dionysius, bishop of Alexandria, A.D. 247–264, did not dare to reject Revelation, but he rather hesitantly suggested that he had heard that there were two tombs of John in Ephesus and that perhaps it was John the Elder rather than the Apostle who wrote Revelation. But since John claimed so vigorously to be "the Elder" (II John 1:1; III John 1:1), it appears to be a weak argument. The tone of John's words to the seven churches is definitely apostolic (Rev. 2–3). No ordinary elder in a local church would address other local churches with that tone of authority.

The church fathers also testify that John ministered in Ephesus. The sequence of seven churches in Revelation 2–3 are in a circuit in the exact order that a conscientious apostle would take in ministering to the churches under his charge. Vincent has documented the large number of words and phrases that John alone used in the NT. The large majority of them are also found in the Gospel and Epistles of John as well (Marvin Vincent, *Word Studies in the New Testament*, II, pp. 575–82). The dominant title applied to the Lord Jesus in Revelation is *Lamb* (ἀρνίον), a very distinctive word that John applies to the Lord twenty-eight times in Revelation (4 × 7), and once to the false prophet (Rev. 13:11). The only other time the word is used in the NT is in John's Gospel (21:15). In all the NT the apostle John is the only one to call Christ *the Word* (John 1:1; Rev. 19:13) and the only one to say that Christ *was pierced*, using a unique verb (ἐκκεντέω, John 19:37; Rev. 1:7). *The overcomer* (ὁ νικῶν) is another term that is well known from the messages to the seven churches (Rev. 2:7, 11, 17, 26; 3:5, 12, 21) and throughout the book (Rev. 5:5; 6:2; 11:7; 12:11; 13:7; 15:2; 17:14; 21:7). In his first Epistle John uses the term again and again (I John 2:13, 14; 4:4; 5:4, 5) and in his Gospel once (John 16:33). In the rest of the NT it is used only in Luke 11:22 and Romans 3:4; 12:21. The verb *worship* (προσκυνέω) is a major theme in Revelation, occurring twenty-four times in Revelation (12 + 12) and in John's Gospel occurring ten times. In the rest of the NT it occurs twenty-five times altogether (in Matthew, Mark, Luke, Acts, and Hebrews). John is the only NT writer to refer to "the first resurrection" (John 5:24–29; Rev. 20:5). The Lord's claim "I am Alpha and Omega" (Rev. 1:11) certainly reminds us of His seven "I am" statements in John's Gospel (6:35; 8:12; 10:9; 10:11; 11:25; 14:6; 15:1).

Date. Early testimony agrees on the reign of Domitian (died in A.D. 96) as the best date for Revelation: Irenaeus (*Against Heresies* V, pp. xxx, 3); Eusebius (*Ecclesiastical History*, III, p. 18); Clement of Alexandria (*Quis*

Dives, p. 42). Many modern writers also agree (Mounce, Swete, Tenney, Walvoord). Other writers will date it earlier in the reign of Nero, largely because they identify the seventh king as Nero (Rev. 17:10), but the context is future. The conditions described in the messages to the seven churches certainly favor the end of the first century, rather than the time of Nero, as Theodor Zahn argued in "The Condition of Affairs in the Church According to Revelation I.—III." (*Introduction to the New Testament*, III, pp. 408–20).

Text. The manuscript evidence for Revelation is full and early.

The papyri: P^{18}, 3rd–4th cent.; P^{24}, 4th cent.; P^{43}, 6th–7th cent.; P^{47}, 3rd cent.; P^{85}, 4th–5th cent.; P^{98}, 2nd cent.

The great uncials: ℵ, 4th cent.; A, 5th cent.; C, 5th cent.

The later manuscripts: 0169, 4th cent.; 0207, 4th cent.; 0163, 5th cent.; 0229, 8th cent.; 046, 051, 052, all 10th cent., and the majority of other manuscripts. A. T. Robertson thought that A was the best of the manuscripts on Revelation (*An Introduction to the Textual Criticism of the New Testament*, p. 85). For a master list see Aland, Barbara and Kurt, Karavidopoulos, Martini, and Metzger, *The Greek New Testament*, 4th ed., Stuttgart: United Bible Societies, 1966, 1993, pp. 903ff.

Purpose. The Book of Revelation sets forth God's eternal purpose, "which must shortly come to pass" (Rev. 1:1). Revelation portrays the grand sweep of the ages that traces the fulfillment of God's plan. From creation ("Thou hast created all things . . . for thy pleasure," Rev. 4:11), to redemption ("Thou hast redeemed us to God by thy blood out of every kindred," Rev. 5:9), to consummation ("The tabernacle of God is with men, he will dwell with them," Rev. 21:3), the book traces the drama of the ages to its perfect climax. God is the great "Alpha and Omega, the beginning and the end" (Rev. 21:6). When God's purpose is fulfilled, the righteous believers will be blessed and satisfied beyond their imagination. "He that overcomes shall inherit all things; and I will be his God, and he shall be my son" (Rev. 21:7). They will have sweet fellowship with God and the privilege of eternal service (Rev. 22:3–6). On the other hand the wicked will be judged and punished in a lake of fire (Rev. 21:8). His plan will be fulfilled in perfect wisdom, justice, and love. It is impossible for man to balance those three attributes.

All this is in complete harmony with OT prophecy. "The Lord of hosts hath sworn, saying, Surely as I have thought, so shall it come to pass; and as I have purposed, so shall it stand" (Isa. 14:24). The Lord will break the power of the Assyrian (Isa. 14:25); He will bring Lucifer down to sheol (Isa. 14:12–15); He will create new heavens and a new earth (Isa. 65:17).

"All flesh [shall] come to worship before me, saith the Lord. And they shall go forth, and look upon the carcases of the men that have transgressed against me: for their worm shall not die, neither shall their fire be quenched" (see Isa. 66:24).

The Lord Jesus taught the same truth. "When the Son of man shall come in his glory, and all the holy angels with him, then shall he sit upon the throne of his glory: and before him shall be gathered all nations: and he shall separate them one from another, as a shepherd divides his sheep from the goats . . . and these shall go away into eternal punishment: but the righteous into life eternal" (Matt. 25:31–32, 46).

The apostle Paul emphasized the same truth. "And we know that all things work together for good to them that love God, to them who are the called according to his purpose. For whom he did foreknow, he also did predestinate to be conformed to the image of his Son, that he might be the firstborn among many brethren" (Rom. 8:28–29). "Having made known unto us the mystery of his will, according to his good pleasure which he has purposed in himself: that in the dispensation [οἰκονομίαν] of the fullness of times he might gather together in one all things in Christ, both which are in heaven, and which are on earth" (Eph. 1:9–10). It was Paul's great glory that he could preach the unsearchable riches of Christ "to illuminate all men as to what is the dispensation [οἰκονομία] of the mystery which has been hidden from the ages in God, who created all things in order that now he might make known to the rulers and authorities in the heavenlies through the church the manifold wisdom of God" (Eph. 3:9–10). The mystery is that the Lord Jesus Christ is the Administrator of the dispensations. The Lord Jesus is the Creator of all things (Col. 1:15–16); He is the Redeemer from all iniquity (Titus 2:14); and at the glorious appearing, He shall be manifested as "our great God and Savior Jesus Christ" (Titus 2:13). He orders the ages to accomplish His great plan. Translations of Ephesians 3:9 have shown an increasing awareness of this administration of Christ. "The dispensation of the mystery" (ASV, 1901); "the administration of the mystery" (NASB, 1960); "the plan of the mystery" (ESV, 2001).

Now let us summarize the changes in method of administration of the dispensations. The idea for this chart came to me originally from James Brookes's *Maranatha*.

The Dispensation	The Covenants	The Change in Method of Administration
1. Conscience	Edenic Adamic Noachian Abrahamic	Spoken revelation
2. Law	Mosaic Palestinian Davidic	Spoken and written revelation
3. The Church	New	Written revelation and the Spirit within
4. The Day of the Lord 　a. Tribulation 　b. Millennium		Spoken and written revelation; the Spirit within, and concrete acts of providential control

Classic Dispensationalism vs. Progressive Dispensationalism.

The old battle line between literal interpreters (premillennialists) and symbolic interpreters (amillennialists and postmillennialists) has become rather ragged. For a clear discussion of the arguments, see the anthology by Wesley R. Willis and John R. Master, eds., *Issues in Dispensationalism* (Chicago: Moody Press, 1994). Anyone who believes in the verbal inerrancy of Scripture must confess that a great deal of the prophetic Scripture must be taken as literal fact. The prophecies of the First Advent were fulfilled in an overwhelmingly literal way. Jesus was born in the little town of Bethlehem, even as the prophet said (Mic. 5:2). He was born of a virgin (Isa. 7:14); they pierced His hands and feet (Ps. 22:16); He was buried with the wicked and the rich (Isa. 53:9). There is therefore an inherent presumption that the prophecies of the Second Advent will also be fulfilled in a literal manner. But there are undoubted figures and symbols in Scripture as well. Jesus said, "I am that bread of life" (John 6:48). He was not a literal loaf of bread, but He could sustain all who will believe on Him (v. 51). He added, "It is the Spirit that makes alive; the flesh profits nothing" (John 6:63). Infidels may sneer at the Book of Revelation as too fantastic for anyone to understand, but Moses Stuart soberly answered, "The original and intelligent readers of this book, beyond all reasonable doubt, could understand the meaning of the writer; else why should he address his work to them?" (*Rev.*, Preface, 1845). Is there a place in Scripture for the idea of God's people, "the Redeemed" of all ages, without distinctions? Yes, John's name for such is "the bride, the Lamb's wife" (Rev. 21:9). Does that mean that individual distinctions between OT and NT believers will disappear? No, for that city of God has gates with the names of the patriarchs on them and foundation stones with the names of the apostles on them (Rev. 21:12–14). The 144,000 Jewish martyrs have their national identity preserved, even as they serve before the throne of God in heaven (Rev. 7:4–15). The idea that the saints in glory have identical appearances comes from cartoons, not from God's Word. God loves individuality and diversity. John stresses that the great multitude that stand before the throne of God come from "all nations, and tribes, and people, and tongues" (Rev. 7:9). We can hardly think of a more diverse group of Jews than the apostles, ranging from a tax collector to a Zealot revolutionary. Yet the Lord loved them all and transformed them into powerful leaders who will always be distinct personalities. God has never created two identical people in the history of the world.

Now we must apply these principles to the prophetic future. Every conservative believer in the Lord Jesus Christ knows that the Bible promises eternal life in heaven in the world to come to everyone who trusts in the Lord Jesus Christ (John 3:16; 6:40; 14:1–4; 20:31). The question that arises is, Will there be a future millennial reign of Christ on the earth for a thousand years? The short answer is yes, Revelation 20:1–6 promises it. However, amillennialists will deny that it will be fulfilled or explain it away as identical with eternity. Thus, we need to examine a longer answer. When God established His covenant with King David, there is no doubt that David took it as a literal kingdom on earth (II Sam. 7:18–29). Of course he had a hope of heaven, of dwelling "in the house of the Lord forever" (Ps. 23:6). But David was astonished that God had spoken "of thy servant's house for a great while to come" (II Sam. 7:19). He was not thinking of heaven but of an earthly kingdom in which his descendants would be chastised if they needed it (vv. 13–14). Isaiah gave a great messianic prophecy, "Behold, a king shall reign in righteousness . . . and a man shall be as an hiding place from the wind, and a covert from the tempest" (Isa. 32:1–2). Here is the great problem of present governments: kings do not rule in righteousness, and there cannot be peace. But when this great King rules, "the work of righteousness shall be peace; and the effect of righteousness quietness and assurance for ever" (Isa. 32:17). Christ is "the Prince of Peace" (Isa. 9:6). This is not a reference to heaven, for the context refers to sowing crops and sending forth "the feet of the ox and the ass" (Isa. 32:20). But the best OT parallel to the teaching of Revelation on the earthly kingdom is the "little apocalypse"

(Isa. 24–27). First, Isaiah sets forth the disasters of the Tribulation period: "Behold the Lord makes the earth empty, and makes it waste, and turns it upside down" (24:1); "the land shall be utterly emptied, and utterly spoiled" (v. 3); "the earth mourns and fades away" (v. 4); "the earth is defiled under the inhabitants thereof" (v. 5.); "therefore the curse devoured the earth" (v. 6). The disasters of the seals and the trumpet judgments do come to mind (Rev. 6–8). Then Isaiah refers to the Jewish remnant: "When thus it shall be in the midst of the land among the people, there shall be as the shaking of an olive tree, and as the gleaning grapes when the vintage is done, They shall lift up their voice, they shall sing for the majesty of the Lord, they shall cry aloud from the sea" (Isa. 24:13–14). That same Jewish remnant can be found in Revelation 7. But then Isaiah refers to the climax of disaster, the Great Tribulation, the last half of Daniel's seventieth week (Dan. 9:27). "Fear, and the pit, and the snare, are upon you, O inhabitant of the earth. And it shall come to pass, that he who flees from the noise of the fear shall fall into the pit; and he that comes up out of the midst of the pit shall be taken in the snare: for the windows from on high are open, and the foundations of the earth do shake. The earth is utterly broken down, the earth is clean dissolved, the earth is moved exceedingly. The earth shall reel to and fro like a drunkard, and shall be removed like a cottage: and the transgression thereof shall be heavy upon it; and it shall fall, and not rise again" (Isa. 24:17–20). This climax of disaster is certainly the "wrath of God" poured out in the bowl judgments (Rev. 16). Then Isaiah described the punishment that the Lord shall visit on the host of the high ones and the kings of the earth upon the earth. "And they shall be gathered together, as prisoners are gathered in the pit, and shall be shut up in the prison, and after many days shall they be visited" (Isa. 24:22). Paul D. Feinberg notes that "Isaiah 24:21–22 teaches that there is a period of confinement before final consignment to hell" (*Issues in Dispensationalism*, p. 233). John reveals that the Lord Jesus shall return in glory, crushing the armies of the Antichrist and slaying his followers (Rev. 19:11–21). But John goes on to explain that the "many days" of Isaiah 24:22 are really a thousand years that the followers of Antichrist are left in their prison while the saints of God enjoy the great reign of peace on earth (Rev. 20). But Isaiah had said "after many days shall they be visited" (Isa. 24:22). God was not through with those wicked people. John now describes the Great White Throne judgment that occurs after the thousand year reign of peace and makes clear that all the wicked dead shall be judged, not just the followers of the Antichrist, and they shall be condemned and cast into an eternal lake of fire (Rev. 20:11–15).

If we were speaking in merely human terms, it would seem that John had taken the "little apocalypse" of Isaiah and expanded it into his marvelous

Revelation. But I believe in the verbal inspiration of Scripture. God revealed to His servant Isaiah in elementary form the sequence of events that would bring the age to a final climax. In keeping with His method of progressive revelation, God later revealed more fully to His servant John the same sequence of events. That sequence is God's plan for the ages, which He has had from the beginning and which He will surely bring to pass in due time.

All of which leads to a serious question for you, the reader. Where do you fit in God's eternal purpose?

(For further discussion see Robert L. Saucy, *The Case for Progressive Dispensationalism*; Craig A. Blaising and Darrell L. Bock, *Dispensationalism, Israel, and the Church*).

The Kingdom of God

The word *kingdom* (βασιλεία) denotes the *reign* or *rule* of God. However, there are many aspects to the rule of God.

1. It may refer to the *providential control* of God over all that exists. King Nebuchadnezzar recognized this when he said to Daniel, "Your God is a God of gods, and a Lord of kings" (Dan. 2:47). Hard-hearted Pharaoh recognized the same when, after the tenth plague, he sent to Moses, "Go, serve the Lord, as you have said" (Exod. 12:31). The psalmist sings, "The Lord sits King forever" (Ps. 29:10); "For the Lord is a great God, and a great King above all gods" (Ps. 95:3).

2. The OT *theocracy* was a preparatory form of God's kingdom (I Sam. 8:7). The Davidic covenant made David and his heirs the legitimate kings of Israel (II Sam. 7:12–16). The Davidic covenant must yet be fulfilled (Luke 1:31–33).

3. The *"mystery"* form of the kingdom is "Christendom," good fish and bad fish caught in the same net (Matt. 13:47–50). The angels will make a separation at the consummation of the age (v. 49). Another image the Lord used was of the sowing of seed and its slow growth until the harvest of judgment (Matt. 13:24–30). The Lord's interpretation shows that the growth period extends all the way to His setting up of the millennial kingdom (Matt. 13:37–43).

4. The NT *church* is another term for the present aspect of the kingdom (Matt. 16:18–19). It includes converted Jews and Gentiles in the same fellowship (Eph. 3:6) and some merely professing "bad fish" like Demas (II Tim. 4:10). It is not brought about by military force (John 18:36) but by conversion (John 3:3) and being led by the Spirit of God (Rom. 8:14).

5. The *Millennium* (Rev. 20:4–6) is a future aspect of the kingdom, which will be set up by military force by angels (Matt. 24:30–31) and in which Christ will prove that He can rule the world in righteousness and peace where all others have failed (Isa. 32:1–17). Death will be known only as a judgment on sin (Isa. 65:20–22). Nothing man can do will bring the eschatological kingdom in; God will establish it by an earth-shaking cataclysm (Dan. 2:44–45).

6. The *eternal kingdom* is the future rule of God, unopposed for all eternity. After the Lord Jesus Christ has ruled the earth for a thousand years, He will present the kingdom to His Father as an accomplished triumph: "Then comes the end, whenever he shall deliver the kingdom to God, even the Father, whenever he shall put down all rule and all authority and power. For it is necessary for him to rule until he shall put all enemies under his feet. The last enemy that shall be destroyed is death" (I Cor. 15:24–26). God shall rule forever, and "His servants shall serve him" (Rev. 22:3).

Cosmic War

The Bible portrays an age-long conflict between God and the Devil, good and evil. The actual battles and wars that are described in the Bible have such attention to detail that they have attracted professional military study (Yigael Yadin, *The Art of Warfare in Biblical Lands*, 2 vols., 1963; Chaim Herzog and Mordechai Gichon, *Battles of the Bible*, rev. ed. 1997). One of the major titles of the true God is "Lord God of hosts [armies]" (Pss. 59:5; 69:6; 80:4; 84:8; 89:8; Isa. 10:23, etc.). The Israelites could sing, "Jehovah is a man of war" (Exod. 15:3). There were times when the Lord provided material help in battle (Josh. 10:10–11; I Sam. 7:10–11). The Garden of Eden was plainly a battle scene (Gen. 3); the Devil was "that original serpent" (Rev. 12:9); but the day is coming when Michael and his angels will sweep the Devil and his angels from the heavenly realm (Rev. 12:7–10). Generation after generation anti-Semitism rears its ugly head; the Devil has a vested interest in destroying God's earthly people (Rev. 7:1–8). But in the coming Millennium they will yet be restored to the Holy Land in peace (Ezek. 40–48). In the initial vision of the Christ of glory, the great broadsword is a striking element and continues to be a vital theme (Rev. 1:16; 2:12, 16; 19:15, 21). The second coming in glory is as clear a scene of war as we have in all of Scripture (Rev. 19:11–21). The Lord Jesus Christ wages war in righteousness (v. 11). His divine word is the sword that crushes the Devil and his armies (v. 15). The saints have nothing to do but follow him in steadfast faithfulness (v. 14). Christ alone is "King of kings, and Lord of lords" (v. 16). But the purpose of His war is peace: a thousand years of peace on earth in the great millennial reign (Rev. 20:4–6) and eternal ages of peace in the glorification that follows (Rev. 21–22). God in His infinite wisdom knew that perfect peace and character could not be formed apart from war and struggle. Thus, the apostle Paul urges believers to take the whole armor of God and the sword of the Spirit and fight against "the world rulers of this darkness, against spiritual wickedness in high places" (Eph. 6:12f.). The day will come when the Lord Jesus Christ shall deliver up the kingdom to God, even the Father; "when he shall have put down all rule and all authority and power. For he must reign, till he hath put all enemies under his feet" (I Cor. 15:24–25). For added thought see "Divine Warrior," Ryken, Wilhoit, and Longman, *Dictionary of Biblical Imagery*, pp. 210–13; "War, Warfare," and "War, Idea of," ISBE, 1988, IV, pp. 1013–21; Paul Bentley Kern, *Ancient Siege Warfare*, Jerusalem, pp. 35ff.

Parallels Between Genesis and Revelation

> I am Alpha and Omega, the beginning and the ending, saith the Lord, which is, and which was, and which is to come, the Almighty. —Revelation 1:8

I. Creation: Genesis	II. Consummation: Revelation
1. God, Heart of the account. Gen. 1:1	1. God. Rev. 1:8; 4:2; 11:15f.; 21:6
2. God the Agent: Lord Jesus. 1:3	2. Jesus. 1:6; 5:5, 9–10
3. God the Spirit. 1:2	3. Spirit. 4:5; 22:17
4. The beginning: Light. 1:3	4. End: Light. 4:3; 21:11, 21, 23; 22:5
5. Separation. 1:4	5. Separation. 22:6–8, 14–15
6. Day and night started. 1:5	6. Day and night ended for saints. 22:5
7. Heaven. 1:8	7. Heaven 21:10
8. Seas. 1:9–10	8. Seas no more. 21:1
9. Plants and trees. 1:11–12; 2:8	9. Plants and trees. 22:2

I. Creation: Genesis (continued)	II. Consummation: Revelation (continued)
10. Light bearers: sun, moon. 1:14–18	10. Sun, moon, etc. 21:23
11. Birds and fish. 1:20–22	11. Birds and fish. 19:17 (Isa. 65:25)
12. Animals, for help. 1:24–25; 2:19f.	12. Animals. 19:11
13. Man. 1:26	13. Man. 21:3–7
14. God's image. 1:26	14. God's image. 22:4
15. Purpose of dominion. 1:26	15. Purpose of dominion fulfilled. 3:21; 5:9f.; 20:6
16. Societal relations: family. 1:27	16. Societal relations. 19:7–10; 21:2, 7, 9
17. God's blessing. 1:28	17. God's blessing. 22:14
18. Everything made was good. 1:31	18. Everything will be good. 21:27
19. God rested. 2:2	19. Man enters into His rest. 6:11; 14:13
20. River out of Eden. 2:10	20. River out of throne. 22:1
21. Man to do useful work. 2:15	21. Man to do useful work. 22:3
22. Tree of life. 2:9	22. Tree of life. 22:2
23. Serpent: attack. 3:1	23. Serpent: influence ended. 12:9; 20:2, 10
24. Curse pronounced. 3:14	24. Curse lifted. 22:3
25. Fellowship with God. 3:8	25. Fellowship with God. 7:15; 21:3

I. Creation: Genesis (continued)	II. Consummation: Revelation (continued)
26. Seed of the woman. 3:15	26. Seed of the woman. 12:1–5
27. Skin: sacrifice necessary. 3:21; 4:4	27. Sacrifice necessary. 12:11; 7:14
28. God clothed them. 3:21	28. God clothed them. 4:4; 6:11; 7:9; 19:14
29. Cherubim and flaming sword. 3:24	29. Cherubim: living beings. 4:6–8
30. Human culture. 4:2, 20–23	30. Culture. 21:12, 14, 24–26
31. True and false worship. 4:3–4	31. True worship. 19:1–6; 21:22 False worship. 13:4; 17:5
32. Sin and violence. 4:7–9	32. Sin ended for saints. 21:4
33. Punishment: fugitive, no home. 4:12	33. No home for the wicked. 14:11; 21:8
34. Deterioration (no evolution). 5:5; 11:22f.	34. Deterioration ended; righteous perfect. 21:4
35. Flood: disaster possible. 6–8; 7:21	35. Disaster accomplished for wicked. 19:19f.; 20:11–15
36. Sons of God influence men. 6:2	36. Spirits influence men. 16:13–16
37. Safety in the ark. 7:1, 16	37. Safety in Christ. 21:27
38. Rainbow: symbol of God's covenant. 9:13–16	38. Rainbow around the throne. 4:3
39. Multitude of nations. 10:1–32	39. Nations redeemed. 7:9; 21:24
40. Building for unity and pride. 11:1–9	40. Building for unity and God's glory. 21:15–21, 23

John's Use of the Old Testament

John's thinking processes are saturated with the language of the Hebrew OT and the Greek Septuagint translation. Although he does not make a single formal quotation, there are hundreds of allusions as he weaves the language of the OT like golden threads through the magnificent tapestry of his Apocalypse. There are times that he draws his phrase from the Septuagint, "the Lord God Almighty" (Amos 3:13; Rev. 1:8). In the same context the phrase "He who is" comes from Exodus 3:14, which John expands into a great confession of the eternal "I am": "He who is and he who was and He who is coming" (Rev. 1:8). Merrill Tenney gives a literal translation of the Greek, "From he who is, and from he was, and from he who is coming" (*Interpreting Revelation*, p. 14). Although this is almost "broken" Greek, it was necessary to convey the profound theological truth of the eternity of God. There is no past participle of the verb "to be" in Greek, and so John used a finite verb to express this glorious truth of the divine nature. Theology was more important than grammar to John! Although he comes back to the Book of Daniel again and again, he has a marvelous memory of the content of the entire OT. Some suggest that John uses the OT out of context (Schussler Fiorenza), but Beale has a thorough rebuttal (*Rev.*, pp. 81–86). We will pay special attention to the OT allusions as we trace John's thought in the commentary that follows.

The Interpretation of Revelation

There have been four major types of interpretation for the Book of Revelation. (Admittedly there have been many minor interpretations, such as John Wick Bowman's view that Revelation is *The First Christian Drama*, dividing it into seven acts of seven scenes each.) The preterist [past] interpreters hold that the book deals entirely with the first century. G. W. Buchanan argues that the seven kings mentioned were Herodians (p. 455), that the ten horns were Roman emperors (p. 458), and that different authors wrote different sections of Revelation, which were "later spliced together by the final editor who organized all of these visions into one anthology" (*The Book of Revelation*, p. 581). R. H. Charles (*The International Critical Commentary*) is another liberal who advocates the preterist view, but this is plainly the voice of unbelief. John, the author, clearly calls his work prophecy (Rev. 1:3). Now these excesses should not cause us to ignore the obvious first century background of the book, which is vital to the understanding of the content.

The historical interpreters hold that Revelation portrays the entire history of the church from the first century to the end. The best-known have been Seventh Day Adventists: E. B. Elliott (*Horae Apocalypticae*, 1862) and Uriah Smith (*Prophecies of Daniel and Revelation*). But if this interpretation is correct, the Lord Jesus Christ could not return until all the events in Revelation were completed. The faith of the church, however, has been that the Lord can return at any moment, and therefore, we should be constantly ready for "the Blessed Hope" (I Cor. 1:7; I Thess. 4:13–17). An obvious objection is that, as the centuries have passed, the identifications have had to be pushed forward so as to make room for later important events (such as the World Wars, etc.). This interpretation has been corrected often enough to make it seem unreliable. It is the least popular of the current views.

The symbolic, or idealist, view holds that Revelation is made up of symbols that portray the eternal conflict between good and evil. One of the best-known advocates of this view is Henry Barclay Swete (*The Apocalypse of St. John*). He presents a masterful analysis of the Greek text of Revelation but just a little help in the interpretation. Gregory K. Beale (*The Book of Revelation*, NIGTC) argues again and again for the symbolic view: The 144,000 symbolize all the redeemed (pp. 412ff.); the last seal and the last trumpet symbolize the last punishment (p. 472); the thousand years are symbolical (pp. 1017ff.). Although there are unquestioned symbols (largely drawn from the OT) in Revelation, the emphasis falls on the specific "things which must shortly come to pass" (Rev. 1:1). If the reference to "the Lamb that had been slain" is to a specific person and a specific event in the history of the world, then the reference to the Lamb opening one of the seals (Rev. 6:1) should be equally specific.

The futurist interpreters hold that most of the book (from 4:1 to the end) refers to future events that will unfold following the Rapture of the church from the earth. Although they recognize that there are many symbols in Revelation, their basic principle is the one that Horatius Bonar wrote in 1879, "Literal, if possible, is, I believe, the only maxim that will carry you right through the Word of God from Genesis to Revelation" (for a longer quotation in context, see Girdlestone, *The Grammar of Prophecy*, pp. 177–79). They love to present these prophetic details in chart form: see Harry Ironside, *Revelation*; Louis T. Talbot, *God's Plan of the Ages*; Clarence Larkin, *Dispensational Truth*, Tim LaHaye, *Prophecy Study Bible*, and LaHaye and Ice, *Charting the End Times*. Since the present author is a futurist, see pages lx–lxi for a prophetic chart. Futurists hold that the seals, trumpets, and bowls are series of judgments of ascending severity during the seven year Tribulation period that follows the Rapture. The Tribulation period will be ended by the revelation in glory (the Second Coming) of the Lord Jesus Christ (Rev. 19:11–16). This will be followed by a literal millennial reign (Rev. 20), and then by the new heaven and new earth. However, Leon Morris sagely notes "that elements from more than one of these views are required for a satisfactory understanding of Revelation" (*Rev.*, p. 20).

Since the Book of Revelation is very complex, this commentary will seek to balance the historical setting in the first century, the symbols and other content drawn from the OT, the prophetic teaching of all the Bible, and the devotional application of God's eternal truth to all ages. Each chapter is written in the light of its setting in the first-century Roman Empire (especially the seven churches); each chapter has a list of timeless practical applications as the idealists note; each chapter reveals John's view of future events, since he called his book "a prophecy" (Rev. 1:3). A. T. Robertson observes that "there is a note of sustained excitement all through the book, combined with high literary skill in the structure of the book in spite of the numerous grammatical lapses" (*Word Pictures in the New Testament*, vol. 6, p. 276). The dialect "I ain't seen it" may be just as accurate and truthful as the more polished "I have not seen it." Anyone who has read the papyri knows that the NT is on a vastly higher plane than the popular speech (See "To a Schoolboy from His Mother," P. Oxy. 930, in Hunt and Edgar, *Select Papyri*, I, p. 334). There is also a definite command to "watch" (Rev. 3:2), which echoes the command of the Lord Jesus Himself (Matt. 24:42). This presupposes that no one will be able to figure out from the contents of Revelation just when the end will come. George Peters argued that "the introduction of those chasms, and the obscurity of certain dates, is *intentional* in order to place us in the commanded position of *watching*" (*The Theocratic Kingdom*, III, p. 98). This leads us to conclude with John's prayer, "Even so, come, Lord Jesus" (Rev. 22:20).

Animals Mentioned in Revelation

John, the fisherman (Matt. 4:21), is highly interested in animals. There are an amazing number of animals mentioned in Revelation. He refers to celestial animals (living beings, living creatures, Rev. 4:6–9; 5:6, 8, 11, 14; 6:1, 3, 5–7; 7:11; 14:3; 15:7; 19:4); wild beasts (6:8); domesticated beasts (18:13); specifically, lion, calf, flying eagle (4:7); lion, lamb (5:5–6); every creature in heaven, and on earth, and under the earth, and in the sea (5:13); four horses (6:2–8); sea creatures (8:9); an eagle flying in mid-heaven (8:13); locusts and scorpions (9:3); battle horses (9:7, 9); lions (9:8); a great eagle (13:14); leopard, bear, lion (13:2); a lamb on Mount Zion (14:1); frogs (16:13); unclean birds (18:2); cattle, sheep, horses (18:13); a white horse (19:11, 14); birds that fly in mid-heaven (19:17); unclean dogs, a symbol for unclean people (22:15). See *Fauna and Flora of the Bible*, United Bible Societies, 1972. There is much help in Peter C. Alden's *National Audubon Society Field Guide to African Wildlife* (New York: Alfred A. Knopf, 1995).

The Significance of Numbers

God the Creator is the Divine Mathematician. He created the heavens and the earth in seven days (Gen. 1:1–2:3). He commanded His people to keep the seventh day as a holy day to Him (Exod. 20:8–11). He commanded His servant Joshua to order seven priests to march around Jericho for seven days, and to do it seven times on the seventh day, and He caused the walls of Jericho to collapse (Josh. 6:1–20). He has a number for every atomic element that He created. The great spiral structures of the atom, the solar system, and the galaxies can all be calculated mathematically. God is the only one who knows the path of every atom and galaxy from creation to chaos, from infinity past to infinity future. Although the apostle John did not know all these modern scientific ideas, he had a special interest in numbers. There can be no doubt that John was counting words. In the ancient world there were seven "sacred" numbers: 3, 4, 7, 10, 12, 40, 70. This is not to say that they were always symbolic. Many times they were used in a merely factual manner. The woman who put leaven in three loaves was not trying to symbolize the Trinity (Matt. 13:33)! When a housewife goes to the trouble of baking bread "from scratch," she does not bake so few loaves that she has to do it all over the next day. But there are some numbers that have symbolic significance in Scripture. Where they do, these guidelines may help.

Number	Explanation
1	Unity, individuality, supremacy, Deut. 6:4.
2	Difference, another (it may be a friend or a foe), Rev. 11:3; Dan. 12:5–7.
3	Divine completeness: tabernacle and temple both had three parts; the Trinity is worshiped by a threefold "Holy," Isa. 6:3; Rev. 4:8; the Aaronic benediction is threefold, Num. 6:22–23.
4	The world or the universe, Isa. 11:12; Rev. 7:1.
5	Half of completion; five wise and five foolish virgins, Matt. 25:2.
6	Limitation, one short of seven; 666, full development of limitation of evil.

Number	Explanation
7	"The" sacred number; perfection; completeness. It occurs over six hundred times in the Bible; fifty-five times in Rev. (ἑπτά); "seventh" five more times (ἕβδομος). (3+4) It was regarded as an important number in the ancient world from Egypt to China.
8	A new beginning; the start of a new week; in music, the octave; in science, the periodic table of chemical elements.
9	The number of judgment, Matt. 27:45–46; Luke 17:17.
10	The round number; the counting number: 10s, 100s, 1,000s, and so forth.
12	The number of the people of God; twelve tribes; twelve apostles.
40	The number of endurance or judgment, Gen. 7:4; Exod. 24:18; Matt. 4:2.
70	An intensified seven (7 × 10). "The frequent use of the number seven is significant in that it is integral to the structure of the entire book" (David E. Aune, "St. John's Portrait of the Church in the Apocalypse" [*Evangelical Quarterly*, Vol. XXXVIII, No. 3, July–September, 1966, p. 133]).

It is not surprising that John organized his Gospel into seven sections:
Prologue: the Word, John 1:1–14.
The witness of John the Baptist, 1:15–34.
The public ministry of Christ, 1:35–12:50.
The private ministry to believers, 13:1–17:26.
The sacrifice of Christ, 18:1–19:42.
The resurrection of Christ, 20:1–31.
Epilogue: Christ the Lord of life, 21:1–25.

John also referred to the "sign" value (σημεῖον) of Christ's miracles seven times in his Gospel (2:11; 4:54; 6:14; 9:16; 11:47; 12:18; 20:30). So it is not a surprise that John's Revelation has a structure of seven sevens.

The First Epistle of John also has a cyclic pattern in its structure (Randy Leedy, "The Structure of I John," *Biblical Viewpoint*, vol. XXVII, no. 1, April, 1993, pp. 11–19; Robert Law, *Tests of Life*; D. Edmond Hiebert, *The Epistles of John*, pp. 14–15).

But it is not just that John was good with numbers but that the Holy Spirit (the sevenfold Spirit) is the Divine Mathematician, who has put together the universe from the atom to the galaxy (and His revealed Word) with mathematical precision.

For further information see "Number Systems and Number Symbolism," *Holman Bible Dictionary*, pp. 1029–31; "Number," ISBE, III, pp. 556–61; "Numbers, Symbolic Meaning of," Elwell, *Evangelical Dictionary of Biblical Theology*, pp. 567–69.

Light, Darkness, and Color. Light is clearly a biblical image for God: "God is light" (I John 1:5). God created light: "God said, Let there be light" (Gen. 1:3). The Lord Jesus is the "light of the world" (John 8:12). The city that God prepares for His redeemed people is radiating with light (Rev. 21:24; 22:5). Darkness is the absence of light (Gen. 1:2). There can be no darkness in God at all (I John 1:5). The Lord Jesus delivered His people from the power of darkness (Col. 1:13). The judgments of God will darken the sun, moon, and stars (Rev. 8:12). Wicked Babylon will be judged until not even the light of a lamp will be left in her (Rev. 18:23). Light has all the colors of the rainbow in it, as any prism can prove. Thus, it is not surprising that the throne of God radiates a rainbow (Rev. 4:3).

Red is the color of blood (II Kings 3:22). Sin is presented as scarlet, red like crimson (Isa. 1:18). The rider on the red horse brings war and murder upon the earth (Rev. 6:4). Wicked Babylon rides on a scarlet beast (Rev. 17:3).

White is the symbol of purity (Rev. 19:8). God's forgiveness turns scarlet sins as white as snow (Isa. 1:18). White robes are given to the Tribulation martyrs (Rev. 6:11; 7:9). The Lord Jesus promises that the overcomer will receive a white stone [his vote] (Rev. 2:17) and will be clothed in white raiment (Rev. 3:5).

Yellow gold is mentioned once in Scripture (Ps. 68:13). Gold has always been symbolic of great wealth (I Kings 10:14–21). Gold is mentioned nine times in Revelation (two different words, 3:18; 17:4; 18:16; 21:18, 21; 9:7; 17:4; 18:12, 16). It is significant that the street of the Celestial City is pure gold, like transparent glass (Rev. 21:21).

Blue is not named in Revelation but is presupposed in the colors of breastplates of jacinth (Rev. 9:17) and some foundations stones (sapphire, chalcedony, Rev. 21:19). It was one of the colors of the tabernacle hangings (Exod. 26:1).

Purple is a red-blue color that was very expensive in the ancient world (Luke 16:19). It is estimated that it took 250,000 mollusks (murex) to produce one ounce of purple dye (ZPEB, I, p. 912). For wicked Babylon to be clothed in purple symbolized the wealth of kings (Esther 8:15; Rev. 17:4).

Green is the color of lush vegetation (Gen. 1:30; Rev. 8:7; 9:4). It is assumed in the emerald light shining from the throne of God (Rev. 4:3), in the emerald foundation stone (Rev. 21:19), and in the leaves of the tree of life (Rev. 22:2). There is a grim variation in the pale horse (Rev. 6:8), which is a pale gray green, the color of gangrene, a symbol of death.

Black is the absence of light. It is the color of mourning (Jer. 14:2), the night (Prov. 7:9), and famine (Rev. 6:5–6). Joel saw the Day of the Lord as a day of darkness and blackness (Joel 2:2–6). John sees the sun turn black in the same Tribulation period (Rev. 6:12).

Main Theme. The Revelation (unveiling) of Jesus Christ

G. Campbell Morgan sees
    I. The Unveiled Person
   II. The Unveiled Power
  III. The Unveiled Purpose
(*The Living Messages of the Books of the Bible*, II, p. 210.)

Key Verses. Revelation 1:1, 19

OUTLINES OF REVELATION

A Bird's Eye View of Revelation

Revelation 1:1–22:21.

Introduction. 1:1–8.
    [Sevenfold]

The Vision of the Glory of Christ. Rev. 1:9–20.
    [Seven characteristics of the Lord]

    I. The Lord and His Seven Churches. Rev. 2–3.

    II. The Lord and the Scene in Heaven. Rev. 4–5.
        [Seven things seen]

    III. The Lord and the Seven Seals. Rev. 6–8:1.
        [Parenthesis: the remnant. Rev. 7:1–17]

    IV. The Lord and the Seven Trumpets. Rev. 8:2–11:19.
        [Parenthesis: the mighty Angel. Rev. 10:1–11]

    V. The Lord and the Seven Personages. Rev. 12:1–13:18.
        [Parenthesis: the 144,000. Rev. 14:1–20]

    VI. The Lord and the Seven Bowls. Rev. 15:1–16:21.
        [Parenthesis: mystery Babylon. Rev. 17:1–18:24]

    VII. The Lord and His Second Coming. Rev. 19:1–20:15.
        [Seven future events]

The Vision of the Glory of Heaven. Rev. 21:1–22:7.
    [Seven new things]

Conclusion. Rev. 22:8–21.
    [Double sevenfold]

Literary Outline of Revelation

The Revelation of Jesus Christ (title and theme)

I. The Lord and His Churches. Rev. 1–3
   A. Introduction. 1:1–3
   B. Salutation. 1:4–8
   C. The Lord of glory. 1:9–18
   D. The commission to write. 1:19–20
   E. The messages to the churches. 2–3
      1. The church in Ephesus. 2:1–7
      2. The church in Smyrna. 2:8–11
      3. The church in Pergamos. 2:12–17
      4. The church in Thyatira. 2:18–29
      5. The church in Sardis. 3:1–6
      6. The church in Philadelphia. 3:7–13
      7. The church in Laodicea. 3:14–22

   [Parenthesis: the scene in heaven. 4:1–11]

II. The Lord and the Seals. 5:1–8:1
   A. The seven-sealed scroll. 5:1–4
   B. The Lion-Lamb. 5:5–7
   C. The worship of the Lamb. 5:8–14
   D. The seven seals. 6:1–8:1
      1. First seal: a white horse, a world conqueror. 6:1–2
      2. Second seal: a red horse, war, and killing. 6:3–4
      3. Third seal: a black horse, famine. 6:5–6
      4. Fourth seal: a pale green horse, death. 6:7–8
      5. Fifth seal: the martyrs under the altar. 6:9–11
      6. Sixth seal: earthquake, the Day of the Lord. 6:12–17

      [Parenthesis: The remnant, 144,000 and the great multitude. 7:1–17]

      7. Seventh seal: silence. 8:1

III. The Lord and the Trumpets. 8:2–11:19
   A. The priestly ministry before God. 8:2–3
   B. The Lord causes the prayers of the saints to ascend before God. 8:4–5
   C. The seven angels prepare to sound the trumpets. 8:6
   D. The seven trumpet judgments. 8:7–11:19
      1. First trumpet: hail, fire, and blood. 8:7
      2. Second trumpet: a great mountain burning with fire. 8:8–9
      3. Third trumpet: a great star fell from heaven. 8:10–11

VII. The Lord and His Coming. 19:7–22:21
    A. The marriage of the Lamb. 19:7–10
    B. The Second Coming in glory. 19:11–16
    C. The end of Armageddon. 19:17–21
    D. The Millennium. 20:1–10
    E. The Great White Throne judgment. 20:11–15
    F. The New Jerusalem. 21:1–27
    G. The new paradise. 22:1–16

    [Parenthesis: the last invitation and warning. 22:17–19]

Epilogue. 22:20–21

The Prophetic Time Outline: Rev. 1:19

    I. The things thou hast seen: The Christ of glory. Rev. 1
    II. The things that are: The seven churches. Rev. 2–3

(The present church age.)

    III. The things that shall be after these things: from the Rapture on. Rev. 4–22
        A. The church in heaven. Rev. 4–5
        B. The Tribulation period. Rev. 6–18
        C. The Second Coming in glory. Rev. 19
        D. The Millennium. Rev. 20
        E. The eternal kingdom. Rev. 21–22

The Chiastic Parallel Outline: The Holy War (Rev. 19:11)

A. The Great General and His Troops. Rev. 1–3
  B. The Beginning of the War. Rev. 4–8:1
    C. The Trumpet Campaign. Rev. 8:2–11
      D. The Leader and the Shock Troops: The Man-Child and the Remnant. (The Lamb and the 144,000). Rev. 12–14
      D'. The Dragon and the Beast Worshipers. Rev. 12–13
    C'. The Bowls of Wrath Campaign. Rev. 15–16
  B'. The Crushing of the Enemy. Rev. 17–18
A'. The Great General and His Victory. Rev. 19–22

My dear friend and colleague, Dr. Ronald Horton, has long pondered John the Apostle, exiled to Patmos, but remembering the words of his Lord, and being privileged to behold a staggering vision of the future.

WONDERING JOHN

"And his disciples came to him for to shew him the buildings of the temple. And Jesus said unto them, See ye not all these things? Verily I say unto you, There shall not be left here one stone upon another that shall not be thrown down" (Matt. 24:1–2)

He stood that hour

And marveled with the rest He marveled not,
As the slant rays of the westering sun
Played lambently upon the towering ranks
Of polished ochre monoliths. Undone

Would be this boasted man's-work. But look now!
A craggy mass, its gilded seams ablaze,
Its gem-encrusted crannies brimming fire,
Is dropping thunderously in smoky haze,

Whilst he amazed, a hundred leagues far off,
Beholds unscrolled the seven-fold end of time
In sunless radiance. From a sea-washed speck
Of rock unrolls a vision so sublime

The ages cower.

THE ISLE — OF —
patmos

NICHOLAS
BAY

CAPE FERRO

APOLLOS COVE

PORT MERIKA

PORT SKALA

MONASTERY OF
ST. JOHN'S RESIDENCE

PATINO~
MONASTERY OF ST. JOHN

PORT GRIKO

PORT STAVROS

jasper*

sapphire

*Revelation 21:19–21

LEFT: *Monastery near the Grotto near Port Skala*

BELOW LEFT: *View from a hill near a cove on Patmos*

BELOW: *The harbor on Patmos*

quartz crystal

ABOVE: *The Temple of Diana (Artemis) at Ephesus*

ABOVE RIGHT: *The Temple of Hadrian at Ephesus*

RIGHT: *Marble street from the theater at Ephesus*

chalcedony

ephesus

emerald

smyrna

ABOVE: *The harbor from Mount Pagos at Smyrna*

RIGHT: *The Forum at Smyrna*

sardonyx

sardius

ABOVE: *View of the Asclepion from the Odeon at Pergamos*

RIGHT: *Column with the sacred serpents from the Temple of Asclepion*

FAR RIGHT: *Ruins of the Church of John at Pergamos*

chrysolyte

thyatira

beryl

imperial topaz

RIGHT: *City wall of Thyatira*

ABOVE: *The Acropolis at Sardis*

sardis

chrysoprasus

ABOVE: *Temple of Artemis at Sardis*

jacinth (lapis lazuli)

BELOW: *City walls at Philadelphia*

RIGHT: *Walls and buildings at Philadelphia*

amethyst

ABOVE: *The theater at Laodicea*

RIGHT: *Ruins of the church of Laodicea*

THE THEOLOGY OF REVELATION

The Book of Revelation is an extremely complex work. "The book is both a word to a specific first-century historical situation and at the same time a vision of the end times" (Donald Guthrie, *New Testament Theology*, p. 812). G. K. Beale holds that "the large amount of symbolic material in Revelation is due primarily to John's theological intention, of identifying his relationship to the situation of the Asia Minor churches with the relationship of the OT prophets and Jesus to the plight of Israel" (Alexander, *et al.*, *New Dictionary of Biblical Theology*, p. 356). Although some charge Revelation with non-Christian ideas (Josephine Massyngberde Ford, *Anchor Bible*, pp. 12, 291), careful study demonstrates a very detailed and orthodox theology, which is deeply rooted in the OT.

The Doctrine of God. John claims that God gave him the contents of the book (Rev. 1:1) and that it is properly called "the Word of God" (1:2). The OT prophets made the same claim (Isa. 1:1–2; Jer. 1:1–4; Ezek. 1:1–3; Dan. 2:27–30). The language John uses sets forth the eternal nature of God (He is and was and is to come, 1:4). The reference to God's throne implies His sovereign rulership over the entire universe (1:4). "The primary theme of the book is the sovereignty of God" (Osborne, *Rev.*, p. 31). He is the Father of the Lord Jesus (1:6). He claims to be eternal, self-existent, the Almighty God (1:8, a major OT title, Gen. 17:1). The scene in heaven reveals that God's throne is central in that realm and that God is a majestic and glorious being (4:1–3). His celestial servants are gathered around Him and constantly celebrate His holiness, power, and eternity (4:4–8). He is worthy of such praise for He is the Creator of all things (4:11). Every created being will ultimately recognize His power and glory (5:13). He is holy and true, and infinitely patient (6:10). He will one day repay wrath on the sins of the wicked (6:17). He is the eternally living God, the Author of life to all (7:2). He provides salvation to His people (7:10). A multitude of mighty angels worship Him (7:11–12). He intends to dwell one day among His people and comfort them (7:15, 17). He is the Creator of all things in heaven and earth (10:6). He shall reign forever over all that exists (11:15). He will repay wrath to the wicked and reward to the righteous (11:18). He is a God of absolute justice (13:10). All beings should reverence, glorify, and worship God (14:7). God will visit wrath on idolaters (14:10; 15:1). God delights in music, for redeemed saints will sing His praises (15:2–4). The glory and power of God fill the heavenly sanctuary (15:8). God's judgments are true and righteous (16:5, 7). Evil men blaspheme God (16:10–11). God shall repay divine wrath to the wicked world system (16:19). God shall fulfill all His words concerning the wicked (17:17). The Lord God is strong in judgment (18:8). God will avenge His servants on wicked Babylon (18:20). The judgments of God are true and righteous (19:2). The Lord God Almighty reigns (19:6). Only God is worthy of worship (19:10; 22:9). The wrath of Almighty God is fierce (19:15). God shall judge all men, small and great (20:12). He shall dwell in the midst of His redeemed people (21:3–4). God has prepared the Holy City, New Jerusalem, for them (21:10). God Himself will be the temple of that city (21:22). The throne of God shall be there; the saints shall see His face (22:1–4). God will judge all people's response to this revelation (22:17–19).

The Names and Titles of Jesus. "The Revelation of Jesus Christ" (1:1) gives us the main theme of the book: it is about Jesus Christ. Revelation presents a very high Christology, setting forth both the divine and human natures of Christ. As God, He is worthy of worship (5:8–12) and as man, He is a Jew (5:5). The names reveal His person.

1. *Lamb* (ἀρνίον) is the dominant title applied to the Lord, occurring twenty-eight times (4 × 7). It is also applied once to the False Prophet, who is "like a lamb" (13:11). The title is introduced properly without the article (5:6), but from then on it is always "the Lamb" (5:8, 12, 13; 6:1, 16; 7:9, 10, 14, 17; 12:11; 13:8; 14:1, 4 [twice], 10; 15:3; 17:14 [twice]; 19:7, 9; 21:9, 14, 22, 23, 27; 22:1, 3). It is a striking truth that the Lord of glory is portrayed as a sacrifice for His people. This a major OT theme (Gen. 22:8–13; Exod. 12:3–7; 29:38–39; Isa. 53:3–12).

2. *Jesus* occurs fourteen times (2 × 7). It is the Greek equivalent of the Hebrew *Joshua*, "Jehovah is salvation." The compound name *Jesus Christ* occurs three times (1:1, 2, 5). *Lord Jesus* occurs twice (22:20, 21). The simple *Jesus* occurs nine times (1:9 [twice]; 12:17; 14:12; 17:6; 19:10 [twice]; 20:4; 22:16).

3. *Christ* occurs seven times. The compound *Jesus Christ* three times (1:1, 2, 5); the simple *Christ* four times (11:15; 12:10; 20:4, 6). Christ is the anointed Messiah, rightful King of His people (Ps. 2:2), true heir of David (Ps. 20:6). The Textus Receptus has the compound seven times (1:1, 2, 5, 9 [twice]; 12:17; 22:21).

4. *Lord* (κύριος) is applied to Christ six times. The simple title *Lord* twice (11:8; 14:13); *Lord of lords* twice (17:14; 19:16); *Lord Jesus* twice (22:20, 21). *Lord of lords* is a title of Jehovah God (Deut. 10:17). *Lord* is also the prophesied title of the Messianic King (Ps. 110:1).

5. *The First and the Last* occurs three times (1:17; 2:8; 22:13). This is a divine title of Jehovah, King of Israel, applied to the Lord Jesus (Isa. 44:6).

6. *The True One* occurs three times (3:7; 6:10; 19:11). This is another divine attribute applied to the Lord Jesus (Jer. 10:10).

7. *The Holy One* is applied to the Lord Jesus twice (3:7; 6:10). This is another name of Jehovah applied to the Lord Jesus (Isa. 6:3; 57:15).

8. *The Faithful Witness* is applied to the Lord Jesus twice (1:5; 3:14). Jehovah is also a Witness (Jer. 29:23).

9. *The Son of man* is applied to the Lord Jesus twice (1:13; 14:14). This is a messianic title drawn from Daniel 7:13.

10. *The Beginning* is applied to the Lord Jesus twice. He is the Beginning of the creation of God (3:14) and He is the Beginning and the End (22:13). In the beginning God created all things (Gen. 1:1). The Lord Jesus was the agent of creation (John 1:1–4).

11. *The Root of David* is applied to the Lord Jesus (5:5) and the *Root and Offspring of David* (22:16). This is another important OT theme (Isa.53:2).

12. *King of kings* occurs twice, always linked to *Lord of lords* (17:14; 19:16). The prophet Isaiah recognized the Lord as a great King (Isa. 6:5; John 12:38–41).

13. *The Lion of the tribe of Judah* is found only once in the entire NT (5:5), but it is a very important OT theme (Gen. 49:9–10; Isa. 31:4; Hos. 11:10).

14. *The Firstborn of the dead* occurs only once in 1:5. The Lord Jesus is the Firstborn in dominion over the dead.

15. *The Ruler of the kings of the earth* occurs in 1:5, which is the only time in the NT that the Lord is called a ruler.

16. *The Son of God* occurs only in 2:18, mentioned with divine attributes. It is a major title in John's Gospel.

17. *A male son* (υἱὸν "αρσεν) a unique phrase, of special interest to royalty, occurs only once in the NT (12:5).

18. *The One who searches the reins and hearts* occurs only once in 2:23. This is an attribute of God (Jer. 17:10).

19. *The One who has the key of David* occurs only once in the NT (3:7). It was an OT symbol of authority (Isa. 22:22).

20. *The One who opens and shuts* occurs only once in the NT (3:7).

21. *The Amen* occurs only once in 3:14.

22. *Faithful* occurs only once (19:11), referring to the conquering Lord. It is an attribute of God (Deut. 7:9).

23. *The Word of God* occurs only once as a title (19:13).

24. *The Alpha and the Omega* occurs only once applied to Christ (22:13); the other occurrences refer to God (1:8; 21:6).

25. *The Bright and Morning Star* occurs only once in the NT (22:16). Balaam's prophecy refers to Him as a "Star" (Num. 24:17).

For a thorough analysis of the meanings of the names and titles applied to the Lord Jesus in the Book of Revelation, see Benjamin B. Warfield, *The Lord of Glory*, "The Witness of the Apocalypse," pp. 286–97. See also "Christology in the Book of Revelation," in Mal Couch, *A Bible Handbook to Revelation*, pp. 104–13.

The Doctrine of the Holy Spirit. John begins his message to the seven churches with a Trinitarian greeting from the eternal Father, from the seven Spirits, and from Jesus Christ (Rev. 1:4–5). This is an anticipation of the throne scene that reveals the Trinity in the center of the courts of heaven (Rev. 4:2–5). The Holy Spirit is manifested as seven lamps, or torches (λαμπάδες), which are blazing before the throne. This is an obvious reference to the messianic prophecy of the Branch of Jesse, who will have the sevenfold Spirit of Jehovah, wisdom, understanding, counsel, might, knowledge, and fear of the Lord resting on Him (Isa. 11:2). John claims to be "in the Spirit on the Lord's day" (Rev. 1:10). That surely means that he was "filled with the Spirit" in preparation to his receiving the great prophetic vision that follows. The Spirit has a special message for each of the seven churches, but only overcomers will benefit. To the church of Ephesus the Spirit promises the tree of life (Rev. 2:7); to the church of Smyrna the Spirit promises protection from the second death (2:11); to the church of Pergamos the Spirit promises hidden manna and a white stone (2:17); to the church of Thyatira the Spirit promises authority over the nations (2:27–29); to the church of Sardis the Spirit promises white raiment and a name in the Book of Life (3:5); to the church of Philadelphia the Spirit promises a new divine name (3:12); to the church of Laodicea the Spirit promises the privilege of sitting with the Lord on the divine throne (3:21).

After this John was "in the Spirit" (4:2) and was spiritually enabled to behold the throne room of heaven, with the seven torches of fire blazing before the throne and identified as "the seven Spirits of God" (4:5). When the third member of the Trinity appears, He is "a Lamb as it had been slain, having seven horns and seven eyes, which are the seven Spirits of God sent forth into all the earth" (5:6). Apparently, the Spirit is the agent of omniscience for the Lamb. The Spirit of life entered into the bodies of the two faithful witnesses and restored them to life (11:11). John hears a voice from heaven commanding, "Write, Blessed are the dead which die in the Lord from henceforth: Yea, saith the Spirit, that they may rest from their labors; and their works do follow them" (14:13). An angel carried John away "in the Spirit" to see mystery Babylon (17:3). Another angel declared to John that "the testimony of Jesus is the spirit of prophecy" (19:10). Another angel carried John away "in the Spirit" to behold holy Jerusalem, descending from God (21:10). In the conclusion it is the Spirit and the bride who give the invitation, "Come. And let him that heareth say, Come" (22:17).

The Doctrine of Salvation. Revelation begins with a clear statement of the redemptive salvation believers have in Christ: Jesus Christ is the one who loved us and washed, or loosed, us from our sins in His own blood (1:5). He has transformed us from poor sinners into kings and priests before God (1:6). The messages to the overcomer in the seven churches make clear the enormous blessings of salvation. The overcomer is the true believer in the Lord Jesus Christ (I John 5:4–5). The Spirit promises the overcomer the right to eat of the tree of life in the midst of the paradise of God (2:7). There is no clearer way of showing the fulfillment of God's original purpose of loving fellowship with man (Gen. 2:9; 3:8, 22). The Spirit promises that the overcomer shall not be hurt by the second death (2:11). The one who believes in the Lord Jesus Christ has everlasting life (John 3:16; 6:47; 17:3). The Spirit promises to give the overcomer hidden manna (supernatural sustenance, Exod. 16:35) and a white stone, the vote of approval (2:17). The Spirit promises the overcomer authority over the nations in spiritual rule (2:26–27) and the gift of the Savior, who is the Morning Star (2:28; II Pet. 1:19). The Spirit promises the overcomer white raiment, his name recorded in the Book of Life, and commendation before the angels (3:5). The Spirit promises to make the overcomer a pillar in God's temple and to give him the name (or character) of God, of the city of God, and of the Lord (3:12). The Spirit promises that the overcomer will share the throne of Christ (3:21–22). All of which are supremely exalted promises.

The celestial company sings praise to the Lamb: "Thou art worthy to take the scroll, and to open the seals thereof: for thou wast slain, and hast redeemed us to God by thy blood out of every kindred, and tongue, and people, and nation" (5:9). The blood of the Lamb bought back His people from slavery to sin. God will have His worshipers from every nation on earth. They shall reign on the earth (5:10). A great multitude from all nations will be saved during "the great tribulation" (7:9–14). Yet, in spite of plagues and judgments, other men will not repent of their murders, use of drugs, fornication, and thefts (9:20–21). When the seventh angel sounded, there is an anticipation of the end: the kingdom of the world became our Lord's (11:15). The saints overcame Satan by the blood of the Lamb (12:10–11). Those who worship the Beast do not have their names written in the Lamb's Book of Life (13:8). The everlasting gospel will still be preached to every nation (14:6). In heaven those who conquer sing the song of Moses and the Lamb (15:2–4). In heaven a great multitude sings a fourfold Alleluia to God (19:1–6). The marriage of the Lamb reveals a bride arrayed in fine linen, which is the righteousnesses of the saints (19:7–8). God's people, and the martyrs killed by the Beast, lived and reigned with Christ a thousand years (20:4). Blessed and holy is the one who has part in the first resurrection

(20:6). John saw a new heaven and a new earth and the New Jerusalem descending from God (21:1–2). The nations of the saved shall walk in the light of that celestial city (21:24). The curse shall be removed and they shall see His face (22:3–4). Character shall be eternally fixed (22:11). The Spirit and the bride give a universal invitation to salvation (22:17).

The Kingdom of Darkness. The word *kingdom* (βασιλεία) occurs six times in Revelation: three times for the kingdom of God (1:9; 11:15; 12:10) and three times for the kingdom of evil (16:10; 17:12, 17). A titanic conflict of the ages is raging, with God on the throne over all (1:4) and Jesus Christ the Ruler of the kings of the earth (1:5), even though they fight against Him. This doctrine has an extensive OT background (Pss. 2:2, 6, 10; 10:16; 47:7; 84:3; Isa. 6:5; Zech. 14:9, 16, 17, etc.). The kingdom of darkness is headed by Satan, the Devil, who was originally named Lucifer (*Light-bearer*, Isa. 14:12ff.), but both *Satan* and *devil* mean *adversary*, or *accuser* (Rev. 12:10). The Devil can use even religious organizations to attack God's people (Rev. 2:9). God's people should not fear the Devil, even though he has the power to cast some of them into prison (2:10). Some of God's people are dwelling where Satan's throne is and may expect persecution (2:13). There are depths of sin in Satan, that, hopefully, God's people will not know (2:24). Ultimately, God will vindicate His people and will bring Satan's followers to bow at their feet (3:9). God reveals the nature of Satan under the image of "a great red dragon" (12:3). His tail casts down a third of the hosts of heaven, which is regularly interpreted as causing the fall of angels (12:4). There is an age-long battle going on between Michael, God's archangel, and the Dragon (12:7; Dan. 12:1). Michael will one day cast out the Dragon from the heavenly realm (12:9). Satan is the original serpent (12:9; Gen. 3:1–7). During the Tribulation period the Devil will be confined to the earth and will persecute the Jews (12:12–13). God will divinely protect His earthly people during this attack (12:14–16). The Dragon continues to make war against the Jews (12:17). The Dragon is the imitator of God. He will raise up a future world dictator (the Antichrist, I John 2:18–22) and give him a throne (13:2). Worldly people will worship this dictator (13:4). Satan will raise up another beast, a religious leader (the counterfeit Holy Spirit), who will speak like the Dragon (13:11). He will put a mark on the foreheads of his followers (13:16–18) to copy the seal of God on the foreheads of the saints (7:3). Evil spirits will proceed from this satanic trinity, the Dragon and the two beasts, to gather men to the Battle of Armageddon (16:13ff.). When the time is right, "an angel" will bind the Devil and cast him into a bottomless pit, where he will fall for a thousand years while the millennial reign celebrates (20:1–3). When the thousand years are expired, Satan will be loosed to test these hothouse plants to prove that even in a perfect environment men will believe the

Devil rather than God (20:7f.). Finally the Devil will be cast into the lake of fire and sulfur for eternal punishment (20:10). The kingdom of God will triumph and will be unopposed for all eternity (22:3).

The Seriousness of Sin. All sin is ultimately directed against a holy God. David confessed, "Against thee, thee only, have I sinned, and done this evil in thy sight" (Ps. 51:4a). In the Ten Commandments the Lord said, "I the Lord thy God am a jealous God, visiting the iniquity of the fathers upon the children unto the third and fourth generation of them that hate me" (Exod. 20:5). The glory of Messiah is that He loves right-eousness and hates wickedness (Ps. 45:7a). The psalmist exhorts the saints, "You that love the Lord, hate evil" (Ps. 97:10). The apostle Paul pronounced the judgment, "Death passed upon all men because all sinned" (Rom. 5:12b). Thus, the Book of Revelation opens with the praise to Jesus Christ, "who loved us and loosed us from our sins in his own blood" (Rev. 1:5b). No one can be saved apart from the death of the Lord Jesus. His sacrifice removes the harm of the second death (Rev. 2:11). Now we understand the reason for the stern judgment against Babylon, the world system. The voice from heaven warns God's people, "Come out of her, my people, that you share not her sins, and receive not of her plagues" (Rev. 18:14b). In God's sight, "Her sins have been piled up even to heaven, and God remembered her unjust deeds" (Rev. 18:5). But sin and evil do not just appear. The Bible recognizes the permanence of unrepented sin. "The one who is unjust, let him be unjust still" (Rev. 22:11). This is the necessity for the lake of fire (Rev. 20:12–15).

Revelation declares what the whole Bible has taught: the conflict of the ages, which started in a garden with a holy God, a crafty serpent, and a sinning mankind (Gen. 3), will come to a triumphant conclusion with the thrice holy God glorified and praised; the old serpent judged and confined to a lake of fire with all his henchmen; and believing mankind redeemed and glorified in the City of God, which is also a garden para-dise. Adolph Saphir referred to "the blessed book of the Revelation. There we have all summed up in this book of the kingdom and this book of the church. There we see the unity of the whole record, which God has given us. He will come again" (*The Divine Unity of Scripture*, p. 214). "Even so, come, Lord Jesus" (Rev. 22:20).

MASTERING THE BOOK OF REVELATION

The believer in the Lord Jesus Christ must not be satisfied with a shallow knowledge of the Scriptures. We are commanded to "search the Scriptures" (John 5:39), meditate on them day and night (Josh. 1:8), and use them for doctrine, reproof, correction, and instruction in righteousness (II Tim. 3:16). It is a good thing for a Christian to study Scripture the way God wrote it: one book at a time. Jacques Ellul maintains "that the Apocalypse must be read as a whole, of which each part takes its import by relation to the whole" (*Apocalypse*, p. 12). But it is also good to study verse by verse so as to digest and absorb that content and the great biblical truths that are in it ("Thy words were found, and I did eat them," Jer. 15:16). Ellul dislikes that method of study, but I strongly disagree. Studying verse by verse forces the reader to follow the thought of the Author. The reader should come to the Book of Revelation with the determination to learn what is in it and to apply its teaching to the life that he lives. He should know the outline of Revelation; he should have a theme to characterize each chapter; he should know each person, place, and major doctrine that is found in each chapter. This commentary seeks to place such information before the reader at the start of every chapter. He should be able to explain the meaning of each chapter and apply its teaching to his own heart relationship with his Savior. This commentary is designed to help the student of Scripture gain a mastery of the Book of Revelation, that its content may master his soul and make him a better servant for the Lord Jesus Christ. When he has so studied Revelation, he will have learned a method of study that he may well apply to the other sixty-five books of Scripture.

ABBREVIATIONS

Arndt and Gingrich—Arndt and Gingrich. *A Greek-English Lexicon of the New Testament and Other Early Christian Literature*. Chicago: The University of Chicago Press, 1957.

ASB—The American Standard Bible, 1901.

AV—The Authorized Version (i.e., the King James Version).

Bengel, *Gnomon*—Bengel, John Albert. *Gnomon of the New Testament*. Vol. 5, "Apocalypse." Edinburgh: T. and T. Clark, 1863.

ESV—The English Standard Version, 2001.

ISBE—*The International Standard Bible Encyclopedia*. 4 vols. Grand Rapids: Eerdmans, 1979–88.

KJV—The King James Version.

LXX—The Septuagint, the Greek translation of the Old Testament.

Moffatt, *Expos. Greek Test.*—Moffatt, James. *Expositor's Greek Testament*. Vol. V, "Revelation." Grand Rapids: Eerdmans, 1951.

Moulton and Milligan—*The Vocabulary of the Greek Testament*. Grand Rapids: Eerdmans, 1963.

NASB—The New American Standard Bible.

NET—New English Translation (Internet). www.netbible.org.

NIV—The New International Version.

NJB—The New Jerusalem Bible.

NKJV—The New King James Version.

NLT—The New Living Translation.

NRSV—The New Revised Standard Version.

NT—The New Testament.

OT—The Old Testament.

p., pp.—page, pages.

Pentecost, *Things*—Pentecost, *Things to Come*. Findley, Ohio: Dunham Publishing Company, 1958.

Rev.—The Book of Revelation.

Robertson, *Word Pictures*—"Robertson," Archibald Thomas. *Word Pictures in the New Testament*, Vol. VI, "Revelation." Nashville: Broadman Press, 1933.

Rpt.—Reprinted.

Trench, *Synonyms*—Trench, Richard Chenevix. *Synonyms of the New Testament*. Grand Rapids: Eerdmans, 1953.

Unger—Unger, Merrill F. *The New Unger's Bible Dictionary*. Chicago: Moody, 1988.

v., vv.—verse, verses.

Vincent, *Word Studies*—Vincent, Marvin R., *Word Studies in the New Testament*. Vol. II. Grand Rapids: Eerdmans, 1946.

ZPEB—*Zondervan Pictorial Encyclopedia of the Bible*. 5 vols. Grand Rapids: Zondervan, 1975.

All other commentaries on Revelation are referred to by the author's last name and *Rev*.

THE DRAMA OF THE AGES

"I am the alpha and the omega, says the Lord God, the one who is and the one who was and the one who is coming, the Almighty" (Rev. 1:8).

Imagine the beginning. The only thing in existence was God: Father, Son, and Holy Spirit. But it is not good to be alone (Gen. 2:18). God desired a bride for His Son. He would have to create one. But it must be a morally worthy one. That would require testing by evil. God created angelic beings of great power. The most beautiful of them became lifted up by pride and fell into sin. He became the adversary, the Devil (Rev. 12:7–12). God created mankind upon a beautiful earth, but the adversary tricked them into rebellion (Gen. 3:1–7). That would mean an age-long struggle of good versus evil, but God would win. The quest would be successful: the Son would seek and save the lost (Luke 19:10). The Son would sacrifice Himself for His bride (John 3:16). The billions and billions of people, redeemed by the blood of the Lamb, would become a suitable bride for the Son (Rev. 21:9). He has prepared a place for His bride (John 14:1–2). He will bring His bride into that place with rejoicing (Rev. 22:1–5). The spiral of the ages will come around, but on an infinitely higher plane.

Imagine the ending. "And his servants shall serve him: And they shall see his face: and his name shall be in their foreheads . . . and they shall reign for ever and ever" (Rev. 22:3–5). The drama of the ages turns out to be a divine comedy. It has a happy ending.

Medallion 1	Introduction	Revelation 1:1–8
Medallion 2	The Christ of Glory	Revelation 1:9–20
Medallion 3	The Seven Churches	Revelation 2:1–3:22
Medallion 4	The Throne in Glory	Revelation 4:1–514
Medallion 5	The Seven Seals	Revelation 6:1–9:11
Medallion 6	The Seven Trumpets	Revelation 8:2–11:19
Medallion 7	The Seven Persons	Revelation 12:1–13:18
Medallion 8	The Seven Bowls	Revelation 15:1–16:21
Medallion 9	Babylon • *The apostate church* • *The corrupt city*	Revelation 17:1–18:24
Medallion 10	The Second Coming in Glory • *Armageddon* • *Millenium Resurrection* • *Great White Throne* • *Gehenna*	Revelation 19:1–20:15
Medallion 11	The New Heaven and Earth	Revelation 21:1–22:5
Medallion 12	Conclusion: Worship God	Revelation 22:6–21

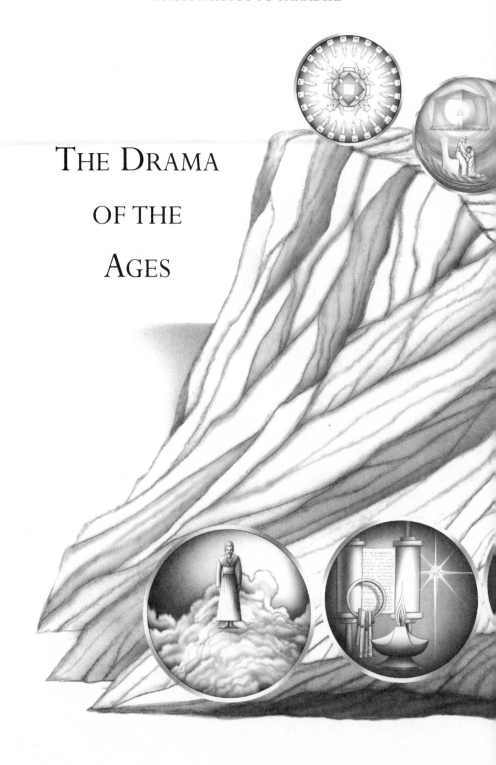

THE DRAMA

OF THE

AGES

Exposition of the
Book of Revelation

Revelation 1:1–8

Revelation 1:9–20

REVELATION 1

The Christ of Glory

Persons

Jesus Christ
  Titles:
    The faithful Witness
    First begotten of the dead
    Prince [Ruler] of the kings
      of the earth
    Alpha and Omega
    The Beginning and the
      Ending
    The First and the Last
    The Son of Man

God the Father
John the Apostle (author)
The sevenfold Spirit

Persons referred to

An angel
The readers

The dead
The kings of the earth

Places mentioned

Asia
Patmos
Ephesus
Smyrna
Pergamos

Thyatira
Sardis
Philadelphia
Laodicea

Doctrines taught

Revelation
The Word of God
Prophecy
Grace
Witness
Sin
The blood of Christ

The Second Coming
Tribulation
Seven golden lampstands
  (= seven churches)
Seven stars (= seven
    angels or messengers)
The resurrection of Christ

1

1 *The Revelation of Jesus Christ, which God gave unto him, to shew unto his servants things which must shortly come to pass; and he sent and signified it by his angel unto his servant John:*
2 *Who bare record of the word of God, and of the testimony of Jesus Christ, and of all things that he saw.*
3 *Blessed is he that readeth, and they that hear the words of this prophecy, and keep those things which are written therein: for the time is at hand.*

Revelation 1 Exposition

I. Introduction. vv. 1–3.

"The Revelation of Jesus Christ, which God gave to him to show to his slaves things which are necessary to come to pass quickly; and he sent officially and communicated by signs through his angel to his slave John" (v. 1). The purpose of the Book of Revelation is to show faithful believ-

---

1:1. "Revelation," or "Apocalypse," is a type of literature that is revealed by a heavenly person (angel, Christ Himself, etc.); it is filled with symbols of animals, human figures, numbers, colors that have spiritual meaning. There is a strong theme of determination: God knows and decrees the course of history. There is usually a cosmic struggle between good and evil, with the end coming at a final crisis with judgment for the wicked and vindication for the righteous. The books of Rev., Dan., and Zech. are biblical examples. Daniel frequently mentioned the power of God in revealing secrets (Dan. 2:19, 22, 28, 29, 30). When John referred to "things which are necessary to come to pass," he used the very idea Daniel conveyed to Nebuchadnezzar about God making known "what shall be in the latter days" (Dan. 2:28, 45). This eternal purpose of God is a major theme of Scripture (Isa. 14:24–27). It is a subject of great comfort to believers (Rom. 8:28–30; Eph. 1:9–12), but to the Devil and evil men, great despair (Rev. 20:10–15). The word God (θεός) occurs 97 times in Rev. Rev. is a God-centered book. It portrays the grand sweep of the ages in fulfilling God's purpose, from Creation (Rev. 4:11), to redemption (Rev. 5:9–10), to the consummation (Rev. 21:3–5). Bengel warns against those teachers who see spiritual truth in Rev. but reject its prophetic meaning. "We ought not to separate the things which God hath joined together, namely, the knowledge of future events, and therefore future times, and repentance, watchfulness, etc." (*Gnomon*, V, p. 183). See ZPEB, "Apocalyptic Literature," I, pp. 200–204; ISBE (1979), "Apocalyptic Literature," I, pp. 151–61; Elwell, Walter, *Evangelical Dictionary of Biblical Theology*, "Apocalyptic," pp. 28–30; Wilder, Amos N., "The Rhetoric of Ancient and Modern Apocalyptic," *Interpretation*, XXV, no. 4, Oct. 1971, pp. 436–53.

Angel (ἄγγελος) occurs 67 times in the Greek text of Rev. God granted the revelation to Jesus Christ, who sent His angel to John to impart it to believers. It is possible that 7 of those times refer to the human messengers of the churches. It is also possible that 2 of those contexts may refer to Christ manifesting Himself in angelic power (8:3–5; 10:1–5). There still remains a large amount of teaching on angelic ministration. Angels are clearly ministering spirits sent forth unto service of those who are about to inherit salvation (Heb. 1:14). Angels miraculously delivered the apostles from prison (Acts 5:19f.; 12:7ff.). Seven angels will pour out the final bowls of wrath on the earth (Rev. 16:1–17).

ers future events. The apostle John was the disciple that Jesus loved, who leaned on His breast at the Last Supper (John 13:23). Now he has been exiled for preaching the Word of God and may have felt that he was "laid on the shelf." But the Lord Jesus manifested to him the infinite love that He has for His faithful slave. It is not by accident that the two greatest prophetic revelations came to men who were exiled and were "greatly beloved" (Dan. 9:23). Both Daniel and John had the "servant's heart." The revelation was the "unveiling" of the Lord Jesus Christ. F. C. Jennings noted that the key to the book is not the church but the Lord Jesus Christ Himself (*Studies in Rev.*, pp. 18–19). In this book He is the person who is revealed in all His glory, but He is also the one who imparted the revelation to John, "His slave." The word *slave* should not be weakened. It was common in the ancient world for a person to sell himself into slavery in a pagan temple to serve an idol. John has given himself in willing service to the Lord of the universe. It was this John "who witnessed to the word

---

Angels are going to come with the Lord when He returns in glory (Matt. 16:27; II Thess. 1:7; Rev. 19:14). See also Rev. 4:6 note. See ZPEB, "Angel," I, pp. 160–66; ISBE (1979), "Angel," I, pp. 124–27; Elwell, Walter, *Evangelical Dictionary of Biblical Theology*, "Angel," pp. 21–23; Ryken, Wilhoit, and Longman, *Dictionary of Biblical Imagery*, "Angel," pp. 23–25.

The key verb *to show* (δείκνυμι) occurs 8 times in Rev. (1:1; 4:1; 17:1; 21:9, 10; 22:1, 6, 8).

Slave (δοῦλος) occurs 14 times in Rev.

1. To show His slaves what must come to pass. 1:1.
2. To His slave John. 1:1.
3. To seduce my slaves to commit fornication. 2:20.
4. Every slave and every free man hid themselves. 6:15.
5. Until we have sealed the slaves of our God. 7:3.
6. He has declared to His slaves the prophets. 10:7.
7. To give reward to Thy slaves the prophets. 11:18.
8. He causes all . . . free men and slaves, to receive a mark. 13:16.
9. They sing the song of Moses, the slave of God. 15:3.
10. He avenged the blood of His slaves at her hand. 19:2.
11. Praise our God, all ye His slaves. 19:5.
12. Birds may eat the flesh of all men, free and slave. 19:18.
13. His slaves shall serve Him. 22:3.
14. He sent His angel to show His slaves the things necessary. 22:6.

The idea *slaves of God* has no thought of coercion, but willing submission and ownership. The reader must put himself back into the culture of the first-century world to understand Rev. Paul argues that all men are either slaves of God or of sin (Rom. 6:15–23). See Ryken, Wilhoit, and Longman, *Dictionary of Biblical Imagery*, "Slave, Slavery," pp. 797–99.

The idea that Christ will come *quickly* occurs 8 times in Rev. (ἐν τάχει, 1:1; 22:6; ταχύ, 2:16; 3:11; 11:14; 22:7, 12, 20).

There are 8 things said *to be necessary* (δεῖ) in Rev. (1:1; 4:1; 10:11; 11:5; 13:10; 17:10; 20:3; 22:6).

of God, and the witness of Jesus Christ and of as many things as he saw" (v. 2). John had borne apostolic witness to the Lord Jesus (Acts 3:1–11) and had been persecuted for it (Acts 4:13). He would hold back nothing of the great revelation that came to him. Revelation is the only book in the Bible that pronounces a special blessing on the reader: "Blessed is the one who reads and they who hear the words of this prophecy and continue keeping the things written in it, for the time is near" (v. 3). In the ancient world, books were expensive and not everyone had a Bible. The scene presupposed is that of a reader in the church who reads to the congregation the precious scroll and of the people who hear, fervently vowing to continue obeying the divine revelation. Every believer should be conscious of the immense blessing and privilege of reading and hearing God's Word. The psalmist has well said, "I will delight myself in thy commandments, which I have loved" (Ps. 119:47). But John remembered that the Israelites who heard Moses read the law promised to do and obey it but did not (Exod. 24:7). Matthew Henry notes that the blessing encourages us to study the book, but far more important is the keeping of the things written in it. "This is the final message of heaven to man" (A. B. Simpson, *Rev.*, p. 9).

1:2. *Witness* (μαρτυρία) occurs 9 times in Rev. It always refers the true witness to Jesus (1:2, 9; 6:9; 11:7; 12:11, 17; 19:10 [twice]; 20:4). John keeps testifying, "I saw" (εἶδον), 46 times in Rev. (1:12, 17; 4:1; 5:1, 2, 6, 11, etc.).

The phrase *word of God* occurs 5 times in Rev. (1:2, 9; 6:9; 19:13; 20:4). In the plural *words* or *sayings* occurs 9 times (17:17; 19:9; 21:5; 22:6, 7, 9, 10, 18, 19), always referring to words of God.

1:3. The word *blessed* (μακάριος, "spiritually happy") denotes "a state of true well-being" (Moulton and Milligan, *Vocabulary*, p. 386). It occurs 7 times in Rev.

1. Blessed are those who read and hear the words of this prophecy. 1:3.
2. Blessed are the dead who die in the Lord. 14:13.
3. Blessed is he that watches and keeps his garments. 16:15.
4. Blessed are those called to the marriage supper of the Lamb. 19:9.
5. Blessed and holy is he that has part in the first resurrection. 20:6.
6. Blessed is he that keeps the sayings of the prophecy of this book. 22:7.
7. Blessed are they that do His commandments. 22:14.

See Ryken, Wilhoit, and Longman, *Dictionary of Biblical Imagery*, "Blessing, Blessedness," pp. 98–99; ISBE (1979), "Bless," I, pp. 523–24; ZPEB, "Bless, Blessing," I, pp. 625–26.

For examples in the papyri of the meaning *read aloud* (ἀναγινώσκω), see Moulton and Milligan, *Vocabulary*, p. 31.

Keeping (τηρέω) God's commands is an important theme in Rev. (1:3; 2:26; 3:3, 8, 10; 12:17; 14:12; 16:15; 22:7, 9). It is also found in John 8:51–52; 14:15, 21, 23, 24; 15:10, etc., and in I John 2:3–5; 3:22, 24, etc. "He that expects to understand what is written must enter upon the study with sincere purpose of heart to keep what is revealed" (Ford Ottman, *The Unfolding of the Ages*, p. 4).

*4 John to the seven churches which are in Asia: Grace be unto you, and peace,
from him which is, and which was, and which is to come; and from the seven Spirits
which are before his throne;*

*5 And from Jesus Christ, who is the faithful witness, and the first begotten of the
dead, and the prince of the kings of the earth. Unto him that loved us, and washed us
from our sins in his own blood,*

*6 And hath made us kings and priests unto God and his Father; to him be glory and
dominion for ever and ever. Amen.*

*7 Behold, he cometh with clouds; and every eye shall see him, and they also which
pierced him: and all kindreds of the earth shall wail because of him. Even so, Amen.*

*8 I am Alpha and Omega, the beginning and the ending, saith the Lord, which is,
and which was, and which is to come, the Almighty.*

II. The Address. vv. 4–8.

"John to the seven churches which are in Asia; grace to you and peace
from the one who is, and the one who was, and the one who is coming,
and from the seven spirits which are before his throne" (v. 4). John calls
his work a *revelation* (apocalypse, ἀποκάλυψις, v. 1), a *prophecy* dealing
with the future (v. 3), and now addresses seven churches in Asia Minor,
demonstrating that it is a *letter* to specific congregations. The conclusion
of Revelation adds three more categories: It is a book of blessing (Rev.
22:7), a book of responsibility for men and angels (Rev. 22:8–9), and
God's final message to the church (Rev. 22:18–19). Plainly, Revelation is
a very complex work. All interpretations that try to reduce it to one thing
are doomed to failure. John prays grace and peace to these congregations
from the triune God. "The one who is and the one who was, and the one
who is coming" is a clear reference to God the Father, the eternal God

---

1:4. The *church* (ἐκκλησία) is mentioned 19 times in the first 3 chapters but only once
afterwards (22:16). This is one of the arguments for the doctrine of the Rapture at 4:1
(Walvoord, *Rev.*, p. 103).

Asia does not refer to the continent but to the Roman province of Asia, which was in
what is now southwestern Turkey.

The threefold formula "the one who is, and who was, and who is to come" occurs 4 times
in Rev. (1:4, 8; 4:8; 11:17). The doctrine of the Trinity (one God in three Persons) is
taught throughout Rev. (1:4–5; 22:1, 16–17).

Throne (θρόνος) is a symbol of authority and power. The word occurs 47 times in Rev.
(76 percent of all NT occurrences). It occurs in reference to God's throne 39 times in
Rev. but only 10 times in the rest of the NT. It also refers to the throne of Satan or the
Beast 3 times (2:13; 13:2; 16:10) and to the thrones of the elders or saints 3 times (4:4;
11:16; 20:4). God's throne is one of holiness (Ps. 47:8) and staggering glory (Rev. 4:2–3;
Isa. 6:1; Ezek. 1:26–28). It is a constant reminder in Rev. of the majestic sovereignty of
God, the Lord of all (Rev. 1:4; 3:21; 4:2–10; 5:1–13; 6:16; 7:9ff.; etc.). See Ryken,
Wilhoit, and Longman, *Dictionary of Biblical Imagery*, "Throne," pp. 868–69; ISBE (1988),
"Throne," IV, pp. 844–45; ZPEB, "Throne," V, pp. 740–41.

(Deut. 33:27), the everlasting God (Gen. 21:33). "The one who is" is the exact Greek phrase of Exodus 3:14 LXX. Jehovah is "a true and faithful witness" (Jer. 42:5). The seven Spirits who are before the throne is a reference to the sevenfold Holy Spirit (Isa. 11:2; Zech. 4:2, 10). "The position of these seven spirits between the Eternal Father and the glorified Christ is unsuitable even for the highest of created spirits in a salutation which is in fact a benediction" (H. B. Swete, *The Holy Spirit in the New Testament*, p. 273). See also "Pneumatology in the Book of Revelation" in Mal Couch, *A Bible Handbook to Rev.*, pp. 114–21. It is significant that the third phrase is not a simple future of *to be* but is "the one who is coming." This concentrates attention on the Second Advent and the love that God has for His people (John 14:2–3). "And from Jesus Christ, the faithful witness, the firstborn from the dead, and the ruler of the kings of the earth. To the one who loved us and loosed us from our sins in his blood" (v. 5). The benediction comes equally from Jesus Christ (v. 5). His deity is assumed,

---

1:5. The great word *faithful* (πιστός) occurs 8 times in Rev. (1:5; 2:10, 13; 3:14; 17:14; 19:11; 21:5; 22:6). It is an attribute of God (I Cor. 10:13). *Faithful witness* is found in Ps. 89:37; Prov. 14:5; Jer. 42:5.

The title *First Begotten* (πρωτότοκος) occurs only here in Rev. It occurs 7 other times in the NT (Luke 2:7; Rom. 8:29; Col. 1:15, 18; Heb. 1:6; 11:28; 12:23).

The word *king* (βασιλεύς) occurs 19 times in Rev.

The word *earth* (γῆ) occurs 82 times in Rev. (a third of all NT references). The basic question in Rev. is who shall rule the earth: Christ, the rightful King; the Dragon, the usurper; or man, who reaches for dominion instead of service.

The verb *to love* (ἀγαπάω) occurs 4 times in Rev. (1:5; 3:9; 12:11; 20:9).

The word *blood* (αἷμα) occurs 19 times in Rev. (1:5; 5:9; 6:10, 12; 7:14; 8:7, 8; 11:6; 12:11; 14:20; 16:3, 4, 6 [twice]; 17:6 [twice]; 18:24; 19:2, 13).

The word *sin* (ἁμαρτία) occurs 3 times in Rev. (1:5; 18:4, 5). The word means literally *missing the mark*. Forgiveness of sin can be found only in Christ (John 1:29). See "Harmartiology in the Book of Revelation" in Mal Couch, *A Bible Handbook to Revelation*, pp. 142–49; Ryken, Wilhoit, and Longman, *Dictionary of Biblical Imagery*, "Sin," pp. 792–93; ZPEB, "Sin," "Sinner," V, pp. 544–47; ISBE (1988), "Sin," IV, pp. 518–25.

We know from the Qumran discoveries that a reader read from the sacred scroll to a roomful of scribes. Once in a while a scribe "heard" a different word from what other scribes heard. The word *loose* (λύω) is very close to the word *wash* (λούω) in pronunciation. Some Greek manuscripts have one word and others have the other. *Loosed* is the reading in P[18], ℵ, A, C, 1611, and other early manuscripts; *washed* is the reading in most later manuscripts. Both ideas are biblically orthodox: wash (Ps. 51:2, 7); loose (Ps. 130:7–8, which is Ps. 129:7–8 LXX; Isa. 40:2 LXX). Both should be treated with respect and not twisted into a truth vs. heresy conflict. Both readings were produced by devout men who were earnestly trying not to make a mistake. But our best efforts are still dogged with slips of the pen (or keyboard)! The doctrine of verbal inspiration is that God imparted His Word to inspired prophets perfectly (Ps. 19:7–9; II Tim. 3:16–17).

not argued. John has already explained that in his Gospel (John 1:1; 8:58; 17:3, 24). Jesus is the faithful witness (μάρτυς, the one who did seal His testimony with His blood, John 8:18; 18:37). He is the firstborn from among the dead, not merely the first to rise but rather the one who has the right of the firstborn over all who will rise from the dead. He is also the ruler of the kings of the earth. The KJV "prince" might be interpreted as one who is less than a king, but the meaning is plainly that He is a King over all other kings, a mighty Emperor over all who exist, "higher than the kings of the earth," even as Psalm 89:27 prophesied of Messiah. Although the kings of the earth set themselves against Him in the days of His earthly humility (Ps. 2:2), He shall yet reign over them all. "Throughout the whole book no theme is more strongly insisted upon than the triumph of God" (Morris, *The Cross in the New Testament*, p. 354). The Lord Jesus is the one who "loves us and loosed us from our sins in his blood" (v. 5). This is exactly what is prophesied that Jehovah shall do for Israel (Ps. 130:7–8; Ps. 129:7–8 LXX; Isa. 40:2 LXX, "her sin has been loosed"). This is the first mention of *blood* (αἷμα), one of the major themes in Revelation (occurring nineteen times). Ironside calls attention to the present tense verb "loves us" and observes "His love is unchanging and eternal" (*The Continual Burnt Offering*, Dec. 26). "And has made us a kingdom, priests to God and His Father, to whom be the glory and the power into the ages of the ages, Amen" (v. 6). It is not accidental that he

---

Although the fate of an individual scroll might be in jeopardy, God has seen to it that His Word is divinely preserved (Jer. 36:1–32). It does not mean that all copies or translations of the Bible are perfect.

1:6. *Kingdom* (βασιλεία) occurs 10 times in Rev. Five times it refers to the kingdom of God (1:6, 9; 5:10; 11:15; 12:10), and 5 times it refers to the kingdom of the world or the "beast" (11:15; 16:10; 17:12, 17, 18). God has always ruled as King (Ps. 93:2); "the Lord is King forever and ever" (Ps. 10:16). Daniel prophesied that in the days of the fourth kingdom "the God of heaven shall set up a kingdom, which shall never be destroyed" (Dan. 2:44). The Lord Jesus portrayed the coming kingdom as a great wedding feast (Matt. 22:2–14), but He made clear that He will determine who will enter that kingdom and who will not (Matt. 25:31–46). See "Kingdom of God," ZPEB, III, pp. 801–9; "Kingdom of God," ISBE (1986), III, pp. 23–29; "Kingdom of God," Ryken, Wilhoit, and Longman, *Dictionary of Biblical Imagery*, pp. 478–81; "Kingdom of God," *Baker's Dictionary of Theology*, pp. 309–14; "Kingdom of God," Elwell, Walter, *Evangelical Dictionary of Biblical Theology*, pp. 451–54.

The word *glory* (δόξα) occurs 17 times in Rev. (1:6; 4:9, 11; 5:12, 13; 7:12; 11:13; 14:7; 15:8; 16:9; 18:1; 19:1, 7; 21:11, 23, 24, 26).

The idea of worship and praise to God appears throughout Rev. (1:6; 4:8–11; 5:8–10, 12–13; 7:12; 11:15–18; 12:10–12; 15:3–4; 19:1–8; 22:3).

1:6–7. The word *amen, so be it* (ἀμήν), occurs 9 times in Rev. (1:6, 7; 3:14; 5:14; 7:12 [twice]; 19:4; 22:20, 21). It is a word that "carries the weight of approval, confirmation, and support of what is said or sung" ("Amen," ZPEB, I, p. 127).

refers first to the redemptive sacrifice of Christ and then to the kingdom that God is establishing. This was God's purpose for His ancient people: "Ye shall be unto me a kingdom of priests, and an holy nation" (Exod. 19:6). Now He has constituted the church a kingdom, a manifestation of His rule over people, and individually we are priests to God. "Each member of this true kingdom is a priest unto God, with direct access to him at all times" (Robertson, *Word Pictures*, VI, p. 287). The apostle Peter has made the priesthood of believers very clear: "You are . . . a holy priesthood" (I Pet. 2:5, 9). Hebrews exhorts us, "Let us offer the sacrifice of praise to God continually" (Heb. 13:15). "Behold, he is coming with the clouds, and every eye shall see him, and those who pierced him; and all the tribes of earth shall mourn for him, truly, Amen" (v. 7). This is a quotation woven together from Daniel 7:13 and Zechariah 12:10, 12. Daniel saw the four world empires as vicious beasts end in a scene of judgment (Dan. 7:2–12). After the destruction of the empires, Daniel saw "one like the Son of man" receive the eternal kingdom of God with universal dominion over mankind (7:13–14). The word *tribes* (KJV *kindreds*) refers dominatingly to the tribes of Israel, both in Zechariah and in Revelation (7:4–8). John refers to a national repentance and conversion of Israel, as does the apostle Paul (Rom. 11:25–26). Spurgeon stresses the literal nature of the appearing of Christ in an eloquent sermon, "He Cometh with Clouds," (Sermon 1989, *The C. H. Spurgeon Collection*, Ages Digital Library). The blessed hope for believers is that the Lord Jesus will come for them. John then hears the voice of God identifying Himself. "I am Alpha and Omega, says the Lord God, the one who is, and the one who was, and the one who is coming, the Almighty" (v. 8). *God's Word to the Nations* translates it "I am the A and the Z, says the Lord God" (p. 1542). The first and last letters of the Greek alphabet tell us that God is the

---

1:7. The regular verb *to come* (ἔρχομαι) is used of the Lord's Second Coming 9 times in Rev. (1:7; 2:5, 16; 3:11; 16:15; 22:7, 12, 20 [twice]).

The word *cloud* (νεφέλη) occurs 7 times in Rev. (1:7; 10:1; 11:12; 14:14 [twice], 15, 16), in each case manifesting heavenly glory.

The verb *pierced* (ἐκκεντέω) occurs only twice in the NT, both by John (here and in John 19:37), both referring to Christ's crucifixion.

1:8. The word *Almighty* (Παντοκράτωρ) occurs 9 times in Rev.

1. The Lord God is the Almighty. 1:8.
2. The 4 living beings say: Holy, holy, holy, Lord God Almighty. 4:8.
3. The 24 elders say: We give thee thanks, O Lord God Almighty. 11:17.
4. The victors over the beast sing: Great are thy works, Lord God Almighty. 15:3.
5. The voice from the altar: Even so, Lord God Almighty. 16:7.
6. The battle of that great day of God Almighty. 16:14.
7. The great multitude: Alleluia: for the Lord God Almighty reigns. 19:6.

*9 I John, who also am your brother, and companion in tribulation, and in the king-
dom and patience of Jesus Christ, was in the isle that is called Patmos, for the word of
God, and for the testimony of Jesus Christ.*
*10 I was in the Spirit on the Lord's day, and heard behind me a great voice, as of a
trumpet,*
*11 Saying, I am Alpha and Omega, the first and the last: and, What thou seest,
write in a book, and send it unto the seven churches which are in Asia; unto Ephesus,
and unto Smyrna, and unto Pergamos, and unto Thyatira, and unto Sardis, and unto
Philadelphia, and unto Laodicea.*

beginning and the end, the originator and consummator of all that exists.
He is the Lord, the Jehovah of the Old Testament, the I AM (Exod. 3:14),
who has always existed and always will exist. He is the first and the last
(Isa. 41:4). He is "the Almighty," who revealed Himself to Abraham
(Gen. 17:1), whose power maintains the host of heaven (Isa. 40:26), of
whom the psalmist says, "Great is our Lord, and of great power" (Ps. 147:5).
"Revelation is the final word on the establishment of the *kingdom of God*"
(Tenney, *Interpreting Rev.*, p. 30).

III. The Experience. vv. 9–11.

John now refers to himself in order to explain how he had received this
great revelation. "I John, your brother and companion in tribulation and
kingdom and patience in Jesus, was in the island that is called Patmos on
account of the word of God and the witness of Jesus" (v. 9). When he

---

8. The winepress of the wrath of Almighty God. 19:15.
9. The Lord God Almighty and the Lamb are the temple of it. 21:22.

In the rest of the NT it occurs only in II Cor. 6:18. In the Greek OT it translates "God of
hosts" (*armies*, Hos. 12:6 [KJV 12:5]; Amos 3:13 LXX). It denotes "not One who can do
anything, but One who holds together and controls all things" (Hort, *Apocalypse of St.
John*, 1:8). See ZPEB, "Almighty," I, p. 108; ISBE (1982), "God, Names of," p. 506.

1:9. *Tribulation* (θλῖψις) occurs 5 times in Rev. (1:9; 2:9, 10, 22; 7:14).

Patience (ὑπομονή), "steadfast endurance," occurs 7 times in Rev.

1. John, our companion in the patience of Jesus Christ. 1:9.
2. To the church of Ephesus: I know . . . thy patience. 2:2.
3. You have patience. 2:3.
4. To the church in Thyatira: I know . . . thy patience. 2:19.
5. To the church of Philadelphia: Because thou hast kept the word of my patience.
   3:10.
6. On nonviolence: Here is the patience and faith of the saints. 13:10.
7. Resisting the mark of Antichrist: here is the patience of the saints. 14:12.

The idea of patient endurance is also found in Rev. 16:15; 17:14; 20:4; 22:7, 11, 14.

Paul prays that believers might be "strengthened with all might . . . unto all patience and
longsuffering with joyfulness" (Col. 1:11).

refs to himself as "I John," he is using the same language that Daniel did three times in his prophecy ("I Daniel," Dan. 7:15; 8:15; 9:2). Although he had apostolic authority, John refers to himself humbly as "your brother and companion." There are three things that all believers will share: tribulation (II Cor. 1:4), the kingdom (Luke 12:32), and the need for patience (Heb. 10:36). To modern readers the island Patmos conjures up images of the beautiful Greek islands, but in the ancient world it had more of the connotation that Siberia had under the rule of Stalin. It was a place where political undesirables were exiled. But John was not sent there for a crime but for his faithfulness to the Word of God and his witness for Jesus. Spurgeon stressed that John "could claim Christ as being dear to him, the companion of his life, the friend of his days. May the Lord teach us more and more how to walk with Jesus and to know his love!" (Sermon 357, "The Christ of Patmos," *The C. H. Spurgeon Collection*, Ages Digital Library). "I was in the Spirit on the Lord's day, and heard behind me a great voice, as of a trumpet" (v. 10). There is a plaintive thought behind "the Lord's day." John was in lonely exile, far from the churches that were on his heart, far from the "little children" he longed to minister to (I John 2:1), but the Lord came to him to bless his soul and to fill him with His Spirit and to impart to him a revelation that would bless God's people to the end of time. On the theological implications of the title *Lord* applied to Christ, see Warfield,

---

Patmos is a small island in the Aegean Sea about 35 miles southwest of Miletus. It extends 10 miles north and south and 6 miles east and west. Eusebius records that John was exiled to Patmos in the 14th year of Domitian (A.D. 95) and later returned to Ephesus (*Ecclesiastical History*, iii, 18–20). For historical background see ZPEB, IV, pp. 619–20; ISBE (1986), III, p. 690 and color plate 61. The *Holman Bible Dictionary* has a color plate of Patmos (p. 1078). Rev. is the only NT book in which the author states the place of writing.

1:10. John is absolutely sure of the authority of the revelation he received. He deliberately repeats the word "I heard" (ἤκουσα) 27 times in Rev. (1:10; 4:1; 5:11, 13; 6:1, 3, 5, 6, 7; 7:4; 8:13; 9:13, 16; 10:4, 8; 12:10; 14:2 [twice], 13; 16:1, 5, 7; 18:4; 19:1, 6; 21:3; 22:8). He is not imagining things; he is listening to the voice of God. Scholars may criticize his claims (Greg Carey, *Elusive Apocalypse: Reading Authority in the Revelation of John*), but all recognize that he does claim it.

J. B. Smith argues that *the Lord's day* refers to the future *day of the Lord*, the prophetic period of God's judgment on the earth (Joel 2:1ff.; *Rev.*, pp. 319–24). Adolph Deissmann proved (*Light from the Ancient East*, p. 357) that the word *lord's* (κυριακῇ) was a regular term for "belonging to the lord Caesar." "The lord's day" would have meant to a Roman an *Imperial holiday*, but here John is claiming the term for the Lord of the universe, Jesus Christ.

Trumpet (σάλπιγξ) is mentioned 6 times in Rev. (1:10; 4:1; 8:2, 6, 13; 9:14). The verb, *to sound a trumpet* (σαλπίζω), is mentioned 10 times (8:6, 7, 8, 10, 12, 13; 9:1, 13; 10:7; 11:15).

12 And I turned to see the voice that spake with me. And being turned, I saw seven golden candlesticks;
13 And in the midst of the seven candlesticks one like unto the Son of man, clothed with a garment down to the foot, and girt about the paps with a golden girdle.
14 His head and his hairs were white like wool, as white as snow; and his eyes were as a flame of fire;
15 And his feet like unto fine brass, as if they burned in a furnace; and his voice as the sound of many waters.
16 And he had in his right hand seven stars: and out of his mouth went a sharp twoedged sword: and his countenance was as the sun shineth in his strength.

The Lord of Glory, pp. 288ff. John heard a great voice, as of a trumpet, one of the most penetrating sounds possible. The words *behind me* show the "unexpected, overpowering entrance of the divine voice" (Vincent, *Word Studies*, II, p. 424). The divine voice said, "What you see write in a book and send it to the seven churches, to Ephesus, and to Smyrna, and to Pergamos, and to Thyatira, and to Sardis, and to Philadelphia, and to Laodicea" (v. 11). They were seven literal cities in Asia Minor, what is now southwestern Turkey. God has directed man's attention to books from earliest times (Gen. 5:1; Exod. 17:14; 24:7; Deut. 17:18; Josh. 1:8). All believers have a continuing responsibility to search the Scriptures (John 5:39). These seven letters not only met the needs of those first-century churches but also continue to meet the needs of all churches and individual believers in them to the end of the age.

IV. The Vision of the Christ of Glory. vv. 12–16.

John records, "And I turned to see the voice which was speaking with me, and having turned, I saw seven golden lampstands" (v. 12). He turned to see the person but saw the symbol of the sustaining power of God. The golden lampstand was prophesied by Zechariah (4:1–2), who saw the golden lampstand with a bowl on top and two olive trees, one on each side. The olives fell into the bowl; the oil went through pipes into the seven lamps, and they burned, entirely untouched by man! The

---

1:11. John is commanded to write (γράψον) 12 times in Rev. (1:11, 19; 2:1, 8, 12, 18; 3:1, 7, 14; 14:13; 19:9; 21:5).

A *little book* (βιβλίον) is mentioned 23 times in Rev. (1:11; 5:1–5, etc.).

1:12. *Lampstand* (λυχνία) occurs 7 times in Rev. (1:12, 13, 20 [twice]; 2:1, 5; 11:4). Moulton and Milligan, *Vocabulary*, p. 383, note that the spelling is found as early as 284 B.C. in the papyri (Classical Greek had λυχνεῖον).

John uses the word *I saw* (εἶδον) as a minor section break between visions throughout Rev. (4:1; 5:1; 6:1, 2, 5, 8, 9, 12; 7:1, 2, 9; 8:2; 9:1; 10:1; 13:1; 14:1, 6, 14; 15:1, 2, 5; 16:13; 17:3, 6; 18:1; 19:11, 17, 19; 20:1, 4, 11, 12; 21:1, 2, 22).

message is that God will supernaturally sustain His people. Thus, His message was "not by might, nor by power, but by my spirit, saith the Lord of hosts" (Zech. 4:6). He will sustain Zerubbabel and He will sustain His church. The tabernacle also had seven lamps (Exod. 25:37). "And in the midst of the lampstands one like the Son of man, clothed with a robe reaching the feet, and girded about the breast with a golden sash" (v. 13). The Lord Jesus promised, "Where two or three are gathered together in my name, there am I in the midst of them" (Matt. 18:20). On the evening of that first Easter day the disciples were huddled together in the Upper Room and Jesus came and stood in the midst and pronounced peace upon them (John 20:19). Harry Ironside observed that the Lord Jesus deserves that central place in every church and in every believer's heart (*Lectures on the Book of Revelation*, p. 28). The Lord Jesus taught that the Father had given Him authority to execute judgment because He was the Son of man (John 5:27). In contrast to the humble clothing the Lord wore on earth, He wears the majestic royal robe of the King of the universe, Lord and High Priest of the church. The golden sash may well symbolize the authority of judgment, for the only other beings who have such a sash are the seven angels of judgment (Rev. 15:6). The title "Son of man" comes from Daniel's vision of "one like the Son of man who came with the clouds of heaven . . . and there was given him dominion, and glory, and a kingdom, that all people, nations, and languages, should serve him" (Dan. 7:13–14). Donald Guthrie argues that Daniel 7 is "the sole pre-Christian source" of the title (*New Testament Theology*, p. 273). "And his head and his hairs were white as wool, white as snow, and his eyes were as a flame of fire" (v. 14). In Daniel 7:9 it was the Ancient of days whose hair was like pure wool. Thus, ideas of deity, holiness, and eternity are involved. Jennings observes that the wisdom of eternity crowns Him (*Studies in Rev.*, p. 40). "Eyes like a flame of fire" implies omniscience. He can see through to the reality of all men and things. Daniel saw "his eyes as lamps of fire" (Dan. 10:6). David knew that God saw him before he was born (Ps. 139:16). "And his feet were like fine bronze as if they had been burned in a furnace, and his voice as the

---

1:13. *Son of man* is applied twice to Christ in Rev. (1:13; 14:14). It is the dominant title He used for Himself in the Gospels (Matt. 8:20; 9:6; 12:8; 13:37; etc.).

The word *man* (ἄνθρωπος) occurs here for the first of 25 times in Rev. (Greek).

1:14. The adjective *white* (λευκός) occurs 15 times in Rev. with the meaning of "purity, holiness" (1:14 [twice]; 2:17; 3:4, 5, 18; 4:4; 6:11; 7:9, 13; 14:14; 19:11, 14 [twice]; 20:11), and once as a counterfeit (6:2).

The word *fire* (πῦρ) occurs 26 times in Rev. Here it refers to the penetrating gaze of the omniscient Son of God, as it does in Rev. 2:18. For fire connected with judgment, see note 8:5, 7, 8.

sound of many waters" (v. 15). Although John had seen the Lord's feet covered with dust from long hikes (John 4:6; cf. Luke 7:38), now he sees the Lord's feet shining like molten bronze. A similar expression is found in the description of the feet of the four living beings in Ezekiel (1:7 LXX), but it is not the same word. A glow so bright that it is hard to look at is plainly the idea. The sound of His voice impressed John as the thunder of surf or the crash of a mighty waterfall. The sound of the wings of the living creatures reminded Ezekiel of the sound of great waters (Ezek. 1:24). "And he was having in his right hand seven stars, and out of his mouth was going a sharp two-edged sword, and his face was as the sun shining in its power" (v. 16). Isaiah declared that the Lord had made his mouth like a "sharp sword" (Isa. 49:2). The verbs change to participles here, stressing the continuous action: He is constantly having in His hand the seven stars and the sword is constantly proceeding from His mouth. The seven stars are identified as the seven messengers (or angels) of the churches (v. 20). Guthrie observes that "no reader can fail to be struck by the tremendous dignity of the account" (*The Relevance of John's Apocalypse*, p. 40).

1:15. The word translated "fine brass" in the KJV (χαλκολίβανον) is found only here and in 2:18 in the Bible, and elsewhere only in writers acquainted with this passage. (See Arndt and Gingrich, p. 883). Since brass (an alloy of copper and zinc) was discovered only by the late Roman empire (3rd cent. A.D.), it is better to think of it as bronze (an alloy of copper and tin). It could be a unique combination of gold and copper. For a careful discussion of the possibilities, see H. B. Swete, *Rev.*, pp. 17–18. The idea in context is certainly the bright glow of molten metal.

1:16. *Stars* (ἀστήρ) are mentioned 14 times in Rev. (1:16, 20 [twice]; 2:1, 28; 3:1; 6:13; 8:10, 11, 12; 9:1; 12:1, 4; 22:16). "Virtually all the biblical star motifs converge in the book of Revelation" (Ryken, Wilhoit, and Longman, *Dictionary of Biblical Imagery*, p. 813).

The *sun* (ἥλιος) is mentioned here for the first of 13 times in Rev. (1:16; 6:12; 7:2, 16; 8:12; 9:2; 10:1; 12:1; 16:8, 12; 19:17; 21:23; 22:5). The last reference is that the sun is not needed in the celestial city because God is there (Rev. 22:5). See Ryken, Wilhoit, and Longman, *Dictionary of Biblical Imagery*, "Sun," p. 827.

The *sharp, two-edged sword* (ῥομφαία) was the great broadsword of the ancient world. It is used once as a symbol of war and violence (6:8) and 5 times as a symbol of the Lord's word of judgment (1:16; 2:12, 16; 19:15, 21). It will ultimately destroy the armies of Antichrist (19:21). It is to be distinguished from the short Roman sword (μάχαιρα), which is a symbol of the power of the empire of the Beast (6:4; 13:10, 14). See Custer, *A Treasury of New Testament Synonyms*, pp. 69–71.

The verb *to shine* (φαίνω) occurs 4 times in Rev. (1:16; 8:12; 18:23; 21:23).

17 And when I saw him, I fell at his feet as dead. And he laid his right hand upon me, saying unto me, Fear not; I am the first and the last:
18 I am he that liveth, and was dead; and, behold, I am alive for evermore, Amen; and have the keys of hell and of death.
19 Write the things which thou hast seen, and the things which are, and the things which shall be hereafter;
20 The mystery of the seven stars which thou sawest in my right hand, and the seven golden candlesticks. The seven stars are the angels of the seven churches: and the seven candlesticks which thou sawest are the seven churches.

V. The Commission. vv. 17–20.

"And when I saw him, I fell at his feet as dead. And he put his right hand upon me, saying, Fear not; I am the First and the Last" (v. 17). The sight of the divine glory is more than an unglorified human being can bear. When Ezekiel saw the glory of the Lord, he fell on his face (Ezek. 1:28). Paul was struck blind on the Damascus road (Acts 9:3–8). Jehovah declared Himself to be the first and the last (Isa. 44:6). The Lord reaches out in compassion to reassure John by saying literally, "Stop fearing." John gives another of the many "I am" statements of the Lord. The Lord has always existed and always will exist. He is changeless in His love for His people. "And [I am] the living one, and I was dead and behold I am living into the ages of the ages, and I have the keys of death and of hades" (v. 18). God promised Eliakim the key of the house of David (Isa. 22:20–22). Here Christ claims the divine title the Living One as His own (Warfield, *The Lord of Glory*, p. 295). God is the "living God"

1:17. For a summary on the verb *to fear* (φοβέομαι), see Rev. 11:18 note.

Kendal Easley notes that Jesus was a Palestinian Jew and therefore "probably had olive skin . . . dark brown eyes . . . black hair and a beard" but that there is little spiritual benefit in such imaginations. But he urges that there is great spiritual benefit in noting what Rev. says of Him, "He stands among the churches, present with His people . . . His robe and golden sash symbolize His role as our High Priest . . . His blazing eyes suggest His presence everywhere at all times" (*Living with the End in Sight*, p. 3).

1:18. The verb *I live* (ζάω) manifests an attribute of the eternal God. He is "the Living One." It occurs 13 times in Rev. (1:18 [twice]; 2:8; 3:1; 4:9, 10; 7:2; 10:6; 13:14; 15:7; 19:20; 20:4, 5). The *living beings* (ζῷα) are powerful archangelic beings, closest to the throne of God (4:6–9, etc.).

The word *key* (κλείς) occurs 4 times in Rev. Twice it symbolizes the authority that the Lord Jesus has: "the keys of death and of hades" (1:18) and "the key of David" (3:7). Twice it refers to delegated authority over the Abyss, the bottomless pit (9:1; 20:1).

The word *death* (θάνατος) occurs 19 times in Rev. (1:18; 2:10, 11, 23; 6:8 [twice]; 9:6 [twice]; 12:11; 13:3 [twice], 12; 18:8; 20:6, 13, 14 [twice]; 21:4, 8).

The word *hades* (ᾅδης) occurs 4 times in Rev. (1:18; 6:8; 20:13, 14). For a summary see Rev. 20:13–14 note.

(Rev. 7:2; Ps. 42:2). All other "gods" are dead idols. Ironside argues that to proclaim the death of Christ is not enough. "It is the resurrection that tells us that His propitiation has been accepted, and God can now justify all who put their trust in Him" (*The Continual Burnt Offering*, Dec. 27). The Lord Jesus submitted to death to atone for the sins of the world, but death could not hold Him. He came forth from the tomb in resurrection power and now holds the symbols of authority, keys, in His hand. He has absolute authority over death and over the realm of the departed spirits, hades (Luke 16:23). He has been through both, and they could not hold Him. "We are never allowed to forget for a moment the over-ruling sovereignty of God" (Morris, *The Cross in the New Testament*, p. 354). Now the Lord gives John the command and commission to write. "Write therefore the things which you saw, and the things which are, and the things which are about to come to pass after these things" (v. 19). This key verse gives the outline for the entire Book of Revelation:

I. The things that you saw: the vision of Christ. chapter 1.
II. The things that are: the seven churches. chapters 2–3.
III. The things that are after these things: the future events after the church age. chapters 4–22.`

The phrase *after these things* (μετὰ ταῦτα) does not occur again until 4:1. "The mystery of the seven stars which you saw upon my right hand and the seven golden lampstands: the seven stars are messengers of the seven churches and the seven lampstands are seven churches" (v. 20). Daniel knew that the God of heaven revealed mysteries (Dan. 2:27–28). The word *messenger* (ἄγγελος) may refer to a literal angel or to a human

---

1:20. Mystery (μυστήριον) occurs 4 times in Rev. (1:20; 10:7; 17:5, 7). A biblical mystery is a divinely revealed truth so profound that there is still some mystery about it. Walvoord comments, "It is significant as indicated in this verse that the revelation embodied in this book, though often in symbols, is designed to reveal truth, not to hide it" (*The Revelation of Jesus Christ*, p. 49). God revealed to Daniel the mystery that He knew the course of all human governments; would permit them and finally destroy them all and establish His own eternal kingdom (Dan. 2:27–44). The Lord Jesus revealed in parables the mystery that God is at work through His servants sowing the seed of the Word, which will result in a harvest of good grain (people) and the casting of other people into fire (Matt. 13:11–30). The apostle Paul revealed the mystery that God was in Christ accomplishing the salvation of all believers through the cross, even though none of the demons or evil men understood what He was doing (II Cor. 2:2–8). Paul made known the fellowship of the mystery of Christ dwelling in the hearts of His people in love (Eph. 1:9–10; 3:8–19). The Book of Rev. shows us Christ holding His servants in His hand (1:20); Christ commanding the seventh angel to sound the trumpet that brings 7 bowls of wrath on human government (10:7; 11:15; 16:1–21); Christ bringing judgment on mystery Babylon, the false church, that He may bring His bride, the true church, into that place of glory and splendor that is His eternal purpose (21:1–22:5). See ZPEB, "Mystery," IV, pp. 327–30; ISBE (1986), "Mystery," III, pp. 451–55; Elwell, Walter, *Evangelical Dictionary of*

messenger. Some expositors (Alford, H. B. Swete, J. B. Smith) argue for the messengers being actual angels, which is not specifically taught elsewhere in Scripture. Others (A. C. Gaebelein, Newell, Walvoord, R. Thomas) argue for the messengers being delegates from the churches or actual pastors of the churches (who may be one and the same). However, angels are never portrayed in Scripture as needing God's comfort. They are beings of immense power whose presence intimidates humans. On the other hand, the picture of the Lord holding the messengers on the palm of His hand is one of the most comforting scenes in all of Scripture for Christian workers. It is also clearly taught elsewhere in Scripture. The Lord upholds a good man with His hand (Ps. 37:23–24); we are the sheep of His hand (Ps. 95:7); "thy right hand shall hold me" (Ps. 139:10); He shall gather the lambs with His arm (Isa. 40:11); underneath are the everlasting arms (Deut. 33:27).

Practical Applications from Revelation 1

1. The Revelation of Jesus Christ: the most important thing in our lives is our relationship with the Lord Jesus Christ (1:1). John begins with Christ (as he does also in his Gospel and First Epistle, John 1:1; I John 1:1). The Lord Jesus is the source of grace and truth for all who believe in Him (John 1:14).
2. Reading the Bible is the great source of blessing and benefit (1:3). The Lord Jesus commanded us to search the Scriptures (John 5:39). His Word is truth that sanctifies us (John 17:17).
3. The Lord Jesus is the faithful witness (1:5). Faithfulness should characterize us as well (Rev. 2:10). Timothy's great virtue was that he was "faithful in the Lord" (I Cor. 4:17).
4. The Lord Jesus is coming again (1:7). The apostle Paul described that blessed hope of meeting the Lord in the air (I Thess. 4:17). We should be constantly looking for the blessed hope (Titus 2:13).
5. The Lord Jesus should be the beginning and the ending of our purposes and ambitions in this life (1:8). We should "seek those things which are above, where Christ sits on the right hand of God" (Col. 3:1b).
6. We should be prepared to endure persecution for the Lord as John did (1:9). Paul urged Timothy to endure hardness as a good soldier of Jesus Christ (II Tim. 2:3).

Biblical Theology, "Mystery," pp. 546–47; Ryken, Wilhoit, and Longman, *Dictionary of Biblical Imagery*, "Ephesians, Letter to the," pp. 240–41.

7. We should be receptive to the influence of the Spirit, especially on the Lord's Day (1:10). He is the Comforter, who will teach us all things (John 14:26).
8. The Son of man was in the midst of the seven lamp stands (1:13). The Lord promised, "Where two or three are gathered together in my name, there am I in the midst of them" (Matt. 18:20).
9. "His eyes were as a flame of fire" (1:14). Hagar's greatest thought was that God was watching her (Gen. 16:13). "The eyes of the Lord are in every place, beholding the evil and the good" (Prov. 15:3).
10. The better we see the Lord, the less confidence we have in ourselves (1:17). When Isaiah saw the Lord, high and lifted up, he cried, "Woe is me!" (Isa. 6:1–5). But the Lord sent him to serve (Isa. 6:8–9).
11. Christ has the keys of hades and death (1:18). No one can die prematurely; no one can resurrect himself. Christ said, "I am the resurrection and the life" (John 11:25).

Prayer

O Lord Jesus, lift up our thoughts to You. Help us to see beyond the busyness of this world to that serene realm where You hold Your servants in Your hand. Give us the courage to bear witness to You before this wicked world. Amen.

Revelation 2–3

REVELATION 2

CHURCHES: EPHESUS TO THYATIRA

Persons

Jesus Christ　　　　　　　　　　The Spirit
    Titles:
        He that holds the seven stars
           in His right hand
        He who walks in the midst of
           the seven golden lampstands
        The First and the Last
        He who was dead and is alive
        He who has the sharp sword
           with two edges
        The Son of God
        He who has eyes like a flame
           of fire and feet like fine brass

Persons referred to

The church of Ephesus

The Devil (Satan)

Those who say they are apostles
  and are not

The church of Pergamos

Antipas the martyr

The Nicolaitans

Balaam

The church of Smyrna

Balac

Those who say they are Jews
  and are not

The church of Thyatira

Jezebel

Places mentioned

Ephesus

Pergamos

Smyrna

Thyatira

Doctrines taught

Service

Suffering

The primacy of love

The second death

Repentance

Faith

Overcoming

The Second Coming

Rewards

1 Unto the angel of the church of Ephesus write; These things saith he that holdeth the seven stars in his right hand, who walketh in the midst of the seven golden candlesticks;

2 I know thy works, and thy labour, and thy patience, and how thou canst not bear them which are evil: and thou hast tried them which say they are apostles, and are not, and hast found them liars:

3 And hast borne, and hast patience, and for my name's sake hast laboured, and hast not fainted.

4 Nevertheless I have somewhat against thee, because thou hast left thy first love.

5 Remember therefore from whence thou art fallen, and repent, and do the first works; or else I will come unto thee quickly, and will remove thy candlestick out of his place, except thou repent.

6 But this thou hast, that thou hatest the deeds of the Nicolaitanes, which I also hate.

7 He that hath an ear, let him hear what the Spirit saith unto the churches; To him that overcometh will I give to eat of the tree of life, which is in the midst of the paradise of God.

Revelation 2 Exposition

I. The Church in Ephesus. vv. 1–7.

The Lord now commands John to write: "To the messenger of the church in Ephesus write: these things says the one who is holding the seven stars in his right hand, who is walking in the midst of the seven golden lampstands" (v. 1). The present participles stress the continuous action of the "holding" and "walking." The Lord never ceases His protection for His messengers or His presence in the midst of His churches. Each of these letters has a threefold application: It is to a literal first-century church that needed spiritual guidance and help, it is to that kind of church that

---

2:1. Perhaps the most helpful chart organizing the content of the 7 churches is that of Merrill Tenney, *Interpreting Revelation*, between pp. 68–69. Bengel argues that these letters are intended to purify the church before the giving of the great prophetic revelation that follows, just as the Lord purified the people at Sinai before giving them the revelation of the law (*Gnomon*, V, p. 205).

"In Paul's day Ephesus was the chief Aegean port of Asia Minor, the gateway to the Orient from Greece and Rome" (Neal, p. 11). The name *Ephesus* means "desirable." For historical background on the city of Ephesus, see Marshall Neal, *Seven Churches*, pp. 11–24; William Ramsay, *The Letters to the Seven Churches of Asia*, pp. 210–50; R. C. Trench, *Commentary on the Epistles to the Seven Churches in Asia*, pp. 74–103; "Ephesus," ZPEB, II, pp. 324–32; "Ephesus," ISBE (1982), II, pp. 115–17; Pfeiffer and Vos, *The Wycliffe Historical Geography of Bible Lands*, pp. 357–65; *Lion Photoguide to the Bible*, "Ephesus," pp. 269ff.; *Bible Lands Photoguide*, CD-ROM by Accordance, for 12 color photos.

The verb *to hold* (κρατέω) implies the power and protection of the Lord on these messengers, but it can also convey the judicial "laying hold" on the Dragon (Rev. 20:2).

has always existed throughout history, and it is for the individual believer who faces parallel situations in his own life. Although some have argued that these churches mark out seven successive periods of church history (J. B. Smith, *Rev.*, pp. 61–62; *Scofield Study Bible*, pp. 1331–32), this is an inference, not the stated teaching of the passage. Ryrie notes that each of the messages to the seven churches ends with an admonition "to the church*es*" [plural] (*Ryrie Study Bible*, p. 1788). That is not to say that church history did not begin with the zeal and service characteristic of the Ephesian church or that it will not end with the general lukewarmness of Laodicea. Walvoord stresses the divine purpose and remarkable progression in the messages (*Rev.*, p. 52). But seven successive ages of church history militates against the doctrine of imminency. Alva J. McClain warns, "Since to the Church, from the day of its birth on Pentecost, the coming of the Lord is always imminent, obviously there could be no chronological chart of ecclesiastical history given in advance" (*The Greatness of the Kingdom*, p. 449). The Lord Jesus may return at any moment; we should always be ready (Matt. 24:42; I Cor. 1:7; James 5:8–9; Rev. 22:20). The apostle Paul makes clear that the church age will end with very grim conditions (II Thess. 2:1–12; I Tim. 4:1–3; II Tim. 3:1–7). The Lord Jesus chose these seven churches because they were the best examples of the truths He was imparting to His people. Vincent observes that the Lord omitted some very important cities in Asia, such as Colossae, Miletus, Hierapolis, Magnesia (*Word Studies in the NT*, II, p. 411). There is a sevenfold pattern in each of the seven messages. Each one begins with the **command** to write; each has then a **characterization** of Christ that fits the message to follow. The command assures us that the messages are not merely John's concerns for the churches but direct messages from the Lord Himself. "These things says the one who holds the seven stars in his right hand, the one who walks in the midst of the seven golden lampstands" (v. 1). There is immense comfort in the fact that Christ is holding the church in the hand of strength and that His presence is always with His churches. There is then a **commendation** for the service of the church. "I know your works and toil, and your patience, and that you are not able to bear evil people, and you test the ones who say they are apostles and are not, and found them liars; and you have patience and you bore on account of my name, and you have not become weary" (vv. 2–3). They were a working church, but

---

2:2. The Lord says *I know* (οἶδα) 7 times in Rev.; 5 times to the churches *I know* your works (2:2, 19; 3:1, 8, 15), *I know* your tribulation (2:9), and *I know* where you dwell (2:13). He *knows* (οἶδα) intuitively, with divine omniscience, as His Father knows (Matt. 6:8); He does not have *to come to know by experience* (γινώσκω) as the churches do (Rev. 2:23 note). See Custer, *A Treasury of New Testament Synonyms*, pp. 106–12.

the second term, *toil* (κόπος), implies very hard labor. There is a promise of rest for all those who toil for the Lord (Rev. 14:13). The word *patience* (ὑπομονή) means steadfast endurance. This is high praise for the earnestness and zeal with which they have served and the determined patience of their continuing steadfastness. They had tested false teachers by the Scriptures and had proved them to be deceivers. What they had done, they did for Christ; their motive was true. "And you have not become weary" shows that their zeal and service continues unabated. But there is also a word of **condemnation**. "But I have against you that you left your first love" (v. 4). Their first fervent love had cooled off. "This is the starting point of all church and individual failure" (Gaebelein, *The Revelation*, p. 34). It was an unconscious process. They were continuing to serve all right, but it was rather through clenched teeth than through the loving adoration they had first felt. Robert Murray McCheyne warns, "It is not a man that has this against you . . . it is Jesus that has this against you; and He is saying unto you, Was I such a small object of love, that ye could only love me one night, that ye could not watch with me one hour?" (*The Seven Churches of Asia*, p. 15). That is a most convicting thought for every saint. We should bow our heads to ask Christ to forgive us and to restore that passionate love that we used to have for Him. There is then a word of **correction**. "Continue remembering therefore from whence you have fallen, and repent, and do the first works; but if not, I am coming to you and I will move your lampstand from its place, if you do not repent" (v. 5). That solemn warning can find illustration in

---

One of the great virtues of the Ephesian church was that they could not bear the evil ones. In modern society the supreme virtue is toleration. The Bible teaches that believers should hold fast to what is good and avoid all appearance of evil (I Thess. 5:21–22). Paul says bluntly that fornicators, idolaters, homosexuals, thieves, extortioners, and other evil-doers "shall not inherit the kingdom of God" (I Cor. 6:9–10).

The only other time *liar* (ψευδής) is found in Rev. is in 21:8, "all liars shall have their part in the lake of fire."

2:3. The word *name* (ὄνομα) occurs 37 times in Rev. Here the *name* stands for the person of Christ. To endure for *His* name is for *His Person*. See Ryken, Wilhoit, and Longman, *Dictionary of Biblical Imagery*, "Name," pp. 582–86; ZPEB, "Name," IV, pp. 360–66; ISBE (1986), "Name," III, pp. 480–83.

The verb *to become weary* (κοπιάω) occurs only here in Rev. The Lord invited those who are weary to come to Him for rest (Matt. 11:28).

2:4. The word for the *love that gives* (ἀγάπη) occurs only here and in 2:19, which attributes this love to the church in Thyatira. See ZPEB, "Love," III, pp. 989–96; ISBE, "Love," III, pp. 173–76.

2:5. The verb *to remember* (μνημονεύω) occurs 3 times in Rev. The Lord gently reminds 2 churches to "remember" to correct their practices (Rev. 2:5; 3:3), but He will "remember" Babylon in fiery judgment (Rev. 18:5).

many churches that no longer exist. They needed to repent, to change their way of thinking and acting. They needed to renew their first works of fervent service. Today the city of Ephesus is gone. "But this you have, that you hate the works of the Nicolaitanes, which I also hate" (v. 6). Even in correction the Lord remembers their virtues. It is a virtue to hate what God hates (Ps. 139:21–22). "Love for Christ will hate without trimming, or dilution, or mitigation, what dishonors or wounds Him" (Jennings, *Rev.*, pp. 66f.). Then follows the **call**. "Let the one who has an ear hear what the Spirit says to the churches" (v. 7). The Lord Jesus regularly exhorted listeners, "He that has ears to hear, let him hear" (Matt. 11:15). But John exhorts with the singular, "If you have even one good ear, listen." It is the Holy Spirit of God who gives this convicting call to the heart of every reader. The language assumes the divine inspiration of Scripture. He concludes with the **challenge**. "To the one who conquers I shall give to eat from the tree of life, which is in the paradise of God" (v. 7). *Paradise* (only here in Rev.) comes from a Persian word that means

---

The verb *to repent* (μετανοέω) occurs 11 times in Rev. (2:5 [twice], 16, 21, 22; 3:3, 19; 9:20, 21; 16:9, 11). Here it is an aorist imperative, "Repent instantly," and "do at once" (Robertson, *Word Pictures*, VI, p. 299).

2:6. The verb *to hate* (μισέω) occurs 4 times in Rev., in every case of something that the Lord hates (2:6 [twice]; 17:16; 18:2). Hating what is evil is a virtue.

The Nicolaitans were a heretical sect mentioned only here and in 2:15 in the Bible. The Lord hates their deeds and classifies them with those who practice idolatry and fornication (2:14–15). For further discussion see "Nicolaitans," ZPEB, IV, pp. 435–36; ISBE (1986), III, pp. 533–34; Alford, *Greek Testament*, IV, pp. 563–65; O. Talmadge Spence, *The Book of Rev.*, pp. 162–66.

2:7. The verb *to conquer* (νικάω) is of special interest to John. Outside of his writings, it occurs in only 3 contexts (Luke 11:22; Rom. 3:4; 12:21). In Rev. John uses the word 17 times: for the true believer who conquers in the 7 churches (Rev. 2:7, 11, 17, 26; 3:5, 12, 21); for the martyrs who conquer in the Tribulation period (Rev. 12:11; 15:2); for all true saints at the consummation (Rev. 21:7); for the Lord Jesus Christ twice (Rev. 5:5; 17:14); and for the Beast (the Antichrist) for his temporary conquests (Rev. 6:2; 11:7; 13:7). In his Gospel he records the Lord's claim "Be of good cheer, I have conquered the world" (John 16:33). In I John he applies it to the believers who conquer the evil one and the world (2:13, 14; 4:4; 5:4, 5). See ISBE (1979), "Conquer," I, p. 761.

The verb *to eat* (ἐσθίω) occurs 6 times in Rev. (2:7, 14, 20; 10:10; 17:16; 19:18).

The word *tree* (ξύλον) occurs 7 times in Rev. (2:7; 18:12 [twice]; 22:2 [twice], 14, 19). The English word *xylem* comes from this Greek word and refers to those plant tissues that convey water and minerals to a tree.

The *tree of life* (Rev. 2:7; 22:2, 14) is a reference to Gen. 2:9; 3:22, 24. The phrase also occurs in Prov. (3:18; 11:30; 13:12; 15:4). It is not possible for a sinful, spiritually dead person to eat of the tree of life. But to one who conquers (overcomes) the right is given. It is specifically promised to all the servants of God in glory (Rev. 22:2). See ZPEB, "Tree of Life," V, pp. 810–11; ISBE (1988), "Tree of Knowledge; Tree of Life," IV, pp. 901–3; Ryken, Wilhoit, and Longman, *Dictionary of Biblical Imagery*, "Tree of Life," pp. 889–90.

8 *And unto the angel of the church in Smyrna write; These things saith the first and the last, which was dead, and is alive;*

9 *I know thy works, and tribulation, and poverty, (but thou art rich) and I know the blasphemy of them which say they are Jews, and are not, but are the synagogue of Satan.*

10 *Fear none of those things which thou shalt suffer: behold, the devil shall cast some of you into prison, that ye may be tried; and ye shall have tribulation ten days: be thou faithful unto death, and I will give thee a crown of life.*

11 *He that hath an ear, let him hear what the Spirit saith unto the churches; He that overcometh shall not be hurt of the second death.*

a royal pleasure park. The tree of life grew only in the Garden of Eden (Gen. 2:9). Redeemed saints will find it again in the paradise that God is preparing for them, but by that time it will be a forest (Rev. 22:2). The Lord promised paradise to the repentant robber (Luke 23:43). The Ephesian church was very privileged. The apostle Paul had spent two full years in a daily preaching ministry there (Acts 19:8–10) and had later ministered to the elders of Ephesus from Miletus (Acts 20:17–38). He also wrote his Epistle to the Ephesians. Marshall Neal notes that the church did not ultimately heed the warning of the Lord and today Ephesus is a deserted place; the lampstand is gone (*Seven Churches*, p. 16). William Ramsay provides maps and photographs to show how the Cayster River silted up the gulf and ruined Ephesus as a harbor (*The Letters to the Seven Churches of Asia*, pp. 212ff.).

II. *The Church in Smyrna. vv. 8–11.*

The Lord **commands**: "And to the messenger of the church in Smyrna write" (v. 8). His words strengthen not only the first century church but all persecuted believers of all time. "Thus says the first and the last, who became dead and lived" (v. 8). It is Jehovah who is the first and the last (Isa. 44:6). The Lord Jesus **characterizes** Himself as Jehovah and as the one who triumphed over death and the grave. He experienced the worst that evil men could do and still accomplished the perfect will of God. Now He exercises all authority over heaven and earth (Matt. 28:18). He is surely able to cause His people to triumph over all that they must suf-

---

2:8. Smyrna (myrrh) was a city with a fine harbor, but it had been sacked by the Lydians in about 600 B.C. and was deserted for 3 centuries. It was ultimately rebuilt and became a powerful city that has continued to this day under the name Izmir. For historical background on the city of Smyrna, see Marshall Neal, *Seven Churches*, pp. 25–36; William Ramsay, *The Letters to the Seven Churches of Asia*, pp. 251–80; R. C. Trench, *Commentary on the Epistles to the Seven Churches in Asia*, pp. 104–19; "Smyrna," ZPEB, V, pp. 462–64; "Smyrna," ISBE (1988), IV, pp. 554–56; Pfeiffer and Vos, *Wycliffe Historical Geography of Bible Lands*, pp. 390–92; *Lion Photoguide to the Bible*, "Smyrna," pp. 276f.

fer. He has much to **commend** in His suffering people. "I know your tribulation and poverty (but you are rich), and the blasphemy of those who say they are Jews, and are not, but are the synagogue of Satan" (v. 9). The word *tribulation* (θλῖψις) refers to the "pressure" that is put on God's saints to betray His will and His Word. The persecutors regarded it as a small thing. "How easy it was to escape poverty, bonds and death by a pinch of incense" (E. M. Blaiklock, *The Seven Churches*, p. 31). The Lord warned us, "In the world you shall have tribulation: but be of good cheer, I have overcome the world" (John 16:33). The word *poverty* (πτωχεία, beggary) denotes the extreme financial loss that results from persecution. The writer to the Hebrews encouraged them, "You took joyfully the spoiling of your goods, knowing in yourselves that you have a better and an enduring substance" (Heb. 10:34). In the aside ("but you are rich") the Lord assures His people that He will provide eternal treasures for them. "The blasphemy of those who say they are Jews, and are not" refers to those who claim to be Jews and yet have no regard for His will. Absalom could pay his vows to Jehovah and still seek to murder his own father (II Sam. 15:7, 14). In the same way there are apostate Christians in liberal churches who claim to be the true church and despise "born again" Christians as the "lunatic fringe." The Lord goes on to command, "Stop fearing the things which you are about to suffer" (v. 10). This is the last time in Scripture that the Lord gives this command. The present imperative implies that they were already afraid. The Lord gave the same assurance to Daniel, "Fear not, Daniel" (Dan. 10:12).

2:9. The noun *blasphemy* (βλασφημία) occurs 5 times in Rev. (2:9; 13:1, 5, 6; 17:3).

2:10. The Devil (διάβολος) is mentioned 5 times in Rev. (2:10; 12:9, 12; 20:2, 10). The word means the "slanderer, adversary," but he is also known as the great dragon, that old serpent, and Satan (Rev. 12:9 note). See Custer, *A Treasury of New Testament Synonyms*, pp. 5–8.

At every stage of life the believer is dogged with hardships and trials, but the Bible provides examples of God's help to encourage us.

David, the young warrior (I Sam. 17:32–54). He was just a ruddy youth; his armor did not fit; he had to face a giant of a warrior; still God enabled him to win.

Benaiah, the mature warrior (I Chron. 11:22). He went down into a pit on a snowy day to slay a lion and God enabled him. He later became captain of the host.

Paul, the old veteran (II Cor. 11:22–33). He was beaten, stoned, and put in prison; endured shipwreck, hunger, thirst, etc. Yet he gloried in his infirmities because God's grace abounded (II Cor. 12:9).

The victor's *crown* (στέφανος) is part of the rewards of the righteous. It occurs 8 times in Rev. (2:10; 3:11; 4:4, 10; 6:2; 9:7; 12:1; 14:14). The 24 elders will have them (Rev. 4:4), as will the Son of Man (Rev. 14:14). It should be distinguished from the imperial crown (see Rev. 12:3 note). However, Moulton and Milligan note that στέφανος has political significance in the papyri (*Vocabulary*, p. 589).

The Devil is the real origin of persecution for believers. "The devil is about to cast some of you into prison in order that you may be tested" (v. 10). The Devil tests only in order to destroy people. But his testing will last only ten days: it is always limited by God's providential control. Daniel was also tested for ten days (Dan. 1:12). "Be faithful unto death, and I will give you the crown of life" (v. 10). *Faithfulness* is one of the attributes of God (I Cor. 1:9) and of Christ (Rev. 1:5) that the believer should emulate. The believer should be faithful until his dying moment, when he will be forever confirmed in righteousness. Persecutors may kill the body, but they cannot touch the soul. The crown of life is surely the fullness of life in the presence of the living God, but there may be a literal crown as well. There is **no** word of **condemnation** about anything to this suffering church. The Lord concludes with His **call** and **challenge,** "He that has an ear, let him hear what the Spirit says to the churches; the one who conquers shall never be harmed by the second death" (v. 11). We need to give careful attention to this spiritual instruction by the Lord. The believer who draws upon the grace of Christ and overcomes can never (double negative) be harmed by the second death, which is eternal separation from God. He will have instead, eternal fellowship with a loving God. Why does a loving God allow persecution? To make His people better and to increase their ability to serve well. Jennings notes that tribulation never separates from the love of Christ; it drives the sheep only "closer to the Shepherd's side" (*Rev.*, p. 79). Peter prays such blessing on the saints: "But the God of all grace, who hath called us unto his eternal glory by Christ Jesus, after that ye have suffered a while, make you perfect, stablish, strengthen, settle you. To him be glory and dominion forever and ever. Amen" (I Pet. 5:10–11).

2:11. The verb *to harm* (ἀδικέω) occurs 11 times in Rev. (2:11; 6:6; 7:2, 3; 9:4, 10, 19; 11:5 [twice]; 22:11 [twice]). God is a just God, who takes notice of all injustice (James 2:10).

2:12. For historical background on the city of Pergamos, see Marshall Neal, *Seven Churches*, pp. 37–52; William Ramsay, *The Letters to the Seven Churches of Asia*, pp. 281–315; R. C. Trench, *Commentary on the Epistles to the Seven Churches in Asia*, pp. 120–42; "Pergamum," ZPEB, IV, pp. 701–4; "Pergamum," ISBE (1986), III, pp. 768–70; Pfeiffer and Vos, *Wycliffe Historical Geography of Bible Lands*, pp. 392–96; *Lion Photoguide to the Bible*, "Pergamum," (pp. 278f.); *Bible Lands Photoguide*, CD-ROM by Accordance, for 5 color photos.

12 And to the angel of the church in Pergamos write; These things saith he which
hath the sharp sword with two edges;
13 I know thy works, and where thou dwellest, even where Satan's seat is: and thou
holdest fast my name, and hast not denied my faith, even in those days wherein
Antipas was my faithful martyr, who was slain among you, where Satan dwelleth.
14 But I have a few things against thee, because thou hast there them that hold the
doctrine of Balaam, who taught Balac to cast a stumblingblock before the children of
Israel, to eat things sacrificed unto idols, and to commit fornication.
15 So hast thou also them that hold the doctrine of the Nicolaitanes, which thing I hate.
16 Repent; or else I will come unto thee quickly, and will fight against them with the
sword of my mouth.
17 He that hath an ear, let him hear what the Spirit saith unto the churches; To him
that overcometh will I give to eat of the hidden manna, and will give him a white stone,
and in the stone a new name written, which no man knoweth saving he that receiveth it.

III. The Church in Pergamos. vv. 12–17.

Pergamos (also spelled Pergamum in some ancient sources) was sixty
miles north of Smyrna, built on a mountaintop thirteen hundred feet
above the Caicus River valley. It was a major center for three different
varieties of idolatrous worship. The great temple and hospital of
Aesculapius, the god of healing, was there. Multitudes of sick people
came hoping for a miracle. The great temple and altar of Zeus, the
supreme god, was there. All pagans worshiped him, regardless of their
local deities. It also had the temple of Caesar Augustus, where every
loyal citizen was expected to offer worship to prove his loyalty to the
empire. Rome did not care what other deities were worshiped as long as
everyone pledged loyalty to Rome. John records the **command** to write
and the **characterization** of the Lord that is especially fitting. "And to
the messenger of the church in Pergamos write: These things says the
one who has the sharp, two-edged sword" (v. 12). The Holy One of Israel
has a mouth like a sharp sword (Isa. 49:2–7). If the ancient world feared
the sword of Rome, the Lord holds a far more powerful sword. His Word
is the sword that will slay the armies of the Antichrist (Rev. 19:15). It is
a two-edged sword: fearsome judgment on the wicked but faithful chas-
tisement on His people. No wrath can fall on them, for He has borne it
all (I Thess. 5:9). The **commendation** is detailed, "I know where you are
dwelling, where the throne of Satan is; and you are holding fast my
name, and you did not deny my faith, even in the days of Antipas, my
faithful witness, who was slain among you, where Satan dwells" (v. 13).

2:12–13. Spurgeon has a powerful and convicting sermon on "Holding Fast the Faith"
(Sermon 2007 in *The C. H. Spurgeon Collection*; Ages Digital Library).
2:13. The verb *to deny* (ἀρνέομαι) occurs twice in Rev. (2:13; 3:8).

They were dwelling permanently in a dangerous place: where Satan's throne is. The seat of false religious worship is the throne of the Devil. Satan tried to get the Lord Jesus to worship him and failed (Matt. 4:9–10). Believers today must hold steadfastly to the Lord just as the believers at Pergamos did. They were holding fast to the Lord's name and did not deny His faith. An outstanding example was Antipas, a believer who was martyred for refusing to worship at Satan's throne. This was a very significant event because Polycarp, bishop of Smyrna, may have heard the Book of Revelation read the first time in Smyrna. He lived to be eighty-six, and in A.D. 155 he, too, was martyred for refusing to worship the emperor. His words were, "86 years have I served Him [Christ] and He never did me wrong. How then can I blaspheme my King and Savior?" It is the glory of the martyrs to choose death rather than to deny Christ. Still, Christ had some words of **condemnation** for Pergamos as well. "However, I have a few things against you, because you have there those who hold the teaching of Balaam, who taught Balak to cast a stumbling block before the sons of Israel, to eat things sacrificed to idols and to commit fornication" (v. 14). Balaam gave the advice to Balak to corrupt Israel so that God could curse them (Num. 22–24). The Israelites fell into sin through Balaam's counsel and God had to judge them (Num. 25; 31:16). It is an ancient trick of the Devil that is still effective. The isolated deeds of the Nicolaitans (Rev. 2:6) became the doctrine of compromise in Pergamos. "Thus you have also those who hold the doctrine of the Nicolaitanes likewise" (v. 15). They were not in control, but their teaching was getting known. We see today a breakdown in separation from worldly practices in our churches. "Sin changes its forms, but not its principles. There are no temples of Diana, and Venus . . . but the temples of Mammon, of Pleasure, of Ambition, rear their alluring fronts and open their wide portals along every walk of life" (James Ramsey, *Rev.*, p. 143). There are people in churches who encourage worldly methods, worldly music, and other practices that will bring God's disapproval on the church. What is Christ's answer? "Repent therefore; but if not, I am coming to you quickly, and I will fight against them with the sword of my mouth" (v. 16).

The word *faith* ($\pi \acute{\iota} \sigma \tau \iota \varsigma$) occurs 4 times in Rev. (2:13, 19; 13:10; 14:12). In each case it refers to faith in the Lord Jesus.

The verb *to kill* ($\dot{\alpha}\pi o\kappa \tau \epsilon \acute{\iota} \nu \omega$) occurs 15 times in Rev. (2:13, 23; 6:8, 11; 9:5, 15, 18, 20; 11:5, 7, 13; 13:10 [twice], 15; 19:21).

2:14. The word *teaching* ($\delta \iota \delta \alpha \chi \acute{\eta}$) occurs 3 times in Rev. (2:14, 15, 24).

The word *stumbling block* ($\sigma \kappa \acute{\alpha} \nu \delta \alpha \lambda o \nu$) occurs only here in Rev.

The verb *to commit fornication* ($\pi o \rho \nu \epsilon \acute{\upsilon} \omega$) occurs 5 times in Rev. (2:14, 20; 17:2; 18:3, 9).

Repent means to change the way you think so thoroughly that you also change the way you act. If these false teachers do not change, Christ will pronounce His Word against them in a way that will be an act of war. Isaiah prophesied that Messiah would smite the earth with the staff of His mouth (Isa. 11:4). In order to end the war of Armageddon the Lord Jesus Christ will return and pronounce His Word, and all the armies of the Beast will die (Rev. 19:11–20). This is a solemn warning indeed. The Lord concludes with the **call** to hear and the **challenge** to overcomers. "Let the one who has an ear hear what the Spirit says to the churches. To the one who conquers I will give the hidden manna, and I will give him a white stone, and upon the stone a new name written, which no one knows except the one who receives it" (v. 17). Just as the Lord provided manna to sustain the Israelites during the forty years of the wilderness wanderings, so He will provide internal sustaining grace to uphold the faithful believer. God always gives great compensation to those who stand for Him and will not compromise. In the ancient world a white stone was a vote of acquittal and approval. A black stone was a vote of condemnation and disapproval. When a body such as the Sanhedrin heard a case presented, they would come to a vote on it. A bowl was passed around, and each member cast into it a white stone or a black stone to indicate approval or disapproval. This is where our idiom "to blackball someone" came from. In the case of voting for candidates for office, sometimes the very names of the candidates were scratched on the stones. Archaeologists have discovered such stones in the ruins of ancient buildings. The Lord Jesus will give His faithful people a vote of approval so specific that their names are on the vote. The name, however, will be a new one, suitable for that realm of eternal glory. Our names in this life have been stained with sin and failure. But in that coming life our new names will shine with the glory and promise of ages of future service. In the Bible the name of a person always reflected his character. When the character of the believer is made perfect, his name must reflect that perfection. Isaiah prophesied that God's people would be called

---

2:16. The verb *to fight against* (πολεμέω) is literally *to do battle*. It occurs 6 times in Rev. (2:16; 12:7 [twice]; 13:4; 17:14; 19:11). See Rev. 9:7 for the related noun *battle*.

2:17. The word for *stone* (ψῆφος) occurs only here in Rev. It has given its name to the modern science of psephology, the study of voting procedures. For examples of ψῆφος meaning "vote" and the verb form ψηφίζω, "to vote, or number with pebbles," see Moulton and Milligan, *Vocabulary*, p. 698. Elsewhere in the NT the regular word for *stone* (λίθος) is used. See Ryken, Wilhoit, and Longman, *Dictionary of Biblical Imagery*, "White," p. 944.

The word *manna* occurs only here in Rev.

The verb *to hide* (κρύπτω) occurs 3 times in Rev. (2:17; 6:15, 16).

18 And unto the angel of the church in Thyatira write; These things saith the Son of God, who hath his eyes like unto a flame of fire, and his feet are like fine brass;
19 I know thy works, and charity, and service, and faith, and thy patience, and thy works; and the last to be more than the first.
20 Notwithstanding I have a few things against thee, because thou sufferest that woman Jezebel, which calleth herself a prophetess, to teach and to seduce my servants to commit fornication, and to eat things sacrificed unto idols.
21 And I gave her space to repent of her fornication; and she repented not.
22 Behold, I will cast her into a bed, and them that commit adultery with her into great tribulation, except they repent of their deeds.
23 And I will kill her children with death; and all the churches shall know that I am he which searcheth the reins and hearts: and I will give unto every one of you according to your works.
24 But unto you I say, and unto the rest in Thyatira, as many as have not this doctrine, and which have not known the depths of Satan, as they speak; I will put upon you none other burden.
25 But that which ye have already hold fast till I come.
26 And he that overcometh, and keepeth my works unto the end, to him will I give power over the nations:
27 And he shall rule them with a rod of iron; as the vessels of a potter shall they be broken to shivers: even as I received of my Father.
28 And I will give him the morning star.
29 He that hath an ear, let him hear what the Spirit saith unto the churches.

by a new name (Isa. 62:2). The Lord Jesus is the good shepherd who has a name for each sheep (John 10:3). If you are His sheep, He has a special name just for you. No one else can know it.

IV. The Church in Thyatira. vv. 18–29.

The city of Thyatira was about forty miles inland from Pergamos; it was originally an outpost of Pergamos against invaders. By NT times it was a major trading center in black wool, bronze, and purple dye (Lydia was from Thyatira, Acts 16:14). The most popular pagan deity in Thyatira was Apollo, the sun god. The Lord gives the **command** to write and the **characterization** of Himself that is fitting. "And to the messenger of the church in Thyatira write: These things says the Son of God, the one who has his eyes as a flame of fire and his feet as fine bronze" (v. 18). The angel who appeared to Daniel had eyes like flaming torches and feet like

---

2:18. For historical background on the city of Thyatira, see Marshall Neal, *Seven Churches*, pp. 53–63; William Ramsay, *The Letters to the Seven Churches of Asia*, pp. 316–53; R. C. Trench, *Commentary of the Epistles to the Seven Churches in Asia*, pp. 143–60; ZPEB, V, pp. 743–44; ISBE (1988), IV, p. 846; Pfeiffer and Vos, *Wycliffe Historical Geography of Bible Lands*, pp. 396–97.

polished bronze (Dan. 10:6). The divine Son has eyes of omniscience and feet of supernatural power to correct the pagan worship and the errors in the church at Thyatira. But He also recognizes the service of many in the church and gives them a **commendation**. "I know your works and love, and faith, and service, and your patience, and your last works more than the first" (v. 19). The Lord knows intuitively (οἶδα) that there were strong believers and diligent workers in Thyatira. He praises them for being a working church, for having the love that gives, for having true faith in Him, for serving (as a deacon would), and for having patience that overcomes against all odds. And He notes that their works were continually increasing. But He also gives a very severe **condemnation** of some of their practices. "However, I have against you that you are permitting that woman Jezebel, who calls herself a prophetess and teaches and leads my slaves astray to commit fornication and to eat things offered to idols" (v. 20). The woman's name was obviously not Jezebel, but the Lord gives her that name of the notorious queen of Ahab, who was a vicious influence in the days of Elijah (I Kings 16:31; 19:1–2). In the ancient world most people were "poor" by modern standards, and the presence of a rich landowner could be an intimidating force in a church. She dissented from the practice of morality and religious separation of the church and yet stayed in it. Her teaching and example were causing others to go astray. The Lord had waited patiently for her to respond. "And I gave her time to repent, and she would not repent from her fornication" (v. 21). The present tense verb implies, "She continued being unwilling to repent." Now the Lord pronounces judgment against her. "Behold I am casting her into a bed and those who commit adultery with her into great tribulation, except they repent of her works" (v. 22). She had chosen a bed of moral sin; the Lord responds by casting her and her lovers into a bed of great tribulation. They might repent, but she will not. "And I will kill her children with death, and all the churches shall know that I am the One who searches the minds and hearts, and I will give to each one of you according to your works" (v. 23). The churches shall *know by experience*. (See Custer, *A Treasury of New Testament Synonyms*, pp. 106–12). God is one who repays every man according to his work (Ps. 62:12). Jehovah searches the heart to give to

---

2:20. The verb *to lead astray* (πλανάω) occurs 10 times in Rev. (2:20; 12:9; 13:14; 18:23; 19:20; 20:3, 8, 10). It is the work of the Devil. He is the one who leads the whole inhabited earth astray (Rev. 12:9). See Custer, *A Treasury of New Testament Synonyms*, pp. 93–96.

2:22. This is the only time that the verb *to commit adultery* (μοιχεύω) occurs in Rev.

2:23. The verb *to know by experience* (γινώσκω) occurs 4 times in Rev. (2:23, 24; 3:3, 9), all referring to human partial knowledge. Compare Rev. 2:2 note.

every man according to his ways (Jer. 17:10). The Lord is not tolerant of moral corruption in His church. Now the Lord gives a **correction** to those who are willing to obey His word. "But I say to you, the remaining ones in Thyatira, as many as have not this teaching, who did not know the depths of Satan (as they say), I will not cast upon you any other burden, except that which you have, hold fast until I come" (vv. 24–25). The command to *hold fast* is repeated to the church of Philadelphia (Rev. 3:11). The verb means to "grasp firmly." Believers must note the need for spiritual effort sustained by the grace of God. The certainty of the second coming of the Lord is assumed. He cannot possibly fail to keep His promise. He concludes with a **challenge** and a **call** to hear. "And the one who is conquering and keeping my works unto the end, to him I will give authority over the nations, and he shall rule them with a rod of iron, as ceramic vessels they shall be shattered" (vv. 26–27). The sense is that He shall rule them as a shepherd rules, but with a rod of iron, almighty power. Jehovah promised this power to the divine Son, "Thou shalt break them with a rod of iron" (Ps. 2:7–9). "Even as I have received from my Father, I also will give to him the morning star" (vv. 27b–28). This is a clear promise to give Himself to His people, because He later identifies Himself as the Morning Star (Rev. 22:16). The apostle Peter also refers to the Morning Star arising in our hearts (II Pet. 1:19). Many different images are applied to the Lord Jesus. He is both the Sun (Mal. 4:2) and the Morning Star. "As the morning star, He is seen

---

The word *minds* (νεφροὺς), used only here in the NT, regularly refers to the kidneys, but here it plainly refers to the mental processes, as it does in the Septuagint (Ps. 7:10; KJV Ps. 7:9, "God trieth the hearts and *reins*").

2:24. The word *deep* (βαθύς) occurs only here in Rev. In the rest of the NT it refers to a very deep Sabbath morning (very early, Luke 24:1); a very deep well (John 4:11); and a very deep sleep (Eutychus, Acts 20:9). Here *depths* refers to the abysmal depravity of Satan. To love murder and lying and the harming of others is despicable sin (John 8:44).

2:25. This verb *to come* (ἥκω) is used only 3 times in Rev. (2:25; 3:3 [twice]), all referring to the Lord's second coming.

2:26. The word *authority* (ἐξουσία) occurs 21 times in Rev. It denotes the right to command. This first reference is to authority over the nations (2:26); the last reference is to authority over the tree of life (Rev. 22:14). The passive voice indicates that God delegates authority (Rev. 6:8; 9:3, etc.). The authority of Christ is of special importance (Rev. 12:10). See Ryken, Wilhoit, and Longman, *Dictionary of Biblical Imagery*, "Authority, Divine and Angelic," pp. 57–59; "Authority, Human," pp. 59–63; ISBE (1979), "Authority," I, pp. 364–71; ZPEB, "Authority," I, pp. 420–21.

2:27. The *rod* (ῥάβδος) is not merely the shepherd's rod (Mic. 7:14 LXX), but it is the royal scepter (Heb. 1:8) of the messianic King (Ps. 2:9). See ISBE (1988), "Rod," IV, pp. 206–7; ZPEB, "Rod," V, pp. 132–33; Ryken, Wilhoit, and Longman, *Dictionary of Biblical Imagery*, "Rod, Staff," pp. 733–34. For a summary of the verb *to shepherd*, see Rev. 12:5 note.

by few; as the sun, He is seen by all. Those who watch not merely for the sun, but for the morning star, properly heed the cautions and injunctions relating to the posture of watching" (Peters, *Theocratic Kingdom*, II, p. 317, n. 2). "He that has an ear, let him hear what the Spirit says to the churches" (v. 29).

Practical Applications from Revelation 2

1. The Lord Jesus Christ is always present with His people (v. 1). God's promise is always "I will never leave thee, nor forsake thee" (Heb. 13:5). [Characterization]
2. Christ views with approval the earnest labors of His people (vv. 2–3). He knows everything that His servants are doing for Him. "For God is not unrighteous to forget your work and labor of love" (Heb. 6:10). [Commendation]
3. The "cooling off" of the believer's love for Christ is a dangerous failure (v. 4). "He that loveth not knoweth not God; for God is love" (I John 4:8). [Condemnation]
4. Believers should repent from their failures and renew their service to God (v. 5). Although John Mark failed on a mission (Acts 13:13), he was yet restored and became profitable for the ministry (II Tim. 4:11). [Correction]
5. It is a virtue to hate what is wrong (v. 6). The Lord Himself hates a number of things (Prov. 6:16). "The fear of the Lord is to hate evil" (Prov. 8:13). [Correction]
6. Fear should have no place in the believer (v. 10). "There is no fear in love; but perfect love casts out fear" (I John 4:18). [Commendation]
7. Believers should confess Christ in the face of an anti-Christian society (v. 13). "He that taketh not his cross, and followeth after me, is not worthy of me" (Matt. 10:38). [Challenge]
8. Christ's provision for the believer is a great comfort (v. 17). There is no man who has left house, or parents, and so forth, for the kingdom of God's sake, who shall not receive manifold more in this present time, and in the world to come life everlasting (Luke 18:30). [Challenge]
9. Christ always repays judgment to the wicked and blessing to His people (vv. 22–23). "Avenge not yourselves, for it is written, Vengeance is mine; I will repay, saith the Lord" (Rom. 12:19). "To the righteous good shall be repayed" (Prov. 13:21). [Consequences]
10. Christ gives Himself to His people (v. 28). Christ gave Himself for our sins that He might deliver us from this present evil world (Gal. 1:4). [Challenge]

Prayer

O mighty Son of God, You see us as we are, yet You love us. Give us grace to hold fast to Your holy Word. Make us hungry for the fruit of the tree of life in the paradise of God. Help us to be faithful to You at all costs. Amen.

REVELATION 3

CHURCHES: SARDIS TO LAODICEA

Person
Jesus Christ
    Titles:
        He that has the seven Spirits of God and the seven stars
        He that is holy and true
        He that has the key of David
        He that opens and no man shuts
        He that shuts and no man opens
        The Amen, the Faithful and True Witness
        The Beginning of the creation of God

Persons referred to
The church of Sardis	The synagogue of Satan
The few who are not defiled	The church of the Laodiceans
The church of Philadelphia	The man who hears
David	

Places
Sardis	New Jerusalem
Philadelphia	Laodicea

Doctrines taught
Responsibility	Crowns
The worthy walk	Heaven
The Second Coming	Pride
Overcoming	Zeal
Reward	Repentance
The hour of temptation	

1 And unto the angel of the church in Sardis write; These things saith he that hath the seven Spirits of God, and the seven stars; I know thy works, that thou hast a name that thou livest, and art dead.

2 Be watchful, and strengthen the things which remain, that are ready to die: for I have not found thy works perfect before God.

3 Remember therefore how thou hast received and heard, and hold fast, and repent. If therefore thou shalt not watch, I will come on thee as a thief, and thou shalt not know what hour I will come upon thee.

4 Thou hast a few names even in Sardis which have not defiled their garments; and they shall walk with me in white: for they are worthy.

5 He that overcometh, the same shall be clothed in white raiment; and I will not blot out his name out of the book of life, but I will confess his name before my Father, and before his angels.

6 He that hath an ear, let him hear what the Spirit saith unto the churches.

Revelation 3 Exposition

I. The Church in Sardis. vv. 1–6.

The city of Sardis was about fifty miles inland, east of Smyrna. Although it had been a rich city, capital of the Lydian empire, it was decaying in the time of the NT. John recorded the **command** to write and the **characterization** of Christ. "And to the messenger of the church in Sardis write: These things says the one who has the seven Spirits of God and the seven stars" (v. 1). The Lord Jesus Christ can minister to His churches the power of the Holy Spirit to accomplish mighty works. He holds His faithful servants in His hand, but the church itself has no spiritual power. There is **no** real **commendation** to the church in Sardis. All that He says is "I know your works, that you have a name that you live, and you are dead" (v. 1b). They had worked for the Lord and had a fine reputation, but they were spiritually dead. The life of God was not empowering the church. In a peculiar way this reflected the history of the city itself. It was located on a precipitous plateau, easily defensible. Yet attackers scaled the heights by night and easily conquered the city (William Ramsay, *The Letters to the Seven Churches of Asia*, p. 355). This is a most convicting thought for any church that has an illustrious past.

3:1. Croesus, famous for his gold, was the king of Sardis who consulted the Delphic Oracle as to whether he should attack Cyrus. The oracle replied, "If you cross the Halys, you will destroy a great empire." He did, but the empire he destroyed was his own. For historical background on the city of Sardis, see Neal, *The Seven Churches*, pp. 64–76; W. M. Ramsay, *The Letters to the Seven Churches of Asia*, pp. 354–68; ZPEB, V, pp. 276–79; ISBE (1988), IV, pp. 336–37; Pfeiffer and Vos, *The Wycliffe Historical Geography of Bible Lands*, pp. 397–400.

What is the present spiritual strength of the church? The Lord pronounces a stinging **condemnation** on the church. "Be watchful and
strengthen the remaining things, which are about to die, for I have not
found your works fulfilled before my God" (v. 2). Isaiah had commanded,
"Strengthen the weak hands" (Isa. 35:3). The word *be watchful* (γρηγορέω)
means "stay awake" or "be alert" (see Custer, *A Treasury of New Testament
Synonyms*, pp. 127–34). The church was not spiritually alert; they were
about to die and were unaware of it. Every church must be on guard
against Satan's attacks and their weakness within. There are many
churches today that are filled with busy committees and classes that have
no spiritual power at all. If the life and power of God does not work in
our churches, nothing will be fulfilled. The Lord also gives them a stern
correction. "Remember therefore how you have received and heard, and
keep holding fast and repent" (v. 3*a*). The Lord Jesus warned the disciples in the Upper Room to remember the word that He had spoken to
them (John 15:20). The church needs to remember God's blessing in the
past, continue holding fast to the precious truths in His Word, and
change the way they are thinking. Believers must never be satisfied with
their spiritual attainments; they must keep on reminding themselves of
the riches of God's grace. God's presence and power must become real to
them. "If, therefore, you will not watch, I shall come as a thief, and you
will never know what hour I shall come upon you" (v. 3*b*). The coming
as a thief is not with malice, but unexpectedly. God will not wait forever
to correct them. Judgment is imminent. "However, you have a few names
in Sardis who did not defile their garments, and they shall walk with me
in white, because they are worthy" (v. 4). There was a remnant of true
believers who had not smeared their garments with filth. Some people
get used to the filth of the world and just wallow in it. But there are a
few who abhor the filth of the world and soon discover that the Lord has
drawn near and is walking with them. Individuals in deteriorating churches
can still stand true. Now he gives a **challenge** to the overcomer. "Thus
the one who conquers shall be clothed in white garments and I will
never blot his name out of the book of life, but I shall confess his name

---

3:2. The command to *be watchful* (γρηγορέω) is a regular reminder for believers (Matt.
24:42; 25:13; I Cor. 16:13; Col. 4:2; I Thess. 5:6; I Pet. 5:8; Rev. 16:15). God watches His
people as a Shepherd (Jer. 31:10), but His people must watch as well, for His coming
(Rev. 3:3) and for the danger of sin (Luke 12:15).

3:3. The word *hour* (ὥρα) occurs 10 times in Rev., always referring to a specific point in
time.

3:4. Walking with God in this life is a good preparation for walking with Him in the next
(Gen. 5:22–24; 6:9; 17:1; Ps. 116:9; Rom. 6:4; Col. 1:10; Rev. 21:24).

7 And to the angel of the church in Philadelphia write; These things saith he that is holy, he that is true, he that hath the key of David, he that openeth, and no man shutteth; and shutteth, and no man openeth;

8 I know thy works: behold, I have set before thee an open door, and no man can shut it: for thou hast a little strength, and hast kept my word, and hast not denied my name.

9 Behold, I will make them of the synagogue of Satan, which say they are Jews, and are not, but do lie; behold, I will make them to come and worship before thy feet, and to know that I have loved thee.

10 Because thou hast kept the word of my patience, I also will keep thee from the hour of temptation, which shall come upon all the world, to try them that dwell upon the earth.

11 Behold, I come quickly: hold that fast which thou hast, that no man take thy crown.

12 Him that overcometh will I make a pillar in the temple of my God, and he shall go no more out: and I will write upon him the name of my God, and the name of the city of my God, which is new Jerusalem, which cometh down out of heaven from my God: and I will write upon him my new name.

13 He that hath an ear, let him hear what the Spirit saith unto the churches.

before my Father and before his angels" (v. 5). Think of the Lord Jesus claiming us as His disciples! It is worth the battle. We must keep on fighting the good fight of faith. David prays that the wicked "be blotted out of the book of the living" (Ps. 69:28 LXX; 68:29). J. William Fuller argues that the verse "promises a unique and honorable eternal identity." For a discussion of different interpretations, see his article, "I Will Not Erase His Name from the Book of Life" (*Journal of the Evangelical Theological Society*, 1983, 26: 297–306). The Lord concludes with His **call**: "Let the one who has an ear hear what the Spirit says to the churches" (v. 6). We must listen carefully to what the Spirit has to say to the churches.

II. The Church in Philadelphia. vv. 7–13.

The Lord gives His solemn **command** to write and gives a **characterization** of Himself that especially fits the church in Philadelphia. "And to the messenger of the church in Philadelphia write: Thus says the Holy

---

3:5. The Book of Life is mentioned 7 times in Rev. (3:5; 13:8; 17:8; 20:12, 15; 21:27; 22:19). Paul is the only other biblical writer to mention it (Phil. 4:3). The Book of Life contains the names of every redeemed saint. It must be distinguished from the books of deeds that record the works of every human being that has ever lived (Rev. 20:12).

The verb *to confess* (ὁμολογέω) occurs only here in Rev. We must remember the Lord's promise, "Whosoever therefore shall confess me before men, him will I confess also before my Father which is in heaven" (Matt. 10:32). See ZPEB, "Confession," I, pp. 937–39; ISBE (1979), "Confess, Confession," I, pp. 759f.

One, the True One, the One who has the key of David, the One who opens and no one shuts, and shuts and no one opens" (v. 7). These are all divine titles. The name of the Lord is Holy (Ps. 99:3, 5, 9). He is "the high and lofty One that inhabiteth eternity, whose name is Holy" (Isa. 57:15 KJV). The Lord will make His holy name known (Ezek. 39:7). The Lord is the true God (Jer. 10:10); the Lord is a true and faithful witness (Jer. 42:5). The Lord promised to give Eliakim, Hezekiah's steward, the authority of government, "And the key of the house of David will I lay upon his shoulder; so he shall open, and none shall shut; and he shall shut, and none shall open" (Isa. 22:22). The Lord Jesus, however, has absolute providential control over His people and the opportunities that arise before them. When He opens a door, all the powers of darkness together cannot shut it. The apostle Paul rejoiced that "a great door and effectual was opened unto me" (I Cor. 16:9). The words that follow are a very encouraging **commendation**. "I know your works; behold I have set before you a door, having been opened, which no one is able to shut, because you have a little power, and you kept my word and did not deny my name" (v. 8). The thought is that the door is permanently standing open. If we do not go through it, it is our fault, not His. The apostle Paul mentions the door that was open for his gospel ministry (II Cor. 2:12). The preaching of the cross is despised by some people, but it is the power of God unto salvation (I Cor. 1:18). Believers may be few in number, but it is the Lord's power that sustains them. *Keeping the Word* means obeying

---

3:7. This is the first of 25 times that the word *holy* (ἅγιος) occurs in Rev. It is applied once to Christ (3:7); 4 times to God (4:8 [3 times]; 6:10); 4 times to Jerusalem (11:2; 21:2, 10; 22:19); once to angels (14:10); and 15 times to men (saints) (5:8; 8:3, 4; 11:18; 13:7, 10; 14:12; 16:6; 17:6; 18:20, 24; 19:8; 20:6, 9; 22:11). This certainly emphasizes the "set apart" nature of God's people. When God manifested His holiness to Isaiah, it was a shattering experience to him (Isa. 6:1–5). It is the blood of Jesus that enables us to enter into the holiest (Heb. 10:19). Believers need to present their bodies as "a living sacrifice, holy, acceptable to God" (Rom. 12:1). See ZPEB, "Holiness," III, pp. 173–83; ISBE (1982), "Holiness, Holy," II, pp. 725–29.

The word *true* (ἀληθινός) occurs 10 times in Rev. (3:7, 14; 6:10; 15:3; 16:7; 19:2, 9, 11; 21:5; 22:6).

The verb *to lock* or *shut* (κλείω) occurs 6 times in Rev. (3:7 [twice], 8; 11:6; 20:3; 21:25). Marshall Neal records that Philadelphia was 28 miles southeast of Sardis and about 75 miles from the coast on a great east-west highway (*Seven Churches*, p. 77). It was the last Christian city in Asia Minor to fall to the Muslim invasion (*Seven Churches*, p. 79). For more historical background on the city of Philadelphia, see Neal, *Seven Churches*, pp. 77–86; W. M. Ramsay, *The Letters to the Seven Churches of Asia*, pp. 391–400; ZPEB, IV, pp. 753–54; ISBE (1986), III, p. 830; Pfeiffer and Vos, *The Wycliffe Historical Geography of Bible Lands*, pp. 400–402.

3:8. *I have set* is literally "I have given," a perf. act. (δέδωκα). The open door is a gift of Christ (A. T. Robertson, *Word Pictures*, VI, p. 317).

it from the heart. They did not deny His name by living a life that contradicted His Word. "Behold, I will give those of the synagogue of Satan, who say they are Jews, but are not, but they lie; behold, I will make them to come and worship before your feet and to know that I loved you" (v. 9). It is a harsh blow to call professing Jews "the synagogue of Satan." The average Jew in Israel today is a secular Jew; he makes no attempt to obey the words of Moses and the prophets. Even rabbinic students spend their time learning the sayings and traditions of the rabbis rather than the actual words of the holy book. The Orthodox rabbis can say this more forcefully than I can. A true Jew submits to the Word of God and obeys it at all costs. God will vindicate those who obey His Word. Of these true Jews Isaiah prophesied that their afflicters will come and bow down before them and recognize Jerusalem as the true city of the Lord (Isa. 59:20; 60:14). "Because you kept the word of my patience, I also will keep you out of the hour of testing, which is about to come on the whole inhabited earth, to test those who are dwelling on the earth" (v. 10). This is a word that requires patience to keep. It is "the teaching which found its central point in the patience of Christ" (Swete, *Rev.*, p. 56). A number of interpreters take the church of Philadelphia to be the true church within the professing church. Within that group are many who take this declaration as a promise of the Rapture to remove the true church before the Tribulation period. The most scholarly defense of this view is Gerald B. Stanton's *Kept from the Hour*. He correctly observes that the passage cannot be limited to a single congregation in a local persecution (pp. 48f.). The trial will fall on the whole inhabited earth, and this church will be kept from the hour, the period of testing. The real purpose of the testing is to try the "earth dwellers," those people who are

---

3:9. For the word *worship* see Rev. 4:10 note.

The word *synagogue* occurs only in Rev. 2:9; 3:9.

3:10. In addition to Stanton's work this view may be found in John Walvoord, *The Rapture Question*; Dwight Pentecost, *Things to Come* (pp. 156–218); and in commentaries on Rev. by Walvoord (pp. 86ff.), Tim LaHaye (pp. 81f.), Robert Thomas (I, pp. 283–90), William Newell (p. 70), Harry Ironside (pp. 72f.), A. C. Gaebelein (pp. 41f.), J. B. Smith (p. 89), and others. See also Walvoord, "Premillennialism and the Tribulation—Part VI: Posttribulationism" in *Bibliotheca Sacra* 112, no. 448, Oct.-Dec. 1955, p. 300. For a face-off between advocates of different views, see *The Rapture: Pre-, Mid-, or Post-Tribulational?* by Archer, Feinberg, Moo, and Reiter.

Those who dwell on the earth (τοὺς κατοικοῦντας ἐπὶ τῆς γῆς) appears only in Rev. (3:10; 6:10; 8:13; 11:10 [twice]; 13:8, 12, 14 [twice]; 17:2, 8). These "earth dwellers" (those settled down on the earth) belong to Satan and will not repent. Their names are not written in heaven (Rev. 17:8). They are a stark contrast to those believers whose hope is in heaven (Phil. 3:20; I Thess. 1:10). The noun form is applied to the poor demon-possessed man who had his dwelling place (κατοίκησις) among the tombs (Mark 5:3).

satisfied with the earth, not God. In contrast the saints belong in glory with the Lord. There is **no condemnation** pronounced on this church. The Lord gives a single word of **correction**. "I am coming quickly; hold fast what you have, that no one take your crown" (v. 11). Believers need to grip tenaciously God's Word, His blessings, the opportunities to serve, and so forth. The *crown* here is the victor's crown, the wreath from winning the games. We should be much more zealous than worldly athletes for an eternal prize. Now the Lord gives a strong **challenge** to the overcomer. "I will make the one who overcomes a pillar in the sanctuary of my God, and he shall never go outside again, and I will write upon him the name of my God, and the name of the city of my God, the new Jerusalem, which comes down out of heaven from my God, and my new name" (v. 12). In contrast to the instability and changeableness of the present world, the overcomer will be made a pillar in God's sanctuary. A pillar is both an element of the structure of a building and an example of beauty. The pillars in Solomon's temple were regarded as so important that they were named (I Kings 7:21). Does this foreshadow the fact that the pillars in God's celestial sanctuary are all named human beings? There are three names that are given to the overcomer. In Scripture, names always indicate the character of the person. Jacob ("Supplanter") became Israel ("Prince with God" or "God rules") when he submitted to the Lord (Gen. 32:27–28). The Lord declares that He will write upon the overcomer "the name of my God"; the very character of God will be stamped on him (holiness, love, righteousness, and so forth). The Lord also puts on him "the name of the city of my God," the character of that heavenly place. The overcomer will be made suitable for dwelling in heaven with God and the angels. Isaiah prophesied of a time when the people of restored Jerusalem will be called by a new name (Isa. 62:2). Ezekiel looked forward to the day when millennial Jerusalem will be named *Jehovah Shammah*, "the Lord is there" (Ezek. 48:35). And the Lord will put on him "my new name," the character of the glorified Christ.

3:12. The Lord pulled back the veil in the account of the rich man and Lazarus (which is not called a parable, Luke 16:19–31). We would tend to bitterly denounce that rich man who could watch a saint of God die of starvation and not help him, but Abraham is beyond such passion. He speaks with kindness and full knowledge ("Son, remember," 16:25). Abraham rejoices that he can provide the comfort that Lazarus never found in this life. He is sure that God has done everything perfectly. This really answers the question "How can saints enjoy heaven when they know the lost are suffering?" They will be transformed into the character of God, perfectly righteous, holy, and serene. The wicked will always be self-centered and dissatisfied.

The word *heaven* (οὐρανός) occurs here for the first of 52 times in Rev. (For a summary of the word *heaven*, see Rev. 21:1 note).

The word *sanctuary* (ναός) occurs here for the first of 16 times in Rev.

14 And unto the angel of the church of the Laodiceans write; These things saith the Amen, the faithful and true witness, the beginning of the creation of God;
15 I know thy works, that thou art neither cold nor hot: I would thou wert cold or hot.
16 So then because thou art lukewarm, and neither cold nor hot, I will spue thee out of my mouth.
17 Because thou sayest, I am rich, and increased with goods, and have need of nothing; and knowest not that thou art wretched, and miserable, and poor, and blind, and naked:
18 I counsel thee to buy of me gold tried in the fire, that thou mayest be rich; and white raiment, that thou mayest be clothed, and that the shame of thy nakedness do not appear; and anoint thine eyes with eyesalve, that thou mayest see.
19 As many as I love, I rebuke and chasten: be zealous therefore, and repent.
20 Behold, I stand at the door, and knock: if any man hear my voice, and open the door, I will come in to him, and will sup with him, and he with me.
21 To him that overcometh will I grant to sit with me in my throne, even as I also overcame, and am set down with my Father in his throne.
22 He that hath an ear, let him hear what the Spirit saith unto the churches.

The overcomer will bear the image of Christ forever. John reminded believers, "We shall be like him, for we shall see him as he is" (I John 3:2). The veil shall be lifted and we shall have the beatific vision. The Lord concludes with the **call,** "Let the one who has an ear hear what the Spirit says to the churches" (v. 13). For a photograph of a synagogue pillar in Capernaum with an inscription dedicated to a named person, see *Holman Bible Handbook* (David S. Dockery, ed.), p. 792.

III. The Church in Laodicea. vv. 14–22.

Ramsay characterizes Laodicea as "the city of compromise . . . the successful trading city, the city of bankers and finance" (*The Letters to the Seven Churches of Asia*, pp. 413–23). It was a little over a hundred miles east of Ephesus, on a great east-west trade route. Because it was a poor position to defend, it survived largely by diplomacy and compromise. John records the **command** to write and the **characterization** of the Lord. "And to the messenger of the church that is in Laodicea write: Thus says the Amen, the faithful and true Witness, the Beginning of the creation of God" (v. 14). *Amen* is probably the most widely known word in the world. As

---

3:14. Marshall Neal observes that Laodicea had no water source and consequently had to bring in water by aqueduct from distant mineral springs. The water was lukewarm and nauseous to the taste (*Seven Churches*, p. 92). "Six miles to the north lay Hierapolis, famed for its hot springs. Ten miles to the east lay Colosse, known for its cold, pure drinking water" (Osborne, *Rev.*, p. 205). For additional historical background see W. M. Ramsay, *The Letters to the Seven Churches of Asia*, pp. 413–23; ZPEB, III, pp. 877–79; ISBE (1986), III, pp. 72–74; Pfeiffer and Vos, *The Wycliffe Historical Geography of Bible Lands*, pp. 377–79; *Lion Photoguide to the Bible*, "Laodicea," pp. 280f.

the appropriate conclusion to prayer, it has been borrowed by all nations. The original Hebrew meant "so be it," "may it be thus confirmed." Here it is a divine title. Delitzsch notes the parallel between this text and Isaiah 65:16. Jehovah is "the God of Amen" (*Isaiah*, II, p. 487). The Lord Jesus Christ is *the Amen*, the one incorruptibly committed to confirming the divine will. He will confirm the will of His Father at all costs (Matt. 26:39–42). The apostle Paul reinforces this. "For all the promises of God in him are yea, and in him Amen, unto the glory of God by us" (II Cor. 1:20). Swete calls attention to the Lord's repeated use of the formula, "Amen, Amen, I say unto you" (*Apocalypse*, p. 59). He is *the faithful and true Witness*, one who will never shade or twist the truth, as He Himself testified (John 8:14–40). It is the Devil who is the father of the lie (John 8:44). The Lord Jesus testified to the nature of His Father (John 8:19, 29, 42; 10:17–18; 15:1, 10, 26); the sinful nature of man (John 3:19; 5:38–40; 8:21, 24, 44); the one way of salvation (John 3:14–17; 5:24; 6:35; 8:12; 14:1–6; 15:5; 17:3). Psalm 89:37 prophesied that the throne of David would be established as a faithful witness in heaven (Ps. 88:38 LXX). He is the *beginning of the creation of God*, that is, the one who originated all creation (John 1:1–3; Col. 1:13–16). The word *beginning* "cannot have meant the earliest and greatest of creatures, but a being above creation" (Gebhardt, *The Doctrine of the Apocalypse*, p. 93). The implication of this characterization is that the Laodiceans were not faithful witnesses and were not speaking all the truth. There is **no commendation** given to this church. The **condemnation**, however, is rather detailed. "I know your works, that you are neither cold nor hot. I would that you were cold or hot" (v. 15). Open unbelief is better than standing for nothing. "Anything would be better than self-satisfied apathy!" (J. I. Packer, *Knowing God*, p. 158). The apostle Peter warns that it is better for the false teachers "not to have known the way of righteousness, than, after they have known it, to turn from the holy commandment delivered to them" (II Pet. 2:21). But the situation in Laodicea was a studied, politic

---

3:15–16. The word *cold* (ψυχρός) occurs only 3 times in these verses and once more in Matt. 10:42, where it refers to cold water. Here it refers to spiritual coldness, a lack of enthusiasm for the things of God.

The word *hot* (ζεστός) occurs only 3 times in the NT, all in this passage. The verb form (ζέω) *to boil* (as in cooking) is applied to Apollos, who was *boiling hot* (fervent) in the Spirit (Acts 18:25). Paul exhorted believers to be *boiling hot* in the Spirit (Rom. 12:11). All of these occurrences refer to fervent spiritual zeal for God.

3:16. The word *lukewarm* (χλιαρός) occurs only here in the NT. A beverage that is neither cold nor hot, especially mineral water, can be sickening to the taste. A normal response would be to *spit it out*, or *vomit it forth* (ἐμέω), only here in the NT. Walvoord holds that this statement "would not be addressed to true believers" ("Contemporary Problems in Biblical Interpretations—Part IV: The Nature of the Church" in

neutrality. "Thus because you are lukewarm and neither hot nor cold, I am about to spit you out of my mouth" (v. 16). The language implies total repudiation. The Lord wants followers such as Joshua, who was thinking about His Word day and night and was eager to obey (Josh. 1:8). "Because you are saying, I am wealthy, and I have become rich, and I have need of nothing, and you do not know that you are wretched and pitiable and poor and blind and naked" (v. 17). It was Hosea who charged Ephraim with claiming to be rich and ignoring their sin (Hos. 12:8). The economic prosperity of Laodicea deceived the church into thinking that it was rich. The Laodiceans were proud of their prosperity in banking and commerce, the export of black wool and eye salve. When an earthquake damaged the city in A.D. 60, they refused help from the Roman Empire and insisted on rebuilding at their own expense (Neal, *Seven Churches*, p. 89). But the Lord advises them to seek help from Him. "I counsel you to buy from me gold that has been burned in the fire in order that you may be rich, and white garments in order that you may be clothed and in order that the shame of your nakedness not be manifested, and anoint your eyes with eyesalve in order that you may see" (v. 18). The Lord can supply them with eternal riches and eyesalve that will give them spiritual vision of the world to come. The white robes He can supply to them (Rev. 6:11) contrast with the black wool they were so proud of. Now the Lord gives them a solemn **correction**. "As many as I love, I convict and chasten; be zealous therefore and repent" (v. 19). "Whom Jehovah loves, he corrects" (Prov. 3:12). Although the church as a whole was in sad condition, the Lord still had warm affection toward individuals within it. He was prepared to convict them and "child-train" them. His goal is to

---

Bibliotheca Sacra 116, no. 464, Oct. 1959, p. 296). It is a most emphatic way of saying that religious neutrality makes the Lord sick. He said, "Whosoever therefore shall be ashamed of me and of my words in this adulterous and sinful generation; of him also shall the Son of man be ashamed, when he cometh in the glory of his Father with the holy angels" (Mark 8:38).

3:17. The Laodiceans were proud of their material goods, but nothing they had was of eternal value. The Lord uses a mournful list of terms to characterize their true condition. They were *wretched* (ταλαίπωρος), the same word Paul used of his unsaved condition (Rom. 7:24); *pitiable* (ἐλεεινός), a word Paul used for those without a resurrection hope (I Cor. 15:19); *poor* (πτωχός), a word for a beggar (Luke 14:13); *blind* (τυφλός) and *naked* (γυμνός), conditions regarded as tragic everywhere.

3:18. The word *eyesalve* (κολλούριον) occurs only here in the NT. See ISBE (1988), "Salve," IV, p. 295.

3:19. This is the only time in the NT that the believer is commanded to be zealous (ζηλεύω). This verse teaches that the Lord has warm affection (φιλέω) for true believers, even as they have for Him (I Cor. 16:22). He is prepared to "child-train" (παιδεύω) them with discipline, firmness, repetition, and divine patience. See ISBE (1988), "Zeal," IV, p. 1175, "Impassioned devotion to a person or cause."

cause them to repent, to change the way they think and act. We have come to the best verse in all the Bible to help us to change. "Behold, I have taken my stand at the door and I am knocking: if any one hears my voice and opens the door, I will come in to him, and will dine with him and he with me" (v. 20). It is the heavenly Bridegroom who knocks and cries, "Open to me, my sister, my love" (Song of Sol. 5:2). The word *behold* tells us to pay special attention to these words. The contrast in tenses is especially convicting. "I have taken my stand" (perfect) tells us that He is always at our heart's door, waiting for us to respond. "I am knocking" (present) implies that He is constantly using the providential happenings of every day, happy or sad, to attract our attention to Himself in praise or petition. (We are so thoughtless and slow to respond.) "And opens the door" implies a conscious invitation, welcoming the Lord into the life situation. "I will come in to him" tells us that the Lord will manifest Himself to the believer with a special sense of His presence. "And will dine with him" reveals the Lord's intention of sweet fellowship in a loving atmosphere. "And he with me" implies the staggering privilege of fellowship with the Lord of the universe. Are we too busy to hear His knock? Will we leave Him standing there? God have mercy upon us! We need to change for the better. We should praise God that He is willing to dwell with one who has a contrite and humble spirit (Isa. 57:15). We need to remember that the Lord Jesus promised to anyone who knocks on His door, "it shall be opened unto you" (Matt. 7:7). He concludes with the **challenge** and the **call**. "To the one who overcomes I will grant to sit with me in my throne, even as I also overcame and sat down with my

---

3:20. John urges believers to have more fellowship "with the Father and with his Son Jesus Christ" (I John 1:3). Paul prays fellowship with the Holy Spirit on believers (II Cor. 13:14). Matthew Henry suggests using the Psalms to maintain our fellowship with God (*The Quest for Communion with God*, p. 1712). He recommends using the morning psalm to begin every day with God. "My voice shalt thou hear in the morning, O Lord; in the morning will I direct my prayer unto thee, and will look up" (Ps. 5:3). He urges conscious prayer at every opportunity. "On thee do I wait all the day" (Ps. 25:5). Like Noah's dove, we find no rest in a defiled world (p. 72). And he suggests closing the day with the evening psalm. "I will both lay me down in peace and sleep: for thou, Lord, only makest me to dwell in safety" (Ps. 4:8). See ZPEB, "Psalms, Book of," IV, pp. 924–47; ISBE (1986), "Psalms," III, pp. 1029–40. Brother Lawrence (*The Practice of the Presence of God*) testified, "I began to live as if there was none but He and I in the world." Spurgeon has a powerful message, "An Earnest Warning About Lukewarmness," in which he says, "The best remedy for backsliding churches is *more communion with Christ*" (Sermon 1185, *The C. H. Spurgeon Collection*, Ages Digital Library). See ZPEB, "Fellowship," II, p. 528; ISBE (1979), "Communion; Fellowship," I, pp. 752–53.

3:21. Even in Laodicea there are overcomers. "The note of triumph throbs through these passages. Christians here and now may be a depressed, down-trodden minority . . . yet they belong to the mighty Conqueror who has won a triumph over all his foes. . . . And when that day comes they will share in the triumph" (Morris, *The Cross in the NT*, p. 356).

Father in his throne" (v. 21). If we will invite Him into our humble heart and home, He will one day invite us into a position of breathtaking majesty in the glorious realm to come. "Let the one who has an ear hear what the Spirit says to the churches" (v. 22). If you have spiritual perception, listen very carefully to what the Spirit is saying to your heart. Each of these letters was written to an actual, historical church at the end of the first century, but each one also applies to that kind of church wherever it may be found in history. Every individual who reads these letters needs to apply them to his own heart and to determine to be that "overcomer" who seeks the blessing of the Lord above all things.

Practical Applications from Revelation 3

1. Believers should avoid at all costs a reputation that is without the internal life to back it up (v. 1). We used to be dead in sins, but now we are alive in Christ (Eph. 2:5). [Caution]
2. We should continue holding fast to the good and keep changing for the better (v. 3). We need to keep giving earnest heed to the things we have learned (Heb. 2:1). [Consistency]
3. We should be zealous to be among the few who have not stained their testimony (v. 4). Few there be that find the way that leads to life (Matt. 7:14). [Challenge]
4. Recognition in heaven is far more important than recognition here (v. 5). "Whosoever shall confess me before men, him shall the Son of man also confess before the angels of God" (Luke 12:8). [Confession]
5. We should go boldly through any door that we know God opens for us (v. 8). The apostle Paul prayed that God would open a door of utterance for him (Col. 4:3). [Confidence]
6. To know that Christ loves us is all that is important (v. 9). It is an eternal truth: "The Lord loves the righteous" (Ps. 146:8). [Commendation]
7. We need to remember the importance of keeping God's Word (v. 10). In keeping the Word there is great reward (Ps. 19:11); the psalmist vows to keep God's statutes (Ps. 119:8, 44). [Confidence]
8. We need to be always ready to meet the Lord (v. 11). Paul warns, "The Lord is at hand" (Phil. 4:5); James also warns, "The coming of the Lord draws nigh" (James 5:8). [Crown]
9. We must remember that God is changing our character (v. 12). Christ will dwell in our hearts by faith (Eph. 3:17). [Change for the better]

10. We must be positively on God's side on every issue (v. 15). Paul exhorts believers to be fervent, "boiling hot in the Spirit" (Rom. 12:11). [Condemnation]
11. We should be aware of our profound need of God's grace and help (v. 17). "If any man thinks that he knows any thing, he knows nothing yet as he ought to know" (I Cor. 8:2). [Condemnation]
12. We must humbly accept God's chastening hand (v. 19). "Whom the Lord loves he chastens" (Heb. 12:6). [Correction]
13. We must be spiritually alert to hear the voice of God (v. 20). "Faith comes by hearing, and hearing by the word of God" (Rom. 10:17). [Challenge]
14. We should remember God's great purpose for our lives (v. 21). "Blessed be the God and Father of our Lord Jesus Christ, who has blessed us with all spiritual blessings in the heavenlies in Christ" (Eph. 1:3). [Challenge]

Prayer

O Lord, You are the faithful and true Witness; enable us to be good witnesses for You. Give us ears to hear Your knock on our heart's door, and give us the desire for that fellowship with You that daily sustains us. Amen.

Revelation 4:1–5:14

REVELATION 4

The Scene in Heaven

Persons

John ("I")   Twenty-four elders
The trumpet voice   The seven Spirits of God
One seated on the   The four living beings
   throne (the Father)

Persons referred to

All created beings

Place

The throne room of heaven

Doctrines taught

Heaven   The holiness of God
The rule of God   The eternality of God
The light of God   The creation of God
The sea of glass

1 After this I looked, and, behold, a door was opened in heaven: and the first voice which I heard was as it were of a trumpet talking with me; which said, Come up hither, and I will shew thee things which must be hereafter.
2 And immediately I was in the spirit: and, behold, a throne was set in heaven, and one sat on the throne.
3 And he that sat was to look upon like a jasper and a sardine stone: and there was a rainbow round about the throne, in sight like unto an emerald.

Revelation 4 Exposition

1. The Throne and the One Sitting on It. vv. 1–3.

"After these things I saw, and behold a door having been opened in heaven, and the first voice that I heard was as a trumpet speaking with me, saying, Come up here, and I will show you things which must come to pass after these things" (v. 1). The phrase *after these things* (μετὰ ταῦτα) refers back to the outline of the book that was given in 1:19, which was the last time the phrase was used. This certainly implies that the glorious events that are now to be described will occur after the close of the church age. John has the privilege of seeing that realm that controls all the events of the universe. Louis Talbot argues that the language presupposes the Rapture of the church and the Judgment Seat of Christ (*God's Plan of the Ages*, pp. 135–36). Gerald B. Stanton holds that the Rapture falls chronologically between Revelation 3 and 4 (*Kept from the Hour*, p. 362). The time that follows on earth is regularly called the Tribulation period (Matt. 24:21), the time of seven years, the last week that Daniel mentioned (Dan. 9:24–27) in which God shall pour out His wrath on unbelieving nations. The true church is not mentioned again until the period is over (Rev. 21:2) and is not named again until 22:16. Jerome Smith warns that this passage is not a reference to the Rapture, for that would make John a type of the church (*The New Treasury of Scripture Knowledge*, p. 1510). Swete mentions that *the door* must be distinguished from the door of opportunity (3:8) and the door of the heart

---

4:1. The Devil has worked hard trying to make men believe that this world is true reality, the whole goal of their existence (Gen. 3:1–6; Luke 12:16–21; I John 2:15–17). He has been stringing gaudy Christmas tree lights in a cemetery. The apostle Paul saw clearly that this world is a temporary place, the light afflictions are but for a moment, and the things that are not seen are the eternal reality of the coming age (II Cor. 4:16–18). John said the same thing in his own way (I John 2:15–17). Spurgeon has a sermon, "A Door Opened in Heaven," in which he says, "Some have doubted whether there will be recognition in heaven: there is no room for doubt, for it is called 'my Father's house;' and shall not the family be known to each other? . . . We are to 'sit down with Abraham, Isaac, and Jacob' but we shall 'know even as we are known'" (Sermon 887, *The C. H. Spurgeon Collection*, Ages Digital Library).

(3:20, *Rev.*, p. 66). This door of revelation opened and John saw reality, the timeless realm of God and the angels. Ezekiel also saw heaven opened and saw a vision of God (Ezek. 1:1). John heard a voice as of a trumpet. He had already heard that voice of the Lord Jesus Christ, speaking to him in the initial vision (1:10–11). Now it commands him, "Come up here, and I will show you things which are necessary to happen after these things." They are necessary because they are the will of God. There is no possibility that John is looking at prophetic delusions. This is the Revelation of the true God. Daniel was also concerned about the things that would happen "hereafter" (Dan. 2:29, 45). "Immediately I was in the Spirit, and behold a throne was set in heaven, and upon the throne [one] who was sitting" (v. 2). This is the eternal throne of God (Ps. 45:6). It is the throne of His holiness (Ps. 47:8). Isaiah saw the Lord "sitting upon a throne, high and lifted up" (Isa. 6:1). Ezekiel saw the throne of the Lord and fell upon his face (Ezek. 1:26–28). Daniel saw the throne of the Ancient of Days with multitudes standing before Him (Dan. 7:9–10). God is always the same; He cannot deteriorate or improve (Heb. 1:12). God's way is perfect (Ps. 18:30). But "God is light" (I John 1:5), and as John continues gazing at the one on the throne, he begins thinking about what kind of light that is. "And the one sitting was like in appearance a jasper stone and a sardius, and a rainbow was around the throne in a circle, like in appearance an emerald" (v. 3). All rainbows are circles, but we can usually see only half or less. The psalmist declared that God covered Himself "with light as a garment" (Ps. 104:2). As John gazes, he thinks of the most ethereal colors that he can: precious stones and the rainbow. Jasper is regularly reddish; a sardius dark red; emeralds are green, but the iridescent rainbow has all the colors of visible light. The human eye can identify millions of colors in visible light, but John is here seeing all sixty-four octaves of electromagnetic radiation, from cosmic rays to radio waves. Beyond this, he is seeing colors of the celestial

---

4:2. The first thing that John sees in heaven is the throne of God with the rainbow; then he notices the 4 living beings. Ezekiel had a vision in reverse order, seeing the 4 living beings, and then above them the throne of God with the rainbow (Ezek. 1:4–28). Ezekiel is overwhelmed by the power of the living beings, but John is fascinated by the one on the throne. *Throne* (θρόνος) is mentioned 44 times in Rev. and only 14 times in the rest of the NT.

4:3. God's words to Noah show that the rainbow is the token of the covenant that God established between Himself and every living creature on earth. There will never again be a universal flood (Gen. 9:11–16). The *rainbow* (ἶρις), mentioned only twice in the NT (Rev. 4:3; 10:1), is the pledge that God is the covenant-keeping God. See Ryken, Wilhoit, and Longman, *Dictionary of Biblical Imagery*, "Rainbow," p. 695.

All 3 of the precious stones mentioned here are also mentioned as foundation stones of the heavenly Jerusalem (Rev. 21:19–20).

4 And round about the throne were four and twenty seats: and upon the seats I saw four and twenty elders sitting, clothed in white raiment; and they had on their heads crowns of gold.

realm that are beyond human description. For the first time in his life he understands what "God is light" means. This is the fulfillment of the Lord's promise, "Blessed are the pure in heart, for they shall see God" (Matt. 5:8). John's vision helps all believers to understand how great God is. "Nowhere in the literature of heavenly visions will one find a more in-spiring presentation of the God who reigns supreme over all" (Mounce, *Rev.*, p. 118).

II. The Twenty-four Elders. v. 4.

"And in a circle around the throne [were] twenty-four thrones, and upon the thrones twenty-four elders sitting, having been clothed in white garments and upon their heads golden crowns" (v. 4). This is the first occurrence of the word *elder* (πρεσβύτερος) in Revelation. There were elders in Israel from earliest times (Exod. 3:16); there were elders in every synagogue (Acts 6:12); the apostles appointed elders (plural) in every church (singular) (Acts 14:23). The elders here are not only rulers but also representatives of the combined people of God. John has said that Christ "has made us kings and priests unto God" (Rev. 1:6). The patriarchs and apostles have been in the presence of God for about two thousand years. We can hardly imagine the transforming effect that would have. They

---

4:4. "As a symbol, twelve is one of the most important numbers in the Bible" (Ryken, Wilhoit, and Longman, *Dictionary of Biblical Imagery*, "Twelve," pp. 900f.) Twelve is the number of the people of God. There were 12 patriarchs and 12 apostles. 12 + 12 = 24. Jennings observes, "Two twelves may point to the redeemed of both dispensations, one company here in their heavenly glories as kings and priests" (*Rev.*, p. 174). Although some commentators hold that they are literal apostles and patriarchs (Victorinus, Matthew Henry, Alford) and others hold that they are symbolic (Ironside, Walter Scott), together, most hold that they represent the combined people of God of all ages (Vincent, II, p. 478; Swete, p. 69; Tenney, *Interpreting Rev.*, p. 190; A. C. Gaebelein, p. 46; LaHaye, p. 117; ZPEB, II, p. 268). Spurgeon calls them "representatives of the great body of the faithful gathered to their eternal rest" and notes that they are "all near the throne" ("The Elders Before the Throne," Sermon 441, *C. H. Spurgeon Collection*, Ages Digital Library). Ottman argues that the Lord promised the 12 apostles that they would sit on 12 thrones as judges (Matt. 19:28, p. 115). Peter called the church "a royal priesthood" (I Pet. 2:9). But there are other interpretations. Some dispensationalists hold that they are the NT church only (J. B. Smith, Walvoord, Dwight Pentecost). Newell "assumes" that they are angels (p. 374); Robert Thomas suggests that they are a special "college of angels" (*Rev.*, I, p. 348). Osborne holds that they are *a ruling class of heavenly beings* (*Rev.*, p. 230). G. K. Beale thinks they represent both angels and the righteous (*Rev.*, p. 322). J. B. Smith declares, "They are not angels because angels are never spoken of as sitting on thrones nor as having crowns on their heads" (*Rev.*, p. 104).

5 And out of the throne proceeded lightnings and thunderings and voices: and there were seven lamps of fire burning before the throne, which are the seven Spirits of God.
6 And before the throne there was a sea of glass like unto crystal: and in the midst of the throne, and round about the throne, were four beasts full of eyes before and behind.

are elders who are kings and priests indeed, exercising authority and priestly ministry in the service of God. The *crown* is the victor's crown (στέφανος), appropriate for human beings who have conquered by the grace of God. The prophet Daniel saw this same scene:

"I kept looking
Until thrones were set up
And the Ancient of Days took His seat" (Dan. 7:9, NASB).

III. The Seven Spirits of God. vv. 5–6a.

"And out of the throne proceeded lightnings and voices and thunders, and seven torches of fire were burning before the throne, which are the seven Spirits of God" (v. 5). The throne of God is a place of awesome power in both sight and sound. Isaiah had the privilege of seeing the Lord "sitting on a throne" (Isa. 6:1). The psalmist has well said, "Great is our Lord, and of great power" (Ps. 147:5). Thunder and lightning are two of the most terrifying phenomena of nature. The psalmist recounts, "The voice of thy thunder was in the heaven: the lightnings lightened the world: the earth trembled and shook" (Ps. 77:18). Jennings notes that between the lightning and the thunder were voices (*Rev.*, p. 175). That implies revelation. The same three phenomena were at the giving of the law at Sinai (Exod. 19:16). The salutation of John (1:4–5) has already made clear that the *seven torches* is a reference to the sevenfold Holy Spirit (Isa. 11:2). There are seven special titles given to Him in the NT. He is the Spirit of truth (John 14:17), the Spirit of holiness (Rom. 1:4), the Spirit of adoption (Rom. 8:15), the Spirit of wisdom and revelation (Eph. 1:17), the Spirit of power and love and of a sound mind (II Tim. 1:7), the Spirit of grace (Heb. 10:29), and the Spirit of prophecy (Rev. 19:10). The word *torch* (λαμπάς) can refer to either a torch or a lamp, but it often has a joyous connotation, as in a torch-lit wedding procession (Matt. 25:1), or as many torches in an upper room for a church service (Acts 20:8). The only other use in Revelation (8:10) refers to "a great star burning as a torch." "And before the throne was as a sea of glass like crystal" (v. 6*a*). Ezekiel looked up toward this scene and saw "the terrible crystal" (Ezek. 1:22 KJV). This

---

4:5. *Lightning* (ἀστραπή) and *thunder* (βροντή) appear together 4 times in Rev. (4:5; 8:5; 11:19; 16:18), but *thunder* appears elsewhere as well (6:1; 10:3, 4 [twice]; 14:2; 19:6). The word *torch* (λαμπάς) occurs twice in Rev. (4:5; 8:10).

7 And the first beast was like a lion, and the second beast like a calf, and the third beast had a face as a man, and the fourth beast was like a flying eagle.

8 And the four beasts had each of them six wings about him; and they were full of eyes within: and they rest not day and night, saying, Holy, holy, holy, Lord God Almighty, which was, and is, and is to come.

is the first mention of a sea in Revelation, but it is a celestial one. The sea was one of the most dangerous things on earth to the ancient world. It swallowed up Pharaoh's army (Exod. 15:1–4). Jonah feared the sea into which he was cast (Jon. 1:15–2:3). Daniel saw four terrible beasts rise up from the sea (Dan. 7:2–3). But here the sea is entirely under the control of God. It is as solid as rock crystal. Later we will learn that light coruscates through the sea and the saints can stand on it without danger (Rev. 15:2). Any architect will explain that a body of water in front of a building will double the beauty of it by reflecting it and at night will double the light that comes from it. The glorious light that comes from the throne will be reflected in the sea and will be an overwhelming sight.

IV. The Four Living Beings. vv. 6b–8.

"And in the midst of the throne, and in a circle around the throne, were four living beings, being filled with eyes before and behind" (v. 6b). The *living beings* (ζῶα) must be sharply distinguished from the wild beasts (θηρία) that appear in Revelation 13:1ff. They are cherubim so close to the Living God that they are called *living beings*. They can be both "in

---

4:6. The apostle Paul provides (Col. 1:16) a hierarchy of angelic beings that includes thrones (θρόνοι), lordships (κυριότητες), rulers (ἀρχαὶ), and authorities (ἐξουσίαι). The biblical doctrine of angels is very complex. Michael is the only named archangel (Jude 9; Rev. 12:7), but Daniel calls him "one of the chief princes" (Dan. 10:13). The only other named angel is Gabriel, who is not called an archangel but who claims to stand in the presence of God (Luke 1:19), certainly a high honor. Where do the "living beings" fit? Some identify them as part of the cherubim. They were guardians of the presence of God (Gen. 3:24); images of cherubim guarded the mercy seat on the ark (Exod. 25:18–20) and were woven into the hangings of the veil and inner tent of the tabernacle so that the presence of God was surrounded by cherubim (Exod. 26:1, 31). Cherubim were also in Solomon's temple (I Kings 6:23) and were engraved on the walls (II Chron. 3:7). The closest parallel may be the living creatures in Ezek. 1:5–25. But there are puzzling differences. Ezekiel's creatures had 4 faces and 4 wings (Ezek. 1:6). They had great wheels with them that were filled with eyes (Ezek. 1:15–18). This implies that they had immense powers of perception. They could go and return as a flash of lightning (Ezek. 1:14). Their position was underneath the throne of God (Ezek. 1:26–28). In a further description they are called cherubim (Ezek. 10:1–2). But it is the seraphim who have 6 wings (Isa. 6:2). Perhaps the solution is that they are spiritual beings, not physical, and can change their appearance at will. We know that angels can look like ordinary human beings (Gen. 18:1–2; 19:1–11; Heb. 13:1–2). Our trouble is that when we think of "man,"

the midst" and "in a circle around" the throne because they are supporting the throne from beneath (Ezek. 1:25–26). This is the reason that the
Hebrew text refers to God "sitting upon the cherubim" (Ps. 80:1; 99:1).
Being filled with eyes implies that they have vastly greater powers of perception than human beings do. It is not an accident that they cry out
"Holy!" (v. 8). They understand the nature of God perfectly. "And the
first living being was like a lion, and the second living being was like a
young bull, and the third living being had the face of a man, and the
fourth living being was like a flying eagle" (v. 7). One had the courage
and powers of destruction of a lion; one had the strength of the young
ox; one had the perception of human nature; one had the speed and distant perception of the eagle. Illustrations from animal life are no more
strange to these mighty spiritual beings than from human life. They are
completely above the physical realm. But this passage shows us that angels differ from one another even as humans do. What a blessing glorification will be when we look at an angel and know his name or look at a
saint and know the name! "And the four living beings, each one of them
having six wings, being full of eyes around and within, have no rest day
or night saying:

> Holy, holy, holy, Lord God, the Almighty, the one who was
> and the one who is and the one who is coming" (v. 8).

Although scholars argue over whether angels can sing, when we consider
that these living beings have been created for the express purpose of
praising the Lord of the universe, can they not fill heaven with the sound
of joyous celebration that would make our best earthly choirs sound like

---

we think of great diversity; when we think of "angel," we think of one thing. There is
probably great diversity. For a more detailed discussion, see "Cherub, Cherubim," ZPEB, I,
pp. 788–90; "Angel," ZPEB, I, pp. 160–66; "Cherub, Cherubim," Unger, *The New Unger's
Bible Dictionary*, pp. 222–23; "Angel," Elwell, *Evangelical Dictionary of Biblical Theology*,
pp. 21–23; Torrey, *What the Bible Teaches*, pp. 501–35; Guthrie, *New Testament Theology*,
p. 885.

4:7. The word *lion* (λέων) occurs 6 times in Rev. (4:7; 5:5; 9:8, 17; 10:3; 13:2); *calf*
(μόσχος) only here; *eagle* (ἀετός) 3 times (4:7; 8:13; 12:14).

4:8. Bengel analyzes the threefold Holy:

> Holy, He who was:
> Holy, He who is:
> Holy, He who is to come.

God is holy in creation, in present providence, and in His consummation. (*Gnomon*, V,
p. 221). The phrase *day and night* occurs 5 times in Rev. (4:8; 7:15; 12:10; 14:11; 20:10).
The living beings do not have even a temporary rest (ἀνάπαυσις) in this celebration.
See Custer, *A Treasury of New Testament Synonyms*, pp. 40–42.

9 And when those beasts give glory and honour and thanks to him that sat on the throne, who liveth for ever and ever,
10 The four and twenty elders fall down before him that sat on the throne, and worship him that liveth for ever and ever, and cast their crowns before the throne, saying,
11 Thou art worthy, O Lord, to receive glory and honour and power: for thou hast created all things, and for thy pleasure they are and were created.

the croaking of frogs by comparison? Reginald Heber (1723–1826) took his keynote from this text when he wrote his famous hymn:

> Holy, Holy, Holy! Lord God Almighty!
> Early in the morning our song shall rise to Thee;
> Holy, Holy, Holy! Merciful and Mighty!
> God in Three Persons, blessed Trinity!

The threefold *Holy* is also the song of the seraphim (Isa. 6:3). They also had six wings (6:2). In heaven the sound was so awesome that the celestial temple trembled (6:4). Isaiah could think only of how inadequate he was even to view such a scene (6:5). These scenes should stir believers to a more serious praise of God in their prayer life. If these living beings spend all their time praising God, can we not spend a few minutes each day doing so? When was the last time that you just praised God for Himself and did not present Him with a list of requests? The word *holy* implies absolute separation from sin. God cannot be tempted with evil (James 1:13). Our whole doctrine of separation comes from this attribute of God. We must be like Him. Filling our minds with the thought and praise of God is certainly the best way to accomplish this purpose (II Cor. 6:14–7:1). The title *Lord God* goes back to creation (Gen. 2:4). *Almighty* ($\pi\alpha\nu\tau\omega\kappa\rho\acute{\alpha}\tau\omega\rho$) is one of the great titles that celebrate God's power. It appears nine times in Revelation. (See note 1:8.) "The one who was and the one who is and the one who is coming" is a title that celebrates the eternity of God. He had no beginning and will have no end. How wonderful that He has called us "unto His eternal glory" (I Pet. 5:10).

V. The Worship of Heaven. vv. 9–11.

"And whenever the living beings give glory and honor and thanksgiving to the one sitting on the throne, who lives into the ages of the ages . . ." (v. 9). The word *whenever* makes clear that it happened every time. The three parts of the praise of the living beings show us how we can improve our own praise of God. To give glory to God is to praise and glorify Him. The psalms do this repeatedly: "How excellent is thy name in all the

---

4:9. For distinctions between *glory* and *honor* see Custer, *A Treasury of New Testament Synonyms*, pp. 9–13.

earth" (Ps. 8:1, 9). "O come, let us worship and bow down: let us kneel before the Lord our maker" (Ps. 95:6). "Praise him according to his excellent greatness" (Ps. 150:2). To honor God is to recognize His true greatness and majesty. "Sing forth the honor of his name" (Ps. 66:2). "O Lord my God, thou art very great; thou art clothed with honor and majesty" (Ps. 104:1). Thanksgiving should be our constant theme. "Let us come before his presence with thanksgiving" (Ps. 95:2). "Enter into his gates with thanksgiving" (Ps. 100:4). "Sing unto the Lord with thanksgiving" (Ps. 147:7). "The twenty-four elders shall fall down before the One sitting on the throne and shall worship the One who lives into the ages of the ages, and shall cast their crowns before the throne, saying . . ." (v. 10). The language comes from the words of Darius concerning the God of Daniel: "He is the living God, and abiding for ages" (Dan. 6:26, Rotherham). These representatives of the saints of all ages shall prostrate themselves before the throne and shall give the worship and praise that all the saints have longed to be able to do. That is certainly the time that such a desire shall be fulfilled. Their worship will never have to be interrupted. They cast their victor's crowns before the throne. God deserves them, for they conquered by the grace and power of God. We will all be able to say with Paul, "I thank Christ Jesus our Lord, who has enabled me" (I Tim. 1:12). Their cry is "You are worthy, our Lord and God, to receive glory and honor and power, because You created all things and on account of Your will they were, and were created" (v. 11). God alone is worthy of supreme worship. The Lord Jesus had warned that only the one

---

4:10. The elders cannot lose their rewards by casting their crowns before the throne of God. They are still kings and priests and shall reign (5:8–10). The Book of Rev. is "a final repository of imagery of worship" (Ryken, Wilhoit, and Longman, *Dictionary of Biblical Imagery*, p. 973). The word *worship* (προσκυνέω) occurs 24 times in Rev. Here the 24 elders worship God; the angels join them in 7:11; they worship God again in 11:16; the heavenly voice directs men to worship Him that made heaven and earth (14:7); the saints in glory cry out that "all nations shall come and worship before Thee" (15:4); the 24 elders and 4 living beings worship God, saying "Alleluia" (19:4); twice the angel commands John to worship God alone (19:10; 22:9). The worst *blasphemy* is the worship of the Dragon and the Beast (13:4). The last reference is the angel's command to John, "Worship God" (22:9). Biblical worship is the praise and honor of the God of the Bible by people submissive to His will. See ISBE (1988), "Worship," IV, pp. 1117–33; ZPEB, "Worship," V, pp. 969–90.

4:11. Alford expresses concern over the English Version "for thy pleasure" they are created. He holds that it "introduces an element entirely strange to the context . . . and inappropriate here" (*Greek Testament*, IV, p. 602). Vincent translates the phrase "because of thy will" (*Word Studies*, II, p. 486). God never does anything for capricious pleasure. He always acts to fulfill His sovereign and holy will. Other translations bring this out. "Because of thy will . . . they were" (A. T. Robertson, *Word Pictures*, VI, p. 331); "Because of Thy will they existed" (NASB); "By your will they existed" (ESV); "Everything . . .

who keeps on doing the will of His Father would enter the kingdom of heaven (Matt. 7:21). God works all things according to the counsel of His will (Eph. 1:11). We need to be "slaves of Christ, doing the will of God from the heart" (Eph. 6:6). God's will encompasses all men and angels and extends from eternity past to eternity future. To put himself in the center of that will is the believer's highest good and greatest benefit. As David prayed, "In thy presence is fullness of joy; at thy right hand there are pleasures for evermore" (Ps. 16:11).

Practical Applications from Revelation 4

1. If a door were opened for you into the spiritual realm this day, where would you go? Up to God and the angels, or down to the wicked and eternal punishment (v. 1)? If you are not sure, will you make sure now?
   A. Accept the Lord Jesus Christ as your Savior from sin (Rom. 3:23). He died that you might not have to (Rom. 5:6).
   B. Believe in Christ's power to save you (Rom. 4:5). He saves by grace, not works (Eph. 2:8).
   C. Call upon Christ to save you (Rom. 10:13). Confess Him before men (Rom. 10:10). Find a Bible-believing church in which to serve Him (Heb. 10:25).
2. Believers should live each day with the sense that God is on the throne and will accomplish His purpose (v. 2). We should trust Him to direct us (Prov. 3:5–6).
3. We should recognize that God is glorious beyond words and worthy of worship (v. 3). We should enter His courts with praise and thanksgiving (Ps. 100:4).
4. We should remember that God will one day give crowns of victory to those who conquer by His grace (v. 4). We should endure temptation faithfully, for the crown awaits us (James 1:12).
5. We should realize that the dangerous sea of today will one day be a sea of glass, on which we may stand to sing God's praise (v. 6; Rev. 15:2–3).
6. The thought of God's holiness should be a controlling factor in our lives (v. 8). We need to ask ourselves, Who shall stand in His holy place? (Ps. 24:3). We should bless His holy name (Ps. 103:1).
7. We should take the time every day to give honor and thanksgiving to God (v. 9). The psalmist gave thanks to God at midnight

---

was created because of your will" (*God's Word to the Nations*). "Because thou didst create all things, and │ by reason of thy will │ they were, and were created" (Rotherham's *Emphasized Bible*, NT, p. 255).

(Ps. 119:62). Paul exhorted us to give thanks always for all things (Eph. 5:20).

8. We should remember that God made all things for His own purpose, not ours (v. 11). The Lord Jesus said, "If any man will do his will, he shall know of the doctrine, whether it be of God, or whether I speak of myself" (John 7:17).

Prayer

Heavenly Father, help us to honor and praise You as You deserve. Cause us to remember that august throne from which You rule the universe. Give us grace to walk in humble submission to Your perfect will. For Jesus' sake. Amen.

THE LION-LAMB

Persons

John ("I")
He that sat on the throne
(the Father)
A strong angel
Jesus Christ
Titles:
The Lion of the tribe of
Judah
The Root of David
The Lamb that had been
slain

The twenty-four elders
The four living beings
The seven Spirits of God
Many angels
Every created being

Persons referred to

David
The saints

Every kindred, tongue, people,
and nation

Places mentioned

Heaven
Earth
Under the earth

Judah
The sea

Doctrines taught

Authority
Prayer
Music in heaven
Redemption

The blood
The kingdom
Worship

1 And I saw in the right hand of him that sat on the throne a book written within and on the backside, sealed with seven seals.

2 And I saw a strong angel proclaiming with a loud voice, Who is worthy to open the book, and to loose the seals thereof?

3 And no man in heaven, nor in earth, neither under the earth, was able to open the book, neither to look thereon.

4 And I wept much, because no man was found worthy to open and to read the book, neither to look thereon.

5 And one of the elders saith unto me, Weep not: behold, the Lion of the tribe of Juda, the Root of David, hath prevailed to open the book, and to loose the seven seals thereof.

Revelation 5 Exposition

1. The Scroll and the Lion. vv. 1–5.

"And I saw upon the right hand of the one sitting on the throne a little scroll, having been written inside and outside, having been sealed with seven seals" (v. 1). "God sits upon the throne of his holiness" (Ps. 47:8). The sovereign Lord of the universe sits enthroned with a little scroll on His right hand. Daniel had seen this same scene with the Ancient of Days on the throne and ten thousand times ten thousand standing before Him (Dan. 7:9–10). Daniel also saw one like the Son of man, who came with the "clouds of heaven" before "the Ancient of days" (Dan. 7:13). "And there was given him dominion, and glory, and a kingdom, that all people, nations, and languages, should serve him: his dominion is an everlasting dominion, which shall not pass away, and his kingdom that which shall

---

5:1. The *right hand* is the place of strength and power (Isa. 63:12). The Lord has already placed His right hand upon John (1:17).

The *little scroll*, or *book* (βιβλίον) is mentioned 7 times in this chapter (vv. 1, 2, 3, 4, 5, 8, 9). It is *little* only in the hand of the Almighty, who holds it. God has been interested in writing a book from the very beginning (Gen. 5:1). God chose to put His revelation in a book and commanded His servants, the prophets, to write (Exod. 17:14; Deut. 31:9; II Chron. 26:22; Isa. 8:1; Jer. 30:2; Hab. 2:2; Rev. 1:11). Thus today we have a "more sure" word of prophecy to which it is well to take heed (II Pet. 1:19). The *little scroll* represents the title deed of the universe, which Christ has redeemed (Seiss, *Apocalypse*, p. 112). Gaebelein called it "the book of the righteous judgments of God" in view of the seal judgments to follow (*Rev.*, p. 47). But there is more involved than merely judgment. Beale holds that it "represents authority in executing the divine plan of judgment and redemption" (*Rev.*, p. 340). Ironside (*Rev.*, p. 89) notes that Jeremiah wrote a title deed of an inheritance on a scroll (Jer. 32:8–12). The breaking of the seals involves the claiming of the inheritance. All these ideas may well be involved. See ZPEB, "Books," I, pp. 637–40; ISBE (1988), "Writing," IV, pp. 1136–60; Ryken, Wilhoit, and Longman, *Dictionary of Biblical Imagery*, "Book," p. 114; "Scroll," pp. 764f.

not be destroyed" (Dan. 7:14). The scroll is plainly the right to rule the eternal kingdom of God. It was "so full of matter that it was written also on the backside" (A. T. Robertson, *Word Pictures*, VI, p. 332). There was no room left for anyone to add to it. "And I saw a strong angel proclaiming with a great voice, Who is worthy to open the little scroll and to loose its seals?" (v. 2). The angel proclaimed like a herald. Good men and angels shrink back from grasping such dominion. The prodigal son declared that he was not worthy of even a good name (Luke 15:21). The apostle Paul declared that sinners are worthy only of death (Rom. 1:32). "And no one in heaven, nor upon the earth, nor under the earth, was able to open the little scroll, nor even to look at it" (v. 3). The statement implies that there are men in all three realms. To *look at* it means facing the blinding light of the presence of God, which, as Paul found out, was too bright for mortal eyes to behold (Acts 9:3–8). Matthew Henry comments on "under the earth," that no fallen angel or spirit of an evil man can read such a scroll. Only the God who wrote it can execute the purpose of the universe. Isaiah describes the inability of man to read the scroll of God (Isa. 29:11–12). "And I was weeping much, because no one was found worthy to open the little scroll, nor even to look at it" (v. 4). No mere human being can look at divine authority. Everything is hopeless without the Ruler of the universe, the one who has the power and holiness to execute the purpose of the universe. The Lord Jesus said, "With God all things are possible" (Matt. 19:26). "And one of the elders says to me, Stop weeping, behold, the Lion of the tribe of Judah, the Root of David, overcame to open the little scroll and its seven seals" (v. 5). The Lord Jesus Christ is

---

5:2. The word *worthy* (ἄξιος) has the moral sense of *fit, deserving* of honor or reward. John the Baptist did not consider himself worthy to serve the Lord, even as a slave (John 1:27). The Lord Jesus declared that the person who does not exalt the Lord Himself above every other human relationship is not worthy of Him (Matt. 10:37–38). The Lord Jesus alone is worthy to receive the scroll (5:12).

5:4. John was weeping unnecessarily. Although there are times when weeping is appropriate for the believer (Matt. 26:75), the NT emphasizes the believer's privilege of rejoicing in Christ (Matt. 5:12; Phil. 3:1; 4:4, 10; I Thess. 5:16; I Pet. 4:13).

5:5. The lion is a terrifying predator. "The lion has roared, who will not fear?" (Amos 3:8). Being cast into a den of lions was the ultimate punishment (Dan. 6:7, 12). But it is a good image for the Lord Jesus, who faced certain death with such courageous strength (Mark 14:48–50). Lions flanked the throne of Solomon (I Kings 10:20). But it must be balanced with the image of the Lamb (5:6). "The Apocalypse expresses this perplexing combination of Suffering Servant and military Messiah by melding the conquering Lion of the tribe of Judah with Lamb that was slain" (Ryken, Wilhoit, and Longman, *Dictionary of Biblical Imagery*, "Lion," p. 515). The doctrine of the Lamb is a major theme in Scripture (Gen. 22:7–8; Exod. 12:3–13; Isa. 53:7; John 1:29, 36; Acts 8:32; I Pet. 1:19). See "Lamb," ISBE (1986), III, pp. 61–62; "Lamb," ZPEB, III, pp. 859–60; Elwell, Walter, *Evangelical Dictionary of Biblical Theology*, "Lamb," pp. 460–61.

6 And I beheld, and, lo, in the midst of the throne and of the four beasts, and in the midst of the elders, stood a Lamb as it had been slain, having seven horns and seven eyes, which are the seven Spirits of God sent forth into all the earth.

7 And he came and took the book out of the right hand of him that sat upon the throne.

the archetypal "Overcomer" (3:21), who will triumph over all mankind's foes and establish the great kingdom of God. He is identified as "the Lion of the tribe of Judah," a clear reference to Genesis 49:9–10. Judah is the lion's whelp from whom the great lawgiver shall come. The Root of David is the same as the prophesied root of Jesse (Isa. 11:1). Walvoord mentions that Roman emperors sealed their wills seven times (*Rev.*, p. 113).

II. The Scroll and the Lamb. vv. 6–7.

"And I saw in the midst of the throne and of the four living beings and in the midst of the elders a lamb, having taken his stand as having been slaughtered, having seven horns and seven eyes, which are the seven spirits of God who have been sent into all the earth" (v. 6). The *as* makes clear that the Lamb is very much alive but has the marks of sacrifice on him. The announcement of a Lion and the appearance of a Lamb are a shock to the reader, but there is a definite revelation intended. To the wicked angels and men, the Lord Jesus is a fearsome danger in their evil pathways, but the blood-washed saints and holy angels cannot see the fearsome qualities of the Lord. They see instead the one who died to redeem them and cherish them. This is a direct reference to the great prophecy of Isaiah: "He is brought as a lamb to the slaughter, and as a sheep before her shearers is dumb, so he opened not his mouth" (53:7ff.). The Lord Jesus is the perfect Redeemer, and hence the number seven is marshaled to emphasize this. He has seven horns (perfect power) and seven eyes (perfect perception). To the unsaved this sounds grotesque, but to the redeemed it has spiritual meaning. The seven eyes symbolize the sevenfold Holy Spirit. The prophets regularly used animals to set forth spiritual truth (Dan. 7:3ff.; 8:3ff.; Zech. 1:8ff.; 6:1ff.; Isa. 11:6ff.; 53:6). "The seven spirits . . . sent into all the earth" is a clear teaching of the omnipresence of God, a constant doctrine (Gen. 16:13; I Kings 8:27; Ps. 139:7–10; Isa. 66:1; Jer. 23:23–24; Acts 7:48–49; 17:27–28; I Tim. 2:1–3). The Holy

---

5:6. Isaiah had such a throne vision: "I saw also the Lord, sitting upon a throne, high and lifted up, and his train filled the temple" (Isa. 6:1). The prophet Micaiah also declared, "I saw the Lord sitting on his throne, and all the host of heaven standing by him on his right hand and on the left" (I Kings 22:19). This is the scene of the permanent assembly of heaven before the divine Ruler of the universe. [See note 1:4.]

For the verb *to slaughter* (σφάζω) see Rev. 13:3 note.

8 *And when he had taken the book, the four beasts and four and twenty elders fell down before the Lamb, having every one of them harps, and golden vials full of odours, which are the prayers of saints.*

9 *And they sung a new song, saying, Thou art worthy to take the book, and to open the seals thereof: for thou wast slain, and hast redeemed us to God by thy blood out of every kindred, and tongue, and people, and nation;*

10 *And hast made us unto our God kings and priests: and we shall reign on the earth.*

11 *And I beheld, and I heard the voice of many angels round about the throne and the beasts and the elders: and the number of them was ten thousand times ten thousand, and thousands of thousands;*

12 *Saying with a loud voice, Worthy is the Lamb that was slain to receive power, and riches, and wisdom, and strength, and honour, and glory, and blessing.*

13 *And every creature which is in heaven, and on the earth, and under the earth, and such as are in the sea, and all that are in them, heard I saying, Blessing, and honour, and glory, and power, be unto him that sitteth upon the throne, and unto the Lamb for ever and ever.*

14 *And the four beasts said, Amen. And the four and twenty elders fell down and worshipped him that liveth for ever and ever.*

Spirit is the Agent of perception for the Son of God. This is part of the mystery of the Trinity. The Lord Jesus is called *Lamb* twenty-eight times in Revelation (5:6, 8, 12, 13; 6:1, 16; 7:9, 10, 14, 17; 12:11; 13:8; 14:1, 4 [twice], 10; 15:3; 17:14 [twice]; 19:7, 9; 21:9, 14, 22, 23, 27; 22:1, 3). Warfield holds that the title *Lamb* "must be looked upon as embodying the seer's favorite mode of conceiving of Jesus and His work" (*The Lord of Glory*, p. 290). The false prophet is called "one like a lamb" (13:11). "And he came and took the scroll out of the right hand of the one who is sitting upon the throne" (v. 7). The word *took* is a dramatic perfect, "He has taken," making the reader a witness to the climax of the ages, which will have eternal results. The Son of God assumes the right to rule all things. He received of His Father that right to rule the kingdom of God (Rev. 2:27). Peter observes that this was foreshadowed on the Mount of Transfiguration (II Pet. 1:16–18). Paul declares that God "has highly exalted him, and given him a name which is above every name, that at the name of Jesus every knee should bow" (Phil. 2:9b–10a). Swete called this scroll "the Book of Destiny" (*Apocalypse*, p. 75).

III. The New Song. vv. 8–14.

"And when he took the little scroll, the four living beings and the twenty-four elders fell down before the lamb, each one having harps and golden bowls full of incense, which are the prayers of the saints" (v. 8). The

---

5:8–9. A *new song* is mentioned twice in Rev. (5:9; 14:3) and 7 times in the OT (Ps. 33:3; 40:3; 96:1; 98:1; 144:9; 149:1; Isa. 42:10). The song of Moses is mentioned in 15:3.

saints have long prayed, "Thy kingdom come" (Matt. 6:10), and now He is going to claim His rightful possession. Incense regularly symbolizes prayer (Exod. 30:7–8; Rev. 8:3). David prayed, "Let my prayer be set forth before thee as incense" (Ps. 141:2). Discouraged believers are sometimes tempted to think that God does not hear their prayers, but this scene assures believers that their prayers are ascending before God. "And they sing a new song, saying, You are worthy to take the little scroll and to open the seals of it, because you were slain and redeemed to God by your blood [those] from every tribe and language and people and nation" (v. 9). This will be the ultimate fulfillment of Psalm 33:2–3, "Praise the Lord with harp: sing unto him with the psaltery and an instrument of ten strings. Sing unto him a new song." The psalmist exhorts, "O sing unto the Lord a new song" (Ps. 96:1). Psalm 98:1 adds, "O sing unto the Lord a new song; for he hath done marvellous things: his right hand, and his holy arm, hath gotten him the victory." The abhorrent modern practice of removing references to the blood of Christ from hymns will be fully corrected in heaven. Redemption by His blood will be the great theme of celebration. One of the astonishments of heaven will be the presence of

---

The word *new* (καινός) means *unused*, as in Matt. 9:17, *unused* wineskins. It does not mean *newly come into existence*, which would be the word νέος. Thus the meaning is that they sing extemporaneously. All these saints will have the musical skills of Bach! See Trench, *Synonyms*, pp. 219–25.

The new song shows that music is a major part of the worship of heaven. The *harps* intimate that there are musical instruments in heaven that will put to shame the grandest pipe organs on earth. The word *harp* (κιθάρα) occurs 3 times in Rev. (5:8; 14:2; 15:2). If the worship of Solomon in dedicating the temple was impressive, with priests and Levites, singers, musicians with cymbals, psalteries and harps, 120 trumpeters, and a vast choir praising God, saying, "For He is good; for his mercy endureth forever" (II Chron. 5:12–14), how much greater will be the celebration in heaven? Johann Sebastian Bach will be highly satisfied, for all his music was dedicated to the glory of God alone. Spurgeon has a powerful sermon on this text, "Jesus, the Delight of Heaven," in which he says, "Jesus is worthy of my life, worthy of my love, worthy of everything I can say of him, worthy of a thousand times more than that, worthy of all the music and harps on earth, worthy of all the songs of all the sweetest singers, worthy of all the poetry of the best writers, worthy of all the adoration of every knee" (Sermon 1225, *The C. H. Spurgeon Collection*, Ages Digital Library). See ZPEB, "Music, Musical Instruments," IV, pp. 311–24; ISBE (1986), "Music," pp. 436–49; Ryken, Wilhoit, and Longman, *Dictionary of Biblical Imagery*, "Music," pp. 576–78.

5:9. Four is the number of the world. This fourfold group (tribe, language, people, and nation) signifies from every part of the world. This kind of group occurs 7 times in Rev. (5:9; 7:9; 10:11; 11:9; 13:7; 14:6; 17:15). Would it be strange if God imparted saving faith to every child who died in infancy, to every insane or feeble-minded person who "never had a chance" to use his mental powers? Abraham was sure that the Judge of all the earth would do right (Gen. 18:25). We may press the verbally inspired Scriptures: every tribe, language, people, and nation will have representatives in heaven by the grace of God. Not a soul there will ever be able to boast that he deserved it.

redeemed saints from every tribe, tongue, people, and nation (as Daniel
had prophesied, Dan. 7:14). The efforts of foreign missionaries are not in
vain. Melchizedek was from the Jebusites (Gen. 14:18; II Sam. 5:6–7);
Moses led Jethro his father-in-law, a Midianite, to the Lord (Exod.
18:1–12); Ruth was a Moabitess (Ruth 1:4); Uriah was from the Hittites
(II Sam. 11:3); Zelek was an Ammonite (II Sam. 23:37); David influenced
Hiram, king of Tyre, for the Lord (I Kings 5:1; II Chron. 2:11–12); Philip
won the treasurer of Ethiopia to the Lord (Acts 8:27–35); Peter won the
Roman centurion Cornelius to the Lord (Acts 10:1–44); Paul won the pro-
consul of Cyprus to the Lord (Acts 13:7–12); Lucius, a prophet in
Antioch, was from Cyrene in North Africa (Acts 13:1). Most Christians
have heard of Nate Saint and Jim Elliott and of their deaths to reach the
Auca Indians, but few people know that Geronimo was converted and
baptized in the Dutch Reformed Church at the Apache Mission in Fort
Sill Military Reservation in 1903 (S. M. Barrett, *Geronimo's Story of His
Life*, p. 211f.). "And you made them to our God a kingdom and priests, and
they shall reign upon the earth" (v. 10). *They shall reign* refers to saints, not
angels. Daniel had prophesied that the kingdom would be given to "the
saints of the most High" (Dan. 7:27). It is not strange that some of these
are saints who sing about themselves in the third person plural, rather than
"we." The Israelites who sing about their deliverance from the Red Sea do
the same thing (Exod. 15:13). A "we" in the present context would include the four living beings, who are not saints. This is the text from
which Edward Perronet (1725–92) drew his famous hymn:

> All hail the power of Jesus' name!
> Let angels prostrate fall;
> Bring forth the royal diadem,
> And crown Him Lord of all.

Stanza 3 stresses the universal acclaim:

> Let every kindred, every tribe,
> On this terrestrial ball,
> To Him all majesty ascribe,
> And crown Him Lord of all.

Craig R. Koester gives a plaintive bleat concerning Christians in main-
line denominational churches who treat Revelation "with the kind of

---

5:10. The verb *to reign as a king* (βασιλεύω) occurs 7 times in Rev. (5:10; 11:15, 17; 19:6;
20:4, 6; 22:5). The weight of evidence for the reading "they shall reign" is very strong
(βασιλεύσουσιν, ℵ, P, 1, 94, 1828, 1854, 2042, 2053, 2073, 2081*, 2344, the Old
Latin, Syriac, and both the Sahidic and Boharic Coptic versions). In contrast "we shall
reign" (βασιλεύσομεν) is found in one old Greek manuscript 2432 (14th cent.), the
Vulgate of Pope Clement, and in authors such as Tyconius, Maternus, Primasius, etc.

uneasy silence that is usually reserved for the more eccentric members of one's extended family" (*Revelation and the End of All Things*, p. 32). He charges that the only time that such Christians hear Revelation is in the wording of the old hymns and lectionaries. "And I saw, and I heard a voice of many angels in a circle around the throne and the living beings and the elders, and the number of them was ten thousand times ten thousand, and thousands of thousands" (v. 11). J. B. Smith notes that the angels are around the elders, and hence, distinguished from them (*Rev.*, p. 117). Daniel had seen millions serving God and hundreds of millions standing before Him (Dan. 7:10). Now John hears this multitude praise the Lamb for seven things. "Saying with a loud voice: Worthy is the Lamb that was slain to receive power, and wealth, and wisdom, and strength, and honor, and glory, and blessing" (v. 12). Every one of these seven attributes is ascribed to the Lord in Scripture elsewhere. The apostle Paul called the Lord Jesus "Christ the power and the wisdom of God" (I Cor. 1:24). In another context he referred to the "Unsearchable wealth of Christ" (Eph. 3:8). Paul referred to "the glory of His strength" when He comes again (II Thess. 1:9). The writer to the Hebrews declared that Jesus was crowned with "glory and honor" when He tasted death for every man (Heb. 2:9). Paul noted that all our spiritual blessings are in Christ (Eph. 1:3). Now the scene enlarges still further to encompass all that exists. "And every creature which is in heaven and upon the earth and under the earth and upon the sea, and all the things in them, I heard saying, To the one sitting upon the throne and to the Lamb be blessing and honor and glory and power into the ages of the ages" (v. 13). This is universal worship and adoration from every being that exists in the universe. Not only does it include all good men and angels in heaven and on the earth, but it may also include the evil men and evil angels under the earth. In the next realm the veil will be lifted, and wicked men and angels will know that God is holy and righteous and that they

---

5:11. "Ten thousand" (μυριάς, μυριάδος) was the largest unit used in the ancient world. It could mean a literal 10,000, or it could mean "an incalculable number." *Myriads* is still with us in that sense, which is probably the best interpretation here.

5:12. For distinctions between *power* (δύναμις) and *strength* (ἰσχύς) see Custer, A *Treasury of New Testament Synonyms*, pp. 27–33.

This is the first of 4 times that wisdom (σοφία) is mentioned in Rev. Here it is an attribute of the Lamb; in Rev. 7:12 it is an attribute of God; in Rev. 13:18 it is needed to understand the number 666; in Rev. 17:9 it is needed to understand the 7 heads of the beast.

This is the first of 3 times that *blessing* (εὐλογία) occurs in Rev. (5:12, 13; 7:12).

5:13. This is the first reference to an earthly *sea* in Rev. The last reference is that there will be no sea in the new earth (Rev. 21:1).

deserve exactly what they are suffering. There will not be a single case of divine injustice. Every being in the universe will have the exact blessing, or punishment, that he deserves. "And the four living beings were saying: Amen. And the elders fell down and worshiped" (v. 14). The Lord of the universe has done all things well, and the four living beings continue saying *Amen*, "So be it!" A more majestic scene cannot be imagined. All readers of this book should ask themselves whether they are among the submissive saints who love to serve and worship God above all things. The KJV translator Lancelot Andrews paraphrased vv. 9–12 in his private devotions (see Alexander Whyte, *Lancelot Andrews and His Private Devotions*, p. 170):

> Glory and blessing, strength and power,
> honour and thanksgiving, riches and holiness,
> praise and wisdom, power and salvation,
> be to our God that liveth for ever,
> that sitteth upon the throne,
> and to the Lamb that was slain.
> Amen: Hallelujah.

Practical Applications from Revelation 5

1. Believers have the privilege of serving the Lord of the universe (v. 1). "The Lord hath prepared His throne in the heavens; and His kingdom ruleth over all" (Ps. 103:19).
2. The messenger of God considers the worthiness of His servants (v. 2). The psalmist asks, "Who shall ascend into the hill of the Lord?" (Ps. 24:3).
3. The Lord Jesus is able to accomplish all the will of God (v. 5). He could say, "I do always those things that please him" (John 8:29).
4. Nothing can be hidden from the Lord; no work is too difficult for Him (v. 6). The *horns* and *eyes* are symbols of power and perception.
5. The prayers of the saints are pleasing (like perfume) before God (v. 8). God is looking for servants who want to please Him (Isa. 56:4–5).

5:13–14. Jennings argues (*Rev.*, p. 193) that the subjects of the 3 choirs are not accidental. The first choir sings of the redemption provided by the Lamb (v. 9). The second sings of the power of the Lamb (v. 12), and the third sings of the universal submission to the rule of the Lamb (v. 13).

5:14. The verb *were saying* (ἔλεγον) is an imperfect tense, which implies repetition. The verb *fell* (ἔπεσαν) is an aorist tense, which implies one time. *They fell down*, "the most profound adoration" (Matthew Henry).

6. God hears the songs of His people (v. 9). "O come, let us sing unto the Lord: let us make a joyful noise to the rock of our salvation" (Ps. 95:1).
7. God's people have a high destiny as kings and priests for God (v. 10). "You are a chosen generation, a royal priesthood" (I Pet. 2:9).
8. The Lord has a vast number of servants doing His bidding (v. 11). Blessed is that servant whom the Lord finds faithful (Matt. 24:46).
9. The Lord is worthy of all that we can give Him (v. 12). The churches of Macedonia first gave their own selves to the Lord (II Cor. 8:5).
10. Every creature in the universe should worship God (v. 13). "Worship the Lord in the beauty of holiness" (Ps. 29:2). "Exalt the Lord our God, and worship at His footstool; for He is holy" (Ps. 99:5).

Prayer

O Lamb of God, slain for me, wash my sinful heart in Your precious blood that I may stand with the company of the redeemed and cry with them, Worthy is the Lamb! Give me grace to praise and serve You as I ought. Amen.

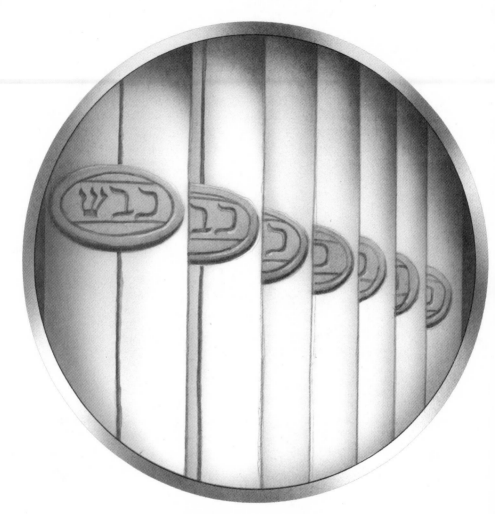

Revelation 6:1–9:11

The Seven Seals

Persons

John ("I")

The Lamb (Jesus Christ)

The four living beings

The rider on the white horse

The rider on the red horse

The rider on the black horse

The rider on the pale [green] horse

The souls of the martyrs

The kings of the earth

The great men

The rich men

The chief captains

The mighty men

Every bond man

Every free man

Places mentioned

The earth

Hades

The altar in heaven

Doctrines taught

The authority of Christ

Antichrist

War

Death

The afterlife

Witness for Christ

Judgment

The wrath of the Lamb

1 And I saw when the Lamb opened one of the seals, and I heard, as it were the noise of thunder, one of the four beasts saying, Come and see.

2 And I saw, and behold a white horse: and he that sat on him had a bow; and a crown was given unto him: and he went forth conquering, and to conquer.

Revelation 6 Exposition

I. The First Seal: A White Horse. vv. 1–2.

"And I saw when the lamb opened one of the seven seals, and I heard one of the four living beings, saying as a voice of thunder, Come" (v. 1). John solemnly declares that he is an eyewitness of this important vision. Only the Lamb has the authority and power to break the seals. One of His divine characteristics is that He "opens and no one shuts" (Rev. 3:7). He has the authority to break the nations with a rod (scepter) of iron (Ps. 2:9). Isaiah wrote of the Rod of Jesse, "But with righteousness shall he judge the poor, and reprove with equity for the meek of the earth: and he shall smite the earth with the rod of his mouth, and with the breath of his lips shall he slay the wicked" (Isa. 11:4). The Lord Jesus Christ alone has the authority to claim His inheritance, crushing the wicked and establishing His kingdom of righteousness on the earth. In each of the series of "sevens" the first four have a close connection, and the last three are added to them. He begins by manifesting His counterfeit, the prince of darkness, the Antichrist. "And I saw, and behold a white horse, and the one sitting upon it having a bow, and a crown was given to him, and he went out conquering and in order that he might conquer" (v. 2).

6:1ff. From this point on Rev. describes the actions of the great King, the Lord Jesus Christ, in claiming His inheritance, breaking the power of the usurper, Satan, ultimately defeating all His foes, and bringing His people finally to the great kingdom reign and heaven itself. This futurist interpretation holds that the Rapture has occurred (4:1) and that the events described in 6:1–19:11 occur in a 7-year period of tribulation, the seventieth week of Dan. 9:27. G. B. Caird, an idealist interpreter, holds that the seals, trumpets, and bowls have an artistic unity "like that of a musical theme with variations, each variation adding something new to the significance of the whole composition" (*Rev.*, p. 106). Although some scholars (Buchanan) hold that all 7 seals are down the edge of the first page of the scroll, it may be better to think of the seals as being at the top of the scroll, so that when a seal is broken, part of the scroll unrolls to reveal the first horseman. Section by section the scroll reveals providential events by which the Lord secures His inheritance (Rev. 8:1). Later, a scroll is seen unrolled in the hand of an angel (Rev. 10:8). Is it the same one?

6:2. This is the only time in the NT that the word *bow* (τόξον) occurs. The horse archers were the "atom bomb" of the ancient world. No one knew how to defend against their attack. The Scythian horse archers were dreaded (Col. 3:11). These savage nomads con-

Zechariah had a vision in which he saw riders on various colored horses (Zech. 1:8). He also saw four chariots pulled by red, black, white, and mixed-colored horses (Zech. 6:1–5). Some have thought that the white horse must indicate the Lord Himself (Newell, *Rev.*, p. 102), but all the seals are terrible disasters; the first one is no exception. The Lord Jesus does appear on a white horse in Revelation 19:11, "but the two riders have nothing in common beyond the white horse" (Swete, *Rev.*, p. 86). Kenneth S. Wuest aptly writes, "The seventieth week of Daniel begins with the rider on the white horse (Antichrist) of 6:2, and closes with the rider on the white horse of 19:11 (Jesus Christ)" ("The Rapture— Precisely When?" *Bibliotheca Sacra*, 114, no. 453, Jan.–Mar., 1957). "The four horsemen of the Apocalypse" present a unified portrait of catastrophe. The four living beings introduce the horsemen to show that judgment ultimately comes from God. Satan is a deceiver who always puts his best foot forward (Gen. 3:1–5). Daniel prophesied of the little horn who had a hypnotic gaze and a mouth boasting great things (Dan. 7:8), who made war against the saints of God and prevailed (Dan. 7:21). He is the prince that shall come, the desolator (Dan. 9:26–27). Here he comes on a white horse, the pseudo-messiah, with a bow and a crown given to him. The bow he brandishes was the symbol of the horse archers, the most feared weapon of the ancient world. Walter Scott suggests that this indicates "a career of unchecked, brilliant, yet almost bloodless victory" for the inauguration of this world ruler (*Rev.*, p. 147). God allows Satan to give the victor's crown to him, along with "his power, his throne, and great authority" (Rev. 13:2). But this is only by the permission of the Lord of the universe (Job 1:12). The ten kings of the confederacy will give their power and authority to the Beast (Rev. 17:12–13). Daniel prophesied

---

quered whole empires. See ISBE (1988), "Scythians," IV, pp. 364–66. The horse meant that they could overtake any enemy; the bow enabled them to strike at a distance and remain out of reach of sword or spear. The Roman Empire, relying on the foot soldiers of the legions, fell in A.D. 455 to the Vandals, but the eastern empire in Constantinople, relying on the horse archers, lasted a thousand years longer. The use of gunpowder ended the advantage.

For the verb *to conquer* (νικάω) see Rev. 2:7 note.

6:2/19:12. The rider on the white horse here has a victor's crown (στέφανος) for a single victory, but when the Lord Jesus returns in Rev. 19:12, He is crowned with many diadems (διαδήματα), the royal crowns of imperial rule. The aorist passive verb form *was given* (ἐδόθη) occurs here for the first time in Rev. It occurs 21 times in Rev. (3 × 7) and in every instance reveals the sovereign control of God over all persons and circumstances in this conflict of the ages (6:2, 4 [twice], 8, 11; 7:2; 8:3; 9:1, 3, 5; 11:1, 2; 13:5 [twice], 7 [twice], 14, 15; 16:8; 19:8; 20:4). There are, of course, many other forms of the verb that occur in Rev.

This is the first of 16 times that the word *horse* (ἵππος) occurs in Rev.

3 And when he had opened the second seal, I heard the second beast say, Come and see.
4 And there went out another horse that was red: and power was given to him that sat thereon to take peace from the earth, and that they should kill one another: and there was given unto him a great sword.

that "he shall speak great words against the most High, and shall wear out the saints of the most High" (Dan. 7:25). He will be the last political ruler of the Western Confederacy, the Beast out of the sea (Rev. 13:1). For a careful discussion of this first rider, see Daniel K. K. Wong, "The First Horseman of Rev. 6," *Bibliotheca Sacra*, 153, no. 610, Apr.–Jun., 1996. Benware makes a strong point that "the tribulation period itself begins when the Antichrist signs a seven-year covenant with the nation of Israel (Dan. 9:27 and Isa. 28:14–22). This covenant is made to guarantee the security of Israel and is *the* event that marks the beginning of the last seven years prior to Christ's return" (Paul N. Benware, *Understanding End Times Prophecy*, p. 246).

II. The Second Seal: A Red Horse. vv. 3–4.

"And when he opened the second seal, I heard the second living being, saying, Come" (v. 3). The immediate result of the advent of this world ruler is not peace, but war. "And another red horse went out, and to the one sitting upon him it was given to take peace from the earth, and that they should slaughter one another, and a great sword was given to him" (v. 4). The sword (μάχαιρα) was the short, heavy sword of the Roman Empire. It must be distinguished from the long broadsword (ῥομφαία) that proceeds from Christ's mouth (Rev. 19:15). Perceptive scholars have long taught the future confederation of such a ten-nation empire (Lactantius, *Divine Institutes*, VII, 16f.; George N. H. Peters, *The Theocratic Kingdom*, II, pp. 649–50; L. Sale-Harrison, *The Resurrection of the Old Roman Empire*, 1928). The Beast may come on the white horse, promising peace, but he succeeds only in plunging the world into war. He

---

6:4. The verb *slaughter* (σφάζω) is a stronger word than just *kill*. It is used for beheading people (II Kings 10:7 LXX). That may be the actual method of execution here (Rev. 20:4). D. Edmond Hiebert notes that σφάζω is another Johannine word used to portray Cain's violent slaughter of his brother, Abel (I John 3:12, *The Epistles of John*, p. 151). The purpose clause here in Rev. actually reveals the Devil's purpose in war: to slaughter human beings. He is a murderer from the beginning (John 8:44) and delights in human destruction and suffering (Job 1:9–2:7).

The only other occurrence of the word *red* (πυρρός) in the NT is in reference to the great red dragon (Rev. 12:3). It is a fitting symbol of the murderous attitude of the Devil, who has from the beginning tried to slay mankind (Gen. 2:17; 3:1ff.).

5 And when he had opened the third seal, I heard the third beast say, Come and see. And I beheld, and lo a black horse; and he that sat on him had a pair of balances in his hand.

6 And I heard a voice in the midst of the four beasts say, A measure of wheat for a penny, and three measures of barley for a penny; and see thou hurt not the oil and the wine.

has great power, but he must constantly use it in order to stay in power. The Lord Jesus Christ warned that the whole period before His return would be characterized by wars and rumors of wars (Matt. 24:6), but He also warned of a great tribulation period of unique severity that would come from the abomination of desolation (Matt. 24:15–21). It will be a period of bloodshed on a scale that the world has never seen (Matt. 24:21). Daniel prophesied that the people of the prince that shall come "shall destroy the city and the sanctuary" (Dan. 9:26); that portion of his prophecy was fulfilled by the Romans in A.D. 70. The Roman prince that shall come (ruler of the same western empire) shall break the covenant in the midst of the week and shall be the abomination that makes desolate (Dan. 9:25–27). Zechariah also saw a red horse (Zech. 1:8) and went on to describe the catastrophic slaughter in Jerusalem (Zech. 14:2).

III. The Third Seal: A Black Horse. vv. 5–6.

"And when he opened the third seal, I heard the third living being saying, Come. And I saw, and behold a black horse, and the one sitting upon him was having a pair of balances in his hand" (v. 5). The balances were a symbol of commerce; both the goods and the money were regularly weighed. In time of war both business and farming suffer. With the destruction of crops and transportation famine stalks the earth. "And I heard as a voice in the midst of the four living beings saying, A measure of wheat for a denarius, and three measures of barley for a denarius, and hurt not the oil and the wine" (v. 6). The denarius was the regular day's wage, for the householder agreed with his laborers for wages of a denarius a day (Matt. 20:2). When enough wheat for a day's meal will sell for a day's wage, you have desperate famine. What about housing or any other expense? If the individuals can get along on very coarse food, barley, they could get enough for three meals. This is terrible inflation that shows the severity of the famine.

6:5. The only other occurrence of the word *black* (μέλας) in Rev. is in v. 12.

6:6. Wheat, barley, oil, and wine are the four ancient staples of Middle Eastern culture. The coin *denarius* (δηνάριον) occurs only here in Rev.

7 And when he had opened the fourth seal, I heard the voice of the fourth beast say, Come and see.

8 And I looked, and behold a pale horse: and his name that sat on him was Death, and Hell followed with him. And power was given unto them over the fourth part of the earth, to kill with sword, and with hunger, and with death, and with the beasts of the earth.

IV. The Fourth Seal: A Pale Green Horse. vv. 7–8.

"And when he opened the fourth seal, I heard a voice of the fourth living being saying, Come" (v. 7). All four of the living beings contributed to the vision. "And I saw, and behold a pale green horse, and the one sitting upon him was named Death, and Hades was following with him. And authority was given to them over the fourth part of the earth, to kill with sword and with famine and with death and by the wild beasts of the earth" (v. 8). The four sore judgments on Jerusalem may be an anticipation of these judgments (Ezek. 14:21). Jeremiah also prophesied a fourfold judgment on his people (Jer. 15:1–4). The word *pale green* (χλωρός) is used for the pale green of spring vegetation (Mark 6:39). The only other two uses in the NT also refer to vegetation (Rev. 8:7; 9:4). Thucydides used it of the appearance of people dying of the plague (II, 49). Homer used it of the face of one blanched with fear (*Iliad*, X, 376). Osborne notes that some would paraphrase the color as "dappled gray," but the meaning is obviously "corpse-colored" (*Rev.*, p. 282). This is a key passage for the doctrine of the afterlife. Death does not end it all; hades follows. In the OT *sheol* was the parallel. The extrabiblical writers agreed. They divided hades into Tartarus, the dark abode of the wicked, and Elysium, the happy abode of the righteous and the heroic. However, they thought that hades was permanent, but Scripture makes clear that it is temporary. The Lord Jesus clearly taught that hades is a place after death in which the wicked and the selfish are tormented, and a separate area, which He called Abraham's Bosom, in which the righteous believers in Scripture will be comforted and find fellowship (Luke 16:19–31). But He also taught that He was going to prepare an eternal abode for resurrected saints in the presence of His Father (John 14:3–6; 17:24). In the same way He taught that the wicked would ultimately be judged and cast into a furnace of fire (Matt. 13:49–50). The Book of Revelation teaches the same thing: the wicked will be judged and hades shall be cast into the lake of fire (Rev. 20:13–14); the righteous will be comforted and wel-

---

6:8. Both *Death* and *Hades* are personifications. A. T. Robertson notes that we cannot tell from the language whether John saw Hades sitting behind Death on the horse or walking behind the horse (*Word Pictures*, VI, pp. 342–43). See Rev. 1:18 note.

9 And when he had opened the fifth seal, I saw under the altar the souls of them that were slain for the word of God, and for the testimony which they held:
10 And they cried with a loud voice, saying, How long, O Lord, holy and true, dost thou not judge and avenge our blood on them that dwell on the earth?
11 And white robes were given unto every one of them; and it was said unto them, that they should rest yet for a little season, until their fellowservants also and their brethren, that should be killed as they were, should be fulfilled.

comed into the city of God with eternal glory (Rev. 21:4–24). It is a solemn thought that these opening judgments of the Tribulation period result in the death of 25 percent of the world's population. No war or plague has come close to that in the history of the world. (But in the sixth trumpet judgment 33 percent more will die, Rev. 9:18).

V. The Fifth Seal: The Martyred Saints Under the Altar. vv. 9–11.

"And when he opened the fifth seal, I saw under the altar the souls of the ones who had been slaughtered on account of the word of God and on account of the witness which they were having" (v. 9). "The Apocalypse everywhere divides sevens into four and three" (Bengel, *Gnomon*, V, pp. 234–35). John has heard each of the four living beings in the previous seals; now he sees the martyrs and soon will hear their voices. The surprise is their position: he sees them under the celestial altar. The writer to the Hebrews explains that the tabernacle was made according to the pattern showed to Moses in the mount (Heb. 8:5). He goes on to argue that it was necessary that the patterns of things in the heavens should be purified with animal sacrifices, "but the heavenly things themselves with better sacrifices than these" (Heb. 9:23). Christ Himself is the perfect sacrifice that appears in the presence of God (Heb. 9:25–26). However, these martyred saints appear under the altar, the place where the fire burned in the OT sacrifices. It was also the place where the blood of the sacrifices was poured out (Lev. 4:7). Now these saints awake in the presence of God under the celestial altar, in fires of glory and praise before the presence of God. Their suffering was an aroma of blessed incense ascending up to the presence of God. The purposes of the altar of incense and the altar of sacrifice seem to be combined in this heavenly altar. "And they cried with a loud voice, saying: How long, O Master, holy and true, are you not judging and avenging our blood on the

---

6:9. The word *altar* (θυσιαστήριον) occurs 4 times in Rev. (6:9; 8:3 [twice]; 9:13).

From the first mention of *altar* (Noah's, Gen. 8:20), to the polluted altar of Malachi (1:7ff.), it is a major OT theme in the worship of God. For background see Ryken, Wilhoit, and Longman, "Altar," *Dictionary of Biblical Imagery*, pp. 20f. See also the golden altar, Rev. 8:3–4 note.

ones dwelling on the earth?" (v. 10). Their loud cry echoes the thunder-ous voices of the four living beings. Their agitation over their own brutal murders is certainly understandable. They are not voicing mere vindic-tiveness; they are crying out for divine justice. They address the Lord as the absolute Master of slaves (δεσπότης). To be a slave of the Lord of the universe is a high honor. The Lord Jesus has already answered their cry: "And shall not God avenge his own elect, who cry day and night unto him, though he bear long with them? I tell you that he will avenge them speedily" (Luke 18:7–8a). God will indeed avenge their blood, but everything in its own time. "And a white robe was given to each one of them, and it was said to them, that they should rest for a short time, until their fellow slaves and their brethren who were about to be killed even as they themselves were, should be fulfilled" (v. 11). These Tribulation martyrs will be given resurrection bodies at the end of the seven-year Tribulation period so that they may reign with the saints of all ages during the thousand-year Millennium (Rev. 20:4). But there will be many more martyrs during the bloody reign of Antichrist (Rev. 13:7–15). Thomas has a valuable excursus on "the imprecatory prayers of the Apocalypse" (*Rev. 1–7*, pp. 517–24).

6:10. The saints often ask the Lord "How long?" (Pss. 13:1; 74:10; 79:5; Isa. 6:11; Zech. 1:12).

The verb *to judge* (κρίνω) occurs 9 times in Rev. (6:10; 11:18; 16:5; 18:8, 20; 19:2, 11; 20:12, 13). God's judgment is good news to the saints but bad news to the wicked. Abraham called God "the Judge of all the earth" (Gen. 18:25). Isaiah foresaw Jerusalem as a place of quiet habitation, "for the Lord is our Judge" (Isa. 33:20–22). The psalmist prophesied that the Lord "cometh to judge the earth: he shall judge the world with right-eousness" (Ps. 96:13). The Lord Jesus declared, "For the Father judges no man, but has committed all judgment to the Son" (John 5:22).

The verb *to avenge* (ἐκδικέω) occurs only twice in Rev. (6:10; 19:2), both times referring to God avenging the death of His martyrs.

6:11. Just as creation was a series of divine acts rather than an instantaneous action (Gen. 1:1–31), so the resurrection will be a series of actions as the apostle Paul has al-ready revealed (I Cor. 15:20–26). He made clear that it will be a bodily resurrection (I Cor. 15:35–44). He also assured God's people that every harmful deed they endure will be thoroughly avenged (Rom. 12:19). It is enough that God's people call to the attention of the Lord their sufferings with the serene trust that God will work out His perfect will and will vindicate them (Acts 4:24–30). See ZPEB, "Resurrection," V, pp. 70–75; Ryken, Wilhoit, and Longman, *Dictionary of Biblical Imagery*, pp. 711–12.

The word *robe* (στολή) occurs 5 times in Rev. (3 times it is a *white robe*, 6:11; 7:9, 13; and twice it is a *washed robe*, 7:14; 22:14).

The only other times the word *fellowslave* (σύνδουλος) occurs in Rev. an angel applies it to himself (19:10; 22:9)!

12 And I beheld when he had opened the sixth seal, and, lo, there was a great earth-
quake; and the sun became black as sackcloth of hair, and the moon became as blood;
13 And the stars of heaven fell unto the earth, even as a fig tree casteth her untimely
figs, when she is shaken of a mighty wind.
14 And the heaven departed as a scroll when it is rolled together; and every mountain
and island were moved out of their places.
15 And the kings of the earth, and the great men, and the rich men, and the chief
captains, and the mighty men, and every bondman, and every free man, hid them-
selves in the dens and in the rocks of the mountains;
16 And said to the mountains and rocks, Fall on us, and hide us from the face of him
that sitteth on the throne, and from the wrath of the Lamb:
17 For the great day of his wrath is come; and who shall be able to stand?

VI. The Sixth Seal: Wrath on the Earth Dwellers. vv. 12–17.

"And I saw when he opened the sixth seal, and there was a great earthquake, and the sun became black as sackcloth of hair, and the whole
moon became as blood" (v. 12). When the Bible calls an earthquake
"great," one wonders what that would be on the Richter scale! The Lord
promised to clothe the heavens with blackness (Isa. 50:3). Earthquake
and the darkening of the heavenly bodies are signs of the Day of the
Lord (Joel 2:10–11). "And the stars of heaven fell to the earth, as a fig
tree casts its unripe figs when shaken by a great wind" (v. 13). This does
not refer to stars like our sun, for if any of them came near the earth, it
would be burned to a crisp. The reference is rather to "shooting stars,"
meteors that fall to earth. There has not been a really impressive meteor
shower for some time, but on November 13, 1833, eyewitnesses testified
that hundreds of meteors could be seen simultaneously. People actually
fell to their knees and begged God for mercy! That will certainly be appropriate during the Tribulation period. Isaiah prophesied that the Day of
the Lord would come with astronomical signs (Isa. 13:9–10). The Lord
Jesus prophesied these same signs for the Tribulation period before His
return in glory (Matt. 24:29–30). "And the heaven departed as a scroll
rolled up, and every mountain and island were moved out of their places"
(v. 14). People who have endured earthquakes or volcanic eruptions can

---

6:12. Earthquakes are mentioned 7 times in Rev. (6:12; 8:5; 11:13 [twice], 19; 16:18
[twice]).

6:13. For a summary on *star* (ἀστήρ) see Rev. 1:16 note.

6:14. The word *mountain* (ὄρος) occurs 8 times in Rev. (6:14, 15, 16; 8:8; 14:1; 16:20;
17:9; 21:10). It is sometimes used for a symbol of a kingdom (Isa. 2:2–3 LXX). This is a
common theme in the prophets (Isa. 40:4; 41:15; Jer. 51:25; Ezek. 38:20–21; Joel
3:17–18). Beale takes this scene as a parallel to the last judgment (*Rev.*, p. 399). See
ISBE (1982), "Hill, Mount," II, pp. 713–16.

testify to the terrifying feeling of the earth moving. There is no question that such disasters have happened in the past, but the worst is yet future. God will remove the false sense of security that lost people have. The sky veiled with clouds and the earth trembling underfoot will remind the earth dwellers that God is angry with their sin and is summoning them to repent. "And the kings of the earth, and the great men, and the captains of thousands, and the rich men, and the strong men, and every slave and every free man hid themselves in the caves and in the rocks of the mountains . . ." (v. 15). "The kings of the earth . . . take counsel together, against the Lord" (Ps. 2:2), but it does them no good. Isaiah proclaimed, "The loftiness of man shall be bowed down . . . and they shall go into the holes of the rocks, and into the caves of the earth, for fear of the Lord, and for the glory of his majesty, when he arises to shake terribly the earth" (Isa. 2:17, 19). Here there are seven social categories from the king to the slave: all of them wish to hide from God. The rich, the military, the strong, all have powers and possessions to trust in, but they are not enough. "What sinners dread most is not death, but the revealed Presence of God" (Swete, *Rev.*, p. 94). The sixth seal anticipates the disasters of the very end. The plagues are intended to crush the arrogance of man. "And they say to the mountains and the rocks, Fall upon us and hide us from the face of the one sitting on the throne, and from the wrath of the Lamb" (v. 16). This was the cry of the sinners in Israel: "they shall say to the mountains, Cover us; and to the hills, Fall on us" (Hos. 10:8). Wicked men know that they are accountable and that they have no excuse. The Lord Jesus also prophesied that people would cry out this way (Luke 23:30). "Because the great day of their wrath came, and who is able to stand?" (v. 17). Nahum asked, "Who can abide in the

---

6:15. The kings of the earth have spoken arrogantly against the Lord—Pharaoh (Exod. 5:2); Nebuchadnezzar (Dan. 3:14–15)—even as Antichrist will (Rev. 13:6), but the Lord will bring them all to account in judgment (Rev. 20:12–15). "The day of the Lord's vengeance" will come (Isa. 34:8).

6:16. There is a humorous Jewish prayer that all men can relate to: "O Lord, give me an excuse!" Rosten, *Leo Rosten's Treasury of Jewish Quotations*, p. 189.

6:16–17. The wrath (ὀργή) of God is mentioned 6 times in Rev. (6:16, 17; 11:18; 14:10; 16:19; 19:15). There are many warnings in Scripture about the wrath of God. Moses charged Israel with provoking the Lord God to wrath by their rebellion (Deut. 9:7). John warned that the unbeliever shall not see life, "but the wrath of God abides on him" (John 3:36). Paul warned that "the wrath of God is revealed from heaven against all unrighteousness and ungodliness of men" (Rom. 1:18). Ps. 2 warned that God will speak to the nations in His wrath (2:1, 5). The writer to the Hebrews warned that "it is a fearful thing to fall into the hands of the living God" (Heb. 10:31). For a clear summary see "Wrath of God," Elwell, *Evangelical Dictionary of Biblical Theology*, pp. 845–46. See also ZPEB, "Wrath," V, pp. 990–95; ISBE (1988), "Wrath, Anger," IV, pp. 1134–35.

fierceness of his anger?" (Nah. 1:6). They are sinners who stand con-demned before God. Malachi proclaimed the coming of the Messenger of the covenant and warned, "Who may abide the day of his coming? and who shall stand when he appears?" (Mal. 3:2). John explained this in his Gospel. "The one who believes in the Son has eternal life; but the one who does not believe in the Son shall not see life, but the wrath of God is abiding on him" (John 3:36).

Practical Applications from Revelation 6

1. The present world system will always have war, famine, and death (vv. 3–8). People should seek the Lord for help. "God is our refuge and strength, a very present help in trouble" (Ps. 46:1).
2. People need to think soberly about their death and the afterlife (v. 8). The beggar was right with God and ready; the rich man was not (Luke 16:19–31).
3. Believers must be ready to sacrifice everything for the Word of God (v. 9). "Therefore I love thy commandments above gold; yea, above fine gold" (Ps. 119:127).
4. There is complete rest from sorrow and suffering in heaven (v. 11). "In thy presence is fullness of joy; at thy right hand there are pleas-ures for evermore" (Ps. 16:11).
5. The catastrophic end of the age is certain to come (v. 12). "Prepare to meet thy God" (Amos 4:12).
6. Even strong men will come to the end of their resources (vv. 14–15). "But my God shall supply all your need according to his riches in glory by Christ Jesus" (Phil. 4:19).
7. A great day of divine wrath is coming (v. 17). "Much more then, being now justified by his blood, we shall be saved from wrath through him [Christ]" (Rom. 5:9).

Prayer

O Lord, the kings of the earth set themselves against You, but Your people look to You to break Satan's rebellion like a potter's vessel. Give us grace that we may serve You with reverence and rejoice with trem-bling. Amen.

REVELATION 7 PARENTHESIS

TRIBULATION SAINTS

Persons

Four angels

The angel with the seal

144,000 sealed servants

A great multitude

The Lamb (Jesus Christ)

All angels

Elders

Four living beings

Persons referred to

12 tribes of Israel

Juda

Reuben

Gad

Aser

Nephthalim

Manasses

Simeon

Levi

Issachar

Zabulon

Joseph

Benjamin

Places mentioned

The four corners of the earth

The sea

The throne in heaven

Doctrines taught

The rule of God

Salvation

Worship

The Great Tribulation

The blood

Comfort

1 And after these things I saw four angels standing on the four corners of the earth, holding the four winds of the earth, that the wind should not blow on the earth, nor on the sea, nor on any tree.

2 And I saw another angel ascending from the east, having the seal of the living God: and he cried with a loud voice to the four angels, to whom it was given to hurt the earth and the sea,

3 Saying, Hurt not the earth, neither the sea, nor the trees, till we have sealed the servants of our God in their foreheads.

Revelation 7 Exposition

I. Salvation During the Tribulation Period. vv. 1–3.

This first parenthesis in the series of sevens provides an answer to a very serious question. Considering the severity of the judgments coming on the earth, can anyone be saved during the Tribulation period? There are two specific answers to this question: the 144,000 and the great multitude that no one could number. "After this I saw four angels having taken their stand on the four corners of the earth, holding the four winds of the earth, that the wind blow not on the earth, nor upon the sea, nor upon any tree" (v. 1). The prophets mention the four winds of heaven (Jer. 49:36; Ezek. 37:9). The idea that there are spiritual beings who can hold back the north, east, south, and west winds is wholly foreign to modern thinking. That is certainly not proof that they do not exist. Some have thought it curious that trees are mentioned in this context. Morris suggests that *trees* symbolize any living thing (*Rev.*, p. 110). But there is no reason that John did not mean literal trees, for in any windstorm the destruction of trees is the great casualty. Daniel also saw the four winds of heaven striving on the great sea (Dan. 7:2). "And I saw another angel rising up from the east, having the seal of the living God, and he cried with a great voice to the four angels to whom it was given to harm the earth and the sea" (v. 2). The phrase *it was given* shows that God was permitting this judgment. The apostle Paul gives us the very inscriptions on the great seal of God.

7:1. "After this I saw" (μετὰ τοῦτο εἶδον) introduces a new, parenthetic vision. It is not part of the 7 seals but is necessary to understand the seals.

This word for *tree* (δένδρον) occurs only 4 times in Rev. (7:1, 3; 8:7; 9:4). For a synonym (ξύλον) see Rev. 2:7 note. In the dry Holy Land trees were especially prized (Ps. 1:3). See Ryken, Wilhoit, and Longman, *Dictionary of Biblical Imagery*, "Tree," pp. 890–92.

7:2. Ezekiel described how the Lord sent an angelic being to Jerusalem to set a mark, a seal (tau, a letter that looked like a small cross +) on the forehead of everyone who mourned over the sins of the land (Ezek. 9:3–4). The sealed ones would be spared, all the rest slaughtered.

4 And I heard the number of them which were sealed: and there were sealed an hundred and forty and four thousand of all the tribes of the children of Israel.

5 Of the tribe of Juda were sealed twelve thousand. Of the tribe of Reuben were sealed twelve thousand. Of the tribe of Gad were sealed twelve thousand.

6 Of the tribe of Aser were sealed twelve thousand. Of the tribe of Nepthalim were sealed twelve thousand. Of the tribe of Manasses were sealed twelve thousand.

7 Of the tribe of Simeon were sealed twelve thousand. Of the tribe of Levi were sealed twelve thousand. Of the tribe of Issachar were sealed twelve thousand.

8 Of the tribe of Zabulon were sealed twelve thousand. Of the tribe of Joseph were sealed twelve thousand. Of the tribe of Benjamin were sealed twelve thousand.

"Nevertheless the foundation of God stands sure, having this seal, The Lord knows them that are his, and, Let every one who names the name of the Lord depart from unrighteousness" (II Tim. 2:19). The obverse declares divine sovereignty and the reverse declares human responsibility. The seal of the believer is nothing less than the Holy Spirit of God ("You were sealed with the Holy Spirit of promise, who is the earnest of our inheritance" Eph. 1:13–14; 4:30). "Saying, Hurt not the earth, nor the sea, nor the trees, until we have sealed the slaves of our God upon their foreheads" (v. 3). The word *slaves* denotes those who have voluntarily devoted themselves to the service of God. There is no judgment that can fall on the earth before the servants of God have His seal of ownership and protection put upon them. Whenever the believer faces disaster, he should remember that there are only two alternatives for him:

1. Protection and deliverance.
2. Promotion to paradise.

This is certainly a great comfort to all true believers. The idea of the seal of God's protection on the people of God comes from Ezekiel 9:4–11.

II. The Saved Remnant of Israel. vv. 4–8.

Although some argue that the 144,000 symbolize the redeemed of all ages (Swete, *Rev.*, p. 98; Beale, *Rev.*, p. 412), the use of the Hebrew

---

7:3. Note the 4 purposes of the disasters of the Tribulation period:

1. To save a great multitude of people. Rev. 7:3–14.
2. To fulfill Daniel's prophecy of the seventieth week. Dan. 9:24–27.
3. To bring the Jews to an end of their human resources. Zech. 14:1–4.
4. To visit God's wrath on the earth dwellers. Rev. 8:13.

The word *forehead* (μέτωπον) occurs 8 times only in Rev. in the NT (7:3; 9:4; 13:16; 14:1, 9; 17:5; 20:4; 22:4). The forehead is an obvious place for an identifying mark. The high priest wore a gold plate on his forehead, inscribed HOLINESS TO THE LORD" (Exod. 28:36). God's mark implies divine protection (Ezek. 9:4). The Beast will demand

names for each tribe, contrasted with the specific mention of the multitude of Gentiles in the following scene, make that highly unlikely. The doctrine of the restored remnant is a major theme in the OT (Isa. 9:6–7; 10:21–23; 46:3–4; Joel 2:18–32; Mic. 5:2–3; Zech. 8:6–8). Ezekiel prophesied in detail of the restored millennial temple and its worship (Ezek. 40–48). "And I heard the number of the ones who have been sealed, a hundred forty-four thousand, having been sealed out of every tribe of the sons of Israel" (v. 4). The number is twelve times twelve thousand, but, lest anyone should think that it is a mere symbol, John gives an itemized list.

> "Out of the tribe of Judah twelve thousand having been sealed,
> Out of the tribe of Reuben twelve thousand,
> Out of the tribe of Gad twelve thousand,
> Out of the tribe of Aser twelve thousand,
> Out of the tribe of Nephthalim twelve thousand,
> Out of the tribe of Manassa twelve thousand,
> Out of the tribe of Symeon twelve thousand,
> Out of the tribe of Levi twelve thousand,
> Out of the tribe of Issachar twelve thousand,
> Out of the tribe of Zabulon twelve thousand,
> Out of the tribe of Joseph twelve thousand,
> Out of the tribe of Benjamin twelve thousand" (vv. 5–8).

This is a very distinctive list, organized by divine logic rather than the order of birth, which is more usual. It begins with the tribe of Judah, which is the most important tribe because of Messiah, who has already been mentioned ("The Lion of the tribe of Judah," Rev. 5:5). The tribes of Manassa and Ephraim are mentioned as Manassa and Joseph, emphasizing the double portion of the inheritance that Jacob promised Joseph

---

"666" on the forehead (Rev. 13:16–18). See Ryken, Wilhoit, and Longman, *Dictionary of Biblical Imagery*, "Forehead," pp. 299f.

The verb *to seal* (σφραγίζω) occurs 8 times in Rev. (7:3, 4 [twice], 5, 8; 10:4; 20:3; 22:10).

7:4. The interpretation that these are literal descendents of Israel has overwhelming support from conservative premillennial commentators: Seiss (p. 161), J. B. Smith (p. 129), Scott (p. 162), A. C. Gaebelein (p. 58), Newell (p. 111), Govett (p. 155), Ironside (pp. 126f.), Walvoord (pp. 141ff.), R. L. Thomas (I, p. 474), Fruchtenbaum, (p. 149), LaHaye (p. 149), etc. Among those who take the 144,000 as a symbolic number, there is a great diversity of opinions. Mounce holds that the numbers are symbolic of the church that is the "eschatological people of God who have taken up Israel's inheritance" (*Rev.*, p. 158). Caird thinks that the numbers refer to future Christian martyrs (*Rev.*, p. 97). Lenski argues that the 144,000 represent the church militant (*Rev.*, p. 245). Beale holds that the 144,000 symbolize the redeemed of all ages (and are identical with the great multitude, *Rev.*, pp. 412ff.). Barclay thinks that the 144,000 were saved in John's own day (*Rev.*, II, 29). See Ryken, Wilhoit, and Longman, *Dictionary of Biblical Imagery*, "Twelve," pp. 900–901.

9 After this I beheld, and, lo, a great multitude, which no man could number, of all nations, and kindreds, and people, and tongues, stood before the throne, and before the Lamb, clothed with white robes, and palms in their hands;
10 And cried with a loud voice, saying, Salvation to our God which sitteth upon the throne, and unto the Lamb.
11 And all the angels stood round about the throne, and about the elders and the four beasts, and fell before the throne on their faces, and worshipped God,
12 Saying, Amen: Blessing, and glory, and wisdom, and thanksgiving, and honour, and power, and might, be unto our God for ever and ever. Amen.
13 And one of the elders answered, saying unto me, What are these which are arrayed in white robes? and whence came they?
14 And I said unto him, Sir, thou knowest. And he said to me, These are they which came out of great tribulation, and have washed their robes, and made them white in the blood of the Lamb.
15 Therefore are they before the throne of God, and serve him day and night in his temple: and he that sitteth on the throne shall dwell among them.
16 They shall hunger no more, neither thirst any more; neither shall the sun light on them, nor any heat.
17 For the Lamb which is in the midst of the throne shall feed them, and shall lead them unto living fountains of waters: and God shall wipe away all tears from their eyes.

(Gen. 48:3–22). A great deal of ink has been spilled over why the tribe of Dan was omitted. Simply, it was necessary to keep the number of tribes at twelve. The idea that Dan was for any reason wiped out is not defensible. When Ezekiel describes the rebuilt millennial city of Jerusalem, one of the twelve gates is named after Dan (Ezek. 48:32). Assuredly Dan's descendants will be there. Even though Israel may break the commandments, God will still establish the Davidic covenant (Ps. 89:31–37).

III. The Great Multitude. vv. 9–17.

"After these things I saw, and behold, a great multitude, which no one was able to count, out of every nation and tribe and people and tongue, having taken their stand before the throne and before the Lamb, having been clothed with white robes, and having palm branches in their hands" (v. 9). Palm branches were associated with the celebration of the feast of the tabernacles (Lev. 23:40), which will be observed in the millennial worship (Zech. 14:19). Here it is part of the worship of heaven. White robes were given immediately to the martyrs of the Tribulation period (Rev. 6:11). Spurgeon commented, "Thus has he chosen white as the

---

7:9. The verb *to count* (ἀριθμέω) occurs only here in Rev. and only in Matt. 10:30; Luke 12:7 in the rest of the NT. The context plainly refers to a vast, incalculable number.
For a summary of the word *robe* (στολή) see Rev. 6:11 note.

symbolic color of his victorious kingdom, and so the redeemed wear it, even the newly born, freshly escaped out of the great tribulation, because they are all of them more than conquerors. They wear the victor garb and bear the palm which is the victor symbol" ("Why the Heavenly Robes Are White," Sermon 1316, *The C. H. Spurgeon Collection*, Ages Digital Library). This scene is the completed group of martyrs from "the great tribulation" (v. 14). In a time of wrath God remembers mercy. "And they cry with a great voice saying, Salvation to our God who sits upon the throne, and to the Lamb" (v. 10). The language echoes the prophecy of the Lord's entrance into Jerusalem (Zech. 9:9). God is the author of the great salvation that these persecuted saints will now enjoy. We must notice that this multinational group can praise God with perfect unity and with an internal sense of the suitability of words to be used. The veil has been lifted so that God's people can communicate perfectly. These newly arrived members are at no disadvantage. The Lord Jesus taught this concerning the whole unseen world (Luke 16:22–31). "And all the angels stood in a circle around the throne, and the elders, and the four living beings, and they fell before the throne upon their faces, and they worshiped God" (v. 11). The "ordinary" angels are here distinguished from the elders and the four living beings. However, it will be an overwhelming sight to behold these mighty beings worshiping God. The angels fall down in reverential awe. Expositors argue over whether angels can sing, but whether this is choric speaking or singing, the effect must be overpowering. When Gabriel spoke, Daniel fell on his face before him (Dan. 8:16–17). Now John hears the angels "Saying, Amen! Blessing, and glory, and wisdom, and thanksgiving, and honor, and power, and strength be to our God into the ages of the ages; Amen" (v. 12). The language parallels the Davidic blessing (I Chron. 29:10–13). The angels ascribe seven categories of praise to God. All of them can be found in Scripture. The psalmist prayed, "Bless the Lord, O my soul" (Pss. 103:1; 104:1). The angels at Bethlehem

---

7:10. The word *salvation* (σωτηρία) occurs 3 times in Rev. (7:10; 12:10; 19:1), in each case a scene of heavenly celebration for the greatness of the salvation provided in Christ. John recorded in his Gospel (4:42) and his First Epistle (4:14) that Christ is the Savior of the world. See "Soteriology in the Book of Revelation" (Mal Couch, *A Bible Handbook to Revelation*, pp. 163–71). The apostles stressed that there is salvation in none other (Acts 4:12); Paul argued that the gospel is the power of God unto salvation to everyone who believes in Christ (Rom. 1:16); the writer of Hebrews declared that the Son of God became the author of eternal salvation to all who obey Him (Heb. 5:9). See ISBE (1988), "Salvation," IV, pp. 287–95; ZPEB, "Salvation," V, pp. 221–32.

7:11. For a summary of the verb *to worship* (προσκυνέω) see Rev. 4:10 note.

7:12. Matthew Henry observes, "We see what is the work of heaven, and we ought to begin it now, to get our hearts tuned for it, to be much in it, and to long for that world where our praises, as well as happiness, will be perfected."

praised God, "Glory to God in the highest" (Luke 2:14). "O Lord . . . in wisdom hast thou made them all" (Ps. 104:24). "O give thanks unto the Lord" (Pss. 105:1; 106:1). "O Lord my God . . . thou art clothed with honor and majesty" (Ps. 104:1). "Great is our Lord, and of great power" (Ps. 147:5). "The Lord is clothed with strength" (Ps. 93:1). We should not leave it to the angels to sing God's praise. "And one of the elders answered, saying to me, These who have been clothed with white robes, who are they and from whence did they come?" (v. 13). The elder asks a leading question in full knowledge that John does not have the answer. "And I said to him, My lord, you know. And he said to me, These are the ones who are coming out of the great tribulation, and they washed their robes and whitened them in the blood of the Lamb" (v. 14). My lord is "an address of reverence as to a heavenly being" (Vincent, Word Studies, II, p. 503). The present tense verb are coming implies that the group is still gathering; the aorist tense washed implies that the only ones showing up in this realm are those washed in the blood of the Lamb. Spurgeon points out that the KJV left out the article the ("Why the Heavenly Robes Are White," p. 690, The C. H. Spurgeon Collection, Ages Digital Library). It does not refer to just any great tribulation, but the Great Tribulation that is prophesied for the end time (Dan. 12:1; Joel 2:10–11; Zech. 14:2; Matt. 24:21). This great multitude from all nations (v. 9) has washed their robes in the blood of the Lamb. That certainly means that they are eternally saved, just as surely as any other saint in heaven. They do not have the honor of the 144,000 witnesses for Christ, but they are definitely saved. We, as well as they, are made nigh by the blood of Christ (Eph. 2:13). The blood of martyrs cannot save; it is the blood of Christ that saves and cleanses from all sin (I John 1:9). "On account of this they are before the throne of God, and they are serving him day and night in his sanctuary, and the one sitting upon the throne shall tabernacle over them" (v. 15). Since they have been saved in the eleventh hour, they are zealous in

---

7:14. The Tribulation period is the 7-year period of Daniel's seventieth week (Dan. 9:24–27). The Great Tribulation is the last half of that 7-year period, in which disaster and persecution rise to unprecedented levels (Dan. 9:27; Rev. 11:15–19:11). But in wrath God remembers mercy, even as Habakkuk prayed (Hab. 3:2). And so the great promise remains true, "For whosoever shall call upon the name of the Lord shall be saved" (Rom. 10:13). Even out of that period of sin and retribution a vast multitude will be saved (Rev. 15:2–4). For carefully reasoned evidence, see Seiss, Apocalypse, pp. 170–79; J. B. Smith, Rev., pp. 133–35; Walvoord, Major Bible Prophecies, pp. 346–53; LaHaye, Rev., pp. 148–62; Mal Couch, Dictionary of Premillennial Theology, "Tribulation, OT References," "Tribulation, the Great," "Tribulation, Various Views of the," pp. 412–17; Merrill Unger, The New Unger's Bible Dictionary, "Tribulation, the Great," pp. 1306–7.

7:15. The verb to serve (λατρεύω) does not refer to menial service but to religious service. It occurs only once more in Rev. (22:3) of the joyous worship service of the redeemed serving God day and night. They may have missed chances to serve here, but they are determined not to miss any opportunities there (in heaven, Seiss, p. 176; Newell, p. 109; J. B. Smith, p. 135; Walvoord, p. 148; LaHaye, p. 161; Scott argues that they serve in the millennial temple, p. 174). Before the throne they rejoice in the privilege of service. "They shall no longer hunger, nor thirst, nor shall the sun fall on them, nor any heat" (v. 16). Isaiah prophesied of protection from hunger, thirst, and the sun in future time (Isa. 49:10). This verse demonstrates the terrible persecution that Antichrist will bring upon those who do not submit to his false religion. The Lord Jesus warned of such persecution in the Great Tribulation: the only hope is to flee into the wilderness, not taking anything with them (Matt. 24:15–21). The sun will *fall*, "glare down" on them. His people will be hungry, thirsty, naked, sick, and in prison (Matt. 25:35–36). John will learn later that no one will be able to buy or sell without state approval by the Antichrist (Rev. 13:17). But now all this is behind them. No evil can touch them. Leon Morris called this "an exquisitely beautiful picture of the bliss of the saved" (*The Cross in the New Testament*, p. 363). "Because the Lamb in the midst of the throne shall shepherd them, and shall lead them to living fountains of waters, and God shall wipe away every tear from their eyes" (v. 17). Isaiah prophesied that the Lord would wipe away tears from all faces (Isa. 25:8). This was the faith of David, "The Lord is my shepherd" (Ps. 23:1). He will not just feed them; He will shepherd them, providing for every need they have. In contrast to the thirst they have experienced, they will have flowing springs of the water of life. Every saint there will be "accepted in the Beloved," having a proper place of service that will be acceptable to all. Never again will discrimination and persecution afflict them.

Practical Applications from Revelation 7

1. No natural disaster can happen without divine permission (v. 1). "Fire, and hail; snow, and vapor; stormy wind fulfilling his word" (Ps. 148:8).
2. God's people have divine protection (v. 3). "Then Satan answered the Lord, and said, Doth Job fear God for nought? hast not thou made an hedge about him, and about his house, and about all that

---

saints in eternity, but often in the NT (Matt. 4:10; Luke 2:37; Acts 24:14; Rom. 1:9; Heb. 12:28, etc.). See Ryken, Wilhoit, and Longman, *Dictionary of Biblical Imagery*, "Servant," p. 774; ISBE (1988), "Servant, Slave," IV, pp. 419–21; ZPEB, "Servant," V, pp. 358–59.

The verb *to tabernacle* (σκηνόω) occurs 4 times in Rev. (7:15; 12:12; 13:6; 21:3). It may mean simply *dwell* (John 1:14), but in this context the root meaning of *tent* surely implies the sheltering protection of God's tabernacling over His people.

he hath on every side? Thou hast blessed the work of his hands, and his substance is increased in the land" (Job 1:9–10).

3. There will be more saved people in heaven than we expect (v. 9). "Cast thy bread upon the waters: for thou shalt find it after many days" (Eccles. 11:1).

4. There will be perfect communication in heaven (v. 10). "Let the saints be joyful in glory" (Ps. 149:5).

5. Believers will see and hear the angelic choirs (vv. 11–12). "And suddenly there was with the angel a multitude of the heavenly host, praising God, and saying, Glory to God in the highest, and on earth peace, good will toward men" (Luke 2:13–14).

6. Our questions will be answered in heaven (vv. 13–14). "Why are ye fearful, O ye of little faith?" (Matt. 8:25–26).

7. Believers will be able to serve God day and night without weariness (v. 15). Compare Isaiah 56:6–7.

8. Believers will be beyond the reach of suffering (v. 16). Lazarus: "now he is comforted" (Luke 16:25).

9. The Lamb shall provide satisfaction and divine comfort to his people (v. 17). "In thy presence is fullness of joy; at thy right hand there are pleasures for evermore" (Ps. 16:11).

Prayer

O God of our salvation, we sing praise to Your holy name for the salvation that Your Son, the Lamb, has brought to His people. We thank You that His precious blood has washed us from our sins and put a new song in our hearts. Amen.

Revelation 8:2–11:19

Trumpet Judgments 1–4

Persons

John ("I")
The seven angels before God
Another angel having a golden
censer (Jesus Christ?)

The angel flying in mid-heaven

Persons referred to

All saints
Many men who died from
wormwood

The inhabiters of the earth

Places mentioned

Heaven
The earth
The sea

The sun
The moon
The stars

Doctrines taught

Intercessory prayer
Judgment

Darkness as a judgment

1 And when he had opened the seventh seal, there was silence in heaven about the space of half an hour.
2 And I saw the seven angels which stood before God; and to them were given seven trumpets.
3 And another angel came and stood at the altar, having a golden censer; and there was given unto him much incense, that he should offer it with the prayers of all saints upon the golden altar which was before the throne.
4 And the smoke of the incense, which came with the prayers of the saints, ascended up before God out of the angel's hand.
5 And the angel took the censer, and filled it with fire of the altar, and cast it into the earth: and there were voices, and thunderings, and lightnings, and an earthquake.
6 And the seven angels which had the seven trumpets prepared themselves to sound.

Revelation 8 Exposition

I. The Seventh Seal and the High Priest. vv. 1–6.

"And whenever he opened the seventh seal, there was silence in heaven for about a half hour" (v. 1). *Whenever* is the only touch of indefiniteness in any of the seals (Alford, IV, p. 642). Habakkuk said, "The Lord is in his holy temple: let all the earth keep silence before him" (Hab. 2:20). But this silence is in heaven. With the breaking of the seventh seal the scroll lies open in the hand of the Lamb, its rightful possessor. Now He will take the steps necessary to claim His inheritance. The seventh of the series introduces a new series of seven. Thus the seven trumpets come out of the seventh seal. Each time the judgments increase in severity. The silence will soon be shattered by the trumpet blasts of judgment to come. "And I saw seven angels who had taken their stand before God, and seven trumpets were given to them" (v. 2). The verb *were given*

8:1. The only other occurrence of *silence* (σιγή) in the NT is in Acts 21:40, of the stunned silence of the angry mob when they heard Paul speak in their own dialect. Jeremiah charged, "The Lord our God hath put us to silence . . . because we have sinned against the Lord" (Jer. 8:14). Zephaniah prophesied, "Hold thy peace at the presence of the Lord God: for the day of the Lord is at hand" (Zeph. 1:7). Although Thomas lists 5 interpretations of the silence, the one he recommends is clearly the best: the silence creates a "hushed expectancy" for the severity of the judgments to follow (R. L. Thomas, *Rev.*, II, p. 3).

8:2. The 7 archangels "of the Presence" is a well-known idea in Jewish literature; in fact, they are named in I Enoch 20:2ff., Uriel, Raphael, Raguel, Michael, Saraqael, Gabriel, and Remiel. Although most are not named in Scripture, the article *the* proves their existence as a specific group. Gabriel claimed to stand in the presence of God (Luke 1:19). "The angel of his presence" is mentioned in Isa. 63:9. Daniel recognized Michael as a "chief prince" (Dan. 10:13).

shows that God is authorizing these trumpet judgments. In the ancient world trumpets were not primarily thought of as musical instruments. The trumpet was principally marked "by loudness; it was primarily an announcement device" (Ryken, Wilhoit, and Longman, A *Dictionary of Biblical Imagery*, p. 900). When the Lord descended to give the Law, "the trumpet sounded long, and waxed louder and louder" (Exod. 19:19). It was not by accident that it was used to signal a cavalry charge. But before these judgments can begin, there is a very important ceremony that must be performed in heaven. "And another angel came and stood at the altar, having a golden censer; and much incense was given to him, that he should offer the prayers of all the saints upon the golden altar before the throne" (v. 3). This angel is not identified, and some have no comment on his nature (Swete), but others will firmly argue that *angel* means angel, and therefore this is a literal angel (Alford, Newell, J. B. Smith, R. L. Thomas). However, there is no angel in Scripture that is portrayed as having the power and authority to cause the prayers of God's saints to ascend up before God. Consequently, others argue that this refers to Christ, appearing not in humble human form but in mighty archangelic appearance as High Priest, causing the prayers of His people to ascend before His Father and answering them in the cataclysmic judgments to follow (Seiss, Scott, Ironside, Gaebelein, Ottman, Govett, Walvoord). For many years God's people have cried out, "Lord . . . how long shall the wicked triumph?" (Ps. 94:3; see also Pss. 13:1; 74:10; Dan. 8:13; Rev. 6:10). "And the smoke of the incense, with the prayers of the saints, ascended up out of the hand of the angel before God" (v. 4). Believers should take their ministry of prayer much more seriously than they commonly do. Spurgeon has a heartfelt sermon on this text, "Preparing for the Week of Prayer" (Sermon 3282, *The C. H. Spurgeon Collection*, Ages Digital Library). When the Bridegroom says, "Let me hear thy voice" (Song of Sol. 2:14), we should certainly speak to Him. This scene reminds us of the words of the Lord Jesus, "And whatever you shall ask in my name, this I will do, that the Father may be glorified in the Son. If you shall ask me anything

---

8:3–4. The golden *altar* (θυσιαστήριον, Rev. 6:9; 8:3 [twice]) stands in the place of the altar of incense in the tabernacle, "before the throne." The altar of sacrifice was outside the tabernacle, just as Calvary was outside of heaven. The text says literally that the angel stood "upon (ἐπί) the altar." The same thing is said of Jehovah (Amos 9:1). Incense was a commanded part of OT ritual (Exod. 30:1–8). It was a symbol of the "fragrance of holiness" (Biedermann, *Dictionary of Symbolism*, p. 184). The use of the censer for the incense was also commanded (Lev. 16:12–13). The word *smoke* (καπνός) occurs 12 times in Rev. (8:4; 9:2 [3 times], 3, 17, 18; 14:11; 15:8; 18:9, 18; 19:3) and only once elsewhere in the NT (Acts 2:19).

The word *prayer* (προσευχή) occurs 3 times in Rev. (5:8; 8:3, 4), each time in the phrase "prayers of the saints."

7 The first angel sounded, and there followed hail and fire mingled with blood, and they were cast upon the earth: and the third part of trees was burnt up, and all green grass was burnt up.

in my name, I will do it" (John 14:13–14). Did He not promise, "If you abide in me, and my words abide in you, you shall ask what you will, and it shall be done unto you" (John 15:7)? He may bear long with His people, but the powers of evil shall be broken in answer to their prayers. "The day of the Lord comes as a thief in the night. For when they shall say, Peace and safety; then sudden destruction comes upon them" (I Thess. 5:3–4). "And the angel took the censer and filled it from the fire of the altar and cast it into the earth, and there were thunders and voices and lightnings and an earthquake" (v. 5). The verb *took* is a dramatic perfect, "has taken," making the reader a witness to the great deed. Events in heaven have immediate effects on earth. To an observer lightning comes before thunder, but many times thunder is heard without any previous perception of lightning. Osborne sees worship and justice intertwined in these events (*Rev.*, p. 348). "And the seven angels who have the seven trumpets prepared themselves to sound" (v. 6). The Lord commanded Joshua to use seven trumpets in the conquest of Jericho (Josh. 6:4). Here the Lord uses seven trumpets to break down the defenses of a wicked world. Joel prophesied the coming of the Day of the Lord: "Blow ye the trumpet in Zion, and sound an alarm in my holy mountain: let all the inhabitants of the land tremble: for the day of the Lord cometh, for it is nigh at hand" (Joel 2:1).

II. The First Trumpet: Hail and Fire. v. 7.

"And the first angel sounded; and there was hail and fire mingled in blood, and it was cast upon the earth; and the third part of the earth was

---

8:5, 7, 8. *Fire* in this context is a manifestation of divine judgment. Fire hurled to earth in v. 5 becomes manifest as hail mingled with fire (v. 7) and a great mountain burning with fire (v. 8). Fire was part of the sixth trumpet judgment as well (9:17–18). Fire will be part of the eternal torment of the beast worshipers (Rev. 14:10). The Devil and all his evil followers will be cast into a lake of fire (Rev. 20:10, 15). Fire "is the fearful antithesis of the kingdom of God. Already Isa. 66:24 speaks of a fire that will not be quenched" (Ryken, Wilhoit, and Longman, *Dictionary of Biblical Imagery*, p. 288). But God manifested Himself to Moses in a burning bush (Exod. 3:2) and led the Israelites as a pillar of fire (Exod. 13:21). During the Millennium God will be a protection, "a wall of fire round about" Jerusalem (Zech. 2:5).

8:6. For a summary of *trumpet* (σάλπιγξ) see Rev. 1:10 note. The original trumpet was a ram's horn (shophar, Josh. 6:4), but the Hebrews knew how to make them out of metal as well (Num. 10:2).This is the first of 7 times that the verb *to prepare* (ἑτοιμάζω) occurs in Rev. (8:6; 9:7, 15; 12:6; 16:2; 19:7; 21:2).

8 *And the second angel sounded, and as it were a great mountain burning with fire was cast into the sea: and the third part of the sea became blood;*
9 *And the third part of the creatures which were in the sea, and had life, died; and the third part of the ships were destroyed.*

burned up, and the third part of the trees was burned up, and all green grass was burned up" (v. 7). The first plague on Egypt turned the waters of the Nile to blood (Exod. 7:17). The seventh plague was hail on all the land of Egypt (Exod. 9:22ff.). The language reminds us of Joel's prophecy, "The fire hath devoured the pastures of the wilderness, and the flame hath burned all the trees of the field" (Joel 1:19). Forest fires and brush-fires have been increasing all over the world, but nothing on this scale. Lightning starts most of them. "Ball" lightning is rare but well documented. The lightning bolt may hit the ground and form a ball of electricity that bounces along, starting fires at each bounce. Hail is another natural disaster that can be very damaging. The thought of forest fires "out of control" is a terrifying situation to those in the path of the fires. But the scale of the fires is without precedent. Premillennial interpreters regularly argue that all this will happen literally (Seiss, Newell, J. B. Smith, Strauss, Walvoord, LaHaye), but Ironside holds that the trees and grass symbolize people. Symbolical interpreters argue that all the details are figurative (Beale, Mounce, Pieters).

III. The Second Trumpet: A Great Burning Mountain. vv. 8–9.

"And the second angel sounded, and as a great mountain burning with fire was cast into the sea, and the third part of the sea became blood" (v. 8). "A great mountain" is a reasonable description of an asteroid, which astronomers identify as a mountain-sized chunk of rock hurtling through space. If such a rock came toward the earth, the friction of the earth's atmosphere would cause it to burn. Astronomers are calculating the orbits of known asteroids to see if any of them would come close enough to strike the earth. If any asteroid struck the ocean, "it could easily produce tidal waves of 600 to 1,000 feet high" (Custer, *The Stars Speak*, p. 132; 2nd ed., p. 148). "And the third part of the creatures that were in the sea and had life, died, and the third part of the ships were destroyed" (v. 9). The impact explosion would produce staggering fish-

---

8:7. This is the first reference to *hail* in Rev. It also occurs in Rev. 11:19; 16:21.

8:8. This is the first of 13 times that the word *blood* ($\alpha\tilde{\iota}\mu\alpha$) occurs in Rev. (8:8; 11:6; 12:11; 14:20; 16:3, 4, 6 [twice]; 17:6 [twice]; 18:24; 19:2, 13). Water turning to blood is an omen of judgment (Exod. 7:19–21). Joel prophesied this very sign about the Day of the Lord (Joel 2:31).

8:9. This is the first reference to *ships* in Rev. It also occurs in Rev. 18:17, 19.

10 And the third angel sounded, and there fell a great star from heaven, burning as it were a lamp, and it fell upon the third part of the rivers, and upon the fountains of waters;
11 And the name of the star is called Wormwood: and the third part of the waters became wormwood; and many men died of the waters, because they were made bitter.

kills and destruction of shipping. Seiss argues that the Mediterranean Sea is the target area. Symbolic interpreters, such as Beale, see the burning mountain as the judgment of a wicked kingdom (p. 476). Daniel refers to the "great sea" (Dan. 7:2, the Mediterranean) and sees four great empires arise from it (Dan. 7:3ff.).

IV. The Third Trumpet: The Star Wormwood. vv. 10–11.

"And the third angel sounded, and a great star, burning like a torch, fell out of heaven, and it fell on the third part of the rivers and the springs of waters" (v. 10). This object is not said to be solid like a rock but like a star, which is made up of gases. It is the rivers and springs in the area that absorb the poisonous gases. "And the name of the star is called Wormwood, and a third of the waters became wormwood, and many men died from the waters, because they were made bitter" (v. 11). The name given to the star is especially thought provoking. It is "Wormwood" (absinthe, ἄψινθος), one of the bitterest substances known. A liquid with one part absinthe to seventy thousand will taste bitter. The plant did grow in Palestine (A. T. Robertson, *Word Pictures*, VI, p. 359). It was not used for a murder weapon because it was so easily detected; it was used for suicide. This passage has special meaning to Russian believers. The Russian word for "Wormwood" is *Chernobyl*, the place of the meltdown of the nuclear reactor in 1986. It is now in the Ukraine. (See *National Geographic Atlas of the World*, 7th ed., p. 86, P-4). The meltdown caused death and physical harm over a wide area. Osborne suggests that this judgment reverses the miracle at Marah (*Rev.*, p. 339). Daniel saw "the little horn" cast some of the stars to the ground (Dan. 8:9).

8:10–11. The head of a comet is made up of ice crystals of well-known poisons (methane, ammonia, etc.). If the head of a comet actually made a direct hit on the earth, some of the poisons could be absorbed by water sources in the area. The so-called Tunguska "meteorite" may be an example. It fell in Siberia on June 30, 1908. The evidence points to an explosion in the atmosphere. All the trees in a 40-mile radius were torn up by the roots and laid down flat like the petals of a flower, but no chunks of rock were ever found in the area of impact. At the center there were trees left standing, but with all their branches stripped off. When the czarist regime finally sent a scientific party to investigate (8 years later), no poisons were detectable (see Custer, *The Stars Speak*, p. 131).

12 And the fourth angel sounded, and the third part of the sun was smitten, and the third part of the moon, and the third part of the stars; so as the third part of them was darkened, and the day shone not for a third part of it, and the night likewise.
13 And I beheld, and heard an angel flying through the midst of heaven, saying with a loud voice, Woe, woe, woe, to the inhabiters of the earth by reason of the other voices of the trumpet of the three angels, which are yet to sound!

V. The Fourth Trumpet: Sun, Moon, and Stars Darkened. vv. 12–13.

"And the fourth angel sounded, and the third of the sun was struck, and the third of the moon, and the third of the stars, in order that the third of them was darkened, and the day did not appear the third part of it and the night likewise" (v. 12). Seiss is clearly wrong in suggesting that the sun, moon, and stars are diminished by a third of their force. The earth would freeze solid in such an event. It is far better to take it as the darkening of the sun, moon, and stars a third of the time (J. B. Smith, Newell, Walvoord). LaHaye suggests sixteen hours of darkness and eight hours of light (*Rev.*, p. 167). Amos prophesied, "And it shall come to pass in that day, saith the Lord God, that I will cause the sun to go down at noon, and I will darken the earth in the clear day" (Amos 8:9). "And I saw, and I heard one eagle flying in mid-heaven, saying with a loud voice: Woe, woe, woe, to the ones dwelling on the earth from the remaining sounds of the trumpet of the three angels who are about to sound" (v. 13). Woe is a common pronouncement of warning, pain, and sorrow (Isa. 5:20; 30:1; Amos 5:18). He gives a threefold *woe* because of the three judgments to come. Plainly, as severe as the four trumpet judgments have been, the three remaining trumpet blasts will be far more catastrophic.

8:12. This is the only time that this verb *to darken* (σκοτίζω) occurs in Rev. Another verb (σκοτόω) is used in Rev. 9:2; 16:10. John uses the related noun *darkness* (σκοτία) in both his Gospel (John 1:5, etc.) and his First Epistle (I John 1:5, etc.). Since God is light (I John 1:5), and darkness is the absence of light, the image has ominous connotations in Scripture. From the thick darkness of the Egyptian plague (Exod. 10:21–22) to the future darkness of the Day of the Lord (Joel 2:1–2), darkness is a reminder of the stern judgment of God on sin. Jude warns the false teachers that they are reserved to the blackness of darkness forever (Jude 13).

8:13. The oldest Greek manuscripts have *eagle* (‫א‬, 1611, 1854, 2053, 2351). The majority have *angel*. It is just as supernatural for an eagle to say something as it is for an angel to speak to you. Perhaps *eagle* was chosen because of the long-range vision of the bird. J. B. Smith argues that *angel* is preferable because angels are the regular messengers of God (*Rev.*, p. 140).

The exclamation *Woe!* (οὐαί) occurs 14 times in Rev. (8:13 [3 times]; 9:12 [twice]; 11:14 [twice]; 12:12; 18:10 [twice], 16 [twice], 19 [twice]). It is an exclamation of calamity and disaster. Here it indicates the severity of the judgments about to fall on the earth. See ISBE (1988), "Woe," IV, p. 1088.

Practical Applications from Revelation 8

1. Modern man tries to avoid silence at all costs (v. 1). But David meditated on God in the night watches (Ps. 63:6).
2. What a privilege these angels have to remain in the presence of God (v. 2). "The upright shall dwell in thy presence" (Ps. 140:13). "Come before his presence with singing" (Ps. 100:2).
3. The prayers of all the saints ascend before God (v. 3). "I sought the Lord, and he heard me" (Ps. 34:4). He hears you too.
4. The smoke of the incense with the prayers of the saints ascended before God (v. 4). "By him therefore let us offer the sacrifice of praise to God continually" (Heb. 13:15).
5. We must be prepared to serve God (v. 6). Believers should be vessels "sanctified, and meet for the master's use, and prepared unto every good work" (II Tim. 2:21).
6. Believers must realize that the present earth cannot be saved (v. 7). It is people who need to be saved (I Cor. 9:22).

Prayer

O Lord, our Intercessor, cause our prayers to ascend before the throne on high. In the midst of the world's tumult help us to seek Your face in a place of quiet trust and perfect peace. We wait for Your blessing. Amen.

The Fifth and Sixth Trumpets

Persons

John ("I")
The fifth angel
The fallen star
The scorpion locusts
The angel of the bottomless pit,
  Abaddon, Apollyon

The sixth angel
The four angels bound in
  Euphrates
The two hundred million man
  army
Unrepentant men

Persons referred to

Men who have not the seal
  of God
Men who desire to die

The third part of men
Demons

Places mentioned

Heaven
Earth

The bottomless pit
The river Euphrates

Doctrines taught

Demonic powers
The condition of unsaved men
The Devil
The restraining power of God

Repentance
Demon and idol worship
Sin

1 And the fifth angel sounded, and I saw a star fall from heaven unto the earth: and to him was given the key of the bottomless pit.

2 And he opened the bottomless pit; and there arose a smoke out of the pit, as the smoke of a great furnace; and the sun and the air were darkened by reason of the smoke of the pit.

3 And there came out of the smoke locusts upon the earth: and unto them was given power, as the scorpions of the earth have power.

4 And it was commanded them that they should not hurt the grass of the earth, neither any green thing, neither any tree; but only those men which have not the seal of God in their foreheads.

5 And to them it was given that they should not kill them, but that they should be tormented five months: and their torment was as the torment of a scorpion, when he striketh a man.

6 And in those days shall men seek death, and shall not find it; and shall desire to die, and death shall flee from them.

7 And the shapes of the locusts were like unto horses prepared unto battle; and on their heads were as it were crowns like gold, and their faces were as the faces of men.

8 And they had hair as the hair of women, and their teeth were as the teeth of lions.

9 And they had breastplates, as it were breastplates of iron; and the sound of their wings was as the sound of chariots of many horses running to battle.

10 And they had tails like unto scorpions, and there were stings in their tails: and their power was to hurt men five months.

11 And they had a king over them, which is the angel of the bottomless pit, whose name in the Hebrew tongue is Abaddon, but in the Greek tongue hath his name Apollyon.

12 One woe is past; and, behold, there come two woes more hereafter.

Revelation 9 Exposition

I. The Fifth Trumpet: The Scorpion Locusts. vv. 1–12.

"And the fifth angel sounded, and I saw a star, having fallen out of heaven unto the earth, and to him was given the key of the bottomless pit" (v. 1). Many expositors identify this fallen star as Satan (Alford, Swete, Seiss, A. C. Gaebelein, J. B. Smith, Ottman, Strauss, Walvoord, Beale, etc.). R. L. Thomas thinks it refers to an unfallen angel; Newell

---

9:1. Moulton and Milligan document the idea of a star symbolizing a personage in ancient literature (*Vocabulary*, pp. 86f.). The *bottomless pit* occurs 7 times in Rev. (9:1, 2, 11; 11:7; 17:8; 20:1, 3). The word *pit* has a bad connotation in the OT. From the slime pits of Siddim (Gen. 14:10) to the pit of destruction (Ps. 55:23), there are bad associations. Lucifer is promised that he shall be brought down "to hell [sheol], to the sides of the pit" (Isa. 14:15; see also Ezek. 28:8–15). The word *bottomless* implies a very deep pit. We know that Satan will be in free fall in it for a thousand years without hitting bottom (Rev. 20:3).

For a summary of the word *key* (κλείς) see Rev. 1:18 note.

holds that it is a fallen angel. The language certainly brings to mind "How art thou fallen from heaven, O Lucifer, son of the morning! how art thou cut down to the ground" (Isa. 14:12). The Lord Jesus said plainly, "I beheld Satan as lightning fall from heaven" (Luke 10:18). The Lord challenged Job concerning His creation, "when the morning stars sang together, and all the sons of God shouted for joy" (Job 38:7). The Hebrew parallelism links together *the morning stars* and *the sons of God* as angelic beings who praise God. Here God gives Satan limited authority, the key to the bottomless pit, the pit of the abyss, which is clearly a prison for evil spirits. The demons were begging the Lord not to send them into "the Abyss" (Luke 8:31). "And he opened the bottomless pit, and smoke went up from the pit, as the smoke of a great furnace, and the sun and the air were darkened from the smoke of the pit" (v. 2). God is a source of light; this pit is a source of darkness. The language reminds us of the destruction of Sodom and Gomorrah, "the smoke of the country went up as the smoke of a furnace" (Gen. 19:28). "And out of the smoke locusts came forth into the earth, and authority was given to them as the scorpions of the earth have authority" (v. 3). Locusts are insects (six legs) primarily known for their ability to eat vegetation (Exod. 10:15); scorpions are arachnids (eight legs) known for their ability to attack and kill anything weaker than they are. God gives them their authority, strictly that of the predator. John Currid argues that the great locust plague of the Exodus (Exod. 10:4ff.) foreshadowed this eschatological judgment (*Exodus*, I, p. 221). "And it was commanded them that they should not harm the grass of the earth, nor any green plant, nor any tree, except the men who do not have the seal of God on their foreheads" (v. 4).

9:2. For a summary of the word *smoke* (καπνός) see Rev. 8:4 note.

For a summary of *sun* (ἥλιος) see Rev. 1:16 note.

The word *air* (ἀήρ) occurs only twice in Rev. (9:2; 16:17).

9:3. Advocates of genetic engineering suggest experiments in blending insects and arachnids (scorpions that fly?). That is enough of a nightmare, but these scorpion locusts are demonic spirits with much greater influence than mere animals. Scorpions are mentioned only here in Rev. (9:3, 5, 10) and only in Luke 10:19; 11:12 in the rest of the NT. The Lord told Ezekiel not to fear his rebellious people, though living among them was like dwelling among scorpions (Ezek. 2:6). The Israelites encountered them in the wilderness wanderings (Deut. 8:15). There is still a valley in the Holy Land leading down to the Dead Sea that is called the valley of the scorpions (Akrabbim). See ZPEB, "Scorpion," V, p. 297; ISBE (1988), "Scorpion," IV, pp. 357–58.

9:4. These evil spirits cannot harm (ἀδικέω) those saints who overcome (Rev. 2:11); they can harm only those who have no spiritual protection from God (9:4). These evil beings cannot kill men; they can cause only spiritual distress (v. 10). For background, see Merrill Unger, *Biblical Demonology*; R. A. Torrey, *What the Bible Teaches* (about the Devil,

Contrary to the physical realm, these locusts ignore green plants and attack people instead. Ezekiel saw the protection of God's seal in his day (Ezek. 9:4f.). This protection shows that they are not insects, but supernatural, demonic adversaries of mankind. However, God limits their ability to attacking spiritually lost people. God's people have His protection. "And who is he that will harm you, if you be followers of the good?" (I Pet. 3:13). "And it was given to them that they should not kill them, but that they should be tormented five months, and their torment was as the torment of a scorpion whenever it strikes a man" (v. 5). The poison of a scorpion sting attacks the nervous system. A person who has been stung on the hand, for instance, will feel the "pins and needles" go up his arm as the poison takes effect. People rarely die from the sting, but the discomfort is acute. "The scorpion ranks with the snake as hostile to man" (A. T. Robertson, *Word Pictures*, VI, p. 362). "And in those days men shall seek death and shall not find it, and they shall desire to die, and death flees from them" (v. 6). The present generation has a consuming desire for comfort and pleasure, but God often uses pain and sorrow to cause men to think of their need for Him. David prayed, "Look upon mine affliction and my pain; and forgive all my sins" (Ps. 25:18). In times of affliction people find out the power of God's Word to impart strength. "This is my comfort in my affliction: for thy word hath quickened me"

---

pp. 513–35); Bernard Schneider, *The World of Unseen Spirits*, and the entertaining (but very serious) *Screwtape Letters* by C. S. Lewis.

This is the last of 13 times that the word *seal* (σφραγίς) occurs in Rev. (5:1, 2, 5, 9; 6:1, 3, 5, 7, 9, 12; 7:2; 8:1; 9:4).

9:5. The verb *strike* (παίω) occurs only here in Rev. John used it to describe Peter's striking off the ear of the high priest's servant (John 18:10). It was also used to describe the blows inflicted on Christ by the servants of the high priest (Matt. 26:68).

The verb *torment* or *torture* (βασανίζω) occurs 5 times in Rev. It is used for very serious torment that the scorpion locusts inflict (9:5); for the plagues the two witnesses inflict (11:10); for birth pangs (12:2); for the eternal wrath of fire and sulfur inflicted on beast worshipers (14:10); and for the lake of fire and sulfur in which the Devil shall be tormented (20:10). The noun *torment* (βασανισμός) occurs 6 times in the NT, all in Rev. (9:5 [twice]; 14:11; 18:7, 10, 15). The Lord Jesus plainly taught the reality of the torment of the wicked in hades (Luke 16:22–24) and in gehenna (Mark 9:43–48). See ISBE (1988), "Torment," IV, p. 880; Ryken, Wilhoit, and Longman, *Dictionary of Biblical Imagery*, "Torment," pp. 876–77.

9:6. All those lost people who think that euthanasia is the solution to their problems are in for a shock. Death is not the end of it all; they are in for worse conditions in the next realm (Luke 16:22–24). The solution is receiving Christ as Savior from sin so that He may forgive, sustain, and take one home to glory in His own good time. "Wherefore let them that suffer according to the will of God commit the keeping of their souls to him in well doing, as unto a faithful Creator" (I Pet. 4:19).

The verb *to desire* (ἐπιθυμέω) occurs only here in Rev.

(Ps. 119:50). "And the appearances of the locusts were like horses having been prepared for battle, and upon their heads were as crowns like gold, and their faces were as faces of men" (v. 7). The language reminds us of Joel's description of battle in the Day of the Lord. "A fire devoureth before them; and behind them a flame burneth: the land is as the garden of Eden before them, and behind them a desolate wilderness; yea, and nothing shall escape them. The appearance of them is as the appearance of horses; and as horsemen, so shall they run" (Joel 2:3–4). The *like* and *as* show us that they were not really horses; their crowns were not really gold; their faces were not really human. They are demonic creatures prepared for this time to afflict mankind. Beginning with this context, there is great emphasis on the age-long battle between God and the Devil, good and evil. The God of light is waging war against the kingdom of darkness, and the creatures of the dark are fighting back. "And they were having hair as the hair of women, and their teeth were as the teeth of lions" (v. 8). They had the appearance of long hair and huge teeth. Their "bite" will cause great spiritual damage. Perhaps their monstrous appearance is meant to terrify their prey. "And they were having breastplates as breastplates of iron, and the sound of their wings was as the sound of many chariots of horses running into battle" (v. 9). Insects have hard thoraxes (breastplates) of chitinous material, but these creatures have breastplates like iron, the hardest known metal of the first century. The sound of their wings was like the sound of a cavalry charge with the rattle of chariot wheels and the thunder of the horses' hooves. "And they have tails like scorpions, and stings, and with their tails their authority was to hurt men five months" (v. 10). The ordinary scorpion sting wears off within a week, but the effect of this sting was much more dreadful.

9:7. The word *battle* (πόλεμος) occurs 9 times in Rev. (9:7, 9; 11:7; 12:7, 17; 13:7; 16:14; 19:19; 20:8). The verb *to do battle* or *wage war* (πολεμέω) occurs 6 times in Rev. (2:16; 12:7 [twice]; 13:4; 17:14; 19:11) and only once in the rest of the NT (James 4:2). The word *army* (στράτευμα) occurs 3 times in Rev. (9:16; 19:14, 19). God is not a pacifist. The Lord of hosts shall destroy Babylon (Isa. 14:22); the Lord of hosts shall break the power of kings and shall reign in Mount Zion (Isa. 24:21–23). It is no wonder that Paul urges Timothy to "endure hardness as a good soldier (στρατιώτης) of Christ Jesus" (II Tim. 2:3). All believers must "put on the whole armor of God, that you may be able to stand against the wiles of the devil" (Eph. 6:11).

The word *gold* (χρυσός) occurs 4 times in Rev. (9:7; 17:4; 18:12, 16). See "Gold," ISBE (1982) II, pp. 520–22; "Gold," ZPEB, II, pp. 771–72; "Gold," Ryken, Wilhoit, and Longman, *Dictionary of Biblical Imagery*, pp. 340–41.

9:9. A chariot (ἅρμα) is mentioned only here in Rev. and only in Acts 8:28–38 in the rest of the NT. For a profound study of this titanic war between God and the Devil, see Donald Grey Barnhouse, *The Invisible War* (Grand Rapids: Zondervan, 1965).

9:10. For the verb *to harm* or *hurt*, see note on Rev. 2:11.

13 And the sixth angel sounded, and I heard a voice from the four horns of the golden altar which is before God,
14 Saying to the sixth angel which had the trumpet, Loose the four angels which are bound in the great river Euphrates.
15 And the four angels were loosed, which were prepared for an hour, and a day, and a month, and a year, for to slay the third part of men.
16 And the number of the army of the horsemen were two hundred thousand thousand: and I heard the number of them.
17 And thus I saw the horses in the vision, and them that sat on them, having breast-plates of fire, and of jacinth, and brimstone: and the heads of the horses were as the heads of lions; and out of their mouths issued fire and smoke and brimstone.
18 By these three was the third part of men killed, by the fire, and by the smoke, and by the brimstone, which issued out of their mouths.
19 For their power is in their mouth, and in their tails: for their tails were like unto serpents, and had heads, and with them they do hurt.
20 And the rest of the men which were not killed by these plagues yet repented not of the works of their hands, that they should not worship devils, and idols of gold, and silver, and brass, and stone, and of wood: which neither can see, nor hear, nor walk:
21 Neither repented they of their murders, nor of their sorceries, nor of their fornication, nor of their thefts.

"They have over them a king, the angel of the abyss; his name in Hebrew was Abaddon [destruction], and in Greek has a name Apollyon [destroyer]" (v. 11). Note in passing that the apostle John is very much at home in both Hebrew and Greek. Comparative word studies are still spiritually fruitful. The death angel of the Exodus is called "the destroyer" (Exod. 12:23). Solomon exclaims, "Hell [Sheol] and destruction [Abaddon] are before the Lord: how much more then the hearts of the children of men?" (Prov. 15:11). Job 26:6 also links Sheol and Abaddon. There is a considerable difference of opinion among expositors over the identity of this personage. Some will argue that he is an otherwise un-known fallen angel under Satan (Seiss, Newell, R. L. Thomas, LaHaye). Others argue that he must be Satan himself (J. B. Smith, Scott, Ironside, Ottman, Strauss, Walvoord). Beale argues that he might be either. "One woe is passed; behold, two woes are yet coming after these things" (v. 12). Plainly, the worst is yet to come.

II. The Sixth Trumpet: The Two Hundred Million Horsemen. vv. 13–21.

"And the sixth angel sounded, and I heard one voice out of the four horns of the golden altar which is before God" (v. 13). The four horns

---

9:11. A good case can be made for the doctrine of the progressive revelation of Satan in Rev. He is introduced as Satan (Σατανᾶς), "Adversary," a being who is behind false

said one thing; John is listening carefully. "Saying to the sixth angel, who has the trumpet, Loose the four angels who have been bound near the river, the great Euphrates" (v. 14). It is *near* the river (ἐπὶ with the dative) as in "near the beautiful gate" (Acts 3:10). These four mighty angels are confined near the border of the east. Alford notes that "there is nothing in the text to prevent 'the great river Euphrates' from being meant literally" (*Greek Testament*, IV, p. 645). The Euphrates was the eastern boundary of the western empires. Not since Tamerlane has any Far Eastern army exploded into the West. "And the four angels were loosed, who were prepared for the hour, and day, and month, and year, in order that they might slay the third part of men" (v. 15). It is a very specific point in time at which the invasion from the East will begin. The result of the invasion will be the slaying of a third of the world's population. Never in the history of the world has a battle led to such a loss of life. When we add the quarter of the world's population slain by the whole series of seal judgments (Rev. 6:2–8), we realize that by this time in the Tribulation period, one half of the world's population has been slaughtered. Zechariah sees two thirds of the Jewish people slain during the Tribulation period, and one third, the converted remnant, preserved (Zech. 13:8–9). "And the number of the army of the horsemen was two

---

religious systems (Rev. 2:9, 13, 24). He is the Devil (διάβολος), "the accuser," who persecutes God's people (Rev. 2:10; 12:9, 12; Job 1:6ff.; John 8:44). He is Apollyon (Ἀπολλύων), "the destroyer," who delights in ruining and hurting people (Rev. 9:11). He is the great red dragon (δράκων), who caused the fall of angels and persecutes the Jewish people, mentioned 13 times only in the NT in Rev. (Rev. 12:3, 4, 7 [twice], 9, 13, 16, 17; 13:2, 4, 11; 16:13; 20:2). He is "that old serpent," who deceives and tempts the whole world (Rev. 12:9, 14, 15; Gen. 3:1–15). He is the ruler of the present world system (Rev. 16:13–14; John 12:31). When the great kingdom reign comes, he will be cast into the bottomless pit, to fall for a thousand years (Rev. 20:1–3). When the thousand years ends, he shall be cast into the lake of fire, where he belongs forever (Rev. 20:10). All who share his evil character shall join him (Rev. 20:11–15; 22:15). See Rev. 12:9 note.

9:13. For a summary of the word *altar* (θυσιαστήριον) see Rev. 6:9 note.

9:14. "The great river Euphrates" is a famous geographical landmark, over 1,700 miles long. It was one of the boundaries of Eden (Gen. 2:14); it was a boundary of the Abrahamic promise of the land (Gen. 15:18). David sought to extend his influence to the Euphrates (I Chron. 18:3). For historical background see Pfeiffer and Vos, *The Wycliffe Historical Geography of Bible Lands*, pp. 2–5, 21–23, 232–33, etc.; ZPEB, II, pp. 416–18; ISBE (1982) II, pp. 202–4; National Geographic Society, *Everyday Life in Bible Times*, pp. 278–80 and map of Bible lands.

9:15–18. *To slay the third part of men.* The old-line liberals used to sneer at the exaggerated numbers in Rev., but with the advent of modern weaponry, nuclear, chemical, and biological, the numbers are horrifyingly sober predictions.

hundred million; I heard the number of them" (v. 16). John assures us that there is no mistake in the vastness of the number. But now John looks more closely at the horses and their riders. "And thus I saw the horses in the vision and the ones sitting on them, having breastplates of fire and hyacinth and sulfur, and the heads of the horses were as heads of lions, and out of their mouths poured fire and smoke and sulfur" (v. 17). The breastplates were the primary colors, red, blue, and yellow; and the smoke that came out of the mouths of the horses was red, blue, and yellow. They are obviously not ordinary horses. Some expositors hold that they symbolize the invasion of Asiatic armies (Scott, Ironside), and Walvoord favors the view that they total a literal two hundred million (Rev., p. 266). Others hold that they are a demonic, infernal cavalry (Seiss, Newell, Strauss). Others hold that there is both a demonic and human invasion pictured here (A. C. Gaebelein). Tenney argues that the human and demonic are so mingled as to be indistinguishable. Ottman holds that they are demon-possessed men. The conclusion is probably that the prophetic portrait is of a literal army from the East of two hundred million men, driven, or possessed, by demons. The Devil is a murderer from the beginning (John 8:44). John reemphasizes what he has already said. "By these three plagues the third of men were killed, from the fire and the smoke and the sulfur which was going out of their mouths" (v. 18). The demons drive the army to slaughter all who are in its path. John considers the demon horses again. "For the authority of the horses is in their mouth and in their tails, for their tails are like serpents, having heads, and with them they do harm" (v. 19). These demonic creatures have authority to harm mankind. Their heads can bite like lions and their tails can bite like serpents. The lion and the scorpion are two of the most deadly killers in the animal world. The hideous appearance of these demonic creatures reflects their cruel, vicious nature. Unsaved people have no protection from such an army. "And the rest of men, who were not killed by these plagues, did not even repent of the works of their hands, that they should not worship the demons and the idols of gold and silver and bronze and stone and wood, which are not able to see, or hear, or walk" (v. 20). Daniel charged Belshazzar with worshiping "gods of silver, and gold, of bronze, iron, wood, and stone, which see not, nor

---

9:16. *200 million* is the largest exact number found in the NT. The blessing on Rebekah has a larger one (Gen. 24:60).

The word *army* (στράτευμα) occurs 4 times in Rev. (9:16; 19:14, 19 [twice]).

9:17. The word *sulfur* (brimstone, θεῖον) occurs 6 times in Rev. (9:17, 18; 14:10; 19:20; 20:10; 21:8).

9:20. The most grievous sin is idolatry. It violates the first and second commandments (Exod. 20:3–4). It violates the great commandment that the Lord Jesus stressed (Matt.

hear, nor know" (Dan. 5:23). Idolatry is a very durable sin. Jehoram
"cleaved unto the sins of Jeroboam the son of Nebat, which made Israel
to sin" (II Kings 3:1–3). It is significant that the worship of demons and
idols are linked together here. Paul also charges that the sacrifices offered
to idols are offered to demons (I Cor. 10:19–21). It does not matter what
materials the idols are made of; they cannot see, hear, or move. The
psalmist ridicules the weaknesses of idols (Ps. 115:4–8). The demons on
the other hand are perceptive, but implacable. "Neither did they repent
of their murders, nor of their use of drugs, nor of their fornication, nor of
their thefts" (v. 21). "Their repentance had been the aim of the plagues"
(Bengel, *Gnomon*, V, p. 245). These idolaters are sunk in their sins,
which are divided into four categories. *Murder* is the violent killing or
harming of people. The *use of drugs* includes drug addicts and magicians,
or witches, who use "potions" to achieve their purposes. *Fornication* is the
widest term for sex sins of all varieties. *Thefts* include robbery, stealing,
and fraud. These hardened sinners will not repent and forsake their sins,
no matter how dreadful world conditions become.

Practical Applications from Revelation 9

1. Believers should be on their guard against demonic influence (v. 2).
The Spirit expressly warns that in the latter days some shall depart
from the faith, giving heed to deceiving spirits and the teachings of
demons (I Tim. 4:1).

22:37–38). It is not limited to worshiping a graven image. An idol can be anything that is
put ahead of God: a person, a possession, a hobby, a habit, a sin, or just selfishness. Moses
classified idolatry as demon worship (Deut. 32:17). The apostle Paul did the same thing
(I Cor. 10:19–20). John closes his first epistle by warning believers, "Keep yourselves from
idols" (I John 5:21).

For a summary of the verb *to repent* (μετανοέω) see Rev. 2:5 note.

9:21. The prophet Samuel rebuked King Saul for the sins of rebellion and stubbornness,
which he equated with the sins of witchcraft and idolatry (I Sam. 15:23). Jehu cried out
against the fornication and witchcraft of Queen Jezebel (II Kings 9:22).

The word *murder* (φόνος) occurs only here in Rev. Exod. 20:13 will never change.

The word translated *use of drugs*, or *witchcraft* (φάρμακον), occurs only here in Rev.

The word *fornication* (πορνεία) occurs 7 times in Rev. (2:21; 9:21; 14:8; 17:2, 4; 18:3;
19:2). The acceptance of false doctrine is called fornication (Rev. 2:21); the false religious church of antichrist is the harlot that causes kings and earth dwellers to commit
fornication that brings God's judgment (Rev. 17:1–5). See also Ryken, Wilhoit, and
Longman, "Adultery," *Dictionary of Biblical Imagery*, pp. 15–16.

The word *theft* (κλέμμα) occurs only here in Rev.

2. We should thank God for His protection (v. 4). "He that dwelleth in the secret place of the most High shall abide under the shadow of the Almighty" (Ps. 91:1).
3. We should realize that death is not the solution to any problem (v. 6). Death is the last enemy (I Cor. 15:26). Christ is the answer: "Greater is he that is in you, than he that is in the world" (I John 4:4).
4. We should keep alert to the Devil's attempts to destroy us (v. 11). Put on the whole armor of God (Eph. 6:13).
5. We should realize that God restrains evil from harming His people (v. 14). "The steps of a good man are ordered by the Lord" (Ps. 37:23).
6. We should recognize the folly of any form of idolatry (v. 20). The rich young ruler put his possessions ahead of the Lord Jesus Himself (Matt. 19:21–22).
7. We should be quick to repent of any wrongdoing (v. 21). David's heart smote him after he had numbered the people (II Sam. 24:10).

Prayer

O Lord, give us a tender heart to flee from sin and to seek Your face. Let all those who seek You rejoice and be glad in You. I am poor and needy: make haste to me, O God; You are my Help and my Deliverer. Amen.

REVELATION 10

THE ANGEL AND THE LITTLE SCROLL

Persons
John ("I")
A mighty angel come down
from heaven (Jesus Christ, 11:3)

Persons referred to

The seventh angel	The prophets

People

Nations	Kings
Tongues	

Places mentioned

Heaven	The sea
The sun	The earth

Doctrines taught

Angels	Prophecy
Creation	Divine revelation
Divine mysteries	

1   And I saw another mighty angel come down from heaven, clothed with a cloud: and a rainbow was upon his head, and his face was as it were the sun, and his feet as pillars of fire:
2   And he had in his hand a little book open: and he set his right foot upon the sea, and his left foot on the earth,
3   And cried with a loud voice, as when a lion roareth: and when he had cried, seven thunders uttered their voices.
4   And when the seven thunders had uttered their voices, I was about to write: and I heard a voice from heaven saying unto me, Seal up those things which the seven thunders uttered, and write them not.
5   And the angel which I saw stand upon the sea and upon the earth lifted up his hand to heaven,
6   And sware by him that liveth for ever and ever, who created heaven, and the things that therein are, and the earth, and the things that therein are, and the sea, and the things which are therein, that there should be time no longer:
7   But in the days of the voice of the seventh angel, when he shall begin to sound, the mystery of God should be finished, as he hath declared to his servants the prophets.

Revelation 10 Exposition

I. The Mighty Angel. vv. 1–7.

"And I saw another mighty angel coming down out of heaven, having been clothed with a cloud, and the rainbow upon his head, and his face was as the sun, and his feet as pillars of fire" (v. 1). John's point of view is now the earth, rather than heaven. He sees an angel with divine attributes coming down from heaven. The angel "is given attributes that are given only to God in the OT or to God or Christ in Revelation" (Beale, *Rev.*, p. 522). The rainbow was on the head of this angel. The only other time that the *rainbow* is mentioned in the NT is the rainbow radiating from the throne of God (Rev. 4:3). The Greek construction, *the rainbow*, makes clear that the article refers back to that previously mentioned rainbow of divine glory. His face was shining as the sun, the same characteristic of the previous vision of Christ (Rev. 1:16), which reminds us not only of the Transfiguration (Matt. 17:2) but also of Paul's words that God "has shined in our hearts, to give the light of the knowledge of the glory of God in the face of Jesus Christ" (II Cor. 4:6). An angel's face is like lightning, rather than the sun (Dan. 10:6). Another hallmark of the Lord Jesus

---

10:1. There is again a parenthesis (Rev. 10:1–11:14) in the series of 7s at the end of the sixth trumpet. The seventh trumpet resumes in 11:15. This parenthesis gives explanations that are necessary in order to understand the events in the series of 7s. Both explanations are about the strong angel and the little scroll.

is that He comes with clouds (Dan. 7:13; Matt. 24:30; Acts 1:9; I Thess. 4:17; Rev. 1:7). His feet have already been noted as being like molten bronze "as if they burned in a furnace" (Rev. 1:15). Here they are like *pillars of fire*, which remind us of the presence of Jehovah as a "pillar of fire" with His people (Exod. 13:21). Many expositors argue that this must be the Lord Jesus Christ (Seiss, Scott, Jennings, Kelly, Ironside, A. C. Gaebelein, Beale). But there are others who argue that the text does not say it is Christ, and therefore, it must be merely a created angel (Newell, J. B. Smith, Walvoord, LaHaye). Beale suggests that he may be the OT "angel of Jehovah" (*Rev.*, p. 523). Hengstenberg advances an extended proof that the Angel of the Lord is a manifestation of the Lord Jesus Christ (*Christology of the Old Testament*, I, pp. 115–30). Osborne argues that he is simply "another mighty angel" (*Rev.*, p. 393). If he were a created angel, he would have delegated authority to claim the earth for God (v. 2). "And he had in his hand a little scroll that had been opened, and he put his right foot upon the sea, and his left foot on the earth" (v. 2). He has in His hand the title deed to the earth, which gives Him the "right to tread" on the earth (Ruth 4:7–9). In His mighty hand it is a "little scroll." The Lord has broken the seals (Rev. 6:1ff.), and now the contents are His to reveal. "The earth is the Lord's, and the fullness thereof; the world, and they that dwell therein" (Ps. 24:1). "And he cried with a great voice, as a lion roars. And when he cried, the seven thunders spoke their voices" (v. 3). "The lion hath roared, who will not fear?" (Amos 3:8). Jeremiah prophesied that "the Lord shall roar from on high" (Jer. 25:30). The loud cry brought reverberations from "the seven thunders." This is probably an allusion to the voice of the Lord in the seven thunders of Psalm 29:3–9. The first reference to thunder (βροντή) in the Book of Revelation (4:5) was a manifestation of divine power from the throne of God. But they were not just noise; they were very articulate pronouncements as they are here. "And when the seven thunders spoke, I was about to write, and I heard a voice from heaven, saying, Seal the things which the seven thunders spoke, and write them not" (v. 4). The aorist imperative

---

10:2. The Lord promised Joshua, "Every place that the sole of your foot shall tread upon, that have I given to you" (Josh. 1:3). There was no danger of the mighty angel sinking into the sea. The Lord Jesus could walk on water as easily as on land (Matt. 14:25). It was all His.

10:3. The verb *roar* (μυκάομαι) occurs only here in the NT. Peter uses a different word when he refers to the roaring of a lion (I Pet. 5:8). *Moo-kaomai* originally referred to the lowing of cattle (Vincent, *Word Studies*, II, p. 514).

Henry M. Morris notes that the rainbow and the thunder both refer back to the Genesis flood (*The Revelation Record*, pp. 178f.).

10:4. For a summary of the word *thunder* (βροντή) see Rev. 4:5 note.

implies "Seal up at once" (A. T. Robertson, *Word Pictures*, VI, p. 372). There are some things that God reveals to His prophets that are not for the rest of mankind to know. When King Saul pried open the door to the future, he was not happy with what he learned (I Sam. 28:15–19). Daniel was twice commanded to "seal the scroll to the time of the end" (Dan. 8:26; 12:4). When he asked further questions, the angel said, "Go thy way, Daniel: for the words are closed up and sealed till the time of the end" (Dan. 12:9). "And the angel which I saw stand upon the sea and upon the earth, lifted up his right hand to heaven" (v. 5). Lifting the hand to heaven is the traditional pose for taking a solemn oath (see Dan. 12:7). He lifted his right hand because the scroll was in his left. "And he swore by the one who lives into the ages of the ages, who created the heaven and the things in it, and the earth and the things in it, and the sea and the things in it, that there shall be delay no longer" (v. 6). This is the response to the question "How long?" in Revelation 6:10 (A. T. Robertson, *Word Pictures*, VI, p. 372). It was Jehovah God who created "heaven and earth, the sea, and all that in them is" (Exod. 20:11). "But in the days of the voice of the seventh angel, whenever he is about to sound, the mystery of God is finished, as he presented the good news to his slaves, the prophets" (v. 7). *His slaves* is not a demeaning term; in first-century culture it refers to the temple slaves who devote their lives to the service of a god. "His servants the prophets" (Zech. 1:6) did not say just whatever they wanted; they delivered the Word of the living God (Isa. 1:10–18; Jer. 1:4–9; Ezek. 3:4; Dan. 2:19–23; Amos 3:1). "Surely the Lord God will do nothing, but he revealeth his secret unto his servants the prophets" (Amos 3:7). A biblical mystery is a divinely revealed truth, so profound

---

10:6. The word *time* (χρόνος) should be translated *delay* here (Arndt and Gingrich, p. 896). Trench identifies time as a "succession of moments" and distinguishes it from a period of time (καιρός). See *Synonyms of the NT*, pp. 209–12; Custer, *A Treasury of NT Synonyms*, pp. xiv–xv; Ryken, Wilhoit, and Longman, *Dictionary of Biblical Imagery*, "Time," pp. 870–72; ISBE (1988), "Time," IV, pp. 852–53. A Heilsgeschichte theologian, Oscar Cullmann, teaches that the advent of Christ is the center of time (*Christ and Time*, pp. 39ff.).

10:7. The verb *is finished* (ἐτελέσθη) is probably a timeless aorist passive.

The verb *hath declared* (KJV) is really *preached the gospel to* (εὐηγγέλισεν, "a rare use of the active," A. T. Robertson, *Word Pictures*, VI, p. 373). The only other time the root verb occurs in Rev., it refers to *preaching* the everlasting gospel (Rev. 14:6). It is the great word in Acts for *preaching the gospel* of Christ (Acts 5:42; 8:4, 12, 25, 35, 40, etc.).

The word *prophet* (προφήτης) occurs 8 times in Rev. (10:7; 11:10, 18; 16:6; 18:20, 24; 22:6, 9), always in the plural of true prophets of God. The false prophet of 19:20 is the word ψευδοπροφήτης. A biblical prophet was a divinely inspired spokesman for God (Moses, Exod. 4:10–17; Elijah, I Kings 17:1–24). See ZPEB, "Prophets and Prophecy," IV, pp. 875–903; ISBE (1986), "Prophet, Prophecy," III, pp. 986–1004; Ryken, Wilhoit, and Longman, *Dictionary of Biblical Imagery*, pp. 670–74.

8 *And the voice which I heard from heaven spake unto me again, and said, Go and take the little book which is open in the hand of the angel which standeth upon the sea and upon the earth.*
9 *And I went unto the angel, and said unto him, Give me the little book. And he said unto me, Take it, and eat it up; and it shall make thy belly bitter, but it shall be in thy mouth sweet as honey.*
10 *And I took the little book out of the angel's hand, and ate it up; and it was in my mouth sweet as honey: and as soon as I had eaten it, my belly was bitter.*
11 *And he said unto me, Thou must prophesy again before many peoples, and nations, and tongues, and kings.*

that there is still an aura of mystery about it. Daniel heard the question "How long shall it be to the end of these wonders?" but he did not understand the answer (Dan. 12:6, 8).

II. The Little Scroll. vv. 8–11.

"And the voice which I heard out of heaven spoke again with me and said, Go, take the scroll, the one which has been opened, in the hand of the angel who is standing upon the sea and upon the earth" (v. 8). *The scroll, the one which has been opened* is a striking link to the seal judgments (Rev. 6:1–12; 8:1). Mercifully, it is a "little scroll" (βιβλαρίδιον, v. 2), because John is going to have to eat it. The image of "eating" God's Word occurs again and again in Scripture. The psalmist exclaimed, "How sweet are thy words unto my taste! yea, sweeter than honey to my mouth!" (Ps. 119:103). Jeremiah declared, "Thy words were found, and I did eat them; and thy word was unto me the joy and rejoicing of mine heart" (Jer. 15:16). "And I went away to the angel, saying to him, Give me the little scroll. And he says to me, Take and eat it, and it shall make your belly bitter, but in your mouth it shall be sweet as honey" (v. 9). "Every revelation of God's purposes, even though a mere fragment, a βιβλαρίδιον, is 'bitter-sweet,' disclosing judgement as well as mercy" (Swete, *Rev.*, p. 131). Thus, the angel warns John of the twofold effect of eating the little scroll. John obeys the command. "And I took the little scroll out of the hand of the angel and ate it up; and it was in my mouth

---

10:8–9. John is commanded twice to *take* (λάβε) the scroll (vv. 8, 9). The only other imperative of the verb *to take* (λαμβάνω) in Rev. is the invitation "And whosoever will, let him *take* the water of life freely" (Rev. 22:17).

10:9. The verb *to make bitter* (πικραίνω) occurs only 3 times in Rev. (8:11; 10:9, 10) and only once in the rest of the NT (Col. 3:19).

The verb *to eat up* (κατεσθίω), literally *to eat down*, occurs 5 times in Rev. (10:9, 10; 11:5; 12:4; 20:9).

as sweet honey, and when I had eaten it, my belly was made bitter" (v. 10). That is a peculiar feature of God's revelation. It is sweet and re-freshing as we read it, but it is terribly convicting in our conscience. God's Word calls us sinners. "For all have sinned, and come short of the glory of God" (Rom. 3:23). It commands us to be perfect even as God is perfect (Matt. 5:48). We know that we are not. Every idle word we speak shall be judged (Matt. 12:36). It compels us to seek God's grace. Seiss ar-gues that the eating of the scroll transfers from the Redeemer to His people all the rights and responsibilities of salvation (*Apocalypse*, p. 228). "And it was said to me, It is necessary for you to prophesy again before many peoples, and nations, and tongues, and kings" (v. 11). Nebuchadnezzar's herald addressed the people, nations, and languages with a command to worship his god (Dan. 3:4–5). The Book of Revelation itself has been a prophecy to all nations of how the world shall come to its appointed end. But it is necessary for all men to repent and believe the gospel. As the apostle Paul phrased it, "For I am not ashamed of the gospel of Christ: for it is the power of God unto salvation to every one that believes; to the Jew first, and also to the Greek" (Rom. 1:16). "For all have sinned, and are coming short of the glory of God" (Rom. 3:23). "But God commends his love toward us, in that, while we were yet sinners, Christ died for us" (Rom. 5:8). "For whosoever shall call upon the name of the Lord shall be saved" (Rom. 10:13). If you, the reader, have never asked the Lord Jesus Christ to save you, now is a good time for you to bow your head to ask Him to save you from your sins. "For the scripture says, Whosoever believes on him shall not be ashamed" (Rom. 10:11). This gospel of salvation is the "devoured" pos-session of God's people. We must share it with others.

Practical Applications from Revelation 10

1. God sends spiritual help to earth, whether we can perceive it or not (v. 1). "The angel of the Lord encampeth round about them that fear him, and delivereth them" (Ps. 34:7).

10:9–10. The word *honey* (μέλι) occurs twice only in these vv. in Rev.

10:10. Ezekiel was also commanded to eat a scroll, in which was written "lamentations, and mourning, and woe" (Ezek. 2:9–10). When he ate it, it was in his mouth "as honey for sweetness" (Ezek. 3:3), but when the Spirit took him away, he went "in bitterness, in the heat of my spirit; but the hand of the Lord was strong upon me" (Ezek. 3:14). There is a sense in which every true preacher has this experience. The scroll (the Word) is open before him. He is not just to preach the message; he is to devour the scroll, to make it part of himself. When he does this, he discovers that he has a message, and it is both sweet and bitter. It is the Word of the living God.

118

2. God uses books to further His purposes (v. 2). Daniel understood by reading books of Scripture the length of the exile (Dan. 9:2).
3. There are some things that we cannot know now; we must walk by faith (v. 4). "Commit thy way unto the Lord; trust also in him; and he shall bring it to pass" (Ps. 37:5).
4. God always acts right on time (never early or late, v. 6). "When the fullness of time was come, God sent forth his Son" (Gal. 4:4).
5. God is bringing all things to a proper conclusion (v. 7). Christ is the Author and Finisher of our faith (Heb. 12:2).
6. We must devour God's revelation in Scripture (v. 9). "How sweet are thy words unto my taste! yea, sweeter than honey to my mouth!" (Ps. 119:103).
7. We should delight ourselves in the sweetness of God's revelation (v. 10). "More to be desired are they than gold, yea, than much fine gold: sweeter also than honey and the honeycomb" (Ps. 19:10).

Prayer

O Lord, I found Your words and did eat them. Your words have become the joy and rejoicing of my heart. Enable me to walk in humble submission to them. Keep me ever mindful of Your perfect will, that I may please You. Amen.

REVELATION 11

TWO WITNESSES

Persons

John ("me")
The angel come down from
    heaven (Jesus Christ)
Two witnesses
The beast who ascends from the
    bottomless pit

People, kindreds, tongues, and
    nations
They that dwell on the earth
Twenty-four elders

Persons referred to

Worshiper in the temple
The Gentiles
Seven thousand earthquake victims

The dead that are to be judged
The prophets
The saints

Places mentioned

The earthly temple
Jerusalem
The earth
The bottomless pit

Sodom
Egypt
Heaven
The temple in heaven

Doctrines taught

Worship
Holiness
Witness for Christ
Judgment
The Cross

The kingdom of God
The rule of God
Wrath
Rewards

1 *And there was given me a reed like unto a rod: and the angel stood, saying, Rise, and measure the temple of God, and the altar, and them that worship therein.*

2 *But the court which is without the temple leave out, and measure it not; for it is given unto the Gentiles: and the holy city shall they tread under foot forty and two months.*

Revelation 11 Exposition

1. The Measurement of the Temple. vv. 1–2.

"And a reed like a rod was given to me, saying: Rise and measure the sanctuary of God, and the altar, and the ones who are worshiping in it" (v. 1). The parenthetic explanation continues. The angel commands John to measure the temple of God. *Measuring* implies divine ownership (Walvoord, *Rev.*, p. 176). This cannot refer to a heavenly temple because the context portrays the Gentiles trampling down the surroundings (v. 2). Seiss observes that "the language is peculiarly Jewish" (*Apocalypse*, p. 236). Zechariah saw a man with a measuring line in his hand to measure Jerusalem (Zech. 2:1–2). It was Ezekiel who was given the privilege of measuring the millennial temple (Ezek. 40:3–4). Mounce observes, "We recognize by now that John makes use of his sources with a sort of sovereign freedom" (*Rev.*, p. 212). But the temple here in Revelation is clearly one that exists in Jerusalem during the seven-year Tribulation period (the third temple). "And the court that is outside the sanctuary leave out, and do not measure it, because it is given to the Gentiles, and they shall tread down the holy city forty and two months" (v. 2). *The holy city* was the usual term for earthly Jerusalem (Matt. 4:5; 27:52f.). God will permit the Gentiles to "tread down" Jerusalem even as the Lord Jesus prophesied (Luke 21:24). Zechariah warned that the possession of Jerusalem was "a burdensome stone for all people: all that burden themselves with it shall be cut in pieces, though all the people of the earth be gathered together

---

11:1. The reed (κάλαμος) will reappear as a golden reed to measure the celestial city (Rev. 21:15–16). In the ancient world the "reed" was 6 cubits long (about 10 feet). See ISBE (1988), "Reed," IV, pp. 63–64; "Measuring Line," III, p. 295; ZPEB, "Reed," V, pp. 51–52.

11:2. The word *court* (αὐλή) occurs only here in Rev. It plainly refers to the court of the temple that the Jews will build before or during the Tribulation period.

The 3½ years, 42 months, and 1,260 days in Dan. and Rev. refer to half of the Tribulation period. Daniel prophesied that the evil prince would confirm a covenant with the Jews for one week of 7 years and at the midpoint would break the covenant and stop the sacrifice (Dan. 9:27). The Lord Jesus prophesied that at that point, the Jews must flee to stay alive (Matt. 24:15–16). No wonder that Jesus wept over the future fate of the city (Luke 19:41–44). For a discussion of Israel's four temples see the frontispiece of Tim LaHaye, *Prophecy Study Bible*. For the OT background for this prophecy see Stephen R. Miller, *Daniel* in the *New American Commentary*, pp. 212–16. Of course, for Roman Catholic interpreters, the number "is probably not meant literally" (Brown, Fitzmyer, and Murphy, *The New Jerome Biblical Commentary*, p. 1007).

3 And I will give power unto my two witnesses, and they shall prophesy a thousand two hundred and threescore days, clothed in sackcloth.

4 These are the two olive trees, and the two candlesticks standing before the God of the earth.

5 And if any man will hurt them, fire proceedeth out of their mouth, and devoureth their enemies: and if any man will hurt them, he must in this manner be killed.

6 These have power to shut heaven, that it rain not in the days of their prophecy: and have power over waters to turn them to blood, and to smite the earth with all plagues, as often as they will.

7 And when they shall have finished their testimony, the beast that ascendeth out of the bottomless pit shall make war against them, and shall overcome them, and kill them.

8 And their dead bodies shall lie in the street of the great city, which spiritually is called Sodom and Egypt, where also our Lord was crucified.

9 And they of the people and kindreds and tongues and nations shall see their dead bodies three days and an half, and shall not suffer their dead bodies to be put in graves.

10 And they that dwell upon the earth shall rejoice over them, and make merry, and shall send gifts one to another; because these two prophets tormented them that dwelt on the earth.

11 And after three days and an half the Spirit of life from God entered into them, and they stood upon their feet; and great fear fell upon them which saw them.

12 And they heard a great voice from heaven saying unto them, Come up hither. And they ascended up to heaven in a cloud; and their enemies beheld them.

13 And the same hour was there a great earthquake, and the tenth part of the city fell, and in the earthquake were slain of men seven thousand: and the remnant were affrighted, and gave glory to the God of heaven.

14 The second woe is past; and, behold, the third woe cometh quickly.

against it" (Zech. 12:3*b*). Daniel prophesied that the evil ruler of the fourth empire would wear out the saints of the most High, and "they shall be given into his hand until a time and times and the dividing of time" (Dan. 7:25). All of this presupposes conditions that we presently see in Jerusalem: it is a divided city, partly controlled by Jews and partly by Gentiles. This is the first specific reference in Revelation to the mid-point of the Tribulation period, three and a half years into the period. Premillennial interpreters regularly argue that the seventh trumpet marks that point, putting the seven seals and seven trumpets in the first half and the seven bowls in the last half of the Tribulation (J. B. Smith, Ironside, LaHaye, Fruchtenbaum).

II. The Two Witnesses. vv. 3–14.

"And I will give to my two witnesses and they shall prophesy a thousand two hundred sixty days, having been clothed in sackcloth" (v. 3). The

---

11:3. What is given is not stated in the Greek text. The KJV and NKJV insert "power"; the NASB and NRSV insert "authority." The ESV renders it "I will grant authority."

speaker must be the Lord Jesus Christ; no mere angel would say, "my two witnesses." This is strong evidence for the identity of the "mighty angel" who is giving this vision to John (Rev. 10:1). It is strange that few commentators have anything to say about this at all. Chapter 11 is central in the book and crucial for the meaning. It has been a theological battleground for the interpretation. Who are the two witnesses? The earliest commentator on Revelation, Victorinus, held that they were Elijah and Jeremiah; the earliest Greek commentator, Oecumenius (along with Tertullian, Irenaeus, etc.), held that they were Elijah and Enoch. (The old idea that these two never died, and so must come back and die, still persists.) But a whole generation of believers will escape death at the Rapture (I Thess. 4:13–18). Among premillennial interpreters there is considerable agreement that one of these is Elijah (Seiss, Scott, Newell, J. B. Smith, Ottman, Strauss). There is no such agreement on the identity of the other. Moses is sometimes mentioned because of the plagues inflicted (J. B. Smith, Thomas, v. 6). Moses and Elijah are linked together at the Transfiguration (Luke 9:30) and in prophecy (Mal. 4:4–6). Walvoord holds that they are two unknown prophets from the Jewish remnant (Rev., p. 179). Ironside thinks they may symbolize the entire Jewish remnant (Rev., p. 192). For symbolic interpreters, they symbolize the whole community of the faithful (Beale, Rev., p. 573). Premillennial interpreters are divided as to whether the 1,260 days refer to the first half of the Tribulation period (J. B. Smith, Ironside, Newell) or the last half (Walvoord, Scott, Jennings, A. C. Gaebelein). The context seems to favor the view that it is the last half, in which the persecution is the most intense and help can come only from God. Daniel prophesied "that it would be for a time, times, and half a time; and as soon as they finish shattering the power of the holy people, all these events will be completed" (Dan. 12:7 NASB). "These are the two olive trees, and the two lampstands, which are standing before the Lord of the earth" (v. 4). The phrase "Lord of the earth" alludes to Zechariah 4:14. Zechariah saw two olive trees dropping olives

---

The NJB renders it "I shall send my two witnesses to prophesy." Rotherham renders it "I will give unto my two witnesses, that they shall prophesy." *God's Word to the Nations* renders it "I will allow my two witnesses . . . to speak."

11:3–12. For a scholarly study of the theme of the two witnesses in the 16th and 17th centuries, see Rodney L. Petersen, *Preaching in the Last Days*, Oxford, 1993. He recounts how some of Luther's followers called Luther "the third Elijah" (p. 105); mentions Heinrich Bullinger's famous series of sermons on Rev. in 1555–56 (pp. 124ff.), and John Foxe's commentary on Rev., in which he identified the two witnesses as the martyrs John Hus and Jerome of Prague (p. 187).

11:4. An *olive tree* (ἐλαία) is mentioned only here in Rev.; *olives*, the fruit, are mentioned in Rev. 6:6; 18:13. In the rest of the NT, olive trees are mentioned only in the rhetorical question of James 3:12 and in Paul's extended illustration of the wild olive tree and the

into a golden lamp stand and oil being carried to the seven lamps that were burning without human aid (Zech. 4:2–6). "This is the word of the Lord unto Zerubbabel, saying, Not by might, nor by power, but by my spirit, saith the Lord of hosts" (Zech. 4:6). These two mighty prophets will be sustained by the power of God alone. "And if anyone wishes to harm them, fire comes forth out of their mouth and eats up their enemies; and if anyone wishes to harm them, thus it is necessary for him to be killed" (v. 5). The Lord told Jeremiah, "I will make my words in thy mouth fire, and this people wood, and it shall devour them" (Jer. 5:14). Elijah (II Kings 1:10ff.) and Moses (Exod. 9:22–24) were certainly examples of prophets who could call down fire from heaven. "These have the authority to shut heaven in order that it rain not during the days of their prophecy, and they have authority over the waters to turn them to blood, and to smite the earth with any plague as often as they will" (v. 6). The Lord will grant them the authority to bring instant judgment upon His foes, even as the OT prophets did (I Kings 13:4–5). Elijah prevented the rain for three and a half years in Israel (I Kings 17:1). Moses turned the water of the Nile into blood (Exod. 7:17). "And whenever they shall finish their witness, the beast, the one who ascends out of the bottomless pit, will make war with them, and will conquer them, and will kill them" (v. 7). Daniel saw the "little horn" make war with the saints and conquer them (Dan. 7:8, 21). Jennings identifies this beast as "the devil-possessed head of the re-vived Roman Empire" (*Rev.*, p. 296). Only when their divinely appointed ministry is completed will he be able to kill them. "And their dead bodies will lie in the street of the great city, which is called spiritually Sodom and Egypt, where also their Lord was crucified" (v. 8). Jeremiah had cried out

---

domestic olive (Rom. 11:17–24). In the 4 Gospels the Mount of Olives is mentioned frequently (Matt. 21:1; 24:3; 26:30; etc.).

This is the seventh and last time that *lampstand* occurs in Rev. See Rev. 1:12 note.

11:5. For a summary of the verb *to kill* (ἀποκτείνω) see Rev. 2:13 note.

11:6. The verb *to rain* (βρέχω) occurs only here in Rev.

11:7. The word *beast* (θηρίον) occurs 37 times in Rev. The first time it referred to the wild beasts of earth (Rev. 6:8), but starting here (36 times, 6 × 6) it refers to a human personality from the Abyss, who personifies the empire (Rev. 17:8), the last world dicta-tor, or his false prophet. Daniel called him *the little horn* (Dan. 7:8), *the prince that shall come* (Dan. 9:26), *the desolator* (Dan. 9:27), *the vile person* (Dan. 11:21), *the willful king* (Dan. 11:36). The Lord Jesus called him *the abomination of desolation* (Matt. 24:15). Paul called him *the man of sin, the son of perdition* (II Thess. 2:3), *the lawless one* (II Thess. 2:8). John called him *the antichrist* (I John 2:22). Satan himself will give him his power and throne (Rev. 13:2). He and his high priest, the False Prophet, will be the first two people cast into the lake of fire (Rev. 19:20).

For a summary of the verb *to conquer* (νικάω) see Rev. 2:7 note.

against the false prophets of Jerusalem that they had become "as Sodom" (Jer. 23:14). Jerusalem under the heel of the Antichrist will be so depraved that it can be called symbolically *Sodom* (the most morally wicked single city in the OT, Gen. 19) and *Egypt* (the nation that enslaved God's people, Exod. 1, and symbol of the wicked world, Acts 7:39; Heb. 11:27). But what makes it the most wicked place in the universe is that it is where the Lord Jesus Christ, the Lord of glory, was crucified. "And they who are from all peoples and tribes and languages and nations shall look upon their dead bodies for three and a half days, and they will not permit their dead bodies to be buried in a grave" (v. 9). Their bodies are allowed to rot in public. Asaph mourned over the defilement of Jerusalem with none to bury the dead bodies (Ps. 79:1–3). Although Jerusalem of the end times may be a cosmopolitan city, the language here hints at the powers of TV to bring news events to the attention of a worldwide audience. The Beast-controlled networks will endlessly portray the gruesome fate of those who resist "the Empire." "And the ones who dwell on the earth shall rejoice over them, and shall be glad and shall send gifts to one another, because these two prophets tormented those who dwell on the earth" (v. 10). The earth dwellers take this world as their portion and care nothing for the next. They will follow the Beast to the end and will be glad to be rid of the judgments of the two prophets of God. They celebrate the prophets' cruel death as though it were a holiday. If they had just heeded these judgmental signs, they could have passed from death to life themselves. "And after the three and a half days, the spirit of life from God entered into them, and they stood upon their feet, and great fear fell upon the ones who were beholding them" (v. 11). Ezekiel prophesied to the dry bones of Israelites and "they lived, and stood up upon their feet" (Ezek. 37:10). The Lord here gives a public vindication to His two faithful servants. The present active participle *were beholding* (θεωροῦντας) implies continued action. They were fascinated by the sight. It is unnerving to the wicked to see the supernatural power of God manifested openly. "And they heard a great voice from heaven, saying to them, Come up here. And they went up into heaven in a cloud, and their enemies beheld them" (v. 12). Perhaps, after three and a half days, it was just in time to be caught live on

---

11:8. The word *dead body* (πτῶμα) is a rather rough word (like the English *corpse* or *carcass*) instead of the normal word for *body* (σῶμα). The wicked will treat the bodies of these prophets with deliberate disrespect.

11:9. This is the only time that the word *tomb* (μνῆμα) occurs in Rev. It is the same word for the Lord's tomb (Luke 24:1).

11:10. For *the earth dwellers* see Rev. 3:10 note.

11:11. The apostle Paul declared, "For the law of the Spirit of life in Christ Jesus has made me free from the law of sin and death" (Rom. 8:2).

*15 And the seventh angel sounded; and there were great voices in heaven, saying,
The kingdoms of this world are become the kingdoms of our Lord, and of his Christ;
and he shall reign for ever and ever.*
*16 And the four and twenty elders, which sat before God on their seats, fell upon
their faces, and worshipped God,*
*17 Saying, We give thee thanks, O Lord God Almighty, which art, and wast, and art
to come; because thou hast taken to thee thy great power, and hast reigned.*
*18 And the nations were angry, and thy wrath is come, and the time of the dead, that
they should be judged, and that thou shouldest give reward unto thy servants the
prophets, and to the saints, and them that fear thy name, small and great; and
shouldest destroy them which destroy the earth.*
*19 And the temple of God was opened in heaven, and there was seen in his temple
the ark of his testament: and there were lightnings, and voices, and thunderings, and
an earthquake, and great hail.*

the evening news. It makes one wonder what the "official explanation" of
that will be! But such things have happened before. Elisha saw the chariot
of fire, and "Elijah went up by a whirlwind into heaven" (II Kings 2:11).
The Lord Jesus went up into heaven in a cloud at the Ascension (Acts
1:9). This calling up of the two martyrs must be distinguished from the
Rapture, which is an instantaneous action (I Cor. 15:52; I Thess. 4:17).
"And in that hour there was a great earthquake, and a tenth of the city
fell, and there were slain in the earthquake seven thousand men, and the
remainder were afraid and gave glory to the God of heaven" (v. 13). In
this context *the city* must refer to Jerusalem. Ezekiel prophesied concerning
the invasion of Gog, "Surely in that day there shall be a great earthquake
in the land of Israel" (Ezek. 38:19). It is possible that the *remainder* refers
to the true *remnant* of Israel, but more likely it refers merely to those not
slain by the earthquake. "The second woe is passed; behold the third woe
is coming quickly" (v. 14). It comes in the form of the seventh trumpet,
which brings the parenthetic passage to a close and resumes the sequence
of sevens.

III. The Seventh Trumpet. vv. 15–19.
"And the seventh angel sounded; and there were great voices in heaven
saying, The kingdom of the world became our Lord's and His Christ's,

---

11:13. There will be 7000 casualties in the earthquake. Contrast the 7000 believers that
God preserved in the days of Elijah (I Kings 19:18; Rom. 11:4).

The God of heaven is a title that occurs only twice in the NT, here and in 16:11. It is
common in the OT (Gen. 24:3, 7; Dan. 2:44; etc.).

and he shall reign into the ages of the ages" (v. 15). The seventh trumpet introduces the last half of the Book of Revelation. Out of it will come the seven bowls of wrath and the consummation of all things. It will be a *woe* to the wicked world and the "goats" who must be removed from it (Matt. 25:41–46). John hears that the diverse kingdoms of the world "became" (ἐγένετο) the unified kingdom of God and His Messiah, and He shall reign without end. This is an anticipation of the final triumph and is a major theme in OT prophecy. The kings of earth may set themselves against the Lord and His Messiah, but the Lord shall have them in derision (Ps. 2:2–4). He shall speak to them in His wrath: "Yet have I set my king upon my holy hill of Zion" (Ps. 2:5–6). "For the kingdom is the Lord's" (Ps. 22:28). "Thy throne, O God, is for ever and ever: the sceptre of thy kingdom is a right scepter" (Ps. 45:6). "The Lord hath prepared his throne in the heavens; and his kingdom ruleth over all" (Ps. 103:19). "Thy kingdom is an everlasting kingdom" (Ps. 145:13). "The kingdom shall be the Lord's" (Obad. 21). But Daniel is very explicit: "And in the days of these [ten] kings shall the God of heaven set up a kingdom, which shall never be destroyed: and the kingdom shall not be left to other people, but it shall break in pieces and consume all these kingdoms, and it shall stand for ever" (Dan. 2:44). "And the twenty-four elders, who were sitting before God upon their thrones, fell upon their faces and worshiped God" (v. 16). The scene in heaven (Rev. 4:1–5) is unchanged by all these catastrophic events on earth. These glorified representatives of the people of God give praise and thanksgiving to the Lord God who is working all things according to the council of His will. "Saying, We give thanks to You, Lord God, the Almighty, the one who is and the one who was, because You have taken Your great power and reigned" (v. 17). The divine titles emphasize the almighty power of God. "The Lord

---

11:15. Adam and Eve heard the voice of the Lord God in the Garden of Eden (Gen. 3:8, 10). "The voice of the Lord is powerful; the voice of the Lord is full of majesty" (Ps. 29:4). The voice of the Lord renders recompense to His enemies (Isa. 66:6). The sound of the wings of the living beings was like the voice of the Almighty (Ezek. 1:24). When Daniel heard the angel, he declared that the voice of his words was like the voice of a multitude (Dan. 10:6). See Ryken, Wilhoit, and Longman, *Dictionary of Biblical Imagery*, "Voice," pp. 918–19.

The word *world* (κόσμος) occurs 3 times in Rev. (11:15; 13:8; 17:8).

For a summary of the verb *to reign as a king* (βασιλεύω) see Rev. 5:10 note.

11:16. God's saints should worship the Lord in the beauty of holiness (Ps. 29:2). David prophesied, "All nations whom thou hast made shall come and worship before thee, O Lord" (Ps. 86:9). For a summary of *worship*, see Rev. 4:10 note.

11:17. The verb *to give thanks* (εὐχαριστέω) occurs only here in Rev. The related noun *thanksgiving* (εὐχαριστία) occurs twice (Rev. 4:9; 7:12). The Lord Jesus gave thanks to His Father (Matt. 26:27; John 11:41); the apostle Paul gave thanks (Rom. 1:8; I Cor. 1:4;

reigneth" (Ps. 99:1). God has "reigned" in that He rescued His prophets and defeated the plans of the Beast. He is certain to accomplish all the rest of His "plan" as well. Robertson suggests that it is an ingressive aorist, "began to reign" (*Word Pictures*, VI, p. 385). "And the nations were wrathful, and the time of your wrath came, and the time of the dead to be judged, and to give reward to your slaves the prophets, and to the saints, and to those who fear your name, both small and great, and to destroy those who are destroying the earth" (v. 18). The song leaps forward to final judgment and the victory of God's people. "He will bless them that fear the Lord, both small and great" (Ps. 115:13). "And the sanctuary of God which is in heaven was opened, and the ark of his covenant in his sanctuary was seen, and there were flashes of lightning, and voices, and thunders, and an earthquake, and great hail" (v. 19). John has the privilege of seeing the ark, the original, the archetype, in the sanctuary of heaven. "At the climactic moment God's heavenly temple appears, and within it is seen the ark of the covenant, God's mobile battle standard" (Ryken, Wilhoit, and Longman, *Dictionary of Biblical Imagery*, "Ark of the Covenant," p. 43). The ark of God was a symbol of the presence of God with His people and the faithfulness of God to His covenant. God will vindicate His people; God will rescue the earth from those who defile His lovely creation; God will keep His covenant and cause His people to triumph.

Eph. 1:16; Phil. 1:3; Col. 1:3; I Thess. 1:2; etc.). Believers are commanded to give thanks "in everything" (I Thess. 5:18).

11:18. For a summary on the *wrath of God*, see Rev. 6:16–17 note. The verb *to be wrathful* (ὀργίζομαι) occurs only here, of the nations being wrathful, and in 12:17, of the Dragon being wrathful.

For a summary of the verb *to judge* (κρίνω) see Rev. 6:10 note.

The verb *to destroy, corrupt,* or *ruin* (διαφθείρω) occurs 3 times in Rev. (of ships being *destroyed* [Rev. 8:9] and in this passage of men who *destroy* the earth being *destroyed* themselves). Paul uses it for men of *corrupt* minds (I Tim. 6:5). It is also used of moths *ruining* clothes (Luke 12:33).

The first 2 times that the verb *to fear* (φοβέομαι) is used in Rev. (1:17; 2:10), it refers to human *terror*, not suitable for believers, but the last 4 times it is used it refers to the *reverential awe* toward God that is very appropriate for all true saints (11:18; 14:7; 15:4; 19:5). "The fear of the Lord is the beginning of wisdom" (Prov. 9:10); "the fear of the Lord is a fountain of life" (Prov. 14:27).

11:19. The *ark* (κιβωτός) of the covenant is mentioned only here in Rev., and only in Heb. 9:4 in the rest of the NT. The first piece of furniture that the Lord commanded the Israelites to make was the ark (Exod. 25:10–22). God promised to commune with Moses from the mercy seat (Exod. 25:22). Hezekiah prayed to God as enthroned upon the ark (II Kings 19:15).

Practical Applications from Revelation 11

1. God rejects things that are defiled (v. 2). "Blessed are the pure in heart: for they shall see God" (Matt. 5:8). "Thy word is very pure" (Ps. 119:140).
2. God sustains the testimony of His witnesses (v. 3). "Cast thy burden upon the Lord, and he shall sustain thee" (Ps. 55:22).
3. God is a God of retribution; He repays wrongs that are done (v. 5). "Vengeance is mine; I will repay, saith the Lord" (Rom. 12:19).
4. God's saints die only when they have finished their ministry (v. 7). "I have finished my course, I have kept the faith" (II Tim. 4:7).
5. The world often rejoices in what is wrong (v. 10). "Rejoice not when thine enemy falleth . . . lest the Lord see it, and it displease him" (Prov. 24:17–18).
6. It should not take a disaster for people to remember God (v. 13). "O Lord God of my salvation, I have cried day and night before thee" (Ps. 88:1).
7. There is wrath or reward waiting for every person (v. 18). "The Son of man . . . shall reward every man according to his works" (Matt. 16:27).

Prayer

O God of heaven, lift our thoughts up to You. Help us to glorify You and to be good witnesses to Your power and majesty. O Lord God Almighty, hasten the day in which Your will shall be done on earth as it is in heaven. Amen.

Revelation 12:1–13:18

REVELATION 12

SEVEN SIGNS: PERSONAGES

Persons

The woman clothed with the
sun (Israel)
The great red dragon, the Devil,
Satan
The stars of heaven (angels)
The Man-Child, the Lamb
(Jesus Christ)

Michael
His angels
Satan's angels
Our brethren
The inhabiters of the earth
The remnant

Persons referred to

All nations

The whole world

Places mentioned

Heaven
The sun
The moon

The wilderness
The earth
The sea

Doctrines taught

The nation Israel
The Devil
The Messiah
Angels
War in heaven
Religious deception

Salvation
Kingdom of God
The blood of the Lamb
Persecution
The remnant

1 And there appeared a great wonder in heaven; a woman clothed with the sun, and the moon under her feet, and upon her head a crown of twelve stars:
2 And she being with child cried, travailing in birth, and pained to be delivered.

Revelation 12 Exposition

I. The Woman Clothed with the Sun. vv. 1–2.

Before the seven bowls of wrath can be introduced, the reader needs an explanation of the seven personages who are involved in this titanic battle. "And a great sign was seen in heaven; a woman clothed with the sun, and the moon under her feet, and upon her head a crown of twelve stars" (v. 1). The vision was drawn from Joseph's dream, in which he saw the sun, moon, and eleven stars bow down to him (Gen. 37:9f.). Beale thinks that the woman represents the believing community, OT and NT (*Rev.,* p. 625). Seiss holds that the woman symbolizes the visible church, and the man-child the invisible church (*Apocalypse,* p. 300). But the symbol plainly refers to the nation of Israel (Ironside, A. C. Gaebelein, J. B. Smith, Walvoord, LaHaye, etc.). Ironside notes that the ark of the covenant has just been seen (Rev. 11:19), an obvious link to earthly Israel. Joseph was to be exalted over the land of Egypt, and his father, mother, and brothers would come in supplication to him. The important thing about the nation of Israel is that the great Messiah would be born through it. The apostle Paul refers to his kinsmen, the Israelites, "to whom belongs the adoption, and the glory, and the covenants, and the giving of the law, and the worship service, and the promises; of whom are the fathers, and out of whom is the Christ according to the flesh, the one who is over all, God blessed into the ages, Amen" (Rom. 9:4–5). "And she was with child, and she was crying with birth pangs, and was being pained to bring forth" (v. 2). There was trauma and pain for Israel to produce the Messiah. But Isaiah prophesied specifically, "Therefore the Lord himself shall give you a sign; Behold, a virgin shall conceive, and bear a son, and shall call his

---

12:1. The word *sign* (σημεῖον) is the usual word for a symbol, a figure of speech. It is used 7 times in Rev. (12:1, 3; 13:13, 14; 15:1; 16:14; 19:20). The Lord Jesus spoke of the sign of His Second Coming (Matt. 24:30; Luke 21:25). The Pharisees were looking for signs from the Lord Jesus (Matt. 12:38–39). The miracles that Moses performed before Pharaoh were signs of God's power (Exod. 4:8–9). See ISBE (1988), "Sign," IV, pp. 505–8; ZPEB, "Sign," V, pp. 429–31.

The previous references to the number *twelve* (δώδεκα) in Rev. all refer to the 12 tribes of Israel (Rev. 7:5–8).

12:2. The verb to *suffer birth pangs* (ὠδίνω) occurs only here in Rev. The verse reminds us of the many women who had trouble in having children: Sarah (Gen. 21:1–2), Rebekah (Gen. 25:21), Rachel (Gen. 35:16–19), Hannah (I Sam. 1:2–7). Both the Lord Jesus and the apostle Paul referred to the beginning of the Tribulation period as the beginning of "birth pangs" (ὠδίν, Mark 13:8; I Thess. 5:3).

3 *And there appeared another wonder in heaven; and behold a great red dragon, having seven heads and ten horns, and seven crowns upon his heads.*
4 *And his tail drew the third part of the stars of heaven, and did cast them to the earth: and the dragon stood before the woman which was ready to be delivered, for to devour her child as soon as it was born.*

name Immanuel" (Isa. 7:14). The virgin Mary was the specific Jewess through whom the Incarnation was accomplished (Matt. 1:20–25).

II. The Great Red Dragon. vv. 3–4.

"And another sign was seen in heaven, and behold a great red dragon, having seven heads and ten horns, and upon his heads seven crowns" (v. 3). This is not a literal dragon; it is the symbol for the Devil, Satan. The symbol is appropriate, for the dragon is a cruel and heartless beast. If Christ bears the crown of the universe, the Devil will outdo Him with seven heads and seven crowns, but he has made himself into a monstrosity of evil in trying. It was Lucifer's purpose to ascend into heaven and exalt his throne above the stars of God (Isa. 14:13), but his desire to be like the most High was not attained (Isa. 14:14). He is a *red* dragon because he is stained with the blood of multitudes that he has slain (John 8:44). Thomas argues that the ten horns are on the seventh head, to agree with Daniel's vision of the final kingdom (Dan. 7:24; *Rev.*, II, p. 123). The image of the ten-horned dragon is stamped upon the fourth kingdom (Dan. 7:7). "And his tail dragged a third of the stars of heaven and cast them to the earth. And the dragon stood before the woman who was about to bring forth, in order that whenever her child was born, he might devour it" (v. 4). Job referred to the creation of God, "when the morning stars sang together, and all the sons of God shouted for joy" (Job 38:7). The Devil caused the fall of a third of the heavenly hosts (note Dan. 8:10; see Seiss, Newell, J. B. Smith). Revelation 12:9 refers to the Devil "and his angels" being cast out. "The dragon stood" shows his intent purpose to destroy the Messiah. "As a

---

12:3. The word *dragon* (δράκων) occurs 13 times in the NT, all in Rev. (12:3, 4, 7 [twice], 9, 13, 16, 17; 13:2, 4, 11; 16:13; 20:2). The great red dragon portrays the hideously deforming power of evil. He who had been the anointed cherub, magnificent in beauty (Ezek. 28:13–15), is now the horrible, monstrous dragon. Asaph said of God, "Thou brakest the heads of the dragons in the waters. Thou brakest the heads of leviathan in pieces" (Ps. 74:13–14).

The word *red* (πυρρός) occurs only here and in Rev. 6:4 in the NT.

The word *crown* is the imperial crown (διάδημα), mentioned only in Rev. 12:3; 13:1; 19:12 in the entire NT. It was "the sign of royalty among the Persians, a blue band trimmed with white, on the tiara, hence a symbol of royalty" (Arndt and Gingrich, p. 181). It should be distinguished from the victor's crown (στέφανος), mentioned in Rev. 2:10; 12:1; etc.

12:4. The verb *to drag* (σύρω) occurs only here in Rev. It always implies the notion of force (Trench, *Synonyms of the NT*, p. 72). Contrast the tender *drawing* (ἑλκύω) power of the Lord Jesus (John 12:32).

5 And she brought forth a man child, who was to rule all nations with a rod of iron: and her child was caught up unto God, and to his throne.

6 And the woman fled into the wilderness, where she hath a place prepared of God, that they should feed her there a thousand two hundred and threescore days.

dragon he is full of cunning and ferocity" (Spurgeon, "The Blood of the Lamb, the Conquering Weapon," Sermon 2043, *The C. H. Spurgeon Collection*, Ages Digital Library). The Devil tried to slay the Lord Jesus during the earthly ministry at Bethlehem by inflaming king Herod with jealousy against Him as a possible rival (Matt. 2:13–16) and at Nazareth by inflaming the mob with religious prejudice against Him (Luke 4:28–30). At Calvary he finally succeeded in slaying the Lord (Luke 22:3; John 13:2), but he did not realize that the death of the Lord would be the atoning sacrifice that would redeem mankind (I Cor. 2:8). All the "dragon's vigilance was futile" (Swete, *Rev.*, p. 151). His malice and trickery succeeded only in helping the Lord of the universe save His people. Vincent notes Milligan's comment that what the Devil tries to do here in destroying the child of Israel is just what Pharaoh did in trying to slay the boys of the Israelite women (Exod. 1:15–22). The crown of Egypt also had a serpent in it (Vincent, *Word Studies*, II, p. 522)!

III. The Man-Child. vv. 5–6.

"And she brought forth a male Son, who is about to shepherd all the nations with a rod of iron. And her child was caught up to God and to His throne" (v. 5). The phrase *a male Son* is not redundant; in the culture of the ancient world, it refers to the proper Heir to the throne of the universe. The phrase *man-child* comes from Isaiah 66:7. The Lord will grant to the Son the power to break the nations with a rod of iron (Ps. 2:9). He will rule all nations as a shepherd with almighty power. In the First Advent He was the good shepherd who gave His life for the sheep (John 10:11–15). His being *caught up* refers to the Ascension (Luke 24:51). At the Second Advent He will be the Chief Shepherd who rewards His sheep (I Pet. 5:4). He will divide the sheep from the goats and will bring His sheep into the kingdom reign (Matt. 25:31–34). "And the woman fled into the desert, where she has a place that has been prepared from God, in order that there they may feed her one thousand two hundred sixty days" (v. 6). This is the time of Jacob's trouble, the same time period as the three and a half years, and the forty-two months, the last half of the Tribulation period (Seiss,

---

12:5. The verb *to shepherd* (ποιμαίνω) occurs 4 times in Rev. (2:27; 7:17; 12:5; 19:15). It also occurs as a prophecy of the Lord's ministry (Matt. 2:6; Mic. 5:2–3 LXX). The Lord Jesus claimed to be the good Shepherd (John 10:1–11). He is indeed "that great shepherd of the sheep" (Heb. 13:20).

12:6. The word *desert* (ἔρημος) occurs 3 times in Rev. (12:6, 14; 17:3). The desert begins just a few miles from Bethlehem, which is 5 miles south of Jerusalem. The idea that the

7 And there was war in heaven: Michael and his angels fought against the dragon; and the dragon fought and his angels,

8 And prevailed not; neither was their place found any more in heaven.

9 And the great dragon was cast out, that old serpent, called the Devil, and Satan, which deceiveth the whole world: he was cast out into the earth, and his angels were cast out with him.

10 And I heard a loud voice saying in heaven, Now is come salvation, and strength, and the kingdom of our God, and the power of his Christ: for the accuser of our brethren is cast down, which accused them before our God day and night.

11 And they overcame him by the blood of the Lamb, and by the word of their testimony; and they loved not their lives unto the death.

12 Therefore rejoice, ye heavens, and ye that dwell in them. Woe to the inhabiters of the earth and of the sea! for the devil is come down unto you, having great wrath, because he knoweth that he hath but a short time.

13 And when the dragon saw that he was cast unto the earth, he persecuted the woman which brought forth the man child.

14 And to the woman were given two wings of a great eagle, that she might fly into the wilderness, into her place, where she is nourished for a time, and times, and half a time, from the face of the serpent.

15 And the serpent cast out of his mouth water as a flood after the woman, that he might cause her to be carried away of the flood.

16 And the earth helped the woman, and the earth opened her mouth, and swallowed up the flood which the dragon cast out of his mouth.

17 And the dragon was wroth with the woman, and went to make war with the remnant of her seed, which keep the commandments of God, and have the testimony of Jesus Christ.

Newell, Ironside, A. C. Gaebelein, J. B. Smith, LaHaye). The Lord Jesus told the Jews that when the temple is desecrated, they should flee into the hill country to hide (Matt. 24:15–16). This is the same territory in which David had to flee from Saul (I Sam. 22:1; 23:26; 24:1). The Jews who will not worship the image of the Beast must flee for their lives. Beale notes that the desert is mentioned repeatedly in Scripture as a place of both trial and protection (Rev., pp. 645f.).

IV. The Archangel Michael. vv. 7–17.

"And there was war in heaven: Michael and his angels waged war against the dragon; and the dragon and his angels waged war" (v. 7). Michael,

---

prepared place is Petra has no biblical grounds; there is no water source at Petra. There are, however, scores of caves throughout the hill country of the south, some of them near water sources.

The verb to nourish (τρέφω) occurs only twice in Rev. (12:6, 14).

12:7. For a summary of the verb to wage war, see Rev. 9:7 note. The angel Michael ("Who is like God?") is mentioned only here in Rev. His very name is a rhetorical challenge to the rebellious Devil. He is called "the archangel" in Jude 9, implying a very special position.

one of the chief princes, came to help the angel who revealed the future to Daniel (Dan. 10:13). The angel referred to him as "Michael your prince" (Dan. 10:21), which implies that Michael had special responsibilities to the Jews. But later the angel states clearly that Michael is "the great prince who stands for the children of your people" (Dan. 12:1). This scene confounds us. How do mighty angelic beings fight with one another? If an angel could slay 185,000 men in one night (II Kings 19:35), how much power do they wield? "And he was not strong enough; neither was their place found any longer in heaven" (v. 8). This certainly means that the Devil's hosts were defeated and swept from the celestial realm. Although the Lord had permitted Satan to enter the celestial realm to accuse believers (Job 1:6ff.), He here rescinds the permission. The Lord wills that the Devil and all his demons will be confined to the earth for the last half of the Tribulation period. "And the great dragon was cast out, the original serpent, the one who is called devil and Satan, the deceiver of the whole inhabited earth, was cast to the earth, and his angels were cast with him" (v. 9). This is the text that proves that *deceiver, dragon, serpent, devil,* and *Satan* all apply to the same evil being,

---

12:8. The verb *to be strong* (ἰσχύω) occurs only here in Rev. Although the Lord Jesus referred to the Devil in His parables as the *strong man* (ἰσχυρός, Matt. 12:29), He shows Himself to be stronger by sweeping the Devil and his angels from the heavenly realm. Unger argues that the Devil's angels are the demons confined to earth with him (*Biblical Demonology*, p. 72). The angels of God justly cry out, "Worthy is the Lamb that was slain to receive . . . *strength*" (ἰσχύς, Rev. 5:12).

12:9. The Devil is called *Satan* 8 times in Rev. (2:9, 13 [twice], 24; 3:9; 12:9; 20:2, 7). The title refers to an adversary (Ps. 109:6). He is called *serpent* 4 times in Rev. (12:9, 14, 15; 20:2). The term *old serpent* (KJV) does not refer to one that is aged or worn out, for there was a word for that (παλαιός). The word here is ἀρχαῖος, which means *going back to the beginning* (ἀρχή), the *original* serpent in the Garden of Eden (Gen. 3:1, see Trench, *Synonyms of the NT*, p. 251). This is the first time of 7 that Satan deceives man or is called *the deceiver* (ὁ πλανῶν) in Rev. (12:9; 13:14; 18:23; 19:20; 20:3, 8, 10). The Lord Jesus called him *the evil one* (ὁ πονηρός), who snatches the good seed from men's hearts (Matt. 13:19, 38). Even so urbane a writer as Jeffrey Burton Russell admits that the idea of the Devil cannot be dismissed as madness (*The Devil*, pp. 258f.) and that he is a mighty person with intelligence and will, whose energies are bent on the destruction of the cosmos and the misery of its creatures (*The Prince of Darkness*, p. 276). Russell states that the NT teaches that demons are "clearly under the generalship of Satan, helping him oppose the kingdom of God. Again, demonology is central, not peripheral, to the teaching of the New Testament" (*The Devil*, p. 237). Osborne notes that the 3 primary characteristics of the Devil are that he is an accuser, a deceiver, and an imitator (*Rev.*, p. 34). Hiebert gives a fine biblical summary ("Satan," ZPEB, V, pp. 282–86); Dwight Pentecost provides a solid exposition (*Your Adversary the Devil*, 191 pp.). Arnold Fruchtenbaum has an interesting appendix on "The Six Abodes of Satan," *The Footsteps of the Messiah*, pp. 382–88. See also Louis Sperry Chafer, *Satan*; Ryken, Wilhoit, and Longman, *Dictionary of Biblical Imagery*, "Satan," pp. 759–61; Van der Toorn, Becking, and Vander Horst, *Dictionary of Deities and Demons in the Bible*, "Satan," pp. 726–32.

the enemy of God and mankind. He was originally created as Lucifer (light bearer), who became lifted up by pride to grasp divine powers (Isa. 14:12–15). "And I heard a great voice in heaven saying, Now salvation came, and the power and the kingdom of our God, and the authority of his Christ, because the accuser of our brethren was cast out, the one who accused them before our God day and night" (v. 10). Satan is a fallen being morally, and here he is removed in presence from the heavenly courts. Jennings observes, "The heavens that have been defiled with the presence of these evil, angelic powers so long, shall know them no more forever" (*Rev.*, p. 330). In part, salvation is deliverance from the malign influence of the Devil and his demons. Although Ezekiel takes up a lamentation against the king of Tyre, the language goes far beyond what is appropriate for any earthly ruler: "Thou sealest up the sum, full of wisdom, and perfect in beauty. Thou hast been in Eden the garden of God; every precious stone was thy covering. . . . Thou art the anointed cherub that covereth; and I have set thee so: thou wast upon the holy mountain of God. . . . Thou wast perfect in thy ways from the day that thou wast created, till iniquity was found in thee . . . thou hast sinned: therefore I will cast thee as profane out of the mountain of God: and I will destroy thee, O covering cherub, from the midst of the stones of fire. Thine heart was lifted up because of thy beauty, thou hast corrupted thy wisdom by reason of thy brightness: I will cast thee to the ground, I will lay thee before kings, that they may behold thee" (Ezek. 28:12–17). Was Satan the very cherub that spread his wings over the presence of God in heaven, or one of two, as the cherubim over the ark of the covenant (Exod. 25:18–20)? No one can be dogmatic, but the possibility is certainly thought provoking. It certainly gives special meaning to the promise of God to destroy the covering cherub (Ezek. 28:16). "And they themselves conquered him because of the blood of the Lamb and because of the word of their witness; and they loved not their lives unto death" (v. 11). Two things gave the saints victory: the atoning blood of the

---

12:10. *The accuser* (ὁ κατήγωρ) is a regular term for one who brings legal charges against someone in a court of law. Satan accused Job (Job 1:6–12; 2:1–7). The Devil can charge us all with much that is true, even as he did the high priest Joshua (Zech. 3:1). Our only hope is the atoning blood of Christ (Rom. 4:24–5:1). John the Baptist understood this when he cried, "Behold the Lamb of God" (John 1:29).

12:10–12. Jacques Ellul notes that these verses are central to the whole book (*Apocalypse*, p. 281, note 4). He sees their meaning as the victory of Christ through the Incarnation, with no regard for a future eschatological war (p. 245).

12:11. For the importance of the believer's witness for Christ, see the author's commentary on Acts, *Witness to Christ* (Acts 1:8 note, pp. 4–6).

For a summary of the verb *to conquer* (νικάω) see Rev. 2:7 note.

Lamb that covered their sins and their testimony to Christ, confessing Him before men as He commanded: "Whosoever therefore shall confess me before men, him will I confess before my Father who is in heaven" (Matt. 10:32). The saints did not shrink back for fear of death. The apostle Paul did not preach Christ the gentle teacher but "Christ crucified" (I Cor. 1:23). The Lord commanded His disciples to take up their cross and follow Him (Matt. 16:24) and then warned, "For whosoever will save his life shall lose it: and whosoever will lose his life for my sake will find it" (Matt. 16:25). Spurgeon has a deeply moving sermon on "The Blood of the Lamb, the Conquering Weapon" (Sermon 2043, *The C. H. Spurgeon Collection*, Ages Digital Library). "On account of this rejoice, you heavens, and you who tabernacle in them. Woe to the earth and the sea, because the devil came down to you having great wrath, because he knows that he has only a little time" (v. 12). The heavens should rejoice because they are forever free from the presence of the Devil. The *little time* refers to the last half of the Tribulation period, three and a half years. All the powers of hell are concentrated on the earth. "Just as the imminent hope should motivate Christians to good works, it motivates Satan to do evil works so that he can cause as much destruction as possible before the end comes" (Beale, *Rev.*, p. 667). Spurgeon preached a famous sermon on "Satan in a Rage," in which he described the fury of the Devil because of how much God was accomplishing. It is when the Devil gathers all his forces to Armageddon that the Lord crushes him (Sermon 1502, *The C. H. Spurgeon Collection*, Ages Digital Library). "And when the dragon saw that he was cast to the earth, he persecuted the woman who had brought forth the man child" (v. 13). "The final

---

12:12. Isaiah tells the heavens to rejoice several times (Isa. 44:23; 49:13). The verb *to rejoice* (εὐφραίνω) is used twice in Rev. for the rejoicing of heaven (12:12; 18:20) and once for the temporary rejoicing of earth dwellers (11:10). A synonym *to exult, rejoice greatly* (ἀγαλλιάω) is used for the rejoicing over the marriage of the Lamb (Rev. 19:7). Abraham rejoiced greatly over the advent of Messiah (John 8:56). Joy is part of the fruit of the Spirit (Gal. 5:22) and will certainly characterize the saints in glory. David prayed, "In thy presence is fullness of joy; at thy right hand there are pleasures for evermore" (Ps. 16:11). God's people should rejoice in the character of God (Ps. 33:1–5). See Ryken, Wilhoit, and Longman, *Dictionary of Biblical Imagery*, "Joy," pp. 464–66; ZPEB, "Joy," III, pp. 714–15; ISBE (1982), "Joy," II, pp. 1140–42.

12:13. The verb *to persecute* (διώκω) occurs only here in Rev. Persecution has been the lot of God's faithful people, from Abel on (Gen. 4:4–8). The Lord Jesus said, "Blessed are those who have been persecuted on account of righteousness, for theirs is the kingdom of heaven. . . . Blessed are you whenever they revile and persecute you. . . . Rejoice and be glad for great is your reward in heaven" (Matt. 5:10–12). Paul had been a persecutor of Christians (Acts 7:58), but after he was converted to Christ, he was persecuted (Acts 9:22–23). He confessed that although he was persecuted, he was not forsaken (II Cor. 4:9). See ZPEB, "Persecution," IV, pp. 704–7; ISBE (1986), "Persecute, Persecution," III,

outpouring of Satanic wrath is the result of his defeat in heavenly battle" (Mounce, *Rev.*, p. 236). Anti-Semitism is always instigated by the Devil. He knows what the Lord Jesus said, "Salvation is of the Jews" (John 4:22). Paul stressed that Christ came through the Jews (Rom. 9:4–5). Paul was prepared to make any sacrifice to reach his people with the gospel (Rom. 9:3). "And to the woman were given the two wings of the great eagle, in order that she might fly into the desert into her place, where she shall be nourished there for a time, and times, and a half a time from the face of the serpent" (v. 14). This verse repeats the promise of verse 6 (1,260 days = three and a half years). The verb *were given* shows that God permits her to flee to the desert. She will find protection in the desert for the last half of the Tribulation period. The Lord reminded Israel at Mount Sinai that He had borne them on eagles' wings and brought them to Himself (Exod. 19:4). The promise still stands, "They that wait upon the Lord shall renew their strength; they shall mount up with wings as eagles" (Isa. 40:31). "And the serpent cast out of his mouth after the woman water as a river in order that he might cause her to be carried away by the river" (v. 15). Flash floods are a very real danger in the desert. The Lord promises His earthly people that the rivers "shall not overflow thee" (Isa. 43:2). "And the earth helped the woman, and the earth opened her mouth and swallowed down the river which the dragon cast out of his mouth" (v. 16). There are examples of sinkholes opening up and draining away whole lakes. Here the earth swallowed the river just as the earth swallowed Korah and his rebellious followers (Num. 16:32). Walvoord argues that the flood is symbolic of "the total effort of Satan to exterminate the nation" (*Rev.*, p. 195). Osborne observes that "this is certainly a flood of lies and deceit as well as persecution in this context" (*Rev.*, p. 483). Beale holds that the flood against the woman is symbolic of persecution against the church (*Rev.*, pp. 676f.). "And the dragon was filled with wrath toward the woman, and went forth to make war with the remnant of her seed who keep the

---

pp. 771–74; Ryken, Wilhoit, and Longman, *Dictionary of Biblical Imagery*, "Persecution," pp. 635–36.

12:14. There is a photograph of some of the caves in the Judean desert in Buchanan, *Rev.*, p. 302.

12:15. The word *river* (ποταμός) occurs 8 times in Rev. (8:10; 9:14; 12:15, 16; 16:4, 12; 22:1, 2). The KJV "flood" is the river at its most dangerous. In Rev. 22 it is the river of life in glory.

The word *carried away by a river* (ποταμοφόρητος) occurs only here in the NT.

12:16. The verb *to help* (βοηθέω) occurs only here in Rev. The Lord Jesus is able to help His people (Heb. 2:18). The cry "Help me!" brings deliverance from the Lord (Matt. 15:25).

commandments of God and have the witness of Jesus" (v. 17). There is an age-long enmity between the Devil and the Jews (Gen. 3:14-15). Daniel saw the little horn wage war against the saints and prevail against them (Dan. 7:21). The Devil hates the Jews because their mere existence is a testimony to the faithfulness of God. This is a clear reference to the *remnant*, the true believers in Israel during this tribulation. "And he stood upon the sand of the sea" (v. 18, Greek; 13:1*a* KJV). The antecedent to the *he* is the Dragon. The sea is the Mediterranean, central to the western empire. The Devil is now ready to call upon his two most zealous servants, the Beast and the False Prophet, to crush the world into submission.

Practical Applications from Revelation 12

1. Sin does not make any person attractive; the longer he lives in sin, the more hideous he becomes (v. 3). As we behold the biblical image of Christ, we are changed into the same image (II Cor. 3:18).
2. The direction of evil is always downward (v. 4). To the "defiled and unbelieving nothing is pure; but even their mind and conscience is defiled" (Titus 1:15).
3. God foresees evil and prepares protection for His people (v. 6). "The steps of a good man are ordered by the Lord: and he delighteth in his way. . . . The Lord upholdeth him with his hand" (Ps. 37:23–24).

12:17. The *remnant of Israel* is a clear OT doctrine. They are true believers who will survive the persecutions of the Tribulation period and will inherit the land during the Millennium. "The remnant of Israel . . . shall stay upon the Lord; . . . The remnant shall return . . . unto the mighty God" (Isa. 10:20–21). "Yet will I leave a remnant, that ye may have some that shall escape the sword among the nations, when ye shall be scattered through the countries" (Ezek. 6:8); "I will surely gather the remnant of Israel" (Mic. 2:12). The NT carries this theme forward (Rom. 9:27; 11:5; Rev. 7:4–15). See ISBE (1988), "Remnant," IV, pp. 130–34; ZPEB, "Remnant," V, pp. 61–62; Elwell, Walter, *Evangelical Dictionary of Biblical Theology*, "Remnant," pp. 669–71; Ryken, Wilhoit, and Longman, *Dictionary of Biblical Imagery*, "Remnant," pp. 703–4.

The *commandments of God* are mentioned twice in Rev. (12:17; 14:12).

For a summary on the *witness* (μαρτυρία) of Jesus see Rev. 1:2 note.

12:18 [KJV 13:1]. The oldest manuscripts have "He stood" (ἐστάθη): P^{47}, ℵ, A, C, 1854, 2344, 2351, the old Latin, Harclean Syriac, and Armenian versions. "I stood" (ἐστάθην) is found in P, 046, 051, and more recent manuscripts.

The word *sand* (ἄμμος) occurs only twice in Rev. (12:18; 20:8). The Lord Jesus warned against building a house on the sand (Matt. 7:26).

4. There is warfare in heaven between good and evil; we are part of it (v. 7). "Put on the whole armor of God, that you may be able to stand against the wiles of the devil" (Eph. 6:11).
5. Deception and trickery characterize the Devil; they should not characterize the believer (v. 9). "We have renounced the hidden things of dishonesty, not walking in craftiness, nor handling the word of God deceitfully; but by manifestation of the truth commending ourselves to every man's conscience in the sight of God" (II Cor. 4:2).
6. The sacrifice of Christ and the word of witness break the power of the Devil (v. 11). "We are more than conquerors through him that loved us" (Rom. 8:37).
7. We should expect the attacks of the Devil and prepare for them (v. 12). "Thy word have I hid in mine heart, that I might not sin against thee" (Ps. 119:11).
8. Obeying God's Word and witnessing for Christ are the best methods of facing the Devil's attack (v. 17). "Therefore endure hardness as a good soldier of Jesus Christ" (II Tim. 2:3).

Prayer

O great Shepherd of the sheep, much we need Your tender care. We praise You for giving Your life for us. You call us by name. Give us ears to hear and cause us to follow You faithfully, for we know You are leading us home. Amen.

The Two Beasts

Persons
The beast out of the sea
The Dragon (Satan)
Beast worshipers

The saints
Earth dwellers
The beast out of the land (earth)

Persons referred to
All kindreds, tongues, and
    nations
The Lamb

All people, small and great, rich
    and poor, free and bond

Places mentioned
The sea
Heaven

The earth

Doctrines taught
The Antichrist
The revived Roman Empire
    (Daniel's fourth empire)
Satan worship
Blasphemy

The cross
Faith
Miracles
The mark of the Beast

1 And I stood upon the sand of the sea, and saw a beast rise up out of the sea, having seven heads and ten horns, and upon his horns ten crowns, and upon his heads the name of blasphemy.

2 And the beast which I saw was like unto a leopard, and his feet were as the feet of a bear, and his mouth as the mouth of a lion: and the dragon gave him his power, and his seat, and great authority.

3 And I saw one of his heads as it were wounded to death; and his deadly wound was healed: and all the world wondered after the beast.

4 And they worshipped the dragon which gave power unto the beast: and they worshipped the beast, saying, Who is like unto the beast? who is able to make war with him?

5 And there was given unto him a mouth speaking great things and blasphemies; and power was given unto him to continue forty and two months.

6 And he opened his mouth in blasphemy against God, to blaspheme his name, and his tabernacle, and them that dwell in heaven.

7 And it was given unto him to make war with the saints, and to overcome them: and power was given him over all kindreds, and tongues, and nations.

8 And all that dwell upon the earth shall worship him, whose names are not written in the book of life of the Lamb slain from the foundation of the world.

9 If any man have an ear, let him hear.

10 He that leadeth into captivity shall go into captivity: he that killeth with the sword must be killed with the sword. Here is the patience and the faith of the saints.

Revelation 13 Exposition

I. The Beast out of the Sea. vv. 1–10.

"And I saw a beast coming up out of the sea, having ten horns and seven heads, and upon his horns ten crowns, and upon his heads names of blasphemy" (v. 1). This vision calls to mind the vision of Daniel, in which

---

13:1. The word *beast* (θηρίον) refers to a vicious, wild beast, not to be confused with the 4 living beings about the throne of God (Rev. 4:6). Daniel saw 4 world empires under the images of wild beasts: the lion, the bear, the leopard, and the fourth beast that had 10 horns (Dan. 7). This beast in Rev. is a second look at Daniel's fourth beast, dreadful, terrible, strong, "and it had great iron teeth" (Dan. 7:7). "In John's day the beast from the sea would have been identified as Rome" (Beale, *Rev.*, p. 684). But there is a blending together of the empire and the last individual head of the empire, the Antichrist. This is a picture of the kingdom of the Antichrist (I John 2:18), the man of sin (II Thess. 2:3–4). Although some argue that the papacy is the Antichrist (Ian Paisley, *Antichrist*), it is better to see a specific future individual who will fulfill all these prophecies.

The word *sea* (θάλασσα) occurs 26 times in Rev. Here it refers to the Mediterranean Sea, central to the Roman Empire. "This passage is first of all a revelation of the revived Roman Empire in its period of worldwide dominion" (Walvoord, *Rev.*, p. 197). The last reference is to the new earth, "there was no more sea" (Rev. 21:1). Daniel saw the 4 winds of heaven striving upon the great sea and the 4 great beasts arising from the sea (Dan. 7:2ff.).

he saw four great beasts rise from the sea (Dan. 7:2ff.), and the fourth beast had ten horns (Dan. 7:7ff.). But the immediate context shows that this beast bears the image of the dragon with its seven heads and ten horns (Rev. 12:3). The Devil is the god of this age, who has blinded the minds of the unbelieving (II Cor. 4:4) and who will bring forth his world ruler "with all power, and signs, and lying wonders" (II Thess. 2:9). The empire and its ruler will be empowered by the Devil himself and will have his character. The ten horns are a confederation of ten kings (Dan. 7:24; Rev. 17:12). They give their power and authority to the Beast (Rev. 17:13). "And the beast which I saw was like a leopard, and his feet were as those of a bear, and his mouth as the mouth of a lion; and the dragon gave him his power and his throne and great authority" (v. 2). This fourth empire will embody the most vicious characteristics of the preceding empires: the lithe speed of the leopard, the huge claws of the bear, and the fearful jaws of the lion. Daniel foresaw "great iron teeth," power such as no natural animal could have (Dan. 7:7). All of these characteristics emphasize the tremendous power that the last worldly empire will exercise. "And one of his heads was as having been slaughtered

---

Isaiah prophesied that Jehovah "shall slay the dragon that is in the sea" (Isa. 27:1). There are cryptic references in the *Pseudepigrapha* to this "beast." First Enoch 90:9–19 draws upon Daniel to portray a "great horn" that afflicts God's sheep (R. H. Charles, *Pseudepigrapha*, II, p. 257). Fourth Ezra 5:7 refers to the "one whom the many do not know will make his voice heard by night; and all shall hear his voice." But it is John in his Epistles who prepares the way to understand this chapter. He declares plainly that this future personage is the Antichrist, who denies the Father and the Son (I John 2:22). John prophesies that Antichrist shall indeed come, but there are many who are already doing his work (I John 2:18). He warns that Antichrist is an arch-deceiver (II John 7). Pentecost provides an exhaustive list of the titles applied in the Bible to the Antichrist (*Things to Come*, pp. 334–35). In his chapter "Antichrist as Head of the Nations," Samuel J. Andrews gave a remarkably perceptive description of the preparation that democracy, socialism, and philosophy will give to the rise of Antichrist (*Christianity and Anti-Christianity in Their Final Conflict*, pp. 264–83). L. Sale-Harrison foresaw the future confederation (*The Resurrection of the Old Roman Empire*). World empire is uniformly set forth by symbols of cruel, dangerous beasts. The Lord Jesus Christ is the only King who can reign in righteousness (Isa. 32:1), and it is only by righteousness that there will be peace on earth (Isa. 32:17). No wonder that the angels sang of peace when the Lord Jesus was born (Luke 2:14). He is the Prince of peace (Isa. 9:6).

For the references to the word *blasphemy* see Rev. 2:9 note.

13:1–4. Vern S. Poythress notes the Devil's counterfeiting skills. Satan produces an unholy trinity of the Dragon, the Beast, and the False Prophet. The Beast is made in the image of the Dragon, paralleling Christ, the image of His Father (*The Returning King*, pp. 16ff.).

13:2. The words *leopard* (πάρδαλις) and *bear* (ἄρκος) occur only here in the NT. For the word *lion* (λέων) see Rev. 4:7 note.

to death, and the wound of his death was healed. And all the earth wondered after the beast" (v. 3). Many expositors argue that vv. 1–3 have to
do with the resurrection of the Roman Empire, the kingdom of the Beast,
and vv. 4–10 refer to the last individual dictator of the empire (Scofield,
Scott, Ironside, Pentecost, Walvoord). He will be the Roman "prince
that shall come" (Dan. 9:26). He will confirm the covenant with the
Jews for one week (the seven-year Tribulation period) and shall break the
covenant at the midpoint and shall seek to annihilate the Jewish people.
The apostle Paul describes him as "the man of sin," who "as God sits in
the temple of God, showing himself that he is God" (II Thess. 2:4). The
Lord Jesus called him "the abomination of desolation spoken through
Daniel the prophet" (Matt. 24:15). John could say, "You have heard that
antichrist is coming" (I John 2:18). Some hold that this last ruler is actually raised from the dead (Seiss, Newell, J. B. Smith). An earlier reference described him as "coming up out of the abyss" (Rev. 11:7). But we
must remember that Satan is skillful at "lying wonders" (II Thess. 2:9).
The Lord Jesus alone holds "the keys of hades and of death" (Rev. 1:18).
Walvoord argues that Satan does have the power to heal, "and apparently
the seemingly fatal wound is healed" (*Prophecy in the New Millennium*,
p. 75). "And they worshiped the dragon, because he gave authority to
the beast, and they worshiped the beast, saying, Who is like the beast,
and who is able to do battle with him?" (v. 4). The rhetorical question is
a parody of the worship of Jehovah in the Song of Moses (Exod. 15:11).
This climaxes the violation of the first two commandments of the
Decalogue (Exod. 20:3–6). There have been Satanists throughout the
world's history, but the Beast will be the most blatant and horrifying of
them all. The Devil will consolidate into his hands the powers of the
world. The Beast will control the armies of the empire; the social, religious, and educational realms; the media; the food supplies; and even the

---

13:3. The verb *to slaughter* (σφάζω) occurs 8 times in Rev. (5:6, 9, 12; 6:4, 9; 13:3, 8;
18:24) and twice in I John 3:12 only in the NT. It is used of the dreadful slaughter of the
Lamb of God to redeem His people (Rev. 5), of the terrible slaughter of people during the
seal judgments (Rev. 6), of the mocking, counterfeit slaughter of the beast here in Rev. 13,
and of the slaughter of martyrs, prophets, and saints in Babylon (Rev. 18; note Ps. 44:22).
There have been enough "after death" experiences recorded to lend credence to such a
claim for the Antichrist (Raymond Moody, *Life After Life*, Atlanta: Mockingbird Books,
1975; *Reflections on Life After Life*, 1977). For a summary of teaching on "The Antichrist,"
see *Dictionary of Premillennial Theology*, ed., Mal Couch, pp. 43–47; Dwight Pentecost,
Things to Come, pp. 332–39; Erich Sauer, *The Triumph of the Crucified*, pp. 115–21; Walter
Elwell, *Evangelical Dictionary of Biblical Theology*, "Antichrist," pp. 27–28; ZPEB,
"Antichrist," I, pp. 178–81.

The verb *to wonder* (θαυμάζω) occurs only here and in Rev. 17:6, 7, 8.

13:4. For a summary of the verb *to worship*, see Rev. 4:10 note.

right of burial. The believers who will not bow the knee to him will be hunted down as criminals. John called him "the antichrist" (I John 2:22). "And a mouth was given to him, speaking great things and blasphemies, and authority was given to him to continue forty-two months" (v. 5). The verb *was given* shows that God gave him his ability in eloquent speech. He may well be the most persuasive speaker for the Devil in the history of the world. For three and a half years, the last half of the Tribulation period, he institutes a reign of terror. He is the "little horn" of Daniel, who had piercing eyes and "a mouth speaking great things" (Dan. 7:8). The piercing gaze and the eloquent speech have been hallmarks of dictators all through history. Think of Hitler! Daniel prophesied, "And he shall speak great words against the most High, and shall wear out the saints of the most High, and think to change times and laws: and they shall be given into his hand until a time and times and the dividing of time" (Dan. 7:25). "And he opened his mouth in blasphemy against God, to blaspheme his name, and his tabernacle, and those who are dwelling [tabernacling] in heaven" (v. 6). He has a satanic hatred of God and does not fear to speak evil of God and of His people. But he really desires to exterminate God's people from the earth. "And it was given to him to make war with the saints and to conquer them; and authority was given to him over every tribe and people and tongue and nation" (v. 7). Walvoord stresses that it is Satan who gives the Beast the power to conquer the saints (*Rev.*, p. 201). But the passive, "authority was given," shows that it is God who permits his rule. Daniel prophesied that the little horn "made war with the saints, and prevailed against them" (Dan. 7:21). Daniel remembered that Nebuchadnezzar had commanded all "people, nations, and languages" to worship his image (Dan. 3:4). There will be no place to hide; no nation will dare to provide sanctuary for the remnant of believers. "And all who are dwelling upon the earth shall worship him, whose names have not been written in the book of life of the Lamb who has been slain from the foundation of the world" (v. 8). Messiah is the Lamb who was led to the slaughter (Isa. 53:7). In every age of the world's history God has had His people on earth, from the Garden of Eden on. The Tribulation period will be no exception. As Tertullian phrased it, "The blood of the martyrs is the seed of the church." Evil men cannot kill the saints of God fast enough. There are always new converts who will pick up the testimony and stand for God. When

---

13:6. The verb *to blaspheme* (βλασφημέω) occurs 4 times in Rev. (13:6; 16:9, 11, 21). The noun *blasphemy* (βλασφημία) occurs 5 times (2:9; 13:1, 5, 6; 17:3).

The word *tabernacle* (σκηνή) occurs 3 times in Rev. (13:6; 15:5; 21:3), all referring to the sanctuary of God.

13:8. For a summary of *the book of life*, see Rev. 3:5 note.

Stephen was martyred, one of his persecutors was Saul, who later was converted and became a greater evangelist for Christ than Stephen could be (Acts 7:59–8:1). A. T. Robertson stresses the perfect tense: "whose names do not *stand written*" (*Word Pictures*, VI, p. 401). Scripture clearly teaches that God has a Book of Life, the roster of the redeemed, which contains the names of every saint who will be in glory. The fact that theologians have difficulty understanding this, and fight theological wars over predestination and free will, does not change the fact of such a book. God is preparing a place for the persons named in that book, and He will not be surprised at the appearance of any saint in glory (Rev. 22:19). "If anyone has an ear, let him hear" (v. 9). When the Lord Jesus spoke of the glorious inauguration of the millennial kingdom, He used the plural: "Then shall the righteous shine forth as the sun in the kingdom of their Father. Who has ears to hear, let him keep hearing" (Matt. 13:43). Here John is saying, if a person has as much as one good ear, let him listen. This suggests "the high importance of the things mentioned" (J. B. Smith, *Rev.*, p. 200). "If anyone leads into captivity, he shall be led into captivity; if anyone kills with the sword, he shall be killed with the sword. Here is the patience and faith of the saints" (v. 10). This is a timeless principle. God commanded mankind to execute the murderer (Gen. 9:6). God promises exact retribution for every evil deed. God declared to the wicked, "To me belongs vengeance and recompence; their foot shall slide in due time" (Deut. 32:35). The wicked may think that they are getting away with evil, but God will cause them to fall in His own good time. The apostle Paul referred to this passage: "Vengeance is mine; I will repay, says the Lord" (Rom. 12:19). God deals in absolute justice with every human being. "Know therefore that the Lord thy God, he is God, the faithful God, which keepeth covenant and mercy with them that love him and keep his commandments to a thousand generations; and repayeth them that hate him to their face, to destroy them: he will not be slack to him that hateth him, he will repay him to his face" (Deut. 7:9–10). This is why the saints of God endure persecution and wait patiently. They believe that God will repay every evil deed. Osborne wisely notes "that these futuristic passages must be understood at three levels: the saints of the 'tribulation period' (the futurist approach), the Christians of John's day (the preterist approach), and believers in our own day (the idealist approach)" (*Rev.*, p. 504).

13:10. For a summary of *patience*, see Rev. 1:9 note; for *faith*, see Rev. 2:13 note.

11 And I beheld another beast coming up out of the earth; and he had two horns like a lamb, and he spake as a dragon.
12 And he exerciseth all the power of the first beast before him, and causeth the earth and them which dwell therein to worship the first beast, whose deadly wound was healed.
13 And he doeth great wonders, so that he maketh fire come down from heaven on the earth in the sight of men,
14 And deceiveth them that dwell on the earth by the means of those miracles which he had power to do in the sight of the beast; saying to them that dwell on the earth, that they should make an image to the beast, which had the wound by a sword, and did live.
15 And he had power to give life unto the image of the beast, that the image of the beast should both speak, and cause that as many as would not worship the image of the beast should be killed.
16 And he causeth all, both small and great, rich and poor, free and bond, to receive a mark in their right hand, or in their foreheads:
17 And that no man might buy or sell, save he that had the mark, or the name of the beast, or the number of his name.
18 Here is wisdom. Let him that hath understanding count the number of the beast: for it is the number of a man; and his number is Six hundred threescore and six.

II. The Beast out of the Land. vv. 11–18.

"And I saw another beast rising up out of the land, and he was having two horns like a lamb and he was speaking like a dragon" (v. 11). He was another wild beast of the same kind as the first beast. This one was rising up out of "the land," which may well refer to the land of Palestine (Matt. 27:45). As the last head of the ecumenical world church he will look like a lamb, but his speech will be the voice of the Devil. In plain language he will be a counterfeit, an evil man masquerading as a "Christ figure." F. F. Bruce notes the satanic trinity here (*Christ and Spirit in the New Testament*, p. 653). As Christ received authority from the Father (Matt. 11:27), so Antichrist receives authority from the Dragon (Rev. 13:4); and as the Holy Spirit glorifies Christ (John 16:14), so the False Prophet glorifies the Antichrist (Rev. 13:12). F. F. Bruce calls him "the Minister of Propaganda" (*International Bible Commentary*, p. 1616). "And he exercises all the authority of the first beast before him, and causes the earth and all the ones dwelling in it to worship the first beast, whose wound of his

---

13:11. *The land* today consists of Israel (8,019 sq. miles; 6,600,000 pop.), the West Bank (2,263 sq. miles; 2,576,000 pop.), and the Gaza Strip (139 sq. miles; 1,107,000 pop.) (*Atlas of the Middle East*, pp. 28–29; 50–51[Washington, D.C.: National Geographic Society, 2003]).

Although some see the False Prophet as nations (Ken Klein, *The False Prophet*), it is better to interpret this text as a specific individual who aids the Antichrist in his wicked purpose.

death was healed" (v. 12). At the end of the first century the emperor cult tried to force the whole empire to worship Caesar along with their other gods. Beale suggests that the worship of Domitian at Ephesus is behind this language (*Rev.*, p. 712). What irony that this last false religious leader will try the same old trick to get mankind to worship a man rather than the true God! "And he will perform great signs, to even cause fire to come down out of heaven to the earth before men" (v. 13). The Jews have a standing warning not to follow a prophet who performs miracles if he tries to lead them away from Jehovah God (Deut. 13:1–5). God has provided a true Prophet (Deut. 18:15) in the person of the Lord Jesus Christ (Acts 3:22–23; 7:37). The apostle Paul specifically warned against "that wicked one . . . whose coming is after the working of Satan with all power and signs and lying wonders" (II Thess. 2:8–9). "And he deceives the ones who dwell on the earth through the signs which were given to him to perform before the beast, saying that the earth dwellers should make an image to the beast, who has the wound of the sword and lived" (v. 14). The earth dwellers are easily manipulated into following the False Prophet's worship of the Beast. The Israelites quickly turned aside to worship the golden calf when Moses was in the mount (Exod. 32:1–4). King Nebuchadnezzar pressured all of his people (except three Jews) to fall down and worship his golden image (Dan. 3:4–7). Modern-day dictators flood their land with photographs of themselves (Hitler, Stalin, etc.). The pictures can become idols of worship. The phrase "the wound of the sword" gives a hint of the assassination attempt against the Antichrist. "And it was granted to him to give spirit to the image of the beast, in order that the image of the beast should speak and should cause that as many as would not worship the image of the beast should be killed"

13:12. The ecumenical world church ("the apostate church," Walvoord, *Rev.*, p. 205) will have room for every religion, sect, and cult, providing that they will also worship the Beast. The one being that they must not worship is the Lord Jesus Christ. *Mystery Babylon* is a vivid picture of that apostate church (Rev. 17:3–6; 18:1–8). The apostle Paul faced the Roman Empire with courage. "I am not ashamed of the gospel of Christ: for it is the power of God unto salvation" (Rom. 1:16). That fidelity cost him his life. We need that same courage.

13:13. When Moses wrought miracles before Pharaoh, the magicians of Egypt copied them (Exod. 7:10–12). For a summary of the word *sign* (σημεῖον) see Rev. 12:1 note. For a summary of the word *fire* (πῦρ) see Rev. 1:14 note.

13:14. The verb *to deceive* (πλανάω) is the regular word *to lead astray*. Satan is the great deceiver (Rev. 12:9). Believers used to be as sheep being led astray (I Pet. 2:25). For a summary of the verb see Rev. 2:20 note.

The word *image* (εἰκών) occurs 10 times in Rev. (13:14, 15 [3 times]; 14:9, 11; 15:2; 16:2; 19:20; 20:4), always *the image of the beast*. The Lord Jesus used the image of a Roman emperor on a coin as an illustration (Matt. 22:20).

(v. 15). Of what demonic nature that "spirit" might be is not revealed. Is the idea of a demon-possessed computer really far-fetched? "And he makes all, small and great, rich and poor, free and slave, to receive a mark upon their right hand, or on their forehead" (v. 16). He will force all classes to receive the mark. This is a public mark of submission to the rule of the Beast. No true believer will receive it. "And that no one might buy or sell, except the one who has the mark, the name of the beast, or the number of his name" (v. 17). By economic warfare the Beast will try to starve out all who will not submit to him. "Here is wisdom. Let the one who has understanding count the number of the beast, for it is the number of a man; and his number is six hundred sixty six" (v. 18). Daniel wrote, "None of the wicked shall understand, but the wise shall understand" (Dan. 12:10). In Scripture, six is the number of man; seven is the divine number. The Antichrist comes short of his claims in all regards. But in all probability the Antichrist will choose this very number (666) because he knows that Bible believers will refuse it. They are the very people he will be hunting for. His edict may well be "If you are loyal to the empire, you will show it by adding three digits to your ID number, 666." If people will not, their number will no longer work.

13:15. The idea that men could make an image of a human being so lifelike that it could not be distinguished from the actual person and had the ability to gesture and speak with a recording of the actual person's voice used to be science fiction, but now it is actual science, audio-animatronics. Such an image could have a remote contact with the database of the empire and could report the past record of any citizen in the empire. The image becomes a major tool of the Devil in the execution of believers.

13:16. The mark of the Beast will symbolize loyalty to the Antichrist and his empire. Such a universal mark is regularly suggested in order to identify fugitive criminals, dead bodies, etc. The OT forbad the printing of any marks on the body by Israelites (Lev. 19:28). See Elwell, *Evangelical Dictionary of Biblical Theology,* "Mark of the Beast," pp. 506–7; ZPEB, "Mark, Sign, Brand," IV, pp. 89–90.

For a summary of the word *forehead* see Rev. 7:3 note.

13:18. An ocean of ink has been spilled over the number 666. Citizens already have Social Security numbers, draft numbers, license numbers, bankcard numbers, etc. One more number is no surprise. Before the invention of Arabic numerals, all alphabetic languages had numeric equivalents to their letters. The early church fathers thought that Nero, the worst despot they could think of, might be revived and come back as the Antichrist. The word *Roman* (λατεῖνος) had the numeric value of 30 + 1 + 300 + 5 + 10 + 50 + 70 + 200 = 666. The Hebrew form of *Nero Caesar* also totaled 666. In contrast, the name *Jesus* (Ἰησοῦς) totals 888, the "New Beginning." For interesting speculations in such numerology, see J. B. Smith, *Rev.,* pp. 206f.; Walvoord, *Rev.,* pp. 209f.; Thomas, *Rev.,* II, pp. 182–88. For examples of Roman practice in numbers, see Deissmann, *Light from the Ancient East,* pp. 276–78. For a factual appraisal of numbers see Ryken, Wilhoit, and Longman, *Dictionary of Biblical Imagery,* "Numbers in the Bible," pp. 599–600. For a cool appraisal of biblical numbers see ISBE (1986), "Number," III, pp. 556–61.

Practical Applications from Revelation 13

1. The Devil can put some wicked people into positions of power (v. 2). Paul refers to that wicked one, "whose coming is after the working of Satan with all power and signs and lying wonders" (II Thess. 2:9).
2. Honoring any man above God is idolatry (v. 4). God charged Eli with honoring "thy sons above me" (I Sam. 2:29). Modern hero-worship is idolatry.
3. God limits the time that worldly people can rule (v. 5). God added to king Hezekiah's life fifteen years (II Kings 20:6).
4. In the end time the Antichrist will attempt to institute universal idolatry in world religion (v. 8). But only the Lord Jesus will have true universal dominion (Dan. 7:13–14).
5. God will repay every wrong that men do (v. 10). "Vengeance is mine; I will repay, says the Lord" (Rom. 12:19).
6. There will be satanic, but false, miracles in the future (v. 13). Paul refers to that wicked one, "whose coming is after the working of Satan with all power and signs and lying wonders" (II Thess. 2:9).
7. The Antichrist will be allowed to kill some faithful believers (v. 15). In the first century King Herod killed the apostle James with the sword (Acts 12:2). His mother's prayer may yet be answered, but martyrdom was not what she was thinking of (Matt. 20:20–21).

Prayer

O Lord Jesus, the Lamb of God, slain from the foundation of the world, we look to You for salvation and grace. Let Your presence sustain us and bring us safely home. May our lives shine with the light of Your love and blessing. Amen.

REVELATION 14

THE LAMB: REDEMPTION AND WRATH

Persons

The Lamb

The 144,000

The four living beings

The elders

An angel

A second angel

A third angel

Beast worshipers

The holy angels

The saints

The Spirit

A fourth angel (v. 15)

A fifth angel (v. 17)

A sixth angel (v. 18)

Persons referred to

The Father

Women

Earth dwellers

All nations

The dead that die in the Lord

Places mentioned

Mount Sion

The throne in heaven

The earth

The sea

Babylon

The place of torment

The city (Jerusalem, v. 20)

Doctrines taught

Worship in song

Redemption

The everlasting gospel

The glory of God

Judgment

Creation

Wrath of God

Eternal torment

The mark of the Beast

Faith in Jesus

The blessed dead

The winepress of the wrath

of God

1 And I looked, and, lo, a Lamb stood on the mount Sion, and with him an hundred forty and four thousand, having his Father's name written in their foreheads.

2 And I heard a voice from heaven, as the voice of many waters, and as the voice of a great thunder: and I heard the voice of harpers harping with their harps:

3 And they sung as it were a new song before the throne, and before the four beasts, and the elders: and no man could learn that song but the hundred and forty and four thousand, which were redeemed from the earth.

4 These are they which were not defiled with women; for they are virgins. These are they which follow the Lamb whithersoever he goeth. These were redeemed from among men, being the firstfruits unto God and to the Lamb.

5 And in their mouth was found no guile: for they are without fault before the throne of God.

Revelation 14 Exposition

1. The Lamb and the 144,000. vv. 1–5.

"And I saw, and behold the Lamb, having taken His stand upon mount Sion, and with him a hundred and forty-four thousand, having his name and the name of his Father written upon their foreheads" (v. 1). In contrast to the worshipers of the Beast, who took his name on their foreheads, here are the martyrs who refused the mark of the Beast and now bear the name of their Lord and His Father forever on their foreheads. They are an elect group that has a special place of honor in heaven (Rev. 7:3–4). Spurgeon notes that they do not have a big *B* for Baptist, or any other denomination, on their forehead! Their heavenly Father's name is on each one ("Heavenly Worship," Sermon 110, *The C. H. Spurgeon Collection*, Ages Digital Library). Ezekiel recorded that the Lord sent an angel into Jerusalem to set a mark on the foreheads of those who mourn over the sins of the people (Ezek. 9:2–4). The mark was the Hebrew letter *tau*, which, in its ancient form, was a cross. Expositors argue over which Mount Sion is intended here. Some (J. B. Smith, *Rev.*, p. 208; Ryrie, *Rev.*, p. 101) argue that this is heavenly Mount Sion (Heb. 12:22), for the 144,000 are singing before the throne of God and before the living beings and elders (v. 3). Others argue that Mount Sion

---

14:1. Mount *Sion* is the celestial one (in contrast with Mt. Sinai) in Heb. 12:22; for the earthly Mount *Sion* see John 12:15; Rom. 9:33; 11:26. In the OT the word is spelled *Zion*: "Yet have I set my King upon my holy hill of Zion" (Ps. 2:6). "Mt. Zion is portrayed as the seat of Yahweh's world government; peace will prevail" ("Zion," Ryken, Wilhoit, and Longman, *Dictionary of Biblical Imagery*, p. 981). See also Pss. 9:11; 14:7; 48:2; 51:18; 74:2, etc. See ZPEB, "Zion," V, pp. 1063–67; ISBE (1988), "Zion," IV, pp. 1198–1200. For photographs south of Zion gate, see Custer, *Stones of Witness*, pp. 98–100.

refers to a specific geographic location in earthly Jerusalem and marks the beginning of the millennial reign (Walvoord, *Rev.*, p. 214; Thomas, *Rev.*, II, p. 190). What complicates the argument is that we have an imperfect perception of the relationship between the celestial realm and the earth. When Jacob slept at the place he named Bethel, he discovered that there was a celestial staircase between heaven and earth (Gen. 28:12–16). That does not mean that it is located at Bethel today. When the Lord Jesus returns to earth at the Second Coming, His feet shall stand in that day on the Mount of Olives, and it shall become a great valley (Zech. 14:4, 16). It is logical that He would move on to Mount Sion and produce the great plain on which 144,000 could stand without crowding in preparation for the great millennial temple yet to be built (Ezek. 46:9), which assumes vast multitudes of constant worshipers. Whatever the Lord will do, will be in clear view of the celestial throne and the elders and living beings and yet be seen on earth as well. "And I heard a voice out of heaven as a voice of many waters and as a voice of great thunder, and the voice which I heard was as harp singers playing on harps with their harps" (v. 2). Ezekiel heard the voice of the Lord as the sound of many waters (Ezek. 43:2). The repetition in v. 2 is strong emphasis on the fact that there are musicians and musical instruments in heaven. The first reference to a harp in Psalms is a command: "Praise the Lord with harp: sing unto him with the psaltery and an instrument of ten strings" (Ps. 33:2). Believers are also commanded, "Sing unto him a new song" (Ps. 33:3). Praising God with the harp is a continuing theme (Pss. 43:4; 57:8; 71:22; 81:1–2; 92:1–3; 98:5; 108:1–2; 147:7; 149:3; 150:3). It is an exciting thought for Christian musicians that their music will never end. "And they sing as a new song before the throne and before the four living beings and the elders, and no one was able to learn the song except the hundred and forty-four thousand, who have been redeemed from the earth" (v. 3). One thing that enduring suffering does for

---

14:2. The word *harp singer* (κιθαρῳδός) occurs only here and in Rev. 18:22 in the NT. It denotes one who sings and accompanies himself on the harp. For the word *harp* (κιθάρα) see the summary in Rev. 5:8–9.

14:3. *They sing as a new song* means extemporizing; they make up the new song as they sing, in perfect harmony. They have greater abilities because they have suffered much. And all heaven listens!

The verb *to redeem*, or *buy* (ἀγοράζω), occurs 6 times in Rev.: 3 times with the commercial meaning *to buy* (3:18; 13:17; 18:11) and 3 times with the theological meaning *to redeem* (5:9; 14:3, 4). Paul uses an intensified form, "Christ *has redeemed* (ἐξαγοράζω) us from the curse of the law" (Gal. 3:13). It was Job's faith, "I know that my Redeemer liveth" (Job 19:25). See ZPEB, "Redeemer, Redemption," V, pp. 49–51; ISBE (1988), "Redeemer, Redemption," IV, pp. 61–63; Ryken, Wilhoit, and Longman, *Dictionary of Biblical Imagery*, pp. 698–700.

6 *And I saw another angel fly in the midst of heaven, having the everlasting gospel to preach unto them that dwell on the earth, and to every nation, and kindred, and tongue, and people,*

7 *Saying with a loud voice, Fear God, and give glory to him; for the hour of his judgment is come: and worship him that made heaven, and earth, and the sea, and the fountains of waters.*

8 *And there followed another angel, saying, Babylon is fallen, is fallen, that great city, because she made all nations drink of the wine of the wrath of her fornication.*

9 *And the third angel followed them, saying with a loud voice, If any man worship the beast and his image, and receive his mark in his forehead, or in his hand,*

the believer is to enlarge his ability to understand how much God's grace has delivered him *from.* The 144,000 will have a featured position before the Lamb. "These are the ones who were not defiled with women, for they are virgins. These are following the Lamb wherever he is going. These were redeemed from mankind, firstfruits to God and to the Lamb" (v. 4). The firstfruits were holy to the Lord; they were the first delicious fruits of springtime (Exod. 23:16, 19; Lev. 23:20; Deut. 18:4). They have already been identified as sealed before God (Rev. 7:4–17). (Although some will argue that they are a different group, LaHaye, *Rev.,* p. 230). Spurgeon declares that the great characteristic of believers is that they follow the Lamb and no other ("The Lamb Our Leader," Sermon 2456, *The C. H. Spurgeon Collection,* Ages Digital Library). "And in their mouth was found no lie; they are blameless" (v. 5). One of the characteristics of Messiah is that there "was [no] deceit in his mouth" (Isa. 53:9). There may be people in the Tribulation period who will try to lie their way out of the Beast's dragnet, but the 144,000 will confess Christ boldly. God says they are blameless. What a tribute!

II. The Heavenly Messages. vv. 6–13.

"And I saw another angel flying in mid-heaven, having the everlasting gospel to proclaim to the ones who are living on the earth, even to every

---

14:4. This is the only time that *firstfruits* (ἀπαρχή) occurs in Rev. The firstfruits were devoted to God (Lev. 19:23–25). The emphasis is on excellence in quality, not merely priority in time (Arndt and Gingrich, p. 80). The 144,000 were holy to the Lord, even as the crops were in OT times (Rom. 11:16). Christ is the supreme Firstfruits to His Father (I Cor. 15:20, 23). Spurgeon uses this vast number to avow his faith that the Lord saves all the children who die in infancy ("Heavenly Worship," Sermon 110, *The C. H. Spurgeon Collection,* Ages Digital Library).

This is the only time that the word *virgin* (παρθένος) occurs in Rev.

14:5. This is the only time that the word *blameless* (ἄμωμος) occurs in Rev.

10 The same shall drink of the wine of the wrath of God, which is poured out without mixture into the cup of his indignation; and he shall be tormented with fire and brimstone in the presence of the holy angels, and in the presence of the Lamb:
11 And the smoke of their torment ascendeth up for ever and ever: and they have no rest day nor night, who worship the beast and his image, and whosoever receiveth the mark of his name.
12 Here is the patience of the saints: here are they that keep the commandments of God, and the faith of Jesus.
13 And I heard a voice from heaven saying unto me, Write, Blessed are the dead which die in the Lord from henceforth: Yea, saith the Spirit, that they may rest from their labours; and their works do follow them.

nation and tribe and tongue and people" (v. 6). The everlasting, or eternal, gospel is certainly the message of salvation through the death of Christ on the cross to atone for the sins of the world. Osborne notes, "Everywhere that εὐαγγέλιον is found in the NT, it implies the gracious offer of salvation" (*Rev.*, p. 535). It was prophesied in the OT (Isa. 53:6–12) and proclaimed (Isa. 55:1–3). The NT writers declared it (John 1:29; 3:16; 6:35; Acts 10:42–43; 13:32–39; I Cor. 15:1–10). The Lord Jesus Himself said, "And this gospel of the kingdom shall be preached in all the world for a witness unto all nations; and then shall the end come" (Matt. 24:14). It should be no surprise that angels see to it that it is proclaimed in the darkest hour of persecution in the world's history. "Saying with a great voice, Fear God and give to him glory because the hour of his judgment came, and worship the one who made heaven and earth and sea and fountains of waters" (v. 7). All mankind should revere and glorify the true God. "Declare his glory among the heathen, his wonders among all people. For the Lord is great, and greatly to be praised: he is to

---

14:6. This is the only time that the word *gospel* (εὐαγγέλιον) occurs in Rev. It is a key word in Paul's Epistles (Rom. 1:1, 9, 16; 15:19; I Cor. 4:15; 9:12, 18; 15:1; II Cor. 2:12; 4:3–4; Gal. 1:6–7; Eph. 1:13; Phil. 1:5, 7; Col. 1:5, 23; I Thess. 2:8–9; II Thess. 1:8; I Tim. 1:11; II Tim. 1:10; Philem. 1:13; etc.).

There is a slight doctrinal hiccup in the old *Scofield Study Bible*, which said the everlasting gospel was only for a short time at the end of the Tribulation (p. 1343). The word *everlasting* has a different denotation. Walvoord distinguishes this everlasting gospel from both the gospel of grace and the gospel of the kingdom (*Rev.*, p. 217). However, both the gospel of grace (Rom. 1:15–18) and the gospel of the kingdom (Matt. 25:41–46) portray the judgment of God on the unbelievers. There is a unity as well as a diversity in the dispensations.

14:7. The verb *to fear* (φοβέομαι) occurs 6 times in Rev. Twice it is a command to believers to "stop fearing" in the sense of being terrified (Rev. 1:17; 2:10), and 4 times it refers to the *awe* and *reverence* that is appropriate for those who trust in God (11:18; 14:7; 15:4; 19:5).

This is the first of 4 times that the word *judgment* (κρίσις) occurs in Rev. (14:7; 16:7; 18:10; 19:2).

be feared above all gods" (Ps. 96:3–4). But instead man reviles and dishonors God in word and actions continually (Gen. 6:5; Rom. 3:11–18). Still, "the Lord . . . cometh to judge the earth: he shall judge the world with righteousness" (Ps. 96:13). The Lord is the one who "made heaven and earth, the sea, and all that in them is" (Exod. 20:11). "And another, second, angel followed, saying, Babylon the great fell, which caused all nations to drink of the wine of the wrath of her fornication" (v. 8). In John's day the *Babylon* everyone would think of was Rome (I Pet. 5:13). But here the angel speaks prophetically of the coming destruction of the city of the Beast (Rev. 17:16; 18:10). Isaiah had prophesied, "Babylon is fallen, is fallen" (Isa. 21:9). God's people may be comforted because her destruction is sure. "And a third angel followed them, saying with a great voice, If anyone worships the beast and his image and receives a mark upon his forehead or upon his hand, even he himself shall drink of the wine of the wrath of God, which is poured out undiluted in the cup of his wrath, and he shall be tormented in fire and sulfur in the sight of holy angels and in the sight of the Lamb" (vv. 9–10). God promises that He will punish the wicked and reward the righteous (Exod. 20:3–6). "The Lord rained on Sodom and Gomorrah brimstone [sulfur] and fire" (Gen. 19:24). Isaiah prophesied that Edom would have its dust turned to sulfur and its land to burning pitch (Isa. 34:9). Babylon is "a golden cup in the Lord's hand, that made all the earth drunken: the nations have drunken of her wine" (Jer. 51:7). Sulfur is regularly found in volcanic regions, such as Sicily, Iceland, Hawaii, and Japan. Although sulfur is naturally yellow, when it is burned, it regularly becomes dark brown and emits a nauseating, choking gas, sulfur dioxide. (O'Donoghue, Michael, *The Encyclopedia of Minerals and Gemstones*, pp. 156–57). Scripture plainly reveals that the final abode of the wicked is a place well worth avoiding.

14:8. Babylon is mentioned 6 times in Rev. (14:8; 16:19; 17:5; 18:2, 10, 21). Some expositors hold that Babylon is a veiled reference to Rome (Swete, A. T. Robertson), but it is probably best to take it as the kingdom of the Beast. Babylon stands "for world power in opposition to God" (Ryken, Wilhoit, Longman, *Dictionary of Biblical Imagery*, p. 69). Her arrogant king mirrors Lucifer himself (Isa. 14:4–12). *Babylon* is both an OT empire and the future empire of the Beast (Rev. 17:5). God will give her a double portion of judgment (Rev. 18:3–6), as the OT prophets foretold (Isa. 47:1ff.; Jer. 50:23ff.). Some scholars hold that ancient Rome fulfilled the prophecy (ISBE [1979], I, p. 391).

14:10. The phrase *wrath of God* occurs here for the first of 7 times in Rev. (14:10, 19; 15:1, 7; 16:1, 19; 19:15). The word *wrath* (θυμός) also refers to the wrath of the Devil (12:12) and the wrath of Babylon's fornication (14:8; 18:3).

The words *fire* (πῦρ) and *sulfur* (θεῖον) occur together 6 times in Rev.: twice referring to the fire and sulfur coming from the mouths of demonic horses (9:17, 18) and 4 times of the lake of fire and sulfur that is the final destination of all evil personages (14:10; 19:20; 20:10; 21:8).

The thought of molten rock, poisonous minerals and gases, the pain of fire, and endless existence should cause one to repent and turn to Christ for His gracious salvation. It is popular in some circles to contradict the Bible and deny that hell exists. But we must remember the words of William G. T. Shedd, "The strongest support of the doctrine of Endless Punishment is the teaching of Christ, the Redeemer of man" (*The Doctrine of Endless Punishment*). Christ taught, "Whosoever shall say, Thou fool, shall be in danger of hell fire [*gehenna*]" (Matt. 5:22). "It is profitable for thee that one of thy members should perish, and not that thy whole body should be cast into hell" (Matt. 5:29). The teaching of Christ on hell is very specific (Matt. 5:30; 10:28; 18:9; 23:15, 33; Mark 9:43, 45, 47; Luke 12:5). "And the smoke of their torment is going up into ages of ages, and they are having no rest day or night, who worship the beast and his image, and if anyone receives the mark of his name" (v. 11). The phraseology emphasizes not only their suffering but also their perception of the eternal continuance of their punishment. Peter L. Berger uses the illustration of a child so engrossed in play that he loses his perception of time and comes home late (*A Rumor of Angels*, pp. 72–75). But here we see that the wicked never lose their sense of the creeping pace of time (day and night) as they suffer forever and ever. "The punishment of the damned is not a temporary measure" (Mounce, p. 274). "With the emphatic 'forever and ever,' it makes the point absolutely clear that this terrible punishment will be their continual eternal destiny" (Osborne, *Rev.*, p. 542; see also his note on 14:11, pp. 547–48). In contrast to the wicked, the righteous will be so enraptured by the glories of heaven that time shall be no more. This passage is one of the strongest in Scripture in defending the reality of hell. R. A. Torrey notes the number of times that fire is mentioned in connection with the future punishment of the wicked (Matt. 7:19–20; 13:30, 41–42; John 15:6; Isa. 66:24; Heb. 6:8; 10:26–27; Rev. 20:15; 21:8; *What the Bible Teaches*, p. 305). "Here is the patience of the saints, the ones keeping the commandments of God and the faith in Jesus" (v. 12). The patient endurance of the saints is logical, for their suffering of persecution or death is soon over, but the suffering of the wicked will be endless. They keep His commandments and will have His good pleasure forever. The faith "in Jesus" is an objective genitive (A. T. Robertson, *Word Pictures*, VI,

---

14:11. For a formal defense of the doctrine of eternal punishment see Robert Peterson, *Hell on Trial: The Case for Eternal Punishment* (1995); Mark Minnick, *The Doctrine of Eternal Punishment* (1996). In a comparative study, *Four Views on Hell*, Walvoord defends a literal hell; Crockett, Hayes, and Pinnock defend divergent views.

14:12. This is the last time that *patience* is mentioned in Rev. For a summary see Rev. 1:9 note.

14 And I looked, and behold a white cloud, and upon the cloud one sat like unto the Son of man, having on his head a golden crown, and in his hand a sharp sickle.
15 And another angel came out of the temple, crying with a loud voice to him that sat on the cloud, Thrust in thy sickle, and reap: for the time is come for thee to reap; for the harvest of the earth is ripe.
16 And he that sat on the cloud thrust in his sickle on the earth; and the earth was reaped.
17 And another angel came out of the temple which is in heaven, he also having a sharp sickle.
18 And another angel came out from the altar, which had power over fire; and cried with a loud cry to him that had the sharp sickle, saying, Thrust in thy sharp sickle, and gather the clusters of the vine of the earth; for her grapes are fully ripe.
19 And the angel thrust in his sickle into the earth, and gathered the vine of the earth, and cast it into the great winepress of the wrath of God.
20 And the winepress was trodden without the city, and blood came out of the winepress, even unto the horse bridles, by the space of a thousand and six hundred furlongs.

p. 413). That faith is not a vague belief but active loyalty and trust. "And I heard a voice out of heaven saying, Write: Blessed are the dead who die in the Lord from now on. Yea, says the Spirit, that they may rest from their weary deeds, for their works are following after them" (v. 13). This is one of the most encouraging words in all the Bible to hard working servants of the Lord. Many times the labors of the saints seem to be in vain, but they often do not see the continuing benefits of what they have tried to do. Many times a pastor will plant a church that seems to remain a poor, struggling work, but after he is gone, men rise up from that congregation to make it a lighthouse of testimony for the Lord and pay tribute to the pastor who would not give up. What a blessing in glory it will be for saints who have given tracts, written hymns, or taught in Christian schools, to meet other saints who benefited by their labors. Spurgeon has a moving sermon on the rewards of the righteous ("A Voice from Heaven," Sermon 1219, The C. H. Spurgeon Collection, Ages Digital Library).

III. The Harvest and the Winepress. vv. 14–20.

"And I saw, and behold a white cloud, and upon the cloud one sitting who was like the Son of man, having upon his head a golden crown and

---

14:13. The verb to rest (ἀναπαύω) occurs only twice in Rev. (6:11; 14:13). It is the Lord Jesus Christ who gives His people rest (Matt. 11:28). The word labor (κόπος) refers to labor so severe it causes one to beat the breast in grief (κόπτω). It occurs only twice in Rev. (2:2; 14:13).

in his hand a sharp sickle" (v. 14). This is a clear reference to the vision of Daniel, "I saw in the night visions, and, behold, one like the Son of man came with the clouds of heaven" (Dan. 7:13). He has the golden victor's crown on His head. In His hand He has a sharp sickle, which may be used for either the wheat harvest (v. 15) or the grape harvest (v. 19). Some expositors hold that the wheat harvest (vv. 14–16) refers to the harvest of good grain, Tribulation saints (Alford, Swete, Scott, Osborne), but most premillennial expositors hold that they both refer to the campaign of Armageddon (Seiss, Newell, J. B. Smith, A. C. Gaebelein, Ottman, Thomas, as well as symbolic interpreters, Morris, Beale, etc.). "And another angel came forth from the sanctuary, crying with a great voice to the one sitting on the cloud: Send your sickle and reap, because the hour to reap came, because the harvest of the earth was ripe" (v. 15). This fourth angel is announcing the will of God: the specific time for reaping has come. He comes from the sanctuary; all judgment comes from the holiness and righteousness of God. Some expositors argue over whether the verb *was dried* (ξηραίνω) means "was ripe" or "was withered." But the harvest of evil, although right on time, is always withered and deadly. Joel saw the gathering of the heathen to the valley of Jehoshaphat: "Put ye in the sickle, for the harvest is ripe: come, get you down; for the press is full, the fats overflow; for their wickedness is great. Multitudes, multitudes in the valley of decision: for the day of the Lord is near in the valley of decision" (Joel 3:13–14). "And the one sitting on the cloud cast his sickle upon the earth and the earth was reaped" (v. 16). The present English idiom for *cast* (ἔβαλεν) is "swung" his sickle. That is a simple way of describing the campaign of Armageddon. Now the Spirit changes the imagery from the wheat harvest to the grape harvest in order to intensify the impact. "And another angel came out from the sanctuary which is in heaven, he himself also having a sharp sickle" (v. 17). This is the fifth angel from the sanctuary who is concerned with reaping. "And another angel came forth out of the altar, one who had authority over fire, and he cried with a great voice to the one who had the sharp sickle, saying: Send your sharp sickle and gather the clusters of the vine of the earth, because her grapes are fully ripe" (v. 18). This is the exact time when the grapes of wrath are

---

14:14. The word *sickle* (δρέπανον) occurs 7 times in Rev. (14:14, 15, 16, 17, 18 [twice], 19) and only in Mark 4:29 in the rest of the NT.

14:18. The words *clusters* (βότρυας, only here in the NT) and *ripe grapes* (σταφυλαὶ, only here and in Matt. 7:16; Luke 6:44 in the NT) are old words that occur together in the words of the butler's dream (Gen. 40:10 LXX).

The verb *to be fully ripe* (ἀκμάζω) occurs only here in the NT. The verb (τρυγάω, *to gather fruit*) occurs only in Rev. 14:18, 19; Luke 6:44 in the NT.

fully ripe that Armageddon comes. The Lord said to Jeremiah, "Therefore prophesy thou against them all these words, and say unto them, The Lord shall roar from on high, and utter his voice from his holy habitation; he shall mightily roar upon his habitation; he shall give a shout, as they that tread the grapes, against all the inhabitants of the earth. A noise shall come even to the ends of the earth; for the Lord hath a controversy with the nations, he will plead with all flesh; he will give them that are wicked to the sword, saith the Lord" (Jer. 25:30–31). "And the angel cast his sickle to the earth and gathered the vine of the earth, and cast it into the great winepress of the wrath of God" (v. 19). The image of God crushing His foes in a winepress of wrath comes from Isaiah 63:1–6. It is the prophesied "day of vengeance" (Isa. 63:4). In the synagogue at Nazareth the Lord Jesus quoted Isaiah 61:1–2 and applied it to Himself (Luke 4:16–21). But He broke off His quotation and did not quote "the day of vengeance" because that referred to this second coming in judgment. "And the winepress was trodden outside the city, and blood came out of the winepress unto the horse bridles for sixteen hundred stadia" (v. 20). The sixteen hundred stadia is a distance of nearly two hundred miles, about the length of Palestine. It is interesting to note that

---

14:19. *The vine of the earth* is a contrast to the Lord's vine (Isa. 5:1–7).

14:20. The idea of blood flowing to the depth of horse bridles is often dismissed as a symbol, but if millions of people are locked in combat in the small area of Palestine, it may be horribly literal in its fulfillment. The valley of Megiddo has been the scene of major battles all through history. For example:

Thothmes III, 1468 B.C.
Amenhotep II, 1429 B.C.
Rameses II, 1350 B.C.
Deborah and Barak vs. Sisera, 13th cent. B.C.
Sargon, 722 B.C.
Sennacharib, 710 B.C.
Pharaoh Necho vs. Josiah, 608 B.C.
Nebuchadnezzar, 606 B.C.
Ptolemy, 197 B.C.
Antiochus Epiphanes, 168 B.C.
Pompey, 63 B.C.
Titus, A.D. 70.
Khosru, A.D. 614.
Omar, A.D. 637.
Crusaders (St. Louis), A.D. 909.
Richard the Lion-Hearted vs. Saladin, A.D. 1187.
Ottoman Turks, A.D. 1616.
(We ought not forget Viscount Allenby of Megiddo, 1918.)
See ZPEB, "Megiddo," IV, pp. 164–76; ISBE (1986), "Megiddo," III, pp. 309–11.

modern warfare in the area has been with Syria and Lebanon in the north and Egypt in the south, but Bosrah in Edom is on the Jordanian, Arabian side to the east. The whole land will be enveloped in the bloodbath. Walvoord suggests that "a 200 mile radius from Jerusalem will be the center of the final carnage where the armies of the world will be gathered at the time of the second coming of Christ" (*Rev.*, p. 223).

Practical Applications from Revelation 14

1. Being right with God brings a spiritual stamp of approval from God (v. 1). "Study [be zealous] to show yourself approved to God, a workman who needs not to be ashamed, rightly dividing the word of truth" (II Tim. 2:15).
2. Some spiritual praise can come only from enduring sufferings (v. 3). "I thank my God always on your behalf, for the grace of God which is given you by Jesus Christ" (I Cor. 1:4).
3. Being devoted to Christ brings special honor in heaven (v. 4). "For the Son of man shall come in the glory of his Father with his angels; and then he shall reward every man according to his works" (Matt. 16:27).
4. All men should glorify and worship God, but only believers actually do (v. 7). "But the manifestation of the Spirit is given to every man to profit withal" (I Cor. 12:7).
5. Sin always brings consequences (vv. 9–10). "Be not deceived; God is not mocked: for whatsoever a man sows, that shall he also reap" (Gal. 6:7).
6. All saints have need of patience (v. 12). "For you have need of patience, that, after you have done the will of God, you might receive the promise" (Heb. 10:36).
7. Those who die in the faith are eternally blessed (v. 13). "For to me to live is Christ, and to die is gain" (Phil. 1:21).
8. There are terrible consequences to all those who reject God (vv. 19–20). "For the wrath of God is revealed from heaven against all ungodliness and unrighteousness of men, who hold down the truth in unrighteousness" (Rom. 1:18).

Prayer

O God of our salvation, we give thanks to You for redeeming us through the blood of the Lamb. Sustain us in our labors. We praise You for the saints' everlasting rest. Help us to serve You well now. For Jesus' sake. Amen.

Revelation 15:1–16:21

The Seven Angels of the Last Plagues

Persons

Seven angels of the last plagues   The four living beings
The victors over the Beast

Persons referred to

Moses   The saints
The Lamb   All nations

Places mentioned

Heaven   The temple in heaven
A sea of glass

Doctrines taught

Angels   The greatness of God
The wrath of God   Judgment
The Beast (Antichrist)   Holiness
Singing in worship

1 And I saw another sign in heaven, great and marvellous, seven angels having the seven last plagues; for in them is filled up the wrath of God.

2 And I saw as it were a sea of glass mingled with fire: and them that had gotten the victory over the beast, and over his image, and over his mark, and over the number of his name, stand on the sea of glass, having the harps of God.

3 And they sing the song of Moses the servant of God, and the song of the Lamb, saying, Great and marvellous are thy works, Lord God Almighty; just and true are thy ways, thou King of saints.

Revelation 15 Exposition

I. The Sign of the Seven Last Plagues. v. 1.

"And I saw another sign in heaven, great and marvelous, seven angels having the seven last plagues, because in them the wrath of God is completed" (v. 1). The main parenthesis is over (Rev. 12–14); the final series of seven judgments is now ready to begin. In them the wrath of God will be finished, brought to an end (ἐτελέσθη). The Lord warned the Israelites four times that He would chastise them seven times for their sins (Lev. 26:18, 21, 24, 28). This is the only sign that is called "great and marvellous," a phrase repeated only in 15:3. The verse sets the stage for the whole vision that follows (15:2–16:21). The vision of the seventh trumpet showed the sanctuary of God open in heaven (Rev. 11:19). The seven bowls of wrath come out of the seventh trumpet. The voice from the sanctuary commands the seven angels to pour out their bowls on the earth (Rev. 16:1).

II. The Scene in Heaven. vv. 2–8.

"And I saw as a sea of glass having been mingled with fire, and the ones who were victorious over the beast, and over his image, and over the number of his name, standing upon the sea of glass, having harps of God" (v. 2). The world empires arose from the sea (Dan. 7:2–3); the beast rose up out of the sea (Rev. 13:1). The wicked are like the ever-restless sea

---

15:1. We must remember that the sea of glass is before the throne of God, shining with all the reflected glory and splendor of God Himself (Rev. 4:6).

The word marvelous (θαυμαστός) occurs only in this context in Rev. (15:1, 3). Peter notes that believers are called out of darkness into His marvelous light (I Pet. 2:9).

For the phrase wrath of God, see Rev. 14:10 note.

15:2. In heaven, all God's people will be in perfect tune, able to sing to God's glory as they had always wished to. Matthew Henry comments, "They extol the greatness of God's works, and the justice and truth of his ways, both in delivering his people and destroying their enemies." They have "harps of God." Does that mean divinely tuned?

4 *Who shall not fear thee, O Lord, and glorify thy name? for thou only art holy: for all nations shall come and worship before thee; for thy judgments are made manifest.*
5 *And after that I looked, and, behold, the temple of the tabernacle of the testimony in heaven was opened:*
6 *And the seven angels came out of the temple, having the seven plagues, clothed in pure and white linen, and having their breasts girded with golden girdles.*
7 *And one of the four beasts gave unto the seven angels seven golden vials full of the wrath of God, who liveth for ever and ever.*
8 *And the temple was filled with smoke from the glory of God, and from his power; and no man was able to enter into the temple, till the seven plagues of the seven angels were fulfilled.*

(Isa. 57:20), but in heaven the sea is under the complete control of God, like solid glass, upon which the saints may safely stand to sing the praises of God. But the sea is shot through with light that coruscates like fire through the sea. It appears like the internal fire of an opal. The fire may well presage the fire of divine judgment about to fall on the wicked world. The victorious remnant that endured the fires of persecution now stands on the fiery sea that shines with the glory of God. They are prepared to sing His praises. "And they sing the song of Moses, the slave of God, and the song of the Lamb, saying,

> Great and marvelous are your works,
> Lord God, the Almighty;
> Righteous and true are your ways,
> King of the nations" (v. 3).

Moses was the servant of God (Exod. 14:31; Num. 12:7; Ps. 105:26; Heb. 3:5). The psalmist exhorted, "O sing unto the Lord a new song; for he hath done marvellous things" (Ps. 98:1). "The works of the Lord are great" (Ps. 111:2; 110:2 LXX). David cried, "Marvellous are thy works" (Ps. 139:14). Isaiah prophesied that the Lord would do a marvelous work

---

15:3. The editors of the Textus Receptus drew *King of saints* from the Latin tradition (only two old Greek manuscripts have it, 296, 2049, and they were unknown to the KJV translators). The manuscript evidence for *King of the nations* (Pss. 72:11; 113:4; Jer. 10:7) and *King of the ages* (Jer. 10:10) is almost evenly divided. Both ideas are orthodox, but *King of the nations* has a better link with the context (v. 4). For a brief list of the manuscript evidence, see Metzger, *A Textual Commentary on the Greek New Testament*, p. 755.

For a summary of *the Almighty* see Rev. 1:8 note.

The great word *righteous* (δίκαιος) occurs for the first time here. It is applied to God 4 times (Rev. 15:3; 16:5, 7; 19:2) and to saints once, in the context of reward (22:11). No man is naturally righteous (Rom. 3:10); he receives righteousness as a gift through faith in Jesus Christ (Rom. 5:17; 10:9–10). See ZPEB, "Righteousness," V, pp. 104–18; Elwell, Walter, *Evangelical Dictionary of Biblical Theology*, "Righteousness," pp. 687–89.

of judgment among His people (Isa. 29:14). It is marvelous insight that they bind together the songs of the past, the song of Moses (Exod. 15:1–19), with spontaneous praise for their own deliverance and victory. What a precious thought of singing the hymns of all ages and all nations to the glory of the one true God. He is the Almighty, the "Lord God of hosts" (Isa. 22:15 LXX), the all-powerful God, but He works invariably according to His holy and just nature, and His ways are true, according to the nature of divine reality and not according to the twisted world of the Dragon. "A God of truth and without iniquity, just and right is he" (Deut. 32:4). Spurgeon has a powerful sermon on the parallels between God's deliverance of Israel at the Red Sea, His deliverance for believers in the present church age, and the final, eschatological deliverance in heaven with songs of triumph ("Israel in Egypt," Sermon 136, *The C. H. Spurgeon Collection*, Ages Digital Library).

"Who shall not fear you, O Lord,
And shall glorify your name?
Because you only are holy,
Because all nations shall come
And shall worship before you,
Because your righteous deeds are made manifest" (v. 4).

These saints view God with profound reverence; they know that all the universe should glorify the God who made it. God is perfectly holy, the source of all blessings (Deut. 28:8) and holiness (Isa. 63:18) for His creatures. David called God "The governor [ruler] among the nations" (Ps. 22:28) and prophesied, "All nations whom thou hast made shall come and worship before thee, O Lord; and shall glorify thy name" (Ps. 86:9). During the millennial reign all nations will literally come before His temple to worship Him (Isa. 2:2–4; Mic. 4:1–3; Zech. 14:16–19). His righteous deeds were made manifest in the days of Moses (Exod. 15:6–11) and in the days of the Lord's public ministry (Acts 2:22ff.) and will be manifested in the coming judgments of the Tribulation (Rev. 19:2–3). "And after these things I saw, and the sanctuary of the tabernacle of witness in heaven was opened" (v. 5). When the glory of the Lord filled the earthly sanctuary, a cloud covered the tent of the congregation (Exod. 40:34). The tables of the law were a testimony, or witness, of the Lord to the sins of the people (Exod. 25:16). Stephen spoke of the tabernacle of witness in the wilderness (Acts 7:44). But here the heavenly sanctuary was

---

15:4. The preacher held that the whole duty of man was to "fear God, and keep his commandments" (Eccles. 12:13). Reverence and obedience toward God remain our responsibility. This word *holy* (ὅσιος) occurs only twice in Rev. (15:4; 16:5), both times applied to God by saints and angels.

opened to witness to the sins of the whole earth. The apostle Paul concluded, "All the world [stands] guilty before God" (Rom. 3:19). In OT times only the high priest could open, and enter, the innermost sanctuary, but here the sanctuary was opened to let seven angels out. "And the seven angels who have the seven plagues came out from the sanctuary, having been clothed in clean, shining linen, and having been girded around the breasts with golden sashes" (v. 6). The OT priests also served with a "holy linen coat" (Lev. 16:4). Are these angels the seven archangels of Jewish tradition (Enoch 20:1–8)? The article *the* implies *the well-known angels*. The *clean, shining clothing* shows that they are holy angels, coming from the holy presence of God. There is not a shred of vindictiveness in what they are about to do. They bring the righteous judgment of God upon the wicked world and the evil Beast who rules it. The golden sash may well symbolize the right to bring judgment (see Rev. 1:13). Osborne suggests that "a golden sash symbolized royalty" and "with 1:13 may indicate that these angels are emissaries of Christ" (*Rev.*, p. 570). "And one of the four living beings gave to the seven angels seven golden bowls filled with the wrath of the God who is living into the ages of the ages" (v. 7). Abraham called on the name of the Lord, "the everlasting God" (El Olam, Gen. 21:33). It is not accidental that these judgments are called *plagues*. There are strong parallels with the Egyptian plagues of the Exodus. Proud Pharaoh is a forerunner of the arrogant Antichrist. Neither is it accidental that the twenty-four elders offered to the Lamb golden bowls filled with incense and the prayers of the saints (Rev. 5:8), and now seven golden bowls filled with the wrath of God are given to the seven angels of judgment. God has heard the prayers of His people and will see to it that proper judgment is poured out upon the persecutors of His people. "Vengeance belongs to me, I will recompense, says the Lord" (Heb. 10:30). "And the sanctuary was filled with smoke from the glory of God and from his power, and no one was able to enter into the sanctuary until the seven plagues of the seven angels should be finished" (v. 8). The wrath of God is kindled against sinful mankind, and no one can prevent the Almighty from pouring out His wrath on the earth. Just as the earthly sanctuary was filled with the smoke of incense (Exod. 30:7–8), so the heavenly sanctuary is filled with smoke until the divine judgments are completed. Isaiah also saw the celestial sanctuary filled with smoke and cried out for cleansing (Isa. 6:4–5).

15:7. The word *bowl* (φιάλη) occurs only in Rev. in the NT. The 24 elders had golden bowls filled with the prayers of the saints (Rev. 5:8), but in this context bowls of wrath are mentioned 10 times (15:7; 16:1, 2, 3, 4, 8, 10, 12, 17; 17:1) and only once more in the book (21:9). The contents of the bowls determine their significance.

Practical Applications from Revelation 15

1. The wrath of God against sin is sure to be fulfilled (v. 1). "For he cometh to judge the earth: with righteousness shall he judge the world, and the people with equity" (Ps. 98:9).
2. The martyrs are unharmed by the persecution they had to endure (v. 2). "Love the Lord, all you his saints! The Lord preserves the faithful but abundantly repays the one who acts in pride" (Ps. 31:23, ESV).
3. The heroes of the past (like Moses) will not be forgotten in glory (v. 3). "The righteous shall be in everlasting remembrance" (Ps. 112:6). No saint will forget Hebrews 11.
4. The praise of God will be the delight of heaven (v. 3). David exhorted, "But let the righteous be glad; let them rejoice before God: yea, let them exceedingly rejoice. Sing unto God, sing praises to his name" (Ps. 68:3–4a).
5. All nations and all saints in glory shall worship God (v. 4). "For the Lord is great, and greatly to be praised. . . . O worship the Lord in the beauty of holiness: fear before him, all the earth" (Ps. 96:4, 9).
6. Judgment on sin as well as blessing on righteousness comes from God (v. 7). "For we are consumed by thine anger, and by thy wrath are we troubled. . . . So teach us to number our days, that we may apply our hearts unto wisdom" (Ps. 90:7, 12).
7. No one can distract God from His purpose of judging sin (v. 8). "He shall judge the world in righteousness" (Ps. 9:8).

Prayer

Dear Lord, put a song in our hearts that we may sing Your praises before men. Help us to add our voices to the worship of all nations who reverence and glorify You. You alone are perfectly holy. Sanctify us for Your service. Amen.

The Bowls of Wrath

Persons

The seven angels

The Beast worshipers

The angel of the waters

The blasphemers of God

The kings of the east

Three unclean spirits

The Dragon (Satan)

The Beast

The False Prophet

The kings of the earth

Jesus Christ ("I")

Persons referred to

Saints

Prophets

A thief

Places mentioned

The temple in heaven

The earth

The sea

The sun

The river Euphrates

The valley of Armageddon

Babylon

Doctrines taught

The wrath of God

The mark of the Beast

The righteousness of God

Judgment

The almighty power of God

Repentance

The Devil

Armageddon

1 And I heard a great voice out of the temple saying to the seven angels, Go your ways, and pour out the vials of the wrath of God upon the earth.

2 And the first went, and poured out his vial upon the earth; and there fell a noisome and grievous sore upon the men which had the mark of the beast, and upon them which worshipped his image.

Revelation 16 Exposition

I. The First Bowl: Wrath on the Earth. vv. 1–2.

"And I heard a great voice out of the sanctuary saying to the seven angels: Go and pour out the seven bowls of the wrath of God into the earth" (v. 1). This voice picks up the theme of judgment from the seventh trumpet (Rev. 11:15–19) and concentrates it into this final series of judgments. It is plainly a divine command to keep going and keep pouring out (present tense) the bowls of wrath. One at a time in close succession all seven angels proceed to do just that. It is a solemn thought that although there are so many legions of angels in heaven (Matt. 26:53), when the time of the final judgments on earth comes, God summons a mere seven angels to come forth and break the power of earth. Jeremiah prayed, "Pour out thy fury upon the heathen that know thee not" (Jer. 10:25). Matthew Henry observes that all that wicked men think belongs to themselves is now given to destruction: "their earth, their air, their sea, their rivers, their cities, all consigned over to ruin, all accursed for the sake of the wickedness of that people." "And the first went and poured out his bowl into the earth, and it became a bad and evil sore upon the ones who have the mark of the beast and who are worshiping his image" (v. 2). The incurable corruption in their hearts now breaks forth into physical maladies. Since it is caused by their sinfulness, there is no medical cure. This bowl is parallel to the sixth Egyptian plague (Exod. 9:8–11). The very word *sore* (ἕλκος) occurs in Exodus 9:9–10 in the Septuagint. The sores caused the Egyptian magicians to flee for they had no ability to withstand them

---

16:1. The verb *to pour out* (ἐκχέω) occurs 9 times in Rev., all in this chapter (16:1, 2, 3, 4, 6, 8, 10, 12, 17).

For a summary of the word *wrath* (θυμός) see Rev. 14:10 note.

16:2. The regular words *bad and evil* (κακὸν καὶ πονηρὸν) become an exercise in ingenuity for translators: "noisome and grievous" (KJV), "a baneful and painful ulcer" (Rotherham), "loathsome and malignant" (NASB), "ugly and painful" (NIV), "disgusting and virulent sores" (NJB), "horrible, painful sores" (NET), "horrible, malignant sores" (NLT), "harmful and painful" (ESV), "bad and malignant sore" (A. T. Robertson, *Word Pictures*, VI, p. 420), "a suppurated wound" (Thayer, p. 204), "a foul and angry sore" (Arndt and Gingrich, p. 251). The modern idea is probably "severe and incurable" sore. The word *sore* (ἕλκος) occurs only twice in Rev. (vv. 2, 11).

3 And the second angel poured out his vial upon the sea; and it became as the blood of a dead man: and every living soul died in the sea.

4 And the third angel poured out his vial upon the rivers and fountains of waters; and they became blood.

5 And I heard the angel of the waters say, Thou art righteous, O Lord, which art, and wast, and shalt be, because thou hast judged thus.

6 For they have shed the blood of saints and prophets, and thou hast given them blood to drink; for they are worthy.

7 And I heard another out of the altar say, Even so, Lord God Almighty, true and righteous are thy judgments.

(Exod. 9:11). The only other occurrence of the word in the NT is in reference to the sores that afflicted the beggar Lazarus (Luke 16:21). Symbolic interpreters treat the sore as a "moral sore" (Scott). Beale argues that the trumpets and the bowls are really the same plagues seen from different viewpoints (*Rev.*, p. 808).

II. The Second Bowl: Wrath on the Sea. v. 3.

"And the second poured out his bowl into the sea, and it became blood as of a dead person, and every living soul that was in the sea died" (v. 3). The idea of the seas becoming like the coagulating blood of a dead person is a grim picture for the conservation movement. Their concerns are not mere hysteria. The selfish pollution of the seas is already having a disastrous effect all over the world. But in this plague God will bring the consequences to everyone's attention. This is a parallel to the first Egyptian plague. Aaron smote the waters of the Nile with the rod of God and the waters turned to blood; the fish in the river died; and the Egyptians could not drink of the water (Exod. 7:19–21). Since the Nile sustained the entire Egyptian culture and economy, it was a catastrophic blow. If the seas become polluted, the entire fishing industry will be wiped out. Many nations depend on the seas for a large portion of their food. The premillennial interpreters defend a literal interpretation (Seiss, Newell, J. B. Smith, Walvoord, etc.). LaHaye stresses the "unbearable stench" and "potential disease" of the situation (*Rev.*, p. 251). The symbolic interpreters take it as referring to moral corruption and apostasy (Scott, Ottman) or spiritual and psychological torment (Beale).

III. The Third Bowl: Wrath on Rivers and Springs. vv. 4–7.

"And the third poured out his bowl into the rivers and springs of waters, and they became blood" (v. 4). The Lord commanded Moses to extend

---

16:3. For a summary of the word *blood* (αἶμα) see Rev. 1:5 note.

8 And the fourth angel poured out his vial upon the sun; and power was given unto him to scorch men with fire.
9 And men were scorched with great heat, and blasphemed the name of God, which hath power over these plagues: and they repented not to give him glory.

the plagues to the streams, rivers, ponds, and all pools of water "that they may become blood" (Exod. 7:19). That plainly included the ponds and canal systems throughout Egypt. Thus, the third bowl turns all the rest of the natural sources of water into blood. There is nothing left that is safe to drink. "And I heard the angel of the waters saying:

> You are righteous, the one who is and who was, the
> Holy One,
> Because you judged these things,
> Because they poured out the blood of saints and prophets;
> And you have given them blood to drink,
> They are worthy (vv. 5–6).

In a tribulation context Isaiah prophesied that the Lord will deliver the remnant of His people and defeat their oppressors: "And I will feed them that oppress you with their own flesh; and they shall be drunken with their own blood, as with sweet wine: and all flesh shall know that I the Lord am thy Saviour and thy Redeemer, the mighty One of Jacob" (Isa. 49:26). The psalmist said, "Righteous art thou, O Lord, and upright are thy judgments" (Ps. 119:137). "The Lord is righteous in all his ways, and holy in all his works" (Ps. 145:17). "And I heard the altar saying: Yea, Lord God Almighty, true and righteous are your judgments" (v. 7). We have already noted that an angel came out of the altar and spoke (Rev. 14:18). All heaven testifies to the true and holy nature of God. He cannot act unjustly or be corrupted. "The judgments of the Lord are true and righteous altogether" (Ps. 19:9).

IV. The Fourth Bowl: Wrath on the Sun. vv. 8–9.

"And the fourth poured out his bowl upon the sun, and it was given to him to scorch men with fire" (v. 8). Premillennial interpreters argue that the sun will literally flare up in heat (Seiss, Newell, J. B. Smith, Walvoord). Symbolic interpreters hold that the sun symbolizes supreme government on earth, which becomes the source of great anguish (Scott,

---

16:5. For a summary of the word *righteous* (δίκαιος) see Rev. 15:3 note.

16:8. The verb *to burn with fire* (καυματίζω) occurs only twice in Rev. (16:8, 9) and only twice in the rest of the NT (Matt. 13:6; Mark 4:6), for the action of the sun on tender plants. For color photographs of the planets and basic astronomical facts, see the author's *Stars Speak*, 2nd ed., 2002.

10 And the fifth angel poured out his vial upon the seat of the beast; and his kingdom was full of darkness; and they gnawed their tongues for pain,
11 And blasphemed the God of heaven because of their pains and their sores, and re-pented not of their deeds.

A. C. Gaebelein). Beale holds that the fire is "likely not literal" (p. 821). Osborne postpones his interpretation until he sees what will really hap-pen (p. 586)! People do not realize what a delicate balance exists in the relation of Earth to the sun. Venus, the next planet closer to the sun has an average temperature of 867 °F; the next planet farther from the sun, Mars, has an average temperature of -85 °F; Earth has an average temper-ature of a pleasant 59 °F. A very slight increase in actual energy being ra-diated from the sun could easily raise the temperature on Earth by a hundred degrees! It is not pleasant to think of what that could do to the air conditioning systems on Earth. "And men were scorched with great heat, and they blasphemed the name of God who has the authority over these plagues, and did not repent to give him glory" (v. 9). They despised the one Being, God, who can control the sun, and would not repent (change their thinking). The highest end for every man is to bring glory to God, but these men give Him blasphemy. Note that true repentance gives glory to God. Sometimes the unsaved will express sorrow that there are consequences to sin, but they have no intention to change and sub-mit to God. Spurgeon has a convicting sermon on such false repentance ("Judgments and No Repentance; Repentance and No Salvation," Sermon 2054, *The C. H. Spurgeon Collection*, Ages Digital Library).

V. The Fifth Bowl: Wrath on the Throne of the Beast. vv. 10–11.

"And the fifth poured out his bowl on the throne of the beast, and his kingdom became darkened, and they gnawed their tongues from the dis-tress" (v. 10). The literal interpreters take it as literal darkness (Seiss, Newell, J. B. Smith, Walvoord); the symbolical interpreters take it as metaphorical darkness (Scott, Strauss, Beale). This is a parallel to the ninth Egyptian plague, in which thick darkness that might be felt covered the land of Egypt (Exod. 10:21–23). The plague was a demonstration that

---

16:9. The verb *to blaspheme* (βλασφημέω) occurs 3 times in this chapter (Rev. 16:9, 11, 21) and only one other time, of the Beast's blasphemy, in Rev. 13:6. Although the verb may refer to reviling or defaming a human being (I Cor. 10:30), it usually denotes irrever-ent language toward God (Mark 3:28–29; John 10:36; Rom. 2:24; I Tim. 1:20; 6:1).

16:10. Out of the 47 times that the word *throne* (θρόνος) is used in Rev., this is the only time that it denotes the throne of the Beast. That will be quickly followed by the great voice from the throne in heaven (v. 17).

The verb *to gnaw, bite like an animal* (μασάομαι) occurs only here in the NT.

12 And the sixth angel poured out his vial upon the great river Euphrates; and the water thereof was dried up, that the way of the kings of the east might be prepared.

the Egyptian sun god Ra could not help them. It lasted only three days, but it was so severe that Pharaoh offered to let the Hebrews go if they would leave their flocks and herds behind (Exod. 10:24). The Beast worshipers will be distressed but still will not leave their sins. "And they blasphemed the God of heaven because of their distresses and because of their sores, but they did not repent from their works" (v. 11). They rejected the very things that could have moved them to God and instead bitterly attacked God. In contrast, "Daniel blessed the God of heaven" (Dan. 2:19). It is no accident that Joel portrays the Day of the Lord as "a day of darkness and of gloominess, a day of clouds and thick darkness, as the morning spread upon the mountains: a great people and a strong; there hath not been ever the like, neither shall be any more after it, even to the years of many generations" (Joel 2:2). He goes on to describe the invading armies and to say, "The earth shall quake before them; the heavens shall tremble: the sun and the moon shall be dark, and the stars shall withdraw their shining" (Joel 2:10). The Devil is the prince of darkness, who leads his followers into thick darkness.

VI. The Sixth Bowl: Wrath on the River Euphrates. v. 12.

"And the sixth poured out his bowl upon the great river, the Euphrates, and its water was dried up, in order that the way of the kings from the east might be prepared" (v. 12). Here there is great agreement that the literal river Euphrates will dry up (Seiss, Newell, J. B. Smith, Scott, Ottman, Strauss, Walvoord, Thomas, Osborne). Probably the reason for this agreement is that the OT prophets repeatedly prophesied that God would dry up the Euphrates, "the river" (Isa. 11:15; Jer. 50:35–38; 51:36; Zech. 10:11). God does this for the remnant, "the redeemed," to pass over (Isa. 51:10–11). A. C. Gaebelein argues that the eastern boundary of the Roman Empire is destroyed. However, Beale still takes it figuratively (p. 827). "The way of the kings of the east" is a definite prophecy of a vast invasion by a coalition of eastern empires. There is no doubt that China, India, Japan, Korea, Indonesia, Pakistan, and others view them-

---

16:11. This is the last time the verb *to repent* (μετανοέω) occurs in Rev. For a summary see Rev. 2:5 note.

16:12. The Euphrates River is named 21 times in Scripture, but the prophets sometimes refer to it simply as "the river" (Isa. 11:15). It was the northeastern boundary of God's covenant with Abraham (Gen. 15:18). For background on the river Euphrates, see Rev. 9:14 note.

13 And I saw three unclean spirits like frogs come out of the mouth of the dragon, and out of the mouth of the beast, and out of the mouth of the false prophet.
14 For they are the spirits of devils, working miracles, which go forth unto the kings of the earth and of the whole world, to gather them to the battle of that great day of God Almighty.
15 Behold, I come as a thief. Blessed is he that watcheth, and keepeth his garments, lest he walk naked, and they see his shame.
16 And he gathered them together into a place called in the Hebrew tongue Armageddon.

selves as important players on the international stage. Some kind of coalition will rebel and come against the empire of the Beast.

Parenthesis: The Origin of Armageddon. vv. 13–16.

"And I saw three unclean spirits like frogs come out of the mouth of the dragon, and out of the mouth of the beast, and out of the mouth of the false prophet" (v. 13). Here, for the first time in Revelation, we see the satanic trinity mentioned in the same verse. The Devil tries to counterfeit the true nature of God. These three monsters of depravity gather the armies of the world together. "For they are spirits of demons, working signs, who go forth upon the kings of the whole inhabited earth to gather them to the war of the great day of God the Almighty" (v. 14). The Lord Jesus warned in the Olivet Discourse that "false messiahs and false prophets shall arise and shall present great signs and wonders" (Matt. 24:24). The Bible clearly teaches that demons incite men to violence, even to men's own harm (Mark 5:1–5). What a contrast to the true Spirit of God, whose fruit is goodness, righteousness, and truth (Eph. 5:9)! The reference to "the kings of the whole inhabited earth" makes clear that it is not merely the kings of the east that are gathering, but every nation on earth will send troops to Palestine for this final "world war." Now John records the voice of the Lord Jesus: "Behold, I am coming as a thief. Blessed is the one who is watching and keeping his garments, lest he walk naked and they see his shame" (v. 15). The picture is that of a householder who is dressed and alert, ready for the thief he knows is coming in the dark. Every believer can apply that to himself in the face of the Devil's attack. The Lord Jesus gave a similar command in the Olivet Discourse: "Keep

---

16:13. The word *frog* (βάτραχος) occurs only here in the NT. The only OT mention of frogs is in reference to the Egyptian plague (Exod. 8:2–13; Pss. 78:45; 105:30).

16:14. The apostle Paul has words of solemn warning against "spirits who lead astray and teachings of demons": their lies and hypocrisy cause some to depart from the Faith (1 Tim. 4:1–2).

For a summary of the word *battle* (πόλεμος) see Rev. 9:7 note.

on watching therefore, because you do not know the day your Lord comes" (Matt. 24:42). But the meaning in this context is plainly that people in the Tribulation period should trust in the Lord and be converted that they may be among the "sheep" (Matt. 25:31–46). "And he gathered them together into the place called in Hebrew Armageddon" (v. 16). The antecedent of he is plainly God the Almighty in v. 14. But J. B. Smith remarks on the synergism of the demons in v. 14 also gathering the armies to this last battle (Rev., p. 235). The word Armageddon, "Mount of Megiddo," has provoked a huge discussion for interpreters (see Vincent, Word Studies, II, p. 542; Osborne, Rev., pp. 594–96). Zechariah mentions the mourning in the valley of Megiddo (Zech. 12:11). Although there is no mountain named Megiddo, the city of Megiddo guards the pass between Mount Carmel toward the Mediterranean and the mountains of Samaria toward the southeast. The great trade route between Damascus and Egypt, the Via Maris, ran right past Megiddo through the pass. Another trade route, the Way of the Mountains, ran from Accho on the coast, past Megiddo, to the city of Samaria, making Megiddo one of the most important crossroads in Palestine. One can stand on the tel of Megiddo and look northeast across the valley of Jezreel (or Esdraelon) twenty miles to the Nazareth escarpment in the north, or one can stand on the Mount of Temptation at Nazareth and look southward across the valley and see that it is a perfect battleground. (For a list of major battles at Megiddo, see Rev. 14:20 note). Alford (Greek Testament, IV, p. 702) directs attention to the reference to the Hebrew language. In the Hebrew text the kings of Canaan came and fought by the waters of Megiddo (Judg. 5:19). The Kishon River flows through the valley, past Mount Carmel, to the sea. Deborah and Barak had to face the army of Sisera in that valley. In the providence of God the waters of the Kishon swept away the chariots of Sisera (Judg. 5:21). In the Hebrew parallelism:

> "They fought from heaven;
> The stars in their courses fought against Sisera" (Judg. 5:20).

In the same way Armageddon will be the last battle on earth, fought and won by the sovereign power of God, before the setting up of the millennial kingdom (Rev. 19:11–21).

16:16. Liberal commentators dismiss the whole idea of "Armageddon": "Probing of John's meaning of the 'battle of Armageddon' thus reveals that we should not be concerned to locate it on a map or give it a date. It is not the prediction of some historical battle" (Boring, Rev., p. 177). Osborne provides a convenient list of interpretations of "Armageddon" (Rev., pp. 594–96). One can stand on the Nazareth escarpment and see Megiddo and Mount Carmel across the valley 30 miles to the south.

17 And the seventh angel poured out his vial into the air; and there came a great voice out of the temple of heaven, from the throne, saying, It is done.

18 And there were voices, and thunders, and lightnings; and there was a great earthquake, such as was not since men were upon the earth, so mighty an earthquake, and so great.

19 And the great city was divided into three parts, and the cities of the nations fell: and great Babylon came in remembrance before God, to give unto her the cup of the wine of the fierceness of his wrath.

20 And every island fled away, and the mountains were not found.

21 And there fell upon men a great hail out of heaven, every stone about the weight of a talent: and men blasphemed God because of the plague of the hail; for the plague thereof was exceeding great.

VII. The Seventh Bowl: Wrath upon the Air. vv. 17–21.

"And the seventh poured out his bowl upon the air, and a great voice came out of the sanctuary from the throne, saying, It has come to pass" (v. 17). The solitary perfect tense verb *It has come to pass* (γέγονεν) is a divinely simple way of showing that the wrath of God has been fully accomplished, with results that will last for all eternity: the power of evil has been broken. This is a parallel to the perfect tense verb in the cry from the cross: "It has been finished" (τετέλεσται, John 19:30), which showed that the atoning sacrifice for sin had been fully accomplished, with results that the redeemed will dwell in heaven for all eternity. It also anticipates the perfect tense verb in Revelation 21:6, "They have come to pass" (γέγοναν), which refers to all God's purposes for the new creation. "And there were lightnings and voices and thunders, and a great earthquake came to pass, such as had not been since men had been on the earth, so mighty an earthquake and so great" (v. 18). The lightning, voices, thunder, and earthquake were all signs at the giving of the Law on Mount Sinai (Exod. 19:16–18). Thus, the Tribulation period reaches its climax in the worst earthquake in the history of the world. Daniel had prophesied that this Tribulation period would be the time of greatest trouble in the history of the world (Dan. 12:1). "And the great city was divided into three parts, and the cities of the nations fell, and great Babylon was remembered before God to give her the cup of the wine of the fury of his wrath" (v. 19). The Lord commanded Jeremiah, "Take the wine cup of this fury at my hand, and cause all the nations, to whom I send thee, to drink it" (Jer. 25:15). Nebuchadnezzar had boasted, "Is not this great Babylon, that I have built?" (Dan. 4:30). In OT times Babylon was the archetypal city of wickedness (Dan. 3:1–23; Isa. 13:1–19).

16:18. For a summary of the word *earthquake* (σεισμός) see Rev. 6:12 note.

In NT times Rome was the city of wickedness but the object of St. Paul's desire for evangelization (Rom. 1:1–32). Both Babylon and Rome were types of the final city of wickedness, Antichrist's capital, which is probably located in Rome (Rev. 17:9). "And every island fled away, and mountains were not found" (v. 20). The disappearance of islands and mountains shows the severity of the judgments upon the earth. The psalmist describes the mighty power of God that delivered Israel from the Egyptian bondage, "The sea saw it, and fled. . . . The mountains skipped like rams, and the little hills like lambs" (Ps. 114:3–4). "And a great hail, about a talent in weight, fell down out of heaven upon men, and men blasphemed God because of the plague of the hail, because the plague was exceedingly great" (v. 21). Isaiah spoke of hailstones as coming judgment (Isa. 28:17; 30:30). In the seventh Egyptian plague the Lord had rained hail, mingled with fire, upon the land of Egypt (Exod. 9:23–24). But the plague here is vastly more severe. A talent was about a hundred pounds in weight. Even small-sized hail can do great damage to roofs and crops, but hail weighing about a hundred pounds would destroy any modern commercial roof. The scene marks the end of the age in which the Second Coming in glory is the next moment (Rev. 19:11–21).

Practical Applications from Revelation 16

1. There are always consequences for sin (v. 2). "Behold, ye have sinned against the Lord: and be sure your sin will find you out" (Num. 32:23).
2. God always judges righteously (v. 5). "He cometh to judge the earth: he shall judge the world with righteousness, and the people with his truth" (Ps. 96:13).
3. God always avenges the harm done to His people (v. 6). "Dearly beloved, avenge not yourselves, but rather give place unto wrath: for it is written, Vengeance is mine; I will repay, says the Lord" (Rom. 12:19).
4. Repentance and submission are the right response to judgment (v. 9). "Except you repent, you shall all likewise perish" (Luke 13:3).
5. Sinful men would rather blame God than change their lifestyle (v. 11). "To day if ye will hear his voice, harden not your heart, as in the provocation, and as in the day of temptation in the wilderness" (Ps. 95:7b–8).

16:21. The heaviest hailstones on record, weighing 2.25 pounds, fell in the Gopalganj district of Bangladesh on April 14, 1986; 92 people died from the stones, *The Guinness Book of Records* (1991).

6. The Devil incites men to attack and destroy one another (v. 14). "He [the Devil] was a murderer from the beginning" (John 8:44).
7. People should always be spiritually prepared for the coming of the Lord (v. 15). "Be also patient; establish your hearts: for the coming of the Lord draws near" (James 5:8).
8. God will judge sin thoroughly (v. 17). "Do you think this, O man, . . . that you shall escape the judgment of God?" (Rom. 2:3). "How shall we escape, if we neglect so great salvation?" (Heb. 2:3).
9. The worldly, sinful life of the wicked will pass away (v. 19). Moses chose "rather to suffer affliction with the people of God, than to enjoy the pleasures of sin for a season" (Heb. 11:25). "The rich man died, and was buried, and in hell he lifted up his eyes, being in torments" (Luke 16:22–23).
10. How much better it would be for men to pray for forgiveness than to blaspheme God (v. 21). "Do you despise the riches of his goodness and forbearance and longsuffering; not knowing that the goodness of God leads you to repentance?" (Rom. 2:4).

Prayer

O Lord, God of righteousness, we give thanks that the wrath we deserved fell upon the holy Lord Jesus, who bore our sins in His body on the cross. Give us grace to so live that people may know that we are redeemed by the blood of the Lamb. Amen.

Revelation 17:1–18:24

REVELATION 17

BABYLON THE SYSTEM

Persons

Seven angels of the bowls
The great whore
The kings of the earth
The Beast

Seven kings
Ten kings
The Lamb

Persons referred to

Harlots
The saints
The martyrs

The earth dwellers
Peoples, multitudes, nations,
    and tongues

Places mentioned

The earth
The wilderness

Babylon
The bottomless pit

Doctrines taught

Judgment
Martyrdom
Perdition
The victory of the Lamb

Election
Faithfulness
The will of God

1 And there came one of the seven angels which had the seven vials, and talked with me, saying unto me, Come hither; I will shew unto thee the judgment of the great whore that sitteth upon many waters:

2 With whom the kings of the earth have committed fornication, and the inhabitants of the earth have been made drunk with the wine of her fornication.

3 So he carried me away in the spirit into the wilderness: and I saw a woman sit upon a scarlet coloured beast, full of names of blasphemy, having seven heads and ten horns.

4 And the woman was arrayed in purple and scarlet colour, and decked with gold and precious stones and pearls, having a golden cup in her hand full of abominations and filthiness of her fornication:

5 And upon her forehead was a name written, MYSTERY, BABLYLON THE GREAT, THE MOTHER OF HARLOTS, AND ABOMINATIONS OF THE EARTH.

6 And I saw the woman drunken with the blood of the saints, and with the blood of the martyrs of Jesus: and when I saw her, I wondered with great admiration.

7 And the angel said unto me, Wherefore didst thou marvel? I will tell thee the mystery of the woman, and of the beast that carrieth her, which hath the seven heads and ten horns.

Revelation 17 Exposition

I. Mystery Babylon. vv. 1–7.

"And one of the seven angels who had the seven bowls came and talked with me, saying, Come, I will show you the judgment of the great harlot who is sitting upon many waters" (v. 1). This chapter is plainly an explanation of things that John has already seen. There is a beautiful literary symmetry to the beginning and ending of the Book of Revelation. Both the beginning and the ending have four parts.

17:1. The word *harlot, prostitute* (πόρνη) occurs here for the first of 5 times in Rev. (17:1, 5, 15, 16; 19:2). The Holy Spirit deliberately chooses an offensive term to describe the unfaithful, false church. He has already charged teachers in the early church with leading His people to commit fornication (Rev. 2:14, 20). The prophets charged Israel with playing the harlot in choosing Baal rather than Jehovah (Jer. 2:20–23). The Lord's fierce denunciation of Aholibah shows His attitude toward sin in His ancient people (Ezek. 23:4–49). He is no less angry toward the false church of the Antichrist. Throughout history organized religion has systematically led people away from the one true God of the Bible and has poured contempt on His divine revelation, Holy Scripture. In every generation there are "religionists" who hide behind religious vestments and pious liturgy to practice sins of the flesh, not knowing that they are treasuring up for themselves wrath in the day of wrath (Rom. 2:5–6). See "Prostitute," Ryken, Wilhoit, and Longman, *Dictionary of Biblical Imagery*, pp. 676–78; ISBE (1982), "Harlot," II, pp. 616–17; ZPEB, "Harlot," III, pp. 34–35

The word *judgment* (κρίμα) occurs 3 times in Rev. (17:1; 18:20; 20:4).

Revelation begins with the following:
1. The introduction (1:1–8).
2. The vision of the Christ of glory (1:9–20).
3. The letters to the seven churches (2–3).
4. The vision of the throne in heaven from which all that follows proceeds (4–5).

In inverse order Revelation now concludes with the following:
1. The vision of judgment on Babylon and the Beast (17:1–19:5).
2. The Second Coming in glory, with the following Millennium and Great White Throne judgment (19:6–20:15).
3. The vision of the new heaven and new earth (21:1–22:5).
4. The conclusion (22:6–21).

One of the angels who poured out the bowls stays with John to explain the meaning of what he has seen. What is "the throne of the beast" (Rev. 16:10)? What is "great Babylon" (Rev. 16:19)? It turns out that there is no simple answer. Babylon was an ancient city, an ancient empire, and a center of false religious worship (Isa. 47:1–13). Yet Isaiah prophesied destruction for it in the eschatological "day of the Lord" (Isa. 13:1–6). That judgment included the eschatological signs in the heavens (Isa. 13:10) and the punishment of the whole world for its evil (Isa. 13:11). The destruction of Babylon "shall be as when God overthrew Sodom and Gomorrah. It shall never be inhabited" (Isa. 13:19–20). Jeremiah also prophesied against Babylon, "O thou that dwellest upon many waters, abundant in treasures, thine end is come, and the measure of thy covetousness" (Jer. 51:13). In John's day Rome was all of these (Rev. 17:9). So the angel reveals to John that the future city/empire/religious system of the Beast shall receive the fury of God's wrath. The literal interpreters agree that this harlot is the false religious system that has existed throughout the world's history and is defiantly opposed to the God of the Bible (Seiss, Scott, Newell, J. B. Smith, Walvoord, Thomas). The exact language used, "Come, I will show you," is paralleled by the angel's words, "Come, I will show you the Bride, the Lamb's wife" (Rev. 21:9). This "harlot" is the vile counterfeit of the true people of God. She sits upon many waters: Babylon had access to the seas through the Euphrates; Rome through its seaport Ostia. The future capital of the Beast will use world religion to dominate the nations. Many interpreters argue that this system includes the papacy, which is indeed centered in Rome (Seiss, Scott, Newell, etc.). "With whom the kings of the earth committed fornication, and the earth dwellers were made drunk with the wine of her fornication" (v. 2). The prophets characterized the

---

17:2. In addition to the 4 times that the word *harlot* (πόρνη) is used in this chapter, the verb *to commit fornication* (πορνεύω) is used in this verse, and the noun *fornication*

sins of Jerusalem (Ezek. 16:26) and Tyre (Isa. 23:17) as fornication. John has already characterized the sins of the churches as fornication (Rev. 2:14, 20). Religious enthusiasm apart from the God of the Bible is always spiritual fornication. The apostate church will love the kings of earth far more than God. The earth dwellers, whose hearts are on earth, will be made drunk by the sensational practices of the church of the Antichrist. "And he carried me away into the desert in the spirit. And I saw a woman sitting upon a scarlet colored beast, being filled with names of blasphemy, having seven heads and ten horns" (v. 3). The woman is the apostate church just described, riding upon the empire of the Beast (Rev. 13:1–2). It is an unholy alliance: the empire supports the apostate church, and the apostate church conforms to the empire's wishes. "And the woman had been arrayed in purple and scarlet and had been adorned with gold and precious stones and pearls, having a golden cup in her hand full of abominations and uncleannesses of her fornication" (v. 4). This is a gross picture of ecclesiastical prostitution. One cannot help but think of the magnificent splendor of St. Peter's Cathedral in Rome, with the faithful lined up by the

---

(πορνεία) is also used twice in this chapter (17:2, 4). Thus, 7 words on the *fornication* (πορν-) root are used in this one chapter to characterize the wicked, apostate church.

For a summary of the "earth dwellers," see Rev. 3:10 note.

17:3. The word *desert* (ἔρημος) occurs only 3 times in Rev. The first 2 times it referred to the literal desert into which the Jewish remnant flees from persecution (12:6, 14), but here it refers to the spiritual desert in which the apostate church dwells (17:3). The Lord will transform the desert into a fruitful place during the Millennium (Isa. 35:1–7).

The word *scarlet* (κόκκινος) occurs 4 times in Rev. (17:3, 4; 18:12, 16). It denotes a bright red, such as the red cloak the Roman soldiers wore (Matt. 27:28).

17:4. The adjective *purple* (πορφυροῦς) occurs only twice in Rev. (17:4; 18:16) and twice in John's Gospel (19:2, 5), all describing purple clothing. It was a very expensive dye made from the Mediterranean shellfish, the purple dye murex (*Bolinus brandaris*). A North American relative, the wide-mouthed purpura, can be found on beaches in south Florida. The animals secrete a purple dye "difficult to remove" (Rehder, *Audubon Society Field Guide to North American Seashells*, p. 524). The noun *purple* (πορφύρα) occurs only in 18:12 in Rev. A quick dip in the dye produced a red color, which was the cloak that the Roman soldiers put on the Lord (Mark 15:17, 20), but it took a long soak in the dye to produce the royal purple the rich man wore (Luke 16:19). Lydia was a dealer in purple cloth (Acts 16:14). Mordecai, as prime minister of Persia, wore a garment of purple linen (Esther 8:15). Interestingly, it was a purple cloth that covered the ashes taken from the altar of sacrifice (Num. 4:13; 4:14 LXX). See ISBE (1986), "Purple," III, p. 1057; ZPEB, "Purple," IV, pp. 960–61.

The verb *to adorn with gold* (χρυσόω) occurs only here and in 18:16 in the NT. Pearls are mentioned 5 times in Rev. (17:4; 18:12, 16; 21:21 [twice]). Paul urges Christian ladies to concentrate on good works rather than gold and pearls (I Tim. 2:9).

The word *abomination* (βδέλυγμα) occurs 3 times in Rev. (17:4, 5; 21:27).

hundreds, waiting to kiss the toe of the image of St. Peter! Jeremiah declared, "Babylon hath been a golden cup in the Lord's hand, that made all the earth drunken: the nations have drunken of her wine; therefore the nations are mad" (Jer. 51:7). An abomination is something that is detestable in the sight of God, such as idolatry. God declared through Ezekiel, "I am broken with their whorish heart, which has departed from me, and with their eyes, which go a whoring after their idols: and they shall loathe themselves for the evils which they have committed in all their abominations" (Ezek. 6:9). "And upon her forehead a name written: Mystery, Babylon the great, mother of harlots and abominations of the earth" (v. 5). "A name captures the essence of the person" (Ryken, Wilhoit, and Longman, *Dictionary of Biblical Imagery*, p. 583). Wicked *Babylon* captures the essence of the apostate church. False religion always draws people away from the worship of the true God. God sees the nature of every being as though a mark were stamped on his forehead. The prophet Nahum used similar language against the wicked city of Nineveh (Nah. 3:4). "And I saw the woman drunken from the blood of the saints and from the blood of the martyrs of Jesus. And I was amazed with great amazement when I saw her" (v. 6). John was "blown out of his mind" when he saw the vileness of the false religious system. The Lord sternly rebuked His sinful people, "Yea, they have chosen their own ways, and their soul delighteth in their abominations. I also will choose their delusions, and will bring their fears upon them" (Isa. 66:3b–4a). "And the angel said to me, Why were you amazed? I will tell you the mystery of the woman and of the beast which is carrying her and has seven heads and ten horns" (v. 7). The holy angel cannot understand why anyone would be amazed at the vileness of sin. Had not Daniel prophesied that "a vile person" would come in peaceably and obtain the kingdom by flatteries (Dan. 11:21)?

17:5. For a brief survey in interpretations of "Babylon," see "Babylon, NT," ZPEB, I, pp. 448–49; "Babylon in the NT," ISBE (1979), I, p. 391; and the extended discussion in Thomas, *Rev.*, II, pp. 281–301.

For a summary of the word *mystery* (μυστήριον) see Rev. 1:20 note.

17:6. The verb *to be drunk* (μεθύω) occurs only here in Rev. It is a terrible picture of the apostate church, drunken with the blood of the martyrs of Jesus. The expression "drunk with blood" was common in the ancient world (Euripides, Josephus, Philo, etc.; see Robertson, *Word Pictures*, VI, p. 431). Drunkenness is one of the sins that exclude from the kingdom of God (Gal. 5:19–21).

8 The beast that thou sawest was, and is not; and shall ascend out of the bottomless pit, and go into perdition: and they that dwell on the earth shall wonder, whose names were not written in the book of life from the foundation of the world, when they behold the beast that was, and is not, and yet is.

9 And here is the mind which hath wisdom. The seven heads are seven mountains, on which the woman sitteth.

10 And there are seven kings: five are fallen, and one is, and the other is not yet come; and when he cometh, he must continue a short space.

11 And the beast that was, and is not, even he is the eighth, and is of the seven, and goeth into perdition.

12 And the ten horns which thou sawest are ten kings, which have received no kingdom as yet; but receive power as kings one hour with the beast.

13 These have one mind, and shall give their power and strength unto the beast.

14 These shall make war with the Lamb, and the Lamb shall overcome them: for he is Lord of lords, and King of kings: and they that are with him are called, and chosen, and faithful.

II. The Meaning of the Beast. vv. 8–14.

"The beast which you saw was, and is not, and is about to ascend out of the abyss, and goes away into ruin, and the earth dwellers, whose names have not been written in the book of life from the foundation of the world, shall be amazed when they see the beast that was, and is not, and shall be" (v. 8). There is no question but that John is expounding and expanding Daniel's prophecy of the four beasts (Dan. 7). The beast in this passage is the beast out of the sea, the last world empire in Daniel's vision (Dan. 7:7), and its last ruler, the little horn (Dan. 7:8), the Antichrist (Rev. 13:1–10). The apostle Paul called the Antichrist "the son of destruction" (II Thess. 2:3). In the only other occurrence, the Lord Jesus referred to Judas by that phrase (John 17:12). "The ascending out of the abyss" may be a reference to the assassination attempt that he will survive (13:3). The Roman Empire itself looked as though it had died about A.D. 400, but it too will be revived. Unsaved people will be

---

17:8. The word *ruin* or *destruction* (ἀπώλεια) occurs only twice in Rev. (17:8, 11). It does not biblically refer to annihilation but to the loss of all that makes life worth living. The rich man died and woke up in hades, suffering in flames (Luke 16:19–23). Sophocles tells the story of Oedipus, the king who killed his father and married his mother (*Oedipus Rex*), but in a later drama portrays him as a blind beggar, at peace with himself and the world (*Oedipus at Colonus*). The courtiers who found him there say, "The gods now sustain whom they once *destroyed*" (the root ὄλλυμι, line 393). Oedipus had not died but had lost the kingship and his power. To the ancient Greeks, that was all that mattered about life. This is why sheol and destruction are often linked together in Scripture (Job 26:6; Prov. 15:11; 27:20). No one should envy the prosperity of the wicked; they will lose everything (Ps. 73:3, 18–19). "The wicked shall be turned into hell" (Ps. 9:17).

amazed by his powers. "Here is the mind that has wisdom. The seven heads are seven mountains, where the woman sits upon them. And there are seven kings" (v. 9). In the first century Rome was certainly considered the city on the seven hills (or mountains: Aventine, Caelian, Capitoline, Equiline, Palatine, Quirinal, and Viminal). Seiss argued that the seven mountains represent seven successive world empires: Egypt, Assyria, Babylon, Persia, Greece, Rome, and the future empire of the Beast (*Apocalypse*, p. 393). Daniel in his day saw four of these empires as wild, vicious beasts: the lion (Babylon), the bear (Medo-Persia), the leopard (Greece), and the dreadful beast with iron teeth (Rome, Dan. 7:3–7). "The five fell; the one is; the other one is not yet come, and whenever he comes, it is necessary for him to remain a little while" (v. 10). The Devil has only a short time (Rev. 12:12), and therefore the Antichrist has only a short time (ὀλίγον). The idea of the empire and of its ruler are bound up together in Revelation. It may then refer to the last head of the empire, the Antichrist. "And the beast which was and is not, even he himself is the eighth, and is of the seven, and he goes away into destruction" (v. 11). Daniel noted his piercing eyes and a "mouth speaking great things" (Dan. 7:8). Daniel added that his "look was more stout than his fellows . . . and the same horn made war with the saints, and prevailed against them" (Dan. 7:20b–21). Thomas argues that he is the seventh king, resuscitated as the eighth (*Rev.*, II, p. 300). "And the ten horns which you saw are ten kings, who have not received a kingdom yet, but they receive authority as kings one hour with the beast" (v. 12). Daniel prophesied, "And the ten horns out of this kingdom are ten kings that shall arise: and another shall arise after them" (Dan. 7:24). The European Union (Common Market) countries have a special interest in commercial and political cooperation that has resulted in a common currency (the euro) and cooperation in military actions. All this is preparation for a much more powerful union that is yet to come. These ten kings will convey their authority to the Beast. "These have one purpose and they shall give their power and authority to the beast" (v. 13). These world leaders are spellbound by the brilliant, charismatic powers of the

---

17:9. This is the last of 4 references to *wisdom* in Rev. For a summary see Rev. 5:12 note.

For a summary of the word *mountain* (ὄρος) see Rev. 6:14 note. On the site of the 7 mountains Vincent observes that, in addition to Rome, Constantinople, Brussels, and Jerusalem have been suggested (*Word Studies*, II, 546). For a formal comparison between world cities in historic periods see Sir Peter Hall, *Cities in Civilization*, "The Imperial Capital, Rome 50 B.C.–A.D. 100" (pp. 621–56).

17:13. The word *purpose* (γνώμη) occurs only in this context in Rev. (17:13, 17). The 10 kings have one purpose in giving their authority to the Beast (17:13), but God granted them that purpose so that He could destroy the unified kingdom of darkness (v. 17).

15 And he saith unto me, The waters which thou sawest, where the whore sitteth, are peoples, and multitudes, and nations, and tongues.
16 And the ten horns which thou sawest upon the beast, these shall hate the whore, and shall make her desolate and naked, and shall eat her flesh, and burn her with fire.
17 For God hath put in their hearts to fulfil his will, and to agree, and give their kingdom unto the beast, until the words of God shall be fulfilled.
18 And the woman which thou sawest is that great city, which reigneth over the kings of the earth.

Antichrist. Daniel wrote of these ten kings and of the "little horn" that will take control of the empire (Dan. 7:20ff.). He mentioned that the "little horn" shall subdue three kings and the others will submit to him (Dan 7:24). "These shall wage war with the Lamb and the Lamb shall conquer them, because he is Lord of lords and King of kings, and the ones who are with him are called and chosen and faithful" (v. 14). I. Howard Marshall notes that titles applied to God in the OT are here deliberately applied to the Lord Jesus (*The Origins of New Testament Christology*, p. 106). The apostle Paul also called the Lord Jesus Christ "the blessed and only Potentate, King of kings, and Lord of lords" (I Tim. 6:15) and in context urged believers to "fight the good fight of faith" (6:12). It was Moses who wrote, "The Lord your God is God of gods, and Lord of lords, a great God, a mighty, and a terrible" (Deut. 10:17). John characterized the saints with the Lord by a unique combination of terms: "called, and chosen and faithful." The Lord Jesus taught that "many are called, but few are chosen" (Matt. 22:14). Peter called the saints "a chosen generation, a royal priesthood" (I Pet. 2:9). Paul urged Timothy to commit the Word "to faithful men, who shall be able to teach others also" (II Tim. 2:2).

III. The Fate of Ecclesiastical Babylon. vv. 15–18.

"And he says to me, The waters which you saw where the harlot sits, are peoples and crowds and nations and tongues" (v. 15). The angel continues his explanation to John. The religion of the empire will dominate the world. Just as ancient Rome demanded that people reverence Caesar and the empire, whatever other gods they might have, so the Beast will demand worship first, whatever other religions people may have. True believers in Christ are easily exposed by such a noose. "And the ten horns which you saw, and the beast, these shall hate the harlot and shall make her desolate and naked, and shall eat her flesh, and shall burn her down

---

17:14. For a summary of the verb *to do battle, wage war* (πολεμέω) see Rev. 2:16 note. For a summary of the word *faithful* (πιστός) see Rev. 1:5 note.

in fire" (v. 16). When the Beast perceives that the apostate church is no longer useful to him, he will order the ten kingdoms to destroy it. The wicked government will eat the wicked church the way that dogs ate the flesh of the wicked queen Jezebel (II Kings 9:36). It will not be the first time that world governments have confiscated and crushed religious organizations for their own profit (the French and Russian revolutions and so forth). "For God put in their hearts to do His purpose, and to have one purpose and to give their kingdom to the beast until the words of God shall have been fulfilled" (v. 17). All the wicked purposes of the Beast, the empire, and the apostate church shall ultimately work out to the accomplishing of God's holy purpose of judging sin and establishing His kingdom on earth. One day the words of God shall be brought to an end (τελέω) by complete fulfillment. David prophesied, "The kings of the earth set themselves, and the rulers take counsel together, against the Lord, and against his anointed, saying, Let us break their bands asunder, and cast away their cords from us" (Ps. 2:2–3). The kings of earth have long rebelled against the rule of God. "And the woman which you saw is the great city which has a kingdom over the kings of the earth" (v. 18). In ancient times that city was Babylon; in John's day it was certainly Rome; in the day of the Antichrist it will be his capital. It is typical of the Antichrist that he will destroy his own capital and the religious organization that supported him if it furthers his diabolical purpose. Charles H. Dyer warns that Saddam Hussein spent years rebuilding the ruins of Babylon, using millions of bricks to rebuild the walls of the procession street, the palace of Nebuchadnezzar, the Ninmach temple, and other ruins (*The Rise of Babylon: Sign of the End Times*, pp. 128–31). Hussein would have liked nothing better than to be a second Nebuchadnezzar, sacking Jerusalem, mutilating Jews, and bringing them as trophies to Babylon (Dan. 1:1–7). Walvoord notes that some people believe that a greatly rebuilt Babylon "will be the capital of the world government of the Great Tribulation" (*Prophecy in the New Millennium*, p. 94).

Practical Applications from Revelation 17

1. God judges religious sin as surely as moral sin (v. 1). The Lord struck down Nadab and Abihu, sons of Aaron, for offering incense contrary to God's commands (Num. 3:4).

17:16. The verb *to hate* (μισέω) occurs only 3 times in Rev. (2:6; 17:16; 18:2). Here it refers to the virulent hatred that the political leaders have for the ecclesiastical "meddlers" who get in their way. Both worldly groups "use" the other for their own ends.

2. Outward adornment never makes up for apostasy from God (vv. 3–4). Peter warned the false teachers of their coming judgment (II Pet. 2:1, 12–17).
3. God governs the rise and fall of empires (v. 8). "All nations before Him are as nothing. . . . [He] bringeth the princes to nothing; He maketh the judges of the earth as vanity" (Isa. 40:17, 23).
4. Wicked rulers shall go into perdition (v. 11). "Thou shalt take up this proverb against the king of Babylon. . . . Hell from beneath is moved for thee to meet thee at thy coming" (Isa. 14:4, 9).
5. Earthly kings rule for a short time; God rules forever (v. 12). The Devil knows that he has but a short time (Rev. 12:12). "Surely thou didst set them in slippery places: thou castedst them down into destruction" (Ps. 73:18).
6. Evil conspiracy can never defeat the Lord (vv. 13–14). "The Lord is known by the judgment which he executeth: the wicked is snared in the work of his own hands" (Ps. 9:16). "I will destroy the wisdom of the wise" (I Cor. 1:19).
7. Faithfulness is a crowning virtue for believers (v. 14). "Who then is a faithful and wise servant, whom his lord has made ruler over his household? . . . Blessed is that servant, whom his lord when he comes shall find so doing" (Matt. 24:45–46).
8. God can use the wicked to bring judgment on other wicked people (v. 16). Zimri murdered Elah to get the kingdom (I Kings 16:8–10), but Omri saw to it that Zimri died (I Kings 16:17–18).
9. God can cause the wicked to unconsciously fulfill His will (v. 17). "Surely the wrath of man shall praise thee" (Ps. 76:10).

Prayer

O Lord of lords, and King of kings, give Your people grace to be separate from the wicked world system and religious compromise. Help us to live for You and to be faithful unto death in the midst of this wicked world. For Your sake. Amen.

BABYLON, THE WORLDLY SETTING

Persons

Another angel
All nations
The kings of the earth
The merchants of the earth
My people

Ship masters
Sailors
Apostles
Prophets
A mighty angel

Persons referred to

Demons
Foul spirits
A queen
A widow
Slaves
Souls of men
Harpers

Musicians
Pipers
Trumpeters
Craftsman
The bridegroom
The bride
Saints

Places mentioned

Heaven
Earth

Babylon
The sea

Doctrines taught

Angelic power
Demons
Wrath
Sin

Judgment
The fleeting nature of riches
Joy in heaven
Martyrdom

1   And after these things I saw another angel come down from heaven, having great power; and the earth was lightened with his glory.

2   And he cried mightily with a strong voice, saying, Babylon the great is fallen, is fallen, and is become the habitation of devils, and the hold of every foul spirit, and a cage of every unclean and hateful bird.

3   For all nations have drunk of the wine of the wrath of her fornication, and the kings of the earth have committed fornication with her, and the merchants of the earth are waxed rich through the abundance of her delicacies.

4   And I heard another voice from heaven, saying, Come out of her, my people, that ye be not partakers of her sins, and that ye receive not of her plagues.

5   For her sins have reached unto heaven, and God hath remembered her iniquities.

6   Reward her even as she rewarded you, and double unto her double according to her works: in the cup which she hath filled fill to her double.

7   How much she hath glorified herself, and lived deliciously, so much torment and sorrow give her: for she saith in her heart, I sit a queen, and am no widow, and shall see no sorrow.

8   Therefore shall her plagues come in one day, death, and mourning, and famine; and she shall be utterly burned with fire: for strong is the Lord God who judgeth her.

Revelation 18 Exposition

I. Warnings Against Babylon. vv. 1–8.

"After these things I saw another angel coming down out of heaven having great authority, and the earth was illuminated from his glory" (v. 1). Swete comments eloquently concerning the angel, "So recently has he come from the Presence that in passing he flings a broad belt of light across the dark earth" (*Apocalypse*, p. 226). The thought that an angel could have such glory as to light up the earth when he came near gives us a different insight into the nature and power of angels. Ezekiel saw the glory of God return to the millennial temple, "and the earth shined with his glory" (Ezek. 43:2). "And he cried with a strong voice saying, Babylon the great fell, fell, and became a dwelling place of demons, and a prison of every unclean spirit, and a prison [cage] of every unclean bird, and a prison [cage] of every unclean and hateful beast" (v. 2). This repeats the cry of the angel in Revelation 14:8 and now expands the declaration. The Devil and

---

18:1. The verb *to illuminate, shine upon* (φωτίζω) occurs only 3 times in Rev. (18:1; 21:23; 22:5). All 3 passages assume a divine light.

18:2. The word *dwelling place* (κατοικητήριον) occurs only here in Rev. and in Eph. 2:22, where it refers to the believer as the permanent dwelling place of God.

The word *prison* (φυλακή) may also mean *garrison*, but in the context here as well as in the other 2 references (Rev. 2:10; 20:7) it must mean *prison*. Peter even used the word for the prison of spirits in the underworld (I Pet. 3:19). The glory of Christ's gospel is that it proclaims release to the prisoners (Luke 4:18). See ZPEB, "Prison," IV, pp. 869–70;

his angels are confined to the earth (Rev. 12:7–9) and now make the wicked Babylon their dwelling place. Isaiah also heard this cry from the horsemen, "Babylon is fallen, is fallen" (Isa. 21:9). "Because all nations have drunk from the wine of the wrath of her fornication, and the kings of the earth committed fornication with her, and the merchants of the earth became rich from the power of her luxury" (v. 3). He singles out the political leaders and the commercial barons who are especially vulnerable to the sensual luxuries of Babylon/Rome/City of Antichrist. If Revelation 17 emphasized the religious corruption of "Babylon," Revelation 18 concentrates on the economic and political powers. The geographic location is probably the same. "And I heard another voice out of heaven saying, Come out of her, my people, in order that you may not share in her sins, and in order that you may not receive her plagues" (v. 4). The pleasures of sin always have catastrophic consequences. The doctrine of separation from sin and compromise is a major theme in Scripture. God commanded His people to depart from sin and to touch no unclean thing (Isa. 52:11). The apostle Paul quoted that passage and applied it to all believers to the end of time (II Cor. 6:14–18). His conclusion was "Having therefore these promises, dearly beloved, let us cleanse ourselves from all filthiness of the flesh and spirit, perfecting holiness in the fear of God" (II Cor. 7:1). He sternly commanded believers to "have no fellowship with the unfruitful works of darkness, but rather reprove them" (Eph. 5:11). He also commanded believers to withdraw from every brother who "broke rank" and did not keep the apostolic teaching (II Thess. 3:6). Jeremiah warned his people to flee Babylon "and deliver ye every man his soul from the fierce anger of the Lord" (Jer. 51:45). "Because her sins reached unto heaven, and God remembered her unrighteous deeds" (v. 5). The image is of sins being piled up until they reached heaven. God is the "righteous judge" (II Tim. 4:8)

ISBE (1986), "Prison," III, pp. 973–75; Ryken, Wilhoit, and Longman, *Dictionary of Biblical Imagery*, "Prison," pp. 663–64.

18:3. The word *luxury* (στρῆνος) occurs only here in the NT. The verb form *to live in sensual luxury* (στρηνιάω) occurs only in Rev. 18:7, 9 in the NT. Trench characterized the root meaning as "the insolence of wealth, the wantonness and petulance from fullness of bread" (*Synonyms of the NT*, p. 201). See ISBE (1986), "Luxury," pp. 187–88.

18:4. The verb *to have fellowship with, share* (συγκοινωνέω) occurs only here in Rev. Paul commended the Philippians for having a share in his grace (Phil. 1:7) and charged the Ephesians to have no share in the unfruitful works of darkness (Eph. 5:11).

18:5. The word *unrighteous deed* (ἀδίκημα) occurs only here in Rev. and only in Acts 18:14; 24:20 in the rest of the NT. This is the only time in Rev. that God is said *to remember* (μνημονεύω) sins. Religious betrayal is a sin to avoid. Three times Rev. declares that God is righteous (Rev. 16:5, 7; 19:2). Paul notes that it is "a righteous thing with God to recompense trouble to them that trouble you" (II Thess. 1:6). God will repay every evil deed done to His people.

and therefore must condemn unrighteous deeds. "Repay to her even as she herself repaid, and double the double according to her works; in the cup which she mixed, mix to her double" (v. 6). The imperative *Repay* is not a command to saints, for it is the Lord God who will judge her (v. 8). The Lord Jesus charged the scribes and Pharisees with doubling their proselytes in sin (Matt. 23:15), but here the Lord doubles the judgment on wicked Babylon. He charges her with arrogant presumption and self-worship. Just as Babylon mixed her intoxicating drinks for others, so now mix for her a double portion. "As much as she glorified herself and lived luxuriously, give her so much torment and sorrow, because she says in her heart, I am sitting as queen, and I am no widow, and I shall never see sorrow" (v. 7). The *never* is a very emphatic double negative "never at any time." Instead, God will pour out sorrow upon her. David urges the saints, "Wait on the Lord" (Ps. 37:34), and goes on to testify, "I have seen the wicked in great power, and spreading himself like a green bay tree. Yet he passed away, and, lo, he was not" (Ps. 37:35–36). "On account of this in one day her plagues shall come, death, and mourning, and famine, and in fire she shall be burned down, because strong is the Lord God who judges her" (v. 8). Isaiah prophesied, "Behold, the Lord God will come with strong hand, and his arm shall rule for him: behold, his reward is with him, and his work before him" (Isa. 40:10). He goes on to rebuke the pride of the daughter of the Chaldeans, "that sayest in thine heart, I am, and none else beside me; I shall not sit as a widow, neither shall I know the loss of children" (Isa. 47:8). These very things will come on the Babylon of the future.

18:6. The verb *to repay double* (διπλόω) occurs only here in the NT. The verb *to mix* (κεράννυμι) occurs only here and in Rev. 14:10 in the NT.

18:7. The word *queen* (βασίλισσα) occurs only here in Rev., and only in reference to the queen of the south (Matt. 12:42; Luke 11:31) and the queen of Ethiopia (Acts 8:27) in the rest of the NT. The OT has striking examples of wicked queens, Jezebel (I Kings 18:4; 19:1–2; 21:5–15) and her daughter Athaliah (II Kings 11:1ff.). See Ryken, Wilhoit, and Longman, *Dictionary of Biblical Imagery*, "Queen," p. 690; ISBE (1988), "Queen," IV, p. 7.

For a summary on the word *torment* see Rev. 9:5 note. The word *sorrow* (πένθος) occurs 3 out of its 4 times in this context in Rev. (18:7 [twice], 8; 21:4).

The word *widow* (χήρα), although common in the NT, occurs only here in Rev. The root meaning is "bereft."

18:8. For a summary on the word *death* (θάνατος) see Rev. 1:18 note.

9 And the kings of the earth, who have committed fornication and lived deliciously with her, shall bewail her, and lament for her, when they shall see the smoke of her burning,
10 Standing afar off for the fear of her torment, saying, Alas, alas, that great city Babylon, that mighty city! for in one hour is thy judgment come.
11 And the merchants of the earth shall weep and mourn over her; for no man buyeth their merchandise any more:
12 The merchandise of gold, and silver, and precious stones, and of pearls, and fine linen, and purple, and silk, and scarlet, and all thyine wood, and all manner vessels of ivory, and all manner vessels of most precious wood, and of brass, and iron, and marble,
13 And cinnamon, and odours, and ointments, and frankincense, and wine, and oil, and fine flour, and wheat, and beasts, and sheep, and horses, and chariots, and slaves, and souls of men.
14 And the fruits that thy soul lusted after are departed from thee, and all things which were dainty and goodly are departed from thee, and thou shalt find them no more at all.
15 The merchants of these things, which were made rich by her, shall stand afar off for the fear of her torment, weeping and wailing,
16 And saying, Alas, alas, that great city, that was clothed in fine linen, and purple, and scarlet, and decked with gold, and precious stones, and pearls!
17 For in one hour so great riches is come to nought. And every shipmaster, and all the company in ships, and sailors, and as many as trade by sea, stood afar off,
18 And cried when they saw the smoke of her burning, saying, What city is like unto this great city!
19 And they cast dust on their heads, and cried, weeping and wailing, saying, Alas, alas, that great city, wherein were made rich all that had ships in the sea by reason of her costliness! for in one hour is she made desolate.

II. The Mourning of Kings and Merchants. vv. 9–19.

"And the kings of the earth, who have committed fornication with her, and lived luxuriously, shall weep and mourn over her, whenever they see the smoke of her burning" (v. 9). The kings had profited from the power and opulence of Babylon, and now they see the danger to themselves in her destruction. "Having taken their stand afar off on account of fear of her torment, saying,

> Woe, woe, the great city,
> Babylon the strong city,
> Because in one hour your judgment has come" (v. 10).

18:10. The word *afar off* (μακρόθεν) occurs only 3 times in Rev., all in this context (18:10, 15, 17). It reminds us of the rich man in hades who saw Abraham *afar off* (Luke 16:23).

The word *judgment* (κρίσις) occurs 4 times in Rev. (14:7; 16:7; 18:10; 19:2).

It is significant that they stand "afar off," which sounds like there is a nuclear or biological element in the destruction. The suddenness of the disaster is also obvious. "And the merchants of the earth shall weep and mourn over her, because no one buys their merchandise any more" (v. 11). The sole concern of these merchants was that they make money. They were prepared to overlook a corrupt government if they could just make a profit. There follows an astonishing list of the things for sale in the ancient world (and will be in the future). The cargo included "merchandise of gold, and silver, and precious stones, and pearls, and fine linen, and purple, and silk, and scarlet, and all citron wood, and every vessel of ivory, and every vessel of most precious wood, and of copper, and of iron, and of marble, and cinnamon, and Indian spice, and incense, and ointment, and frankincense, and wine, and oil, and fine flour, and wheat, and cattle, and sheep, and horses, and carriages, and bodies and souls of men" (vv. 12–13). The list ranges from precious metals and gems, through luxury items of all kinds, to the iniquitous slave trade. Swete calls it "human live stock" (*Rev.*, p. 235). Although the word for *slave* (δοῦλος) is common in the NT, this is the only verse in the NT of the KJV in which the word *slave* occurs, yet δοῦλος does not occur in this verse. The word here is *soul* (ψυχή). Osborne notes that the purpose of this long list is to show what God condemns, "ostentatious, self-centered materialism" (*Rev.*, p. 647). "And the fruit your soul lusted for departed from you, and all things rich and splendid departed from you, and they

---

18:11. The word *merchandise* (γόμος) means literally the *cargo* or *freight* of a ship. It occurs only 2 times in Rev. (18:11, 12) and only in Acts 21:3 in the rest of the NT.

18:12. The word *fine linen* (βύσσινος) occurs 4 times in the NT, all in Rev. (18:12, 16; 19:8, 14), always referring to the highest grade of linen; the last two references to the robes of the saints in glory. See "Linen," ZPEB, (1975) III, pp. 937–39; "Linen," ISBE (1986) III, pp. 139–41.

Some words are unique: *silver* (ἄργυρος) occurs only here in Rev.; *silk* (σιρικός) was a very costly import from the Far East, only here in the NT; *citron wood* (ξύλον θύϊνον), aromatic wood, only here in the NT; *ivory* (ἐλεφάντινος) only here in the NT. King Solomon made a great throne of ivory (I Kings 10:18). *Marble* (μάρμαρος) occurs only here in the NT. It is mentioned in the palace of King Ahasuerus (Esther 1:5) and in the rich materials used in the temple (I Chron. 29:2). For a summary on the word *gold*, see Rev. 9:7 note.

18:13. The word *cinnamon* (κιννάμωμον) occurs only here in the NT. The word *Indian spice* (ἄμωμον) is sometimes merely transliterated (*amomum*) and refers to an otherwise unidentified spice from India (Arndt and Gingrich, p. 47; Swete, *Rev.*, p. 234). It occurs only here in the NT. The word *incense* (θυμίαμα) is the regular word that occurs 4 times in Rev. (5:8; 8:3, 4; 18:13). The word *frankincense* (λίβανος) occurs only here and in Matt. 2:11 in the NT. It was a costly perfume. The word *carriage* (ῥέδη) refers to a 4-wheeled vehicle (Moulton and Milligan, *Vocabulary*, p. 563).

shall never, never find them any more" (v. 14). There is a rare triple negative in the last clause. For all eternity these enemies of God and mankind shall find nothing to enjoy or control. The flames of gehenna await them. The Lord Jesus Christ Himself warned all men to flee the flames of gehenna at all costs (Matt. 5:22, 29, 30; 10:28; 18:9; 23:15). He would not have spoken so severely if there were not just cause (John 8:40, 45). "And the merchants of these things, who were made rich from her, shall stand afar off on account of fear of her torment, weeping and mourning" (v. 15). Again there is great stress on the distance these merchants keep between themselves and Babylon. Its fiery end is so dangerous that they keep afar off from the burning. "Saying:

> Woe, woe, the great city,
> Which was clothed in fine linen, and purple, and scarlet,
> And was adorned with gold and with precious stones and
> with pearls,
> Because in one hour so great wealth was laid waste"
> (vv. 16–17a).

It is the ten horns, the confederation of kings, who lay ecclesiastical Babylon waste (Rev. 17:16). But the members of business and transportation mourn over the loss of such a source of income. "And every ship owner, and all who sail anywhere, and sailors, and as many as work the sea, stood afar off, and were crying when they saw the smoke of her burning, saying, What is like the great city!" (vv. 17b–18). Their single, most

---

18:14. The word *fruit* (ὀπώρα) occurs only here in the NT. It is actually an old Greek word for the rising of the star Sirius in late summer (when fruit would ripen). See Arndt and Gingrich, p. 580.

The word *lust* (ἐπιθυμία) can be a neutral term for *desire* (Phil. 1:23), but here it plainly refers to the lust for luxurious possessions. James warns that lust leads to temptation (James 1:14). Paul warns against homosexual lust (Rom. 1:24, 26) and worldly lust (Titus 2:12). The matched pair of adjectives of similar sound expresses the luxury: *rich* (λιπαρὰ) only here in the NT, and *splendid* (λαμπρὰ), in Rev. elsewhere only of the glory of heaven, Rev. 19:8; 22:1, 16. See *Holman Bible Dictionary*, "Lust," p. 903; Elwell, *Evangelical Dictionary of Biblical Theology*, "Lust," pp. 500–501; Harrison, *Baker's Dictionary of Theology*, "Concupiscence," p. 133; "Desire," pp. 164–65.

18:15. The noun *fear* (φόβος) occurs only 3 times in Rev., always of the fear of unbelievers (11:11; 18:10, 15). Believers are told not to fear (Rev. 1:17; 2:10).

18:17. The verb *to lay waste* (ἐρημόω) occurs 3 times in Rev. (17:16; 18:17, 19).

The word *ship owner*, or *pilot* (κυβερνήτης), occurs only here in Rev. and only in Acts 27:11 in the rest of the NT. The word *sailor* (ναύτης) occurs only here in Rev. and only in Acts 27:27, 30 in the rest of the NT. A. T. Robertson notes that the idiom *to work the sea* goes back as far as Hesiod (*Word Pictures*, VI, p. 443). See ISBE (1988), "Ships, Boats," IV, pp. 482–89; ZPEB, "Ships," V, pp. 410–15; Ryken, Wilhoit, and Longman, *Dictionary of Biblical Imagery*, "Ship, Shipwreck," pp. 785–86.

20 Rejoice over her, thou heaven, and ye holy apostles and prophets; for God hath avenged you on her.
21 And a mighty angel took up a stone like a great millstone, and cast it into the sea, saying, Thus with violence shall that great city Babylon be thrown down, and shall be found no more at all.
22 And the voice of harpers, and musicians, and of pipers, and trumpeters, shall be heard no more at all in thee; and no craftsman, of whatsoever craft he be, shall be found any more in thee; and the sound of a millstone shall be heard no more at all in thee;
23 And the light of a candle shall shine no more at all in thee; and the voice of the bridegroom and of the bride shall be heard no more at all in thee: for thy merchants were the great men of the earth; for by thy sorceries were all nations deceived.
24 And in her was found the blood of prophets, and of saints, and of all that were slain upon the earth.

opulent source of income is gone. "And they were casting dust upon their heads, and were crying, weeping and mourning, saying,

> Woe, woe, the great city in which all who have ships in the sea were made rich out of her costly things, because in one hour she was laid waste" (v. 19).

When Ezekiel described the mourning of the mariners over the destruction of Tyre, he said that they cried bitterly and "cast up dust upon their heads" (Ezek. 27:30).

III. The Heavenly Rejoicing. vv. 20–24.

> "Rejoice over her, heaven, and the saints and the apostles and the prophets, because God judged your judgment on her" (v. 20).

The people of God had suffered persecution and discrimination from Babylon and had already judged Babylon as a wicked city, and God now has executed His judgment on it with poetic justice and divine finality.

18:19. The word *dust* (χοῦς) occurs only here in Rev. and only in Mark 6:11 in the rest of the NT.

The word *costly things* (τιμιότης), literally *costliness*, is an abstract term "for concrete abundance of costly things" (Arndt and Gingrich, p. 826).

18:20. For a summary of the verb *to judge* (κρίνω) see Rev. 6:10 note. The word *judgment* (κρίμα) occurs 3 times in Rev. (17:1; 18:20; 20:4).

18:21. The word *millstone* (μύλινος) occurs only here in the NT. The more common term for *millstone* (μύλος) occurs in Rev. 18:22 and in Matt. 18:6; 24:41; Mark 9:42. The Gospels make clear that it is "an ass-drawn" (μύλος ὀνικός) millstone, not the kind a housewife would use. See ISBE (1986), "Mill, Millstone," III, pp. 355–56; ZPEB, "Mill, Millstone," IV, pp. 226–27.

The old word *violence* (ὅρμημα) occurs only here in the NT. Moulton and Milligan suggest "with a rush," like an eagle's dive as in Deut. 28:49 LXX (*Vocabulary*, p. 458).

The NT apostles and the OT prophets are obvious examples of people persecuted by the world system, Babylon. The prophets' warnings are now fulfilled (Isa. 13:19; Jer. 51:8–9; Mic. 4:10; Zech. 2:7–9). "And a strong angel took up a stone like a great millstone and cast it into the sea, saying, Thus with violence the great city Babylon shall be cast down, and shall never be found again" (v. 21). This is the third time that a "strong angel" is mentioned in Revelation (5:2; 10:1; 18:21). The angel provides a vivid illustration for the sudden, catastrophic end of Babylon. He takes up a "strong stone" and hurls it into the sea. Millstones more than six feet in diameter have been found in the Holy Land. Such a stone would cause a mighty splash. In a similar way Babylon will violently disappear into the murky waters of the past and will have no counterpart in the glorious kingdom that follows. The action of the angel seems to parallel the command of Jeremiah to Seraiah, to bind the scroll of judgment to a rock and cast it into the Euphrates, and say, "Thus shall Babylon sink, and shall not rise from the evil that I will bring upon her" (Jer. 51:64). "And the voice of harp singers, and musicians, and flute players, and trumpeters, shall never be heard in you again; and no craftsman, of whatever trade, shall ever be found in you again; and the sound of a millstone shall never be heard in you again" (v. 22). The bustling sounds of celebration and commerce are forever silenced in ruined Babylon. There will be no food for anyone to prepare. "And the light of a lamp shall never shine in you again; and the voice of the bridegroom and the bride shall never be heard in you again; because your merchants were the great men of the earth; because by your sorcery all the nations were led astray" (v. 23). The cheerful pleasures of human life are forever

---

18:22. The word *harp singer* (κιθαρῳδός) denotes a person who sings and accompanies himself on the harp. It occurs only twice in the NT, both in Rev. (14:2; 18:22). The word *musician* (μουσικός) occurs only here in the NT. *Flute player* (αὐλητής) occurs only here and in Matt. 9:23 in the NT. The word *trumpeter* (σαλπιστής) occurs only here in the NT. See ZPEB, "Music, Musical Instruments," IV, pp. 311–24; ISBE (1986), "Music," III, pp. 436–49.

The word *craftsman* (τεχνίτης) occurs 4 times in the NT (Acts 19:24, 38; Heb. 11:10; Rev. 18:22).

18:23. For the verb *to shine* (φαίνω) see Rev. 1:10 note.

The word *bridegroom* (νυμφίος) occurs only here in Rev.

The word *bride* (νύμφη) occurs 4 times in Rev. (once as a human illustration, 18:23; and 3 times as the bride of Christ, 21:2, 9; 22:17). The fact that the voice of the bridegroom and bride shall be heard no more signals "the end of a civilization" (Ryken, Wilhoit, and Longman, *Dictionary of Biblical Imagery*, p. 121).

The word *sorcery* (φαρμακεία) occurs only here and in 9:21 in Rev. It can refer to *magic* or to *magic potions* or *drugs*.

For the verb *to lead astray* (πλανάω) see Rev. 2:20 note.

removed from Babylon. Her sorcery poisoned the world and now only judgment remains. No sound of a wedding celebration shall ever rise from Babylon again. No home in Babylon will ever be cheered by the light of a lamp again. "And in her was found the blood of prophets, and saints, and of all those slaughtered upon the earth" (v. 24). The word *slaughtered* is a vivid expression of the way that the world has treated the prophets and saints. From the martyrdom of Abel (Gen. 4:8–16) to the martyrdom of Stephen (Acts 7:54–60), the Bible has clearly portrayed how the world has ruthlessly slain God's people. Only God can properly comfort His people. But Babylon, the world system, has slaughtered many billions of people, saved and lost alike, and God will bring her down in violent destruction to a fitting catastrophic end.

Practical Applications from Revelation 18

1. We cannot see that an angel can light up the earth; we have much to look forward to in heaven (v. 1). No wonder the psalmist said, "I will lift up mine eyes unto the hills, from whence cometh my help. My help cometh from the Lord, which made heaven and earth" (Ps. 121:1–2).
2. The world system gathers evil men and demons to itself (v. 2). David warned, "The kings of the earth set themselves, and the rulers take counsel together, against the Lord, and against his anointed, saying, Let us break their bands asunder, and cast away their cords from us. He that sitteth in the heavens shall laugh" (Ps. 2:2–4a).
3. Believers must be separate from the world so that they do not share the world's judgments (v. 4). Paul exhorts, "Having therefore these promises, dearly beloved, let us cleanse ourselves from all filthiness of the flesh and spirit, perfecting holiness in the fear of God" (II Cor. 7:1).
4. God will repay all evil deeds (v. 6). God promises, "Vengeance is mine; I will repay, says the Lord" (Rom. 12:19).
5. God judges sin (v. 8). "The ungodly shall not stand in the judgment, nor sinners in the congregation of the righteous" (Ps. 1:5).
6. Those who trust in their riches will regret it (v. 11). "Riches profit not in the day of wrath: but righteousness delivereth from death" (Prov. 11:4).
7. God will avenge His servants (v. 20). "Shall not God avenge his own elect, who cry day and night to him, though he bears long

---

18:24. For a summary of the verb *to slaughter* (σφάζω) see Rev. 13:3 note. This is the last occurrence of the verb in Scripture.

with them? I tell you that he will avenge them speedily" (Luke 18:7–8*a*).

8. All the happy times the wicked now enjoy will come to an end one day (v. 22). "The noise of them that rejoice endeth, the joy of the harp ceaseth. . . . all joy is darkened, the mirth of the land is gone" (Isa. 24:8, 11).

Prayer

O Lord, deliver Your people from worldliness. Help us to keep focused on Your pathway and Your service. Cause us to remember that we are pilgrims on our way home to Your Presence and the place You are preparing for us. Amen.

Revelation 19:1–20:15

REVELATION 19
FOUR ALLELUIAS; THE SECOND COMING

Persons

Much people in heaven
The great whore
The twenty-four elders
The four living beings
Jesus Christ
Titles
    The Lamb
    Faithful
    True
    The Word of God
    King of kings
    Lord of lords
    He that sat upon the horse

His wife
The armies in heaven
The nations
And angel standing in the sun
The Beast
The kings of the earth
The False Prophet

Persons referred to

Servants of God
Kings
Captains

Mighty men
Beast worshipers
The remnant of the armies

Places mentioned

Heaven
The earth

The sun
A lake of fire

Doctrines taught

Worship of God
Salvation
Judgment
Martyrdom
The reign of God
The marriage of the Lamb
Righteousness
The testimony of Jesus

Prophecy
The Second Coming
Divine war
The Word of God
The wrath of Almighty God
The Antichrist (Beast)
Hell (lake of fire)

1 And after these things I heard a great voice of much people in heaven, saying, Alleluia; Salvation, and glory, and honour, and power, unto the Lord our God:
2 For true and righteous are his judgments: for he hath judged the great whore, which did corrupt the earth with her fornication, and hath avenged the blood of his servants at her hand.
3 And again they said, Alleluia. And her smoke rose up for ever and ever.
4 And the four and twenty elders and the four beasts fell down and worshipped God that sat on the throne, saying, Amen; Alleluia.
5 And a voice came out of the throne, saying, Praise our God, all ye his servants, and ye that fear him, both small and great.
6 And I heard as it were the voice of a great multitude, and as the voice of many waters, and as the voice of mighty thunderings, saying, Alleluia: for the Lord God omnipotent reigneth.
7 Let us be glad and rejoice, and give honour to him: for the marriage of the Lamb is come, and his wife hath made herself ready.
8 And to her was granted that she should be arrayed in fine linen, clean and white: for the fine linen is the righteousness of saints.
9 And he saith unto me, Write, Blessed are they which are called unto the marriage supper of the Lamb. And he saith unto me, These are the true sayings of God.
10 And I fell at his feet to worship him. And he said unto me, See thou do it not: I am thy fellowservant, and of thy brethren that have the testimony of Jesus: worship God: for the testimony of Jesus is the spirit of prophecy.

Revelation 19 Exposition

1. The Fourfold Alleluia. vv. 1–10.

"And after these things I heard as a great voice of a huge crowd in heaven, saying, Alleluia; Salvation and glory and power be to our God" (v. 1).

The phrase *after these things* (μετὰ ταῦτα) regularly marks an important new section of the book (4:1; 7:1; etc.). Osborne notes the striking contrast between the lamentations of the world (Rev. 18:10–19) and the celebration in heaven over God's judgment (*Rev.*, p. 662). It is significant that the scene of the Second Coming begins with celestial praise to God. The time has finally come in which God will take over the rebellious world and rule in sovereign power. The *huge crowd* of Revelation 7:9 referred to the Tribulation martyrs, but here it refers to the saints of all ages. The heavenly hosts cry out, "Alleluia," *Praise ye Jehovah*, the word of constant

---

19:1. For the wide-ranging influence of the doctrine of the Second Coming, see the series of fervent sermons by I. M. Haldeman, *Why I Preach the Second Coming*. This is the third and last time that the word *salvation* (σωτηρία) occurs in Rev. (7:10; 12:10; 19:1). In each case it is in praise to God for having rescued His people.

praise in the Psalms (Pss. 104:35; 105:45; 106:1, 48; 111:1; 112:1; 113:1, 9; 116:19; 117:2; 135:1, 21; 146:1, 10; 147:1, 20; 148:1 [twice], 14; 149:1, 9; 150:1, 6). These four occurrences here are the only time in the KJV that the word is transliterated instead of translated. God has provided salvation for His people (Isa. 49:26; Luke 1:47; Titus 1:3). David exhorts, "Give unto the Lord, O ye mighty, give unto the Lord glory and strength" (Ps. 29:1). All men should attribute glory and power to the Living God. "Because true and righteous are His judgments; because He judged the great harlot who corrupted the earth by her fornication, and He avenged the blood of His slaves at her hand" (v. 2). David sang, "The judgments of the Lord are true and righteous altogether" (Ps. 19:9). "Righteous art Thou, O Lord, and upright are Thy judgments" (Ps. 119:137 NASB). The voice from the altar repeated this idea (Rev. 16:7). Moses prophesied that the Lord "will avenge the blood of his servants" (Deut. 32:43). The true saints in glory praise God for judging the counterfeit church, the harlot, on earth. The apostate church has corrupted the earth by her spiritual fornication with the world and has shed the blood of the true servants of God. The verb *to corrupt* (φθείρω) occurs only here in Revelation and reminds us of Paul's pronouncement of judgment, "If any man corrupt the temple of God, him shall God corrupt" (I Cor. 3:17). "And a second time they said,

Alleluia;
And her smoke continues going up into the ages of the ages"
(v. 3).

Isaiah prophesied that in the day of the Lord's vengeance the smoke of the land of Idumea shall go up forever (Isa. 34:8–10). This is a clear anticipation of hell, the lake of fire, with its eternal smoke of torment (Rev. 14:11; 19:20; 20:10, 15). Osborne contrasts this smoke of torment going up with the smoke of incense, the prayers of the saints going up in Revelation 8:4 (*Rev.*, p. 665). The Lord Jesus Himself warned, "And if your right hand cause you to stumble, cut it off and cast it from you; for it is profitable for you that one of your members perish and not that your whole body be cast into Gehenna" (Matt. 5:30). "And the twenty-four elders and the four living beings fell down and worshiped God who sits upon the throne, saying,

Amen, alleluia" (v. 4).

19:2. For the verb *to avenge* (ἐκδικέω) see Rev. 6:10 note.

19:3. This is the last occurrence of the word *smoke* in Rev. See Rev. 8:3–4 note.

19:4. This is the seventh time that the word *Amen* has appeared in Rev.

The words are a phrase from Psalm 106:48. It is a convicting thought to note how frequently the inhabitants of heaven return to the worship and praise of God and how rare such worship is on earth, even among true believers. "And a voice came out from the throne, saying,

> Praise our God
> All you his slaves
> And you who fear him,
> Both the small and the great" (v. 5).

"He will bless them that fear the Lord, both small and great" (Ps. 115:13). A direct command should certainly move believers, willing servants of God, to a greater praise and worship of God in their private devotions and in their public worship. Whether they are important or unimportant in the world's eyes makes no difference. God is no respecter of persons. He listens to all His people. "And I heard as a voice of a great crowd, and as a voice of many waters, and as a voice of powerful thunders, saying:

> Alleluia,
> Because the Lord our God, the Almighty, reigned" (v. 6).

Zechariah prophesied, "The Lord shall be king over all the earth" (Zech. 14:9). The time has come for God to take His great power and reign, intervening in the affairs of men. His people respond with a voice of thunderous praise.

> "Let us rejoice and exult and give glory to him, because the marriage of the Lamb came, and his wife made herself ready" (v. 7).

"This is the day the Lord hath made; we will rejoice and be glad in it" (Ps. 118:24). Weddings are times of rejoicing, but the marriage of the Lamb and His bride is a time of greatest exultation. Spurgeon exclaimed, "There is joy in heaven in the presence of the angels of God over one sinner that repenteth; but when all these repenting sinners are gathered together into one perfect body, and married to the Lamb, what will be the infinite gladness?" ("The Marriage of the Lamb," Sermon 2096, *The C. H. Spurgeon Collection*, Ages Digital Library). It will be the fulfillment of the passionate love expressed in the Song of Solomon:

19:6–9. "The wedding feast of the Lamb is the ultimate Thanksgiving dinner, where the promises made in Isaiah 25 are finally realized: no more mourning, or crying, or pain, or death. It is a glorious family reunion, when God and God's people will be brought together, reconciled wholly and completely," Sara Covin Juengst, *Breaking Bread*, p. 99.

"My beloved responded and said to me,
'Arise, my darling, my beautiful one,
And come along.
'For behold, the winter is past,
The rain is over and gone.
'The flowers have already appeared in the land;
The time has arrived for pruning the vines,
And the voice of the turtledove has been heard in our land'"
(Song of Sol. 2:10–12 NASB).

Hosea prophesied that the day would come when Israel would call Jehovah "my husband" (Hos. 2:16). Paul described the church as the bride of Christ (Eph. 5:23–24). But here the bride is the combined people of God of all ages, as her dwelling place makes clear (Rev. 21:12–14). Christ clearly portrayed Himself as the Bridegroom (Matt. 9:15). "And to her was granted that she should be clothed with fine linen, bright and clean, for the fine linen is the righteous deeds of the saints" (v. 8). It will be a marvelous experience in heaven to recognize people who have prayed for you, and you had not even known about it. Paul prophesied, "For it is necessary for us all to be made manifest before the judgment seat of Christ in order that each one may receive for the things which he did through the body, whether good or worthless" (II Cor. 5:10). If the deeds are worthless, they must be purged away by fire (I Cor. 3:12–15), but if they are good, he will receive reward in that all will know his deeds. "And he says to me, Write: Blessed are the ones who have been called to the marriage supper of the Lamb. And he says to me: These are the true words of God" (v. 9). Leon Morris notes that the phrase *marriage supper* implies "the joy of heaven" (*The Cross in the NT*, p. 363). The marriage supper is the great thousand-year kingdom reign of the Lord on earth (Isa. 24:22–25:9). The angel assures John that his words are the true words of God: a good angel cannot lie. Just as Ezekiel fell on his face before Jehovah, John is so overwhelmed by what the angel has showed him that he falls before the angel in reverence. "And I fell before his feet to

---

19:8. The word *righteous deed* (δικαίωμα) occurs twice in Rev., once of the righteous deeds of God being manifested (15:4) and here of the righteous deeds of the people of God being manifested. Paul revealed God's promise that we shall *fully know*, even as we are *fully known* (ἐπιγινώσκω, I Cor. 13:12). The veil shall be lifted (II Cor. 3:16). At the judgment seat of Christ we must all *be made manifest* (φανερόω) in order that the good things we have practiced in the body might be known and the worthless things forever removed (II Cor. 5:10). Throughout eternity the fine linen will be seen by all.

19:9. This is the fourth of 7 benedictions in Rev. See Rev. 1:3 note. The word *supper* (δεῖπνον) occurs only twice in Rev. (19:9, 17). It referred to the evening meal, which to the Jew meant the beginning of the new day. Compare the Lord's Supper (I Cor. 11:23–26). For the word *true* (ἀληθινός) see Rev. 3:7 note.

11 And I saw heaven opened, and behold a white horse; and he that sat upon him was called Faithful and True, and in righteousness he doth judge and make war.
12 His eyes were as a flame of fire, and on his head were many crowns; and he had a name written, that no man knew, but he himself.
13 And he was clothed with a vesture dipped in blood: and his name is called The Word of God.
14 And the armies which were in heaven followed him upon white horses, clothed in fine linen, white and clean.
15 And out of his mouth goeth a sharp sword, that with it he should smite the nations: and he shall rule them with a rod of iron: and he treadeth the winepress of the fierceness and wrath of Almighty God.
16 And he hath on his vesture and on his thigh a name written, KING OF KINGS, AND LORD OF LORDS.

worship him. And he says to me, See you do it not; I am your fellow-slave, and of your brethren who have the witness of Jesus; worship God, for the witness of Jesus is the spirit of prophecy" (v. 10). All true believers in Christ are fellow slaves of the Lord (Matt. 18:28; the Lord Jesus interpreted the king as His Father, v. 35), and the angel is happy to class himself among them, although he is greater in power. Witness to Jesus the Savior is not true unless it includes the truth that He is also the coming divine King. The idea of a merely human Jesus is a liberal invention and not a true portrait of the biblical Jesus. He said of himself, "Truly, truly, I say to you, you shall see the heaven opened and the angels of God ascending and descending upon the Son of man" (John 1:51).

II. The Second Coming of Christ in Glory. vv. 11–16.

"And I saw heaven opened, and behold a white horse, and the one sitting upon him being called faithful and true, and in righteousness he judges and wages war" (v. 11). Ezekiel also saw the heavens opened and

---

19:11. The word *horse* (ἵππος) occurs 16 times in Rev. (6:2, 4, 5, 8; 9:7, 9, 17 [twice], 19; 14:20; 18:13; 19:11, 14, 18, 19, 21) and only once in the rest of the NT (James 3:3). Expositors regularly take the white horse to be a symbol (of vindication, Beale, p. 950, etc.), but is it not proper to examine the subject more thoroughly? In the Lord's lifetime, He is described as riding only the colt of an ass (Matt. 21:2–7), but the prophecies stand that He will one day ride a royal charger (Ps. 45:4; Rev. 19:11). Is there a celestial equivalent of the noble steed (or pets in general)? Is there some truth to the old Greek myth of Pegasus, the horse the gods rode? When God created living creatures of all kinds, He saw "that it was good" (Gen. 1:25). If God has filled this world with so many thousands of different species of animals and plants, is it logical to think that in a greater realm there will be only angels and humans? There is something in the divine nature that loves small creatures, for that is what we are in relation to the divine nature. The Lord Jesus declared that He loved us (John 13:34). Is it a surprise that we love small creatures, dogs, cats, etc.?

beheld visions of God (Ezek. 1:1). Just as often in human experience the bridegroom is called away from his bride to wage the just war to make life safe for his bride, so here the heavenly Bridegroom rides forth to crush the enemies of His people and to make the great kingdom of God secure from the attacks of the enemies of God. The Antichrist had appeared on a white horse, but the colors quickly deteriorated into darker hues (Rev. 6:1–8). John has already called the Lord Jesus *faithful and true* (Rev. 3:14). Here He acts in perfect righteousness to remove evil from the earth. He wages war against the enemies of righteousness. Satan had offered Christ a victory of compromise, but the Lord rejected it (Matt. 4:8–10, A. T. Robertson, *Word Pictures*, VI, p. 451). Thomas marshals a considerable argument for the Lord Jesus returning as a Warrior-Prince to subjugate His enemies and secure His kingdom (*Rev. 8–22*, pp. 381–84). The Lord Jesus had prophesied such a scene of triumphant glory at His return: "Then shall appear the sign of the Son of man in heaven: and then shall all the tribes of the earth mourn, and they shall see the Son of man coming in the clouds of heaven with power and great glory" (Matt. 24:30). John goes on to describe this great King: "And his eyes were as a flame of fire, and upon his head many diadems, and having a name written which no one knew except He himself" (v. 12). His eyes could see the true nature of every man. John had already testified that He "needed not that any man should testify of man: for he knew what was in man" (John 2:25). He knew that His disciples murmured at His teaching (John 6:61). On His head were many imperial diadems, symbols of the right to rule all nations. It was prophesied that all nations should serve Him and call Him blessed (Ps. 72:11, 17). Some believers may be puzzled by the thought of many crowns stacked on His head, but the imperial crown in the ancient world was a thin linen band, and thus the "crowns" of the nations would take the appearance of a turban on His head (see Rev. 12:3 note). His name is a divine characterization of His Person that only God could truly appreciate. The Father alone knows how great His Son really is. The Father ranks Him above all other human beings in Matthew 3:17. Spurgeon has an eloquent sermon on

---

The child's question at the death of a pet, "Will I see my doggie in heaven?" is a very serious theological question. The answer must be that if the presence of pets in the world to come will increase the joy of the saints, they will be there. God has promised, "No good thing will he withhold from them that walk uprightly" (Ps. 84:11). This world is His footstool; the next is His throne. We may be sure that it is filled with more delightful things than we can now imagine. The number of animals mentioned in the Book of Rev. is surprising. (See Introduction, p. xxiii.)

19:12. This is the third and last time that the word *diadem* (διάδημα) occurs in Rev. (12:3; 13:1; 19:12). The first two uses refer to the Devil's attempts to usurp the rule of the world, but here it denotes Christ's proper rule over all kingdoms.

"The Savior's Many Crowns" (Sermon 281, *The C. H. Spurgeon Collection*, Ages Digital Library). "And he has been clothed with a garment dipped in blood, and his name has been called the Word of God" (v. 13). The garment dipped in blood is not a reference to the Crucifixion, but rather to the victorious conquest of His foes as the prophecy of Isaiah described. "Who is this that cometh from Edom, with dyed garments from Bozrah? . . . Wherefore art thou red in thine apparel, and thy garments like him that treadeth in the winefat? I have trodden the winepress alone; and of the people there was none with me: for I will tread them in mine anger, and trample them in my fury; and their blood shall be sprinkled upon my garments, and I will stain all my raiment. For the day of vengeance is in mine heart, and the year of my redeemed is come" (Isa. 63:1–4). He does not have to take a literal sword in hand and slay His foes one at a time. He is the Word of God (John 1:1; I John 2:14; Rev. 1:2; John is the only NT writer to apply the phrase to Christ personally). All He has to do is to utter the word, Die! and the armies of the Antichrist are dead bodies. He could create the universe with a word (Gen. 1:3; John 1:3–5), and He can destroy the armies of Antichrist with a word as well. "And the armies that are in heaven were following him upon white horses, having been clothed with fine linen, white and clean" (v. 14). They do not come to fight but to share in the glorious victory of their great King. The white linen is the clothing of the bride, pure and spotless (vv. 7–8), in contrast with the gaudy splendor of the apostate church (Rev. 17:4). "And from His mouth comes a sharp sword so that with it He may smite the nations; and He will rule them with a rod of iron; and He treads the wine press of the fierce wrath of God, the Almighty" (v. 15 NASB). He will rule the nations with a shepherd's rod, but one of iron. David prophesied concerning Messiah and the nations, "Thou shalt break them with a rod of iron; thou shalt dash them in pieces like a potter's vessel" (Ps. 2:9). His Word is the weapon that slays His enemies, the great broadsword in contrast with the short sword of the Roman Empire. The OT prophesied of Messiah that "with the breath of

---

19:13. This is the only time that the verb *to dip* or *dye* (βάπτω) occurs in Rev. Some manuscripts have the verb *to sprinkle* (ῥαίνω) here.

19:14. This is the only time in Rev. that the word *army* (στράτευμα) refers to the armies of the Lord; the other 2 occurrences refer to worldly armies (9:16; 19:19). However, the idea is presupposed in Rev. 12:7.

19:15. For a summary on the great *broadsword* (ῥομφαία) see Rev. 1:16 note. The *rod of iron* (ῥάβδος) is mentioned 3 times in Rev. (2:27; 12:5; 19:15). It was not only a symbol of power (Ps. 2:9) but also the scepter of the kingdom (Ps. 45:6), as the writer to the Hebrews notes (Heb. 1:8).

The verb *to smite* (πατάσσω) occurs only twice in Rev. (11:6; 19:15), both times of the judgment of God, as prophesied (Isa. 11:4).

17 And I saw an angel standing in the sun; and he cried with a loud voice, saying to all the fowls that fly in the midst of heaven, Come and gather yourselves together unto the supper of the great God;
18 That ye may eat the flesh of kings, and the flesh of captains, and the flesh of mighty men, and the flesh of horses, and of them that sit on them, and the flesh of all men, both free and bond, both small and great.
19 And I saw the beast, and the kings of the earth, and their armies, gathered together to make war against him that sat on the horse, and against his army.
20 And the beast was taken, and with him the false prophet that wrought miracles before him, with which he deceived them that had received the mark of the beast, and them that worshipped his image. These both were cast alive into a lake of fire burning with brimstone.
21 And the remnant were slain with the sword of him that sat upon the horse, which sword proceeded out of his mouth: and all the fowls were filled with their flesh.

his lips shall he slay the wicked" (Isa. 11:4). His shepherd's staff is almighty power. "And he has upon his garment and upon his thigh a name written: KING OF KINGS AND LORD OF LORDS" (v. 16). The apostle Paul applied that title to the Lord Jesus as the blessed and only Potentate (I Tim. 6:15). Vincent suggests that the name is on the royal robe draped over the thigh of the rider (*Word Studies*, II, p. 558).

III. The Battle of Armageddon. vv. 17–21.

"And I saw one angel standing in the sun, and he cried with a great voice, saying to all the birds who are flying in mid-heaven: Come, gather together to the great supper of God in order that you may eat the flesh of kings, and the flesh of captains of thousands, and the flesh of strong men, and the flesh of horses, and of those sitting on them, and the flesh of all, both free and slave, and small and great" (vv. 17–18). The irony is that the lowly vultures and other scavengers get the first course of the great supper, cleaning up the carnage in preparation for the great kingdom to follow. Ezekiel saw a similar gathering of vultures after the defeat of Gog (Ezek. 39:17–20). An angel is a spiritual being and cannot be harmed by being in or near the sun. John now gives a brief summary of the actual capture of the evil leaders of this godless army. "And I saw the beast, and the kings of the earth, and their armies, having gathered together to make war with the one sitting on the horse and with his army" (v. 19). David prophesied the gathering of the kings of the earth against the Lord and His Anointed (Ps. 2:2–3). The Beast, the Antichrist, and the wicked kings who are confederate with him are really fighting against the Lord

---

19:16. There are many titles applied to the Lord Jesus in Rev. (see Introduction, p. 1).
19:17. For the word *supper* (δεῖπνον) see Rev. 19:9 note.

Jesus, not merely His earthly people. But now the Beast's time has come. The Lord Jesus is ready to deal with him. "And the beast was seized, and with him the false prophet who made the signs before him, by which he led astray the ones who received the mark of the beast, and the ones who worshiped his image; the two of them were cast alive into the lake of fire which burns with sulfur" (v. 20). These two monsters of depravity are "caught in the act," judged, and cast while still alive into the lake of fire (hell). They will be the first persons sent into that place of eternal punishment and will suffer a thousand years longer than anyone else. The rest of the wicked dead are in sheol, or hades, awaiting the Great White Throne judgment. "And the remainder were slain with the sword of the one sitting upon the horse, which [sword] proceeded out of his mouth, and all the birds were gorged with their flesh" (v. 21). This is the conclusion of the Battle of Armageddon (Rev. 16:16), an ignominious end of the kingdom of darkness. God's people can now take over the earth under the rule of the great King, the Lord Jesus Christ, as Daniel prophesied: "And in the days of these kings shall the God of heaven set up a kingdom, which shall not be destroyed: and the kingdom shall not be left to other people, but it shall break in pieces and consume all these kingdoms, and it shall stand for ever" (Dan. 2:44). The millennial reign, which follows, is a test case to show that the Lord Jesus Christ can reign in perfect peace and righteousness where all others miserably failed. "Behold, a king shall reign in righteousness . . . and the work of righteousness shall be peace; and the effect of righteousness quietness and assurance for ever" (Isa. 32:1, 17).

Practical Applications from Revelation 19

1. Believers should never forget to praise God for His salvation and continual blessings (v. 1). "Bless the Lord, O my soul, and forget not all his benefits" (Ps. 103:2).
2. God will avenge the persecution inflicted on His people (v. 2). "Dearly beloved, avenge not yourselves, but rather give place unto wrath: for it is written, Vengeance is mine; I will repay, saith the Lord" (Rom. 12:19).
3. Both the small and the great have reason to praise God (v. 5). "He will bless them that fear the Lord, both small and great" (Ps. 115:13).
4. Believers should think of the clean garments that they will have in heaven (v. 8). "Having therefore these promises, dearly beloved, let

---

19:20. The verb *to seize* (πιάζω) is the regular word *to arrest as a criminal* (John 7:32; 10:39; Acts 12:4).

us cleanse ourselves from all filthiness of the flesh and spirit, perfecting holiness in the fear of God" (II Cor. 7:1).

5. Men should worship God only (v. 10). The Lord Jesus quoted the
command, "Thou shalt worship the Lord thy God, and him only
shalt thou serve" (Matt. 4:10; Deut. 6:13).

6. Believers should be like their Lord, faithful and true (v. 11).
"Moreover it is required in stewards, that a man be found faithful"
(I Cor. 4:2). The Lord prizes a good and faithful servant (Matt.
25:19–21).

7. All men should remember that the wrath of God is very real
(v. 15). "But the Lord is the true God, he is the living God, and an
everlasting king: at his wrath the earth shall tremble, and the nations shall not be able to abide his indignation" (Jer. 10:10).

8. God is high above all earthly kings (v. 16). Daniel said, "Blessed be
the name of God for ever and ever: for wisdom and might are his:
and he changeth the times and the seasons: he removeth kings, and
setteth up kings" (Dan. 2:20–21).

9. Fighting against God is a hopeless task (vv. 19–20). "Woe to him
that striveth with his Maker! Let the potsherd strive with the pot-
sherds of the earth" (Isa. 45:9).

10. There is eternal retribution for the wicked (v. 20). "The wicked
shall be turned into hell, and all the nations that forget God"
(Ps. 9:17).

Prayer

Alleluia to our God. Help us to celebrate Your greatness, for You are worthy of glory and praise. We praise You for the coming marriage of the
Lamb and the coming victory of the Lamb. You alone are King of kings
and Lord of lords. Amen.

REVELATION 20

MILLENNIUM AND THE THRONE

Persons

An angel

Satan

Saints

Martyrs

Jesus Christ

The Beast

The wicked dead

The False Prophet

Persons referred to

The nations

Priests

Gog and Magog

Places mentioned

Heaven

The bottomless pit

The earth

The sea

The millennial city

The lake of fire

Hades

Doctrines taught

Angels

The Devil

The Millennium

Judgment

The Word of God

The first resurrection

The second death

Satanic deception

Eternal retribution

Hell

1 And I saw an angel come down from heaven, having the key of the bottomless pit and a great chain in his hand.
2 And he laid hold on the dragon, that old serpent, which is the Devil, and Satan, and bound him a thousand years,
3 And cast him into the bottomless pit, and shut him up, and set a seal upon him, that he should deceive the nations no more, till the thousand years should be fulfilled: and after that he must be loosed a little season.

Revelation 20 Exposition

1. The Binding of Satan. vv. 1–3.

"And I saw an angel coming down out of heaven, having the key of the bottomless pit, and a great chain in his hand" (v. 1). When the time comes to arrest Satan and stop his reign of terror, it does not take a delegation of archangels. "An angel" is sufficient in God's power. The angel has the key to the bottomless pit (authority to put beings in or let them out) and a great chain in his hand. This is the passage over which the symbolic interpreters manifest great mirth over the idea that a spirit could be bound with a literal chain. But the God who can create a spirit can also create something that can bind a spirit (and we are not thinking of anything metallic). Walvoord notes that a chain is intended to make a person inactive (*Rev.*, p. 291), but the Devil is certainly not inactive in the present age. Culver defines the Millennium as the period from the resurrection of the just to the resurrection of the unjust, the thousand years that Satan is bound (Robert Culver, *Daniel and the Latter Days*, p. 28). "And he seized the dragon, the old serpent, who is the devil and

20:1. This chapter is the battleground between the literal (premillennial) interpreters and the symbolic (amillennial and postmillennial) interpreters. For a comparison of the major positions see Robert G. Clouse, *The Meaning of the Millennium: Four Views* (G. E. Ladd, historic premillennialism; H. A. Hoyt, dispensational premillennialism; L. Boettner, postmillennialism; A. A. Hoekema, amillennialism). For a chapter-by-chapter comparison of interpretations see Steve Gregg, *Revelation: Four Views, A Parallel Commentary*. For a formal defense of the literal view see Paul Lee Tan, *The Interpretation of Prophecy*; Charles L. Feinberg, *Premillennialism or Amillennialism?* (reprinted as *Millennialism: The Two Major Views*, 1980). Perhaps the most fervent presentation of amillennialism is by Geerhardus Vos, *The Pauline Eschatology*, but he does not draw his main arguments from the Book of Rev. Even a hard-core skeptic such as Bart D. Ehrman candidly admits that the Book of Rev. clearly teaches a 1000-year reign of Christ on the earth; he just does not believe it will happen (*The New Testament*, p. 400).

For a summary of the word *key* (κλείς) see Rev. 1:18 note.

The word *chain* (ἄλυσις) occurs only here in Rev. Every other reference in the NT refers to a literal chain (Mark 5:3, 4 [twice]; Luke 8:29; Acts 12:6, 7; 21:33; 28:20; Eph. 6:20; II Tim. 1:16).

Satan, and bound him a thousand years" (v. 2). "The old serpent" refers to *the original serpent* (Gen. 3:1). Satan has always stood at the right hand, suggesting an evil way for man (Zech. 3:1). An unnamed angel arrests the evil leader of darkness and binds him for a thousand years—the period of the great millennial reign on earth. The phrase *thousand years* (χίλια ἔτη) occurs six times in six verses (Rev. 20:2–7). This is certainly repetition for emphasis and not an accident. The phrase occurs only in Revelation 11:3; 12:6; 14:20; II Peter 3:8 in the rest of the NT. (A different word for *thousand* [χιλιάς] occurs elsewhere in the NT.) A thousand years is a brief time for the Lord (Ps. 90:4), but it is a substantial time for a reign of peace on earth. "And cast him into the bottomless pit, and

---

20:2. The premillennial interpreters argue that it is a literal abyss and a literal 1000 years (Seiss, Newell, Scott, Ironside, A. C. Gaebelein, Alva McClain, Charles C. Ryrie, Tim LaHaye, etc.). For a brief comparison of millennial views see Walvoord, *Rev.*, pp. 282–90; Merrill Unger, *The New Unger's Bible Dictionary*, "Millennium," pp. 854–55; Couch, *Dictionary of Premillennial Theology*, "Millennium, Doctrine of the," pp. 259–62. As distinguished an expositor as John Albert Bengel (1687–1752) argues for the literal 1000 years between the destruction of the Beast and the last day (*Gnomon*, V, pp. 364ff.). The symbolic interpreters exercise considerable ingenuity in explaining away these terms. William Milligan thought that the 1000 years symbolized the completeness of Satan's binding (*Expositor's Bible*, VI, p. 337). F. E. Hamilton thought it symbolized the entire period between the two advents of Christ (*The Basis of Millennial Faith*, pp. 115–39). Hoekema holds that the literal Millennium could be fulfilled in the new heaven and not on earth (*The Bible and the Future*, pp. 274–87). Beale argues that the intermediate reign "is now the church age and the reign takes place in heaven, though 1:6 and 5:10 show that it also takes place on earth among those who are regenerate" (*Rev.*, p. 1021). The early church fathers, however, were overwhelmingly premillennial. Those who taught a literal 1000-year reign of Christ on the earth include the following:

Barnabas: *Epistle of Barnabas*, XV; Papias (quoted in Eusebius's *Ecclesiastical History*, III, 39, 12); Justin Martyr: *Dialogue with Trypho the Jew*, pp. 32–34, 39, 64, 80; Irenaeus: *Against Heresies* (iv, 21, 1; v, 28, 3; v, 32, 1, classing the amillennialists with heretics!); Hypolytus: *Treatise on Christ and Antichrist*, pp. 63–66; Victorinus: *On the Creation of the World: Commentary on the Apocalypse of the Blessed John* (but all of his words on chapter 20 were removed by Damasus, a friend of St. Augustine); Methodius: *Banquet of the Ten Virgins*; Tertullian: *Against Marcion*, iii, 25; iv, p. 35; Commodianus: *The Instructions*, pp. 41–44, 80; Cyprian of Carthage: *Exhortations to Martyrdom*, pp. 11, 12; Lanctantius: *The Divine Institutes*, vii, 22; vii, p. 24. There were many other fathers who taught a literal, political kingdom on the earth but just did not mention the time period: Clement of Rome, Polycarp, *The Didache*, Hegesippus, Novatian, *The Martyrdom of Polycarp*, *The Constitutions of the Holy Apostles*.

J. B. Smith notes that there are 21 cardinal numbers in Rev., all literal in meaning: 1, 2, 3, 3½, 4, 5, 6, 7, 10, 12, 24, 42, 144, 1,000, 1,260, 1,600, 7,000, 12,000, 144,000, 100,000,000, 200,000,000 (*Rev.*, p. 269). We could add 666, but it might be a symbol.

For a summary of the word *devil* (διάβολος) see Rev. 2:10 note.

For a summary of the word *serpent* (ὄφις) see Rev. 12:9 note.

The verb *to bind* (δέω) occurs only twice in Rev. (9:14; 20:2), both of angelic beings.

locked him in, and put a seal upon him, in order that he might not deceive the nations again until the thousand years should be ended. After
these things, it is necessary for him to be loosed a short time" (v. 3).
Isaiah had prophesied that the Lord would punish the inhabitants of the
earth for their iniquity and punish "that crooked serpent" for his evil
(Isa. 26:21–27:1). Satan was cast out of heaven in Revelation 12:9; now
for a thousand years the vile deceit and trickery of the Devil's tempta-
tions shall be removed from the earth. The seal of God cannot be broken: Satan is confined for the entire thousand years. The prophets
describe the transformation of all nations during that time: "Behold, a
king shall reign in righteousness, and princes shall rule in judgment"
(Isa. 32:1). The Jewish remnant from Assyria to Egypt will return to the
land (Isa. 27:12–13). "Many people shall go and say, Come ye, and let
us go up to the mountain of the Lord, to the house of the God of Jacob;
and he will teach us of his ways, and we will walk in his paths: for out of
Zion shall go forth the law, and the word of the Lord from Jerusalem.
And he shall judge among many nations, and shall rebuke many people:
and they shall beat their swords into plowshares, and their spears into
pruning hooks: nation shall not lift up sword against nation, neither shall
they learn war anymore" (Isa. 2:3–4). "And they shall teach no more
every man his neighbor, and every man his brother, saying, Know the
Lord: for they shall all know me, from the least of them unto the greatest
of them, saith the Lord: for I will forgive their iniquity, and I will remember their sin no more" (Jer. 31:34). "And it shall come to pass, that every
one that is left of all the nations which came against Jerusalem shall
even go up from year to year to worship the King, the Lord of hosts, and
to keep the feast of tabernacles" (Zech. 14:16). The world has not yet
seen such universal worship of the one true God, Jehovah. Spurgeon
gave his testimony to his faith in a coming literal millennial reign of
Christ on the earth:

20:3. "'The bottomless pit' mentioned several times in the Apocalypse is not (I believe)
named in any other Book of Holy Scripture. To us Christians it is revealed 'for our admonition, upon whom the ends of the world are come.' Whatever other idea we may form of
the bottomless pit, whatever other feature we may think to detect within its undefined
horror, two points stand out unmistakably: as a pit it is a place into which to fall; as bottomless, it appears to be one within which to fall lower and lower for ever and ever"
Christina Rossetti, *Time Flies: A Reading Diary* (1885). Quoted in Kent and Stanwood,
eds. *Selected Prose of Christina Rossetti*, p. 313. Miss Rossetti has correctly perceived the
helpless condition that Satan will be in for 1000 years. Anyone who has "had a fall"
knows the feeling of not being able to catch a support. Satan will be in helpless freefall for
a 1000 years, unable to interfere with the glorious millennial reign that will be going on.
For a summary of the verb *to lock* (κλείω) see Rev. 3:7 note.

4 And I saw thrones, and they sat upon them, and judgment was given unto them: and I saw the souls of them that were beheaded for the witness of Jesus, and for the word of God, and which had not worshipped the beast, neither his image, neither had received his mark upon their foreheads, or in their hands; and they lived and reigned with Christ a thousand years.

5 But the rest of the dead lived not again until the thousand years were finished. This is the first resurrection.

6 Blessed and holy is he that hath part in the first resurrection: on such the second death hath no power, but they shall be priests of God and of Christ, and shall reign with him a thousand years.

"We believe that the Jews will be converted, and that they will be restored to their own land. We believe that Jerusalem will be the central metropolis of Christ's kingdom; we also believe that all nations shall walk in the light of the glorious city which shall be built at Jerusalem. We expect that the glory which shall have its center there, shall spread over the whole world, covering it as with a sea of holiness, happiness, and delight. For this we look with joyful expectation" ("The Lamb—the Light," Sermon 583, *The C. H. Spurgeon Collection*, Ages Digital Library).

II. The Millennial Reign. vv. 4–6.

"And I saw thrones, and they sat upon them, and judgment was given to them, and [I saw] the souls of the ones who were beheaded on account of the witness of Jesus and on account of the word of God, and who had not worshiped the beast, neither his image, and who had not received his mark upon their foreheads or upon their hands; and they lived and reigned with Christ a thousand years" (v. 4). The *they* who sit upon

---

20:4. It is well to remember Henry Alford's impassioned words on this text: "It will have been long ago anticipated by the readers of this commentary, that I cannot consent to distort words from their plain sense and chronological place in the prophecy, on account of any considerations of difficulty, or any risk of abuses which the doctrine of the millennium may bring with it. Those who lived next to the apostles, and the whole Church for 300 years, understood them in the plain literal sense: and it is a strange sight in these days to see expositors who are among the first in reverence of antiquity, complacently casting aside the most cogent instance of consensus which primitive antiquity presents. As regards the text itself, no legitimate treatment of it will extort what is known as the spiritual interpretation now in fashion. If, in a passage where *two resurrections* are mentioned, where certain ψυχαὶ ἔζησαν [souls lived] at the first, and the rest of the νεκροὶ ἔζησαν [dead lived] only at the end of a specified period after that first,—if in such a passage the first resurrection may be understood to mean *spiritual* rising with Christ, while the second means *literal* rising from the grave;—then there is an end of all significance in language, and Scripture is wiped out as a definite testimony to anything. If the first resurrection is

thrones are plainly the saints of all ages (Seiss, A. C. Gaebelein, Thomas, Osborne), specifically joined by the martyrs of the Tribulation period who would not receive the mark of the Beast, who now reign for the thousand years of peace on earth, even as the twenty-four elders had prophesied (Rev. 5:10) and Daniel had prophesied long before: "Until the Ancient of days came, and judgment was given to the saints of the most High; and the time came that the saints possessed the kingdom" (Dan. 7:22). Did not the apostle Paul ask, "Do you not know that the saints shall judge the world?" (I Cor. 6:2). This will be the fulfillment of those portraits of the OT prophets who describe the universal kingdom of Jehovah over people who still must use plows and pruning hooks (Isa. 2:2–4). "Behold, a king shall reign in righteousness, and princes shall rule in judgment. . . . Blessed are ye that sow beside all waters, that send forth thither the feet of the ox and the ass" (Isa. 32:1, 20). The saints will make sure that the world does not go in the direction that the Devil and the legions of his demons took it. We can hardly imagine life in which rulers govern indeed for the benefit of all the people; in which businesses are run for the benefit of all, and not the rapacious few; in which there is not a single dangerous product on the market. For a thousand years the Lord Jesus will prove that He can rule this world in perfect righteousness and peace, for He is the Righteous One (Acts 3:14) and the Prince of peace (Isa. 9:6). That will be the day of instantaneous answers to prayer: "And it shall come to pass, that before they call, I will answer; and while they are yet speaking, I will hear" (Isa. 65:24). The Lord will tame the whole animal creation: "The wolf and the lamb shall feed together, and the lion shall eat straw like the bullock: and dust shall be the serpent's meat. They shall not hurt nor destroy in all my holy mountain, saith the Lord" (Isa. 65:25). All these texts presuppose a transformed earth and not the glory of heaven. In the Millennium there will be no infant death:

---

spiritual, then so is the second . . . but if the second is literal, then so is the first, which in common with the whole primitive Church and many of the best modern expositors, I do maintain, and receive as an article of faith and hope" (*Alford's Greek Testament*, IV, pp. 732–33).

We might also remember Berkhof's admission in his reference to the resurrection, the final judgment, and the end of the world, "There is not the slightest indication that they are separated by a thousand years, except this be found in Rev. 20:4–6" (*Systematic Theology*, p. 714).

The verb *to behead* (πελεκίζω) occurs only here in the NT. A. J. Gordon noted that the martyrs were literally beheaded, and therefore this resurrection must be literal ("The First Resurrection" in *Premillennial Essays of the Prophetic Conference of 1878*, Chicago: Revell, 1879, rpt. Klock & Klock, 1981, p. 80).

For a summary of the word *throne* (θρόνος) see Rev. 1:4 note.

For a summary of the verb *to reign as a king* (βασιλεύω) see Rev. 5:10 note.

"There shall be no more thence an infant of days, nor an old man that
hath not filled his days: for the child shall die an hundred years old; but
the sinner being an hundred years old shall be accursed" (Isa. 65:20).
The unsaved shall have a hundred-year probation period. If they do not
get saved during that time, God will smite them with the plague under a
curse of judgment (Zech. 14:18). This will be the reign "with the rod of
iron" (Ps. 2:9). If there will never be a literal reign of peace on earth,
there would always be a lingering suspicion that even God could not rule
this present world perfectly. The Lord Jesus will prove otherwise for a
thousand years by fulfilling the angelic song, "Glory to God in the highest, and on earth peace, good will toward men" (Luke 2:14). "And the
rest of the dead lived not until the thousand years were ended. This is
the first resurrection" (v. 5). The first resurrection is the resurrection of
the righteous (John 6:39–40). It is a resurrection "out from among the
dead" (ἐκ νεκρῶν, Phil. 3:11). "The rest of the dead" refers to the unsaved, wicked dead, who have rejected Christ (John 10:24–26). The Lord
Jesus promised that He would raise the righteous to a resurrection of life,
and the evildoers to a resurrection of judgment (John 5:28–29). "Blessed
and holy is the one who has part in the first resurrection; upon these the
second death has no authority, but they shall be priests of God and of
Christ, and shall reign with him the thousand years" (v. 6). The saints of
all ages who trusted in Christ for salvation shall reign with Him for a
thousand years, even as the Lord promised (Matt. 24:45–47; Rev. 3:21).
Those who are holy, "set apart" for God here, will be "set apart" in the
world to come for increased service. The Lord Jesus specifically promised
the apostles that they would reign over the twelve tribes of Israel
(Matt. 19:28). In a messianic context Isaiah prophesied, "They shall re-
pair the waste cities, the desolations of many generations. And strangers
shall stand and feed your flocks, and the sons of the alien shall be your
plowmen and your vinedressers. But you shall be named the Priests of the

---

20:5. The phrase *the dead* occurs 5 times in Rev. 20 (vv. 5, 12 [twice], 13 [twice]). It is
clear that although they have lost their physical bodies, they are still conscious, moral beings that are responsible before God. The wicked dead will have a thousand years to
think over their selfish, evil deeds before facing the Great White Throne judgment. They
thought they were clever enough to get away with it all, but they were not. The dead in
Christ are with Him and will return with Him (I Thess. 4:14ff.).

For a wide-ranging survey of the millennial kingdom see Girdlestone, R. B., *The Grammar
of Prophecy*, pp. 141–49; Herman Hoyt, *The End Times*, pp. 167–92; Ryken, Wilhoit, and
Longman, *Dictionary of Biblical Imagery*, "Millennium," pp. 551–54; Rene Pache, *The
Future Life*, "The Marriage Feast of the Lamb," pp. 244–57; Dwight Pentecost, *Things to
Come*, pp. 467–546; John Walvoord, *Major Bible Prophecies*, "The Millennial Kingdom,"
pp. 389–406.

20:6. For a summary of the 7 uses of the word *blessed* (μακάριος) see Rev. 1:3 note.

7 And when the thousand years are expired, Satan shall be loosed out of his prison,

8 And shall go out to deceive the nations which are in the four quarters of the earth, Gog and Magog, to gather them together to battle: the number of whom is as the sand of the sea.

9 And they went up on the breadth of the earth, and compassed the camp of the saints about, and the beloved city: and fire came down from God out of heaven, and devoured them.

10 And the devil that deceived them was cast into the lake of fire and brimstone, where the beast and the false prophet are, and shall be tormented day and night for ever and ever.

Lord: men shall call you the Ministers of our God: ye shall eat the riches of the Gentiles, and in their glory shall ye boast yourselves" (Isa. 61:4–6). Spurgeon has a powerful sermon on Revelation 20:4–6, in which he avoids prophetic questions but emphasizes two great truths: Scripture teaches a literal first resurrection of believers in Christ to joy and blessedness in the world to come; and Scripture also teaches a literal resurrection of the wicked dead to damnation and eternal suffering ("The First Resurrection," Sermon 391, *The C. H. Spurgeon Collection*, Ages Digital Library).

III. The Loosing of Satan. vv. 7–10.

"And when the thousand years shall be ended, Satan shall be loosed out of his prison" (v. 7). This is one of the most difficult passages in Revelation. When there has been a thousand years of peace and blessing on the earth, why would God release the Devil again? It is because God intends to prove that the trouble is with man. In a society of peace and prosperity man is still ready to follow the Devil rather than God. It is not circumstances that drive a person to sin; it is his own sinful nature (Rom. 3:10–18). In the midst of millennial blessings, man is ready to listen to the Devil's lies. Whether it is Eden (Gen. 3) or the Millennium (Rev. 20), human nature has not changed. Osborne notes, "God allows Satan and his followers to have one last gasp, yet the purpose there is to prove beyond any doubt that the hold of depravity over the sinner is total" (*Rev.*, p. 717). "And he shall go forth to lead astray the nations that are in the four corners of the earth, Gog and Magog, to gather them together to war, of whom their number was as the sand of the sea" (v. 8). Gog and

---

20:7. For a summary on *Satan* see Rev. 12:9 note.

The apostle Peter also mentioned spirits in prison (I Pet. 3:19).

20:8. The Gog and Magog mentioned in Ezek. 38–39 referred to a northern confederacy of nations that attack Israel (and the Beast's empire) just before the midpoint of the Tribulation period. Their defeat by fighting and providential disasters probably emboldens

Magog were names of the ancient enemies of Israel (Ezek. 38–39, which refers to a battle during the Tribulation period). Here they are applied to this huge multitude that comes against the Holy City at the end of the Millennium. It is the last revolt of sinful men, but there is no war allowed. The thousand years of peace and prosperity have led to a huge increase in the world's population. The abundant harvests will support it (Amos 9:13–15). "And they went up upon the broad place of the earth and encircled the camp of the saints, and the beloved city, and fire came down out of heaven and consumed them" (v. 9). Jerusalem is the beloved city (Ps. 87:2–3). The final exam was over and man had flunked again. There is no excuse left. God has been infinitely patient, but time has come to an end. "And the devil who led them astray was cast into the lake of fire and sulfur, where the beast and the false prophet are, and they shall be tormented day and night into the ages of the ages" (v. 10). Satan will sink into the center of that ball of fire, where the heat and pressure are most extreme, where the stench of burning sulfur is most foul; and there he will be imprisoned forever. There he can ponder how well the universe will get along without him. The word *torment* informs us that spirits can suffer. For a spirit who delighted to cause pain and suffering to people (Job 1:6–2:7; Luke 13:16; 22:31), it is appropriate that he be inflicted with suffering equal to that of billions of human beings that he deceived. There are degrees of punishment in hell (Luke 12:47–48). The phrase *day and night* shows that the punishment is constant and without end (inversely parallel to the praises of the living beings, Rev. 4:8).

---

the Beast to institute the Great Tribulation of the last 3½ years. Beale thinks that this is a recapitulation of the same battle described in Rev. 16:14–16 and 19:17–21 (*Rev.*, pp. 1022–23). See "Gog," ISBE (1982) II, pp. 519–20; "Gog and Magog," ZPEB, II, p. 770.

20:9. The verb *to encircle* (κυκλεύω) occurs only here in the NT. See Moulton and Milligan, *Vocabulary*, p. 363, for parallels in the papyri. The rest of the NT uses a classical Greek synonym (κυκλόω) in John 10:24; Luke 21:20; Acts 14:20; Heb. 11:30. Joshua used encirclement to capture the city of Ai (Josh. 8:10–22).

Jerusalem of the Millennium is "the beloved city," but the Jerusalem that comes down out of heaven is the truly "holy city" (Rev. 21:2, 10).

For a summary of the verb *to eat down*, or *up* (κατεσθίω), see Rev. 10:9 note.

20:10. For a summary of the verb *to torment* (βασανίζω) see Rev. 9:5 note. Isaiah cries out, "The sinners in Zion are afraid; . . . who among us shall dwell with everlasting burnings?" (Isa. 33:14). Robert Govett notes that the idea of eternal torment destroys the interpretation that wicked beings are merely annihilated (*Eternal Suffering of the Wicked*, p. 57).

For a summary of the word *sulfur* (θεῖον) see Rev. 9:17 note.

This is the last time the verb *to lead astray* (πλανάω) occurs. For a summary see Rev. 2:20 note.

11 And I saw a great white throne, and him that sat on it, from whose face the earth and the heaven fled away; and there was found no place for them.
12 And I saw the dead, small and great, stand before God; and the books were opened: and another book was opened, which is the book of life: and the dead were judged out of those things which were written in the books, according to their works.
13 And the sea gave up the dead which were in it; and death and hell delivered up the dead which were in them: and they were judged every man according to their works.
14 And death and hell were cast into the lake of fire. This is the second death.
15 And whosoever was not found written in the book of life was cast into the lake of fire.

IV. The Great White Throne Judgment. vv. 11–15.

"And I saw a great white throne and the one who is sitting upon it, from whose face the earth and the heaven fled, and no place was found for them" (v. 11). The temporal "stage props" of the present earth and heaven will no longer be needed (II Cor. 4:18–5:1). The psalmist prophesied that God created the heavens and the earth, and "they shall perish, but thou shalt endure" (Ps. 102:26). The apostle Peter prophesied that "the day of the Lord shall come as a thief, in which the heavens shall pass away with a great noise, and the elements shall be loosed with fervent heat" (II Pet. 3:10), which is a reasonable description of the atomic dissolution of all things. Daniel prophesied, "I kept looking until thrones were set up, and the Ancient of days took His seat" (Dan. 7:9 NASB). The great throne of God fills the universe. It is white in absolute purity and holiness. The Lord Jesus made clear who is on that throne: "For the Father judges no one, but has given all judgment to the Son, in order that all men should honor the Son, even as they honor the Father. The one who does not honor the Son does not honor the Father who sent him" (John 5:22–23). The writer to the Hebrews reveals that the Son is enthroned at the right hand of the Father for the express purpose of making His enemies His footstool (Heb. 1:3–13). The spirits of all the wicked dead must stand before that throne. They are suspended in space before the throne. There is no place to stand and no place to hide. "And I saw the dead, the great and the small, having taken their stand before the throne; and the books were opened; and another book was opened, which is the book of life, and the dead were judged out of the things written in the books, according to their works" (v. 12). Daniel also saw

---

20:11. For a summary of the word *throne* (θρόνος) see Rev. 1:4 note.

20:12. If you, the reader, realize that you will stand among the lost in that day of judgment, will you turn now to the Lord Jesus Christ and ask Him to forgive you your sins? There is a simple ABC of salvation:

the books opened in judgment (Dan. 7:10). The wicked are blotted out of the Book of Life and not written with the righteous (Ps. 69:27–28). Scripture is very clear that if anyone is judged by his works for salvation, "There is none righteous, no not one . . . there is none that seeks after God . . . there is none that does good, no, not one" (Rom. 3:10–12). Paul concludes, "Now we know that what things soever the law says, it says to them who are under the law: that every mouth may be stopped, and all the world may become guilty before God" (Rom. 3:19). The world's "great" will stand before that throne. Pharaoh, who asked, "Who is the Lord, that I should obey his voice?" (Exod. 5:2), will find out. Pilate, who condemned the Lord to crucifixion in full knowledge of His innocence (Matt. 27:22–26), will have to face Him again. The "small" will also be there. The foot soldiers who spit on the Lord and smote Him in the face with the jeer, "Prophesy to us you Messiah, Who is he that smote you?" (Matt. 26:68), will find out that He knew exactly who they were. All the wicked who are before Him will know that every charge against them is true and right, and they have no excuse. "And books were opened." Are these "books" the minds of men? Does the human mind operate like a "little black box" that records every experience? Does each sinner remember every evil deed he has done, every vile word he has spoken, every wicked thought he has harbored? Everyone who is before that throne will understand that his condemnation is right and just in view of his "works." There are degrees of punishment as well as of reward. "And that slave, who knew his lord's will and did not prepare and do his will shall be beaten with many stripes. But the one who knew not and did things worthy of stripes, shall be beaten with few; and to whom much is given, they shall ask much" (Luke 12:47–48). "And the sea gave up the dead which were in it; and death and hades gave up the dead which were in them, and they were judged each one according to their works" (v. 13). One of the great "fears" of the ancient world was to be lost at

---

Ask the Lord Jesus to forgive you and cleanse you from your sins. He that asks will receive (Matt. 7:7–8).

Believe on Him as the only Savior (Acts 16:31).

Call upon Him for salvation. "Whosoever shall call upon the name of the Lord shall be saved" (Rom. 10:13).

Now you need to read the Bible with eyes of faith, seeking to learn how you can live to please Him (II Tim. 3:16–17).

20:13. This is the last time the verb to judge (κρίνω) occurs in Rev. For a summary see Rev. 6:10 note.

20:13–14. These are the last 2 references to hades (ᾅδης) in Rev. (Rev. 1:18; 6:8; 20:13, 14). Hades is the unseen realm of the departed, not the eternal "hell." The Lord Jesus revealed that in OT times the dead, both the righteous and the wicked, were in view of

sea, where there could be no burial, no "closure" that seemed satisfying. But God has not overlooked a single person, wherever he has died. Death released the bodies of these wicked people; hades released the souls, and reunited they stand before God in this judgment. The bodies are not glorified and the souls are not forgiven. Their works condemn them. "And death and hades were cast into the lake of fire. This is the second death, the lake of fire" (v. 14). The idea of annihilation is a man-made myth. There is not a single verse in Scripture that teaches that a spirit that God has created can pass out of existence. The Lord Jesus taught that a believer who dies may expect angels to escort his spirit to a place of comfort and fellowship with other saints (Luke 16:22, 25). He also clearly taught that the wicked person may expect to be in a place of torment, bitter regrets, and unsatisfied wishes (Luke 16:22–31). The

---

one another, but kept separate (Luke 16:22–26). But the blood of Christ now brings all saints into the presence of His Father (Heb. 10:19–22). Now we may draw near in prayer; at death we draw near in presence. To be absent from the body is to be present with the Lord (II Cor. 5:8). Hades is still the place to which the wicked dead go after death, to await the judgment of the Great White Throne. In the article "Hell," Ryken, Wilhoit, and Longman note that the general view of the NT is that "hell is punishment experienced as suffering in body and soul (Matt. 10:28; Rom. 2:8–9; Jude 7)" *Dictionary of Biblical Imagery*, pp. 376–77.

20:14–15. *The lake of fire* is the eternal hell that God has prepared for evildoers. It was specifically prepared for the Devil and his angels, but wicked people will also be cast into it (Matt. 25:41–46). The Beast and the False Prophet are the first to be cast into it (Rev. 19:20); then, a 1000 years later, the Devil will be cast in (Rev. 20:10); then all sinful people who have rejected Christ (Rev. 20:12–15). These 3 stages have been emphasized by literal interpreters from Seiss (*Apocalypse*, p. 450) to Osborne (*Rev.*, p. 715). The Lord Jesus clearly taught continued existence in the world to come (Matt. 12:31–32), a resurrection to life or condemnation for all who are in the grave (John 5:28–29), and warned again and again of the dangers of hell fire in gehenna (Matt. 5:22, 29, 30; 10:28; 18:8–9; 23:15, 33; Mark 9:43, 45, 47; Luke 12:5; James 3:6). For a formal defense of the doctrine of hell see John Blanchard, *What Ever Happened to Hell?* David George Moore, *The Battle for Hell*, John H. Gerstner, *Repent or Perish*, Robert Govett, *Eternal Suffering of the Wicked*, Harry Buis, *The Doctrine of Eternal Punishment*, Ajith Fernando, *Crucial Questions About Hell*, and Mark Minnick, *The Doctrine of Eternal Punishment*. In his sermon "Divine Retribution," Jonathan Edwards gave a list of the good and important ends that will be obtained by the eternal punishment of the wicked (see Roberts, Richard Owen, ed., *Salvation in Full Color*, pp. 345–50). For a scholarly study of the OT doctrine of death and the afterlife, see Philip S. Johnston, *Shades of Sheol*, especially "Resurrection from Death," pp. 218ff. Those who teach annihilationism overlook two important truths: (1) There is no Scripture that teaches that any spirit, human or angelic, can ever disappear or pass out of existence. But on the contrary there are many passages that teach that the spirit of man will survive death: II Sam. 12:16–23; Eccles. 12:7; Mark 9:47–48; II Cor. 5:1–4, 8; Rev. 14:9–11; 22:11. (2) There is no Scripture that teaches that a holy God could overlook or compromise with sin. God, by His nature, must love the righteous and punish the wicked (Exod. 20:5–6). The Lord Jesus taught that He would do just that (Matt. 25:31–46).

Bible clearly teaches conscious, eternal punishment for the wicked men and angels. There will be degrees of punishment appropriate for every sinner. "And if anyone was not found written in the book of life, he was cast into the lake of fire" (v. 15). This construction is a first class condition, assumed true: he was not found, and he was cast. This is the judgment of the wicked dead of all ages. A. T. Robertson noted that "there is no room here for soul sleeping, for an intermediate state, for a second chance, or for annihilation of the wicked" (*Word Pictures*, VI, p. 465). The OT clearly taught that Jehovah God can kill and can make alive (Deut. 32:39). Isaiah prophesied to his people,

> "Your dead will live;
> Their corpses will rise.
> You who lie in the dust, awake and shout for joy"
> (Isa. 26:19*a* NASB).

The angel said to Daniel, "Many of them that sleep in the dust of the earth shall awake, some to everlasting life, and some to shame and everlasting contempt" (Dan. 12:2). Spurgeon has a powerful, eloquent sermon "The Great White Throne" (Sermon 710, *The C. H. Spurgeon Collection*, Ages Digital Library). This solemn scene of judgment is in Scripture to cause people to recognize that they are moral beings who are responsible to God and who will one day stand before Him and hear exactly what He thinks of them. It is the blood of Christ alone that can cleanse us from all sin (I John 1:7). Without Christ as our advocate, we have no hope for the life to come (I John 2:1–2). May God help you, the reader, to trust Christ as the perfect Savior from your sins (John 3:16).

Practical Applications from Revelation 20

1. Every moral being will face moral accountability before God (v. 2). "So then every one of us shall give account of himself to God" (Rom. 14:12).
2. God will see to it that His people will ultimately rule all things (v. 4). "Know you not that we shall judge angels?" (I Cor. 6:3).

20:15. *The book of life* (βίβλος τῆς ζωῆς) is mentioned twice in Rev. (3:5; 20:15). A *little book of life* is also mentioned (βιβλίον τῆς ζωῆς), perhaps the same one (13:8; 17:8; 20:12; 21:27). See ISBE (1979), "Book of Life," I, p. 534; ZPEB, "Book of Life," I, p. 637; Ryken, Wilhoit, and Longman, *Dictionary of Biblical Imagery*, "Book," p. 114.

Theologians may argue free will or predestination over this verse, but the whole context teaches that every human being will get exactly what he chooses, God or sin, and God's will shall be done perfectly in each case. *How* remains a mystery to all but God.

3. The saints will one day be kings and priests to God (v. 6). "Humble yourselves therefore under the mighty hand of God, that he may exalt you in due time" (I Pet. 5:6).
4. Sinners quickly return to their evil ways (vv. 7–8). "But it is happened to them according to the true proverb, The dog is turned to his own vomit again; and the sow that was washed to her wallowing in the mire" (II Pet. 2:22).
5. God decrees eternal consequences for sin (v. 10). "Be sure your sin will find you out" (Num. 32:23).
6. All mankind must face God for good or for ill (v. 12). "Prepare to meet thy God, O Israel" (Amos 4:12).
7. To be judged by your works means condemnation (vv. 13–14). "For by the works of the law shall no flesh be justified" (Gal. 2:16).
8. To have one's name in the Lamb's Book of Life is the most important thing in the world (v. 15). "For what is a man profited, if he shall gain the whole world, and lose his own soul? or what shall a man give in exchange for his soul?" (Matt. 16:26).

Prayer

Dear heavenly Father, we still pray, "Thy kingdom come. Thy will be done in earth, as it is in heaven." Hasten that day when Your dear Son will reign supreme over this world and all mankind shall live in obedience to Your will. Amen.

Revelation 21:1–22:5

THE NEW HEAVEN AND EARTH

Persons

John (the author)
The Father
The Lamb
The bride, the Lamb's wife
One of the seven angels

The twelve tribes of Israel
The twelve apostles of the Lamb
The nations of the saved
The kings of the earth

Persons referred to

A bride and her husband
He that overcomes
The fearful
The unbelieving
The abominable
Murderers
Whoremongers

Sorcerers
Idolaters
All liars
Twelve angels of the gates
They that are written in the
    Lamb's Book of Life

Places mentioned

New heaven
New earth
Sea
Heaven
Earth

New Jerusalem
The lake of fire
A high mountain
The sun
The moon

Doctrines taught

Heaven
The presence of God
Divine comfort
Retribution for sin

Hell
The beauties of heaven
The glory of God
The Lamb's Book of Life

1 *And I saw a new heaven and a new earth: for the first heaven and the first earth were passed away; and there was no more sea.*

2 *And I John saw the holy city, new Jerusalem, coming down from God out of heaven, prepared as a bride adorned for her husband.*

Revelation 21 Exposition

I. The Vision of the New Heaven and New Earth. vv. 1–2.

"And I saw a new heaven and a new earth. For the first heaven and the first earth passed away, and the sea is no more" (v. 1). The Lord God had promised, "Behold, I create new heavens and a new earth," so splendid that "the former shall not be remembered, nor come into mind" (Isa. 65:17), but went on to describe millennial conditions (Isa. 65:19–25). The prophesied "times of restitution of all things" (Acts 3:21) must come. The old material universe is gone, for "the heavens shall pass away with great noise, and the elements, being on fire, shall be loosed" (II Pet. 3:10). "But according to his promise, we look for new heavens and a new earth, in which dwells righteousness" (II Pet. 3:13). The sun and the moon are not needed, "but the Lord shall be unto thee an everlasting light, and thy God thy glory" (Isa. 60:19). The sea was the place of origin for the Antichrist, "the beast from the sea" (Rev. 13:1). "The troubled sea," which

---

21:1. The existence of heaven is not argued but assumed, as it is elsewhere in Scripture. Jacob was astounded to see what a busy place heaven was (Gen. 28:12); David assumed that he would have fellowship with his dead child in the heavenly realm (II Sam. 12:23); Moses and Elijah returned and talked with the Lord Jesus about future events (Luke 9:30–31); the Lord Jesus said that resurrected saints will be like angels in heaven (Matt. 22:30–32); the Lord said that there would be personal fellowship and celebration in heaven (Matt. 26:29); the Lord said that His personal fellowship with His people could never be broken (Matt. 28:20). Will we see Father Abraham still welcoming the saints into the presence of God and comforting them (Luke 16:22–23)? In contrast with the fragile vegetation of earth, heaven is portrayed with the imagery of permanent jewels (Isa. 54:11–14; Rev. 21:18–21). It is the dwelling place of God, and therefore absolutely inde-structible. The Lord Jesus referred to it as a definite place, not merely a mental state (John 14:2). It is a higher realm than earth; men must look up to heaven (Luke 18:13); God looks down upon the earth (Ps. 14:2). It is the presence of God that makes heaven what it is. Isaiah begs God to look down from heaven "from the habitation of thy holi-ness and of thy glory" (Isa. 63:15). See ZPEB, "Heaven," III, pp. 60–64; Ryken, Wilhoit, and Longman, *Dictionary of Biblical Imagery*, "Heaven," pp. 370–72; ISBE (1982), "Heaven," II, pp. 654–55.

Some have suggested that during the millennial reign, the celestial city will descend into the material universe and will be visible as a satellite city suspended over the earth (Walvoord, *Major Bible Prophecies*, pp. 414–15).

Note that there are 7 things that will **not** be in the new creation: 1. No sea (v. 1). 2. No tears (v. 4). 3. No death (v. 4). 4. No sorrow (v. 4). 5. No crying (v. 4). 6. No pain (v. 4). 7. No curse (22:3), nothing to harm the perfect bliss of God's people.

3 And I heard a great voice out of heaven saying, Behold, the tabernacle of God is with men, and he will dwell with them, and they shall be his people, and God himself shall be with them, and be their God.

4 And God shall wipe away all tears from their eyes; and there shall be no more death, neither sorrow, nor crying, neither shall there be any more pain: for the former things are passed away.

5 And he that sat upon the throne said, Behold, I make all things new. And he said unto me, Write: for these words are true and faithful.

6 And he said unto me, It is done. I am Alpha and Omega, the beginning and the end. I will give unto him that is athirst of the fountain of the water of life freely.

7 He that overcometh shall inherit all things; and I will be his God, and he shall be my son.

8 But the fearful, and unbelieving, and the abominable, and murderers, and whore-mongers, and sorcerers, and idolaters, and all liars, shall have their part in the lake which burneth with fire and brimstone: which is the second death.

cannot rest (Isa. 57:20), will be forever stilled; the only sea in heaven is one as calm as glass (Rev. 4:6). There will be no place in heaven from which evil may arise. The new heaven will be vastly greater than anything we can imagine now. "And I saw the holy city, new Jerusalem, coming down from God out of heaven, having been prepared as a bride having been adorned for her husband" (v. 2). The wedding dress is often the most magnificent clothing that a woman will ever wear. It is a beautiful picture of the love lavished upon the bride by the heavenly Bridegroom, who will provide all that she needs and much more. The Holy City is the place that God has prepared for His people. The Lord Jesus promised that He would go to prepare a place for His people (John 14:2–3). His purpose is that they may be with Him forever (John 14:3). Earthly Jerusalem was called the holy city (Matt. 4:5), but it will be desolate in this age (Jer. 19:8). The millennial Jerusalem will be greatly blessed (Isa. 52:1f.), but this celestial holy city will be "the city of the living God, the heavenly Jerusalem" (Heb. 12:22), forever undefiled, a holy and beautiful place in which the love of God may be manifested eternally to His people. If God prepares the place so lavishly, how will He adorn His people? Osborne argues that new Jerusalem is both a place and a symbol of the people in the place, even as Babylon the great is (*Rev.*, p. 733).

II. The New People of God. vv. 3–8.

"And I heard a great voice out of the throne, saying, Behold, the tabernacle of God is with men, and he shall tabernacle with them, and they

---

21:2. The word *bride* (νύμφη) occurs 4 times in Rev. (18:23 [a joy removed from Babylon]; 21:2, 9; 22:17 [eternal joy with God]).

themselves shall be his peoples, and God himself, their God, shall be with them" (v. 3). The striking plural word *peoples* reveals that this is not merely the fulfillment of Jewish hopes but the consummation of the hopes of all God's saints of all ages. Matthew Henry comments, "Their souls shall be assimilated to him, filled with all the love, honor, and delight in God which their relation to him requires, and this will constitute their perfect holiness; and he will be their God: *God himself will be their God*; his immediate presence with them, his love fully manifested to them, and his glory put upon them, will be their perfect happiness." The prophetic name of Christ, *Emmanuel* ("God with us," Matt. 1:23), is now made reality. Here is the fulfillment of God's age-long purpose. God walked in the Garden of Eden with Adam and Eve (Gen. 3:8); Enoch walked with God (Gen. 5:22–24); God commanded Abraham to walk before Him (Gen. 17:1); God's purpose in the tabernacle was that He might dwell among His people (Exod. 25:8); the pinnacle of the psalmist's desire was to dwell in the secret place of the Most High (Ps. 91:1); Elijah stood in the presence of the Lord of hosts (I Kings 18:15); God promised that He would dwell "in the high and holy place, with him also that is of a contrite and humble spirit" (Isa. 57:15). The Lord promised the daughter of Zion, "I come, and I will dwell in the midst of thee" (Zech. 2:10). The Lord Jesus ordained twelve "that they should be with him" (Mark 3:14). Every believer should cultivate the sense of the Presence of God in his daily living. "And He shall wipe away every tear from their eyes, and death shall be no more, neither sorrow nor crying nor pain shall be any more, because the first things passed away" (v. 4). In a millennial context

---

The verb *I adorn* (κοσμέω) occurs only twice in Rev. (21:2, 19).

This is the last of 7 things said *to be prepared* (ἑτοιμάζω) in Rev. (8:6; 9:7, 15; 12:6; 16:12; 19:7; 21:2).

This is the only time that the word *husband* (man, ἀνήρ) occurs in Rev. God ordained husband and wife in a family (Gen. 1:26–28) because He intended to care for His people in just such a loving relationship. Isaiah cried out, "For thy Maker is thine husband; the Lord of hosts is his name; and thy Redeemer the Holy One of Israel; the God of the whole earth shall he be called" (Isa. 54:5). In the Song of Sol. the passionate love of the bridegroom for the bride has always been taken to represent the infinite love of God for His people (Song of Sol. 2:10, 14). See also "Husband," Ryken, Wilhoit, and Longman, *Dictionary of Biblical Imagery*, pp. 413–15.

21:3. This is the last of 3 times that the word *tabernacle* (σκηνή) occurs in Rev. (13:6; 15:5; 21:3). This is the last of 4 times that the verb *to tabernacle, dwell* (σκηνόω) occurs in Rev. (7:15; 12:12; 13:6; 21:3), making 7 times for the word root. There is an interesting use of the intensified form *to dwell* (κατασκηνόω) in Zech. 2:14 LXX, 2:10 KJV.

21:4. Vincent describes the word *sorrow* as "manifested grief," or "mourning" (*Word Studies*, II, p. 563). This is the second and last time in Rev. that God is said to wipe away the *tears* of the saints (7:17; 21:4). The word *crying* (κραυγή) occurs only here in Rev. This is the third and last time that the word *pain* (πόνος) occurs in Rev. (16:10, 11; 21:4).

the Lord promises to wipe away every tear (Isa. 25:6–8), but in glory
God's people shall be beyond the reach of any human affliction. Sorrow
shall be unknown in heaven. "Weeping may endure for a night, but joy
cometh in the morning" (Ps. 30:5b). The apostle Paul confessed, "we
ourselves are groaning in ourselves, waiting for the adoption, the redemption of our body" (Rom. 8:23b). There will be a divine serenity for God's
people in the knowledge that God has done all things well. "And the
one who is sitting upon the throne said, Behold, I make all things new,
and he says, Write, because these words are faithful and true" (v. 5). The
Lord makes heaven and earth *new* in the sense of pristine splendor, in
contrast with the shattered and worn-out earth of the Tribulation period.
Christ has already declared Himself to be "the Amen, the faithful and
true Witness" (Rev. 3:14). He would not deceive us. The new heaven
and earth will be perfect. Spurgeon has a powerful salvation message on
this text, "A New Creation" (Sermon 3467, *The C. H. Spurgeon
Collection*, Ages Digital Software). "And he said to me, They have been
finished. I am the Alpha and the Omega, the beginning and the end. I
will give to the one who thirsts of the fountain of the water of life freely"
(v. 6). The purposes of God for the ages have now been brought to consummation. The titles apply equally to God the Trinity and to the Lord
Jesus, the Agent of the Trinity. The Lord Jesus was the one who said,
"Let there be light" (Gen. 1:3; John 1:3–5). Note that this is a universal
promise, just as He promised, "And this is the will of him that sent me,
that every one who sees the Son, and believes on him, may have everlasting life: and I will raise him up at the last day" (John 6:40). He also
promised, "I go to prepare a place for you. And if I go and prepare a place
for you, I will come again, and receive you unto myself; that where I am,
there you may be also" (John 14:2b–3). Salvation is always presented as a
free gift to one who thirsts for it. The psalmist cries out to God, "My soul
thirsteth for God, for the living God: when shall I come and appear before God?" (Ps. 42:2). "O God, thou art my God; early will I seek thee;
my soul thirsteth for thee, my flesh longeth for thee in a dry and thirsty
land, where no water is" (Ps. 63:1). The prophet Isaiah cries out, "Ho,
every one that thirsteth, come ye to the waters, and he that hath no
money; come ye, buy, and eat; yea, come, buy wine and milk without

---

21:5. The word *new* (καινός) is the word for *unused, not worn out*, rather than the word
νέος, which means *recently come into existence*. See Trench, *Synonyms*, p. 220.

21:6. This is the third of 4 times that the phrase *the Alpha and the Omega* occurs in Rev.
(1:8, 11; 21:6; 22:13).

This is the fifth and last time that the word *fountain* (πηγή) occurs in Rev. (7:17; 8:10;
14:7; 16:4; 21:6).

The phrase *water of life* occurs 3 times in Rev. (21:6; 22:1, 17).

money and without price" (Isa. 55:1). God will thoroughly satisfy the spiritual thirst of every true believer. Spurgeon has a deeply moving salvation message on this text, "Good News for Thirsty Souls" (Sermon 1549, *The C. H. Spurgeon Collection*, Ages Digital Library). "The one who conquers shall inherit these things, and I shall be God to him, and he himself shall be my son" (v. 7). *The one who conquers* refers back to the sevenfold conqueror of Revelation 2–3. God promises not merely survival after death, but a very personal relationship with Himself for every believer who conquers the wicked one by the grace of Christ. "In all these things we are more than conquerors through him that loved us" (Rom. 8:37). Paul reminds us that we are "joint heirs with Christ" (Rom. 8:17), "heirs according to the hope of eternal life" (Titus 3:7). "But to the cowards and unbelievers and to the abominable, and to murderers, and to fornicators, and to drug users, and to idolaters, and to all liars, their part shall be in the lake that burns with fire and sulfur, which is the second death" (v. 8). The *cowards* are not merely faint-hearted; they are people who fear to take God at His word, hence the Lord's word to His disciples, "Why are you cowardly?" (Matt. 8:26). They are unbelievers in His promises; "strangers from the covenants of promise" (Eph. 2:12). They are *practicing abominable deeds* (βδελύσσομαι), which Paul warned against (Rom. 2:22) and which reminds us of the abominations of the harlot Babylon (Rev. 17:4–5). They are *murderers* liable to the judgment (Matt. 5:21). They are *fornicators* who shall not inherit the kingdom of God (I Cor. 6:9). The *drug users* (φάρμακοι) may be sorcerers who poison others or addicts who worship a drug that poisons them (only here and in Rev. 22:15 in the NT, although there are cognates, Rev. 9:21; 18:23). The *idolaters* are those who worship any god except the one true God of the Bible, Jehovah (Exod. 20:3–6; Matt. 22:37). "And all liars" have lied against the Holy Spirit, the Spirit of truth (Acts 5:3–4; John 14:17). They follow their father the Devil, who was the father of lies (John 8:44). All these sinners shall have their portion in the lake that burns with fire and sulfur, which the Lord Jesus warned against so solemnly (Matt. 5:22, 29–30). The first death is physical death; the second death is eternal suffering in the lake of fire. The Lord does not desire this for anyone; He is "not willing that any should perish, but that all should come to repentance" (II Pet. 3:9). If

---

21:7. This is the last of 15 times that the verb *to conquer* (νικάω) occurs in Rev. For a summary see Rev. 2:7 note.

The verb *to inherit* (κληρονομέω) occurs only here in Rev. The inheritance of the saints is a great theme in the NT (Matt. 5:5; I Cor. 6:9, 10; 15:50; Gal. 4:30; 5:21; Heb. 1:14; 6:12; 12:17; I Pet. 3:9). If God gives His only begotten Son to His people, what will He withhold from them (John 3:16)?

21:8. This is the last reference to *fire* and *sulfur* in Scripture. See Rev. 14:10 note.

9 And there came unto me one of the seven angels which had the seven vials full of the seven last plagues, and talked with me, saying, Come hither, I will shew thee the bride, the Lamb's wife.

10 And he carried me away in the spirit to a great and high mountain, and shewed me that great city, the holy Jerusalem, descending out of heaven from God,

11 Having the glory of God: and her light was like unto a stone most precious, even like a jasper stone, clear as crystal;

12 And had a wall great and high, and had twelve gates, and at the gates twelve angels, and names written thereon, which are the names of the twelve tribes of the children of Israel:

13 On the east three gates; on the north three gates; on the south three gates; and on the west three gates.

14 And the wall of the city had twelve foundations, and in them the names of the twelve apostles of the Lamb.

15 And he that talked with me had a golden reed to measure the city, and the gates thereof, and the wall thereof.

16 And the city lieth foursquare, and the length is as large as the breadth: and he measured the city with the reed, twelve thousand furlongs. The length and the breadth and the height of it are equal.

17 And he measured the wall thereof, an hundred and forty and four cubits, according to the measure of a man, that is, of the angel.

18 And the building of the wall of it was of jasper: and the city was pure gold, like unto clear glass.

19 And the foundations of the wall of the city were garnished with all manner of precious stones. The first foundation was jasper; the second, sapphire; the third, a chalcedony; the fourth, an emerald;

20 The fifth, sardonyx; the sixth, sardius; the seventh, chrysolite; the eighth, beryl; the ninth, a topaz; the tenth, a chrysoprasus; the eleventh, a jacinth; the twelfth, an amethyst.

21 And the twelve gates were twelve pearls; every several gate was of one pearl: and the street of the city was pure gold, as it were transparent glass.

you, the reader, do not know Christ as your Savior, now is the time that you should ask Him to save you from your sins. Man is a spirit; he cannot just disappear. He must live somewhere forever. Choose God.

III. The Bride, the Lamb's Wife, Holy Jerusalem. vv. 9–21.

"And one of the seven angels who had the seven bowls that were filled with the seven last plagues came and spoke with me, saying, Come, I will show you the bride, the wife of the Lamb" (v. 9). The angel used the

---

21:9. God's people as the *bride* or *wife* of the Lord is a beautiful picture of God's loving care for His people. This is the last time that the word *wife* (literally *woman*, γυνή) occurs in Rev.

exact phraseology to show John the great harlot, the false church (Rev. 17:1). The same angel who could pour out the wrath of God can also announce blessing and celebration. They are servants of God for whatever purpose He wills. The bride has become "the wife of the Lamb," the permanent consort of the Lamb. She is the combined people of God of all ages. Believers sometimes wonder what it will be like to actually know the patriarchs and apostles, the kings and prophets, mentioned in Scripture, but it will probably be a greater delight to come to know the lesser persons, like Bezaleel and Aholiab, who designed and built the tabernacle (Exod. 31:1–6), or Shiphrah and Puah, the midwives who braved the wrath of Pharaoh to save the Hebrew children (Exod. 1:15–17), or the unnamed man who was healed by the apostles (Acts 4:14), or the unnamed widow who cast in her two mites to the Lord (Mark 12:42). We shall all know them! "And he carried me away in the Spirit to a great and high mountain, and showed me the city, the holy Jerusalem, coming down out of heaven from God" (v. 10). This is metonymy: the angel offers to show John the bride, but what John sees is the city where the bride will live. In the visions of God Ezekiel was also brought to a very high mountain from which to view the millennial city and its temple (Ezek. 40:2). But here John has the privilege of seeing the eternal city of God. This city is a precious gift of God to His dearly loved people. God started man out in a beautiful garden, but sin blighted it (Gen. 2:15; 3:1–7). People have always been attracted to the benefits of a great city (Gen. 4:17; 11:4; Dan. 4:29–30), but the sins of the city God judges (Isa. 27:10–11). This great, celestial city combines the beauties of the garden with the security of the city, something man has long tried to do but failed. The secret of success is God. His presence is central to this celestial city, and His presence pervades the entire city. In worldly cities God is shut out or confined to little enclaves called churches. And the worldly city rots. "It is a place where culture subverts religion for its own purposes rather than advancing the glory of God" ("City," Ryken, Wilhoit, and Longman, *Dictionary of Biblical Imagery*, p. 151). This celestial city is incapable of deterioration, for God is there. "Having the glory of God; her radiance was like a most precious stone, as a jasper stone, clear as crystal" (v. 11). When Isaiah had his vision of the glory of the Lord, he heard the seraphim celebrate the holiness of God and cry, "the whole earth is full of his glory" (Isa. 6:3). In the

---

21:10. The Holy City is a direct creation of God, the great link between the celestial heavens and the material universe, both able to perceive the glory of God during the Millennium. At the end of the millennial reign, the material universe will also be glorified, but the city will go on radiating the glory of God forever.

21:11. The word *radiance* (φωστήρ) occurs only here and in Phil. 2:15 in the NT. In Phil. 2:15 true believers are a source of God's radiance for the cosmos.

Millennium the glory of God will fill the temple (Ezek. 43:2–5), but in this celestial city His glory permeates everything. Great worldly cities, such as Rome, Athens, London, Paris, are built on the glory of men, but the great characteristic of this city is that it is filled with the glory of God. The earthly jasper stone is a variety of quartz that is not transparent; it is opaque. The language shows that the city is related to things we already know, but they are transformed into beauty and transparency that is unknown on earth. The light of God can shine right through everything that is in the celestial city. There is nothing that can cast a shadow. That does not mean that the city is not real; it means that the Presence of God fills every part of the city with His approval and makes it permanent. No saint can ever disappear from that city, which is his eternal home. "Having a wall great and high; having twelve gates, and at the gates twelve angels, and names having been written, which are the names of the twelve tribes of the sons of Israel" (v. 12). The guardian angels make sure that no evil can enter the Holy City. The prophet Ezekiel saw the millennial city of Jerusalem with twelve gates and the names of the twelve tribes on the gates (Ezek. 48:31–35). There are two levels of reference here. John saw the celestial city shining with eternal glory, but that light also shone into the material universe so that the nations walk in the light of it (Rev. 21:24). During the Millennium the earthly Jerusalem will be the center of God's worship on earth (Ezek. 40–48), but those saints will not be glorified until the end of the Millennium. The purpose of the Millennium is to prove that the Lord Jesus can reign perfectly on the earth, fulfilling Isaiah 32, although all others have failed. "On the east three gates, and on the north three gates, and on the south three gates, and on the west three gates" (v. 13). The east is named first because the east was considered the

---

For a summary of the word *glory* (δόξα) see Rev. 1:6 note.

The word *jasper* (ἴασπις) occurs only in this context (vv. 11, 18, 19) and 4:3 in the NT. It is usually a dark reddish quartz, although it may have green, yellow, brown, white, or clear quartz swirled through it.

The verb *to be clear as crystal* (κρυσταλλίζω) occurs only here in the NT; the noun occurs in Rev. 4:6 and 22:1.

21:12. The word *wall* (τεῖχος) is the regular word for a city wall (Acts 9:25; II Cor. 11:33; Heb. 11:30). It occurs 6 times in this context only in Rev. (21:12–19).

The word *gate* (πυλών) occurs 10 times in this context (Rev. 21:12–25) and once in Rev. 22:14. In the ancient world the gate of a city was a great protection (Deut. 3:5; Josh. 2:5; Neh. 1:3; Ps. 122:2; Isa. 26:2). Without gates and walls, a city was open to attack from all enemies (Jer. 49:31–32). The gate was the primary target of attack by any foe (Ezek. 21:15). During the millennial reign, the gates of Zion will remain open day and night (Isa. 60:11). See "Gate," ZPEB, II, pp. 655–57; "Gate," ISBE (1982), II, p. 408.

21:13. God has not walled Himself off from people; He has invited them to come to Him from wherever they are. "Look unto me, and be ye saved, all the ends of the earth: for

"front" of any edifice. The Hebrew word for *east* (*qadîm*) also meant *front* (Ezek. 40:6; 42:15). There are gates on every side to show that there is a way to God from wherever a person is. But there is one limitation. The Lord Jesus said, "I am the door: by me if any man enter in, he shall be saved" (John 10:9). The Lord Jesus alone can bring the believer safely through the gate. "And the wall of the city has twelve foundations, and upon them the twelve names of the twelve apostles of the Lamb" (v. 14). The combined names of the patriarchs (v. 12) and the apostles show that this city is the dwelling place for the people of God throughout the ages. It is the city that Abraham looked for (Heb. 11:10). This is what Paul called "the riches of the glory of his inheritance in the saints" (Eph. 1:18). The apostles were foundational to the church, as both the Lord and the apostle Paul taught (Matt. 16:18; Eph. 2:20). The description so far has left a question: Is this just a beautiful picture, or is it an actual place? "And the one who was speaking with me was having a golden measuring reed, in order that he might measure the city and its gates, and its wall" (v. 15). The big question that faces interpreters in this passage is "Is this city a symbol, or is it an actual place?" No one measures a symbol. The angel measures the city and its details to remove all doubt: the city is as real as the capital of any nation on earth, but it is huge, beyond any person's experience. Did not the psalmist say, "All nations shall serve him" (Ps. 72:11)? There will be representatives from "all nations, and tribes, and people, and languages" who will stand before Him, crying, "Salvation" (Rev. 7:10). The resurrection body of the Lord Jesus was just as real as the merely physical bodies of the disciples (Luke 24:39). The Lord invited Thomas to touch His body and prove it (John 20:27–28). "And the city lies foursquare and the length of it and the breadth are equal. And he measured the city with the reed at twelve thousand stadiums [stadions];

I am God, and there is none else" (Isa. 45:22). But they must come through an appointed gate. The Lord Jesus said, "Enter in through the narrow gate" (Matt. 7:13a). Dr. Harry Hager said of the city of God, "Because the quadrangle has twelve gates and there are three gates on each side, we may be assured it will be the greatest of all convocations, a gathering from all generations and from all peoples that have ever populated this globe in all of the centuries and in all of the dispensations" ("The City of God," *Great Preaching on Heaven*, p. 211, ed. Curtis Hutson).

21:14. The word *apostle* (ἀπόστολος), "one sent officially," occurs 3 times in Rev.: false apostles in 2:2; apostles and prophets in 18:20; and the Twelve here in 21:14. The Lord Jesus Christ sent the Twelve forth to do His work (Matt. 10:1–6; John 17:18).

The word *foundation* (θεμέλιος) occurs 3 times in vv. 14 and 19 in Rev.

21:15. The word *reed* (κάλαμος) occurs 3 times in Rev. (11:1; 21:15, 16).

The verb *to measure* (μετρέω) occurs 3 times in 3 verses (vv. 15, 16, 17) and in Rev. 11:1, 2 only in Rev.

the length and the breadth and the height of it are equal" (v. 16). Thus, the great city is a gigantic cube. It is not an accident that the inmost sanctuary of the tabernacle was a cube marked off by a veil (Exod. 26:31–34) and that the inmost sanctuary of the temple was also a cube (II Chron. 5:7–9). God planned all along that His throne would be in the midst of a cubic sanctuary. In that vast cube there will be ample room for great companies of saints and angels to praise God, but they will all know one another; no one will be lost in the crowd. Paul clearly referred to the realm of perfection when he said, "Then shall I know even as also I am known" (I Cor. 13:12). "And he measured the wall of it, a hundred forty-four cubits, the measure of a man, that is, of the angel" (v. 17). The real question is whether the angel was the same size as John. The fact that twice John fell at his feet to worship him (Rev. 19:10; 22:8) implies that he was much more impressive looking. Any attempt to limit this cubit to eighteen or nineteen inches is a mere guess. The foundations will be impressive by celestial standards, not merely human size. The wall reveals divine protection. It is not the divine will that any evil thing pass through, under, or over that wall. God's redeemed people will enjoy serene peace forever. "And the building of the wall of it was jasper, and the city was pure gold, like transparent glass" (v. 18). Nothing in the city can cast a shadow. God's glory shines unhindered through it all. "Though an angel stand between you and the throne, he can cast no shadow on you" (Anon.). The most precious things in human society will be everyday surroundings in that blessed realm. "The foundations of the wall of the city have been adorned with every precious stone: the first foundation, jasper; the second, sapphire; the third, chalcedony; the fourth, emerald; the fifth, sardonyx; the sixth, sardius; the seventh, chrysolyte; the eighth, beryl; the ninth, topaz; the tenth, chrysoprasus; the eleventh, jacinth; the twelfth, amethyst" (vv. 19–20). Abraham

---

21:16. There are some expositors who think that the city will be a pyramid (Larkin, *Dispensational Truth*, pp. 146–48).

The word *stadium* or *stadion* (στάδιον) can refer to an arena (I Cor. 9:24) or to the length of the arena, approximately 200 yards, about an eighth of a mile (see ZPEB, V, p. 915; Arndt and Gingrich, *Lexicon*, p. 771). Thus, the heavenly city is approximately 1500 miles on a side. Today it is impossible to see a person who is 1500 miles away, even if we had a direct line of sight; but if Abraham could see all the way to the inside of hades (Luke 16:24–26), there will surely be no problem for the saints in glory to see and recognize every other saint in glory.

21:18. The word *building* (ἐνδώμησις) occurs only here in the NT.

The word *glass* (ὕαλος) occurs only here and in v. 21 in the NT.

21:19. The word *foundation* (θεμέλιος) occurs only in 21:14, 19 in Rev. but is common elsewhere in the NT (Luke 6:48, 49; Rom. 15:20; I Cor. 3:10–12; etc). See also "Foundation" ISBE (1982) II, pp. 355–56.

"looked for the city which has the foundations, whose Builder and Maker is God" (Heb. 11:10). These foundations are obviously well worth looking for. Just as King Solomon brought "costly stones" for the foundation of the temple (I Kings 5:17), the Lord creates gemstones of staggering value for the foundation of His holy city. The average human being has seen only very small pieces of a few of these precious stones. The thought of vast foundation stones of these gems is beyond present human experience. When we think of foundation stones, we think of having to get out of a building to see them. But the heavenly city is transparent, with the light of God shining through it all. Saints will be well aware of the magnificent gemstones on which the city rests. The Lord is here revealing to His people that He will take the most precious things in this realm and use them lavishly to decorate the eternal home of His bride. There is not

---

21:19–20. The foundation stones will make a magnificent sight:
1. Jasper: deep reddish quartz (silicon dioxide). Only in Rev. 4:3; 21:11, 18, 19 in the NT. It is the first gemstone mentioned in Rev.
2. Sapphire: deep blue corundum (the red variety is ruby). Only here in NT.
3. Chalcedony: usually a pale blue variety of microcrystalline quartz. Only here in the NT.
4. Emerald: bright green beryl (beryllium aluminum silicate). Only here in the NT.
5. Sardonyx: banded sard and carnelian quartz (silicon dioxide). Only here in the NT.
6. Sardius: brownish red quartz (silicon dioxide). Only here and Rev. 4:3 in the NT.
7. Chrysolite: an old name for a gold stone; now thought to be peridot or apatite. Only here in the NT.
8. Beryl: aquamarine; sea blue variety (beryllium aluminum silicate). Only here in the NT.
9. Topaz: imperial topaz is usually a warm yellow (aluminum fluorsilicate). Only here in the NT.
10. Chrysoprase: apple green chalcedony (silicon dioxide). Only here in the NT.
11. Jacinth: a deep blue stone, probably lapis lazuli; the finest comes from Afghanistan (silicate of sodium, calcium, and aluminum). Only here in the NT.
12. Amethyst: deep purple quartz (silicon dioxide). Only here in the NT.

See Chesterman, Charles. *The Audubon Society Field Guide to North American Rocks and Minerals*. New York: Alfred A. Knopf, 1978.

Pough, Frederick. *A Field Guide to Rocks and Minerals*. Boston: Houghton Mifflin Co., 1960.

Hurlbut, Cornelius. *Dana's Manual of Mineralogy*. 16th ed. New York: John Wiley and Sons, 1956.

Most of these stones were also in the high priest's breastplate (Exod. 28:17–20). All were highly prized in the ancient Middle East. Some of these stones adorned the anointed cherub (Lucifer) before his fall (Ezek. 28:13–14).

Osborne lists the twelve stones, the stones of the high priest's breastplate, and the stones of the zodiac, and gives some of the theories that have been proposed for them, which cannot be either proved or disproved (*Rev.*, pp. 756–59).

22 And I saw no temple therein: for the Lord God Almighty and the Lamb are the temple of it.
23 And the city had no need of the sun, neither of the moon, to shine in it: for the glory of God did lighten it, and the Lamb is the light thereof.
24 And the nations of them which are saved shall walk in the light of it: and the kings of the earth do bring their glory and honour into it.
25 And the gates of it shall not be shut at all by day: for there shall be no night there.
26 And they shall bring the glory and honour of the nations into it.
27 And there shall in no wise enter into it any thing that defileth, neither whatsoever worketh abomination, or maketh a lie: but they which are written in the Lamb's book of life.

one thing in this life that the believer will look back upon and wish that he had. It is like the successful businessman who discovers in his attic the little box of trinkets and stones that he had saved as a child. There is not a one that he would care to keep now. So the saint in glory will not wish for a single thing that he had in this life. That blessed city will satisfy the longings of every human heart. "And the twelve gates were twelve pearls; each one of the gates were out of one pearl. And the broad place of the city was pure gold, as transparent glass" (v. 21). People tend to think of a city gate as a rectangular space, flat on the bottom, into which they could walk. No one, however, is going to walk into the heavenly city. We do know that the angels carried Lazarus into Abraham's bosom (Luke 16:22). Saints who die are said to "fly away" (Ps. 90:10). The gates are said to be pearls. Since a pearl is round, it is logical to think of the gates as round, perhaps spherical. Mother-of-pearl, with its coruscating colors, is a beautiful thought for the gates of heaven.

IV. The New Sanctuary. vv. 22–27.
"And I saw no sanctuary in it, for the Lord God, the Almighty, and the Lamb, are the sanctuary of it" (v. 22). The Presence of God fills the entire city. Every believer will forever live in the Presence of God. There will be no break in the fellowship of God forever. Job's plaintive cry will be answered, "Oh that I knew where I might find him! that I might come even to his seat" (Job 23:3). The longing of Isaiah will be fulfilled, "Oh

---

21:21. The word *pearl* (μαργαρίτης) occurs here for the last time in Rev. (17:4; 18:12, 16; 21:21).

The word *broad place* (πλατεῖα) occurs 3 times in Rev. (11:8; 21:21; 22:2), referring to the plaza or broad boulevard of a city.

This is the last of 5 times that gold (χρυσίον) is mentioned in Rev. (3:18; 17:4; 18:16; 21:18, 21).

21:22. This is the last time that the word *sanctuary* (ναός) occurs in Rev.

that thou wouldest rend the heavens, that thou wouldest come down, . . . that the nations may tremble at thy presence" (Isa. 64:1, 2). David had that sense of the Presence of God: "Whither shall I go from thy spirit? or whither shall I flee from thy presence? If I ascend up into heaven, thou art there: if I make my bed in hell [sheol], behold, thou art there. If I take the wings of the morning, and dwell in the uttermost parts of the sea; even there shall thy hand lead me, and thy right hand shall hold me" (Ps. 139:7–10). The practice of the Presence of God will be normal life in that blessed city. Today all believers need to obey His command, "Abide in me, and I in you" (John 15:4). "And the city had no need of the sun, nor of the moon, to shine in it, for the glory of God illuminated it, and the Lamb is the lamp of it" (v. 23). "God is light" (I John 1:5). The Lord Jesus claimed, "I am the light of the world" (John 8:12). In the celestial city we shall see His true glory. The sun and the moon are God's provisions for human needs in this physical realm, but they are poor substitutes for His glory. The immediate Presence of God will be the domi-

---

21:23. Rene Pache lists the characteristics of heaven:
1. Glory. The Lord prayed, "Father, I desire that they also whom thou hast given me be with me where I am, that they may behold my glory" (John 17:24).
2. Holiness. God said, "I dwell in the . . . holy place." Before Him the seraphim cry unceasingly: "Holy, holy, holy, is Jehovah of hosts!" (Isa. 57:15; 6:3).
3. Beauty. "Out of Zion, the perfection of beauty, God has shined forth" (Ps. 50:2). "Thine eyes shall see the king in his beauty" (Isa. 33:17).
4. Immortality. God "only has immortality" (I Tim. 6:16).
5. Light. "Jehovah will arise upon thee, and his glory shall be seen upon thee. And nations shall come to thy light . . . Jehovah will be unto thee an everlasting light, and thy God thy glory" (Isa. 60:2, 3, 19).
6. Unity. "God will complete the execution of His eternal plan 'to sum up all things in Christ, the things in heaven and the things upon the earth'" (Eph. 1:10).
7. Perfection. "He who began a good work in you will perfect it until the day of Jesus Christ" (Phil. 1:6). "We shall be like him, for we shall see him even as he is" (I John 3:2).
8. Love. "I made known unto them thy name . . . that the love wherewith thou lovest me may be in them and I in them" (John 17:26).
9. Joy. "Jehovah thy God in the midst of thee is mighty; he will save, he will rejoice over thee with joy; he will rest in his love, he will joy over thee with singing" (Zeph. 3:17).
10. Consolation. "Blessed are they that mourn: for they shall be comforted" (Matt. 5:4). God is "the God of all comfort" (II Cor. 1:3).
11. Perfect happiness. "Nine times Jesus declared 'blessed' [happy] those who suffer when they live in this world according to His law" (Matt. 5:3–11). "God shall wipe away all tears from their eyes" (Rev. 7:17).
12. Eternity. Now we must number our days, since we have so few of them (Ps. 90:12), but there the elect will enjoy eternal life (John 3:16) and will "reign for ever and ever" (Rev. 22:5). (From *The Future Life*, pp. 347–57.)

nating illumination of the world to come. "And the nations shall walk through the light of it, and the kings of the earth shall carry their glory into it" (v. 24). David prophesied in a millennial context that "all the kings of the earth shall praise thee, O Lord [Jehovah]" (Ps. 138:4). But there is no question that many literal kings and queens have already professed faith in Christ as Savior, and no doubt there will be literal kings and queens in heaven worshiping Christ. It is significant that human culture will continue in heaven, but at a greatly exalted level. The Book of Revelation shows us that there will be in heaven music (Rev. 5:8–9), literature (Rev. 15:3), architecture (Rev. 21:12–13), pageantry (Rev. 5:6–14), but all centered in God (Rev. 22:3). Everything in heaven will perfectly reflect the will of God (Matt. 6:10). "And the gates of it shall never be shut by day, for there shall be no night there" (v. 25). The gates of the heavenly city shall stand open for all eternity. The powers of darkness will never be able to face the light of God that radiates from the city. Isaiah expresses it under the image of the Shepherd. "Behold, the Lord God will come with strong hand, and his arm shall rule for him: behold, his reward is with him, and his work before him. He shall feed his flock like a shepherd: he shall gather the lambs with his arm, and carry them in his bosom, and shall gently lead those that are with young" (Isa. 40:10–11). There will never be a dark and somber day in that city. "And they shall bring the glory and honor of the nations into it" (v. 26). The best aspects of human civilization will be found in that city, but none of the vices and flaws of human life. The psalmist desired to come before the presence of God with thanksgiving (Ps. 95:2). He wrote concerning the messianic King, "all nations shall serve him" (Ps. 72:11). "And nothing that is impure, or makes an abomination or lie, shall ever enter into it, except the ones who have been written in the book of life of the Lamb" (v. 27). Only saints who have been washed in the blood of the Lamb will be in that city (Rev. 1:5–6). His word to all others will be "I never at any time knew you. Depart from me, you who are continually working lawlessness" (Matt. 7:23). To have one's name written in the

---

21:24. Pache also raises the question of what will become of family relationships. His answer is that "heart relationships will not be changed. We shall meet again our husbands and wives and our parents and children, and we shall love them even more than we did on earth" (*The Future Life*, p. 359). But the love of God will be paramount in every saint's heart (Matt. 22:37–38).

21:25. There can be no darkness at all in the presence of the God who is light (I John 1:5). The saints will never have need of the light of a lamp or of the sun (Rev. 22:5). Night is useful now only because people need to rest; in glory no one will ever get tired.

21:26. All patriotic zeal will find its ultimate fulfillment in the worship and service of the Lord Jesus Christ, "KING OF KINGS AND LORD OF LORDS" (Rev. 19:16).

Lamb's Book of Life is far more important than any success or possession in this life. Spurgeon has a ringing message on this text (v. 27), "The Barrier: the Word of Exclusion" (Sermon 1590, *The C. H. Spurgeon Collection*, Ages Digital Library).

Practical Applications from Revelation 21

1. The world is going to pass away; only what honors Christ will last (v. 1). The apostle John warns, "And the world passes away, and the lust thereof: but he that does the will of God abides forever" (I John 2:17).
2. God is preparing a glorious, eternal home for His people (v. 2). The Lord Jesus said, "I go to prepare a place for you" (John 14:2).
3. God intends to dwell with His people (v. 3). "For thus saith the high and lofty One that inhabiteth eternity, whose name is Holy; I dwell in the high and holy place, with him also that is of a contrite and humble spirit, to revive the spirit of the humble, and to revive the heart of the contrite ones" (Isa. 57:15).
4. There will be no sorrow or pain in that heavenly city (v. 4). "Your sorrow shall be turned into joy . . . I will see you again, and your heart will rejoice, and your joy no man takes from you" (John 16:20, 22).
5. The thirsty soul will be satisfied (v. 6). Jesus said, "If any man thirst, let him come unto me, and drink" (John 7:37).
6. Unbelieving sinners will be cast into fire (v. 8). "The wicked shall be turned into hell, and all the nations that forget God" (Ps. 9:17).
7. God's place for believers is a place of light and glory (v. 11). "The Lord shall be unto thee an everlasting light, and thy God thy glory" (Isa. 60:19*b*).
8. We will have fellowship with OT and NT saints alike (vv. 12, 14). "Many shall come from the east and the west, and shall sit down with Abraham, and Isaac, and Jacob, in the kingdom of heaven" (Matt. 8:11).
9. God will take the most precious things here and make them abundant in that city (vv. 18–19). "The silver is mine, and the gold is mine, saith the Lord of hosts" (Hag. 2:8).
10. The saints will have direct fellowship with God (v. 22). "Make thy face to shine upon thy servant; and teach me thy statutes" (Ps. 119:135).

21:27. This is the last of 3 times that the word *abomination* (βδέλυγμα) occurs in Rev. (Rev. 17:4, 5; 21:27).

11. There can be no darkness in that city (v. 25). "God is light, and in him is no darkness at all" (I John 1:5b).
12. No evil thing can ever enter that city (v. 27). "The face of the Lord is against them that do evil" (Ps. 34:16).

Prayer

Dear God, blessed Holy Trinity, Father, Son, and Holy Spirit, thank You for loving us so much that You would make us a bride for Your dear Son. Make us all we should be to please You forever. Mold us into His perfect image that our will may be conformed to His to the glory of God. Amen.

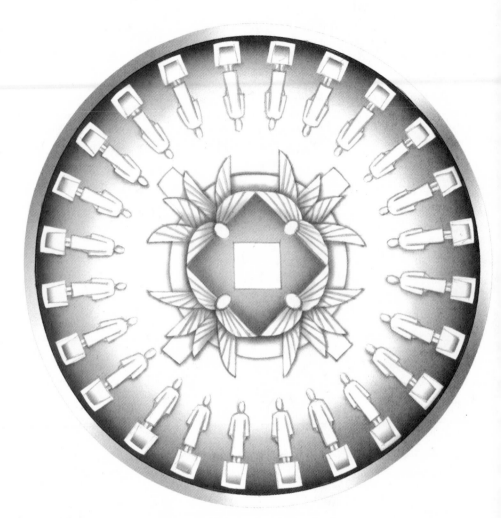

Revelation 22:6–21

REVELATION 22

THE NEW PARADISE

Persons

Jesus Christ
  Titles:
    The Lamb
    Alpha and Omega
    The Beginning and the End
    The First and the Last
    The Root and Offspring of
      David
    The bright and morning Star
    Lord Jesus

His servants
His angel
The Spirit
The Bride
John (the author)

Persons referred to

The nations
The holy prophets
He that keeps the saying
  of this book
The unjust
The filthy
The righteous
The holy
Dogs

Sorcerers
Whoremongers
Murderers
Idolaters
Whoever loves and makes a lie
David
He that hears
He that thirsts

Places mentioned

Heaven
The sun

The Holy City
The gates of the city

Doctrines taught

The rule of God
The curse
Service
The Presence of God
Prophecy
Worship
Sin
Righteousness

Holiness
Rewards
The invitation
The water of life
Judgment
The Second Coming
Grace

253

1 And he shewed me a pure river of water of life, clear as crystal, proceeding out of the throne of God and of the Lamb.

2 In the midst of the street of it, and on either side of the river, was there the tree of life, which bare twelve manner of fruits, and yielded her fruit every month: and the leaves of the tree were for the healing of the nations.

3 And there shall be no more curse: but the throne of God and of the Lamb shall be in it; and his servants shall serve him:

4 And they shall see his face; and his name shall be in their foreheads.

5 And there shall be no night there; and they need no candle, neither light of the sun; for the Lord God giveth them light: and they shall reign for ever and ever.

6 And he said unto me, These sayings are faithful and true: and the Lord God of the holy prophets sent his angel to shew unto his servants the things which must shortly be done.

7 Behold, I come quickly: blessed is he that keepeth the sayings of the prophecy of this book.

Revelation 22 Exposition

I. The New Paradise. vv. 1–7.

"And he showed me a river of water of life, clear as crystal, coming out of the throne of God and of the Lamb" (v. 1). Seiss notes that God's redemption moves in a great circle (*Apocalypse*, p. 503). Human history begins in a paradise with a tree of life and here ends in a paradise with the tree of life. But it is not a mere circle; it is a spiral, for the paradise here is on an infinitely higher plane. The paradise of God in Eden (Gen. 3) was only a small foretaste of the true paradise that the Lord God was planning for all eternity. "In the first paradise there were only two persons to behold the beauty and taste the pleasures of it, but in this second paradise whole cities and nations shall find abundant delight and satisfaction" (Matthew Henry). The true paradise is growing within the celestial city, the true "garden city" that mankind has dreamed of but could never attain. God commanded Israel to make garments for the priests "for glory and for beauty" (Exod. 28:40). God has exercised divine ingenuity in creating a place in which His people will be enraptured by the spectacular beauty and wonder of their surroundings. Now people travel for miles to see a national park or a nature reserve, but in that paradise God's people will be living in the midst of the most spectacular scenery imaginable. In that celestial city the water of life flows from the throne

---

22:1. The word *river* (ποταμός) occurs 8 times in Rev. (8:10; 9:14; 12:15, 16; 16:4, 12; 22:1, 2), but only in Rev. 22 does it refer to the celestial river.

The word *crystal* (κρύσταλλος) occurs only in Rev. 4:6; 22:1 in the NT. *Clear as crystal* "conveys the idea of sparkling brilliance" (Morris, *Rev.*, p. 248).

254

of God and of the Lamb, bringing abundance of life and joy to all God's redeemed people. The Lord Jesus promised the Samaritan woman that He could supply water that would spring up into everlasting life (John 4:14). There is something about the sight of a great river, the sound of rushing rapids, that is refreshing to all who remember it. During the millennial reign living waters shall flow from the temple to the Dead Sea (Ezek. 47:1–10; Zech. 14:8; Joel 3:18). Osborne notes that in Genesis the river flowed out of Eden, but here in paradise it flows out of the throne of God (*Rev.*, p. 769). "In the midst of the broad place of it and on both sides of the river was the tree of life, which bears twelve fruits, according to each month it is bearing its fruit, and the leaves of the tree were for the healing of the nations" (v. 2). David Baron refers to Ezekiel 47:1–12 and observes that John transfers "Ezekiel's imagery of the earthly but glorified Jerusalem during the millennial period . . . to the heavenly Jerusalem" (*The Visions and Prophecies of Zechariah*, p. 506). All those precious memories of the "walk in the woods" and the sight of "the sylvan forest" will have their fulfillment in this blessed city. But there will be constant variety: the trees bear different kinds of fruit in succession. Swete notes that the fruit of the tree will be life supporting (Gen. 3:22, *Rev.*, p. 299). The leaves will be for the healing of the nations. For the first thousand years the millennial reign will be going on down on the earth. The leaves may have specific value for those millennial saints. The single tree of Eden will become a forest. Some trees sprout new trunks from their roots so that a whole forest of trees may have organic connection to a single parent tree (such as quaking aspen; see Little, Elbert, *The Audubon Society Field Guide to North American Trees*, p. 326). We should note that the words *river* and *tree* both conjure up the idea of homes for multitudes of creatures in our present world. Shall there be trees in heaven, but no birds singing in them, no butterflies floating by, no chipmunks scampering up and down? I am not arguing for the existence of smelly animals in heaven, only calling attention to the eagle flying in mid-heaven with very intelligent words to say (Rev. 8:13) and to the fact that the Lord and all His saints will have horses to ride that will

---

22:2. For a summary of the *tree of life* see Rev. 2:7 note. The Lord knows what refreshes the hearts of His people. Most people have the experience of tasting an apple that reminds of "that apple tree that I loved as a child." But some love peaches, cherries, apricots, pears, plums, oranges, grapefruits, limes, lemons, dates, figs, kiwis, mangos, guavas, and other fruits. But the fruits will be beyond anything we have tasted here. No one will be dissatisfied in heaven.

This is the last of 8 times that the word *river* (ποταμός) occurs in Rev. (8:10; 9:14; 12:15, 16; 16:4, 12; 22:1, 2).

The word *healing* (θεραπεία) occurs only here and in Luke 9:11; 12:42 in the NT.

be the delight of every equestrian (Rev. 19:11–14). No pet lover should ever fear that he will be disappointed in heaven. The earth, with all its multitude of creatures, is only the footstool; heaven is the throne with a vastly greater variety of inhabitants. For a list of animals mentioned in Revelation, see Introduction, p. xxiii. "And there shall be no curse there. And the throne of God and of the Lamb shall be in it, and his slaves shall render worship-service to him" (v. 3). The word *throne* shows us that this is the majestic center of God's control of the universe. The Lord Jesus could refer to His enthronement at the right hand of His Father as "sitting at the right hand of power" (Matt. 26:64). If Solomon's throne was impressive (I Kings 10:18–20), the throne of God will be overwhelming. David longed for that day when he would "come and appear before God" (Ps. 42:2*b*). Spurgeon comments, "Certainly it is most true of the celestial city, as well as of the millennial city, that the throne of God and of the Lamb shall be in it" ("The Throne of God and of the Lamb," Sermon 1576, *The C. H. Spurgeon Collection*, Ages Digital Library). "And they shall see his face, and his name shall be upon their foreheads" (v. 4). The Lord Jesus promised that the pure in heart will be blessed, for they shall see God (Matt. 5:8). The saints by then will be perfectly conformed to the image of their Lord and Savior. The character of Christ shall be stamped upon the countenance of the believer. "We shall be like him, for we shall see him as he is" (I John 3:2). The Lord invited His people to seek His face (Ps. 27:8). The saints who have longed to see Him shall be fully satisfied (Ps. 63:1–2). Now we see through a glass, dimly, but the day will come when we shall see him face to face (I Cor. 13:12). God's original purpose for mankind, that they should serve and worship Him,

---

22:3. This is the only occurrence of this word *curse* (κατάθεμα) in the NT. The rest of the NT uses *anathema* (ἀνάθεμα), Rom. 9:3; I Cor. 12:3; etc.

For a summary of the verb *to perform worship-service* (λατρεύω) see Rev. 7:15 note. For the idea of *worship and praise* to God see Rev. 1:6 note.

This is the last of 39 times that the word *throne* (θρόνος) occurs in Rev. For a summary see Rev. 1:4 note.

22:4. The very name of God will be on the forehead of the redeemed, in contrast to the beast worshipers, who have 666 on their foreheads (Rev. 13:16–18).

Spurgeon notes that the words "They shall see his face" imply five things:

    Certain salvation
    Clear knowledge of Him
    Conscious favor
    Close fellowship
    Complete transformation

("The Heaven of Heavens," Sermon 824, *The C. H. Spurgeon Collection*, Ages Digital Library).

will be perfectly fulfilled (Exod. 20:5; Deut. 10:12). But we shall also come "to the spirits of just men made perfect" (Heb. 12:23). It is not surprising that the old saints urged a determined meditation on the joys and glories of heaven. "Such fixed considerations as these of things above will serve as notable helps to draw and keep thy heart heavenward, and may mightily move thee to delight in God, and to hold it the sweetest life upon earth to walk with him in the ways of purity and peace" (Robert Bolton, *General Directions for a Comfortable Walking with God*, p. 72, A.D. 1626). "And there shall be no night there, and they have no need of the light of a lamp, or the light of the sun, because the Lord God shines upon them, and they shall reign into the ages of the ages" (v. 5). The apostle Paul assures believers, "If we suffer, we shall also reign with him" (II Tim. 2:12a). A. T. Robertson observes, "Reign eternally in contrast with the limited millennial reign of 20:4, 6" (*Word Pictures*, VI, p. 481). The saints will never grow tired or need to sleep. Their future will be a victorious reign throughout eternity. The glory of God will be their blessing forever. Daniel saw that the saints of the Most High will possess the kingdom into "the age of the ages" (Dan. 7:18b, Heb.). "And he said to me, These words are faithful and true, and the Lord God of the spirits of the prophets sent his angel to show to his slaves the things which are necessary to come to pass quickly" (v. 6). This statement shows that the angel has fulfilled the initial promise (Rev. 1:1). The apostle Peter explained, "For prophecy was never borne by the will of man, but men spoke from God, being borne along by the Holy Spirit" (II Pet. 1:21). The things are necessary to come to pass because God said they would. The writer to the Hebrews declared, "For yet a little while, the one who is coming will come and will not waste time" (Heb. 10:37). Now the Lord Jesus Himself promises, "And behold, I am coming quickly. Blessed is the one who is keeping the words of the prophecy of this book" (v. 7). Here the Lord repeats His initial promise of blessing (Rev. 1:3). It is not for us to know the time (Acts 1:7), but He will come at the exact right time in His Father's will. The psalmist cried out to God, "O that my ways were directed to keep thy statutes" (Ps. 119:5). The Lord Jesus said to the

---

22:5. This is the last of 7 times that the verb *to reign* (βασιλεύω) occurs in Rev. For a summary see Rev. 5:10 note.

This is the last of 8 times that the word *night* (νύξ) occurs in Rev. (4:8; 7:15; 8:12; 12:10; 14:11; 20:10; 21:25; 22:5).

22:6. The phrase *faithful and true* occurs 3 times in Rev. (3:14; 19:11; 22:6).

For the phrase *the spirits of the prophets* see I Cor. 14:32. Only the spiritual nature of the prophets could understand the revelation given to them.

22:7. John has already written, "Whoever shall keep his word, truly in this one the love of God has been perfected" (I John 2:5).

8 *And I John saw these things, and heard them. And when I had heard and seen, I fell down to worship before the feet of the angel which shewed me these things.*
9 *Then saith he unto me, See thou do it not: for I am thy fellowservant, and of thy brethren the prophets, and of them which keep the sayings of this book: worship God.*
10 *And he saith unto me, Seal not the sayings of the prophecy of this book: for the time is at hand.*
11 *He that is unjust, let him be unjust still: and he which is filthy, let him be filthy still: and he that is righteous, let him be righteous still: and he that is holy, let him be holy still.*
12 *And, behold, I come quickly; and my reward is with me, to give every man according as his work shall be.*
13 *I am Alpha and Omega, the beginning and the end, the first and the last.*
14 *Blessed are they that do his commandments, that they may have right to the tree of life, and may enter in through the gates into the city.*
15 *For without are dogs, and sorcerers, and whoremongers, and murderers, and idolaters, and whosoever loveth and maketh a lie.*
16 *I Jesus have sent mine angel to testify unto you these things in the churches. I am the root and the offspring of David, and the bright and morning star.*
17 *And the Spirit and the bride say, Come. And let him that heareth say, Come. And let him that is athirst come. And whosoever will, let him take the water of life freely.*
18 *For I testify unto every man that heareth the words of the prophecy of this book, If any man shall add unto these things, God shall add unto him the plagues that are written in this book:*
19 *And if any man shall take away from the words of the book of this prophecy, God shall take away his part out of the book of life, and out of the holy city, and from the things which are written in this book.*
20 *He which testifieth these things saith, Surely I come quickly. Amen. Even so, come, Lord Jesus.*
21 *The grace of our Lord Jesus Christ be with you all. Amen.*

disciples, "If you love me, keep my commandments" (John 14:15). The person who *continues keeping* (present tense) the words of this book will be blessed indeed. Every believer should cherish this final revelation of God to His people.

II. The Conclusion. vv. 8–21.

Just as John began his book with a sevenfold introduction, so he formally closes with a double sevenfold conclusion, reinforcing what he has said. He takes many of the themes of the introduction and enlarges and applies them in this conclusion.

1. The testimony of John. "And I John am the one who heard and saw these things. And when I heard and saw them, I fell down to worship before the feet of the angel who showed these things to

me" (v. 8). John identified himself in the introduction (Rev. 1:1).
He is overwhelmed by the power of the angel and the glorious revelation he has given to John. John knows that he has seen the purpose of the universe and its glorious consummation. But he forgets
that the majestic angel is just a servant of the Lord, as he is. We
must not judge John too harshly for this lapse. If we had seen that
angel towering over us, looking at us with eyes that could see our
inmost soul, we would sympathize with John.

2. The angelic correction. "And he says to me: See, you do it not; I
am your fellow-slave, and of your brethren the prophets, and of the
ones who are keeping the words of this scroll; worship God" (v. 9).
God alone is worthy of worship. The Devil and evil angels will receive worship (Matt. 4:8–10), but not a good angel. The Lord Jesus
quoted the law to the Devil, "Thou shalt worship the Lord thy
God, and him only shalt thou serve" (Matt. 4:10b). The psalmist
urges, "O worship the Lord in the beauty of holiness: fear before
him, all the earth" (Ps. 96:9). God has ordained "that at the name
of Jesus every knee should bow" (Phil. 2:10a). This is the ultimate
purpose for the creation of man (Exod. 24:1–12).

3. The angelic command. "And he says to me, Seal not the words of
the prophecy of this scroll, for the time is near" (v. 10). Daniel had
to seal up his scroll of prophecy because the time was not right for
full revelation (Dan. 12:4). But now the person who reads God's
Word should understand it (Matt. 24:15). God's blessing rests on
the reader (Rev. 1:3). "This book is to be left open for all to read
(1:3; 13:18; 17:9; 22:7, 18)" (A. T. Robertson, *Word Pictures*, VI,
483).

4. The permanent choice. "Let the one who is unjust be unjust still,
and let the one who is filthy be filthy still, and let the one who is
righteous be righteous still, and let the one who is holy be holy
still" (v. 11). The unjust are morally filthy. Daniel had foreseen

---

22:8. If the sight of an angel moves men to worship, what will the sight of the everlasting
God of the universe be like?

22:9. This is the last of 24 times that the word *worship* (προσκυνέω) occurs in Rev. For a
summary see Rev. 4:10 note.

22:10. This is the last of 8 times that the verb *to seal* (σφραγίζω) occurs in Rev. (7:3, 4
[twice], 5, 8; 10:4; 20:3; 22:10).

22:11. The word *filthy* (ῥυπαρός) occurs only here and in James 2:2 in the NT.
This is the last time that the word *righteous* (δίκαιος) occurs in Rev., and the only time
that it is applied to saints. For a summary see Rev. 15:3 note.

For a summary of the word *holy* (ἅγιος) see Rev. 3:7 note. Both the noun form and the
verb form *to make holy, sanctify* (ἁγιάζω) occur together here only in Rev.

that the wicked would continue to do wickedly (Dan. 12:10). But Joshua's challenge to his people still rings true: "Choose you this day whom ye will serve . . . but as for me and my house, we will serve the Lord" (Josh. 24:15). The moral choices that people make in this life have eternal consequences. There is no second chance. "The states of both the evil and the good are now fixed forever" (A. T. Robertson, *Word Pictures*, VI, p. 483). Elijah said to his people, "How long halt ye between two opinions? If the Lord be God, follow him: but if Baal, then follow him" (I Kings 18:21).

5. The reward. "Behold, I am coming quickly, and my reward is with me to recompense to each one as his work is" (v. 12). This verse repeats the promise of the introduction (Rev. 1:7). Isaiah had prophesied that the Lord God shall come and "his reward is with him" (Isa. 40:10b; compare Jer. 14:10). That is the will of His Father: "Your Father who sees in secret shall himself reward you openly" (Matt. 6:4). Robert Klund sees the heavily emphasized coming of Christ (Rev. 22:12, 17 [3 times], 20 [twice]) as the climax of the plot of the whole book of Revelation (*The Plot of Revelation 4–22*, pp. 217–18).

6. The identification. "I am the Alpha and the Omega, the first and the last, the beginning and the end" (v. 13). Jehovah claimed, "I am the first, and I am the last; and beside me there is no God" (Isa. 44:6). The Lord Jesus is claiming divine titles. He is the Creator of all things (John 1:3), and He is the Consummator of all things (Dan. 9:27; Rev. 19:11). To the devout believer Christ must be everything. "Christ is sovereign over all and therefore the one who has authority over the destiny of everyone" (Osborne, *Rev.*, p. 789). Spurgeon has an eloquent sermon of meditations on "Alpha and Omega" (Sermon 546, *The C. H. Spurgeon Collection*, Ages Digital Library).

7. The benediction on the redeemed. "Blessed are the ones who wash their robes, that they may have right to the tree of life, and may enter in through the gates into the city" (v. 14). The tree of life was in the original Garden of Eden (Gen. 2:9), but only those washed in the blood of the Lamb are pure enough to enter that Holy City and eat from the tree of life (which is now a forest, Rev. 22:2).

22:12. The word *reward* (μισθός) occurs only here and in 11:18 in Rev.

22:13. "I am Alpha and Omega" occurs 3 times only in the NT (Rev. 1:8; 21:6; 22:13); "the first and the last" occurs 4 times (Rev. 1:11, 17; 2:8; 22:13); "the Beginning and the End" occurs twice (Rev. 21:6; 22:13).

22:14. The phrase "who wash their robes" occurs twice in Rev. 7:14; 22:14 in the NT. The phrase has stronger manuscript support than "who do his commandments." See Metzger, *A Textual Commentary on the Greek New Testament*, p. 767.

REVELATION 22   THE NEW PARADISE

8. The warning against sin. "Outside are the dogs, and the drug users, and the fornicators, and the murderers, and the idolaters, and every one who loves and practices a lie" (v. 15). The *dogs* are plainly unclean people (Matt. 7:6; Phil. 3:2; II Pet. 2:21–22), not animals, for all the other categories are people. The *drug users* may be sorcerers or addicts; the *fornicators* are any category of sexual sinners (Matt. 5:27–28); the *murderers* are those who kill people (even those who for shrewd reasons refrain, Matt. 5:22); the *idolaters* are those who put anything above the true God (Phil. 3:19). *One who loves and practices a lie* certainly characterizes the Devil (John 8:44) and false religious teachers (I Tim. 4:1–2). True believers "hate every false way" (Ps. 119:104, 128).

9. The testimony of Jesus. "I, Jesus, sent my angel to testify these things to you upon the churches. I am the root and offspring of David, the shining morning star" (v. 16). "The root of David" is a reference to the prophecies of the messianic King (Isa. 11:1, 10). The mystery is that He could be both the origin and the offspring of David. Balaam prophesied that "a Star shall rise out of Jacob" (Num. 24:17). The picture of the "shining morning star" is a beautiful prophecy of the advent of the Lord Jesus, who will usher in the new day of God's kingdom on earth. *The morning star* (usually a planet) is the last bright star that rises before the dawn of a new day. The apostle Peter applies the expression to the Lord Jesus: "We have also a more steadfast prophetic word, to which you do well to take heed, as to a lamp shining in a dark place, until the day dawns, and the morning star arises in your hearts" (II Pet. 1:19).

10. The invitation. "And the Spirit and the bride say, Come. And let the one who hears say, Come. And let the one who is thirsty come; let the one who is willing take the water of life as a gift" (v. 17). The language reminds us of the Lord's invitation, "Come to me, all

---

22:15. The word *dog* (κύων) is "a term of reproach" (Moulton and Milligan, *Vocabulary*, p. 366). The dog was an unclean animal (I Kings 21:23; Prov. 26:11). Although little children could smuggle little dogs (κυνάριον), *puppy*, into a house (Matt. 15:26–27), the pampered house pet of modern society was rare in the ancient world. There is a mosaic floor in a villa in Pompei that portrays a house dog with a jeweled collar and the words *Cave Canem*, "Beware of the dog!" Trained hunting dogs were pictured on Egyptian wall paintings (see Ryken, Wilhoit, and Longman, *Dictionary of Biblical Imagery*, "Dogs," pp. 213–14).

This is the last occurrence of the word *sorcerer* (φάρμακος). Albert A. Bell Jr. suggests that the word referred to "those who supplied drugs to induce abortions" (*Exploring the New Testament World*, p. 249).

22:16. The word *shining* (λαμπρός) is used of the celestial river (Rev. 22:1) as well as of the robe of an angel (Acts 10:30).

you who labor and are burdened, and I will give you rest" (Matt. 11:28). The OT parallel is Isaiah's sweeping invitation, "Ho, every one that thirsteth, come ye to the waters, and he that hath no money; come, buy, and eat; yea, come, buy wine and milk without money and without price" (Isa. 55:1). After the beautiful vision of heaven (Rev. 22:1–5), it is logical to invite people to come to the Lord. It is the responsibility of believers (the bride) to invite other people to come to the Lord. When Andrew found the Lord Jesus, he first sought his brother, Simon Peter, and led him to the Lord (John 1:40–42). Philip invited Nathaniel, "Come and see" Jesus (John 1:46). The writer to the Hebrews exhorted, "Let us therefore come boldly to the throne of grace, that we may obtain mercy, and find grace to help in time of need" (Heb. 4:16). Spurgeon has a powerful sermon balancing God's will and man's will in salvation (Rev. 22:17; Rom. 9:16, "God's Will and Man's Will," Sermon 442, *The C. H. Spurgeon Collection*, Ages Digital Library).

11. The warning against adding to Scripture. "I testify to every one who hears the words of the prophecy of this book: If any one adds to them, God will add upon him the plagues that have been written in this book" (v. 18). Swete argues that this is the personal testimony of the Lord Jesus to the reader (*Rev.*, p. 311). It is not mere error that is meant, but "deliberate falsification" (Swete). The person who dares to add to the Bible is arrogating to himself divine authority. God will judge him as surely as He will judge the Devil (Rev. 20:10). The plagues of Revelation are acts of divine judgment. The Lord Jesus preauthenticated every part of the NT (Theodore Roberts, *The Faithful and True Witness*, pp. 50–58).

12. The warning against omission from Scripture. "And if anyone takes away from the words of the book of this prophecy, God shall take away his part from the tree of life, and from the holy city, of the things which have been written in this book" (v. 19). There is no clearer way of saying that anyone who deletes anything from God's holy Word will have his name deleted from the roster of the re-

---

22:17. This is the last time that the word *bride* occurs in Rev. For a summary see Rev. 18:23 note.

Spurgeon has a number of sermons based on this text: "Come and Welcome," Sermon 279; "The Two 'Comes,'" Sermon 1331; "The Double 'Come,'" Sermon 1608; "The Oft-Repeated Invitation," Sermon 2685, *The C. H. Spurgeon Collection*, Ages Digital Library.

22:18. The Lord God warned, "Woe unto the foolish prophets, that follow their own spirit, and have seen nothing!" (Ezek. 13:3).

22:19. As I have written years ago, "If it is dangerous to add to or to take away from this book, does this not presuppose that this book is infallible and divinely authoritative?

deemed. Jehovah warned Moses, "Whatever I command you, you shall be careful to do; you shall not add to nor take away from it" (Deut. 12:32 NASB). When wicked king Jehoiakim burned the scroll of Jeremiah, he did not understand that he was burning up his chance of heaven (Jer. 36:21–31). But to the person who regards His Word with awe and reverence, the Lord says, "To this man will I look, even to him that is poor and of a contrite spirit, and trembleth at my word" (Isa. 66:2b). The psalmist said it well, "Therefore I love thy commandments above gold; yea, above fine gold" (Ps. 119:127).

13. "Come, Lord Jesus" (v. 20). This whole book is a revelation from the Lord Jesus Christ (Rev. 1:1). He earnestly testifies these things (Rev. 1:2). In the light of eternity He is coming quickly and will accomplish all His will upon the earth and its inhabitants. Believers, along with John, should pray that the Lord come quickly, that His will may be done on earth as it is in heaven (Matt. 6:10). "The next thing for every Christian to be looking for in this world is the coming of Christ to fulfil what is written in this Book" (Seiss, *Apocalypse*, p. 523). All divine promises are blessings, but the last is special. The apostle Paul urges believers to be "looking for that blessed hope and glorious appearing of our great God and Savior Jesus Christ" (Titus 2:13). "But they that wait upon the Lord shall renew their strength; they shall mount up with wings as eagles; they shall run, and not be weary; and they shall walk, and not faint" (Isa. 40:31). Blackstone observes that the verse closes with the "yearning cry of the Spirit 'Even so, come Lord Jesus'" (*Jesus Is Coming*, p. 131).

14. The last benediction. "The grace of the Lord Jesus be with all" (v. 21). Some early manuscripts (א) add "with all saints," which is certainly the intent of the words. Many have noted that the OT concludes with a curse (Mal. 4:6), but the NT ends with a blessing.

Why would it be wrong to take away the errors in a book? In this case it must be because there are none to remove" (1968, Stewart Custer, *Does Inspiration Demand Inerrancy?* p. 59).

22:20. The believer should wait patiently for the Lord that he might be ready to welcome Him when He comes (Matt. 24:42–46). "Wait on the Lord, and keep his way" (Ps. 37:34).

Thiselton argues that the imperative *Come* in this context "seems to confirm the imperative" of the parallel Aramaic in I Cor. 16:22 (Anthony Thiselton, *The First Epistle to the Corinthians*, p. 1352).

22:21. The word *grace* (χάρις) occurs twice in Rev. John began by praying grace upon the reader (Rev. 1:4) and now closes by again praying grace upon all the saints (22:21). In the same way the apostle Paul begins and ends every epistle with a prayer of grace on the readers (Rom. 1:7; 16:24; I Cor. 1:3; 16:23; II Cor. 1:2; 13:14; Gal. 1:3; 6:18; Eph. 1:2;

"John could not finish his book without mentioning that name which was dearest of all names to him" ("Till We Meet Again," Sermon 1628, *The C. H. Spurgeon Collection*, Ages Digital Library). It is wonderful that Jesus (through John) ends this marvelous Revelation with a prayer of grace upon every true believer. It should encourage us all to receive the Word with all readiness of mind and to search the Scriptures daily (Acts 17:11). This whole chapter lends itself to practical applications.

When A. T. Pierson comes to the end of his chapter "The Mystery of History" he observes, "Notwithstanding all this perversity of man, there is a divine progression through the ages and dispensations, never one backward step on God's part, however many on man's" (*The Bible and Spiritual Life*, p. 438). God's perfect will for man and for the universe shall be accomplished. Redeemed mankind shall yet be the holy bride of the divine Son of God.

May God bless every reader of this book.

Practical Applications from Revelation 22

1. God is constantly pouring out grace and strength to His people (v. 1). "God is able to make all grace abound toward you; that you, always having all sufficiency in all things, may abound to every good work" (II Cor. 9:8).
2. Beautiful trees will have eternally beneficial effects for God's people (v. 2). From Eden to eternity trees are part of man's existence; they even had a part in our redemption (I Pet. 2:24).
3. One day believers will be able to serve God perfectly (v. 3). God is perfecting the saints "till we all come in the unity of the faith, and of the knowledge of the Son of God, unto a perfect man, unto the measure of the stature of the fullness of Christ" (Eph. 4:13).
4. In heaven believers will be able to see God perfectly (v. 4). "Blessed are the pure in heart: for they shall see God" (Matt. 5:8).
5. Saints shall have positions of responsibility forever (v. 5). "You have made us unto our God kings and priests: and we shall reign on the earth" (Rev. 5:10).
6. God is always faithful and true (v. 6). "God is faithful, who will not suffer you to be tempted above that you are able; but will with the temptation also make a way to escape, that you may be able to bear it" (I Cor. 10:13b).

6:24; Phil. 1:2; 4:23; Col. 1:2; 4:18; I Thess. 1:1; 5:28; II Thess. 1:2; 3:18; I Tim. 1:2; 6:21; II Tim. 1:2; 4:22; Titus 1:4; 3:15; Philem. 3, 25). See "Grace," ZPEB, II, pp. 799–804.

7. Obedience to God always brings blessings (v. 7). "If you consent and obey, you will eat the best of the land" (Isa. 1:19 NASB).
8. All knowledge of God should lead believers to worship (v. 8). "That you might be filled with the knowledge of his will . . . that you might walk worthy of the Lord . . . giving thanks unto the Father" (Col. 1:9, 10, 12).
9. Worshiping God is the most important thing we can do (v. 9). "O worship the Lord in the beauty of holiness: fear before him, all the earth" (Ps. 96:9).
10. The Bible is meant to be understood (v. 10). "Think about what I say; for the Lord shall give you understanding in all things" (II Tim. 2:7).
11. Our actions in this world fix our eternal destiny (v. 11). "For if you live after the flesh, you shall die: but if you through the Spirit do mortify the deeds of the body, you shall live" (Rom. 8:13).
12. God rewards His people (v. 12). "The judgments of the Lord are true and righteous altogether . . . and in keeping of them there is great reward" (Ps. 19:9b, 11).
13. God originated all things and will bring all things to consummation (v. 13). "God created the heaven and the earth" (Gen. 1:1). "Behold, I create new heavens and a new earth" (Isa. 65:17a).
14. Obedience to God is the open door to heaven (v. 14). "Hope to the end for the grace that is to be brought to you at the revelation of Jesus Christ; as obedient children" (I Pet. 1:13b–14a).
15. Sinners would never feel at home in the presence of a holy God (v. 15). "The way of the wicked is as darkness" (Prov. 4:19). "Men loved darkness rather than light, because their deeds were evil" (John 3:19b).
16. Jesus is our guiding star to God (v. 16). "Jesus says to him, I am the way, the truth, and the life: no man comes to the Father, but by me. . . . He that has seen me has seen the Father" (John 14:6, 9b).
17. If a person wants God and heaven, the door is open (v. 17). "Whosoever shall call upon the name of the Lord shall be saved" (Rom. 10:13).
18. Counterfeiting God's Word is a very dangerous practice (v. 18). "Woe unto them that call evil good, and good evil; that put darkness for light, and light for darkness! . . . Therefore as the fire devoureth the stubble, and the flame consumeth the chaff, so their root shall be as rottenness, and their blossom shall go up as dust: because they have cast away the law of the Lord of hosts, and despised the word of the Holy One of Israel" (Isa. 5:20, 24).
19. Trying to destroy God's Word is a sure way of going to hell (v. 19). "Because they have despised the law of the Lord, and have not kept

his commandments, and their lies caused them to err, after the which their fathers have walked: but I will send a fire upon Judah, and it shall devour the palaces of Jerusalem" (Amos 2:4b–5).

20. Every believer should long to see the Lord Jesus (v. 20). "O God, thou art my God; early will I seek thee: my soul thirsteth for thee, my flesh longeth for thee in a dry and thirsty land, where no water is; to see thy power and thy glory, so as I have seen thee in the sanctuary" (Ps. 63:1–2).

21. The grace of God is our greatest single need (v. 21). The apostle Paul could confess, "But by the grace of God I am what I am: and his grace which was bestowed upon me was not in vain; but I labored more abundantly than they all: yet not I, but the grace of God which was with me" (I Cor. 15:10).

Prayer

Dear Lord Jesus, thank You for giving us this revelation of Your love. Thank You for preparing a place for us. Thank You for Your promise of eternal privilege of service. Keep our hearts fixed upon You. Help us to live rejoicing in You. "Even so, come, Lord Jesus." Amen.

Epilogue

Jonathan Edwards's meditations on the work of redemption provide a fitting conclusion for this commentary.

"All the church shall enter with Christ their glorious Lord into the highest heaven, and there shall enter on the state of their highest and eternal blessedness and glory. . . .

Christ will bring them into his chambers in the highest sense. He will bring them into his Father's house, into a world not like that which they have left. Here Christ will bring them, and present them in glory to his Father. . . .

And then the Father will accept them, and own them all for his children, and will welcome them to the eternal and perfect inheritance and glory of his house, and will on this occasion give more glorious manifestations of his love than ever before. . . .

And now shall be the marriage of the Lamb in the most perfect sense.

This shall be the day of the gladness of Christ's heart, wherein he will greatly rejoice, and all the saints shall rejoice with him. Christ shall rejoice over his bride, and the bride shall rejoice in her husband, in the state of her consummate and everlasting blessedness, of which we have a particular description in the 21st and 22nd chapters of Revelation.

And now the whole work of redemption is finished. We have seen how it has been carrying on from the fall of man to this time. But now it is complete with respect to all that belongs to it. Now the top-stone of the building is laid.

And now Christ the great Redeemer shall be most perfectly glorified, and God the Father shall be glorified in him, and the Holy Ghost shall be most fully glorified in the perfection of his work on the hearts of all the church. . . .

And who can conceive of the triumph of those praises which shall be sung in heaven on this great occasion. . . .

Now shall the praises of that vast and glorious multitude be as mighty thunderings indeed!"

ALLELUIA; FOR THE LORD GOD OMNIPOTENT REIGNETH.

(Jonathan Edwards, *The Work of Redemption* in Edwards's *Works*, Vol. I, pp. 504ff.)

BIBLIOGRAPHY ON REVELATION

Although some expositors do not follow any one system of interpretation, we have tried to put each commentary into its dominant method of interpretation among the four main systems. We recommend the futurist interpreters. Those works of great value for the expositor we have marked with an asterisk(*).

Preterist Commentaries

Adams, Jay E. *The Time Is at Hand.* Nutley, N.J.: Presbyterian and Reformed, 1966, 1976. 123 pp.

An amillennial interpretation of eschatology. He holds that the Book of Revelation is symbolical and preterist (p. v); wishes to call his position "realized millennialism" (p. 9); attacks premillennialists for teaching an imperfect golden age (p. 13); misrepresents the premillennial position (p. 18); claims, "Over against the bifurcated and diplopic premillennial scheme, realized millennialism is a consistent and orderly system" (p. 41); presents his view as a totally symbolical view (pp. 41–45); gives a preterist interpretation of Revelation (pp. 46–55).

Allen, Cady H. *The Message of the Book of Revelation.* New York: Abingdon-Cokesbury Press, 1939. 180 pp.

Amillennial studies on the Apocalypse. He stresses apocalyptic literature (pp. 15–20); holds Johannine authorship (pp. 23–24); says that the purpose of Revelation is to comfort believers in times of persecution (p. 25); identifies 666 with Nero (pp. 47–48); claims that chapter 13 depicts Roman emperor worship (p. 63); teaches that the theme of Revelation is the struggle and victory over evil (pp. 27, 92).

Ashcraft, Morris. *Revelation* in Vol. XII of *The Broadman Bible Commentary*, ed. Clifton J. Allen. Nashville: Broadman Press, 1972. Pp. 240–361.

An amillennial exposition. He rejects Johannine authorship (p. 247); argues for the preterist interpretation of Revelation 1:1, 3 (pp. 257–58); teaches that the first seal judgment repeats itself throughout history (p. 285); says that the measuring of the temple symbolizes safety for the children of God (p. 302); insists that there must be more than two witnesses in chapter 11 (pp. 304, 307); rejects a literal Armageddon (p. 328).

Bruce, F. F. *The Revelation to John* in *A New Testament Commentary*, ed. G. C. D. Howley, F. F. Bruce, H. L. Ellison. Grand Rapids: Zondervan, 1969. Pp. 629–66.

A brief amillennial exposition. He says that the date of writing is sometime between A.D. 69 and A.D. 96 (p. 629); gives the preterist interpretation of 1:1 (p. 633); does not commit himself on the author-ship (p. 634); connects the seal judgments with imperial Rome (p. 643); holds that the Great Tribulation is the church age (pp. 646, 649); claims that the flood out of the dragon's mouth relates to an unidentifiable event of the Jewish war (A.D. 66–70, p. 252); interprets 13:3 according to the Nero legend but refrains from interpreting 666 (p. 652); teaches that the reign for Christians has already begun (p. 661).

Dana, H. E. *The Epistles and Apocalypse of John*. Kansas City, Kans.: Central Seminary Press, 1947. 161 pp.

Brief amillennial notes. He emphasizes the historical background and apocalyptic literature (p. 87); gives the preterist interpretation of 1:1 (p. 99); associates the woman with Israel (p. 132); identifies the first beast with Domitian (p. 134); believes that John used the Nero legend (p. 135); asserts that Armageddon is not a literal, future event (p. 142); says that Revelation describes the Roman persecutions and God's judgment on imperial Rome (p. 149); holds that Antichrist is a principle, not a person (p. 149).

Dean, J. T. *Visions and Revelations*. Edinburgh: T. and T. Clark, 1911. 265 pp.

Devotional messages. He thinks the sixth seal symbolizes the social revolution associated with the fall of Rome (p. 70); sees repeated ful-fillments of prophecy (pp. 71, 115, 189–90); connects chapters 8 and 9 with the national decay of the Roman Empire (p. 97); calls the first beast the pagan and persecuting power of the Roman Empire (p. 142); regards Babylon as the attitude of antagonism against God (p. 206).

Ezell, Douglas. *Revelations on Revelation*. Waco, Tex.: Word Books, 1977. 124 pp.

A liberal interpretation of Revelation. He commends the preterist in-terpretation (pp. 16–17); sees contradictions between Daniel and Rev-elation (p. 23); applies the privileges of Israel to the present church (p. 31); quotes the Apocrypha to give meaning to silence (pp. 45–46); argues that the seals, trumpets, and bowls refer to different aspects of the same time period (pp. 43, 54–55); holds that the great multitude and the 144,000 are the same group (p. 59); thinks that the woman in Revelation 12 symbolizes the ideal people of God in both Testaments (p. 69); holds that the thousand-year reign is just one brush stroke (p. 88) and not primarily a time symbol at all; instead it symbolizes the messianic rest (p. 95); treats Revelation 21–22 as symbols and "lan-guage stretching" (p. 101).

Hailey, Homer. *Revelation: An Introduction and Commentary.* Grand Rapids: Baker, 1979. 438 pp.

A conservative amillennial commentary. He says the purpose of Revelation is to prepare people for persecution (pp. 18, 52); teaches that the Tribulation lasted from A.D. 64 to A.D. 313 (pp. 26–27, 210); holds that the theme is the conflict between good and evil (p. 51); argues that Revelation was fulfilled soon after John wrote (p. 186); maintains that the sixth seal symbolizes the destruction of the Roman Empire (p. 197); claims that the winepress refers to the present judgment of the wicked (p. 317); connects Armageddon with the fall of Rome (p. 388); insists that the thousand years symbolize the victory of Christianity, which began with Constantine (p. 392).

Hobbs, Herschel H. *The Cosmic Drama: An Exposition of Revelation.* Waco, Tex.: Word Books, 1971. 212 pp.

An amillennial Baptist exposition. He stresses the apocalyptic nature of the book (p. 14); argues that the whole book is symbolical (pp. 25, 77); insists that the trumpets relate to the fall of Rome (pp. 103–7); holds that the first beast is Domitian (p. 127); says that John used the Nero legend (p. 128); connects the second beast with Roman emperor worship (p. 131); believes that the thousand years symbolize completeness (p. 184).

Minear, Paul S. *I Saw a New Earth.* Washington, D.C.: Corpus Books, 1968. 385 pp.

A thoughtful analysis based on idealist-preterist opinions. He lists his presuppositions (p. 6); commends a measure of honest doubt in studying Revelation (p. 18); lists titles of Christ (p. 33); argues the seven angels are angels, not men (pp. 41–42); holds that opposition in the seals is by false Christians, not persecutors (pp. 79–81) and thinks the four horsemen discipline the church, not the world (p. 266); rejects identification of the beast as Nero (pp. 127, 247ff.); thinks Babylon is the unfaithful within the church (pp. 147–52); rejects all millennial views (pp. 160–61); holds that numbers are temporal symbols that cannot be identified in solar years (p. 177); thinks that the modern church would not have included Revelation in the canon (p. 189); disparages Luke as a historian (pp. 205f.); examines special topics in Revelation: suffering (pp. 201ff.), sovereignties in conflict (pp. 228ff.), kings of the earth (pp. 235ff.), death and resurrection of the sea beast (pp. 247ff.), heaven (pp. 270ff.), and so forth. He concludes with an annotated translation of Revelation (pp. 300–65) and a bibliography (pp. 367–84).

Pieters, Albertus. *Studies in the Revelation of St. John.* Grand Rapids: Eerdmans, 1950. 367 pp.

A highly symbolical Reformed commentary. He holds to apostolic authorship (p. 22); rejects the historical and futurist views (pp. 43–63); advocates the preterist view but admits he cannot find first-century events that correspond to Revelation (pp. 64, 67, 128); argues for a spiritual meaning of the entire book (pp. 68–69); thinks that he has seen the bottomless pit in chapter 9 opened twice—the two world wars (p. 130); says the woman in chapter 12 symbolizes the church (p. 153); claims that the battle in heaven (chapter 12) is purely spiritual (p. 173); denies a future Antichrist (p. 194); calls the resurrection (chapter 20) a symbol of regeneration (p. 279); argues for a symbolical interpretation of the Millennium (p. 308).

Roberts, J. W. *The Revelation to John.* Austin, Tex.: Sweet Publishing Co., 1974. 203 pp.

A synchronous preterist interpretation. He argues that the sixth seal cannot refer to the end of the world (pp. 68–69); criticizes the interpretation of the 144,000 as literal Israelites and claims they represent Christians of John's day who faced the great tribulation (pp. 71, 73); associates the first beast with imperial Rome under Domitian and the second beast with Roman emperor worship (p. 96); advocates the Nero legend to explain 13:3 (p. 109); takes the bowls as judgments on imperial Rome (p. 127); believes that 19:11–21 symbolizes "a war waged spiritually and fought in the courtrooms of the Roman magistrates" (p. 164); says the Millennium refers to the triumph of the gospel after the fall of Rome in A.D. 476 (p. 171).

Scott, C. Anderson. *The Book of the Revelation.* London: Hodder and Stoughton, n.d. 337 pp.

An amillennial commentary. He emphasizes apocalyptic literature (pp. 2–19); claims that John must have written before A.D. 70 because the temple (chapter 11) is still standing (pp. 209–10); identifies 666 with Nero (p. 241); hesitates in fully equating chapter 18 with the fall of pagan Rome (p. 277).

Stuart, Moses. *A Commentary on the Apocalypse.* 2 vols. Andover, Mass.: Allen, Morrill and Wardwell, 1845. 504 pp.

The classic representative of the preterist position. He teaches that chapters 4–11 portray the fall of Jerusalem and chapters 12–19 portray the fall of Rome (II, 5); holds to a Neronian date of writing (II, 5); argues against seeking detailed historical connections with John's prophecy (II, 139–50); takes the first four seals as any war against a persecuting power (II, 159); calls the two hundred million horsemen a hyperbole (II, 195); believes that the two witnesses remained in Jerusalem to preach repentance to their countrymen as the Romans took the city (II, 227); gives postmillennial interpretations (II, 354).

Summers, Ray. *Worthy Is the Lamb.* Nashville: Broadman Press, 1951. 224 pp.

An amillennial Baptist commentary. He emphasizes apocalyptic literature (pp. 3–26); relates the first seal to the heathen conquest of imperial Rome (p. 140); identifies the martyred saints as those slain during the Domitian persecutions (p. 142); views the first four trumpets as natural calamities that fell on the Roman Empire (p. 156); says the sixth trumpet portrays the Parthian invasion of Rome (p. 159); calls the first beast the Roman emperor and the second beast emperor worship (pp. 173–78); connects Armageddon with the fall of Rome (pp. 190, 199); rejects a literal Millennium (pp. 203–4).

Wieand, David J. *Visions of Glory.* Elgin, Ill.: Brethren Press, 1979. 132 pp.

A popularized preterist interpretation. He condemns Hal Lindsay's "pop-eschatology" (p. 1); holds that Revelation has an ancient worldview of a three-storied universe (p. 3); charges the futurist interpretation with overemphasizing the future and neglecting the past (p. 7); recommends preterist principles of interpretation (pp. 7ff.); quotes liberal authors with approval (pp. 12, 21, 34, etc.); claims that only one item in Revelation 11 is to be interpreted literally: the city Jerusalem (p. 60); thinks the two witnesses prophesy for 1,266 days (p. 61); holds that the glorious mother is the church (p. 61); thinks Armageddon is a symbol of the last battle between good and evil (p. 88); thinks the thousand years are not literal (p. 108) and the heavenly city is a symbolic portrait of an idealized Jerusalem (p. 117).

Continuous Historical Commentaries

Barnes, Albert. *Notes on the New Testament, Explanatory and Practical Revelation.* 1852; rpt. Grand Rapids: Baker, 1949. 464 pp.

An interesting but outdated postmillennial exposition. He thinks that the fifth seal refers to the Diocletian persecutions (pp. 161–62, 284–304); holds that the sixth seal is the Goth and Huns' invasion of imperial Rome (p. 167); claims that the fifth trumpet refers to the rise of Mohammedanism (p. 216); considers that the measuring of the temple symbolizes the true church during the Reformation (p. 272); argues for the year-day theory (p. 273); says that the saints in 13:7 relate to the Waldenses and Albigenses (p. 324); believes that the bowl judgments portray the French Revolution (pp. 359–61).

Carroll, B. H. *The Book of Revelation in an Interpretation of the English Bible*. New York: Revell, 1913. 358 pp.

A postmillennial exposition. He defends the Johannine authorship (p. 17); claims that 1:7 refers to Christ's ascension (p. 42); interprets the first trumpet as the heathen invasions of imperial Rome (p. 134); thinks that the star Wormwood refers to the establishment of the papacy (p. 136); holds to the year-day theory (p. 138); identifies the woman as the true church in the wilderness during the Middle Ages (p. 164); believes that the Man-Child represents the martyrs during the persecution of Decius (p. 170); asserts that the Battle of Armageddon has been in progress since A.D. 250 (pp. 227, 231, 233).

Elliott, E. B. *Horae Apocalypticae*. 4 vols. London: Seeley, Jackson, and Halliday, 1862. 638, 481, 455, 604 pp.

The classic representative of the continuous historical view. He associates the wrath of the Lamb of the sixth seal with the fall of paganism during the time of Constantine (I, 251); interprets the fourth trumpet as the fall of Rome in A.D. 476 (I, 383); believes that the locusts in chapter 9 depict the Arab invasions of Christian Rome (I, 448–49); advocates the year-day theory (I, 463); says that the Man-Child stands for the children of the church, not Christ (III, 11); thinks that the dragon in chapter 12 is Maximin, not Satan (III, 19); teaches that the seventh trumpet symbolizes the French Revolution (III, 291).

Glasgow, James. *The Apocalypse Translated and Expounded*. Edinburgh: T. and T. Clark, 1872. 611 pp.

An old historical commentary. He argues that 1:7 does not refer to a visible coming of the Lord (p. 124); holds that the seal judgments refer to the destruction of Jerusalem in A.D. 70 (pp. 81–82, 216); considers the fourth trumpet to depict the Roman Empire under Constantine (pp. 249–50); says that the fallen star (9:1) is Mohammed (p. 251); thinks that the sixth trumpet symbolizes the Crusades (p. 265); applies the year-day theory to the Millennium and says that the Millennium will last for 360,000 years (p. 477).

Newton, Sir Isaac. *Observations upon the Prophecies of Daniel, and the Apocalypse of St. John*. London: J. Darby and T. Brown, 1733. Reprinted in part II of Sir William Whitla, *Sir Isaac Newton's Daniel and the Apocalypse*. London: John Murray, 1922. Pp. 295–351.

An old historical exposition. He associates the fifth seal with the victory of Constantine (p. 323); thinks the Man-Child is the Christian empire under Constantine (p. 324); teaches the year-day theory (p. 326); says the fourth trumpet depicts the fall of Rome in A.D. 476 (p. 335); believes that the fifth and sixth trumpets relate to the rise of Mohammedanism (pp. 340, 342).

Idealist and Synchronous Historical Commentaries

Alford, Henry. *The Apocalypse of John* in Vol. IV of *The Greek Testament.*
4 vols. London: Longmans, Green, and Co., 1894. Pp. 545–750.
Concise comments on the Greek text. He defends Johannine authorship (p. 229); interprets the four horsemen as personifications of the
conquering kingdom (p. 618); holds that the locust judgment will take
place immediately prior to the Second Advent (p. 644); suggests that
the beast wounded unto death (13:3) refers to the ruin of pagan Rome
and the healing of the beast refers to the establishment of the Christian Roman empire (p. 675); argues for a literal Armageddon (p. 702)
and for a literal resurrection and millennium (p. 732).

Auberlen, Carl August. *The Prophecies of Daniel and the Revelations of St.
John,* trans. Adolph Saphir. Andover, Mass.: W. F. Draper, 1857. 459 pp.
Old but helpful premillennial studies. He defends the inerrancy of
Scripture (p. viii); holds that John wrote Revelation before A.D. 70
(pp. 235); maintains that the identification of the woman, the harlot,
and the two beasts is the key to the book (p. 234); says that John out-
lined the major epochs of church history in chapters 6 through 19
(p. 262, 294); interprets the harlot as apostate Christendom
(pp. 274–75, 292–93, 315); defends the literalness of a future Jewish
kingdom (pp. 325–26, 344, 346); distinguishes between the two resurrections (p. 331); maintains distinction between Israel and the church
until the Millennium (p. 349).

Barclay, William. *The Revelation of John.* 2 vols. Philadelphia: Westminster Press, 1959. 231, 297 pp.
Liberal commentary, but rich in word studies; a reverent treatment.
He denies that John the apostle wrote Revelation (I, 16); the seven
spirits denote the Holy Spirit (I, 146); the twenty-four elders symbolize the faithful people of God (I, 194); gives symbolic-preterist interpretations (II, 2–3); thinks John believed in a square, flat earth (II,
22); holds the 144,000 were saved in John's day (II, 29); links Antichrist with Nero (II, 78, 116, 133); holds that the first beast is the
Roman Empire and that the woman Babylon is also Rome (II, 109,
177); attacks premillennialism (II, 238–45); argues that there are
many ways to God (II, 269).

Beale, Gregory K. *The Book of Revelation* in *The New International Greek
Testament Commentary.* Grand Rapids: William B. Eerdmans, 1999.
1245 pp.
He dates the book from after A.D. 70 up to 95 (p. 27); holds to a sym-
bolical idealist interpretation (pp. 48–49); links major themes in the
OT and Revelation (pp. 88ff.); argues that solecisms are signals for OT

allusions (pp. 100f.); attacks the chronological outline in 1:19 for not being symbolical enough (p. 161); argues that Revelation is not merely a futurology but also a redemptive-historical and theological psychology for the church's thinking (p. 177); takes the seven churches as all churches (pp. 186f.); thinks that Christ reigned as king by conquering sin and death by the cross (p. 193); declares that 3:10 does not refer to a rapture from the Tribulation period (pp. 290f.); holds that the four living beings are likely symbolic (p. 330) and that the seven-sealed book symbolizes judgment and redemption (p. 340); notes that Scripture does not imply universal salvation (p. 403); thinks that the four winds are equivalent to the four horsemen (p. 406); takes the 144,000 as symbolical of all the redeemed and identical with the great multitude (pp. 412–24); argues that the Great Tribulation is a present reality (pp. 433f.); stresses the figurative nature of the trumpets (p. 488); argues that the locusts produce a spiritual famine (p. 500); declares that the two hundred million horsemen must be figurative (p. 509); holds that the forty-two months are not literal but figurative for the Tribulation period and may refer to the Roman siege of Jerusalem (pp. 565f.); thinks that the two witnesses represent the whole community of faith (p. 573); argues that the death of the two witnesses does not mean literally that the whole church is martyred (p. 590); thinks that, since the martyrdom of the two witnesses is symbolical, so is their resurrection (p. 597); states that "prophets" refers to the whole church (p. 617); holds that the woman in Revelation 12 refers to the people of God, before and after Christ's advent (p. 627); suggests that the three-and-a-half-year tribulation commences at Christ's ascension and lasts to His return (p. 646); argues that the Devil is barred from heaven only in a limited sense (p. 655); holds that the image of the beast is any substitute for God in any age (p. 711); defends the idea of eternal, conscious suffering for the wicked (pp. 762–65); thinks that the "sea of glass" connotes cosmic evil (p. 789); thinks that the trumpets and bowls are the same things and that the burden of proof lies on those trying to make a difference (p. 809); holds that the "sore" is a metaphor (p. 814); says the seven mountains are figurative but do not mean Rome (p. 868); stresses the conscious, enduring punishment of the Beast and his prophet (p. 969); notes that postmillennialism and amillennialism are more consistent with his own symbolic interpretations (p. 973); argues that the binding of Satan is not universal (p. 985); thinks that the Millennium is enjoyed by deceased saints during the church age (p. 991); discounts Alford's famous defense of two literal resurrections (p. 1004); argues for a general judgment (p. 1031); holds that the new heaven and earth are not a literal new creation but figurative (p. 1040); declares that "some interpret

21:10–22:5 as a literal description of an actual physical city. But this is highly improbable" (p. 1062); holds that the size of the cubic city shows the figurative idea of the completeness of God's people (p. 1073); thinks that the 144,000 are not a remnant but a symbol for all of God's people (p. 1076); holds that the new heavens and earth are equivalent to the new city alone (p. 1109). Such a commentary is very little help to one who believes in a literal, future fulfillment of prophecy.

Blaney, Harvey J. S. *Revelation* in Vol. VI of *The Wesleyan Bible Commentary*, ed. Charles W. Carter. Grand Rapids: Eerdmans, 1966. Pp. 399–523.

Brief Arminian notes. He accepts the Johannine authorship (p. 415); emphasizes the apocalyptic nature of Revelation (p. 409); holds to a synchronous arrangement of the seal, trumpet, and bowl judgments (p. 446); says that the seals typify the continuing struggle between the church and the world (p. 447); interprets the three and a half years as the Christian age (p. 471); claims that there have been several historical appearances of the Beast, "the incarnation of evil" (p. 505); spiritualizes the thousand years (pp. 506–7).

Caird, George Bradford. *A Commentary on the Revelation of St. John the Divine*. New York: Harper and Row, Publishers, 1966. 326 pp. (Harper Commentary Series).

Liberal commentary based on symbolic imagery; doubts Johannine authorship but dates it about A.D. 95; denies threefold division of Revelation (p. 26); says on 4:1: prophet "is transported from earth to heaven in a prophetic rapture" (p. 60); explains sea of glass by Tiamat (p. 65); separates rider on white horse from Revelation 19 (p. 80); denies literal nature of first resurrection (p. 254); says on Gog and Magog: even when progress reaches the Millennium, "men must remember that they still have no security except in God" (p. 257); concludes with a chapter on the theology of Revelation (pp. 289–301).

Carpenter, W. Boyd. *The Revelation*. The Layman's Handy Commentary Series, ed. Charles J. Ellicott. 1903; rpt. Grand Rapids: Zondervan, 1957. 280 pp.

A popular amillennial exposition. He prefers Johannine authorship (p. 8); teaches that John's prophecies find multiple fulfillments throughout human history (pp. 13–14); sees many comings of the Lord (p. 15); considers Revelation as a symbolical unfolding of the conflict between good and evil (p. 18); claims that the mission of Christianity is to slowly eliminate wars, disease, death, and persecution (p. 80); holds to a synchronous arrangement of the three series judgments (p. 107).

Easley, Kendall H. *Revelation* in the *Holman New Testament Commentary*. Nashville: Broadman and Holman, 1998. 438 pp.

A commentary based on the NIV, advocating the PreWrath Rapture. He holds that the white stone is an admission ticket (p. 40); argues for a posttribulation view (p. 58); cannot think of anything the gems symbolize (p. 75); takes the twenty-four elders as an unknown class of heavenly beings (pp. 76, 83).

Erdman, Charles R. *The Revelation of John*. Philadelphia: Westminster Press, 1936. 168 pp.

Brief devotional studies. He regards John's prophecy as generic rather than specific (pp. 72, 124); says the seal judgments characterize the whole church age (p. 72); treats the trumpets as divine judgments that precede the return of Christ (p. 85); holds that the two witnesses represent the church in its divine mission (p. 93); considers Babylon as the worldly and godless spirit in any period (p. 111); maintains that 19:11–16 refers to the yet future return of Christ (p. 140).

Franzman, Martin H. *The Revelation to John*. St. Louis: Concordia Publishing House, 1976. 148 pp.

A brief Lutheran exposition. He argues that the theme of Revelation is the conflict between good and evil (pp. 17, 84–85); says that the temple in chapter 11 symbolizes the church (p. 78); holds that Jerusalem represents any place men reject God (pp. 80–81); considers the woman in chapter 12 to be the people of God (p. 88); takes Armageddon as "any great climactic conflict" (p. 112); maintains that the saints have already risen and are now reigning with Christ (p. 130).

Hendriksen, W. *More Than Conquerors*. Grand Rapids: Baker, 1940. 285 pp.

A popular amillennial exposition. He considers John's purpose is to comfort the militant church in her struggle against evil (p. 11); divides the book into seven sections, each spanning the entire church age (pp. 25, 28); claims that the seal, trumpet, and bowl judgments recur repeatedly (p. 55); refers the first seal to Christ and the spread of the gospel (p. 118); calls the 144,000 the entire church militant (p. 134); suggests that the sixth trumpet denotes war anytime war occurs (p. 147); says that Armageddon symbolizes every battle in which the Lord intervenes in behalf of His people (p. 196); identifies the Millennium as the church age (pp. 228–29).

Hengstenberg, E. W. *The Revelation of St. John*, trans. Patrick Fairbairn. 2 vols. Edinburgh: T. and T. Clark, 1851. 487, 508 pp.

An old amillennial exposition. He attacks the continuous historicists (I, 41, 248); regards the sixth seal as the overthrow of world governments and maintains that the seal is fulfilled whenever governments fall (I, 274); thinks the star in 9:1 represents various rulers who appear in history (I, 352); believes that the measuring of the temple symbolizes the preservation of the church and that the three and a half years symbolize the whole course of world history (I, 395–96); argues that the beasts in chapter 13 cannot be individuals (II, 83); suggests that the sore of the first bowl judgment is the "eruptive distemper" that affects people during this age (II, 156).

Hoeksema, Herman. *Behold, He Cometh! An Exposition of the Book of Revelation.* Grand Rapids: Reformed Free Publishing Association, 1969. 726 pp.

An exhaustive Reformed commentary. He defends apostolic authorship (p. 2); relates 1:19 with 4:1, saying that 4:1 is future from John's viewpoint (p. 151); attacks the futurist school (pp. 155, 187); takes the sixth seal literally, arguing that no symbolical interpretation of the passage is necessary (p. 236); says the whole church age is depicted by the seven seals (p. 229); believes that the two hundred million horsemen represent a future war (p. 326); thinks the temple in chapter 11 symbolizes the church (pp. 368–69); interprets the first four trumpets and bowls literally (pp. 302, 532).

Kalamos. *Prophetical Suggestions.* London: Deigby, Long and Co., 1906. 760 pp.

The author follows the continuous historical interpretation of Revelation (p. 2); has intricate charts, starting with the first seal, emperor Augustus, and so forth.

Lange, John Peter. *Revelation* in *Lange's Commentary on the Holy Scriptures*, trans. Philip Schaff. Grand Rapids: Zondervan, n.d. 446 pp.

A premillennial exposition. He defends apostolic authorship (p. 58); argues that the Second Coming is the theme of the book (p. 93); holds that the sixth seal is the final judgment (p. 167); believes that the twelve tribes symbolize the NT church (p. 182); thinks the trumpet judgments refer to the church militant and to her spiritual conflicts (p. 197); connects the three and a half years with the "pilgrimage of Christianity through the world" (p. 224); identifies the woman in chapter 12 with spiritual Israel (pp. 223, 237).

Lawrence, J. B. *A New Heaven and a New Earth.* New York: The American Press, 1960. 165 pp.

A brief Baptist commentary. He states the theme of the book is the battle between Christ and Satan for control of the earth (pp. 15, 85); interprets "shortly" in 1:1 to mean that the prophecies were shortly to begin to be fulfilled (p. 21); cautions against symbolizing every detail in the book (p. 53); views the Rapture as taking place at the sixth seal (p. 94); refrains from stating his millennial position (p. 149).

Lee, William. *The Revelation of St. John* in Vol. 4 (NT) of *The Holy Bible with an Explanatory and Critical Commentary*, ed. F. C. Cook. New York: Charles Scribner's Sons, 1901. Pp. 405–844.

A helpful contribution. He states that the Second Coming is the central theme of Revelation (pp. 502, 576); provides numerous additional notes, such as the Lord's Day (pp. 510–11), the measuring of the temple (pp. 646–47), the forty-two months (pp. 647–50), the two witnesses (pp. 650–52), Antichrist (pp. 689–91), and the premillennial advent (pp. 778–91); says that John's visions depict a general survey of the progress of the church during this age (p. 571); lists various interpretations (pp. 582–84, 608, 614, 618–22, 697–700); spiritualizes 19:11–16 (p. 784) and the thousand years (p. 792).

Lenski, R. C. H. *The Interpretation of St. John's Revelation*. Minneapolis: Augsburg Publishing House, 1943. 675 pp.

An amillennial Lutheran exposition. He defends apostolic authorship (p. 5); upholds divine inspiration (pp. 27, 36); denies that 1:19 represents the structural key to the book (p. 80); says that the 144,000 stands for the church militant and that the great multitude stands for the church triumphant (p. 245); interprets all numbers symbolically (pp. 503, 564); takes 19:11–21 as the future second coming (p. 550); symbolizes the thousand years (p. 573).

McDowell, Edward A. *The Meaning and Message of the Revelation*. Nashville: Broadman Press, 1951. 224 pp.

An amillennial Baptist commentary. He does not commit himself on authorship (p. 13); argues that the phrase "the time is at hand" (1:3) does not refer to the Second Advent (p. 24); says that the first seal depicts anyone who sets out to conquer the world (p. 89); relates the sixth seal to the end of the age (p. 91); teaches that the 144,000 stand for the new Israel of God who are spiritually secure but not physically safe (p. 97); calls the Great Tribulation the earthly experience of the people of God during any age (p. 99); maintains that the kingdom in 11:15 began with the Incarnation (p. 122); finds a counterpart to the bowl judgments in the fall of Nazi Germany (p. 164); spiritualizes the Second Advent (19:11–21) and the thousand years (pp. 183–86, 190).

Mauro, Philip. *Of Things Which Soon Must Come to Pass*. Grand Rapids: Eerdmans, 1933. 623 pp.

A Plymouth Brethren exposition from a historical perspective. He argues that every symbol is explained somewhere in the Bible (p. 3); says the arrangement of Revelation is topical rather than chronological

(p. 5); insists that Revelation refers to events during the church age
(p. 24); interprets the first seal as the spread of the gospel (p. 190);
treats the sixth seal as the future day of judgment (p. 235); attacks the
continuous historical view (pp. 265–66); frequently cites Hengstenberg (pp. 275, 351–53, 368, 392); believes that the fifth trumpet is the
rise of Mohammedanism (p. 313); holds that the Millennium began in
Constantine's era (p. 596).

Milligan, William. *The Book of Revelation* in *The Expositor's Bible*. London: Hodder and Stoughton, 1889. 392 pp.

The representative commentary from the idealist point of view. He interprets the sixth seal as "every great crisis in human history" (p. 107);
views the woman in chapter 12 as the Christian church (p. 198); identifies the 1260 days with the present dispensation (p. 212); thinks the
first beast symbolizes the godless influence of the world (p. 224); rejects a chronological sequence of visions (p. 259); takes the thousand
years to be symbolical of completeness (p. 337).

Morris, Leon. *The Revelation of St. John*. Grand Rapids: Eerdmans, 1969.
263 pp.

A symbolical amillennial exposition. He divides the book into three
sections based on 1:19 (p. 56); teaches that God's wrath during the
sixth seal concerns the end time (p. 111); tends toward a synchronous
arrangement of the visions (p. 119); stresses divine intervention
(p. 124); thinks the locusts symbolize the preaching of the gospel
(p. 125); identifies the temple in chapter 11 as the church (p. 146);
associates the two witnesses with the testimony of the church (p. 149);
believes that the seal, trumpet, and bowl judgments symbolize all of
human history until the end (p. 187).

Plummer, A. *Revelation* in Vol. 22 of *The Pulpit Commentary*, eds. H. D.
M. Spence and Joseph S. Exell. N.d.; rpt. Grand Rapids: Eerdmans,
1950. 591 pp.

A thorough amillennial exposition. He defends apostolic authorship
(p. ii); holds to an early date of writing (p. iii); believes that John's
prophecies are fulfilled repeatedly throughout the church age (p. 185);
teaches that the sixth seal depicts the end of the age (p. 189); calls the
sixth trumpet "spiritual evils which afflict the ungodly in this life"
(p. 288); associates the two witnesses with the elect church of both
Testaments (p. 289); thinks that the Great Tribulation means all the
tribulations the redeemed face in this life (p. 209); says the conflict in
19:11–16 takes place throughout history (p. 449).

Ramsey, James B. *The Book of Revelation*. Edinburgh: Banner of Truth Trust, 1873. 518 pp.

Spiritual applications on the first eleven chapters of Revelation. He maintained that visions were designed "to produce a good moral and religious impression on the minds of the men of that and of coming generations" (p. xxiv).

Richardson, Donald W. *The Revelation of Jesus Christ*. Richmond: John Knox Press, 1957. 195 pp.

An amillennial exposition. He rejects a literal interpretation of numbers (p. 33); claims that John's purpose is to give a philosophy of history (pp. 34, 96) that is neither chronological nor detailed (pp. 45, 136); thinks the first seal depicts "Christ or the victorious march of God's truth" throughout history (p. 79); says the sixth seal, the sixth trumpet, and the harvest portray the end of the age (pp. 85, 100, 126); takes the temple in chapter 11 as the preservation of the church and the two witnesses as the testimony of the church (pp. 103–4); associates the first beast with any godless political system (p. 114); believes that 19:11–21 refers to the First Advent (p. 152) and that the triumph in chapter 19 is won by the preaching of the gospel (p. 155); symbolizes the thousand years (p. 168).

Robbins, Ray Frank. *The Revelation of Jesus Christ*. Nashville: Broadman Press, 1975. 260 pp.

An amillennial Baptist commentary. He leaves the question of authorship open (p. 17); claims John's purpose is to set forth a symbolical portrayal of history between the two advents (p. 22); objects to 1:19 as being the outline of the book (p. 49); interprets the sixth seal as the consequences of sin anytime man sins (p. 108); thinks that the men fleeing from the wrath of God (6:16) refer to men during this age who are trying "to escape from a guilty conscience" (p. 108); holds that the three and a half years depict the duration of the church on earth (pp. 135–36); says that the kingdom (11:15) refers to the eternal rule of God in men's hearts (p. 143); views the harvest as God's adding to the church (p. 174); teaches that 19:11–16 represents Christ's continuing conquests over evil (p. 215).

Swete, Henry Barclay. *Commentary on Revelation*. 1911; rpt. Grand Rapids: Kregel Publications, 1977. Original title *The Apocalypse of St. John*. 338 pp.

Helpful comments on the Greek text. He is uncertain on the authorship (p. clxxxv); connects 1:19 with 4:1 (p. 21); says the sixth seal symbolizes social revolutions that precede the end (p. 92); identifies the 144,000 with the whole number of the faithful (p. 99); believes that the Great Tribulation is a time of crisis that everyone must endure

(p. 102); associates the two witnesses with the testimony of the church (p. 134); holds that the woman in 12:1–2 is the Jewish church and that the persecuted woman is the Christian church (pp. 148–49); says John used the Nero legend (p. 163); connects the second beast with emperor worship (p. 170); interprets 19:11–16 as Christ converting the lost throughout this age (p. 254); symbolizes the thousand years (p. 260).

Torrance, Thomas F. *The Apocalypse Today*. Grand Rapids: Eerdmans, 1959. 155 pp.

Brief devotional studies. He prefers apostolic authorship (p. 5); maintains that the seals symbolize world history (p. 43); believes that the sixth seal refers to earthquakes in the souls of men and to thunders of God's voice in their ears (p. 48); interprets the wrath of God as "the wrath of sacrificial love" (p. 49); associates the sealing of the 144,000 with baptism (pp. 54–56); thinks the fifth trumpet portrays the poisoning of the atmosphere when men reject the gospel (p. 62); symbolizes the thousand years (p. 133).

Wernecke, Herbert H. *The Book of Revelation Speaks to Us*. Philadelphia: Westminster Press, 1954. 176 pp.

A brief amillennial commentary. He tends to favor apostolic authorship (p. 22); believes that John's visions portray the conflict between the first-century church and imperial Rome, which represents the ensuing spiritual conflict now being fought and which awaits the ultimate triumph of Christ (p. 24); supports a synchronous interpretation of John's visions (pp. 76, 86, 119); argues that the sixth seal cannot be literal (p. 81); views the trumpets as calamities that recur repeatedly (p. 86); identifies the first beast as the Roman Empire and as any godless political power in general (p. 108); spiritualizes the Millennium (p. 148).

Wilcock, Michael. *I Saw Heaven Opened: The Message of Revelation*. Downers Grove, Ill.: InterVarsity Press, 1975. 223 pp.

An amillennial commentary. He leaves the question of authorship open (p. 23); claims "soon" in 1:1 refutes the futurist position (p. 32); teaches that the fulfillment of John's prophecies is a lengthy process covering the entire church age (p. 33); rejects a literal interpretation of numbers (pp. 59–60); thinks that the first five seals and trumpets have come true repeatedly throughout history (p. 97); associates the sixth trumpet with tanks, planes, cancer, road accidents, malnutrition, and terrorist bombs (p. 99); takes the 1260 days as symbolical for the church age (pp. 119, 130).

Futurist Commentaries

Ainslie, Edgar. *The Dawn of the Scarlet Age*. Philadelphia: Sunday School Times Company, 1954. 150 pp.

A warm-hearted premillennial exposition. Holds that Revelation is a book of endings (p. 2); calls the Lord Jesus "the Priest of Patmos Isle" (p. 16); holds that the seven churches are ages of church history (pp. 34ff.), the door opened marks the Rapture (4:1, pp. 54f.), the twenty-four elders represent the redeemed of all ages (p. 62), the four horses represent human agencies under the control of satanic powers (p. 71); argues that death does not end it all for either the righteous or the wicked (pp. 79f.); holds that the revived Roman empire will be the most scarlet, sinful empire the world has ever seen (p. 105); says the scarlet woman will be the apostate church formed by papal Rome, apostate Protestantism, and the lukewarm professors of Laodicea (p. 121); holds that the Great White Throne is the judgment of unbelievers for whom there is no annihilation, but instead eternal fire (p. 141); concludes with the seven perfect things of heaven (pp. 148ff.).

Barnhouse, Donald Grey. *Revelation*. Grand Rapids: Zondervan, 1971. 432 pp.

A thorough premillennial exposition. He identifies the seven spirits as the Holy Spirit (p. 22); argues that hades had two divisions (p. 31); holds that the twenty-four elders are representatives of Israel and the church (p. 91), that the four living beings are cherubim (p. 95), that the two witnesses are Elijah and Moses (pp. 199, 202); thinks that the woman clothed with the sun is spiritual Israel (p. 217); holds that the first beast in Revelation 13 is both Antichrist and the empire (pp. 235ff.) and that both may be killed and restored (p. 238); quotes R. A. Torrey on eternal punishment (p. 269); attacks the idea that Babylon on the Euphrates must be rebuilt and destroyed again (pp. 334–35); holds that the bride includes both OT and NT believers (p. 400); concludes with an appendix arguing for a literal interpretation of the Millennium (pp. 417–32).

Beasley-Murray, G. R. *The Book of Revelation*. New Century Bible. London: Marshall, Morgan and Scott, 1974. 352 pp.

A nondispensational premillennial exposition. He stresses apocalyptic literature (p. 12); does not commit himself on the authorship (p. 37); holds that 1:19 presents the three divisions of the book but that 4:1 and following is not entirely future (p. 68); interprets the 144,000 as the whole Christian community (p. 140); says that Jerusalem in chapter 11 symbolizes the world in opposition to God (p. 179); thinks that the temple in chapter 11 refers to the true church (p. 182); identifies the woman as the people of God (p. 197); employs the Nero legend to interpret chapter 13 (p. 211); does not try to interpret 19:11–21 except by saying that it pictures Christ's judgment on His enemies (p. 284).

Bengel, John Albert. *Revelation* in Vol. V of *Gnomon of the New Testament.* Edinburgh: T. and T. Clark, 1863. Pp. 172–389.

He gives a careful argument for a literal millennial reign (pp. 364ff.).

Bullinger, E. W. *The Apocalypse or "The Day of the Lord."* 3rd ed. London: Eyre and Spottiswoode, 1935. 741 pp.

An ultradispensational futurist commentary. He claims that his conclusions are different from any other work ever published on Revelation (p. i); teaches that the Day of the Lord is the key to the book (pp. ii–iii); argues that nothing in the book relates to the church age (p. 63); holds that the seven churches are future Jewish assemblies on earth after the rapture of the church (p. 71); condemns those who base their exposition on 1:19 (p. 159).

Criswell, Wallie Amos. *Expository Sermons on Revelation.* 5 vols. Grand Rapids: Zondervan, 1962, 1963, 1964, 1965, 1966. 184, 184, 214, 189, 183 pp.

Careful expositions by a master preacher. He evaluates the four major interpretations of Revelation, commending the futurist (I, 23–31); defends John, son of Zebedee, as the author (I, 44–47); discusses the meaning of numbers (I, 56–84); holds that "He cometh" is the sublime theme of the whole Bible (I, 96); recounts persecutions believers have suffered (1, 126–39); takes the seven messengers to be men, not angels (II, 28–29); maintains that the churches are seven periods of church history, but they also coexist (II, 39–44); attacks the liquor business (II, 123f.); argues for the pretribulation Rapture (III, 17–20); identifies the four living beings as cherubim (II, 42ff.); estimates two hundred million horsemen would form a troop a mile wide and eighty-seven miles long (III, 191); declines to guess who the two witnesses are (IV, 42); holds that the Antichrist will be specially attractive (IV, 106); thinks that the bride is the NT church (V, 28); argues that only saints will enter the Millennium (V, 144); holds that the Laodicean period has already begun (V, 167f.).

DeBurgh, William. *An Exposition of the Book of Revelation.* 2 parts in 1 vol. Dublin: Richard M. Tims, 1834. 100, 265 pp.

Old but valuable lectures. He does not view the seven churches as chronological (I, 17); divides Revelation according to 1:19 (II, 2); argues for a literal interpretation (II, 4); symbolizes Israel (II, 121); claims that the woman's giving birth refers to the Second Advent

(II, 124); attacks postmillennial interpretations (II, 145, 161); defends a literal thousand years and a premillennial return of the Lord (II, 214–16); stresses imminency (II, 259).

DeHaan, M. R. *Revelation*. Grand Rapids: Zondervan Publishing House, 1946. 308 pp.

A thorough-going dispensational treatment, consistently premillennial. He holds that the second beast of Revelation 13 is the Antichrist and that he is Judas Iscariot (p. 184); the beast in Revelation 17 is the revived Roman Empire and the scarlet woman is the apostate church (p. 255).

Erdman, W. J. *Notes on the Revelation*. New York: Revell, 1930. 102 pp.

A brief midtribulational interpretation. He divides the book into two sections, chapters 1–11, 12–22 (p. 20); argues that the 144,000 represent the church that is granted safety during the Tribulation (p. 47); holds that the woman represents Israel (p. 63); identifies the first beast as the man of sin (p. 66); regards the Rapture as taking place before the bowls (p. 77).

Falwell, Jerry, Edward Hindson, and Woodrow Kroll, eds. *Revelation* in *Liberty Bible Commentary*. New York: Thomas Nelson, 1978. Pp. 743–801.

A premillennial commentary. They argue that "the Lord's day" is not Sunday but the prophetic Day of the Lord (p. 750); think that each church is symbolic of an age of church history (p. 752); argue for a pretribulation rapture (p. 757); make the twenty-four elders the raptured church (p. 758); identify chapters 6–19 as the Tribulation period (p. 760); hold that the 144,000 are Jews (p. 762); argue that no one who has heard the gospel before the Rapture will be able to be saved during the Tribulation (p. 763); maintain that Apollyon is Lucifer (p. 766), that the forty-two months denote the last half of the Tribulation (p. 769), that the beast out of the sea is Antichrist (p. 774), that Babylon is the future world church (p. 783), that there is a literal hell (pp. 791, 794), and that there will be a literal Millennium (p. 792).

Fausset, A. R. *Revelation* in Vol. VI of *A Commentary Critical, Experimental and Practical*, ed. Jamieson, Faussett, and Brown. 1869; rpt. Grand Rapids: Eerdmans, 1945. Pp. 655–731.

A conservative premillennial exposition. He holds that the twenty-four elders are heads of OT and NT believers (p. 673) and the four living creatures are cherubim (p. 673); holds the 144,000 to be literal Israelites (p. 680); identifies the two witnesses with Moses and Elijah (p. 689), the beast of Revelation 13 with Antichrist, the little horn of Daniel (p. 698); holds mystery Babylon to be the apostate church with a location in Rome (pp. 709, 715); teaches a Millennium, defending it from OT passages (pp. 721–22).

Gaebelein, Arno C. *The Revelation*. New York: Our Hope. 1915. 225 pp.

A popular dispensational commentary. He holds that the seven churches are prophetic of the church age (p. 33); calls the earthquakes of the sixth seal symbols of the end-time shaking of civil and governmental powers (p. 56); interprets the temple of chapter 11 as a restored Jewish temple but says that the inner court symbolizes the faithful remnant and the outer court symbolizes apostate Israel (pp. 68–69); maintains that the flight of the woman represents the persecution of Israel during the Tribulation (p. 78).

Govett, Robert. *The Apocalypse, Expounded by Scripture*. London: Chas. J. Thynne, 1920. 629 pp.

A literal interpretation of Revelation. He divides the book on the basis of 1:19 (p. 21); holds to the doctrine of imminency (p. 22); argues for a literal interpretation (pp. 24, 143); says some of the church will go through the Tribulation (pp. 67, 78); thinks the rider on the first horse in chapter 6 is Christ (p. 130); gives nine arguments why the 144,000 must refer to Israel (p. 155); advocates an end-time return of Nero and interprets 666 as Nero (pp. 350–58); teaches that a literal Babylon will reappear (p. 422); suggests that Satan will be visible when he is tossed down to earth, therefore the chain can be literal (p. 505); argues for a literal resurrection and literal Millennium (pp. 509–10, 526, 533).

Harris, Keith. *The Unveiling*. Columbia, S.C.: The Olive Press, 1999. 490 pp.

An exhausting study of Revelation. He is a premillennialist (p. 8) and a pretribulationist (p. 18). He believes that Christ transported the righteous from paradise to the sea of glass beneath God's throne (p. 27); gives six different interpretations of each of the seven churches (pp. 33–34); holds that the sardine stone was reddish brown (p. 110), that the seven lamps of fire represent the church from Pentecost to the Rapture (p. 118), that the 144,000 will consist of both male and female witnesses (p. 162), and that the star angel in 9:1 is the same one who binds Satan (20:1–3, p. 185).

Hoste, William. *The Visions of John the Divine*. Kilmarnock, Scotland: John Ritchie, Ltd., n.d. 192 pp.

A futurist interpretation. He holds that the angels of the churches are literal angels (p. 18), John's translation (4:1) represents the Rapture (p. 38), the twenty-four elders are the overcomers of chapters 1–2 (p. 40), the four living beings portray the church as sharing in responsibility and government (p. 45); holds that the little scroll is the title deed of the earth (p. 56); says the four horsemen are great movements on earth (p. 56); thinks that a gigantic meteor struck Siberia, digging a trench, and lies buried in a crater (none of which exist, p. 66); holds that the two witnesses are Moses and Elijah (p. 79) and mystery Babylon is Rome (p. 136); defends a literal thousand-year reign with both earthly and heavenly aspects, but not a single one of the wicked dead have a part in it (p. 159); attacks annihilationism (p. 163); holds that the Great White Throne is the judgment of the wicked dead (p. 166).

Hoyt, Herman A. *The Revelation of the Lord Jesus Christ*. Winona Lake, Ind.: Brethren Missionary Herald Company, 1966. 108 pp.

Brief popular exposition. He sees the purpose of Revelation to bless the reader (p. 20); warns against contradicting the imminent return, but still sees general periods of church history in the seven churches (pp. 28–29); argues for the necessity of the rapture of the church at the close of Revelation 3 (pp. 32–34); identifies the twenty-four elders as the church (p. 35); maintains that one of the two witnesses is Elijah and "Moses may be the other" (p. 57); holds that the Antichrist will be killed and restored to life (pp. 70–71); thinks that Babylon will be rebuilt (pp. 81–82); takes the bride to be the church only (p. 91); thinks the city is for the church alone (p. 105).

Ironside, H. A. *Lectures on the Book of Revelation*. New York: Loizeaux Brothers, 1920, 1951. 366 pp.

Popular dispensational messages. He believes that 4:1 symbolizes the Rapture (p. 80); says that the martyrs of the fifth seal are believing Jews during the Tribulation (p. 112); takes the sixth seal as a symbol of the breaking up of society (p. 114); identifies the 144,000 with Israel (p. 126); argues that the woman of chapter 12 must be Israel, not the church (pp. 209, 212); maintains that the second beast is Antichrist (p. 236); holds to a pretribulation rapture and to a literal Millennium (pp. 258, 334).

Jennings, Samuel W. *Alpha and Omega: Studies in the Book of Revelation*. Greenville, S.C.: Ambassador Productions, 1996. 336 pp.

The largest part of the book deals with the seven churches (pp. 41–166). He defends the pretribulation rapture (p. 183); stresses the age-long struggle between the Man-Child and the Dragon (p. 238); notes the ministry of angels (pp. 283f.); suggests that there are three books of judgment (p. 297); warns against prophetic scholars who draw attention to themselves rather than to the Lord Jesus (p. 302).

Kelly, William. *Lectures on the Book of Revelation*. London: G. Morrish, n.d. 502 pp.

An old Plymouth Brethren exposition. He holds to a pretribulation rapture (p. 126); symbolizes the sixth seal (p. 148); connects the

144,000 with Israel but symbolizes the number (p. 155); says the locusts symbolize false doctrine (p. 188); believes that the two witnesses may be symbolical of hundreds of witnesses (p. 229); identifies the woman with Israel (p. 249); considers the second beast to be Antichrist.

Kuyper, Abraham. *The Revelation of St. John*, trans. John Hendrik de-Vries. Grand Rapids: Eerdmans, 1935. 360 pp.

An amillennial futurist commentary. He argues for a synchronous arrangement of the visions and a figurative meaning of the numbers in Revelation (p. 9); takes the sixth seal literally (p. 26); identifies the rider on the first horse with Christ (p. 75); connects the 144,000 with the elect (p. 197); attacks millennialism (pp. 270–77).

Ladd, George Eldon. *A Commentary on the Revelation of John*. Grand Rapids: Eerdmans, 1972. 308 pp.

A nondispensational futurist commentary. He casts doubt on the traditional apostolic authorship (p. 8); says that the correct interpretation is a combination of the preterist and futurist views (p. 14); believes that the first beast is both imperial Rome and the future Antichrist, or any other demonic power that plagues the church (p. 14); takes the Great Tribulation primarily as future but claims it may also denote any tribulation the church faces (p. 14); gives posttribulational interpretations (p. 165); identifies the 144,000 and the woman with the church (pp. 114, 166); rejects the interpretation of 666 as Nero (pp. 186–87); objects to a symbolical interpretation of the Second Coming in 19:11–21 (p. 252); upholds premillennialism (p. 261).

LaHaye, Tim. *Revelation Illustrated and Made Plain*. Grand Rapids: Zondervan, 1973, 1975. 326 pp.

A dispensational interpretation. He places the midpoint of the Tribulation between the trumpets and the bowls (p. 3); gives an outline for Revelation (pp. 4–5); holds that the seven churches show seven periods of history (p. 8); teaches a pretribulation rapture at 4:1 (p. 76); holds that the twenty-four elders are angels and the four living creatures are seraphim (pp. 81, 83); thinks the seals cover the first quarter of the Tribulation (twenty-one months, p. 98); argues that more people will be saved in the Tribulation than during the entire church age (p. 118); holds that the two hundred million horsemen are "demonlike evil spirits" (p. 140); maintains that the two witnesses will be Moses and Elijah (p. 152); thinks the Antichrist will die and be resurrected (pp. 174, 180); holds that there are two different groups of 144,000 (p. 194); argues that Babylon must be rebuilt and destroyed again (pp. 199, 239); holds that the bride is the NT church only; the OT saints are the guests (pp. 252, 254).

————. *Revelation Unveiled*. Grand Rapids: Zondervan, 1999. 378 pp.

A premillennial, pretribulation rapture commentary. He provides parallels between Genesis and Revelation (pp. 16–17); identifies the Philadelphian church as the church from A.D. 1750 to the Rapture (p. 78); lists Rapture passages vs. Second Coming passages (p. 102); holds that the twenty-four elders represent Israel and the church (p. 120); suggests that the seven-sealed scroll is the title deed to the earth (p. 125); stresses that the 144,000 preach the same gospel that Paul preached (p. 153); holds that the two-hundred-million-man army is made up of evil spirits (p. 174); argues that the two witnesses are Elijah and Moses (p. 186); thinks that the Beast will be killed and raised from the dead to parallel Christ's life (p. 217); stresses the eternal suffering of the damned (p. 240); holds that it is religious Babylon in Revelation 17 and commercial Babylon in Revelation 18 (pp. 260, 278); maintains that the friends of the Bridegroom are not the church but all the rest of the believing dead from Adam to the resurrection of Christ (p. 296); holds that OT saints will be resurrected at the end of the Tribulation period (p. 326); concludes with a brief bibliography (pp. 377–78).

Lang, G. H. *The Revelation of Jesus Christ*. London: Paternoster Press, 1948. 420 pp.

A dispensational exposition, filled with odd and private interpretations. He warmly commends the English RV (p. 12); discusses the interweaving of the literal and figurative elements in Revelation (pp. 17ff.); denies a secret rapture; teaches a partial rapture and a posttribulation rapture (pp. 28–29, 40, 243); argues that the twenty-four elders are angelic powers (pp. 127–31); confuses the beast with the king of the north (p. 157); states that the two witnesses "may be Enoch and Elijah" (p. 185); interprets the woman as the church and the man-child as overcoming believers (p. 201); suggests that both the Beast and the False Prophet may be killed and brought back to life (pp. 223, 225); identifies the Antichrist with Gog (p. 290); denies that the lake of fire is material (p. 353).

Lindsey, Hal. *There's a New World Coming*. Santa Ana, Cal.: Vision House Publishers, 1973. 308 pp.

A popular futurist treatment. He claims that the meaning of Revelation is clear only in light of current events (pp. 21–23); holds that the seven churches represent periods of church history (p. 41); uses the parable of the fig tree to approximate the time of the Rapture (pp. 78–79); interprets the sixth seal as a nuclear exchange (p. 110); associates the locusts as Cobra helicopters (pp. 138–39); identifies the sixth trumpet with Red Chinese soldiers (p. 140); says the two eagle wings symbolize aircraft from the Sixth Fleet (p. 179).

Meyer, Nathan M. *From Now to Eternity.* Winona Lake, Ind.: BMH Books, 1976. 216 pp.

Warm-hearted sermons from Revelation. He identifies the seven spirits as seven angels (p. 16), the seven churches as seven periods of history (p. 43), and the twenty-four elders as symbols of the redeemed (p. 78); teaches the pretribulation rapture (p. 67); holds that the first beast of Revelation 13 is the Antichrist, killed and restored to life (pp. 102–3); identifies Babylon as Rome (p. 143), the bride as the NT church (p. 152), the bottomless pit as the center of the earth (p. 170).

Morris, Henry M. *The Revelation Record.* Wheaton, Ill.: Tyndale House Publishers, 1983. 521 pp.

A futurist interpretation. He notes the hundreds of already fulfilled OT prophecies (p. 20), the numerous sevens (pp.28f.); argues that *angels* must be literal (p. 44); holds the hour of temptation is the great tribulation (p. 73); thinks that the sun and moon will be reduced by a third of their power (p. 150); does not think that Abaddon is Satan (p. 164); argues that the two witnesses are Elijah and Enoch (p. 194); holds that literal Babylon will be rebuilt (p. 239); does not identify brimstone (p. 269); holds that the seven angels of judgment are symbolic (p. 283); tries to give a scientific explanation for the death of oceans (p. 298); holds that the Lord will return on a symbolic white horse (p. 391); holds to a literal lake of fire for the eternal abode of the wicked (p. 401).

Mounce Robert H. *The Book of Revelation.* Grand Rapids: Eerdmans, 1977. 426 pp.

A technical nondispensational commentary. He tentatively recognizes the apostle John as the author (p. 31); interprets the first seal as military conquests in general (p. 154); says the 144,000 is symbolical of believers who are about to enter the Tribulation (p. 168); dwells upon the sources of the symbols and visions (pp. 203–4); treats the temple and two witnesses of chapter 11 as symbols of the witnessing church during the Tribulation (pp. 218, 223); identifies the woman as Israel and the persecuted woman as true Israel (pp. 237, 245); says that 19:11–21 refers to the final conflict between Christ and Antichrist (p. 317).

Newell, William R. *The Book of Revelation.* Chicago: Grace Publications, 1935. 405 pp.

A popular dispensational exposition. He interprets "shortly" in 1:1 as denoting imminency (pp. 4–5); divides the book on the basis of 1:19 (pp. 31, 84); takes the first seal as referring to Christ (p. 102); sees the 144,000 as Jews during the Tribulation (pp. 112–13); argues for a literal interpretation (p. 123); treats the locusts as literal (p. 131); identifies the woman as Israel (p. 170); insists that the two beasts in chapter 13 are persons (pp. 183–84); gives nine reasons that the first beast is Antichrist (pp. 195–201); teaches a literal Babylon (pp. 263, 268, 272); holds to a pretribulation rapture (p. 382).

Newton, Benjamin Wills. *Thoughts on the Apocalypse*. London: Houston and Sons, 1904. 515 pp.

An old Plymouth Brethren exposition. He asserts that the personal return of Christ is not the main theme of Revelation (p. 45); holds that the prophetic judgments from chapter 6 on are always at hand (p. 51); maintains that the two witnesses and Antichrist are individuals (p. 194); believes that the temple in chapter 11 symbolizes true believers (p. 203); interprets all of chapter 12 as future, calling the man-child the future saints of Jerusalem (pp. 225, 240); identifies the woman in chapter 12 as Christianity during the reign of Antichrist (p. 226); lists eleven reasons the first beast is not the pope (pp. 275–77).

Osborne, Grant R. *Revelation* in *Baker Exegetical Commentary on the New Testament*. Grand Rapids: Baker Book House, 2002. 869 pp.

A perceptive premillennial commentary, but with considerable attention to symbolic interpretations. He provides a thorough introduction (pp. 1–49); portrays the Devil as the accuser, deceiver, and imitator (p. 34); lists seven interpretations of the "white stone" (p. 149); prefers the view that the elders are angelic beings (p. 229); holds that the seven-sealed scroll is a contract deed containing the redemptive plan and future history of God's creation (p. 249); sees seven major themes in the three cycles of judgment of seals, trumpets, and bowls (pp. 270ff.); holds that the mighty angel of Revelation 10 is not Christ (p. 393); thinks that the woman clothed with the sun represents Israel and the church (p. 456); argues that the beast from the sea is the Antichrist (p. 491); has a considerable discussion of 666 (pp. 518–21); holds that the scorching heat of the sun is a solar flare (p. 586); lists many interpretations of Armageddon (pp. 594–96); holds that Babylon represents "blasphemous religion that seduces the nations" (p. 610); argues for a premillennial coming of Christ (pp. 688–94) but recognizes the viability of the other two views (p. 697); concludes with a thorough bibliography (pp. 801–24) and indexes of subjects, authors, and writings (pp. 825–69).

Ottman, Ford C. *The Unfolding of the Ages*. Glasgow, Scotland: Pickering and Inglis, 1905. 511 pp.

A thorough dispensational exposition. He stresses that the Lord is the ruler of the kings of the earth (p. 10); holds that the seven churches show moral features from the first century to the Second Coming (p. 20); identifies the twenty-four elders as OT and NT saints and the living beings as cherubim (pp. 116, 120); holds that the trumpet judgments are directed against the land of Palestine (pp. 202–3); thinks the two hundred million horsemen are demons (p. 237); identifies the two witnesses as Moses and Elijah (p. 267), the first beast of Revelation 13 as the Antichrist (p. 322), and the scarlet woman as the apostate church (p. 378); holds that Babylon on the Euphrates must be rebuilt and destroyed again (pp. 394f.); argues that both the church and redeemed OT saints are in a bridal relation to Christ (p. 411) but still claims the church dwells in the bridal city, but Israel upon earth (p. 447).

Pettingill, William L. *The Unveiling of Jesus Christ.* 8th ed. Findlay, Ohio: Fundamental Truth Publishers, 1939. 132 pp.

Dispensational messages. He gives the structural plan of Revelation (p. 5); identifies the seven spirits as the Holy Spirit (pp. 6–7); holds the seven churches represent seven successive phases of the professing church (p. 13); thinks that the seven seals, trumpets, and vials are parallel descriptions of the Tribulation period (pp. 31–32); holds that Babylon refers to the false church and to Rome (pp. 72–73); identifies the twenty-four elders as the church and the guests as OT saints (p. 85); attacks the idea of a general resurrection (p. 99); argues that the New Jerusalem is situated over the earth (p. 119).

Phillips, John. *Exploring Revelation.* Chicago: Moody Press, 1974. 282 pp.

A premillennial exposition. He holds that the seven stars are forces that shape man's destiny (p. 36); sees a chronological sequence in the churches, identifying today's church as Laodicea (pp. 435–47); devotes about a third of the book to chapters 1–3; does not mention the Rapture or the beginning of the Tribulation at 4:1; holds that the most deadly animal on earth is the rat (p. 117); finds both literal and symbolic interpretations (pp. 128–29); notes that the Beast must control the "revived Roman Empire" and the Middle East (p. 143); identifies the Beast's seven-year pact with Daniel's tribulation (p. 154); suggests that the Beast may be killed and restored to life (pp. 177, 221); calls the False Prophet the Antichrist (p. 181); thinks the distance between Dan and Beersheba is two hundred miles (p. 195); prophesies the rebuilding and overthrow of Babylon (p. 209); charts the organization of the Roman Catholic Church (p. 215); lists the crimes of the Inquisition (p. 220); identifies the bride as the church from Pentecost to the Rapture (p. 241); thinks that some glorified saints will be on the earth during the Millennium (p. 256); portrays the New Jerusalem as a literal city hovering over the earth, a satellite suspended over earthly Jerusalem (p. 268).

Ryrie, Charles Caldwell. *Revelation. Everyman's Bible Commentary.* Chicago: Moody Press, 1968. 127 pp.

Brief popular exposition. He gives four interpretations of Revelation, recommending the futurist (pp. 8–9); uses 1:19 to outline the book

(p. 16); argues for the pretribulation rapture (pp. 29–39); takes the twenty-four elders as representatives of the church only (p. 36); thinks days will be shortened to sixteen hours long (p. 59); refuses to identify the two witnesses (p. 76); holds that Antichrist will actually die and be restored to life (p. 83); identifies mystery Babylon with Rome (p. 102); holds that both Israel and the church will be in the heavenly Jerusalem (p. 120).

Sadler, M. F. *The Revelation of St. John the Divine.* London: George Bell and Sons, 1898. 298 pp.

A helpful premillennial commentary by an evangelical Anglican. He holds to apostolic authorship (p. xv); emphasizes the doctrine of imminency (pp. xvi–xix, 70–72); utterly rejects the preterist system (p. xxviii); identifies the 144,000 as Jews (p. 89); believes that the Jewish temple will be rebuilt (p. 131); holds that the two witnesses are heavenly beings (p. 134); takes the three and a half years literally (pp. 138, 169); explains why the woman refers to the church (p. 153); interprets Babylon as apostate Christendom, not simply as Romanism (p. 223); rejects the amillennial interpretation of the thousand years (p. 256).

Scott, Walter. *Exposition of the Revelation of Jesus Christ.* London: Pickering and Inglis, n.d. 456 pp.

An old Plymouth Brethren exposition. He says that 1:19 is the key to the book (p. 7); holds to a pretribulation rapture (p. 12); views the seven churches as periods of church history (p. 55); argues that the first seal is not Christ (p. 147); associates the 144,000 with Israel (p. 162); teaches that the two witnesses refer to Jews during the future Tribulation period but says that there could be more than two (p. 230); identifies the woman in chapter 12 with Israel (p. 247); interprets the first beast as the revived Roman Empire (p. 269); takes the thousand years literally (p. 398).

*Seiss, Joseph A. *The Apocalypse.* 1865; rpt. Grand Rapids: Zondervan, n.d. 536 pp.

Powerful messages from Revelation. He stresses the deity of Christ (p. 46); warns against Laodicean lukewarmness (p. 64); teaches a partial rapture: holds that the twenty-four elders are the senior company of raptured saints (pp. 104–5); interprets the judgments literally (pp. 191ff.); attacks spiritualism (p. 214); identifies the two hundred million horsemen as infernal cavalry (p. 219); errs on chapter 12: holds that the woman is the visible church and the man-child the true church (pp. 297, 300); stresses the literal nature of the binding of Satan (p. 446) and the literal thousand-year reign (p. 474); holds that the New Jerusalem will be suspended over the earth (p. 497).

Simcox, William Henry. *The Revelation of St. John the Divine*. Cambridge: Cambridge University Press, 1890. 176 pp.

A brief premillennial commentary. He accepts apostolic authorship (p. xxiii); dates the book A.D. 68–70 (p. xxxix); finds multiple fulfillments of the first four seals throughout the present dispensation (p. 41); relates the sixth seal to the Second Coming (p. 47); believes Moses and Elijah are the two witnesses (p. 71); associates the woman in chapter 12 with Israel (p. 74); thinks the woman fleeing into the wilderness refers to the Christians fleeing to Pella before the fall of Jerusalem in A.D. 70 (p. 79); teaches a future, personal antichrist (p. 82); argues for a literal thousand years and two literal resurrections (p. 124).

Simpson, A. B. *Heaven Opened*. Nyack, N.Y.: Christian Alliance Publishing Co., 1899. 299 pp.

Popular exposition of Revelation. He emphasizes Jesus as king (pp. 30f.); holds that the beast out of the sea represents a universal empire (p. 115); holds to a literal millennial reign: a world without a devil, without a prison, and so forth (pp. 241f.).

*Smith, Jacob Brubaker. *A Revelation of Jesus Christ*. Scottdale, Penn.: Herald Press, 1961. 369 pp.

A very thorough futurist interpretation. He discusses the names of the Lord (pp. 1ff.); lists many symbols that are interpreted (pp. 18f.); draws the outline from 1:19 (p. 56); interprets the judgments literally (pp. 139ff.); identifies Abaddon with Satan (p. 145); notes Revelation 10 and 11 as the midpoint of the Tribulation (p. 149); thinks 666 refers to Nero (p. 207); stresses that the thousand years are literal (p. 269); the editor (Yoder) holds that the unity of believers is seen in the foundations and gates (p. 293); stresses imminency (p. 301); concludes with a number of appendices (pp. 309–63).

Spence, O. Talmadge. *The Book of Revelation*. Dunn, N.C.: Foundations Press, 2001. 171 pp.

A brief futurist exposition. He argues that Jesus revealed the book and that the book reveals Jesus (p. 2); holds that the seven messengers were pastors (p. 9); traces the rise of the Roman Catholic Church (p. 14); stresses the unique nature of the Tribulation period (p. 41); identifies mystery Babylon with Romanism (pp. 104f.); has an appendix on Nicolaitanism (pp. 162ff.).

Strauss, Lehman. *The Book of the Revelation*. Neptune, N.J.: Loizeaux, 1964. 381 pp.

Expository messages with beautifully logical alliteration. He holds that the twenty-four elders are representative of both OT and NT saints (p. 132); thinks the four living beings are symbols of redeemed men

(p. 135); calls the locusts "infernal cherubim" (p. 190); identifies the two witnesses as Elijah and Enoch (pp. 215–16); holds that the first beast of Revelation 13 refers to both the empire and the personal Antichrist and both may be "killed" and restored (pp. 248–50); defends the premillennial position (pp. 329–31).

Talbot, Louis T. *The Revelation of Jesus Christ*. Grand Rapids: Eerdmans, 1937, 1946. 254 pp.

A dispensational interpretation. He gives parallels between Genesis and Revelation (pp. 11–12); uses 1:19 to outline the book (pp. 20–21); lists titles of Christ (p. 34); thinks the seven churches are periods of church history (p. 40); holds that the twenty-four elders are OT and NT saints (p. 71); links the seal judgments with the Olivet Discourse and Daniel's seventy weeks (pp. 90–91); thinks the two witnesses will be Moses and Elijah (p. 148); holds that Babylon refers to Rome, not to a rebuilt Babylon (pp. 214–16); includes a fold-out prophetic chart.

Tatford, Frederick A. *Prophecy's Last Word*. London: Pickering and Inglis Ltd., 1947. 270 pp.

A futurist exposition of Revelation with color illustrations of the Holy Land. He identifies the calling up in 4:1 as the Rapture of the church (p. 75); suggests that the rider on the white horse symbolizes the imperial ruler after the Rapture (p. 86); holds that the 144,000 refer to the Jewish remnant (pp. 96f.); argues that the beast out of the sea is the culmination of Gentile dominion (p. 147), the harlot is the papacy (p. 198), the Millennium is a literal thousand-year reign of Christ (p. 222), the Great White Throne is the judgment of all the wicked dead (p. 224).

*Tenney, Merrill C. *Interpreting Revelation*. Grand Rapids: Eerdmans, 1957. 220 pp.

Not a commentary but a study of special topics. He defends John, an early disciple, as author (p. 15); gives background in history (pp. 20f.), society (pp. 22ff.), religion (pp. 23f.), and the OT (pp. 101f.); examines the structure of the book (pp. 32ff.); has a chart on the "sevens" (p. 38); gives a brief survey of the contents (pp. 42ff.); has a thorough study of the seven churches (pp. 50–69); contrasts Babylon and New Jerusalem (p. 91); discusses the Christology of Revelation (pp. 117ff.), the chronology (pp. 135ff.), the different millennial views (pp. 147ff.); has help on the symbolism (pp. 186ff.); gives extensive bibliography (pp. 207–11).

Tenney, Merrill C. *The Book of Revelation: Proclaiming the New Testament*. Grand Rapids: Baker Book House, 1963. 116 pp.

Homiletical material from Revelation. He has some interesting subjects: "The Man at the Door" (3:20), "The Lamb and the Book"

(5:1–12), "The Harvest of Earth" (14:14–19) in which he sees two harvests. Premillennial.

Thomas, Robert L. *Revelation 1–7; Revelation 8–22.* Chicago: Moody Press, 1992, 1995. 524, 690 pp.

A thorough premillennial commentary. He defends apostolic author-ship (I, 2ff.); dates Revelation about A.D. 95 (I, 23); interprets "his slaves" as all Christian readers (I, 53); identifies the overcomer as a regenerated believer (I, 151); stresses the pretribulational removal from the hour of trial (I, 283–90); holds that the twenty-four elders are angelic beings (I, 347), that the little scroll represents the counsels of God (I, 378), that the rider on the white horse in Revelation 6:2 is the world ruler of Revelation 13 (I, 422). He argues for a single altar in heaven (II, 9), a literal interpretation of the judgments (II, 17), the demonic nature of the scorpion locusts (II, 30); stresses that the two hundred million is a part of the vision and not just an estimate (II, 47). He holds that the seven bowls come out of the sev-enth trumpet (II, 115); argues for the literal chronological sequence of Revelation 19–22 (II, 381f.) and a literal thousand year millennium (II, 408ff.); denies that the new heaven and earth are a picture of the present age of the Christian church (II, 438); provides an excursus on the kingdom of Christ in the Apocalypse (II, 545ff.).

Tow, Timothy. *Coming World Events Unveiled.* Singapore: Christian Life Publishers, 1995. 144 pp.

He stresses that Revelation is an opened book, not a closed one (p. 11); argues that Smyrna represents any church that suffers for Christ (p. 17); holds that the twenty-four elders represent the twelve patriarchs and twelve apostles (pp. 25–26); thinks that the rider on the white horse is an angel of peace (p. 31); argues for the premillen-nial coming of Christ (pp.112ff.); includes hymns on the coming of Christ (pp. 132ff.).

Van Ryn, August. *Notes on the Book of Revelation.* Kansas City, Kans.: Walterick Publishers, n.d. 228 pp.

Highly individualistic interpretations from a basically premillennial view. He holds the seven churches give a consecutive history of the dispensation of grace (p. 15); attacks the Roman Catholic Church (p. 40); holds that the twenty-four elders are the raptured church (pp. 73–74); thinks that the seals, trumpets, and vials run concurrently (p. 87); mistakenly identifies Jaffa with Haifa (p. 113); makes the three and a half days identical with three and a half years of the Tribu-lation period and makes the two witnesses the Jewish remnant (p. 127); denies that there is a temple in heaven (pp. 181f.); holds that the bride is the church, the guests are OT saints (p. 205).

*Walvoord, John F. *The Revelation of Jesus Christ.* Chicago: Moody, 1966. 347 pp.

A careful futurist commentary. He stresses that Christ is the main theme of the book (p. 7); defends apostle John as author (pp. 11ff.); surveys the theology of Revelation (pp. 30ff.); often gives different opinions without deciding which is right (pp. 42, 52, 58f.); holds that the twenty-four elders represent the church (p. 107); teaches a pretribulation rapture (p. 139); argues for a literal interpretation (pp. 153f.); holds that the scorpion locusts are hordes of demons (p. 160); thinks that the two witnesses are unknown future prophets (p. 179); does not think that the False Prophet is a Jew (p. 205); holds that the everlasting gospel is not the gospel of grace (p. 217); discusses the millennial views at length (pp. 282ff.); argues for premillennialism (pp. 300f.); holds that both Israel and the church will be in the heavenly city (p. 322).

Weidner, Revere F. *Annotations on the Revelation of St. John the Divine* in *The Lutheran Commentary,* ed. Henry E. Jacobs. New York: The Christian Literature Co., 1898. 365 pp.

A literal premillennial Lutheran commentary. He defends the apostolic authorship (p. x); sees a threefold division of the book based on 1:19 (p. 22); takes chapter 6 as future events just prior to the Second Advent (p. 83); relates the 144,000 to literal Israel (p. 96); argues that the Great Tribulation immediately precedes the Lord's return (p. 102); cites various interpretations (pp. 111, 113, 119, 132, 145, 167, 336–49); believes that the Jewish temple will be rebuilt (p. 138); identifies the woman in chapter 12 as the OT church (p. 154); claims that the meaning of 666 will not be solved until Antichrist comes (p. 188); argues for literal interpretations (pp. 214, 222, 224); holds to a literal thousand years (p. 283).

Critical Commentaries

Barker, Margaret. *The Revelation of Jesus Christ.* Edinburgh: T and T Clark, 2000. 447 pp.

A reinterpretation of Revelation in the light of Josephine Ford's commentary (p. xiii). She thinks the Gnostic texts about Jesus are correct (p. 4); holds that Jesus as high priest took away sickness (p. 7); thinks that resurrection was the process by which one became a son of God (p. 8); thinks that the words of Revelation were already ancient when John wrote his book (p. 57); thinks that Revelation had the same myths as Ugarit (p. 60); holds that the seven horns of the Lamb mean that He has been transfigured by the sevenfold light of day one of creation (p. 63); thinks that Revelation is similar to Ezekiel because both were written by temple priests (p. 67); thinks that Revelation was not written in Greek but translated by an Asian Christian (p. 73); holds that it is really a collection of prophecies, some pre-Christian (p. 76); thinks that the seven lamps were in the temple and the later vision of the throne was the holy place (p. 82).

Beckwith, Isbon T. *The Apocalypse of John.* 1919; rpt. Grand Rapids: Baker, 1967. 794 pp.

A critical amillennial exposition on the Greek text. He says that Revelation was a "tract for the times" (p. 208); believes that historical predictions in Revelation do not need to be fulfilled (p. 306); suggests that 13:3 and 17:8 refer to Nero (p. 406); divides the book on the basis of 1:19 (p. 443); maintains that John's prophecy is entirely spiritual (p. 519); says that the Great Tribulation is the period of woes to come before the end (p. 545); applies the three and a half years to the period of the domination of evil before the end (p. 598); identifies the woman with the believers of both Testaments (p. 622); includes over four hundred pages of introduction.

Boring, M. Eugene. *Revelation in Interpretation: A Bible Commentary for Teaching and Preaching.* Louisville: John Knox Press, 1989. 236 pp.

A liberal, preterist interpretation. He studies Revelation because it was accepted by the early church (p. 5); holds that it was written by John, a Christian prophet, not the apostle (pp. 10, 34); says John wrote to his own time and expected the "end" to come soon (p. 24); argues that the visions of Revelation are literary compositions based on John's visionary experience, not merely reports of what he "actually" saw (p. 27); dates Daniel 165 B.C.E. (p. 38); defends the preterist view, dismissing the idealist and historical views, and attacking the premillennial futurist view as "dangerous" (pp. 49–50); holds that Revelation does not teach a doctrine of the Second Coming or "Millennium," but presents pictures that point to eternal realities (p. 53); thinks that interpreters should not try to fit John's surrealistic pictures into logical and chronological confines of a space-time world (p. 57); holds that John made errors (p. 73); divides the book into three parts: God speaks to the church in the city (pp. 63–97), God judges the "great city" (pp. 99–189), God redeems the "holy city" (pp. 191–231).

Bratcher, Robert G. *A Translator's Guide to the Revelation of John.* New York: United Bible Societies, 1984. 204 pp.

He illustrates all translation by the RSV and the TEV, favoring the latter (pp. 1, 7). He recommends "white as an egret's feather" for "snow" (p. 15); has no explanation for a white stone (p. 27); thinks that Genesis describes the sky as a solid dome (p. 59); holds that wormwood was not poisonous, people only thought so (p. 71); suggests changing the order of the text (p. 120); admits that the TEV drops out phrases

(p. 140); thinks that the foundation stones are partly above ground (p. 179); holds that Revelation is filled with inconsistencies (p. 181).

Case, Shirley Jackson. *The Revelation of John*. Chicago: University of Chicago Press, 1919. 419 pp.

A cynical, unbelieving interpretation. He recounts typical apocalypses (pp. 57ff.); argues that an unknown John wrote Revelation (pp. 201–2); identifies the twenty-four elders as astral deities of Babylonian origin (p. 251); holds the seven horns and seven eyes of the Lamb are probably "ornamental" (p. 257); pictures an angel coming through an opening in the "bell-shaped vault of the sky" (p. 269); sees the locusts as an "ancient mythological fancy" (p. 281); identifies the woman clothed with the sun as a "strange astral mother" of the Lord (p. 304), the first beast of Revelation 13 as a future ruler of the Roman Empire (p. 311), and the harlot as Rome (p. 340); calls the ten kings a "fanciful feature" (p. 346); thinks that John describes the heavenly city with "the most brilliant phraseology that his own imagination could devise" (p. 376); holds that John thought the world would end in the early second century (p. 389).

Charles, Robert Henry. *The Revelation of St. John*. 2 vols. *International Critical Commentary*. Edinburgh: Clark, 1920. 564, 497 pp.

A very critical preterist-idealist interpretation. He holds the author is John the Seer, not the elder (I, xxii); argues that the seven spirits and the twenty-four elders are angels (I, 11–13, 130); favors preterist interpretation of the seals (I, 160); thinks the text "is corrupt or the writer confused beyond all precedent" (I, 169); thinks four trumpets are "colourless and weak repetitions" of seals (I, 220); gives naturalistic explanations for the rain of blood (I, 233); holds that Revelation 12 was originally neither Christian nor Jewish (I, 229f.); thinks the dragon came from Babylonian mythology (I, 317); holds the first beast in Revelation 13 is the Roman Empire (I, 345); thinks there are interpolations in Revelation (II, 2–3); identifies the harlot with Rome (II, 55); thinks the text deranged (II, 58); takes the thousand-year reign to be an innovation of the first century (II, 142–43); calls the text of Revelation 20–22 "incoherent and self-contradictory" (II, 144); rearranges the order of the text (II, 180f.); concludes with many critical notes on the Greek text (II, 236-385).

Collins, Adela Yarbro. *Revelation* in *The New Jerome Biblical Commentary*. Raymond Brown, Joseph Fitzmeyer, Roland Murphy, eds. Englewood Cliffs, N.J.: Prentice Hall, 1990. Pp. 996–1016.

She does not think it was written by one of the Twelve (p. 997); thinks that the doxology may reflect early Christian liturgy (p. 1000); suggests that the seven stars may allude to the Little Dipper, the

Pleiades, or to the seven planets (p. 1001); denies that the promise of protection to Philadelphia implies rescue from the sufferings of the end time (p. 1003); thinks that the praise given to the Lamb recalls the honors given to the Roman emperor (p. 1004); holds that the white robes were symbols of the glorified bodies of the righteous dead (p. 1005); holds that the beast from the sea is "a mythic symbol" (p. 1009); notes that the thousand-year reign has been controversial, but it probably refers to an earthly messianic reign (p. 1014).

Dusterdieck, Friedrich. *Critical and Exegetical Handbook to the Revelation of John*, trans. Henry E. Jacobs, in *Meyer's Commentary on the New Testament*. New York: Funk and Wagnalls, 1887. 494 pp.

An exhaustive critical exegesis of the Greek text. He defends the inspiration of the book (p. iv); emphasizes that the central message of Revelation is the ever-impending personal return of the Lord (pp. 27, 45); denies the Johannine authorship (p. 83); maintains that the seals are signs of the Lord's return (pp. 224, 225, 228, 232); takes the sixth seal literally (p. 232); interprets the 144,000 as literal Jews (pp. 248–50); says that the trumpets are threatening signs preceding the Second Advent (p. 268); argues for literal interpretations (pp. 269, 284, 288, 291); denies that prophecy must be fulfilled (pp. 327–28, 341–42); states that John erred in thinking that the Roman Empire would perish with Domitian (p. 437).

Eller, Vernad. *The Most Revealing Book of the Bible: Making Sense out of Revelation*. Grand Rapids: Eerdmans, 1974. 214 pp.

A decalendarizing approach to Revelation. He spiritualizes the contents of the book (p. 13); stresses imminency (pp. 17–24); says we are living in the eschaton John prophesied (pp. 32, 117); thinks the wrath of God is God's justice in letting the wicked experience the consequence of their own sin (p. 141); maintains that 13:8 and 17:9–17 were later additions by an interpolator (pp. 159, 166).

Ezell, Douglas. *Revelations on Revelation*. Waco, Tex.: Word Books, 1977. 124 pp.

A huge oversimplification of Revelation by taking everything symbolically. He attacks obsession with the future (pp. 17f.); orients Revelation to the first-century world and OT interpretation alone (pp. 19f.); makes the seals, trumpets, and bowls all refer to the same thing (pp. 40ff.); quotes from the Apocrypha to prove that silence refers to the end of history (p. 46); holds that the 144,000 are the redeemed of all ages (pp. 59–60); thinks that the Antichrist rules from the cross to the consummation (p. 82); takes the thousand-year reign to symbolize the rest of God's rule (pp. 95–96); thinks that Revelation 21–22 stretches language to the breaking point (p. 101); concludes that John is not seeking to unfold the future (p. 111); chart 4 makes ten different terms refer to the time from the Cross to the end.

Fiorenza, Elizabeth Schussler. *Invitation to the Book of Revelation.* Garden City: Image Books, 1981. 223 pp.

A popular treatment of Revelation by a well-known feminist.

Ford, Josephine Massyngberde. *Revelation. The Anchor Bible.* Garden City, N.Y.: Doubleday, 1975. 504 pp.

A very critical interpretation by a Roman Catholic. She holds to multiple authorship (at least three: John the Baptist and his disciples, pp. 3–4, 28–46); thinks Jesus is not the central figure of Revelation (p. 7); does not think Revelation 4–22 is a Christian work at all (p. 12); denies that the "Spirit" refers to the Holy Spirit (p. 19); sees the structure of Revelation as a series of sixes (pp. 48–50); thinks the light around the throne is taken from the idea of the sun chariot in non-Jewish literature (p. 79); Z. C. Hodges is the only premillennialist she quotes (pp. 104–5); takes the seven-sealed scroll to be a marriage or divorce document (p. 165); sees no Christological reference in the Man-Child caught up (p. 20); thinks "the blood of the martyrs of Jesus" is an interpolation (p. 279); holds "the Lamb" is "the apocalyptic war figure of the non-Christian literature" (p. 291); thinks that 20:1–3; 21:9–27 refer to "Millennial Jerusalem" (pp. 329–46); classes premillennialists with Mormons, Adventists, Jehovah's Witnesses, and so forth (p. 351).

Garrett, Susan R. *Revelation* in *Women's Bible Commentary.* Carol A. Newsome and Sharon H. Ringe, eds. Louisville, Ky.: Westminster/John Knox, 1992. Pp. 377–82.

A liberal feminist interpretation. She thinks that Revelation is full of "bizarre, psychedelic imagery that allows many interpretations" (p. 377); argues that the three main feminine symbols in Revelation (the bride, Babylon, the woman clothed with the sun) reflect "the male-centered culture of the first century: women are caricatured as virgins, whores, or mothers" (p. 377). The author is not John the apostle but "a figure unmentioned elsewhere in extant early Christian literature" (p. 378).

Gonzalez, Catherine Gunsalus, and Justo L. Gonzalez. *Revelation.* Louisville, Ky.: Westminster John Knox Press, 1997. 149 pp.

A commentary on the NRSV that draws upon both preterist and futurist interpretations (p. 11). They hold that it is unlikely that John the apostle was the author (p. 4); think that the white stone means victory (p. 29); argue that Revelation was a fan-folded book (p. 42); declare that the seven seals are not successive stages but images (p. 53); assume that the mighty angel is Gabriel (p. 69); hold that forty-two months, three and a half years, and so forth, mean transitory time (p. 72); think that the woman in chapter 12 represents the people of God, Mary, Israel, the church (p. 77); teach that the sacraments of baptism and the eucharist sustain the church (p. 79); hold that no one can know what the 666 means (p. 90); do not know where Harmageddon is; it may be symbolic (p. 107); suppose that Babylon represents the Rome of the Caesars (p. 113); do not settle what the Millennium or the two resurrections mean (pp. 130–32); conclude with the eucharist (pp. 147–48).

Kiddle, Martin. *The Revelation of St. John. Moffatt New Testament Commentaries*. London: Hodder and Stoughton, 1940. 460 pp.

Liberal preterist interpretation. He thinks Revelation is filled with "incoherent imaginations" (p. xix); is uncertain of authorship (pp. xxxivff.); identifies the seven spirits with the Holy Spirit (p. 67); but questions this later (pp. 99–100); holds that the temple in heaven, and so forth are merely ideas (pp. 71–72); holds that the source of the twenty-four elders is the twenty-four star gods of Babylonian mythology (p. 84); claims that the locusts seem a weird fairy tale to us but a reality to John's readers because "fire-spouting monsters were common figures in mythology" (p. 164); interprets the temple in Revelation 11 to be the church and the two witnesses to be symbols of militant believers (pp. 180–84); charges that John "is composing freely" (p. 234); blood for two hundred miles is symbolical (p. 295); speaks of the "strange concomitants" of the Millennium (p. 395); holds that much of the description of the heavenly city is symbolical (p. 425).

Lilje, Hanns. *The Last Book of the Bible*. Philadelphia: Muhlenberg, 1957. 286 pp.

A liberal Lutheran interpretation, blending idealist, preterist, and futurist ideas. He argues that history must have an end (pp. 16f.); holds that both the messengers and the twenty-four elders are angels (pp. 64, 107); thinks that John believed in the earth as a disk (p. 134); calls literalist interpretations of the trumpets "wooden" (p. 142); holds that the temple symbolized the church (p. 161); thinks that the woman crowned with the sun is the church (p. 177); takes the 1,600 stadia to be the whole earth (p. 208); holds that only the martyrs of the Beast reign (p. 248); treats the thousand years symbolically (p. 249); holds that the "lake of fire" means no more than that God's will has triumphed (p. 254); thinks that the design of the heavenly Jerusalem is patterned after earthly Babylon (p. 267).

Moffatt, James. *Revelation* in Vol. V of *The Expositor's Greek Testament*. Grand Rapids: Eerdmans, 1951. Pp. 281–494.

Liberal preterist interpretation. He argues for an unknown John as author (p. 323); identifies the seven spirits as seven angels (pp. 337–38); sees a source for the four horsemen in "Semitic folk-lore" (p. 388); calls the two hundred million horsemen a "semi-mythical, semi-historical pageant" (p. 409); sees parallels to the woman clothed with the sun in Babylonian myths (p. 423); identifies Babylon with Rome (pp. 451f.); holds that the saints are the bride and the guests (p. 464); calls John's portrait of Christ a grim, implacable conqueror (p. 470); thinks the thousand years have led to more "unhappy fantasies" than any other passage (p. 473); refers to the "mythological background" of the heavenly Jerusalem (p. 482).

Preston, Ronald H., and Anthony T. Hanson. *The Revelation of Saint John the Divine*. London: SCM Press, 1949. 145 pp.

Liberal commentary, deny that John of the Gospel and Revelation are the same (p. 25); suggest that an editor added passages (p. 129). They admit that it teaches a Millennium but deny that anything is to be taken literally (p. 129). There is an interesting section on the OT in Revelation (pp. 34–42).

Reddish, Mitchell G. *Revelation*. Smyth and Helwys Bible Commentary. Macon, Ga.: Smyth and Helwys Publishing, 2001. 472 pp.

A critical, symbolic interpretation with numerous illustrations and sidebars. He does not mention the Rapture in an obvious text (p. 77); commends a liberation theology interpretation (p. 82, note); calls John's stern language against Jews "sub-Christian" (p. 87); holds that chapters 4–22 are not in historical or chronological sequence (p. 90); declares that Revelation is not a blueprint for the future (p. 91, 154); thinks that John's visions are like a good joke, "if they have to be explained, they are not worth it!" (p. 92); holds that the twenty-four elders are probably angelic attendants (p. 96); quotes whole pages from Martin Luther King Jr. (p. 117); states concerning seals, trumpets, and bowls, "the reader must avoid a rigid, chronological interpretation" (p. 121); thinks that the 144, 000 and the great multitude both symbolize the church, the new Israel (pp. 146, 152); quotes Marcus Borg with approval (p. 171); claims that John is a "skilled storyteller" (p. 177); refers to Second Isaiah (p. 184); holds that the one wrong way to take the demonic invasion is literally (p. 186); thinks that apocalyptic literature is like a horror movie, not to be taken literally or factually (p. 189); holds that the temple in Revelation 11, Sodom, Egypt, and Jerusalem are all symbolic (pp. 206–12); argues that John recast an old Apollo myth as Christ's conflict with the Dragon (pp. 231–32); holds that belief in a personal Satan is not a required doctrine in Christian faith (p. 246).

Rissi, Mathias. *Time and History*. Richmond, Va.: John Knox, 1966. 147 pp.
A very critical study of Revelation and its time periods. He thinks the silence comes from the creation myth in II Esdras 6:39 (p. 4); holds that the blood-soaked robes of Christ refer to the Lamb and are a sign of forgiving grace (pp. 12–13); argues that an existence outside of time is not seen in Revelation (p. 32); holds that the seven spirits are proved to be the Holy Spirit by 1:4 (p. 58); identifies the raising of the two witnesses with the Rapture (p. 103); teaches an imminent coming (p. 111); holds that numbers refer to the end time, not to any length of time (p. 117); argues that the second death cannot mean dissolution into nothingness (pp. 123–24); teaches universal salvation (pp. 133f.).

Rist, Martin, and Lynn H. Hough. *Revelation* in Vol. XII of *The Interpreter's Bible*. New York: Abingdon, 1957. Pp. 347–613.
An unbelieving preterist interpretation. They claim that everything John wrote denies that he knew anything about the human Jesus (p. 357); think that John thought the end of the age would be about A.D. 100 (p. 365); hold that John believed in a three-story universe (p. 401); admit they do not know what the twenty-four elders signify (p. 402); suggest the silence in heaven is to permit God to hear the prayers of the saints (p. 425); refer to the "myth of malicious locusts" (p. 432); hold that the two witnesses are Moses and Elijah (p. 445) and the woman clothed with the sun is a celestial queen of heaven (p. 453); think that John contradicted Paul and Peter in teaching that the Roman Empire was evil and satanic (p. 461); hold that the harlot is the goddess Roma (p. 489) and that the binding of Satan has a mythological base (p. 518); think that the heavenly Jerusalem is an inconsistent description of a city with "astral speculations" (p. 533).

Scott, E. F. *The Book of Revelation*. New York: Scribner's Sons, 1939. 191 pp.
A liberal preterist interpretation. He thinks Revelation is a "treasure-house of primitive myth and speculation" (p. 7); claims the author is an unknown John, not the apostle (pp. 31ff.); denies that John was a real prophet; he spoke of his own time (pp. 51ff.); claims that John made little attempt to be consistent (p. 64); holds that the meaning of the passage on the two witnesses is "probably lost beyond recovery" (p. 68); regards Revelation 12 as "wild and incoherent" (p. 71); identifies Revelation 17–18 as the fall of Rome (pp. 85ff.); thinks that life in the heavenly city "would soon become wearisome. The prospect of an

eternity spent in such conditions would be almost intolerable"
(pp. 100–101).

Thompson, Leonard L. *Revelation* in *Abingdon New Testament Commentaries*. Nashville: Abingdon, 1998. 207 pp.

A liberal preterist interpretation, although he admits that from 19:11 on, the visions are truly eschatological (pp. 60, 175). He holds that the author was an otherwise unknown John from Asia (p. 22); thinks that John does not present doctrines but sense perceptions (p. 37); argues that the seven spirits and seven torches before the throne are seven archangels (p. 49); denies that there was any persecution of Christians in John's time (p. 57); imagines that John saw an apparition (p. 65); thinks that the white stone was an amulet (p. 72); does not know whether *zygon* means "yoke" or "scale" (p. 102); claims that John modeled the heavenly temple after the Jerusalem temple (p. 114); states that the locusts in 9:3 are clearly demonic creatures (p. 118); claims that John never calls himself a prophet (in spite of Revelation 1:3, p. 125); holds that the enthronement of the sea beast parodies the enthronement of the Lamb (p. 137); thinks that even Paul spoke of an interim messianic reign in I Corinthians 15:22–28 (p. 178); maintains that John thought that Messiah and at least some of His followers will reign for a thousand years (p. 180); thinks that it is typical of "utopian buildings and cities, as well as fairy tale castles and castles in the sky," that the walls, foundation stones, and gates of the New Jerusalem are built of precious stones (p. 183).

Works on the Seven Churches

Barclay, William. *Letters to the Seven Churches*. New York: Abingdon, 1957. 111 pp.

A two-part study of each of the seven churches: background information and then an exposition of the text. He gives word studies (pp. 20, 50, 84, etc.); describes the Caesar worship at Smyrna (pp. 28–29) and the Asklepios worship at Pergamos (pp. 42–43); lists the meanings of the white stone (pp. 53–54); warns against compromise (pp. 60–61) and against loving a system more than Christ (p. 74); links the continual flight of the Philadelphians with the promise to go out no more (p. 82); suggests that the term *lukewarm* refers to the evil-tasting mineral springs (p. 98).

Best, W. E. *Diminishing Spirituality in Local Churches*. Houston, Tex.: South Belt Grace Church, 1986. 147 pp.

Studies in Revelation 2 and 3. He believes that the aorist tense renders commands "more authoritative" (p. 21); attacks amillennialism (p. 23); holds that the seven lampstands "represent all the assemblies of Jesus Christ during the church age" (p. 25); compares the salutations to the churches (pp. 32ff.), the commendations of the churches (pp. 53ff.), the condemnations of the churches (pp. 65ff.), and promises to the overcomers (pp. 109ff.).

Blaiklock, E. M. *The Seven Churches*. London: Marshall, Morgan and Scott, n.d. 78 pp.

A reverent exposition of Revelation 2–3. He sees fulfillment both in the ancient Roman oppression and in the future world ruler (p. 9); describes the desolate condition of Ephesus today (pp. 14f.); holds that the Nicolaitans had worked out a compromise with the pagan world (p. 20); notes that Smyrna claimed to be the birthplace of Homer (p. 26); describes the great altar of Zeus at Pergamum (p. 34); holds that being faithful in Thyatira meant loss and humiliation for believers (p. 51); notes that there are still five Christian churches in Philadelphia (p. 65).

Hort, Fenton J. A. *The Apocalypse of St. John: I–III*. London: Macmillan, 1908. 92 pp.

A critical commentary on the Greek text of Revelation 1–3. He argues that John the son of Zebedee wrote the Book of Revelation but during the years A.D. 64–70 (pp. x–xii); traces the theme of giving in John (p. 5); holds that the seven spirits were divine (p. 11); discusses the term *paradise* (p. 24); identifies the throne of Satan with the serpent worship in Pergamum (p. 27).

Kelshaw, Terence. *Send This Message to My Church*. Nashville: Thomas Nelson, 1984. 199 pp.

Contemporary messages on the seven churches by one who has traveled through Asia Minor. He quotes Bonhoeffer, Moltmann, and Barth (p. 17); holds that the message to Ephesus was repent for the loss of love for Christ (p. 65); in Smyrna urges hiding Scripture in the mind to be able to endure pressure of the world (p. 76); in Pergamos holds that Satan's throne was the altar of Zeus (p. 94); in Thyatira warned against Jezebel, false leader in the church (pp. 112f.); at Sardis describes a dead church and the need for repentance (pp. 126, 142).

Lee, Sang Chan. *The Seven Churches of Asia*. Seoul, Korea: Doo Rae Village Publishing Company, 1989. 440 pp.

A conservative exposition of Revelation 2–3, all written in Korean. He includes foldout charts on the kings of Israel and Judah as well as material on the seven churches following p. 236. There are also photos of the locations of the churches and maps.

Loane, Marcus L. *They Overcame*. Grand Rapids: Baker, 1971, 1981. 133 pp.

Expository messages on the first three chapters of Revelation. He defends salvation by the blood of the Lamb (p. viii); gives idealist interpretations (pp. 1–2); holds that the seven spirits are the Holy Spirit (p. 11); thinks that John labored in a marble quarry (p. 22); stresses that God limits persecution against His people (p. 52); interprets "Jezebel" as the wife of the minister (p. 71); links the "hour of trial" with frequent earthquakes (p. 97); concludes with notes on "the Sea," "Eden and Zion," and "Yea and Amen" (pp. 121–33).

Martin, Hugh. *The Seven Letters.* Philadelphia: Westminster, 1956. 123 pp.

Liberal messages on Revelation 1–3. He denies that the apostle John was the author (pp. 9–10); gives preterist interpretations (pp. 13–14); holds that the NT does not speak of "eternal torment" but only of "eternal consequences" (p. 63); argues that the "bitter condemnation" of Revelation is not the whole message of the NT (p. 85).

McCheyne, Robert Murray. *The Seven Churches of Asia.* Geanies House, Fearn, Scotland: Christian Focus Publications, 1986. 95 pp.

Warm-hearted, devotional sermons on Revelation 2–3.

Meinardus, Otto F. A. *St. John of Patmos and the Seven Churches of the Apocalypse.* New Rochelle, N.Y.: Caratzas, 1979. 154 pp.

A Greek Orthodox interpretation of the messages to the seven churches. He gives many traditions from nonbiblical sources (pp. 4–11, 41, etc.); refers to the "Holy Virgin Mary" (p. 58); provides historical background for each of the churches (pp. 33ff., etc.); has photographs of each city (pp. 32, 60, 90, etc.).

Morgan, G. Campbell. *A First Century Message to Twentieth Century Christians.* New York: Revell, 1902. 217 pp.

Devotional messages on the seven churches. He warns against tolerating people in the church who tend toward pernicious teaching and moral laxness (p. 102); states that "truth never excuses sin" (p. 106); warns against the claims of inspiration in some modern cults (Jezebel, p. 122); warns against formalism (p. 142); cries out against a lack of compassion in the church today (p. 153); teaches a pretribulation rapture (p. 172); describes how an atheist made General Booth evangelistic (p. 197); warns that the church of Laodicea had everything except Jesus Christ (p. 208).

*Neal, Marshall. *Seven Churches: God's Revelation to the Church Today.* Greenville, S.C.: Bob Jones University Press, 1977. 102 pp.

A very helpful exposition of the messages to the seven churches. He gives the general characteristics of each letter (pp. 5–6); attacks the idea that they refer to consecutive church ages (p. 10); provides interesting historical sidelights (p. 16); warns against the dangers of compromise

(p. 49); identifies the morning star as Christ (p. 62); warns against over-confidence (p. 69); shows the need for real repentance (pp. 97–98); the work is especially valuable because Dr. Neal has visited each location and can describe the circumstances of each place (pp. 92–93); there are beautiful color photos of each city following p. 24.

Plumptre, E. H. *The Epistles to the Seven Churches of Asia*. London: Hodder and Stoughton, 1877. 218 pp.

Messages on the seven churches. He defends John the apostle as author (pp. 2–3); urges being intolerant of evil but tolerant of all besides (p. 64); argues that the "lake of fire" is a state of enduring pain (p. 100); thinks that the white stone was a ticket for a banquet (pp. 127–28); shows the unity between Paul and John (pp. 178–79); suggests that John may have heard the Lord Jesus literally knock at a door during the earthly ministry (p. 213).

*Ramsay, Sir William. *The Letters to the Seven Churches of Asia*. London: Hodder and Stoughton, 1906. 446 pp.

Strong study of the historical and archeological background. He argues that the NT Epistles are both true letters and literary ones (p. 26); urges importance of geographic surroundings for interpretation (p. 41); discusses the symbolism (pp. 57–73); holds that John had absolute authority (p. 79); thinks that John's penalty was banishment with hard labor (p. 85); thinks that all seven churches were on the principal circuit road of the province (p. 183); argues that John addressed specific churches, yet the whole universal church has found truth in these words (p. 200); recounts the history and geography of each city, then expounds the biblical text: Ephesus (pp. 210–50).

Smith, Hamilton. *The Addresses to the Seven Churches*. Oak Park, Ill.: Bible Truth Publishers, n.d. 128 pp.

Sermons on Revelation 2–3. He maintains the deity of Christ (pp. 5, 18); identifies the seven spirits as the Holy Spirit (p. 9); thinks that the seven churches portray seven consecutive church ages (pp. 29–30); describes the twofold attack of the Devil (pp. 54f.); thinks that Jezebel refers to the worldly ecclesiastical system (pp. 77f.); sees Sardis as the anti-Catholic Protestant system (pp. 90–91).

Stott, John R. W. *What Christ Thinks of the Church*. Grand Rapids: Eerdmans, 1958. 128 pp.

Expository messages on Revelation 1–3. He defends John, son of Zebedee, as the author (p. 19); quotes Bonhoeffer with approval (pp. 42–43); urges a balance of love and truth (pp. 53–54); holds that the two fundamentals of the deity of Christ and His saving work on the cross must not be negotiated away (p. 56); warns against being "nominal Christians" (p. 86); identifies the seven spirits as the Holy Spirit (p. 94); urges personal trust in Christ (p. 110).

Trench, Richard Chenevix. *Commentary on the Epistles to the Seven Churches in Asia*. London: MacMillan, 1883. 249 pp.

An exposition of Revelation 2–3. He holds that the seven spirits refer to the Holy Spirit (pp. 8–9, 162); thinks the seven churches are typical of leading aspects of all churches (p. 29) but attacks the idea of seven consecutive ages of church history (pp. 236ff.); discusses sacred numbers (pp. 62–69); holds that Christ is the touchstone of doctrine (p. 80); traces the history of paradise (pp. 101–2); discusses meats offered to idols (pp. 128f.); combines the meanings of the hidden manna and the new stone (pp. 140–42); faults Augustine for his doctrine of predestination (p. 177) and others for ideas of irresistible grace (p. 224); stresses that Christ was not the first created being but rather the Source of all creation (p. 204); identifies the "gold" as faith (pp. 214ff.).

Other Works on Revelation

Augustine, St. *The City of God* in *Basic Writings of Saint Augustine*. Vol. 2. New York: Random House, 1948. Pp. 1–663.

In Book XXII, chapter 30, he discusses heaven, the resurrection body, and so forth (pp. 660ff.). "There we shall rest and see, see and love, love and praise. This is what shall be in the end without end" (p. 663).

Bauckham, Richard. *The Theology of the Book of Revelation*. Cambridge: Cambridge University Press, 1993. 169 pp.

He identifies Revelation as "apocalyptic prophecy," but it is also a circular letter (pp. 6, 12); it is filled with symbols, most of which are not explained (p. 9); holds that the seven churches symbolize all churches (p. 16); states that "Revelation is saturated with verbal allusions to the Old Testament" (p. 18); demonstrates that it teaches the Trinity and that all worship must be theocentric (pp. 23, 33); holds that Revelation is "the most powerful piece of political resistance literature from the period of the early empire" (p. 38); refers to Deutero-Isaiah (pp. 55–56); includes Christ in the eternal being of the one true God (p. 58); argues that the worship of Jesus is proof of His deity (p. 60); stresses three major symbolic themes: the messianic war, the eschatological Exodus, and the witness (pp. 67–73); holds that the rule of Christ in the church cannot be the ultimate goal of Christ's victory (p. 75); thinks that the great multitude are martyrs (p. 77); claims the two witnesses represent the church (p. 84); holds to a millennium, but not a literal one (p. 108); teaches that biblical prophecy both addresses the prophet's contemporaries and raises hopes that continue to direct later readers (p. 152); thinks that the picture of a truly universal anti-Christian state is merely hyperbole (p. 155).

Beasley-Murray, G. R., Hershel Hobbs, and Ray Frank Robbins. *Revelation: Three Viewpoints.* Nashville: Broadman Press, 1977. 248 pp.

Lectures on Revelation by three well-known Baptists. Beasley-Murray defends the generally premillennial view while recommending authors such as Rissi, Caird, and Ladd (pp. 12–13). He holds that the preterite, futurist, historical, and symbolic views all have elements of truth in them (pp. 13–14). Hobbs advocates amillennialism while recommending his own book, that of Ray Summers, and others (p. 73). He holds that the thousand years symbolize the time from the Ascension to Christ's coming again (p. 137). Robbins describes how he has successively held the premillennial, postmillennial, and amillennial views but now calls himself simply an apocalyptic interpreter (p. 147).

Bewes, Richard. *The Lamb Wins.* Ross-shire, Great Britain: Christian Focus Publications, 2000. 156 pp.

A huge oversimplification of Revelation: the whole book means only that Christ wins. Bewes is a parallelist interpreter: each series of churches, seals, trumpets, bowls, and so forth runs from the time of Christ to the end (pp. 17ff.); he admits that he is an amillennialist but just does not like the title (p. 135); he has kind words for the liberal Bonhoeffer (pp. 95, 131); calls Karl Barth the greatest theologian of the twentieth century (p. 145). Of course the Lamb wins, but the Book of Revelation means much more than just that.

Blevins, James L. *Revelation as Drama.* Nashville: Broadman Press, 1984. 192 pp.

He interprets Revelation as a drama in seven acts of seven scenes each and provides diagrams for stage settings and an actual script. He suggests illuminated windows to illustrate the seven scenes. He is a pan-millennialist: all the views are good; just do not fight over them (pp. 131–33).

Bowman, John Wick. *The First Christian Drama.* Philadelphia: Westminster Press, 1955, 1968. 159 pp.

A brief explanation of the Book of Revelation, treating it as a drama. He does not know who John was (p. 14); arranges the book into seven acts of seven scenes each (pp. 15f.); holds that the twenty-four elders and the 144,000 are the church (pp. 43, 53); thinks that the locust-horsemen symbolize a world culture attempting to destroy God's rule (p. 67); thinks that the Great Tribulation began at the Incarnation and will last to the end of the world (p. 79); holds that the thousand years are not literal (p. 135).

Boyer, Paul. *When Time Shall Be No More*. Cambridge, Mass: Harvard, 1992. 468 pp.

A study of prophecy belief in modern American culture. He notes that most Christians throughout history have believed in an eschatological consummation (p. ix) and that prophecy is linked to a religious belief system (p. x); observes that there are eight million committed premillennialists in America (p. 2); discusses the interpretation of Ezekiel, Daniel, Mark 13, Revelation (pp. 21–45); gives a history of prophetic thought (pp. 46–79); reviews "The Premillennial Strand" (pp. 80–112); cites W. M. Smith (p. 118f.), M. R. DeHaan (pp. 124f.), Hal Lindsey (pp. 126f.); has photos of premillennial charts and leaders (between pp. 144–45, 280–81); admits that the premillennial position has continuing strength in the "vast subculture of late 20th-century U.S. evangelicalism" (p. 339).

Bruce, Frederick F. *Revelation* in *The International Bible Commentary*. Grand Rapids: Zondervan, 1986. Pp. 1593–1629.

Bruce, Frederick F. "The Spirit in the Apocalypse." In *Christ and Spirit in the New Testament*. Lindars and Smalley, eds. Cambridge: Cambridge University Press, 1973. Pp. 333–44.

Essays in honor of C. F. D. Moule. Bruce weaves the references in Revelation into a definite doctrine of the Spirit and concludes with the invitation "Come" (p. 344).

Buchanan, George Wesley. *The Book of Revelation: Its Introduction and Prophecy*. Vol. 22 of *The Mellen Biblical Commentary*. Lewiston, New York: Edwin Mellen Press, 1993. 697 pp.

An intertextual commentary that draws upon the language of the OT and Jewish apocalyptic literature. He argues that financial practices govern Revelation, not theology (pp. 4–5); denies that there is a spiritual kingdom unrelated to geographical territory (p. 11); argues that Revelation was written by false prophets just before the temple burned in A.D. 70 (p. 21); uses Sinaiticus as his text (p. 29); claims that the writer thought he was near the end of the three and a half years (p. 35); admits that Revelation definitely predicted future events (p. 39); translates "I was in the spirit" as "I was day-dreaming" (p. 57); holds that "John" wrote only chapters 1–3, other prophets wrote the rest (p. 79); holds that the 144,000 were an elite group of Christian monks (p. 190); argues that the Great Tribulation refers to Maccabean times (p. 199); refers to Second Isaiah (p. 288); suggests that Vespasian may be the Dragon (p. 307); interprets the seven heads as the Herodian dynasty (pp. 318f.); thinks that the slain lamb was Antigonus (p. 326); attacks the practice of indiscriminate, symbolical interpretation (pp. 349f.); thinks that "Jesus" was added to the text to

Christianize a Jewish document (pp. 376, 530); says "blood to the horse bridles" shows exaggeration (p. 387); thinks that the cherubim looked like bats (p. 398); argues that the Mount of Megiddo is a real place (p. 423); holds that the author thought all his prophecies would happen in A.D. 69–70 (p. 432); suggests that the seven kings were Herods (p. 455); argues that the Millennium was thought to be a thousand years of historical time (p. 518); holds that Jesus was only legally God (p. 569); claims that the rabbis and the NT writers got ideas from their imagination and from Scripture (p. 587); says, "In some way all of this seemed reasonable to the author" (p. 600); thinks that 22:6–21 was the work of another editor (p. 615).

Carey, Greg. *Elusive Apocalypse*. Macon, Ga.: Mercer University Press, 1999. 209 pp.

Reading authority in the Revelation to John. He holds that Revelation is an example of resistance literature (p. 1); notes the difference between liberationist interpretations and millennarian views (pp. 4–5); seeks to find how John constructs his authority (p. 6); classes liberals as "scholarly" and premillennialists as "popular" but is willing to study both (pp. 25–30); holds that John used classical rhetorical methods to gain authority (p. 45); admits that the person he terms "John" is his own construct (p. 93); sees three genres in Revelation: apocalypse, prophecy, and letter (pp. 96–100); holds that John will admit no dissent from his message (pp. 112–17); in the messages to the seven churches and in Revelation 22:12ff. the risen Christ Himself is the speaking voice (p. 138); argues that the city where the Lord was crucified signified Rome (p. 144); admits he has followed Fiorenzas' practice (p. 167); confesses that his postmodern conclusions are contradictory and unsatisfactory (pp. 184–85).

Chappell, Clovis G. *Sermons from Revelation*. New York: Abingdon-Cokesbury Press, 1943.

Sermons mostly on the seven churches. Catchy titles: "The Cold Church," "The Rich Church," "Jezebel's Church," "How They Won," and so forth.

Clouse, Robert G. *The Meaning of the Millennium: Four Views*. Downers Grove, Ill.: InterVarsity Press, 1977. 223 pp.

G. E. Ladd defends historic premillennialism (pp. 17ff.), with responses by others (pp. 41ff.); Herman A. Hoyt defends dispensational premillennialism (pp. 63ff.), with responses (pp. 93ff.); L. Boettner defends postmillennialism (pp. 117ff.), with responses (pp. 143ff.); A. A. Hoekema defends amillennialism (pp. 155ff.), with responses (pp. 189ff.). Clouse concludes with a postscript (pp. 209ff.) and a select bibliography (pp. 217ff.).

Coleman, Robert E. *Songs of Heaven*. Old Tappan, N.J.: Revell, 1980. 159 pp.

A devotional exposition of fourteen passages in Revelation as songs. He admits that some of them are not said to be sung (p. 17); does not settle millennial views (p. 22); explains the threefold holy (p. 33); holds that the twenty-four elders symbolize OT and NT saints (p. 39); emphasizes that the blood is mentioned 460 times in the Bible (p. 48); *amen* appears 126 times in the NT (p. 89); commends Billy Graham (pp. 116–17).

Couch, Mal, gen. ed. *A Bible Handbook to Revelation*. Grand Rapids: Kregel, 2001. 328 pp.

A dispensational introduction to the study of Revelation. There are helpful discussions of its importance (pp. 15ff.), its interpretation (pp. 36ff.), its literary structure (pp. 69ff.), and the theology of the book (pp. 81ff.), including Christology (pp. 104ff.), pneumatology (pp. 114ff.), hamartiology (pp. 142ff.), angelology (pp. 150ff.), soteriology (pp. 163ff.), Israelology (pp. 172ff.), and the Rapture (pp. 187ff.). They conclude with a hundred pages of verse-by-verse background information to help in the exposition of the book (pp. 199ff.).

Cox, Clyde C. *Footprints of the Great Tribulation*. Cleveland, Tenn.: Pathway Press, 1961. 128 pp.

An imaginative reconstruction of the events of the Tribulation period through the deeds of "Nicholas Marx," the Antichrist (and relative of Karl).

Dumbrell, William J. *The End of the Beginning*. Grand Rapids: Baker Book House, 1985. 200 pp.

A study in Revelation 21–22 and the OT. He first presents the New Jerusalem in Revelation 21–22 (pp. 1ff.) and then surveys the OT teaching in Isaiah (pp. 5–22); Lamentations (pp. 22–23); Ezekiel (pp. 24–25); Zechariah (pp. 25–27) as well as the NT teaching (pp. 27–31). He then argues that the new temple is God Himself (pp. 35–36); shows parallels between Revelation 21–22 and Ezekiel 40–48 (pp. 37–38) and other parallels with Exodus (pp. 38–40), the Davidic covenant (pp. 50–52), and Ezekiel's new temple (pp. 55–59). He presents the new covenant in connection with Jeremiah 31:31–34 (pp. 78–87), the new Israel (pp. 119ff.), and the new creation (pp. 165ff.). He concludes that the gospel has to do not merely with personal renewal but with a total worldview of a new creation (p. 196).

Easley, Kendell. *Living with the End in Sight*. Nashville: Holman Bible Publishers, 2000. 100 pp.

Popular meditations on the Book of Revelation, based on the Holman Christian Standard Bible translation. He has brief notes on the meaning of the word *Almighty* (p. 5), *victor* (p. 9); draws illustrations from the movie *Titanic* (p. 11) and the TV *Gunsmoke* (p. 37); uses the "Four Spiritual Laws" (pp. 16f.); characterizes the scroll of Revelation 5 as "God's judgment scroll" (p. 22); warns against the moral filth on the Internet (p. 45); refers to Frank Peretti's novels (p. 50); provides color illustrations of scenes in Revelation (following p. 54); calls Babylon the "devil in a red dress" (p. 73).

Ellul, Jacques. *Apocalypse.* New York: Seabury Press, 1977. 285 pp.

A book that is not a commentary but attempts "to discern the specificity of the Apocalypse" (p. 11). He avoids other commentaries, multiple interpretations, and deciphering symbols. Instead he seeks to discern the movement of the Apocalypse from a beginning to an end (p. 12). The Apocalypse deals with "the ultimate in Tillich's sense" (p. 24); Ellul deals with the "septenaries" in the Apocalypse (pp. 36ff.); holds that the keystone of the book is Revelation 8:1–14:5 (pp. 65ff.).

Farrer, Austin. *A Rebirth of Images.* Boston: Beacon Press, 1949. 350 pp.

A study of the literary symbolism in the Apocalypse. He thinks the author is an unknown John, not the apostle, but a friend of Timothy (p. 23). He blends together Jewish traditions, first-century culture, literary symbols, and the images in Revelation (p. 176). He provides a chart of images on p. 350.

Foster, Ivan. *Shadow of the Antichrist.* Belfast: Ambassador Productions, 1996. 242 pp.

Popular, devotional sermons on Revelation. He warns against the sin of pride (p. 33); identifies the one on the throne as Christ (4:2, p. 52), the twenty-four elders as OT and NT saints (p. 55), the seven lamps as the Holy Spirit (p. 56), the rider on the white horse as Christ (6:2, p. 68), the mighty angel as Christ (10:1, p. 106), the forty-two weeks as the final three and a half years of this age (p. 115), the woman as the church of Christ (12:1, p. 122), the child born as overcomers in the church (p. 125), the first beast as the Antichrist (13:1, p. 134), and the false prophet as a false religious leader from Israel (p. 143). He denies that the beast is Roman Catholicism (p. 154 and Appendix, pp. 237–40); teaches an eternal hell (pp. 154–55); stresses that the bowls are poured out in the last half of the Tribulation period (p. 166); holds that compromising believers cannot see the need to separate from the false church (p. 177); holds that literal Babylon on the Euphrates will be rebuilt (pp. 189f.); teaches a literal bodily resurrection and a literal thousand-year millennial reign (p. 207).

Fruchtenbaum, Arnold G. *The Footsteps of the Messiah*. Tustin, Calif.: Ariel Ministries Press, 1983, 1999. 471 pp.

Subtitled "A Study of the Sequence of Prophetic Events," it is in reality an extremely detailed commentary on Revelation. He makes the signing of the seven-year covenant between Israel and Antichrist the beginning of the Tribulation period (pp. 36, 86); has a minute chart of the Tribulation period that is sure to provoke discussion (p. 120); has a chart of the campaign of Armageddon (p. 254); holds that Ezekiel 40–48 deals with the millennial temple (p. 323; has an interesting appendix on the six abodes of Satan (pp. 382ff.).

Fuller, Robert C. *Naming the Antichrist*. New York: Oxford University Press, 1995. 232 pp.

Subtitled "The History of an American Obsession," it is actually a bitter, vitriolic attack on the futurist interpretation of prophecy. He charges that this apocalyptic worldview "presupposes a literal interpretation of ancient biblical writings and postulates an overtly supranaturalist vision of reality in which angelic beings are expected to intervene in worldly events" (p. 7); stresses that the antichrist in I John is merely a human heretic (p. 17); admits that John may have known the supernatural character of Antichrist but did not stress it (p. 19); thinks that the author of Daniel was an unknown person from the second century "B.C.E." (p. 22); lumps together literal interpreters of Revelation and those who oppose bar codes and the Susan B. Anthony dollar (p. 25); quotes with approval the slur by George B. Shaw that the Book of Revelation is "a curious record of the visions of a drug addict" (p. 27). He concludes that the apocalyptic interpretations have resisted good organizations and have refused to be a part of an inclusive worldview (p. 200).

Gebhardt, Hermann. *The Doctrine of the Apocalypse*. Edinburgh: T. and T. Clark, 1878. 440 pp.

A thorough survey of the doctrinal teaching of Revelation. He holds to Johannine authorship (p. 9); discusses the name of God, His nature, His works, angels, heaven, Satan, the Abyss, earth and its inhabitants, the Person and work of Christ, the Spirit, the gospel, the saints, the churches; holds to a personal Antichrist (p. 273) and a thousand-year reign (p. 277), but he speaks of it in almost postmillennial language (p. 283). He discusses many other prophetic subjects and makes a number of comparisons between the doctrines of Revelation and doctrines of the Gospel and Epistles of John.

Godet, Frederic. *Studies on the New Testament*. New York: E. P. Dutton and Co., 1873. 398 pp.

In his "Essay upon the Apocalypse" (pp. 294–399) he likens the Apocalypse to an epic poem such as Job (p. 294); sees its main theme as "Christ will return" (p. 298); holds that the seal is "the emblem of an event still hidden, but divinely decreed"; the trumpet is "a manifestation of will which calls for speedy realization"; the vial poured out "is the image of a decree as identified with its execution" (p. 305). He concludes with "the Apocalypse is the crown of the New Testament and of the whole Bible" (p. 397).

Govett, Robert. *The Locusts, the Euphratean Horsemen, and the Two Witnesses*. 1852; rpt. Miami Springs, Fla.: Conley and Schoettle Publishing Co., Inc. 1985. 145 pp.

He attacks the symbolical interpretations of his day (pp. 3ff.); accepts the reality of miracles and literal interpretation, which "brings us into harmony with the rest of God's word" (p. 6). He attacks the idea that the "Mahometans" fulfill Revelation (pp. 11ff.); shows the incongruity of Elliott's interpretations (pp. 70ff.); holds that the angel descending in Revelation 10 is the Lord Jesus (p. 77); argues that the city where the Lord was crucified refers indeed to Jerusalem (pp. 113f.); concludes that the preterist view is absurd (p. 145).

Gregg, Steve. *Revelation: Four Views*. Nashville: Thomas Nelson. 1997. 528 pp.

After an introduction and chapters 1–3 of Revelation, each two-page spread gives four different interpretations: quotations from the historicist, preterist, futurist, and spiritualizing interpretations. The editor is neutral.

Guinness, H. Grattan. *The Approaching End of the Age*. London: Morgan and Scott, 1918. 372 pp.

A defense of the historical approach. He holds to a premillennial return of Christ (pp. vii, 40–56); says that the church will go through the Tribulation (p. 47); argues for a literal Second Advent (p. 52); claims that Revelation outlines the great events of church history (p. 90); criticizes the futurist position (p. 102); attacks a literal approach (pp. 104–10); defends the year-day theory (pp. 239–49); dates the end of the times of the Gentiles at A.D. 1924 (pp. 328, 337).

Guthrie, Donald. *The Relevance of John's Apocalypse*. Grand Rapids: Eerdmans, 1987. 121 pp.

He provides a brief history of interpretation (pp. 12ff.); holds that the author's mind was so saturated with the OT that he was not conscious of following any particular sources (p. 20); thinks that there is symbolism in the book but that Farrar went too far (p. 23); surveys the visions and titles of Christ in Revelation (pp. 40–53); notes that parallels between Revelation and John's Gospel are remarkable (p. 56); concludes that the Christology of Revelation should not be overlooked by modern theology (p. 60); holds that there is no doctrine of the church in Revelation, that it sheds much light on conditions in the church, past and present (p. 67); argues that Revelation teaches conflict both in the earthly realm and in the heavenly (p. 95); concludes that Revelation is the only NT book that is "detailed and specific concerning the winding up of the present age" (p. 117).

Haldeman, I. M. *The Coming of Christ.* Atlanta: The Granary, n.d. 325 pp.

A reprint of a famous defense of the premillennial view by a leader of early Fundamentalism. He holds that the scarlet woman is the professing church in its final development (p. 108); argues that the course of this world is downward (pp. 113ff.); says the Bridegroom comes at midnight (p. 121); argues that the kingdom will be set up only by the power of the King (pp. 161ff.); concludes that the coming of the Lord must be premillennial (pp. 224, 238, etc.); urges the imminency of His coming (pp. 267ff.).

Hocking, David. *The Coming World Leader.* Portland, Ore.: Multnomah Press, 1988. 319 pp.

A futurist interpretation of Revelation. He lists thirty-two titles of Christ in Revelation (pp. 18–19); holds that the seven spirits are seven angels (8:2; p. 26); argues that the angels of the churches are literal angels (p. 44); defends the imminence of Christ's return (p. 92); devotes 102 pages to Revelation 1–3; thinks that the twenty-four elders are the completed church (p. 108); holds that the rider on the white horse is the Antichrist (p. 129); argues that anyone who has heard the gospel before the Rapture will not be able to be saved in the Tribulation period (p. 147); favors Moses and Elijah as the two witnesses (p. 182); holds that the first beast in Revelation 13 is the Antichrist (p. 205); defends the eternal punishment of the wicked (p. 221); thinks that the bride is the NT church only (p. 269); holds that the New Jerusalem will sit on the earth (p. 296); concludes with a thorough bibliography (pp. 315–19).

Hurnard, Samuel F. *Revelation: The Book with a Blessing.* London: Marshall, Morgan, and Scott, 1930. 154 pp.

A devotional book that stresses the blessing of studying Revelation. He notes that Revelation sets Christ forth as the faithful witness three times (p. 12); holds a general futurist interpretation (p. 13); thinks that the Philadelphian church may be raptured (p. 30); denies that I Thessalonians 4:16ff. teaches a pretribulation rapture (p. 96); distinguishes the millennial reign from the eternal state (p. 127); adds yet another period, the dispensation of the fullness of times, between the Millennium and eternity (p. 135).

Hurtgen, John E. *Anti-Language in the Apocalypse of John.* Lewiston, N.Y.: Edwin Mellen Press, 1993. 172 pp.

A sociological study of the language of John's Revelation, a published doctoral dissertation. He holds that John was an unknown person writing as part of an oppressed minority (pp. 20ff.), his language resisted the social and religious practices of his time (p. 26), the scenes of worship reinforce the community's vision (p. 31); paints a dualistic struggle between God vs. Satan (p. 37); cites Malina's view that Revelation expected a restructuring of the world imminently (p. 46); holds that "anti-language is the language of social resistance" (p. 51); holds that anti-language is pathological (p. 61); gives examples from the underworld of Calcutta in which there are forty-one words for "police" (p. 63); applies his anti-language ideas to Revelation 11:19–15:4 (pp. 89ff.).

Jenkins, Ferrell. *The Old Testament in the Book of Revelation.* Grand Rapids: Baker, 1972. 151 pp.

A critical investigation of OT quotations in Revelation. He summarizes the OT quotations and allusions in Revelation (p. 24); discusses apocalyptic literature (pp. 33–47); surveys the most frequently quoted OT books (pp. 49–71); lists the OT passages referred to in the description of Christ (pp. 73–93); explains the divine titles in Revelation (pp. 95–107) and OT imagery in Revelation (pp. 109–27); concludes that there are 348 allusions in Revelation (p. 129); gives a thorough bibliography (pp. 133–41).

Keith, Alexander. *The Harmony of Prophecy.* New York: Harper and Brothers Publishers, n.d. 439 pp.

An attempt to illustrate the teaching of Revelation by cross-references. Oftentimes this is done effectively (pp. 46–51). He holds to a general resurrection and general judgment (p. 41).

Kistemaker, Simon J. *The Book of Revelation.* Grand Rapids: Baker Books, 2001. 635 pp.

A symbolic interpretation. He holds that the warning of Jesus in 22:18–19 is a copyright notice (p. 3); emphasizes the polarities in the book: Christ vs. Satan, light vs. darkness, life vs. death, love vs. hatred, heaven vs. hell (p. 6); defends John the apostle as author (p. 26); lists the strong points and weaknesses of premillennial and amillennial views (pp. 44–48); holds that the throne and the seals are symbolic (p. 182); thinks that the great city where Jesus was crucified symbolizes the world (p. 334); holds that the woman clothed with the sun is a symbol of God's covenant people, OT and NT (p. 355); thinks that the three and a half years, forty-two months, and 1,260 days all refer to the entire time in which the gospel is proclaimed until Jesus returns (p. 382); argues that the binding of Satan and the thousand-year reign are symbols (pp. 534–36).

Koester, Craig R. *Revelation and the End of All Things*. Grand Rapids: Eerdmans, 2001. 209 pp.

He favors the symbolic interpretation of Revelation (p. 26); pays special attention to the songs drawn from Revelation (pp. 32ff.); thinks that the thousand years point to a reality that lies beyond time (p. 181).

Lotz, Anne Graham. *The Vision of His Glory*. Dallas: Word Publishing, 1996. 363 pp.

A series of devotional meditations aimed at ladies' Bible studies. She defends her father's use of "rock" and "rap" groups to reach young people (p. 29); describes total surrender to Jesus as falling at His feet as dead (p. 40); urges finding hope through listening to Jesus (p. 61); attacks abortion (pp. 75–76).

Ludwigson, R. *A Survey of Bible Prophecy*. Grand Rapids: Zondervan, 1951, 1973. 187 pp.

A dictionary of prophetic terms and ideas. He covers "Antichrist" (pp. 13ff.), "Armageddon" (pp. 27ff.), "Babylon" (pp. 31ff.), "Gog and Magog" (pp. 57ff.), the millennial views (pp. 94ff., 103ff., 115ff.).

Metzger, Bruce M. *Breaking the Code*. Nashville: Abingdon Press, 1993. 144 pp.

Brief comments on the symbolic meaning of Revelation. He holds that the seven churches represent the whole church (p. 23), the seven spirits refer to the Holy Spirit (p. 23), the vision of Christ is not to be taken literally (p. 27); holds that the messengers of the churches were guardian angels (p. 30); argues that the Philadelphian believers will be kept in and not from trouble (p. 42); holds that the seven seals and the seven trumpets "essentially tell the same thing" (p. 56); claims that the silence in heaven is so that prayers may be heard (p. 62); calls Revelation 11 one of the most perplexing sections of Revelation (p. 68); thinks that the temple refers to God's people, not a building (p. 69); denies that Revelation is a time chart of the last days (p. 71); holds that the woman clothed with the sun is a personification of the ideal community of God's people (p. 74); argues that fire and brimstone are symbols of the self-imposed suffering of those who turn away from God (pp. 78f.); holds that the bowl judgments must not be taken literally (p. 82); lists the millennial views, favoring the amillennial (pp. 94–95); thinks that the heavenly city is a symbol, a perfect cube, which, if literal, would be "architecturally preposterous" (pp. 100f.).

Moorehead, William G. *Studies in the Book of Revelation.* Pittsburgh: United Presbyterian Board of Publication, 1908. 153 pp.

Not a commentary but studies in topics. He defends Johannine authorship (pp. 9f.); discusses symbolism (pp. 15–19), systems of interpretation (pp. 20–26), and the plan of the book (pp. 27–40); thinks the seals, trumpets, and vials run parallel (p. 33); gives three different outlines for Revelation (pp. 41–45); objects to seeing seven consecutive ages in the seven churches (pp.. 52f.); thinks the twenty-four elders refer to the idealized people of God (pp. 58–60); suggests that Islam may fulfill some prophecies at the end (pp. 83f.); argues that the head that dies is Rome; the revived head is the empire of Antichrist (p. 97); identifies the first beast as Antichrist (pp. 100f.); holds that the vials cover the last three and a half years of the Tribulation period (p. 109); thinks that mystery Babylon will be Romanism with other apostates (pp. 122–23).

Mulholland, M. Robert Jr. *Revelation.* Grand Rapids: Francis Asbury Press [Zondervan], 1990. 376 pp.

He holds that the visions of Revelation are synchronous, not sequential (p. 33); sees twelve sections in Revelation (p. 55); stresses the power of the liturgy (pp. 78f.); claims that the seven churches represent the totality of the church (p. 90); thinks that Christ is the door opened in heaven (p. 140); argues that the rider on the white horse is either Christ or an antichrist figure (pp. 168f.); holds that the five months have no calendar meaning (9:5–6, p. 194); states that the two hundred million horsemen represent the inescapable presence of God (p. 198); thinks that the witness of Jesus is the death of martyrs such as Bishop Oscar Romero, slain while celebrating the Eucharist, or Martin Luther King Jr., and so forth (p. 207); claims that the woman in 12:1 represents God (pp. 215–17); holds that the False Prophet symbolizes the values and dynamics of the Beast (p. 232), that fire and brimstone are images of the holiness of God (p. 249), that the thousand years are not calendar years but the entire period between the Cross and the consummation (pp. 307f.), that the New Jerusalem is not a future event but a present reality "continually coming down" from God (pp. 41, 321); argues that there is redemptive purpose for New Jerusalem in the midst of fallen Babylon (p. 332).

Niles, Daniel T. *As Seeing the Invisible.* New York: Harper and Brothers, 1961. 192 pp.

He holds that "John" is a poet, not to be interpreted literally (p. 9); says the author is unknown, not an apostle (pp. 21–22); thinks that

Christ will come in a series of crises, but also at the end (p. 34); claims that the cherubim carried the throne on their backs (p. 55); argues that there is no such thing as the tragedy of pure evil (p. 65); holds that the Dragon tries to destroy with a flood of lies (p. 76); declares that every time the church sets herself free from worldly alliances, it is given to her to reign with Christ a thousand years (p. 91); analyzes the book as a daily liturgy for the festal year (pp. 101–15); concludes with brief theological meditations (pp. 117–80); recommends liberal commentaries (pp. 185–86).

Oecumenius. *Complete Commentary of Oecumenius.* H. C. Oskier, ed. Ann Arbor: University of Michigan, 1928.

He was the first-known Greek exegete to expound Revelation (tenth cent.). See Schaff, *History of the Christian Church,* IV, p. 589.

Palmer, Earl F. *The Communicator's Commentary: 1, 2, 3, John and Revelation.* Waco: Word, 1982. Pp. 93–259.

A talk-through on the NKJV text. He quotes Bonhoeffer with approval (p. 114); on the four living beings he declares, "Individual parts in themselves are baffling, but the large scene is what we must try to see" (p. 159). Don't expect too much.

Pate, C. Marvin, ed. *Four Views on the Book of Revelation.* Grand Rapids: Zondervan, 1998. 252 pp.

Kenneth Gentry defends the preterist view (pp. 35ff.); Sam Hamstra defends the idealist view (pp. 93ff.); Marvin Pate defends the progressive dispensationalist view (pp. 133ff.); Robert Thomas defends the classical dispensationalist view (pp. 177ff.).

Patrides, C. A., and Joseph Wittreich, eds. *The Apocalypse in English Renaissance Thought and Literature.* Ithaca, N.Y.: Cornell University Press, 1984. 452 pp.

McGinn and Reeves trace the developing ideas of apocalypticism; Pelikan notes that Luther called the pope the Antichrist in the Smalcald Articles, settling the Lutheran position (p. 86); Capp documents Alsted and Mede as defenders of millennialism (p. 101); Sandler shows how Spenser's *Faerie Queene* used the Apocalypse as a moral allegory applied to Elizabethan times (pp. 148–71); Wittreich demonstrates how Shakespeare applied the Apocalypse to events in the time of King James (pp. 175–200); Patrides examines Milton's many references to the Revelation (pp. 207–31); Korshin documents Isaac Newton and John Bunyan as millennialists (pp. 242, 256, note 44); Stein traces the influence of millennial ideas in New England (pp. 266ff.); Tuveson shows the millennial ideas underlying the Communist Manifesto (pp. 323ff.); Abrams surveys the vast influence of Revelation in modern times (pp. 342ff.); concludes with a bibliography of 1,757 titles on Revelation and apocalyptic literature.

Petersen, Rodney L. *Preaching in the Last Days*. Oxford: Oxford University Press, 1993. 318 pp.

The theme of "Two Witnesses" in the sixteenth and seventeenth centuries. He begins with a brief exegesis of the text (pp. 5–8); mentions early interpreters such as the Venerable Bede (p. 28); surveys the dawn of Reformation preaching (pp. 59ff.); shows that Anabaptists held that the witnesses were Elijah and Enoch (p. 97), that Luther saw himself at the end of history, but not as Elijah (p. 105), that Heinrich Bullinger was for Revelation because it was the revelation of Christ (p. 126); discusses the first Protestant commentaries by Lambert (pp. 130ff.) and Sebastian Meyer (pp. 154ff.); shows that Thomas Brightman held that the two prophets symbolized holy Scripture and the assemblies of the faithful (p. 202); holds that Joseph Mede held a twofold view that the witnesses symbolized the faithful throughout history and also a future specific fulfillment, close to the modern millennial view (pp. 208–10); shows that Cotton Mather also held that only the Lord's imminent return will bring victory, very close to the modern premillennial view (p. 229); provides a thorough bibliography (pp. 265–301).

Phillips, J. B. *The Book of Revelation*. New York: Macmillan, 1957. 50 pp.

Phillips's translation of the book. He questions the authorship of Revelation (p. 1); recommends the use of commentaries (p. 2); includes a bibliography of largely liberal commentaries (pp. 49–50).

Pickering, Ernest. *The Glories of the Lamb*. Clarks Summit, Pa.: Baptist Bible College and School of Theology, 1978. 60 pp.

Six messages portraying the glory of Christ as seen in the Book of Revelation. He expounds the blood of the Lamb (Rev. 5:6–9), His worship (Rev. 5:4–12), His wrath (Rev. 6:16), His marriage (Rev. 19:7), His conquest (Rev. 17:14–17), and His city (Rev. 21:2).

Poythress, Vern S. *The Returning King*. Phillipsburg, N.J.: P and R Publishing, 2000. 213 pp.

A guide to the Book of Revelation. He provides a very perceptive introduction (pp. 11–66) and a very brief commentary (pp. 69–198). He likens the throne room scene to an airport control tower that controls the universe (pp. 97–98); holds that the twenty-four elders are angelic beings (p. 103), the 144,000 symbolize "the fullness of the people of God" (p. 118), the woman clothed with the sun represents OT saints, but Mary included (p. 134); suggests that hell is endless punishment for evil (pp. 151, 176); thinks that Babylon represents "the seductions of the world" (p. 159); argues that Revelation 20:1–15 is "the seventh and last cycle of judgments, each of which leads up to the Second Coming" (p. 179).

Richard, Pablo. *Apocalypse: A People's Commentary of the Book of Revelation.* Maryknoll, N.Y.: Orbis Books, 1998. 184 pp.

Not a verse-by-verse commentary but a Roman Catholic preterist interpretation that advocates liberation theology (pp. 2–4). He specifically rejects "every kind of fundamentalist, dispensational, or neoconservative interpretation of Revelation" (p. 5); refers to Second and Third Isaiah (p. 9); begins his interpretation with the peasant insurrection of the Maccabees (p. 10); stresses the pluralistic nature of early Christianity (p. 12); calls Colossians/Ephesians "post-Pauline tradition" (p. 13); thinks that apocalyptic arose against an imperial slave-based mode of production (p. 24); holds that apocalyptic eschatology is eminently historical and political (p. 29); argues that apocalyptic vision combines symbols and myths into a single view (p. 30); classes Revelation 4:1–19:10 as the present moment, "the community in the midst of the world" (p. 35); claims that Jesus standing at the door knocking does not refer to an individual but to a community opportunity (p. 63); thinks that the twenty-four elders "symbolize liberated humankind" (p. 66), the two witnesses symbolize the whole church (p. 91); calls the woman and the dragon "myths" (p. 101); says Satan gave power to the Beast, so he stands behind the Roman Empire and present empire (p. 108); argues that the answer to "who is like God?" is "everyone" (p. 109); holds that the thousand-year reign is not purely spiritual but is a utopia within history, established after the empire has been abolished (pp. 156–57); declares that the Book of Revelation has a decisive influence, especially in the Third World in the reconstruction of liberating theologies (p. 173).

Scroggie, W. Graham. *The Great Unveiling.* 1925; rpt. Grand Rapids: Zondervan, 1979. 143 pp.

An introduction to Revelation. He shows the relationship between Revelation and Daniel and Genesis (pp. 25–27); gives chapter content of Revelation (pp. 31–40); stresses Christ in Revelation (pp. 43–52); discusses literal and symbolical interpretations (pp. 57–62); evaluates different interpretations (pp. 99–103); examines the structure of the book (pp. 107–16); gives study questions on Revelation (pp. 119–29), synthetic studies (pp. 131–33), and an analysis on Revelation (pp. 135–40); concludes with a chart of the plan of Revelation (pp. 142–43).

Stedman, Ray C. *God's Final Word.* Grand Rapids: Discovery House, 1991. 359 pp.

Premillennial comments on Revelation. He declares that Revelation is "the scariest book in the Bible" (p. 1); thinks the seven churches are a history of the church (p. 19); calls Sardis "the church of the Zombies" (p. 67); claims Laodicea as the present church age (p. 103); calls the four living beings "weird" and "bizarre" (p. 121); identifies Revelation 6–19 with Daniel's seventieth week (pp. 140ff.); calls the 144,000 "Christ's Commandos" (p. 160); titles Revelation 9 "All Hell Breaks Loose" (p. 185); teaches the pretribulation rapture (p. 224); thinks that the Man-Child snatched up to heaven refers to the rapture of the church (p. 234); calls the second beast Antichrist (p. 251) and Babylon "the dragon lady" (p. 287); thinks the rider on the white horse is like the Lone Ranger (p. 311); defends the thousand-year reign (pp. 320ff.).

Stonehouse, Ned B. *The Apocalypse in the Ancient Church.* Amsterdam: Oosterbaan and Le Cointre, 1929. 160 pp.

A history of the acceptance of the Book of Revelation as authoritative and canonical. He documents its acceptance by Papias (second quarter of the second century, p. 8), Irenaeus (pp. 8–10), Justin Martyr (pp. 10–11, 46f.), Theophilus (p. 81, note 155), the Muratorian Canon (pp. 82f.), Tertullian (pp. 86–92), Hippolytus (pp. 99–109), Origen (pp. 117–23), Athanasius (pp. 142ff.), Commodian, Lactantius, Victorinus (p. 146), Augustine (p. 149).

Taylor, Preston A. *Revelation: Past, Present, Future.* Ann Arbor, Mich.: Cushing-Malloy, Inc., 1989. 291 pp.

Practical sermons on Revelation. He is premillennial but avoids discussing the systems (pp. 255f.); warns against a day of coming judgment (p. 263).

*Tenney, Merrill C. *Interpreting Revelation.* Grand Rapids: Eerdmans, 1957. 220 pp.

Not a commentary but a study of special topics. He defends John, an early disciple, as author (p. 15); gives background in history (pp. 20f.), society (pp. 22ff.), religion (pp. 23f.), and the OT (pp. 101f.); examines the structure of the book (pp. 32ff.); has a chart on the "sevens" (p. 38); gives a brief survey of the contents (pp. 42ff.); has a thorough study of the seven churches (pp. 50–69); contrasts Babylon and New Jerusalem (p. 91); discusses the Christology of Revelation (pp. 117ff.), the chronology (pp. 135ff.), the different millennial views (pp. 147ff.); has help on the symbolism (pp. 186ff.); gives an extensive bibliography (pp. 207–11).

Van Hartingsveld, L. *Revelation.* Grand Rapids: Eerdmans, 1985. 103 pp.

An independent interpretation by a Reformed pastor. He stresses sacred numbers (p. 3); notes the precise composition of Revelation (pp. 5–6); thinks the seven spirits are seven angels (p. 11); notes parallels between Revelation 1:9–20 and Daniel 10:2–21 (pp. 14–15);

thinks the 144,000 is not literal but refers to a group of Christians (p. 33); calls the woman of 12:1 mother of Messiah, but not Mary (p. 48); thinks Ar Mageddon is the valley of decision (p. 68); holds that the woman on the beast is Rome (p. 72); warns against not taking the Millennium literally (pp. 99f.).

Wall, Robert W. *Revelation* in *New International Biblical Commentary*. Peabody, Mass.: Hendrickson Publishers, 1991. 295 pp.

A commentary that stresses the symbolical nature of Revelation (p. 15). He denies that John the apostle wrote it (p. 8); warns against the Fundamentalist attitude of over-defending the canonicity of Revelation (pp. 28–29); recommends a canonical critical interpretation that sets forth the "theo-logic" of Revelation (pp. 36–40); argues that Revelation does contain a prediction of the future of God's salvation (p. 53); has no comment on the hour of trial or the Tribulation period (pp. 84, 88); holds that the twenty-four elders are not literal people but symbols of the Christian community (p. 93); thinks that the four living beings are angelic (p. 94); argues that the seal and trumpet judgments do not depict a sequence of future historical events but rather together they symbolize God's response to the Lamb's exaltation (p. 109); identifies the four horsemen with the four living creatures (p. 109); maintains that the Great Tribulation refers to salvation history not literal history (p. 120); thinks that the Euphrates symbolizes the vulnerability of the Roman Empire (p, 132), the temple and holy city symbolize God's people (pp. 143–44), the two witnesses symbolize renewal for God's people (p. 144), the woman in chapter 12 symbolizes God's people (p. 159), the first beast symbolizes universal secular power (p. 168). He denies that Armageddon is a literal place (p. 200); stresses that the visions of the Lord's coming are not chronological (p. 227); holds that the robe dipped in blood refers to Christ's own blood (p. 231); argues that "a 1000 years" does not refer to chronological years and has sharp words for those who use this passage as a litmus test for orthodoxy (p. 234); holds that the Christian hope is not a heavenly place but a transformed human existence (p. 243); thinks that the twelve gates symbolize the universal character of God's salvation (p. 252).

Walvoord, John F., and John E. Walvoord. *Armageddon: Oil and the Middle East Crisis*. Grand Rapids: Zondervan, 1974. 207 pp.

Reasonable guesses about the future of the Middle East crisis. They recount the history of the Arab-Israeli conflict (pp. 27ff.) and the Arab oil blackmail (pp. 43ff.); give a chart of events in Jerusalem from 605 B.C. to 1974 (pp. 97f.); hold that Russia will be excluded from future Middle East affairs (pp. 121ff.); describe the rise of Antichrist (pp. 133f.), the disasters of the Tribulation period (pp. 147ff.), and the coming of the Lord in glory (pp. 185ff.).

Wiersbe, Warren W. *Be Victorious*. Wheaton, Ill.: Victor Books, 1985. 156 pp.

Brief premillennial comments on Revelation. He stresses that it is a Christ-centered book (p. 22); sees the Rapture at 4:1 (p. 49); holds that the twenty-four elders are the complete people of God (p. 51); teaches a seven-year Tribulation period (p. 61); holds that the fallen star is probably Satan (p. 80); argues that the first beast is Antichrist (13:1, p. 103); stresses a literal thousand-year reign (p. 139); warns of a literal hell (p. 143).

Wishart, Charles Frederick. *The Book of Day*. New York: Oxford University Press, 1935. 63 pp.

Brief studies on the Apocalypse. He argues for the symbolical meaning of the numbers in Revelation (p. vii); insists that three and a half and thousand are not measures of duration (pp. vii–viii); says the literary form is pure poetry (p. 2); asserts that Revelation portrays the continuing conflict between the forces of good and evil (p. 3); teaches that there may be many meanings to a particular passage (p. 8); believes that the dominant theme might be the coming of the Lord but claims that the Lord comes repeatedly anytime the afflicted are comforted (pp. 12–13); divides the book into seven synchronous sections (pp. 30, 35–36, 40).

Periodicals and Encyclopedia Articles

Aune, David E. "St. John's Portrait of the Church in the Apocalypse." *Evangelical Quarterly*, vol. XXXVIII, no. 3 (July–Sept. 1966): 131–49.

Beale, G. K. "Revelation (Book)." *New Dictionary of Biblical Theology*, pp. 356–63. T. Desmond Alexander, ed. Downers Grove, Ill.: InterVarsity Press, 2000.

He stresses the images of suffering and victory, the throne, the new creation, the New Jerusalem, and others with little regard for future events.

Beers, V. Gilbert. *The Victor Handbook of Bible Knowledge*. Wheaton, Ill.: Victor Books, 1981. Pp. 616–17.

Very brief notes on the seven churches with seven photographs and a map showing their locations.

Biblical Viewpoint. vol. XVI, no. 1 (April 1982).

Focus on Revelation. "The Interpretation of Revelation," "The Revelation of Jesus Christ" (Rev. 1:9–18); "The Seven Churches of Asia"

(Rev. 2–3); "The Throne Set in Heaven" (Rev. 4:1–11); "The Worthiness of the Lamb" (Rev. 5); "The Six Seals" (Rev. 6); "The Lesson of the Little Scroll" (Rev. 10); "The King Takes Possession" (Rev. 11); "The Two Beasts" (Rev. 13); "Annotated Bibliography on Revelation."

Biblical Viewpoint. vol. XVI, no. 2 (Nov. 1982).

Focus on Revelation. "The Pulpit of Patmos"; "Principles of Worship and Judgment" (Rev. 14); "The Wrath of God from Heaven" (Rev. 16); "The Religion That Opposes God" (Rev. 17); "Babylon the Great Is Fallen" (Rev. 18); "The Revelation of Jesus Christ" (Rev. 19); "The Thousand Years and the Throne" (Rev. 20); "Attraction to Eternity" (Rev. 21); "The Prophetic Epilogue" (Rev. 22:6–21); "Annotated Bibliography on Revelation."

Cockburn, Andrew. "21ˢᵗ Century Slaves," *National Geographic*, vol. 204, no. 3 (Sept. 2003): 2–25.

A documentation of literal slave trade in modern society.

Drinkard, Joel F. Jr. "Number Systems and Number Symbolism." *Holman Bible Dictionary*. Trent C. Butler, gen. ed., pp. 1029–31. Nashville: Holman Bible Publishers, 1991.

Fuller, J. William. "I Will Not Erase His Name from the Book of Life" (Rev. 3:5). *The Journal of the Evangelical Theological Society* 26 (1983): 297–306.

"The unfaithful Christian . . . will find that even as he on earth was ashamed of Christ's ὄνομα, Christ will in heaven be ashamed of his (Matt. 10:33; 2 Tim. 2:12)."

Hiebert, D. Edmond. "Satan." *Zondervan Pictorial Encyclopedia of the Bible*, vol. V, pp. 282–86. Grand Rapids: Zondervan Publishing House, 1975.

Kevan, Ernest Frederick. "Millennium." *Baker's Dictionary of Theology*. Everett F. Harrison, ed., pp. 351–55. Grand Rapids: Baker Book House, 1960.

A brief survey of the three major views. He gives an amillennial conclusion.

Ladd, G. E. "Revelation, Book of." *The International Standard Bible Encyclopedia*, vol. IV, pp. 171–77. G. W. Bromiley, ed. Grand Rapids: Eerdmans, 1979.

He leaves the question of authorship undecided; surveys the interpretations, arguing for a moderate futurist view; discusses the problem of evil and the pouring out of the wrath of God. His bibliography is overwhelmingly liberal.

MacLeod, David J. "The Fourth 'Last Thing': The Millennial Kingdom of Christ (Rev. 20:4–6)." *Bibliotheca Sacra*, vol. 157, no. 625 (Jan.–Mar. 2000: 44–67.

He gives arguments for the reign of Christ on earth.

McCall, Thomas S. "How Soon the Tribulation Temple?" *Bibliotheca Sacra*, vol. 128, no. 512 (Oct. 1971): 341–51.

Rainbow, Paul A. "Revelation, Theology of." *Evangelical Dictionary of Biblical Theology*, pp. 682–85. Walter A. Elwell, ed. Grand Rapids: Baker Books, 1996.

He stresses the solidarity of Revelation with the rest of the NT books in their message of the crucified and risen Christ; defends the mutual relation of the present and the future but concludes with an amillennial interpretation of eschatology.

Rissi, Mathias. "The Kerugma of the Revelation to John." *Interpretation*, vol. XXII, no. 1 (Jan. 1968): 3–17.

"John does not predict specific historical events, as is the case in the Jewish apocalypticism. He rather interprets the true meaning and nature of the history with which he is concerned in terms of a traditional imagery long since known and taken over particularly from the OT" (p. 5).

Rosscup, James E. "The Overcomer of the Apocalypse." *Grace Theological Journal*, vol. 3, no 2 (Fall 1982): 261–86.

He argues cogently that the *overcomer* must refer to every born again believer and not merely "super-saints."

Ryken, Leland, James Wilhoit, and Tremper Longman III, eds. *Dictionary of Biblical Imagery*. Downers Grove, Ill.: InterVarsity Press, 1998. 1058 pp.

A thorough study of Bible symbols, images, metaphors, and figures of speech.

Sloan, Robert B. "Revelation, Book of." *The Holman Bible Dictionary*, pp. 1183–91. Trent C. Butler, ed. Nashville: Holman Bible Publishers, 1991.

He provides an extensive chart listing the amillennial, historical premillennial, and dispensational premillennial interpretations.

Smith, Wilbur M. "The Contested Word of God." *Bibliotheca Sacra*, vol. 131, no. 523 (Oct.–Dec. 1974).

Sweet, John. "Revelation, The Book of." *The Oxford Companion to the Bible*, pp. 651–55. Bruce M. Metzger, ed. New York: Oxford, 1993.

He regards Revelation as a "bewildering kaleidoscope of scenes" but organizes it as four groups of seven. Although he questions its unity, he concludes that "it is best to try to make sense of what we have on its own terms."

Tenney, M. C. "Revelation, Book of the." *The Zondervan Pictorial Encyclopedia of the Bible*, vol. V, pp. 89–99. M. C. Tenney, ed. Grand Rapids: Zondervan, 1975.

He defends the unity of the book, Johannine authorship; gives an analytical outline, an evaluation and history of interpretation, and the theology of the book.

Townsend, Jeffrey L. "The Rapture in Revelation 3:10." *Bibliotheca Sacra*, vol. 137, no.547 (July–Sept. 1980).

He argues that the verse describes the result of the Rapture, not the Rapture itself, but it does show removal from the time period.

Unger, Merrill F. "Revelation, Book of the." *The New Unger's Bible Dictionary*, pp. 1077–79. R. K. Harrison, ed. Chicago: Moody Press, 1988.

Walvoord, John F. "Christ's Coming to Reign." *Bibliotheca Sacra*, vol. 123, no. 491 (July 1966): 195–203.

He argues from Revelation 20:1–3 that Satan is bound during the Millennium and "all demonic activity will cease" (p. 202).

———. "Contemporary Problems in Biblical Interpretation—Part IV: The Nature of the Church." *Bibliotheca Sacra*, vol. 116, no. 464 (Oct. 1959).

———. "The Millennial Kingdom and the Eternal State." *Bibliotheca Sacra*, vol. 123, no. 492 (Oct. 1966): 291–300.

———. "Premillennialism and the Tribulation—Part VI: Posttribulationism." *Bibliotheca Sacra*, vol. 112, no. 448 (Oct. 1955).

———. "The Prophecy of the Ten-Nation Confederacy." *Bibliotheca Sacra*, vol. 124, no. 494 (Apr. 1967): 99–105. He compares four major passages: Daniel 2, 7; Revelation 13, 17.

———. "Will Israel Build a Temple in Jerusalem?" *Bibliotheca Sacra*, vol. 125, no. 498 (Apr. 1968): 99–106.

He argues yes.

Wilder, Amos N. "The Rhetoric of Ancient and Modern Apocalyptic." *Interpretation*, vol. XXV, no. 4 (Oct. 1971).

Wong, Daniel K. K. "The First Horseman of Revelation 6." *Bibliotheca Sacra*, vol. 153, no. 610 (Apr.–June 1996).

Wuest, Kenneth S. "The Rapture—Precisely When?" *Bibliotheca Sacra*, vol. 114, no. 453 (Jan.–Mar. 1957).

Bibles and Testaments

Aland, Barbara and Kurt, Johannes Karavidopoulos, Carlo Martini, and Bruce Metzger. *The Greek New Testament*. 4th revised edition. Stuttgart: Deutsche Bibelgesellschaft, 1966, 1993. 918 pp.

The Holy Bible: English Standard Version. Wheaton, Ill.: Crossway Bibles, 2002. 1328 pp.

The International Inductive Study Bible. NAS. Eugene, Ore.: Harvest House Publishers, 1977. 2206 pp.

Kittel, Rudolf. *Biblia Hebraica*. Stuttgart: Privileg. Wurtt. Bibelanstalt, 1937, 1954. 1434 pp.

LaHaye, Tim. *Prophecy Study Bible*. N.p.: AMG Publishers, 2000. 1576 pp. and color charts.

A helpful study Bible from a premillennial, dispensational viewpoint. There are many explanatory notes as well as major articles on such themes as dispensations, fallen angels, the future temples, Satan, Gog and Magog, Daniel's seventy weeks, hell, the Rapture, heaven, the Battle of Armageddon, and so forth.

Nestle, Eberhard, and Kurt Aland. *Novum Testamentum Graece*. 26th ed. Stuttgart: Deutsche Bibelstiftung, 1898, 1979. 779, 78 (intro.) pp.

Rahlfs, Alfred. *Septuaginta*. [The OT in Greek.] Stuttgart: Privilegierte Wurttembergische Bibelanstalt, 1935. 2 vols. 1184, 941 pp.

Rotherham, Joseph Bryant. *The Emphasized Bible*. Grand Rapids: Kregel Publications, rpt. 1959. 920, 272 (intro.) pp.

Ryrie, Charles Caldwell. *The Ryrie Study Bible*. Chicago: Moody Press, 1976. 2006 pp.

Scofield, C. I. *The Scofield Study Bible*. New York: Oxford University Press, 1909, 1945. 1362 pp.

Works on Heaven

Baxter, Richard. *The Saints' Everlasting Rest*. 2 vols. London: Griffith, Farran and Company, 1887. 289, 319 pp.

An old classic. He shows the four preparations for rest: the coming of Christ, our resurrection, justification, coronation (pp. 30ff.); the joy of seeing God face to face (p. 64); the rest from suffering, doubts, and fears (p. 77); the rest from Satan's attacks (p. 78); rest from un-Christian-like quarrels (p. 83); the eternal nature of the rest (pp. 92f.); the greatness of the loss of the wicked (pp. 190ff.); stresses the motivations to a heavenly life (vol. 2, pp. 156ff.); exhorts to the duty of meditating on the coming rest (pp. 216ff.); lists the advantages of meditating on heaven (pp. 262ff.).

Bounds, Edward M. *Heaven: A Place, a City, a Home.* Grand Rapids: Baker, n.d. 151 pp.

Devout meditations by a great saint. He stresses that heaven is a continuing, prepared, holy city (pp. 40–41); holds that it is also a state of perfected knowledge (p. 77); concludes with the idea of reunion in heaven (pp. 147–51).

Bunyan, John. *The Holy City—The New Jerusalem.* In *The Complete Works of John Bunyan.* Vol. I, pp. 280–337. Marshallton, Del.: National Foundation for Christian Education, rpt. 1968.

An exposition of Revelation 21:10–22:4. Although there is an allegorizing style, there are also helpful, devotional comments. After giving symbolic interpretations of the twelve gates, he argues soberly for the restoration of literal Israel in the light of Romans 11 (p. 296).

Gilmore, John. *Probing Heaven.* Grand Rapids: Baker, 1989. 466 pp.

A book of questions and answers on heaven. He begins with simple ones, such as, Isn't Revelation too difficult? There are ways of understanding (pp. 33ff.). Is there a heaven? The Bible says yes (pp. 55ff.). Who will be in heaven? (pp. 125ff.). He goes on to more inferential questions: Sex in heaven? (pp. 219ff.); humor in heaven? (pp. 245ff.); growth in heaven? (pp. 278ff.); ownership in heaven? (pp. 295ff.); and so forth. Many will have some questions about his answers.

Hutson, Curtis, ed. *Great Preaching on Heaven.* Murfreesboro, Tenn.: Sword of the Lord Publishers, 1987. 256 pp.

Eloquent sermons on heaven by famous preachers. "Heaven Is a Place," Billy Sunday (pp. 83ff.); "The Wedding in the Sky," William Biederwolf (pp. 109ff.); J. Wilbur Chapman, "And the Twelve Gates Were Twelve Pearls" (pp. 117ff.); Harry Hager, "The City of God," (pp. 209ff.).

Lawson, Steven J. *Heaven Help Us!* Colorado Springs: NavPress Publishing Group, 1995. 197 pp.

Popular sermons drawn from texts in Revelation. He has topics such as "I've Seen Fire and I've Seen Reign" (pp. 27ff.); contrasts the wild crowd waiting to see Michael Jordan with the few people waiting for church to begin (pp. 48ff.); holds that the only man-made thing in heaven will be the nail prints in Jesus' hands (p. 77); describes an ovation given to Billy Graham and argues that Jesus Christ will have a greater one (pp. 88f.); invites the reader to come to Christ (p. 117).

Lockyer, Herbert. *The Gospel of the Life Beyond.* Westwood, N.J.: Revell, 1967. 110 pp.

Presents the progressive revelation of immortality in the NT (pp. 21ff.); location of the saints' everlasting rest (pp. 47ff.); occupations of the occupants of heaven (pp. 58ff.); recognition in heaven: George MacDonald: "Shall we be greater fools in Paradise than we are here?" (p. 65); relationships in heaven: "Heaven is not a sphere of ethereal, implied, cold, unsocial and formless spirits, but a home of saints with glorified bodies having a perpetual interchange of perfect love and affection" (p. 69).

Mascall, Eric L. *Grace and Glory*. New York: Morehouse-Barlow, 1961. 90 pp.

Paraphrases Augustine on heaven: "There we shall rest, see, love, praise. Behold what shall be in the end and shall not end" (p. 11); organizes the book on these ideas; refers to saints as characterized by intensity (p. 77), vastness (p. 78), permanence (p. 80), utter satisfaction (p. 82).

McDannell, Colleen, and Bernhard Lang. *Heaven: A History*. New Haven: Yale University Press, 1988. 411 pp.

A history of the images Christians use to describe what happens after death and in the final state (p. xiii); they discuss ancient Near Eastern myths (pp. 2ff.) and apocalypticism (pp. 11ff.); think that belief in a resurrection came from Zoroaster (p. 12); think that the Sadducees were prosperous and did not want heaven (p. 20); hold that the Gospels were written "by second- or third-generation Christians who had no personal knowledge of Jesus himself" (p. 25); claim that Paul gave Jewish apocalyptic concepts new meaning by infusing them with Christian ideas (p. 34); referring to John on Patmos, they claim, "Although his vision seems quite fantastic to us, what he saw was largely based on tradition" (p. 39); the scene in heaven was "laid out like a big synagogue" (p. 41); "John's visions reveal a decidedly theocentric heaven" (p. 43); they go on to recount the thought of Irenaeus and Augustine (pp. 47ff.), medieval writers (pp. 69ff.), Renaissance writers (pp. 111ff.), the Reformers (pp. 145ff.), Swedenborg (pp. 181ff.), and conclude with contemporary thought (pp. 307ff.); say, "Fundamentalists base their views exclusively on the Bible" (p. 336); record Scofield's view (p. 337), Hal Lindsey's view (p. 339), and Hans Jonas (p. 346), and other skeptics.

Moody, Dwight Lyman. *Heaven*. New York: Revell, 1880. 119 pp.

Subtitled "Where It Is, Its Inhabitants, and How to Get There, Its Hope"; tells about the preacher who said he thought of heaven as a great shining city, vast walls, domes, spires, angels, but unknown; his little brother died and there was one little fellow that he knew; then another brother died, other friends; four of his own children he laid to rest; he could not see any more the walls and domes and spires; he thought of the people; "now it seems to me that I know more people in heaven than I do on earth" (pp. 30–31).

Powell, Ivor. *Heaven: My Father's Country*. Grand Rapids: Kregel, 1995. 141 pp.

A brief survey of biblical teaching on heaven. He shows that heaven is the place of God (p. 10); that it is called a city, implying population (p. 21); angels are said to be there (p. 25); believers in Christ go to God when they die (p. 42); Christ is our High Priest in heaven (p. 54); all there will understand the language (p. 61); only what you give here will you keep in heaven (p. 78); only John wept in heaven (p. 93); argues that New Jerusalem will be the greatest city ever built (p. 99).

Sanders, J. Oswald. *Heaven: Better by Far*. Grand Rapids: Discovery House, 1993. 154 pp.

A book of questions and answers about heaven. He quotes famous authors on heaven: Graham Scroggie (p. 33), Henry Alford (p. 38); attacks the idea of soul sleep (p. 46); holds that children and the mentally handicapped who die are saved by the grace of Christ (pp. 51–55); denies universalism (pp. 112–15); favors a symbolic interpretation of Revelation (p. 136).

Schilder, K. *Heaven, What Is It?* Grand Rapids: Wm. B. Eerdman's Publishing Company, 1950. 118 pp.

A philosophical discussion of the Reformed view of heaven. He attacks neoplatonism (p. 14); holds that the coming Day of the Lord will bring the world out of misery into blessedness (p. 23); argues that heaven must be a place (pp. 29f.); holds that the New Jerusalem is the instituted church (p. 40); assumes that Adam met angels (p. 50); thinks that we may not recognize one another in heaven but will know one another (p. 66); suggests that if man had kept the covenant, "the first human pair would also have multiplied to the full number of humanity ordained to life" (p. 91); observes that the old economy labored toward rest; the new economy begins with rest (p. 101).

Scroggie, W. Graham. *What About Heaven?* Westwood, N.J.: Revell, 1940. 145 pp.

Devotional comfort for believers, written after the death of his wife. He describes pagan views of heaven (pp. 18ff.); gives the OT views (pp. 26ff.); sets forth the NT revelation of the believer's persistence (pp. 47ff.) and consciousness (pp. 52ff.); stresses that heaven is a place (pp. 56ff.); holds that there will be perfect knowledge (p. 67) and clear memory there (pp. 73ff.); gives the teaching on the Parousia (pp. 82ff.), the judgment (p.103), and rewards (pp. 108f.); discusses the resurrection (pp. 85ff.), arguing for full recognition of those in heaven (pp. 93ff.) and the ability to make progress in perfection (pp. 112ff.); identifies the twenty-four elders as OT and NT saints (p. 121).

Smith, Wilbur M. *The Biblical Doctrine of Heaven*. Chicago: Moody Press, 1968. 317 pp.

An investigation of the subject of heaven. He discusses liberal objections to the doctrine, the meaning of the terms, heaven as the abode of God, the angels, the redeemed, the intermediate state, the meaning of our inheritance, "Occupations of the Redeemed in Heaven" (pp. 190–201); gives many comments on the "New Heavens and New Earth" and "the Holy City." There are some appendixes on great hymns about heaven and so forth. He admits evolutionary time periods (p. 43); identifies the kingdom of heaven with the kingdom of God (p. 131).

Watts, Isaac. *The World to Come*. 1739, 1745: rpt. Chicago: Moody, 1945. 448 pp.

Puritan sermons on the life to come. He preached on the end of time: the end of time for service, for hope, for preparation for the next life, and so forth (pp. 89ff.), surprise in death (pp. 137ff.), the wrath of the Lamb (pp. 186ff.), no night in heaven: no need for sleep, activities never interrupted, no danger from evil men at night, and so forth (pp. 217ff.), no pain among the blessed (pp. 265ff.), the punishments of hell (pp. 355ff.).

Zoller, John. *Heaven*. Grand Rapids: Eerdman Printing Company, 1968. 443 pp.

Fervent meditations on heaven by a well-known radio preacher. He interprets the Bible literally (p. 3); argues that the justice of God demands that there be life after death (pp. 14f.); shows that the Bible clearly teaches it (II Cor. 5:1–2; Ps. 23:4, p. 22); David's child (II Sam. 12:15–23, p. 33); Lazarus (John 11:11–45, pp. 34–36); discusses the doctrine of sheol-hades (pp. 42f.); argues that heaven is a place (pp. 54ff.); discusses the beauty of heaven (pp. 90ff.); argues that believers will have perfect understanding (pp. 133ff.); concludes with a call for decision to receive Christ as Savior (p. 442).

Works on Hell

Benton, John. *How Can a God of Love Send People to Hell?* Welwyn, Saskatchewan: Evangelical Press, 1985. 96 pp.

A popular survey. He demonstrates why God is angry with man (pp. 11–19); lists current opinions on punishment (pp. 20–37); gives Jesus' teaching on hell (pp. 38–56); demonstrates the seriousness of sin (pp. 57–75); concludes with a fervent appeal to seek God's forgiveness for sin (pp. 76–93).

Blanchard, John. *Whatever Happened to Hell?* Darlington, Col.: Evangelical Press, 1993. 336 pp.

A formal defense of the biblical doctrine of hell. He defends the biblical teaching (pp. 19ff.); discusses the words *hades, gehenna*, and so forth (pp. 33–43; 130–42); defends the idea of life after death (pp. 63ff.) and the idea of a day of judgment (pp. 98ff.); attacks conditional immortality (pp. 210ff.); explains how to avoid hell (pp. 267ff.).

Buis, Harry. *The Doctrine of Eternal Punishment.* Grand Rapids: Baker Book House, 1957. 148 pp.

He provides a systematic portrait of the teaching on hell in the OT (pp. 1ff.), in literature of the intertestamental period (pp. 16ff.), and in the NT (pp. 33–52). He notes that the Lord taught that punishment in hell will take place in a "furnace of fire" (Matt. 13:4ff., p. 36); argues that if Jesus is God, He taught the truth (pp. 41–42). He shows that Paul taught the same doctrine (pp. 43ff.), as did Peter (pp. 45f.) and John in the Revelation (pp. 46ff.). He also traces the doctrine through church history (pp. 53ff.) and answers the denials of universalism (pp. 112ff.) and annihilationism (pp. 123ff.).

Crockett, William, ed. *Four Views on Hell.* Grand Rapids: Zondervan, 1992. 190 pp.

John Walvoord defends the literal interpretation (pp. 11ff.); William Crockett advocates the metaphorical view (pp. 43ff.); Zachary J. Hayes sets forth the Roman Catholic purgatorial view (pp. 91ff.); and Clark Pinnock advocates the conditional immortality view (pp. 135ff.). There are responses to the views by each of the participants.

Fernando, Ajith. *Crucial Questions About Hell.* Wheaton, Ill.: Crossway Books, 1991. 190 pp.

He warns against the pluralism of the day and eastern religious thinking (pp. 22ff.); explains that the Bible teaches that it is a place of punishment and separation and that there are degrees of punishment (pp. 26ff.); he refutes annihilationism (pp. 37ff.); stresses the eternality of hell (pp. 45ff.); attacks universalism (pp. 53ff.) and reincarnationism (pp. 77ff.); holds that God will not violate man's free will (pp. 87ff.); balances God's wrath with His love (pp. 105ff.); shows that universalists take Scripture out of context and use unwarranted assumptions in interpretation (pp. 113ff.); holds that we should talk about hell to rescue men from it (pp. 125ff.); provides ideas for preaching the message of judgment (pp. 149ff.).

Gerstner, John H. *Repent or Perish.* Ligonier, Pa.: Soli Deo Publications, 1990. 218 pp.

A trenchant defense of the biblical doctrine of hell. He argues that all men are sinners who deserve to go to hell (pp. 4ff.); shows how the

Lord Jesus is the one who tells us the most about hell (pp. 15ff.); traces the history of the denial of hell (pp. 32ff.); specifically answers the arguments of Fudge (pp. 66ff.); expounds Jesus' teaching about hell (pp. 125ff.) and Paul's teaching on hell (pp. 163ff.); describes the day of judgment (pp. 188ff.); describes how to repent (pp. 196ff.).

Govett, Robert. *Eternal Suffering of the Wicked*, and *Hades*. Miami Springs, Fla.: Schoettle Publishing Co., 1871, rpt. 1989. 181, 22 pp.

He defends the doctrine from the Scriptures, distinguishing the judgment of the nations from the Great White Throne judgment (pp. 3ff.); traces the words *eternal, punishment*, and so forth through Scripture (pp. 6ff.); argues that punishment is a process (pp. 15ff.) and that *eternal punishment* does not mean *instant annihilation* (pp. 20ff.); argues that fire is prepared for the Devil and his angels, who cannot be materially burned up (pp. 26f.); argues that annihilation would be the end of punishment (p. 34); holds that millennial saints will look upon the wicked in literal fire (p. 37); stresses that the wrath of God *abides* on the wicked (pp. 38ff.); notes that the worship of the Beast will be literal and so the torment with fire and brimstone should be literal (pp. 48ff.); argues that when the Devil is cast into the lake of fire, the Beast and the False Prophet are still there (p. 52). His shorter work on the biblical doctrine of hades is bound with it.

Minnick, Mark. *The Doctrine of Eternal Punishment*. Woodridge, Ill.: Preach the Word Ministries, Inc., 1996. 41 pp.

A formal defense of the biblical teaching on hell. He notes that a denial of the doctrine attacks the deity of the Lord Jesus (p. 5); distinguishes between hades and gehenna (pp. 10f.); defines the characteristics of brimstone, sulfur (p. 21); defends the eternality of hell (pp. 31ff.).

Moore, David George. *The Battle for Hell*. New York: University Press of America, Inc., 1995. 102 pp.

He notes the current disappearance of belief in hell (p. 3), the opinions of evangelicals like Clark Pinnock, who hold to annihilationism (p. 5); evaluates the objections to the doctrine of hell (pp. 18ff.); argues that God would be unjust to annihilate Himmler in view of the sufferings of the Jews at Auschwitz (pp. 28f.); charges that the rejection of hell is an emotional reaction rather than biblical faith (pp. 45ff.); warns against the self-centeredness of modern Christianity (pp. 63ff.); concludes with a thorough bibliography (pp. 77–94).

Munsey, William Elbert. *Eternal Retribution*. Wheaton, Ill.: Sword of the Lord Publishers, 1951. 128 pp.

Eloquent sermons on the necessity of punishment for sin. He argues for the resurrection of both the righteous and the wicked (pp. 11ff.);

holds that sin must be judged by a holy God (pp. 31ff.); holds that there will be future rewards for the righteous and future punishment for the wicked (pp. 53ff.); argues that the punishment of the wicked must be eternal (pp. 65ff.); stresses the awfulness of eternal punishment (pp. 79ff.); ponders the meaning of outer darkness (pp. 93ff.); urges people to receive salvation in Christ (pp. 105ff.).

Peterson, Robert A. *Hell on Trial.* Phillipsburg, N.J.: Presbyterian and Reformed, 1995. 258 pp.

"The Case for Eternal Punishment." As in a courtroom he introduces the witness of the OT (pp. 21ff.), the witness of the Redeemer (pp. 39ff.), the witness of the apostles (pp. 77ff.), the witness of church history (pp. 97ff.); then deals with false witnesses: universalism (pp. 139ff.), annihilationism (161ff.), and so forth. He then argues the case for eternal punishment (pp. 183ff.).

Pusey, E. B. *What Is of Faith as to Everlasting Punishment?* London: Rivingtons, 1881. 290 pp.

A formal answer to Frederick Farrar's denial of the eternal nature of hell. He documents Farrar's attacks on Jonathan Edwards, Moody, Spurgeon for preaching the doctrine of hell (p. 2); argues that universalism is only a human theory, not the teaching of Scripture (p. 17); says Farrar denied that he was a universalist but yet taught the elements of it (p. 27); charges Farrar with using emotional appeals rather than the clear teaching of Scripture (p. 45); documents the teaching of Jewish authorities on gehenna (pp. 51ff.).

Shedd, William G. T. *The Doctrine of Endless Punishment.* New York: Charles Scribner's Sons, 1887. 201 pp.

He gives a history of the doctrine (pp. 1ff.); devotes most of his interest to the biblical argument (pp. 12–117); holds that "the strongest support for the doctrine of endless punishment is the teaching of Christ, the Redeemer of man" (p. 12); argues that the omniscient Christ who gave the warnings of Matthew 25:31–46 "could neither have believed nor expected that all men without exception will eventually be holy and happy" (p. 13); then goes on to quote and expound the many passages in which Christ taught of hell and everlasting punishment (pp. 15ff.). He also gives the rational argument that a good God must punish evil (pp. 118ff.).

Vincent, Thomas. *Fire and Brimstone.* Morgan, Pa.: Soli Deo Gloria, 1999, rpt. from 1670 ed. 241 pp.

A Puritan study of the fire and brimstone visited on Sodom and Gomorrah (pp. 1ff.), the fire and brimstone from an eruption of Mount Etna (pp. 53ff.), and the fire and brimstone prophesied upon the wicked in hell (pp. 98ff.). He notes that fire came down from heaven on Sodom rather than ascending up (p. 27); defends the existence of hell (pp. 101ff.); argues that just as the glory of the New Jerusalem will far surpass all metaphors, so the fire and torment of hell will far surpass all metaphorical interpretations (p. 108); holds that hell fire is such, that the bodies of the wicked, "though they shall be tormented by it, shall never be consumed by it" (p. 113); argues that hell will be a dark fire (Matt. 25:30, p. 115); stresses that Jesus Christ is the only deliverer from the wrath to come (pp. 155ff.).

Electronic Media

Bible Lands Photoguide. Accordance.

The C. H. Spurgeon Collection. The Metropolitan Tabernacle Pulpit. Ages Digital Library.

The Theological Journal Library, Version 2. *Bibliotheca Sacra.*

Other Works Cited

Alden, Peter C. *National Audubon Society Field Guide to African Wildlife.* New York: Alfred A. Knopf, 1995. 988 pp.

Allis, Oswald T. *Prophecy and the Church.* Philadelphia: Presbyterian and Reformed, 1945. 339 pp.

An amillennial interpretation of prophecy.

Andrews, Samuel J. *Christianity and Anti-Christianity in Their Final Conflict.* Chicago: Moody Press, 1898, 1937.

A thought-provoking study on the preparation of the world for the coming of the Antichrist. He covers the biblical teaching (pp. 1–68), modern philosophy (pp. 139ff.), humanism (pp. 159ff.), modern biblical criticism (pp. 169ff.), modern science (pp. 185ff.), socialism (pp. 221ff.), and so forth.

Archer, Gleason, Paul Feinberg, Douglas Moo, and Richard Reiter. *The Rapture.* Grand Rapids: Zondervan, 1984. 268 pp.

Reiter gives a brief history of the rapture positions (pp. 9ff.); Feinberg presents the pretribulation position (pp. 45ff.); Archer gives the midtribulation view (pp.113ff.); Moo gives the posttribulation view (pp. 169ff.). There are responses to each view.

Arndt, William, and Wilbur Gingrich. *A Greek-English Lexicon of the New Testament.* Chicago: University of Chicago Press, 1957. 909 pp.

This is the most helpful Greek-English lexicon that is currently available.

Barnhouse, Donald Grey. *The Invisible War*. Grand Rapids: Zondervan, 1965. 288 pp.

A study of the biblical doctrine of the age-long war between God and the Devil. He holds that the Devil fell between Genesis 1:1 and 1:2 (pp. 15f.), and that the creation of man was the first step in overthrowing Satan (pp. 73f.); the creation of man meant a three-way battle for supremacy (pp. 84ff.), which he calls "triangular warfare" (p. 97); he paints an exciting picture of angelic warfare (pp. 130ff.); holds that the conclusion of Revelation describes the actual victory of Christ over the Devil (pp. 287–88).

Baron, David. *The Visions and Prophecies of Zechariah*. London: Morgan and Scott, 1918. 554 pp.

A careful exposition of Zechariah by a converted rabbi. He provides technical and devotional explanations. He is especially helpful on the messianic prophecies.

Barrett, S. M. *Geronimo's Story of His Life*. 1905; rpt. Williamstown, Mass.: Corner House Publishers, 1980. 216 pp.

Geronimo joined the Dutch Reformed Church and was baptized in the summer of 1903 (p. 211).

Bell, Albert A. Jr. *Exploring the New Testament World*. Nashville: Thomas Nelson, 1998. 322 pp.

A helpful book on NT background. He documents the Judaic influence (pp. 19ff.), "the powers that be" (pp. 57ff.), Roman law (pp. 91ff.), Greco-Roman religion (pp. 123ff.), philosophy (pp. 161ff.), society (pp. 185ff.), personal relations (pp. 221ff.), and so forth.

Benware, Paul N. *Understanding End Times Prophecy*. Chicago: Moody Press, 1995. 343 pp.

A survey of the covenants (pp. 17ff.); the millennial positions (pp. 77ff.); the rapture views (pp. 157ff.); Daniel's seventieth week (pp. 243ff.); coming judgments and resurrections (pp. 269ff.); death (pp. 293ff.); an overview of the Book of Revelation (pp. 311ff.); and a chart of the prophecies of Daniel (p. 325).

Berger, Peter L. *A Rumor of Angels*. New York: Doubleday and Co., 1969. 129 pp.

A rediscovery of the supernatural in modern society. He holds that liberal Protestantism has conceded too much and shows a lack of character (p. 12); says modern theologians relativize the past yet think that they are immune to relativization (p. 51); says angels and demons can go right on existing despite the inability of modern man to perceive them (p. 52); gives arguments for the divine world from order, play (pp. 72–75), hope (pp. 75ff.), damnation (pp. 81ff.), and humor (pp. 86f.).

Berkhof, Louis. *Systematic Theology*. Grand Rapids: Eerdmans, 1949. 784 pp.

A traditional conservative Reformed theology. He is an amillennialist (p. 708).

Biedermann, Hans. *Dictionary of Symbolism*. New York: Facts on File, 1989, 1992. 465 pp.

A popular explanation of major symbols, including some biblical ones: angel, blood, cube, incense, lamb, lion, and so forth.

Black, David Alan, and David S. Dockery, eds. *Interpreting the New Testament*. Nashville: Broadman and Holman, 2001. 565 pp.

An anthology on methods and issues. Boyd Luter contributes the chapter on "Interpreting the Book of Revelation" (pp. 457–80), a very helpful contribution.

Blackstone, W. E. *Jesus Is Coming*. Chicago: Fleming H. Revell, 1908. 252 pp.

A fervent defense of the pretribulational, premillennial coming of the Lord Jesus Christ. He argues exclusively from the wording of Scripture.

Blaising, Craig A., and Darrell L. Bock. *Dispensationalism, Israel and the Church*. Grand Rapids: Zondervan, 1992. 402 pp.

A presentation of progressive dispensationalism (pp. 380ff.). They discuss literal interpretation (pp. 31ff.); argue for present and future forms of the kingdom, visible and invisible (pp. 45–46); hold that the kingdom was not postponed but always coming in two phases (p. 60); think that two new covenants are a defenseless position (p. 91); defend the idea of the universal church (p. 124); argue that national Israel must be converted (Rom. 11, p. 229); hold that the Sermon on the Mount is applicable to all ages (p. 263); see three stages of fulfillment of Revelation 21–22: preliminary blessing at the First Advent; millennial blessings by the Second Advent; ultimate golden age of eternal blessing (pp. 290–92).

Bock, Darrell L. "The Kingdom of God in New Testament Theology," in *Looking into the Future*. David W. Baker, ed. Grand Rapids: Baker Book House, 2001. Pp. 28–60.

He argues for a "both/and" view of the kingdom: it is present and it will be future (pp. 45ff.); argues that the imagery of Revelation 21–22 "looks back to the Garden of Eden and forward to the New Jerusalem" (p. 54).

Bolton, Robert. *General Directions for a Comfortable Walking with God.* Morgan, Pa.: Soli Deo Gloria Publications, 1626, rpt. 1995. 444 pp.

A Puritan exhortation toward "heavenly meditation" (p. 78). He warns not only against drunkenness but against "excessive sleep" as well (p. 229); he also warns against an undervaluing of God's mercies (p. 399).

Brookes, James. *Maranatha.* New York: Revell, 1889.

An early American advocate of the premillennial, pretribulation rapture of the saints.

Buchanan, George Wesley. *New Testament Eschatology.* Lewiston, N.Y.: Mellen Biblical Press, 1993. 297 pp.

He discusses eschatology in financial metaphors of debt and merit (pp. 1ff.); sabbatical eschatology (pp. 26ff.); eschatology in cycles: Cullmann, Daniel, and so forth (pp. 58ff.); kingdom eschatology (pp. 90ff.); says the author of the Beatitudes saw the land as the reward of the meek (p. 106); holds that Jesus thought the kingdom would come within a year of His death (p. 111); concludes that all references to the kingdom in the OT or that Jesus referred to are to the literal Davidic kingdom (p. 119); thinks that Daniel saw fulfillment in Judas the Maccabee (pp. 121–60); tries to "demythologize" the NT teaching into a fulfillment in A.D. 70 (pp. 161–91); holds that after A.D. 70, Jewish and Christian writers understood eschatology to be political fulfillment in the land of Palestine (pp. 192–224); evaluates Muslim and Christian millennial views in the light of this (pp. 225–53). He includes a thorough annotated bibliography of works cited (pp. 254–70).

Chafer, Louis Sperry. *Satan.* Chicago: Moody, 1919. 180 pp.

He covers the career of Satan, the satanic system, the satanic host, Satan's motives and methods, the man of sin, modern devices, and so forth.

Charles, R. H. I Enoch in *The Apocrypha and Pseudepigrapha of the Old Testament.* II, pp. 163–281. Oxford: Clarendon Press, 1913.

Visions and revelations of the future. The same vision that Jude 14–15 referred to.

Chesterman, Charles W. *The Audubon Society Field Guide to North American Rocks and Minerals.* New York: Alfred A. Knopf, 1978. 851 pp.

Full-color illustrations of the specimens.

Connolly, R. Chris. *Millennium Superworld.* Rochester, N.Y.: Megiddo Press, 1997. 157 pp.

An argument for an earthly Millennium (pp. 25ff.). He sees a coming of Elijah, Tribulation before the Lord Jesus reigns (pp. 30ff.); argues that the Lord will rule from Jerusalem (pp. 60ff.); suggests subjects that will not be taught in the Millennium (pp. 74f.) and others that will be taught (pp. 77ff.); thinks that glorified saints will be mingled among the unglorified (p. 113); believes that the consciousness of the wicked will end in extinction (p. 121).

Conyers, A. J. *The Eclipse of Heaven*. Downers Grove, Ill.: InterVarsity Press, 1992. 202 pp.

A plea for rediscovering the hope of a world beyond. He quotes Martin Buber's comment that the present hour is an eclipse of the light of heaven and of God (p. 11); quotes P. T. Forsythe, "If within us we find nothing over us we succumb to what is around us" (p. 20); teaches that salvation comes by grace (p. 35); stresses that eternal life means worship (p. 54); notes how reading the Scriptures changed Jurgen Moltmann (p. 59); argues for the need of self-transcendence (pp. 73ff.); warns that a fragmented "Christian" society is too compromised to render help (p. 122); urges a longing for heaven (pp. 159f.); concludes with "Only heaven can prevent theology from becoming psychology" (p. 193).

Couch, Mal, ed. *Dictionary of Premillennial Theology*. Grand Rapids: Kregel, 1996. 442 pp.

Helpful articles on amillennialism (pp. 37ff.), dispensationalism (pp. 96ff.), various judgments (pp. 225ff.), kingdom of God, of heaven (pp. 230f.), rapture (pp. 233ff.), Millennium (pp. 259ff.), and many other topics.

Cullmann, Oscar. *Christ and Time*. Philadelphia: Westminster, 1964.

Heilsgeschichte theologian argues that Christ's advent is the center of time (p. 82).

Culver, Robert D. *Daniel and the Latter Days*. Westwood, N.J.: Revell, 1954. 221 pp.

A survey of the millennial positions (pp. 19ff.) and a premillennial interpretation of the Book of Daniel (pp. 93–212). It includes a fold-out chart of the Book of Daniel.

Currid, John D. *Exodus*. 2 vols. Auburn, Mass.: Evangelical Press, 2000. 415, 398 pp.

He uses Genesis 3:15 as the theme of Exodus (I, 17ff.); sees parallels in Egyptian mythology to the miracles in Exodus (I, 101); takes Exodus 19:1 as a major break in the text and outlines accordingly (II, 13ff.); gives practical applications of the law (II, 50f.).

Custer, Stewart. *Does Inspiration Demand Inerrancy?* Nutley, N.J.: Craig Press, 1977. 120 pp.

The thesis of the author is that the teaching of the Bible does demand the doctrine of inerrancy. He provides answers to the "alleged errors" (pp. 93ff.).

————. *The Stars Speak.* 2nd ed. Greenville, S.C.: BJU Press, 2002. 212 pp.

Devotional studies in the biblical references to the sun, moon, stars, planets, and other heavenly bodies. Illustrated by color photographs from the Hubble Space Telescope.

————. *Stones of Witness.* Greenville, S.C.: BJU Press, 2002. 236 pp.

Images of the Holy Land from Dan to Beersheba and on to the Red Sea. There is an accompanying interactive CD-Rom with 635 color photos of the Holy Land.

————. *Tools for Preaching and Teaching the Bible.* 2nd ed. Greenville, S.C.: BJU Press, 1979, 1998. 400 pp.

Recommended books for the pastor: concordances, atlases, commentaries, books on prophecy, cults, ethics, and so forth.

————. *Treasury of New Testament Synonyms.* Greenville, S.C.: BJU Press, 1975. 143 pp.

An investigation of thirty-two different groups of Greek synonyms to bring out distinctions in meaning. It covers such words as *burden, devil, power, righteousness, soul, trickery.*

————. *Witness to Christ.* Greenville, S.C.: BJU Press, 2000. 463 pp.

A commentary on the Book of Acts. It is an exposition with maps and photographs.

Deissmann, Adolph. *Light from the Ancient East.* New York: Harper, 1922. 535 pp.

A very technical study of the Koine Greek background of the NT. He provides numerous examples of NT words and phrases illustrated by the papyri and inscriptions.

Dockery, David S. *Holman Bible Handbook.* Nashville: Holman Bible Publishers, 1992. 894 pp.

Helpful notes on the Book of Revelation (pp. 783–804).

Dyer, Charles H. *The Rise of Babylon: Sign of the End Times.* Wheaton, Ill.: Tyndale House, 1991. 236 pp.

He gives a brief history of Babylon (pp. 47ff.); portrays its OT conquest of Israel (pp. 67ff.); has photographs of the huge rebuilding program under Saddam (between pp. 128–29); argues that the OT prophecies of Babylon's destruction have never been completely fulfilled but will yet happen (pp. 161ff.).

Edwards, Jonathan. *The Work of Redemption* in Edwards, *Works*, New York: Robert Carter and Brothers, 1869. Pp. 295–516.

A history of God's redemption of mankind from Genesis to Revelation.

Ehrman, Bart D. *The New Testament and Other Early Christian Writings.* New York: Oxford University Press, 1998. 412 pp.

A liberal survey and reader of canonical works and extrabiblical ones: Gospels of Matthew and Thomas; the Revelation of John and the Apocalypse of Peter, and so forth.

Eusebius. *Ecclesiastical History.* Kirsop Lake, ed. Loeb Classical Library. 2 vols. London: Wm. Heinemann Ltd., n.d.

Feinberg, Charles L. *Premillennialism or Amillennialism?* Wheaton, Ill.: Van Kampen Press. N.d. 354 pp.

A formal defense of the premillennial interpretation and refutation of amillennialism.

Girdlestone, R. B. *The Grammar of Prophecy.* Grand Rapids: Kregel, 1955. 192 pp.

He discusses prophetic forms of thought (pp. 48ff.), recurrent prophetic formulae (pp. 54ff.), the prophetic use of names (pp. 81ff.), the structure of the Apocalypse (pp. 110ff.), the Parousia and the Millennium (pp. 141ff.), Christ and Antichrist (pp. 150ff.), and so forth.

God's Word to the Nations. Grand Rapids: World Publishing, Inc., 1995.

A modern translation of the Bible.

Grenz, Stanley J. *The Millennial Maze.* Downers Grove, Ill.: InterVarsity, 1992. 239 pp.

He surveys four views: dispensationalism (pp. 91ff.); historic premillennialism (post trib., pp. 127ff.); amillennialism (pp. 149ff.); postmillennialism (pp. 65ff.), here in the order in which he personally traveled through them (pp. 10–11).

Guthrie, Donald. *New Testament Theology.* Downers Grove, Ill.: InterVarsity, 1981. 1064 pp.

He believes that the NT is authoritative and normative (p. 33); stresses the Book of Revelation in teaching the Ascension (p. 398); holds that the seven spirits of God refers to the perfection of the Spirit (p. 569); thinks that the Revelation portrays the church as the true Israel of God (p. 786); argues that its presentation of the consummation of human history is valuable "because it is the only treatment of the theme within the NT" (p. 812).

Haldeman, I. M. *Why I Preach the Second Coming.* New York: Revell, 1919. 160 pp.

A series of sermons drawn from a message at the World's Conference on Christian Fundamentalism on May 30, 1919. He argues that the Second Coming is the one future event most often recorded in the Bible (pp. 11ff.), that it is bound up with every fundamental doctrine (pp. 50ff.), that only at the coming of Christ will redemption be complete (pp. 55ff.), that only at the coming of Christ will the church be exalted to her position of rulership (pp. 70ff.).

Hall, Peter, Sir. *Cities in Civilization.* New York: Pantheon Books, 1998. 1169 pp.

A formal comparison among world cities in different historic periods. On the theme of the establishment of the urban order he uses Rome as the example: "The Imperial Capital, Rome 50 B.C.–A.D. 100" (pp. 621–56).

Hamilton, Floyd E. *The Basis of Millennial Faith.* Grand Rapids: Eerdmans Publishing Company, 1952. 162 pp.

A defense of the amillennial position.

Hengstenberg, E. W. *Christology of the Old Testament.* 4 vols. Grand Rapids: Kregel, 1872, rpt. 1956.

A scholarly and reverent study of the OT messianic prophecies.

Henry, Matthew. *The Quest for Communion with God.* Grand Rapids: Eerdmans, 1712, rpt. 1954. 110 pp.

A fervent exhortation to begin every day with God (Ps. 5:3, pp. 9ff.), to spend the day with God (Ps. 25:3, pp. 39ff.), to close the day with God (Ps. 4:8, pp. 72ff.).

Herzog, Chaim, and Mordechai Gichon. *Battles of the Bible.* New York: Random House, 1978, 1997. 320 pp.

An examination of the battles in the Bible in the light of modern strategy and tactics. They cover the battles of Abraham, Joshua, the judges, the kingdom, and so forth. There are many maps with battle plans (Gibeah, Michmash, pp. 69, 71), David's Rephaim campaign (pp. 80f.), the Assyrian conquest (p. 144), and so forth. There are many photos, some in color.

Hiebert, D. Edmond. *The Epistles of John.* Greenville, S.C.: Bob Jones University Press, 1991. 371 pp.

A warm-hearted, conservative exposition, written in full knowledge of the Greek text and the commentary literature. He defends Johannine authorship (pp. 3–16); teaches a premillennial interpretation of Antichrist (pp. 109ff.); urges the imminency of Christ's return (p. 137).

Hoekema, Anthony A. *The Bible and the Future.* Grand Rapids: Eerdmans Publishing Company, 1979. 343 pp.

He gives a critique of dispensational premillennialism (pp. 194–222); provides an amillennial interpretation of Revelation 20 (pp. 223ff.).

Hoyt, Herman A. *The End Times.* Chicago: Moody Press, 1969. 256 pp.

Premillennial studies in the Second Coming (pp. 49ff.), the Antichrist (pp. 115ff.), the Tribulation (pp. 133), the Millennium (pp. 167ff.), and other subjects.

Hunt, A. S., and C. C. Edgar. *Select Papyri.* Cambridge: Harvard University Press, 1932, 1952. 452 pp.

Greek text and translations of nonliterary papyri, covering agreements, wills, letters, invitations, Christian prayers, and so forth.

Hurlbut, Cornelius. *Dana's Manual of Mineralogy.* 16th ed. New York: John Wiley and Sons, 1956.

A standard textbook on mineralogy.

Ice, Thomas, and Randall Price. *Ready to Rebuild.* Eugene, Ore.: Harvest House, 1992. 288 pp.

A survey of the arguments and movements that are for the rebuilding of the Jewish temple (the third temple). They give a history of the place and describe the current interest in rebuilding (pp. 101ff.); show the temple vessels and harps remade (pp. 105ff., 113); describe the most zealous group, the Temple Mount Faithful (pp. 120–23); describe the attempt to lay the four-ton cornerstone (pp. 124ff.); provide photos of the third temple models, the gold menorah, the ark, the cornerstone, the tunnel under the western wall, and so forth (pp. 132f.); give diagrams for suggested locations for the temple (pp. 154ff.) and also give the official governmental position that only Messiah can rebuild the temple (pp. 174ff.). They conclude with a premillennial picture of the prophetic future (pp. 230ff.).

Ironside, H. A. *The Continual Burnt Offering.* New York: Loizeaux Brothers, 1941. (No pagination.)

Comforting meditations for every day in the year, drawn from Genesis to Revelation.

James, William T., gen. ed. *Foreshocks of Antichrist.* Eugene, Ore.: Harvest House, 1997. 418 pp.

An anthology by diverse writers on the preparation of the world for Antichrist. James warns against the world order schemers who change A.D. to C.E. (common era) in despite of Christ (p. 31); Berit Kjos quotes the feminist Naomi Goldenberg: "God is going to change. We women . . . will change the world so much that He won't fit anymore"

(p. 45); and he quotes Federico Mayor, "The 21st Century city will be a city of social solidarity" (p. 51); Grant Jeffrey attacks the unbiblical heresies that the Roman Catholic Church has taught (pp. 99ff.); David Webber warns that the World Wide Web is open to large-scale attacks (p. 130); Zola Levitt warns that the "peace process" in Israel leads to war, which the Antichrist will use to introduce his "seven-year peace plan" (p. 176); he also attacks progressive dispensationalism (p. 182); Chuck Missler warns of China's military build-up (p. 194); Christopher Corbett warns that America is being absorbed by global concerns that center in lands of the Roman Empire (pp. 204f.); Dave Breese attacks the atheism of Russia (p. 233); Paul Feinberg argues that Armageddon will be a full-scale war (p. 261); Arno Froese holds that Europe will be the head of the last Gentile world empire (p. 298); John Walvoord defends the pretribulation rapture (pp. 362f.).

Johnston, Philip S. *Shades of Sheol*. Downers Grove, Ill.: InterVarsity Press, 2002. 288 pp.

A study of death and the afterlife in the OT. He covers the OT references to death, resurrection, the underworld from an evangelical viewpoint. He notes especially Psalms 16, 49, 73 (pp. 200ff.), and Job 19 (p. 209).

Juengst, Sara Covin. *Breaking Bread*. Louisville, Ky.: Westminster/John Knox, 1992. 113 pp.

Devotional meditations for women on the biblical background of food preparation.

Kern, Paul Bentley. *Ancient Siege Warfare*. Bloomington: Indiana University Press, 1999. 419 pp.

A survey of ancient military practices. He covers the Middle East, Israel, and so forth (pp. 29ff.).

Klein, Kenneth B. *The False Prophet*. Eugene, Ore.: Winterhaven Publishing House, 1992. 224 pp.

A detailed argument that the False Prophet and his two horns are really the United States and Great Britain, who will bring in the new world order of the Devil (pp. 203–4).

Klund, Robert W. *The Plot of Revelation 4–22*. Ann Arbor, Mich.: Proquest Information and Learning Company, 2002. 309 pp.

A dissertation accepted by the faculty of Dallas Theological Seminary. A study examining the literary plot of the Book of Revelation.

LaHaye, Tim, and Thomas Ice. *Charting the End Times*. Eugene, Oreg.: Harvest House, 2001. 141 pp.

Premillennial, dispensational charts of the end times.

Larkin, Clarence. *Dispensational Truth*. Philadelphia: Rev. Clarence Larkin Est., 1918, 1920. 176 pp.

Premillennial, dispensational charts on Revelation and many other subjects.

Law, Robert. *Tests of Life*. Edinburgh: T. and T. Clark, 1913. 422 pp.

Not a verse-by-verse commentary but a study of major topics in I John. He groups most of his thought around three great tests—of righteousness, of love, and of faith—but he also discusses the doctrines of Christ, sin, propitiation, eternal life, and so forth.

Lawrence, Brother. *The Practice of the Presence of God*. New York: Revell. 1895, rpt.

A devotional classic by a cook in an ancient monastery.

Lewis, C. S. *The Screwtape Letters*. New York: Macmillan, 1951. 160 pp.

A humorous, but very serious, collection of letters from a head demon to his nephew, telling him how best to betray the man he is tempting.

Liddon, H. P. *The Divinity of Our Lord and Saviour Jesus Christ*. London: Longmans, Green, and Co., 1892. 585 pp.

A classic defense of the deity of Christ by a very devout scholar. He argues that "to the beloved disciple the Divinity of his Lord was not a scholastic formula, nor a pious conjecture. . . . It was nothing less than a fact of personal experience" (p. 278).

Lion Photoguide to the Bible. Tring, Herts, England: Lion Publishing, 1972, 1973, 1983. 287 pp.

Photographs by David Alexander, including Ephesus (pp. 269f.), Smyrna (pp. 276f.), Pergamum (pp. 278f.), Laodicea (pp. 280f.).

Little, Elbert L. *The Audubon Society Field Guide to North American Trees*. New York: Alfred A. Knopf, 1980. 714 pp.

Marshall, I. Howard. *The Origins of New Testament Christology*. Downers Grove, Ill.: InterVarsity Press, 1976. 132 pp.

A technical study in the NT doctrine of Christology. He explains the doctrine in the light of both liberal and conservative opinions, but he does defend the deity of Christ (p. 123).

McCall, Thomas S., and Zola Levitt. *Israel and Tomorrow's Temple*. Chicago: Moody, 1973, 1977. 159 pp.

A discussion of the four temples that have or will exist on the temple mount in Jerusalem. They note the day that the Jews retook the temple mount (6/7/1967, p. 22); describe the coins and weights found at the temple site (p. 28); hold that the millennial temple will have memorial sacrifices (p. 33); note that the Jews' right to pray on the temple mount is illegal yet there are legal challenges (pp. 49–55); think that the Jerusalem Great Synagogue may be a half-way house (pp. 56f.); note that the synagogue's foundation stone was laid on 6/24/1969 (p. 61); give a chart of Israel's four temples (p. 78); identify the Tribulation temple as in the *naos* (pp. 80–81); provide a brief history of the first and second temples (pp. 90ff.); think that Justinian's church was at the Aksa mosque (p. 126); give a premillennial chart of the future (p. 140).

McClain, Alva J. *The Greatness of the Kingdom*. Grand Rapids: Zondervan, 1959, 1974. 556 pp.

Metzger, Bruce M. *A Textual Commentary on the Greek New Testament*. New York: United Bible Societies, 1971. 775 pp.

A companion volume to the Greek NT, explaining the choices of the editors in difficult textual variations.

Miller, Stephen R. *Daniel* in *The New American Commentary*. N.p.: Broadman and Holman, 1994. 348 pp.

A conservative, premillennial exposition of the Book of Daniel. He provides numerous parallels with Revelation (pp. 213ff.).

Minear, Paul S. *New Testament Apocalyptic*. Nashville: Abingdon Press, 1981. 157 pp.

An examination of apocalyptic ideas in Scripture. He gives Harris's Law: "Any philosophy that can be put into a nutshell belongs there" (p. 25); provides guidelines for interpreting apocalyptic literature (pp. 31, 45, 61ff.); discusses the prophet's gift and discernment (p. 34), invisible warfare (p. 42), God and light (pp. 53f.); refers to the myth of origins (p. 57); organizes the vision of heaven (Rev. 4:1–8:1, pp. 67–77).

Moody, Raymond A. Jr. *Life After Life*. Atlanta: Mockingbird Books, 1975. 129 pp.

After-death experiences of people who were later revived and remembered what happened while they had no vital signs. He cites Isaiah 26:19; I Corinthians 15:35–52 (pp. 79–81).

———. *Reflections on Life After Life*. New York: A Bantam/Mockingbird Book, 1977. 148 pp.

Further testimonies of people who have had "after death" experiences. He does not discount the idea of a final judgment or hell (pp. 36–37).

Morris, Leon. *Apocalyptic*. Grand Rapids: Eerdmans, 1972. 87 pp.

A brief discussion of apocalyptic literature. He covers the meaning of revelation (pp. 19ff.), the setting for the literature (pp. 23ff.), symbolism involved (pp. 34ff.), the pessimistic worldview (pp. 37ff.), the shaking of the foundations (pp. 39ff.), the ultimate triumph of God (pp. 41ff.), the dualism of good and evil (pp. 47ff.), the question of pseudonymity (pp. 50ff.), stress on wisdom (pp. 57ff.), prediction (pp. 61ff.), the irresponsibility of the apocalyptists (pp. 70f.), apocalyptic and the NT (pp. 72ff.), the Revelation of St. John (pp. 78ff.).

―――. *The Cross in the New Testament.* Grand Rapids: Eerdmans, 1965. 454 pp.
A careful study that traces the doctrine of salvation through the NT. He stresses the need for conversion (p. 17); defends the idea of propitiation against C. H. Dodd's attacks (pp. 225ff.); stresses that Revelation gives "an exquisitely beautiful picture of the bliss of the saved" (p. 363). The work will suggest many sermons to the preacher.

Moulton, James Hope, and George Milligan. *The Vocabulary of the Greek New Testament.* Grand Rapids: Eerdmans, 1963. 705 pp.
A thorough listing of the words of the Greek NT that are also found in the papyri. They provide helpful background.

National Geographic Society. *Atlas of the Middle East.* Washington D.C.: National Geographic Society, 2003. 96 pp.
Maps and a brief list of current statistics for lands of the Middle East.

―――. *Everyday Life in Bible Times.* Washington D.C.: National Geographic Society, 1967. 448 pp.
Popular biblical background.

O'Donoghue, Michael. *The Encyclopedia of Minerals and Gemstones.* New York: G. P. Putnam's Sons, 1976. 304 pp.
He covers crystals (pp. 24ff.), geology (pp. 42ff.), the mineral kingdom (pp. 148–287), and identification tables (pp. 289ff.).

Pache, Rene. *The Future Life.* Chicago: Moody Press, 1962. 376 pp.
A warm-hearted meditation on death (pp. 35ff.), the world of the spirits (pp. 99ff.), the Resurrection (pp. 163ff.), eternal perdition (pp. 261ff.), and heaven (pp. 329ff.).

Packer, J. I. *Knowing God.* Downers Grove, Ill.: InterVarsity Press, 1973. 256 pp.
A practical and devotional study of the biblical doctrine of God. He stresses that God has revealed Himself in His Word (p. 15); warns that the purpose must not be learning about God but communing with God (pp. 18f.); argues that we learn about God through Jesus Christ (p. 27); holds that there is only one true God (pp. 38ff.) and that Christ is God incarnate (pp. 45ff.); defends the doctrine of the Trinity (pp. 57ff.); discusses the attributes of God (pp. 67ff.), the wrath of God (pp. 134ff.), and the heart of the gospel (pp. 161ff.).

Paisley, Ian R. K. *Antichrist.* Belfast: Martyrs Memorial Productions, n.d. 71 pp.

A reprinting of J. A. Wylie's argument that the papacy is the Antichrist. He lists the many "Reformation Worthies" who held this view, from Huss and Wycliffe to Foxe, Bullinger, and many others (p. 11). He provides many striking arguments, including the number 666 (p. 67).

Pentecost, J. Dwight. *Things to Come.* Findlay, Ohio: Dunham, 1958. 663 pp.

A thorough premillennial study of eschatology. He defends the pretribulational rapture (pp. 193–218; discusses Daniel's seventy weeks (pp. 239ff.), the campaign of Armageddon (pp. 340ff.), and other prophetic events.

————. *Your Adversary the Devil.* Grand Rapids: Zondervan, 1969. 191 pp.

He covers the fall of Satan (pp. 11ff.), the hierarchy of Satan (pp. 30ff.), Satan the deceiver (pp. 48ff.), the perverter (pp. 56ff.), the imitator (pp. 66ff.), the lawless one (pp. 76ff.), the rebel (pp. 85ff.), the roaring lion (pp. 93ff.), and so forth.

Peters, George N. H. *The Theocratic Kingdom.* 3 vols. Grand Rapids: Kregel, 1957.

A grand sweep of premillennial prophecy.

Petersen, Rodney Lawrence. *Preaching in the Last Days.* Oxford: Oxford University Press, 1993. 318 pp.

A scholarly study of the theme of "the two witnesses" in the literature of the sixteenth and seventeenth centuries.

Pfeiffer, Charles F., and Howard Vos. *The Wycliffe Historical Geography of Bible Lands.* Chicago: Moody Press, 1967. 588 pp.

Historical background and maps on Palestine, Asia Minor, Greece, Italy, and others.

Pierson, Arthur T. *The Bible and Spiritual Life.* Los Angeles: The Biola Book Room, 1923. 483 pp.

A fascinating book on the nature of the Bible and its power to transform man.

Porter, R. F., S. Christensen, and P. Schiermacker-Hansen. *Field Guide to the Birds of the Middle East.* London: T and A D Poyser, Ltd., 1996. 460 pp. (U.S. ed., San Diego: Academic Press, Inc., n.d.)

Pough, Frederick H. *A Field Guide to Rocks and Minerals.* The Peterson Field Guide Series. Boston: Houghton Mifflin Company, 1960. 349 pp. Black-and-white and color illustrations.

Roberts, Richard Owen. *Salvation in Full Color.* Wheaton, Ill.: International Awakening Press, 1994. 362 pp.
An anthology of twenty sermons by Great Awakening preachers, including Timothy Dwight, Gilbert Tennent, John Witherspoon, George Whitefield, concluding with Jonathan Edwards's "Divine Retribution" (Matt. 25:46, pp. 331ff.), and Asahel Nettleton's, "The Final Warning" (pp. 353ff.).

Roberts, Theodore. *The Faithful and True Witness.* London: Marshall Brothers, Ltd., 1928. 167 pp.
A study of the teaching of the Lord Jesus Christ on the binding authority of every part of Scripture, including the Book of Revelation (p. 58).

Robertson, Archibald Thomas. *An Introduction to the Textual Criticism of the New Testament.* Nashville: Broadman Press, 1925. 300 pp.
———. "Revelation," in Vol. VI of *Word Pictures in the New Testament.* Pp. 267–488.
A very helpful study of the words of the Greek New Testament. He gives historical background as well as precise meanings.

Rossetti, Christina. *Time Flies: A Reading Diary,* quoted in Kent and Stanwood, eds. *Selected Prose of Christina Rossetti.* P. 313.

Rosten, Leo. *Leo Rosten's Treasury of Jewish Quotations.* New York: Bantam Books, 1972, 1980. 654 pp.
"If one man says, 'You're a donkey,' don't mind; if two say so, be worried; if three say so, get a saddle" (p. 186); "Do not neglect study because of your pleasures, or even for your occupation" (p. 438).

Russell, Jeffrey Burton. *A History of Heaven: The Singing Silence.* Princeton, N.J.: Princeton University Press, 1997. 220 pp.
He discusses the teaching about heaven from Ezekiel on (pp. 14ff.); holds that individuality is not lost in heaven (p. 41); holds that the body of Christ really encompasses the Carpenter's body—resurrection body—the Eucharist—the Ecclesia (p. 47); thinks that the Book of Revelation sets forth symbols of the temple, the throne, the garden, drawn from the tabernacle, the city, paradise (p. 51); surveys the patristic references to heaven (pp. 55ff.); recounts what believers have regarded as orthodoxy (pp. 65ff.); notes that Tertullian taught the Millennium (p. 67); gives Origen's fourfold interpretation (pp. 70ff.); describes Augustine's opposition to the Millennium (p. 78f.); recounts

fictional journeys to heaven (pp. 101–13); traces the spirit of devotion (pp. 114ff.), the attempt of Aquinas to rationalize heaven (pp. 125ff.), and the experiences of mysticism (pp. 141ff.). He spends two chapters explaining Dante's *Divine Comedy* in detail (pp. 151–85). He concludes with a plea for universalism (pp. 188–89).

―――. *The Devil.* Ithaca, N.Y.: Cornell University Press, 1977. 276 pp.

He wrestles with the problem of evil (pp. 17ff.); searches history for the Devil (pp. 36ff.); thinks that the idea of the Devil arose after the exile (pp. 174ff.); but gives a clear picture of the NT doctrine: "The Devil is not a peripheral concept that can easily be discarded without doing violence to the essence of Christianity. He stands at the center of NT teaching that the Kingdom of God is at war with the kingdom of the Devil" (p. 222).

―――. *The Prince of Darkness.* Ithaca, N.Y.: Cornell University Press, 1988.

Radical evil and the power of God in history.

Ryle, J. C. *Shall We Know One Another in Heaven.* Greenville, S.C.: Ambassador Productions, 1996. 88 pp.

An anthology of eloquent, stirring sermons on heaven. Ryle argues that God, bringing those that sleep with Jesus, implies mutual recognition of saints (p. 51); D. L. Moody exclaims that we shall be satisfied when we gaze upon Jesus (p. 14); C. H. Spurgeon preached upon a joyful invitation, "Come Up Hither" (p. 26); Billy Sunday argued that heaven is a great home circle; it would be strange if people at home did not know one another (p. 65); R. M. M'Cheyne held that "Blessed are the dead" implies fullness of joy in heaven (p. 76).

Sale-Harrison, L. *The Resurrection of the Old Roman Empire.* New York: Hephzibah House, 1928, 1934. 130 pp.

He expounds Daniel's fourth kingdom (pp. 21ff.); shows the constant attempt at federation in Europe (pp. 43ff.); stresses the importance of Turkey (pp. 75ff.); prophesies ancient Rome's resurrection (pp. 92ff.).

Saphir, Adolph. *The Divine Unity of Scripture.* London: Hodder and Stoughton, 1892. 361 pp.

A warm-hearted defense of the power and unity of the Scriptures.

Saucy, Robert L. *The Case for Progressive Dispensationalism.* Grand Rapids: Zondervan Publishing House, 1993. 336 pp.

An attempt to bring dispensational and nondispensational theology into speaking terms with each other. Nondispensationalists emphasize simple unity in history (p. 22); dispensationalists emphasize earthly and heavenly objectives in history (pp. 24f.). He notes that the prophets call for an earthly as well as heavenly future for Jerusalem (pp. 230ff.); argues that there is room for both a future earthly city and a heavenly one (pp. 292ff.); argues that the Book of Revelation teaches both (p. 295).

Sauer, Erich. *The Triumph of the Crucified.* London: Paternoster Press, 1951. 207 pp.
A survey of the NT teaching on the twofold coming of Christ for His people. He teaches a pretribulation rapture of the church (pp. 101ff.).

Schneider, Bernard N. *The World of Unseen Spirits.* Winona Lake, Ind.: BMH Books, 1975. 157 pp.
He gives the biblical teaching on angels (pp. 13ff.), the Devil (pp. 55ff.), demons (pp. 101ff.), spiritism (pp. 125ff.); discusses life after death (pp. 145ff.).

Smith, Jerome H. *The New Treasury of Scripture Knowledge.* Nashville: Thomas Nelson, 1992. 1660 pp.
The most complete system of Bible cross-references in existence. There is no text; just cross-references and helps.

Smith, Uriah. *The Prophecies of Daniel and the Revelation.* Nashville: Southern Publishing Association, 1944. 830 pp.
Seventh-Day Adventist propaganda.

Sophocles. *Oedipus Rex, Oedipus at Colonus.* F. Storr, trans. London: William Heinemann, Ltd., 1962.

Stanton, Gerald B. *Kept from the Hour.* Miami Springs, Fla.: Schoettle Publishing Co., 1991. 423 pp.

Swete, Henry Barclay. *The Holy Spirit in the New Testament.* Grand Rapids: Baker, 1910, rpt. 1964. 417 pp.
A thought-provoking survey of the NT teaching about the Holy Spirit. He holds that the seven spirits of God refer to the one Holy Spirit of God (p. 274).

Talbert, Layton. *Not by Chance.* Greenville, S.C.: BJU Press, 2001. 322 pp.
Devotional meditations on God's overruling providence.

Talbot, Louis T. *God's Plan of the Ages.* Grand Rapids: Eerdmans, 1936. 199 pp.
A premillennial interpretation of God's plan from eternity to eternity, illustrated with a fold-out chart. He answers the question, Why are people judged at the end of the Millennium? Children will be born during the Millennium; not all will be converted. Thus there must be a judgment (p. 189).

Tan, Paul Lee. *The Interpretation of Prophecy*. Winona Lake, Ind.: BMH Books, Inc., 1974. 435 pp.

A formal defense of the literal method of interpreting biblical prophecy. He gives principles of prophetic interpretation (pp. 96ff.); notes the progress of revelation (pp. 111ff.); covers symbols and types (pp. 152ff.); has appendixes on the New Jerusalem (pp. 285ff.), the millennial sacrifices (pp. 293ff.), and other subjects.

Thayer, Joseph Henry. *A Greek-English Lexicon of the New Testament*. New York: Harper, 1886. 727 pages.

Thiselton, Anthony C. *The First Epistle to the Corinthians*. NIGTC. Grand Rapids: Eerdmans, 2000. 1446 pp.

A very technical commentary on the Greek text of I Corinthians. He lists as many interpretations as possible, liberal and conservative, on every verse.

Torrey, Reuban Archer. *What the Bible Teaches*. New York: Revell, 1898, 1933. 539 pp.

A thorough presentation of what the Bible teaches in propositions about God (pp. 13ff.), Christ (pp. 68ff.), the Holy Spirit (pp. 225ff.), man (pp. 293ff.), angels (pp. 501ff.), the Devil (pp. 513ff.).

Tregelles, Samuel Prideaux. *The Hope of Christ's Second Coming*. London: Sovereign Grace Advent Testimony, 1864, rpt. 1964. 104 pp.

An early textual scholar defends the premillennial position but attacks the idea of a secret rapture.

Trench, Richard Chenevix. *Synonyms of the New Testament*. Grand Rapids: Eerdmans, 1880, rpt. 1953. 405 pp.

A study of more than a hundred groups of synonyms, with careful distinctions among them.

Unger, Merrill. *Biblical Demonology*. Wheaton, Ill.: Van Kampen Press, 1952. 250 pp.

He defends the reality of demons (pp. 35ff.), demon possession (pp. 77ff.), magic (pp. 107ff.), divination (pp. 119ff.), necromancy (pp. 143ff.), and so forth.

United Bible Societies. *Fauna and Flora of the Bible*. N.d. 207 pp.

Van der Toorn, Karel, Bob Becking, and Pieter van der Horst, eds. *Dictionary of Deities and Demons in the Bible*, 2nd ed. Leiden: Brill, 1999. 960 pp.

A list of supernatural beings mentioned in the Bible. Although there is strong liberal bias in the work, the article on "Satan" (pp. 726–32) provides valuable historical information.

Vincent, Marvin R. *Word Studies in the New Testament.* 4 vols. Grand Rapids: Eerdmans, 1887, rpt. 1946.

He covers Revelation in vol. II, pp. 405–574. He stresses that the Hebrews regarded seven as a sacred number (pp. 410ff.); argues that John needed to be in the Spirit because reason cannot comprehend the infinite (pp. 422f.).

Vos, Geerhardus. *Pauline Eschatology.* Grand Rapids: Baker, 1930, rpt. 1979. 374 pp.

A formal defense of the amillennial position.

Walvoord, John F. *Major Bible Prophecies.* Grand Rapids: Zondervan, 1991. 450 pp.

A brief study of thirty-seven biblical prophecies, including those dealing with the Great Tribulation (pp. 346ff.), Armageddon (pp. 354ff.), the second coming of Christ (pp. 360ff.), the first resurrection (pp. 376ff.), the millennial kingdom (pp. 389ff.), the Great White Throne judgment (pp. 407ff.), the new heaven and new earth (pp. 413ff.).

————. *Prophecy in the New Millennium.* Grand Rapids: Kregel, 2001. 176 pp.

A brief survey and updating of prophetic subjects at the turn of the millennium. He covers prophecies fulfilled in the twentieth century (pp. 11ff.), the Rapture (pp. 27ff.), the judgment seat of Christ (pp. 43ff.), the United States of Europe (pp. 51ff.), Israel in the new Millennium (pp. 59ff.), Antichrist and the coming world government (pp. 69ff.), the impending Day of the Lord (pp. 79ff.), the second coming of Christ (pp. 97ff.), and so forth.

————. *The Rapture Question.* Grand Rapids: Zondervan, 1957. 204 pp.

He covers the doctrines of the church (pp. 19ff.), the Tribulation period (pp. 41ff.), imminency (pp. 75ff.), the partial rapture (pp. 105ff.), posttribulationism (pp. 127ff.), midtribulationism (pp. 171ff.), and fifty arguments for pretribulationism (pp. 191ff.).

Warfield, Benjamin B. *The Lord of Glory.* Grand Rapids: Zondervan, 1907 rpt. 332 pp.

A proof of the deity of the Lord Jesus Christ drawn from the titles applied to Him in Scripture. He specifically draws upon Revelation for proof (pp. 286ff.). He stresses the accumulated designations applied to Him in Revelation (pp. 292ff.).

West, Nathaniel, ed. *Premillennial Essays of the Prophetic Conference of 1878.* Chicago: Revell, 1879, rpt. Klock and Klock, 1981. 528 pp.

Powerful messages by A. J. Gordon, "The First Resurrection," Bishop Nicholson, "The Gathering of Israel," James Brookes, "The Coming of the Lord in Its Relation to Christian Doctrine" (one hundred points to his sermon!), Nathaniel West, "History of the Premillennial Doctrine," and so forth.

Whyte, Alexander. *Lancelot Andrews and His Private Devotions.* Edinburgh: Oliphant, 1896. 232 pp.

A translation and interpretation of the tear-stained prayers of this famous translator of the KJV.

Willis, Wesley R., and John R. Master, eds. *Issues in Dispensationalism.* Chicago: Moody Press, 1994. 271 pp.

An anthology evaluating differing positions in dispensationalism. C. C. Ryrie gives a brief update on the discussion (pp. 15ff.); Thomas D. Ice surveys dispensational hermeneutics (pp. 29ff.); John Walvoord sets forth the classic position on biblical kingdoms (pp. 75ff.); John Master covers the new covenant (pp. 93ff.); Zane Hodges discusses a dispensational understanding of Acts 2 (pp. 167ff.) and so forth.

Yadin, Yigael. *The Art of Warfare in Biblical Lands.* 2 vols. New York: McGraw Hill, 1963.

A famous general provides a survey of warfare in the Middle East from earliest history to the fall of Judah in 586 B.C.

Zahn, Theodor. *Introduction to the New Testament.* 3 vols. Grand Rapids: Kregel Publications, 1953. 564, 617, 539 pp.

He sees a contemporary-historical interpretation of Revelation for the first century, as well as a futurist interpretation (III, 436–49).

Scripture Index

Pseudepigrapha

Subject Index